Comprehensive Compound Interest Tables

Michael Sherman

Contemporary Books, Inc.
Chicago

41194

Acknowledgments

Computer Analyst: David R. Warren
Edited and designed by Thomas D. Kinsey, Marketing and
  Computer Consultant

About the Author

Michael Sherman, Ph.D.

EXPERIENCE: 15 Years Computer Research, Theoretical and Applied Mathematics

SPECIALIST IN: Financial Mathematics
Real Estate Finance

SPECIFIC PROJECTS INCLUDE:

- Consultant to Major California Financial Institutions

- Consulting Mathematician to:
  - Federal Reserve Board
  - Federal Trade Commission
  - California Department of Real Estate
  - California Department of Corporations
  - Courts of the State of California
  - Federal Deposit Insurance Corp.
  - Federal Home Loan Bank
  - Legal Aid Society

- Author and Holder of 12 copyrights on Real Estate Publications

- Author of 6 papers published in:
  - Real Estate Review
  - Real Estate Syndication Digest
  - California Real Estate Magazine

- Speaker & Lecturer to:
  - Property Improvement Lenders' Council
  - California Independent Finance Association

EDUCATION: PhD Case Institute of Technology
MS Stanford University
BS New York University

The purpose of this book is to show how time affects the value of invested money. Our tables and explanations are appropriate for people in business, finance, real estate, or in any aspect of investment analysis. This handy pocket guide is also useful to students in the investment field. No advanced mathematical skills are required to understand these tables. You need only the ability to read and follow directions.

Since people in diverse professions and financial positions are often intimidated by successive columns of fractional numbers, our tables offer a simple approach. We present the following six different effects of time on money. Then for clarity and for easy use, we have placed each of the different effects of time on money, into sections.

Section 6. Partial Payment to Amortize $1.00, page 146

Each respective section explains the use of each concept and includes practical questions. Also, each section is separated into four compounding periods: monthly, quarterly, semi-annual, and annual. In each period, the interest is either compounded or calculated according to the duration of the period.

The above categories include the use of $1.00 as the simplest monetary factor for calculation of value. However, if your investment is greater than $1.00, simply multiply the table factor given, by the dollar amount invested.

Your first and most important job in correctly using these tables, will be to select the appropriate section for analysis of your investment. This should be an easy task after careful reading of the summaries within each classification.

Section 1. Future Value of $1.00:

This represents the growth of $1.00 including interest over a designated period of time. In this section it is important to understand that the date of your original $1.00 investment constitutes the beginning of the investment period. The factors presented in this section are based on the fact that no additional investments may be made, and that the future growth of this fund depends upon the interest paid. These factors are based on the assumption that no funds will be withdrawn at any point, for the duration of the investment.

In this section, the following four (4) periods are presented in detail: monthly, quarterly, semiannual, and annual.

Monthly:

The factors presented on pages 8 through 15 will indicate the value of a $1.00 investment at the end of each stated monthly interval. That is, the original $1.00 plus the interest earned for each monthly period. The interest is compounding each month. This is interest earned on interest.

Example A

If you invest $1250.00 on a certain date, what will be the value of that investment in 20 years? We assume an earned annual interest of 8%, and a monthly compounding.

Turn to page 8 and locate the 8.0% column. Proceed down that column until you locate the point where the 20 year row intersects the 8.0% interest column. The number is 4.926803 for each $1.00 invested. So, to determine your answer, multiply 4.926803 by $1250. The correct answer is $6,158.50. That is, the value of that $1250 investment is $6,158.50 in 20 years.

Note: If your investment period is less than 4 years, we have provided all the $1.00 amounts for each monthly period. Over 4 years, only the annual figures are provided.

Quarterly:

The factors presented on pages 16 through 21, will indicate

the value of a $1.00 investment at the end of each stated quarterly interval. That is, the original $1.00 plus the interest earned for each quarterly period. The interest is compounding each quarter. This is interest earned on interest.

Example B

You deposit $500.00 in the credit union every quarter. What is the value of that account at the end of 2 years or eight quarters? Assume an interest rate of 7.0% and quarterly compounding.

Turn to page 16 and locate the 7.0% column. Proceed down that column until you locate the point where the 8 quarters row intersects the 7% interest column. The number is 1.148882 for each $1.00 invested. So, to determine your answer, multiply 1.148882 by $500.00. The correct answer is $574.44. That is, the value of that $500.00 account is $574.44 in 2 years (or eight quarters).

Note: For investments of 14 years and more, only the annual amounts are shown.

Semiannual:

The factors on pages 22 through 25 cover semiannual compounding (or the interest being compounded every 6 months). They are used the same way as the monthly or quarterly tables.

Annual:

The factors on pages 26 through 33 cover annual compounding (or the interest being compounded every year). They are used the same way as the monthly, quarterly, and semiannual tables.

In case you want to know how it is done, here's the formula . . .

$$S = (1 + i)^n$$
S = The future value of $1.00
i = interest rate per period
n = number of compounding periods

SECTION 1

MOS	7.00% ANNUAL RATE	8.00% ANNUAL RATE	9.00% ANNUAL RATE	10.00% ANNUAL RATE	10.25% ANNUAL RATE	10.50% ANNUAL RATE	MOS
1	1.005 833	1.006 667	1.007 500	1.008 333	1.008 542	1.008 750	1
2	1.011 701	1.013 378	1.015 056	1.016 736	1.017 156	1.017 577	2
3	1.017 602	1.020 134	1.022 669	1.025 209	1.025 845	1.026 480	3
4	1.023 538	1.026 935	1.030 339	1.033 752	1.034 607	1.035 462	4
5	1.029 509	1.033 781	1.038 067	1.042 367	1.043 444	1.044 522	5
6	1.035 514	1.040 673	1.045 852	1.051 053	1.052 357	1.053 662	6
7	1.041 555	1.047 610	1.053 696	1.059 812	1.061 346	1.062 881	7
8	1.047 631	1.054 595	1.061 599	1.068 644	1.070 411	1.072 182	8
9	1.053 742	1.061 625	1.069 561	1.077 549	1.079 555	1.081 563	9
10	1.059 889	1.068 703	1.077 583	1.086 529	1.088 776	1.091 027	10
11	1.066 071	1.075 827	1.085 664	1.095 583	1.098 076	1.100 573	11
12	1.072 290	1.083 000	1.093 807	1.104 713	1.107 455	1.110 203	12
13	1.078 545	1.090 220	1.102 010	1.113 919	1.116 915	1.119 918	13
14	1.084 837	1.097 488	1.110 276	1.123 202	1.126 455	1.129 717	14
15	1.091 165	1.104 804	1.118 603	1.132 562	1.136 077	1.139 602	15
16	1.097 530	1.112 170	1.126 992	1.142 000	1.145 781	1.149 574	16
17	1.103 932	1.119 584	1.135 445	1.151 516	1.155 568	1.159 632	17
18	1.110 372	1.127 048	1.143 960	1.161 112	1.165 438	1.169 779	18
19	1.116 849	1.134 562	1.152 540	1.170 788	1.175 393	1.180 015	19
20	1.123 364	1.142 125	1.161 184	1.180 545	1.185 433	1.190 340	20
21	1.129 917	1.149 740	1.169 893	1.190 383	1.195 558	1.200 755	21
22	1.136 508	1.157 404	1.178 667	1.200 303	1.205 770	1.211 262	22
23	1.143 138	1.165 120	1.187 507	1.210 305	1.216 070	1.221 860	23
24	1.149 806	1.172 888	1.196 414	1.220 391	1.226 457	1.232 552	24
25	1.156 513	1.180 707	1.205 387	1.230 561	1.236 933	1.243 337	25
26	1.163 260	1.188 579	1.214 427	1.240 816	1.247 498	1.254 216	26
27	1.170 045	1.196 502	1.223 535	1.251 156	1.258 154	1.265 190	27
28	1.176 870	1.204 479	1.232 712	1.261 582	1.268 901	1.276 261	28
29	1.183 736	1.212 509	1.241 957	1.272 095	1.279 739	1.287 428	29
30	1.190 641	1.220 592	1.251 272	1.282 696	1.290 670	1.298 693	30
31	1.197 586	1.228 730	1.260 656	1.293 385	1.301 695	1.310 056	31
32	1.204 572	1.236 921	1.270 111	1.304 163	1.312 814	1.321 519	32
33	1.211 599	1.245 167	1.279 637	1.315 031	1.324 027	1.333 083	33
34	1.218 666	1.253 468	1.289 234	1.325 990	1.335 337	1.344 747	34
35	1.225 775	1.261 825	1.298 904	1.337 040	1.346 743	1.356 514	35
36	1.232 926	1.270 237	1.308 645	1.348 182	1.358 246	1.368 383	36
37	1.240 118	1.278 705	1.318 460	1.359 417	1.369 848	1.380 357	37
38	1.247 352	1.287 230	1.328 349	1.370 745	1.381 548	1.392 435	38
39	1.254 628	1.295 812	1.338 311	1.382 168	1.393 349	1.404 618	39
40	1.261 947	1.304 450	1.348 349	1.393 686	1.405 251	1.416 909	40
41	1.269 308	1.313 147	1.358 461	1.405 300	1.417 254	1.429 307	41
42	1.276 712	1.321 901	1.368 650	1.417 011	1.429 360	1.441 813	42
43	1.284 160	1.330 714	1.378 915	1.428 819	1.441 569	1.454 429	43
44	1.291 651	1.339 585	1.389 256	1.440 726	1.453 882	1.467 155	44
45	1.299 185	1.348 516	1.399 676	1.452 732	1.466 301	1.479 993	45
46	1.306 764	1.357 506	1.410 173	1.464 838	1.478 825	1.492 943	46
47	1.314 387	1.366 556	1.420 750	1.477 045	1.491 457	1.506 006	47

YRS	7.00% ANNUAL RATE	8.00% ANNUAL RATE	9.00% ANNUAL RATE	10.00% ANNUAL RATE	10.25% ANNUAL RATE	10.50% ANNUAL RATE	MOS
4	1.322 054	1.375 666	1.431 405	1.489 354	1.504 196	1.519 184	48
5	1.417 625	1.489 846	1.565 681	1.645 309	1.665 830	1.686 603	60
6	1.520 106	1.613 502	1.712 553	1.817 594	1.844 832	1.872 472	72
7	1.629 994	1.747 422	1.873 202	2.007 920	2.043 069	2.078 825	84
8	1.747 826	1.892 457	2.048 921	2.218 176	2.262 607	2.307 919	96
9	1.874 177	2.049 530	2.241 124	2.450 448	2.505 736	2.562 260	108
10	2.009 661	2.219 640	2.451 357	2.707 041	2.774 990	2.844 630	120
11	2.154 940	2.403 869	2.681 311	2.990 504	3.073 177	3.158 118	132
12	2.310 721	2.603 389	2.932 837	3.303 649	3.403 406	3.506 153	144
13	2.477 763	2.819 469	3.207 957	3.649 584	3.769 119	3.892 543	156
14	2.656 881	3.053 484	3.508 886	4.031 743	4.174 130	4.321 515	168
15	2.848 947	3.306 921	3.838 043	4.453 920	4.622 662	4.797 761	180
16	3.054 897	3.581 394	4.198 078	4.920 303	5.119 391	5.326 491	192
17	3.275 736	3.878 648	4.591 887	5.435 523	5.669 496	5.913 488	204
18	3.512 539	4.200 574	5.022 638	6.004 693	6.278 712	6.565 175	216
19	3.766 461	4.549 220	5.493 796	6.633 463	6.953 392	7.288 680	228
20	4.038 739	4.926 803	6.009 152	7.328 074	7.700 570	8.091 918	240
21	4.330 700	5.335 725	6.572 851	8.095 419	8.528 036	8.983 675	252
22	4.643 766	5.778 588	7.189 430	8.943 115	9.444 417	9.973 707	264
23	4.979 464	6.258 207	7.863 848	9.879 576	10.459 268	11.072 844	276
24	5.339 430	6.777 636	8.601 532	10.914 097	11.583 170	12.293 109	288
25	5.725 418	7.340 176	9.408 415	12.056 945	12.827 841	13.647 852	300
26	6.139 309	7.949 407	10.290 989	13.319 465	14.206 259	15.151 893	312
27	6.583 120	8.609 204	11.256 354	14.714 187	15.732 794	16.821 663	324
28	7.059 015	9.323 763	12.312 278	16.254 564	17.423 364	18.675 491	336
29	7.569 311	10.097 631	13.467 255	17.957 060	19.295 594	20.733 595	348
30	8.116 497	10.935 730	14.730 576	19.837 399	21.369 005	23.018 509	360

8

FUTURE VALUE OF $1

MOS	10.75% ANNUAL RATE	11.00% ANNUAL RATE	11.25% ANNUAL RATE	11.50% ANNUAL RATE	11.75% ANNUAL RATE	12.00% ANNUAL RATE	MOS
1	1.008 958	1.009 167	1.009 375	1.009 583	1.009 792	1.010 000	1
2	1.017 997	1.018 417	1.018 838	1.019 259	1.019 679	1.020 100	2
3	1.027 116	1.027 753	1.028 389	1.029 026	1.029 664	1.030 301	3
4	1.036 318	1.037 174	1.038 031	1.038 888	1.039 746	1.040 604	4
5	1.045 601	1.046 681	1.047 762	1.048 844	1.049 927	1.051 010	5
6	1.054 968	1.056 276	1.057 585	1.058 895	1.060 207	1.061 520	6
7	1.064 419	1.065 958	1.067 500	1.069 043	1.070 588	1.072 135	7
8	1.073 954	1.075 730	1.077 508	1.079 288	1.081 071	1.082 857	8
9	1.083 575	1.085 591	1.087 609	1.089 631	1.091 657	1.093 685	9
10	1.093 282	1.095 542	1.097 806	1.100 074	1.102 346	1.104 622	10
11	1.103 076	1.105 584	1.108 098	1.110 616	1.113 140	1.115 668	11
12	1.112 958	1.115 719	1.118 486	1.121 259	1.124 039	1.126 825	12
13	1.122 928	1.125 946	1.128 972	1.132 005	1.135 045	1.138 093	13
14	1.132 988	1.136 267	1.139 556	1.142 853	1.146 159	1.149 474	14
15	1.143 138	1.146 683	1.150 239	1.153 805	1.157 382	1.160 969	15
16	1.153 378	1.157 194	1.161 023	1.164 863	1.168 715	1.172 579	16
17	1.163 710	1.167 802	1.171 907	1.176 026	1.180 158	1.184 304	17
18	1.174 135	1.178 507	1.182 894	1.187 296	1.191 714	1.196 147	18
19	1.184 654	1.189 310	1.193 984	1.198 675	1.203 383	1.208 109	19
20	1.195 266	1.200 212	1.205 177	1.210 162	1.215 166	1.220 190	20
21	1.205 974	1.211 214	1.216 476	1.221 759	1.227 065	1.232 392	21
22	1.216 777	1.222 317	1.227 880	1.233 468	1.239 080	1.244 716	22
23	1.227 678	1.233 521	1.239 391	1.245 288	1.251 212	1.257 163	23
24	1.238 676	1.244 829	1.251 011	1.257 222	1.263 464	1.269 735	24
25	1.249 772	1.256 239	1.262 739	1.269 271	1.275 835	1.282 432	25
26	1.260 968	1.267 755	1.274 577	1.281 435	1.288 328	1.295 256	26
27	1.272 264	1.279 376	1.286 526	1.293 715	1.300 943	1.308 209	27
28	1.283 661	1.291 104	1.298 588	1.306 113	1.313 681	1.321 291	28
29	1.295 161	1.302 939	1.310 762	1.318 630	1.326 544	1.334 504	29
30	1.306 763	1.314 882	1.323 050	1.331 267	1.339 533	1.347 849	30
31	1.318 470	1.326 935	1.335 454	1.344 025	1.352 649	1.361 327	31
32	1.330 281	1.339 099	1.347 974	1.356 905	1.365 894	1.374 941	32
33	1.342 198	1.351 374	1.360 611	1.369 909	1.379 268	1.388 690	33
34	1.354 222	1.363 762	1.373 367	1.383 037	1.392 774	1.402 577	34
35	1.366 354	1.376 263	1.386 242	1.396 291	1.406 411	1.416 603	35
36	1.378 594	1.388 879	1.399 238	1.409 672	1.420 183	1.430 769	36
37	1.390 944	1.401 610	1.412 356	1.423 182	1.434 088	1.445 076	37
38	1.403 404	1.414 458	1.425 597	1.436 821	1.448 131	1.459 527	38
39	1.415 976	1.427 424	1.438 962	1.450 590	1.462 310	1.474 123	39
40	1.428 661	1.440 509	1.452 452	1.464 492	1.476 629	1.488 864	40
41	1.441 460	1.453 713	1.466 069	1.478 526	1.491 087	1.503 752	41
42	1.454 373	1.467 039	1.479 813	1.492 696	1.505 688	1.518 790	42
43	1.467 402	1.480 487	1.493 686	1.507 001	1.520 431	1.533 978	43
44	1.480 547	1.494 058	1.507 690	1.521 443	1.535 318	1.549 318	44
45	1.493 810	1.507 754	1.521 824	1.536 023	1.550 352	1.564 811	45
46	1.507 192	1.521 575	1.536 091	1.550 743	1.565 532	1.580 459	46
47	1.520 694	1.535 522	1.550 492	1.565 605	1.580 861	1.596 263	47

YRS	10.75%	11.00%	11.25%	11.50%	11.75%	12.00%	MOS
4	1.534 317	1.549 598	1.565 028	1.580 608	1.596 341	1.612 226	48
5	1.707 630	1.728 916	1.750 462	1.772 272	1.794 349	1.816 697	60
6	1.900 521	1.928 984	1.957 867	1.987 176	2.016 918	2.047 099	72
7	2.115 200	2.152 204	2.189 847	2.228 140	2.267 095	2.306 723	84
8	2.354 129	2.401 254	2.449 313	2.498 323	2.548 303	2.599 273	96
9	2.620 047	2.679 124	2.739 522	2.801 268	2.864 392	2.928 926	108
10	2.916 002	2.989 150	3.064 117	3.140 948	3.219 689	3.300 387	120
11	3.245 388	3.335 051	3.427 171	3.521 817	3.619 056	3.718 959	132
12	3.611 980	3.720 979	3.833 243	3.948 870	4.067 960	4.190 616	144
13	4.019 982	4.151 566	4.287 428	4.427 707	4.572 546	4.722 091	156
14	4.474 072	4.631 980	4.795 428	4.964 608	5.139 720	5.320 970	168
15	4.979 454	5.167 988	5.363 619	5.566 613	5.777 245	5.995 802	180
16	5.541 923	5.766 021	5.999 132	6.241 617	6.493 849	6.756 220	192
17	6.167 928	6.433 259	6.709 945	6.998 471	7.299 340	7.613 078	204
18	6.864 644	7.177 708	7.504 979	7.847 101	8.204 743	8.578 606	216
19	7.640 061	8.008 304	8.394 214	8.798 635	9.222 451	9.666 588	228
20	8.503 067	8.935 015	9.388 810	9.865 552	10.366 395	10.892 554	240
21	9.463 557	9.968 965	10.501 252	11.061 842	11.652 233	12.274 002	252
22	10.532 541	11.122 562	11.745 503	12.403 194	13.097 564	13.830 653	264
23	11.722 276	12.409 652	13.137 180	13.907 196	14.722 173	15.584 726	276
24	13.046 401	13.845 682	14.693 751	15.593 574	16.548 297	17.561 259	288
25	14.520 096	15.447 889	16.434 754	17.484 440	18.600 932	19.788 466	300
26	16.160 258	17.235 500	18.382 041	19.604 591	20.908 173	22.298 139	312
27	17.985 688	19.229 972	20.560 054	21.981 831	23.501 603	25.126 101	324
28	20.017 316	21.455 242	22.996 132	24.647 333	26.416 719	28.312 720	336
29	22.278 432	23.938 018	25.720 850	27.636 052	29.693 422	31.903 481	348
30	24.794 959	26.708 098	28.768 409	30.987 181	33.376 565	35.949 641	360

FUTURE VALUE OF $1

MOS	12.25% ANNUAL RATE	12.50% ANNUAL RATE	12.75% ANNUAL RATE	13.00% ANNUAL RATE	13.25% ANNUAL RATE	13.50% ANNUAL RATE	MOS
1	1.010 208	1.010 417	1.010 625	1.010 833	1.011 042	1.011 250	1
2	1.020 521	1.020 942	1.021 363	1.021 784	1.022 205	1.022 627	2
3	1.030 939	1.031 577	1.032 215	1.032 853	1.033 492	1.034 131	3
4	1.041 463	1.042 322	1.043 182	1.044 043	1.044 904	1.045 765	4
5	1.052 094	1.053 180	1.054 266	1.055 353	1.056 441	1.057 530	5
6	1.062 835	1.064 150	1.065 468	1.066 786	1.068 106	1.069 427	6
7	1.073 684	1.075 235	1.076 788	1.078 343	1.079 900	1.081 458	7
8	1.084 645	1.086 436	1.088 229	1.090 025	1.091 823	1.093 625	8
9	1.095 717	1.097 753	1.099 791	1.101 834	1.103 879	1.105 928	9
10	1.106 903	1.109 188	1.111 477	1.113 770	1.116 068	1.118 370	10
11	1.118 202	1.120 742	1.123 286	1.125 836	1.128 391	1.130 951	11
12	1.129 617	1.132 416	1.135 221	1.138 032	1.140 850	1.143 674	12
13	1.141 149	1.144 212	1.147 283	1.150 361	1.153 447	1.156 541	13
14	1.152 798	1.156 131	1.159 473	1.162 823	1.166 183	1.169 552	14
15	1.164 566	1.168 174	1.171 792	1.175 421	1.179 060	1.182 709	15
16	1.176 455	1.180 342	1.184 242	1.188 154	1.192 079	1.196 015	16
17	1.188 464	1.192 638	1.196 825	1.201 026	1.205 241	1.209 470	17
18	1.200 596	1.205 061	1.209 541	1.214 037	1.218 549	1.223 077	18
19	1.212 853	1.217 614	1.222 393	1.227 189	1.232 004	1.236 836	19
20	1.225 234	1.230 297	1.235 381	1.240 484	1.245 607	1.250 751	20
21	1.237 741	1.243 113	1.248 506	1.253 922	1.259 361	1.264 821	21
22	1.250 377	1.256 062	1.261 772	1.267 507	1.273 266	1.279 051	22
23	1.263 141	1.269 146	1.275 178	1.281 238	1.287 325	1.293 440	23
24	1.276 035	1.282 366	1.288 727	1.295 118	1.301 539	1.307 991	24
25	1.289 062	1.295 724	1.302 420	1.309 148	1.315 910	1.322 706	25
26	1.302 221	1.309 221	1.316 258	1.323 331	1.330 440	1.337 587	26
27	1.315 514	1.322 859	1.330 243	1.337 667	1.345 131	1.352 634	27
28	1.328 943	1.336 639	1.344 377	1.352 158	1.359 983	1.367 852	28
29	1.342 510	1.350 562	1.358 661	1.366 807	1.375 000	1.383 240	29
30	1.356 215	1.364 630	1.373 097	1.381 614	1.390 182	1.398 801	30
31	1.370 059	1.378 845	1.387 686	1.396 581	1.405 532	1.414 538	31
32	1.384 045	1.393 208	1.402 430	1.411 711	1.421 051	1.430 451	32
33	1.398 174	1.407 721	1.417 331	1.427 004	1.436 742	1.446 544	33
34	1.412 447	1.422 385	1.432 390	1.442 464	1.452 606	1.462 818	34
35	1.426 866	1.437 201	1.447 609	1.458 090	1.468 645	1.479 274	35
36	1.441 432	1.452 172	1.462 990	1.473 886	1.484 861	1.495 916	36
37	1.456 146	1.467 299	1.478 534	1.489 853	1.501 257	1.512 745	37
38	1.471 011	1.482 583	1.494 244	1.505 993	1.517 833	1.529 764	38
39	1.486 028	1.498 027	1.510 120	1.522 308	1.534 593	1.546 973	39
40	1.501 198	1.513 631	1.526 165	1.538 800	1.551 537	1.564 377	40
41	1.516 522	1.529 398	1.542 381	1.555 470	1.568 669	1.581 976	41
42	1.532 004	1.545 329	1.558 768	1.572 321	1.585 989	1.599 773	42
43	1.547 643	1.561 427	1.575 330	1.589 355	1.603 501	1.617 771	43
44	1.563 442	1.577 691	1.592 068	1.606 573	1.621 207	1.635 971	44
45	1.579 402	1.594 126	1.608 984	1.623 977	1.639 107	1.654 375	45
46	1.595 525	1.610 731	1.626 079	1.641 570	1.657 206	1.672 987	46
47	1.611 812	1.627 510	1.643 356	1.659 354	1.675 504	1.691 808	47
YRS							
4	1.628 266	1.644 463	1.660 817	1.677 330	1.694 005	1.710 841	48
5	1.839 318	1.862 216	1.885 394	1.908 857	1.932 606	1.956 645	60
6	2.077 725	2.108 803	2.140 340	2.172 341	2.204 814	2.237 765	72
7	2.347 035	2.388 043	2.429 759	2.472 194	2.515 362	2.559 275	84
8	2.651 251	2.704 258	2.758 313	2.813 437	2.869 652	2.926 977	96
9	2.994 899	3.062 345	3.131 295	3.201 783	3.273 843	3.347 509	108
10	3.383 090	3.467 849	3.554 712	3.643 733	3.734 964	3.828 460	120
11	3.821 598	3.927 048	4.035 384	4.146 687	4.261 035	4.378 512	132
12	4.316 943	4.447 052	4.581 054	4.719 064	4.861 203	5.007 593	144
13	4.876 494	5.035 913	5.200 509	5.370 448	5.545 905	5.727 056	156
14	5.508 572	5.702 748	5.903 727	6.111 745	6.327 047	6.549 887	168
15	6.222 579	6.457 884	6.702 035	6.955 364	7.218 213	7.490 939	180
16	7.029 133	7.313 011	7.608 292	7.915 430	8.234 901	8.567 195	192
17	7.940 231	8.281 371	8.637 093	9.008 017	9.394 788	9.798 082	204
18	8.969 423	9.377 958	9.805 010	10.251 416	10.718 047	11.205 816	216
19	10.132 016	10.619 750	11.130 854	11.666 444	12.227 687	12.815 805	228
20	11.445 301	12.025 975	12.635 980	13.276 792	13.949 959	14.657 109	240
21	12.928 811	13.618 407	14.344 631	15.109 421	15.914 815	16.762 961	252
22	14.604 609	15.421 703	16.284 328	17.195 012	18.156 421	19.171 370	264
23	16.497 620	17.463 783	18.486 312	19.568 482	20.713 757	21.925 805	276
24	18.635 998	19.776 269	20.986 051	22.269 568	23.631 296	25.075 983	288
25	21.051 547	22.394 964	23.823 808	25.343 491	26.959 770	28.678 761	300
26	23.780 193	25.360 417	27.045 289	28.841 716	30.757 061	32.799 166	312
27	26.862 519	28.718 543	30.702 382	32.822 810	35.089 201	37.511 568	324
28	30.344 369	32.521 339	34.853 991	37.353 424	40.031 524	42.901 021	336
29	34.277 126	36.827 686	39.566 985	42.509 410	45.669 975	49.064 802	348
30	38.720 488	41.704 262	44.917 276	48.377 089	52.102 603	56.114 160	360

SECTION 1

MOS	13.75% ANNUAL RATE	14.00% ANNUAL RATE	14.25% ANNUAL RATE	14.50% ANNUAL RATE	14.75% ANNUAL RATE	15.00% ANNUAL RATE	MOS
1	1.011 458	1.011 667	1.01 875	1.012 083	1.012 292	1.012 500	1
2	1.023 048	1.023 469	1.023 891	1.024 313	1.024 734	1.025 156	2
3	1.034 770	1.035 410	1.036 050	1.036 690	1.037 330	1.037 971	3
4	1.046 627	1.047 490	1.048 353	1.049 216	1.050 081	1.050 945	4
5	1.058 620	1.059 710	1.060 802	1.061 894	1.062 988	1.064 082	5
6	1.070 750	1.072 074	1.073 399	1.074 726	1.076 054	1.077 383	6
7	1.083 019	1.084 581	1.086 146	1.087 712	1.089 280	1.090 850	7
8	1.095 428	1.097 235	1.099 044	1.100 855	1.102 669	1.104 486	8
9	1.107 980	1.110 036	1.112 095	1.114 157	1.116 223	1.118 292	9
10	1.120 676	1.122 986	1.125 301	1.127 620	1.129 943	1.132 271	10
11	1.133 517	1.136 088	1.138 664	1.141 245	1.143 832	1.146 424	11
12	1.146 505	1.149 342	1.152 185	1.155 035	1.157 892	1.160 755	12
13	1.159 642	1.162 751	1.165 868	1.168 992	1.172 124	1.175 264	13
14	1.172 930	1.176 316	1.179 712	1.183 117	1.186 531	1.189 955	14
15	1.186 369	1.190 040	1.193 721	1.197 413	1.201 116	1.204 829	15
16	1.199 963	1.203 924	1.207 897	1.211 882	1.215 880	1.219 890	16
17	1.213 713	1.217 970	1.222 241	1.226 526	1.230 825	1.235 138	17
18	1.227 620	1.232 179	1.236 755	1.241 346	1.245 954	1.250 577	18
19	1.241 686	1.246 555	1.251 441	1.256 346	1.261 269	1.266 210	19
20	1.255 914	1.261 098	1.266 302	1.271 527	1.276 772	1.282 037	20
21	1.270 305	1.275 811	1.281 339	1.286 891	1.292 465	1.298 063	21
22	1.284 860	1.290 695	1.296 555	1.302 441	1.308 352	1.314 288	22
23	1.299 583	1.305 753	1.311 952	1.318 179	1.324 434	1.330 717	23
24	1.314 474	1.320 987	1.327 531	1.334 107	.340 713	1.347 351	24
25	1.329 535	1.336 399	1.343 296	1.350 227	1.357 193	1.364 193	25
26	1.344 770	1.351 990	1.359 247	1.366 542	1.373 875	1.381 245	26
27	1.360 179	1.367 763	1.375 388	1.383 055	1.390 762	1.398 511	27
28	1.375 764	1.383 720	1.391 721	1.399 767	1.407 857	1.415 992	28
29	1.391 528	1.399 864	1.408 248	1.416 681	1.425 162	1.433 692	29
30	1.407 472	1.416 196	1.424 971	1.433 799	1.442 679	1.451 613	30
31	1.423 600	1.432 718	1.441 892	1.451 124	1.460 412	1.469 759	31
32	1.439 912	1.449 433	1.459 015	1.468 658	1.478 363	1.488 131	32
33	1.456 411	1.466 343	1.476 341	1.486 405	1.496 535	1.506 732	33
34	1.473 099	1.483 450	1.493 872	1.504 365	1.514 930	1.525 566	34
35	1.489 978	1.500 757	1.511 612	1.522 543	1.533 551	1.544 636	35
36	1.507 051	1.518 266	1.529 562	1.540 940	1.552 401	1.563 944	36
37	1.524 319	1.535 979	1.547 726	1.559 560	1.571 482	1.583 493	37
38	1.541 785	1.553 899	1.566 105	1.578 405	1.590 798	1.603 287	38
39	1.559 452	1.572 028	1.584 703	1.597 477	1.610 352	1.623 328	39
40	1.577 320	1.590 368	1.603 521	1.616 780	1.630 146	1.643 619	40
41	1.595 394	1.608 922	1.622 563	1.636 316	1.650 183	1.664 165	41
42	1.613 674	1.627 693	1.641 831	1.656 088	1.670 467	1.684 967	42
43	1.632 164	1.646 683	1.661 327	1.676 099	1.690 999	1.706 029	43
44	1.650 866	1.665 894	1.681 056	1.696 352	1.711 785	1.727 354	44
45	1.669 782	1.685 330	1.701 018	1.716 850	1.732 825	1.748 946	45
46	1.688 915	1.704 992	1.721 218	1.737 595	1.754 125	1.770 808	46
47	1.708 267	1.724 883	1.741 657	1.758 591	1.775 686	1.792 943	47

YRS							
4	1.727 841	1.745 007	1.762 339	1.779 841	1.797 512	1.815 355	48
5	1.980 979	2.005 610	2.030 542	2.055 779	2.081 324	2.107 181	60
6	2.271 202	2.305 132	2.339 561	2.374 497	2.409 948	2.445 920	72
7	2.603 945	2.649 385	2.695 608	2.742 628	2.790 459	2.839 113	84
8	2.985 436	3.045 049	3.105 840	3.167 833	3.231 049	3.295 513	96
9	3.422 817	3.499 803	3.578 504	3.658 959	3.741 205	3.825 282	108
10	3.924 277	4.022 471	4.123 101	4.226 227	4.331 910	4.440 213	120
11	4.499 203	4.623 195	4.750 577	4.881 441	5.015 882	5.153 998	132
12	5.158 359	5.313 632	5.473 545	5.638 237	5.807 849	5.982 526	144
13	5.914 084	6.107 180	6.306 539	6.512 363	6.724 860	6.944 244	156
14	6.780 527	7.019 239	7.266 303	7.522 010	7.786 659	8.060 563	168
15	7.773 909	8.067 507	8.372 129	8.688 187	9.016 108	9.356 334	180
16	8.912 825	9.272 324	9.646 245	10.035 163	10.439 677	10.860 408	192
17	10.218 599	10.657 072	11.114 263	11.590 968	12.088 015	12.606 267	204
18	11.715 675	12.248 621	12.805 693	13.387 978	13.996 612	14.632 781	216
19	13.432 081	14.077 855	14.754 533	15.463 588	16.206 561	16.985 067	228
20	15.399 948	16.180 270	16.999 959	17.860 991	18.765 442	19.715 494	240
21	17.656 118	18.596 664	19.587 105	20.630 076	21.728 350	22.884 848	252
22	20.242 827	21.373 768	22.567 978	23.828 467	25.159 076	26.563 691	264
23	23.208 503	24.565 954	26.002 496	27.522 721	29.131 485	30.833 924	276
24	26.608 666	28.234 683	29.959 698	31.789 716	33.731 105	35.790 617	288
25	30.506 969	32.451 308	34.519 129	36.718 246	39.056 966	41.544 120	300
26	34.976 393	37.297 652	39.772 439	42.410 872	45.223 737	48.222 525	312
27	40.100 611	42.867 759	45.825 226	48.986 057	52.364 190	55.974 514	324
28	45.975 552	49.269 718	52.799 159	56.580 627	60.632 060	64.972 670	336
29	52.711 201	56.627 757	60.834 424	65.352 625	70.205 359	75.417 320	348
30	60.433 657	65.084 661	70.092 540	75.484 592	81.290 203	87.540 995	360

FUTURE VALUE OF $1

MONTHLY COMPOUNDING

MOS	15.25% ANNUAL RATE	15.50% ANNUAL RATE	15.75% ANNUAL RATE	16.00% ANNUAL RATE	16.25% ANNUAL RATE	16.50% ANNUAL RATE	MOS
1	1.012 708	1.012 917	1.013 125	1.013 333	1.013 542	1.013 750	1
2	1.025 578	1.026 000	1.026 422	1.026 844	1.027 267	1.027 689	2
3	1.038 612	1.039 253	1.039 894	1.040 536	1.041 178	1.041 820	3
4	1.051 811	1.052 676	1.053 543	1.054 410	1.055 277	1.056 145	4
5	1.065 177	1.066 273	1.067 370	1.068 468	1.069 567	1.070 667	5
6	1.078 714	1.080 046	1.081 380	1.082 715	1.084 051	1.085 388	6
7	1.092 423	1.093 997	1.095 573	1.097 151	1.098 731	1.100 313	7
8	1.106 305	1.108 128	1.109 952	1.111 779	1.113 609	1.115 442	8
9	1.120 365	1.122 441	1.124 520	1.126 603	1.128 689	1.130 779	9
10	1.134 603	1.136 939	1.139 280	1.141 625	1.143 974	1.146 327	10
11	1.149 022	1.151 624	1.154 233	1.156 846	1.159 465	1.162 089	11
12	1.163 624	1.166 500	1.169 382	1.172 271	1.175 166	1.178 068	12
13	1.178 412	1.181 567	1.184 730	1.187 901	1.191 080	1.194 267	13
14	1.193 387	1.196 829	1.200 280	1.203 740	1.207 209	1.210 688	14
15	1.208 553	1.212 288	1.216 033	1.219 790	1.223 557	1.227 335	15
16	1.223 912	1.227 947	1.231 994	1.236 053	1.240 126	1.244 211	16
17	1.239 466	1.243 808	1.248 164	1.252 534	1.256 919	1.261 318	17
18	1.255 217	1.259 873	1.264 546	1.269 235	1.273 940	1.278 662	18
19	1.271 169	1.276 147	1.281 143	1.286 158	1.291 191	1.296 243	19
20	1.287 323	1.292 630	1.297 958	1.303 307	1.308 676	1.314 067	20
21	1.303 683	1.309 327	1.314 994	1.320 684	1.326 398	1.332 135	21
22	1.320 251	1.326 239	1.332 253	1.338 293	1.344 359	1.350 452	22
23	1.337 029	1.343 370	1.349 739	1.356 137	1.362 564	1.369 020	23
24	1.354 020	1.360 721	1.367 454	1.374 219	1.381 016	1.387 845	24
25	1.371 228	1.378 297	1.385 402	1.392 542	1.399 717	1.406 927	25
26	1.388 654	1.396 100	1.403 585	1.411 109	1.418 671	1.426 273	26
27	1.406 301	1.414 133	1.422 007	1.429 924	1.437 882	1.445 884	27
28	1.424 173	1.432 399	1.440 671	1.448 989	1.457 354	1.465 765	28
29	1.442 272	1.450 901	1.459 580	1.468 309	1.477 089	1.485 919	29
30	1.460 601	1.469 642	1.478 737	1.487 887	1.497 091	1.506 350	30
31	1.479 163	1.488 625	1.498 146	1.507 725	1.517 364	1.527 063	31
32	1.497 960	1.507 853	1.517 809	1.527 828	1.537 912	1.548 060	32
33	1.516 997	1.527 329	1.537 730	1.548 199	1.558 738	1.569 346	33
34	1.536 275	1.547 057	1.557 913	1.568 842	1.579 846	1.590 924	34
35	1.555 799	1.567 040	1.578 360	1.589 760	1.601 239	1.612 799	35
36	1.575 570	1.587 281	1.599 076	1.610 957	1.622 923	1.634 975	36
37	1.595 593	1.607 783	1.620 064	1.632 436	1.644 900	1.657 456	37
38	1.615 871	1.628 551	1.641 327	1.654 202	1.667 175	1.680 246	38
39	1.636 406	1.649 586	1.662 870	1.676 258	1.689 751	1.703 350	39
40	1.657 202	1.670 893	1.684 695	1.698 608	1.712 633	1.726 771	40
41	1.678 262	1.692 476	1.706 807	1.721 256	1.735 825	1.750 514	41
42	1.699 590	1.714 337	1.729 208	1.744 206	1.759 331	1.774 583	42
43	1.721 189	1.736 480	1.751 904	1.767 462	1.783 155	1.798 984	43
44	1.743 062	1.758 910	1.774 898	1.791 028	1.807 302	1.823 720	44
45	1.765 214	1.781 629	1.798 194	1.814 909	1.831 776	1.848 796	45
46	1.787 647	1.804 642	1.821 795	1.839 108	1.856 581	1.874 217	46
47	1.810 365	1.827 952	1.845 706	1.863 629	1.881 722	1.899 988	47

YRS	15.25%	15.50%	15.75%	16.00%	16.25%	16.50%	
4	1.833 371	1.851 563	1.869 931	1.888 477	1.907 204	1.926 112	48
5	2.133 354	2.159 847	2.186 663	2.213 807	2.241 282	2.269 092	60
6	2.482 422	2.519 461	2.557 045	2.595 181	2.633 878	2.673 145	72
7	2.888 605	2.938 950	2.990 162	3.042 255	3.095 245	3.149 146	84
8	3.361 250	3.428 284	3.496 641	3.566 347	3.637 427	3.709 909	96
9	3.911 231	3.999 093	4.088 909	4.180 724	4.274 581	4.370 526	108
10	4.551 201	4.664 940	4.781 497	4.900 941	5.023 343	5.148 777	120
11	5.295 886	5.441 651	5.591 396	5.745 230	5.903 263	6.065 610	132
12	6.162 419	6.347 684	6.538 478	6.734 965	6.937 315	7.145 702	144
13	7.170 738	7.404 571	7.645 978	7.895 203	8.152 499	8.418 123	156
14	8.344 042	8.637 429	8.941 068	9.255 316	9.580 541	9.917 123	168
15	9.709 326	10.075 557	10.455 524	10.849 737	11.258 727	11.683 046	180
16	11.298 003	11.753 134	12.226 501	12.718 830	13.230 876	13.763 425	192
17	13.146 625	13.710 027	14.297 449	14.909 912	15.548 478	16.214 252	204
18	15.297 726	15.992 741	16.719 179	17.478 455	18.272 045	19.101 493	216
19	17.800 798	18.655 526	19.551 106	20.489 482	21.472 690	22.502 860	228
20	20.713 433	21.761 665	22.862 711	24.019 222	25.233 979	26.509 903	240
21	24.102 644	25.384 974	26.735 242	28.157 032	29.654 119	31.230 471	252
22	28.046 411	29.611 562	31.263 709	33.007 667	34.848 518	36.791 623	264
23	32.635 472	34.541 877	36.559 217	38.693 924	40.952 800	43.343 038	276
24	37.975 413	40.293 086	42.751 688	45.359 757	48.126 345	51.061 052	288
25	44.189 095	47.001 870	49.993 053	53.173 919	56.556 454	60.153 398	300
26	51.419 484	54.827 664	58.460 974	62.334 232	66.463 232	70.864 801	312
27	59.832 937	63.956 450	68.363 207	73.072 600	78.105 343	83.483 564	324
28	69.623 030	74.605 175	79.942 701	85.660 875	91.786 758	98.349 325	336
29	81.015 017	87.026 910	93.483 551	100.417 742	107.864 694	115.862 206	348
30	94.271 004	101.516 858	109.317 978	117.716 787	126.758 941	136.493 572	360

FUTURE VALUE OF $1

MOS	16.75% ANNUAL RATE	17.00% ANNUAL RATE	17.25% ANNUAL RATE	17.50% ANNUAL RATE	17.75% ANNUAL RATE	18.00% ANNUAL RATE	MOS
1	1.013 958	1.014 167	1.014 375	1.014 583	1.014 792	1.015 000	1
2	1.028 112	1.028 534	1.028 957	1.029 379	1.029 802	1.030 225	2
3	1.042 462	1.043 105	1.043 748	1.044 391	1.045 035	1.045 678	3
4	1.057 013	1.057 882	1.058 752	1.059 622	1.060 492	1.061 364	4
5	1.071 767	1.072 869	1.073 971	1.075 075	1.076 179	1.077 284	5
6	1.086 727	1.088 068	1.089 410	1.090 753	1.092 097	1.093 443	6
7	1.101 896	1.103 482	1.105 070	1.106 660	1.108 251	1.109 845	7
8	1.117 277	1.119 115	1.120 955	1.122 798	1.124 644	1.126 493	8
9	1.132 872	1.134 969	1.137 069	1.139 173	1.141 280	1.143 390	9
10	1.148 685	1.151 048	1.153 414	1.155 785	1.158 161	1.160 541	10
11	1.164 719	1.167 354	1.169 995	1.172 641	1.175 292	1.177 949	11
12	1.180 977	1.183 892	1.186 813	1.189 742	1.192 677	1.195 618	12
13	1.197 461	1.200 664	1.203 874	1.207 092	1.210 318	1.213 552	13
14	1.214 176	1.217 673	1.221 180	1.224 696	1.228 221	1.231 756	14
15	1.231 124	1.234 923	1.238 734	1.242 556	1.246 388	1.250 232	15
16	1.248 308	1.252 418	1.256 541	1.260 676	1.264 825	1.268 986	16
17	1.265 732	1.270 161	1.274 604	1.279 061	1.283 533	1.288 020	17
18	1.283 400	1.288 155	1.292 926	1.297 714	1.302 519	1.307 341	18
19	1.301 314	1.306 403	1.311 512	1.316 639	1.321 785	1.326 951	19
20	1.319 478	1.324 911	1.330 365	1.335 840	1.341 337	1.346 855	20
21	1.337 896	1.343 680	1.349 489	1.355 321	1.361 177	1.367 058	21
22	1.356 571	1.362 716	1.368 888	1.375 086	1.381 312	1.387 564	22
23	1.375 506	1.382 021	1.388 565	1.395 140	1.401 743	1.408 377	23
24	1.394 706	1.401 600	1.408 526	1.415 485	1.422 478	1.429 503	24
25	1.414 174	1.421 456	1.428 774	1.436 128	1.443 518	1.450 945	25
26	1.433 913	1.441 593	1.449 312	1.457 071	1.464 870	1.472 710	26
27	1.453 928	1.462 015	1.470 146	1.478 320	1.486 538	1.494 800	27
28	1.474 223	1.482 727	1.491 279	1.499 879	1.508 527	1.517 222	28
29	1.494 800	1.503 733	1.512 717	1.521 752	1.530 840	1.539 981	29
30	1.515 665	1.525 036	1.534 462	1.543 945	1.553 484	1.563 080	30
31	1.536 821	1.546 640	1.556 520	1.566 460	1.576 463	1.586 526	31
32	1.558 273	1.568 551	1.578 895	1.589 305	1.599 781	1.610 324	32
33	1.580 024	1.590 772	1.601 591	1.612 482	1.623 444	1.634 479	33
34	1.602 078	1.613 308	1.624 614	1.635 997	1.647 458	1.658 996	34
35	1.624 441	1.636 163	1.647 968	1.659 856	1.671 827	1.683 881	35
36	1.647 115	1.659 342	1.671 658	1.684 062	1.696 556	1.709 140	36
37	1.670 106	1.682 850	1.695 688	1.708 621	1.721 651	1.734 777	37
38	1.693 418	1.706 690	1.720 063	1.733 539	1.747 117	1.760 798	38
39	1.717 055	1.730 868	1.744 789	1.758 819	1.772 959	1.787 210	39
40	1.741 022	1.755 389	1.769 870	1.784 469	1.799 184	1.814 018	40
41	1.765 324	1.780 257	1.795 312	1.810 492	1.825 797	1.841 229	41
42	1.789 965	1.805 477	1.821 120	1.836 895	1.852 804	1.868 847	42
43	1.814 950	1.831 055	1.847 299	1.863 683	1.880 210	1.896 880	43
44	1.840 284	1.856 994	1.873 854	1.890 862	1.908 021	1.925 333	44
45	1.865 971	1.883 302	1.900 790	1.918 437	1.936 244	1.954 213	45
46	1.892 017	1.909 982	1.928 114	1.946 414	1.964 885	1.983 526	46
47	1.918 426	1.937 040	1.955 831	1.974 800	1.993 948	2.013 279	47
YRS							**MOS**
4	1.945 204	1.964 482	1.983 946	2.003 599	2.023 442	2.043 478	48
5	2.297 241	2.325 733	2.354 573	2.383 765	2.413 312	2.443 220	60
6	2.712 988	2.745 417	2.794 439	2.836 065	2.878 301	2.921 158	72
7	3.203 975	3.259 747	3.316 478	3.374 184	3.432 883	3.492 590	84
8	3.783 820	3.859 188	3.936 041	4.014 408	4.094 319	4.175 804	96
9	4.468 603	4.568 860	4.671 346	4.776 108	4.883 198	4.992 667	108
10	5.277 316	5.409 036	5.544 016	5.682 335	5.824 076	5.969 323	120
11	6.232 386	6.403 713	6.579 712	6.760 511	6.946 240	7.137 031	132
12	7.360 303	7.581 303	7.808 891	8.043 262	8.284 618	8.533 164	144
13	8.692 346	8.975 441	9.267 696	9.569 405	9.880 870	10.202 406	156
14	10.265 457	10.625 951	10.999 026	11.385 120	11.784 683	12.198 182	168
15	12.123 265	12.579 975	13.053 792	13.545 352	14.055 315	14.584 368	180
16	14.317 293	14.893 329	15.492 416	16.115 470	16.763 446	17.437 335	192
17	16.908 388	17.632 089	18.386 607	19.173 247	19.993 370	20.848 395	204
18	19.968 411	20.874 484	21.821 471	22.811 211	23.845 625	24.926 719	216
19	23.582 227	24.713 129	25.898 015	27.139 450	28.440 120	29.802 839	228
20	27.850 060	29.257 669	30.736 111	32.288 935	33.919 866	35.632 816	240
21	32.890 270	34.637 912	36.478 029	38.415 493	40.455 431	42.603 242	252
22	38.842 640	41.007 538	43.292 614	45.704 514	48.250 247	50.937 210	264
23	45.872 251	48.548 485	51.380 255	54.376 566	57.546 941	60.901 454	276
24	54.174 056	57.476 150	60.978 776	64.694 069	68.634 892	72.814 885	288
25	63.978 295	68.045 538	72.370 430	76.969 232	81.859 231	87.058 800	300
26	75.556 871	80.558 550	85.890 197	91.573 505	97.631 591	104.089 083	312
27	89.230 900	95.372 601	101.935 637	108.948 818	116.442 916	124.450 799	324
28	105.379 608	112.910 833	120.978 582	129.620 953	138.878 743	148.795 637	336
29	124.450 855	133.674 202	143.579 004	154.215 454	165.637 430	177.902 767	348
30	146.973 553	158.255 782	170.401 487	183.476 557	197.551 891	212.703 781	360

SECTION 1

MOS	18.25% ANNUAL RATE	18.50% ANNUAL RATE	18.75% ANNUAL RATE	19.00% ANNUAL RATE	19.25% ANNUAL RATE	19.50% ANNUAL RATE	MOS
1	1.015 208	1.015 417	1.015 625	1.015 833	1.016 042	1.016 250	1
2	1.030 648	1.031 071	1.031 494	1.031 917	1.032 341	1.032 764	2
3	1.046 322	1.046 967	1.047 611	1.048 256	1.048 901	1.049 546	3
4	1.062 235	1.063 107	1.063 980	1.064 853	1.065 727	1.066 602	4
5	1.078 390	1.079 497	1.080 605	1.081 714	1.082 823	1.083 934	5
6	1.094 791	1.096 139	1.097 489	1.098 841	1.100 194	1.101 548	6
7	1.111 440	1.113 038	1.114 638	1.116 239	1.117 843	1.119 448	7
8	1.128 344	1.130 197	1.132 054	1.133 913	1.135 775	1.137 639	8
9	1.145 504	1.147 621	1.149 742	1.151 866	1.153 994	1.156 126	9
10	1.162 925	1.165 314	1.167 707	1.170 104	1.172 506	1.174 913	10
11	1.180 611	1.183 279	1.185 952	1.188 631	1.191 315	1.194 005	11
12	1.198 566	1.201 521	1.204 483	1.207 451	1.210 426	1.213 408	12
13	1.216 795	1.220 045	1.223 303	1.226 569	1.229 843	1.233 125	13
14	1.235 300	1.238 854	1.242 417	1.245 990	1.249 572	1.253 164	14
15	1.254 087	1.257 953	1.261 830	1.265 718	1.269 617	1.273 528	15
16	1.273 159	1.277 346	1.281 546	1.285 758	1.289 984	1.294 222	16
17	1.292 522	1.297 039	1.301 570	1.306 116	1.310 677	1.315 254	17
18	1.312 179	1.317 035	1.321 907	1.326 796	1.331 703	1.336 626	18
19	1.332 135	1.337 339	1.342 562	1.347 804	1.353 066	1.358 347	19
20	1.352 395	1.357 956	1.363 539	1.369 144	1.374 771	1.380 420	20
21	1.372 962	1.378 891	1.384 845	1.390 822	1.396 825	1.402 852	21
22	1.393 843	1.400 149	1.406 483	1.412 844	1.419 232	1.425 648	22
23	1.415 041	1.421 735	1.428 459	1.435 214	1.441 999	1.448 815	23
24	1.436 561	1.443 653	1.450 779	1.457 938	1.465 131	1.472 358	24
25	1.458 409	1.465 910	1.473 447	1.481 022	1.488 634	1.496 284	25
26	1.480 589	1.488 509	1.496 470	1.504 471	1.512 514	1.520 598	26
27	1.503 106	1.511 457	1.519 852	1.528 292	1.536 777	1.545 308	27
28	1.525 966	1.534 759	1.543 600	1.552 490	1.561 430	1.570 419	28
29	1.549 173	1.558 419	1.567 719	1.577 071	1.586 478	1.595 939	29
30	1.572 734	1.582 445	1.592 214	1.602 042	1.611 928	1.621 873	30
31	1.596 652	1.606 841	1.617 092	1.627 407	1.637 786	1.648 228	31
32	1.620 935	1.631 613	1.642 360	1.653 175	1.664 058	1.675 012	32
33	1.645 587	1.656 767	1.668 021	1.679 350	1.690 753	1.702 231	33
34	1.670 613	1.682 309	1.694 084	1.705 940	1.717 875	1.729 892	34
35	1.696 020	1.708 245	1.720 554	1.732 950	1.745 433	1.758 003	35
36	1.721 814	1.734 580	1.747 438	1.760 389	1.773 432	1.786 570	36
37	1.748 000	1.761 322	1.774 742	1.788 261	1.801 881	1.815 602	37
38	1.774 584	1.788 475	1.802 472	1.816 576	1.830 786	1.845 106	38
39	1.801 573	1.816 048	1.830 636	1.845 338	1.860 155	1.875 089	39
40	1.828 972	1.844 045	1.859 239	1.874 556	1.889 995	1.905 559	40
41	1.856 787	1.872 474	1.888 290	1.904 236	1.920 314	1.936 524	41
42	1.885 026	1.901 341	1.917 795	1.934 387	1.951 119	1.967 993	42
43	1.913 694	1.930 654	1.947 760	1.965 015	1.982 418	1.999 972	43
44	1.942 798	1.960 418	1.978 194	1.996 127	2.014 220	2.032 472	44
45	1.972 345	1.990 641	2.009 103	2.027 733	2.046 531	2.065 500	45
46	2.002 341	2.021 330	2.040 495	2.059 838	2.079 361	2.099 064	46
47	2.032 793	2.052 492	2.072 378	2.092 452	2.112 717	2.133 174	47

YRS							
4	2.063 708	2.084 135	2.104 759	2.125 583	2.146 609	2.167 838	48
5	2.473 492	2.504 132	2.535 146	2.566 537	2.598 311	2.630 471	60
6	2.964 644	3.008 748	3.053 540	3.098 968	3.145 063	3.191 833	72
7	3.553 322	3.615 099	3.677 936	3.741 852	3.806 865	3.872 995	84
8	4.258 893	4.343 618	4.430 010	4.518 103	4.607 929	4.699 521	96
9	5.104 566	5.218 949	5.335 871	5.455 388	5.577 556	5.702 435	108
10	6.118 161	6.270 678	6.426 965	6.587 114	6.751 219	6.919 378	120
11	7.333 022	7.534 353	7.741 168	7.953 617	8.171 850	8.396 025	132
12	8.789 113	9.052 685	9.324 104	9.603 603	9.891 420	10.187 801	144
13	10.534 335	10.876 963	11.230 722	11.595 879	11.972 831	12.361 955	156
14	12.626 100	13.068 938	13.527 212	14.001 456	14.492 225	15.000 089	168
15	15.133 219	15.702 606	16.293 293	16.906 072	17.541 765	18.201 222	180
16	18.138 168	18.867 015	19.624 991	20.413 254	21.233 007	22.085 501	192
17	21.739 798	22.669 119	23.637 964	24.648 004	25.700 982	26.798 714	204
18	26.056 590	27.237 428	28.471 520	29.761 257	31.109 135	32.517 763	216
19	31.230 553	32.726 348	34.293 455	35.935 259	37.655 304	39.457 300	228
20	37.431 890	39.321 402	41.305 876	43.390 065	45.578 956	47.877 787	240
21	44.864 605	47.245 499	49.752 216	52.391 377	55.169 950	58.095 269	252
22	53.773 207	56.766 471	59.925 687	63.260 020	66.779 138	70.493 240	264
23	64.450 757	68.206 120	72.179 458	76.383 375	80.831 200	85.537 031	276
24	77.248 510	81.951 101	86.938 913	92.229 182	97.840 181	103.791 282	288
25	92.587 467	98.465 988	104.716 423	111.362 218	118.428 292	125.941 129	300
26	110.972 224	118.308 975	126.129 127	134.464 421	143.348 675	152.817 920	312
27	133.007 576	142.150 745	151.920 360	162.359 199	173.512 953	185.430 422	324
28	159.418 407	170.797 139	182.985 456	196.040 777	210.024 578	225.002 680	336
29	191.073 542	205.216 389	220.402 829	236.709 632	254.219 195	273.019 957	348
30	229.014 322	246.571 848	265.471 410	285.815 282	307.713 505	331.284 485	360

FUTURE VALUE OF $1

MOS	19.75% ANNUAL RATE	20.00% ANNUAL RATE	21.00% ANNUAL RATE	22.00% ANNUAL RATE	23.00% ANNUAL RATE	24.00% ANNUAL RATE	MOS
1	1.016 458	1.016 667	1.017 500	1.018 333	1.019 167	1.020 000	1
2	1.033 188	1.033 611	1.035 306	1.037 003	1.038 701	1.040 400	2
3	1.050 192	1.050 838	1.053 424	1.056 014	1.058 609	1.061 208	3
4	1.067 476	1.068 352	1.071 859	1.075 375	1.078 899	1.082 432	4
5	1.085 045	1.086 158	1.090 617	1.095 090	1.099 578	1.104 081	5
6	1.102 903	1.104 260	1.109 702	1.115 167	1.120 653	1.126 162	6
7	1.121 055	1.122 665	1.129 122	1.135 611	1.142 132	1.148 686	7
8	1.139 506	1.141 376	1.148 882	1.156 431	1.164 023	1.171 659	8
9	1.158 260	1.160 399	1.168 987	1.177 632	1.186 334	1.195 093	9
10	1.177 323	1.179 739	1.189 444	1.199 222	1.209 072	1.218 994	10
11	1.196 700	1.199 401	1.210 260	1.221 208	1.232 246	1.243 374	11
12	1.216 396	1.219 391	1.231 439	1.243 597	1.255 864	1.268 242	12
13	1.236 416	1.239 714	1.252 990	1.266 396	1.279 934	1.293 607	13
14	1.256 765	1.260 376	1.274 917	1.289 613	1.304 467	1.319 479	14
15	1.277 449	1.281 382	1.297 228	1.313 256	1.329 469	1.345 868	15
16	1.298 474	1.302 739	1.319 929	1.337 332	1.354 950	1.372 786	16
17	1.319 845	1.324 451	1.343 028	1.361 850	1.380 920	1.400 241	17
18	1.341 567	1.346 525	1.366 531	1.386 817	1.407 388	1.428 246	18
19	1.363 647	1.368 967	1.390 445	1.412 242	1.434 363	1.456 811	19
20	1.386 091	1.391 784	1.414 778	1.438 133	1.461 855	1.485 947	20
21	1.408 903	1.414 980	1.439 537	1.464 499	1.489 874	1.515 666	21
22	1.432 092	1.438 563	1.464 729	1.491 348	1.518 430	1.545 980	22
23	1.455 661	1.462 539	1.490 361	1.518 690	1.547 533	1.576 899	23
24	1.479 619	1.486 915	1.516 443	1.546 532	1.577 194	1.608 437	24
25	1.503 971	1.511 697	1.542 981	1.574 886	1.607 423	1.640 606	25
26	1.528 724	1.536 891	1.569 983	1.603 758	1.638 232	1.673 418	26
27	1.553 884	1.562 506	1.597 457	1.633 161	1.669 632	1.706 886	27
28	1.579 459	1.588 548	1.625 413	1.663 102	1.701 633	1.741 024	28
29	1.605 454	1.615 024	1.653 858	1.693 592	1.734 248	1.775 845	29
30	1.631 877	1.641 941	1.682 800	1.724 641	1.767 487	1.811 362	30
31	1.658 735	1.669 307	1.712 249	1.756 260	1.801 364	1.847 589	31
32	1.686 035	1.697 128	1.742 213	1.788 458	1.835 890	1.884 541	32
33	1.713 784	1.725 414	1.772 702	1.821 246	1.871 078	1.922 231	33
34	1.741 990	1.754 171	1.803 725	1.854 636	1.906 941	1.960 676	34
35	1.770 661	1.783 407	1.835 290	1.888 637	1.943 490	1.999 890	35
36	1.799 803	1.813 130	1.867 407	1.923 262	1.980 741	2.039 887	36
37	1.829 424	1.843 349	1.900 087	1.958 522	2.018 705	2.080 685	37
38	1.859 534	1.874 072	1.933 338	1.994 429	2.057 397	2.122 299	38
39	1.890 139	1.905 306	1.967 172	2.030 993	2.096 830	2.164 745	39
40	1.921 247	1.937 061	2.001 597	2.068 228	2.137 019	2.208 040	40
41	1.952 868	1.969 346	2.036 625	2.106 145	2.177 979	2.252 200	41
42	1.985 009	2.002 168	2.072 266	2.144 758	2.219 723	2.297 244	42
43	2.017 679	2.035 538	2.108 531	2.184 079	2.262 268	2.343 189	43
44	2.050 886	2.069 463	2.145 430	2.224 120	2.305 628	2.390 053	44
45	2.084 640	2.103 954	2.182 975	2.264 896	2.349 819	2.437 854	45
46	2.118 950	2.139 020	2.221 177	2.306 419	2.394 858	2.486 611	46
47	2.153 824	2.174 671	2.260 048	2.348 703	2.440 759	2.536 344	47

YRS							
4	2.189 273	2.210 915	2.299 599	2.391 763	2.487 540	2.587 070	48
5	2.663 023	2.695 970	2.831 816	2.974 388	3.124 012	3.281 031	60
6	3.239 290	3.287 442	3.487 210	3.698 938	3.923 333	4.161 140	72
7	3.940 259	4.008 677	4.294 287	4.599 987	4.927 172	5.277 332	84
8	4.792 915	4.888 145	5.288 154	5.720 528	6.187 857	6.692 933	96
9	5.830 083	5.960 561	6.512 041	7.114 030	7.771 105	8.488 258	108
10	7.091 689	7.268 255	8.019 183	8.846 983	9.759 449	10.765 163	120
11	8.626 302	8.862 845	9.875 138	11.002 078	12.256 539	13.652 830	132
12	10.492 999	10.807 275	12.160 633	13.682 146	15.392 543	17.315 089	144
13	12.763 641	13.178 294	14.975 081	17.015 070	19.330 937	21.959 720	156
14	15.525 642	16.069 495	18.440 904	21.159 883	24.277 024	27.850 234	168
15	18.885 328	19.594 998	22.708 854	26.314 358	30.488 635	35.320 831	180
16	22.972 037	23.893 966	27.964 576	32.724 445	38.289 572	44.795 355	192
17	27.943 093	29.136 090	34.436 678	40.696 008	48.086 486	56.811 341	204
18	33.989 865	35.528 288	42.406 679	50.609 416	60.390 076	72.050 517	216
19	41.345 134	43.322 878	52.221 252	62.937 697	75.841 708	91.377 477	228
20	50.292 054	52.827 531	64.307 303	78.269 105	95.246 853	115.888 735	240
21	61.175 052	64.417 420	79.190 541	97.335 191	119.617 072	146.974 937	252
22	74.413 086	78.550 028	97.518 346	121.045 710	150.222 748	186.399 758	264
23	90.515 777	95.783 203	120.087 925	150.532 031	188.659 306	236.399 964	276
24	110.103 025	116.797 184	147.880 992	187.201 119	236.930 388	299.812 315	288
25	133.928 875	142.421 445	182.106 467	232.802 670	297.552 290	380.234 508	300
26	162.910 542	173.667 440	224.253 063	289.512 604	373.685 140	482.229 295	312
27	198.163 726	211.768 529	276.154 038	360.036 884	469.297 629	611.583 346	324
28	241.045 555	258.228 656	340.066 940	447.740 637	589.373 890	775.635 561	336
29	293.206 839	314.881 721	418.771 800	556.808 724	740.173 316	983.693 435	348
30	356.655 615	383.963 963	515.692 058	692.445 423	929.556 851	1247.561 128	360

QTRS	6.50% ANNUAL RATE	7.00% ANNUAL RATE	7.50% ANNUAL RATE	8.00% ANNUAL RATE	8.50% ANNUAL RATE	9.00% ANNUAL RATE	QTRS
1	1.016 250	1.017 500	1.018 750	1.020 000	1.021 250	1.022 500	1
2	1.032 764	1.035 306	1.037 852	1.040 400	1.042 952	1.045 506	2
3	1.049 546	1.053 424	1.057 311	1.061 208	1.065 114	1.069 030	3
4	1.066 602	1.071 859	1.077 136	1.082 432	1.087 748	1.093 083	4
5	1.083 934	1.090 617	1.097 332	1.104 081	1.110 863	1.117 678	5
6	1.101 548	1.109 702	1.117 907	1.126 162	1.134 468	1.142 825	6
7	1.119 448	1.129 122	1.138 868	1.148 686	1.158 576	1.168 539	7
8	1 137 639	1.148 882	1.160 222	1.171 659	1.183 196	1.194 831	8
9	1.156 126	1.168 987	1.181 976	1.195 093	1.208 339	1.221 715	9
10	1.174 913	1.189 444	1.204 138	1.218 994	1.234 016	1.249 203	10
11	1.194 005	1.210 260	1.226 715	1.243 374	1.260 239	1.277 311	11
12	1.213 408	1.231 439	1.249 716	1.268 242	1.287 019	1.306 050	12
13	1.233 125	1.252 990	1.273 149	1.293 607	1.314 368	1.335 436	13
14	1.253 164	1.274 917	1.297 020	1.319 479	1.342 298	1.365 483	14
15	1.273 528	1.297 228	1.321 339	1.345 868	1.370 822	1.396 207	15
16	1.294 222	1.319 929	1.346 114	1.372 786	1.399 952	1.427 621	16
17	1.315 254	1.343 028	1.371 354	1.400 241	1.429 701	1.459 743	17
18	1.336 626	1.366 531	1.397 067	1.428 246	1.460 082	1.492 587	18
19	1.358 347	1.390 445	1.423 262	1.456 811	1.491 109	1.526 170	19
20	1.380 420	1.414 778	1.449 948	1.485 947	1.522 795	1.560 509	20
21	1.402 852	1.439 537	1.477 135	1.515 666	1.555 154	1.595 621	21
22	1.425 648	1.464 729	1.504 831	1.545 980	1.588 201	1.631 522	22
23	1.448 815	1.490 361	1.533 046	1.576 899	1.621 951	1.668 231	23
24	1.472 358	1.516 443	1.561 791	1.608 437	1.656 417	1.705 767	24
25	1.496 284	1.542 981	1.591 075	1.640 606	1.691 616	1.744 146	25
26	1.520 598	1.569 983	1.620 907	1.673 418	1.727 563	1.783 390	26
27	1.545 308	1.597 457	1.651 299	1.706 886	1.764 273	1.823 516	27
28	1.570 419	1.625 413	1.682 261	1.741 024	1.801 764	1.864 545	28
29	1.595 939	1.653 858	1.713 804	1.775 845	1.840 052	1.906 497	29
30	1.621 873	1.682 800	1.745 937	1.811 362	1.879 153	1.949 393	30
31	1.648 228	1.712 249	1.778 674	1.847 589	1.919 085	1.993 255	31
32	1.675 012	1.742 213	1.812 024	1.884 541	1.959 865	2.038 103	32
33	1.702 231	1.772 702	1.845 999	1.922 231	2.001 512	2.083 960	33
34	1.729 892	1.803 725	1.880 612	1.960 676	2.044 045	2.130 849	34
35	1.758 003	1.835 290	1.915 873	1.999 890	2.087 481	2.178 794	35
36	1.786 570	1.867 407	1.951 796	2.039 887	2.131 839	2.227 816	36
37	1.815 602	1.900 087	1.988 392	2.080 685	2.177 141	2.277 942	37
38	1.845 106	1.933 338	2.025 674	2.122 299	2.223 405	2.329 196	38
39	1.875 089	1.967 172	2.063 656	2.164 745	2.270 653	2.381 603	39
40	1.905 559	2.001 597	2.102 349	2.208 040	2.318 904	2.435 189	40
41	1.936 524	2.036 625	2.141 768	2.252 200	2.368 181	2.489 981	41
42	1.967 993	2.072 266	2.181 926	2.297 244	2.418 505	2.546 005	42
43	1.999 972	2.108 531	2.222 838	2.343 189	2.469 898	2.603 290	43
44	2.032 472	2.145 430	2.264 516	2.390 053	2.522 383	2.661 864	44
45	2.065 500	2.182 975	2.306 975	2.437 854	2.575 984	2.721 756	45
46	2.099 064	2.221 177	2.350 231	2.486 611	2.630 723	2.782 996	46
47	2.133 174	2.260 048	2.394 298	2.536 344	2.686 626	2.845 613	47
48	2.167 838	2.299 599	2.439 191	2.587 070	2.743 717	2.909 640	48
49	2.203 065	2.339 842	2.484 926	2.638 812	2.802 021	2.975 107	49
50	2.238 865	2.380 789	2.531 518	2.691 588	2.861 564	3.042 046	50
51	2.275 247	2.422 453	2.578 984	2.745 420	2.922 372	3.110 492	51
52	2.312 219	2.464 846	2.627 340	2.800 328	2.984 473	3.180 479	52
53	2.349 793	2.507 980	2.676 603	2.856 335	3.047 893	3.252 039	53
54	2.387 977	2.551 870	2.726 789	2.913 461	3.112 661	3.325 210	54
55	2.426 782	2.596 528	2.777 917	2.971 731	3.178 805	3.400 027	55

YRS							
14	2.466 217	2.641 967	2.830 002	3.031 165	3.246 354	3.476 528	56
15	2.630 471	2.831 816	3.048 297	3.281 031	3.531 215	3.800 135	60
16	2.805 665	3.035 308	3.283 430	3.551 493	3.841 072	4.153 864	64
17	2.992 526	3.253 422	3.536 700	3.844 251	4.178 118	4.540 519	68
18	3.191 833	3.487 210	3.809 507	4.161 140	4.544 740	4.963 166	72
19	3.404 415	3.737 797	4.103 357	4.504 152	4.943 531	5.425 154	76
20	3.631 154	4.006 392	4.419 872	4.875 439	5.377 316	5.930 145	80
21	3.872 995	4.294 287	4.760 803	5.277 332	5.849 165	6.482 143	84
22	4.130 943	4.602 871	5.128 032	5.712 354	6.362 417	7.085 522	88
23	4.406 070	4.933 629	5.523 587	6.183 236	6.920 706	7.745 066	92
24	4.699 521	5.288 154	5.949 654	6.692 933	7.527 984	8.466 003	96
25	5.012 517	5.668 156	6.408 585	7.244 646	8.188 549	9.254 046	100
26	5.346 359	6.075 464	6.902 917	7.841 838	8.907 078	10.115 444	104
27	5.702 435	6.512 041	7.435 380	8.488 258	9.688 655	11.057 023	108
28	6.082 226	6.979 990	8.008 914	9.187 963	10.538 815	12.086 247	112
29	6.487 312	7.481 565	8.626 689	9.945 347	11.463 575	13.211 275	116
30	6.919 378	8.019 183	9.292 116	10.765 163	12.469 480	14.441 024	120

FUTURE VALUE OF $1

QTRS	9.50% ANNUAL RATE	10.00% ANNUAL RATE	10.50% ANNUAL RATE	11.00% ANNUAL RATE	11.50% ANNUAL RATE	12.00% ANNUAL RATE	QTRS
1	1.023 750	1.025 000	1.026 250	1.027 500	1.028 750	1.030 000	1
2	1.048 064	1.050 625	1.053 189	1.055 756	1.058 327	1.060 900	2
3	1.072 956	1.076 891	1.080 835	1.084 790	1.088 753	1.092 727	3
4	1.098 438	1.103 813	1.109 207	1.114 621	1.120 055	1.125 509	4
5	1.124 526	1.131 408	1.138 324	1.145 273	1.152 257	1.159 274	5
6	1.151 234	1.159 693	1.168 205	1.176 768	1.185 384	1.194 052	6
7	1.178 575	1.188 686	1.198 870	1.209 129	1.219 464	1.229 874	7
8	1.206 567	1.218 403	1.230 341	1.242 381	1.254 523	1.266 770	8
9	1.235 223	1.248 863	1.262 637	1.276 546	1.290 591	1.304 773	9
10	1.264 559	1.280 085	1.295 781	1.311 651	1.327 695	1.343 916	10
11	1.294 592	1.312 087	1.329 796	1.347 721	1.365 867	1.384 234	11
12	1.325 339	1.344 889	1.364 703	1.384 784	1.405 135	1.425 761	12
13	1.356 816	1.378 511	1.400 526	1.422 865	1.445 533	1.468 534	13
14	1.389 040	1.412 974	1.437 290	1.461 994	1.487 092	1.512 590	14
15	1.422 030	1.448 298	1.475 019	1.502 199	1.529 846	1.557 967	15
16	1.455 803	1.484 506	1.513 738	1.543 509	1.573 829	1.604 706	16
17	1.490 378	1.521 618	1.553 474	1.585 956	1.619 077	1.652 848	17
18	1.525 775	1.559 659	1.594 252	1.629 570	1.665 625	1.702 433	18
19	1.562 012	1.598 650	1.636 101	1.674 383	1.713 512	1.753 506	19
20	1.599 110	1.638 616	1.679 049	1.720 428	1.762 775	1.806 111	20
21	1.637 089	1.679 582	1.723 124	1.767 740	1.813 455	1.860 295	21
22	1.675 970	1.721 571	1.768 356	1.816 353	1.865 592	1.916 103	22
23	1.715 774	1.764 611	1.814 776	1.866 303	1.919 228	1.973 587	23
24	1.756 523	1.808 726	1.862 413	1.917 626	1.974 406	2.032 794	24
25	1.798 241	1.853 944	1.911 302	1.970 361	2.031 170	2.093 778	25
26	1.840 949	1.900 293	1.961 473	2.024 546	2.089 566	2.156 591	26
27	1.884 672	1.947 800	2.012 962	2.080 221	2.149 641	2.221 289	27
28	1.929 433	1.996 495	2.065 802	2.137 427	2.211 443	2.287 928	28
29	1.975 257	2.046 407	2.120 030	2.196 206	2.275 022	2.356 566	29
30	2.022 169	2.097 568	2.175 680	2.256 602	2.340 429	2.427 262	30
31	2.070 195	2.150 007	2.232 792	2.318 658	2.407 716	2.500 080	31
32	2.119 363	2.203 757	2.291 403	2.382 421	2.476 938	2.575 083	32
33	2.169 697	2.258 851	2.351 552	2.447 938	2.548 150	2.652 335	33
34	2.221 228	2.315 322	2.413 280	2.515 256	2.621 409	2.731 905	34
35	2.273 982	2.373 205	2.476 629	2.584 426	2.696 775	2.813 862	35
36	2.327 989	2.432 535	2.541 641	2.655 498	2.774 307	2.898 278	36
37	2.383 279	2.493 349	2.608 359	2.728 524	2.854 068	2.985 227	37
38	2.439 882	2.555 682	2.676 828	2.803 558	2.936 123	3.074 783	38
39	2.497 829	2.619 574	2.747 095	2.880 656	3.020 536	3.167 027	39
40	2.557 152	2.685 064	2.819 206	2.959 874	3.107 377	3.262 038	40
41	2.617 885	2.752 190	2.893 210	3.041 271	3.196 714	3.359 899	41
42	2.680 059	2.820 995	2.969 157	3.124 905	3.288 619	3.460 696	42
43	2.743 711	2.891 520	3.047 097	3.210 840	3.383 167	3.564 517	43
44	2.808 874	2.963 808	3.127 084	3.299 138	3.480 433	3.671 452	44
45	2.875 585	3.037 903	3.209 169	3.389 865	3.580 496	3.781 596	45
46	2.943 880	3.113 851	3.293 410	3.483 086	3.683 435	3.895 044	46
47	3.013 797	3.191 697	3.379 862	3.578 871	3.789 334	4.011 895	47
48	3.085 375	3.271 490	3.468 584	3.677 290	3.898 277	4.132 252	48
49	3.158 652	3.353 277	3.559 634	3.778 415	4.010 353	4.256 219	49
50	3.233 670	3.437 109	3.653 074	3.882 322	4.125 650	4.383 906	50
51	3.310 470	3.523 036	3.748 968	3.989 086	4.244 263	4.515 423	51
52	3.389 094	3.611 112	3.847 378	4.098 785	4.366 285	4.650 886	52
53	3.469 585	3.701 390	3.948 372	4.211 502	4.491 816	4.790 412	53
54	3.551 987	3.793 925	4.052 016	4.327 318	4.620 956	4.934 125	54
55	3.636 347	3.888 773	4.158 382	4.446 320	4.753 808	5.082 149	55

YRS							QTRS
14	3.722 710	3.985 992	4.267 539	4.568 593	4.890 480	5.234 613	56
15	4.089 167	4.399 790	4.733 585	5.092 251	5.477 607	5.891 603	60
16	4.491 698	4.856 545	5.250 527	5.675 932	6.135 222	6.631 051	64
17	4.933 853	5.360 717	5.823 922	6.326 514	6.871 787	7.463 307	68
18	5.419 533	5.917 228	6.459 937	7.051 667	7.696 780	8.400 017	72
19	5.953 022	6.531 513	7.165 408	7.859 938	8.620 818	9.454 293	76
20	6.539 028	7.209 568	7.947 922	8.760 854	9.655 791	10.640 891	80
21	7.182 718	7.958 014	8.815 893	9.765 034	10.815 018	11.976 416	84
22	7.889 773	8.784 158	9.778 652	10.884 315	12.113 416	13.479 562	88
23	8.666 429	9.696 067	10.846 551	12.131 889	13.567 694	15.171 366	92
24	9.519 537	10.702 644	12.031 072	13.522 461	15.196 565	17.075 506	96
25	10.456 624	11.813 716	13.344 952	15.072 422	17.020 990	19.218 632	100
26	11.485 956	13.040 132	14.802 317	16.800 042	19.064 447	21.630 740	104
27	12.616 613	14.393 866	16.418 836	18.725 684	21.353 231	24.345 588	108
28	13.858 571	15.888 135	18.211 892	20.872 046	23.916 796	27.401 174	112
29	15.222 785	17.537 528	20.200 761	23.264 426	26.788 130	30.840 262	116
30	16.721 290	19.358 150	22.406 830	25.931 024	30.004 182	34.710 987	120

QTRS	12.50% ANNUAL RATE	13.00% ANNUAL RATE	13.50% ANNUAL RATE	14.00% ANNUAL RATE	14.50% ANNUAL RATE	15.00% ANNUAL RATE	QTRS
1	1.031 250	1.032 500	1.033 750	1.035 000	1.036 250	1.037 500	1
2	1.063 477	1.066 056	1.068 639	1.071 225	1.073 814	1.076 406	2
3	1.096 710	1.100 703	1.104 706	1.108 718	1.112 740	1.116 771	3
4	1.130 982	1.136 476	1.141 989	1.147 523	1.153 077	1.158 650	4
5	1.166 326	1.173 411	1.180 532	1.187 686	1.194 876	1.202 100	5
6	1.202 773	1.211 547	1.220 375	1.229 255	1.238 190	1.247 179	6
7	1.240 360	1.250 923	1.261 562	1.272 279	1.283 074	1.293 948	7
8	1.279 121	1.291 578	1.304 140	1.316 809	1.329 586	1.342 471	8
9	1.319 094	1.333 554	1.348 155	1.362 897	1.377 783	1.392 813	9
10	1.360 315	1.376 894	1.393 655	1.410 599	1.427 728	1.445 044	10
11	1.402 825	1.421 643	1.440 691	1.459 970	1.479 483	1.499 233	11
12	1.446 664	1.467 847	1.489 314	1.511 069	1.533 114	1.555 454	12
13	1.491 872	1.515 552	1.539 578	1.563 956	1.588 690	1.613 784	13
14	1.538 493	1.564 807	1.591 539	1.618 695	1.646 280	1.674 301	14
15	1.586 571	1.615 663	1.645 254	1.675 349	1.705 957	1.737 087	15
16	1.636 151	1.668 173	1.700 781	1.733 986	1.767 798	1.802 228	16
17	1.687 281	1.722 388	1.758 182	1.794 676	1.831 881	1.869 811	17
18	1.740 008	1.778 366	1.817 521	1.857 489	1.898 287	1.939 929	18
19	1.794 384	1.836 163	1.878 862	1.922 501	1.967 099	2.012 677	19
20	1.850 458	1.895 838	1.942 274	1.989 789	2.038 407	2.088 152	20
21	1.908 285	1.957 453	2.007 826	2.059 431	2.112 299	2.166 458	21
22	1.967 919	2.021 070	2.075 590	2.131 512	2.188 870	2.247 700	22
23	2.029 416	2.086 755	2.145 641	2.206 114	2.268 216	2.331 989	23
24	2.092 835	2.154 574	2.218 056	2.283 328	2.350 439	2.419 438	24
25	2.158 237	2.224 598	2.292 916	2.363 245	2.435 643	2.510 167	25
26	2.225 681	2.296 897	2.370 301	2.445 959	2.523 935	2.604 298	26
27	2.295 234	2.371 546	2.450 299	2.531 567	2.615 427	2.701 960	27
28	2.366 960	2.448 622	2.532 997	2.620 172	2.710 237	2.803 283	28
29	2.440 928	2.528 202	2.618 485	2.711 878	2.808 483	2.908 406	29
30	2.517 207	2.610 368	2.706 859	2.806 794	2.910 290	3.017 471	30
31	2.595 869	2.695 205	2.798 216	2.905 031	3.015 788	3.130 627	31
32	2.676 990	2.782 800	2.892 656	3.006 708	3.125 111	3.248 025	32
33	2.760 646	2.873 241	2.990 283	3.111 942	3.238 396	3.369 826	33
34	2.846 916	2.966 621	3.091 205	3.220 860	3.355 788	3.496 194	34
35	2.935 882	3.063 036	3.195 533	3.333 590	3.477 435	3.627 302	35
36	3.027 629	3.162 585	3.303 382	3.450 266	3.603 492	3.763 326	36
37	3.122 242	3.265 369	3.414 871	3.571 025	3.734 119	3.904 651	37
38	3.219 812	3.371 493	3.530 123	3.696 011	3.869 480	4.050 867	38
39	3.320 431	3.481 067	3.649 265	3.825 372	4.009 749	4.202 775	39
40	3.424 195	3.594 201	3.772 428	3.959 260	4.155 103	4.360 379	40
41	3.531 201	3.711 013	3.899 747	4.097 834	4.305 725	4.523 893	41
42	3.641 551	3.831 621	4.031 363	4.241 258	4.461 808	4.693 539	42
43	3.755 349	3.956 149	4.167 422	4.389 702	4.623 548	4.869 547	43
44	3.872 704	4.084 723	4.308 072	4.543 342	4.791 152	5.052 155	44
45	3.993 726	4.217 477	4.453 470	4.702 359	4.964 831	5.241 610	45
46	4.118 530	4.354 545	4.603 774	4.866 941	5.144 806	5.438 171	46
47	4.247 234	4.496 068	4.759 152	5.037 284	5.331 305	5.642 102	47
48	4.379 960	4.642 190	4.919 773	5.213 589	5.524 565	5.853 681	48
49	4.516 834	4.793 061	5.085 816	5.396 065	5.724 831	6.073 194	49
50	4.657 985	4.948 835	5.257 462	5.584 927	5.932 356	6.300 939	50
51	4.803 547	5.109 673	5.434 901	5.780 399	6.147 404	6.537 224	51
52	4.953 658	5.275 737	5.618 329	5.982 713	6.370 247	6.782 370	52
53	5.108 460	5.447 198	5.807 948	6.192 108	6.601 168	7.036 709	53
54	5.268 099	5.624 232	6.003 966	6.408 832	6.840 461	7.300 585	54
55	5.432 727	5.807 020	6.206 600	6.633 141	7.088 427	7.574 357	55
YRS							
14	5.602 500	5.995 748	6.416 073	6.865 301	7.345 383	7.858 396	56
15	6.336 329	6.814 023	7.327 087	7.878 091	8.469 789	9.105 134	60
16	7.166 276	7.743 974	8.367 456	9.040 291	9.766 316	10.549 667	64
17	8.104 932	8.800 840	9.555 547	10.373 941	11.261 311	12.223 376	68
18	9.166 536	10.001 942	10.912 333	11.904 336	12.985 155	14.162 620	72
19	10.367 190	11.366 967	12.461 770	13.660 500	14.972 879	16.409 525	76
20	11.725 110	12.918 284	14.231 209	15.675 738	17.264 877	19.012 903	80
21	13.260 893	14.681 319	16.251 891	17.988 269	19.907 726	22.029 308	84
22	14.997 837	16.684 965	18.559 488	20.641 953	22.955 134	25.524 267	88
23	16.962 269	18.962 061	21.194 739	23.687 116	26.469 029	29.573 702	92
24	19.184 051	21.549 926	24.204 168	27.181 510	30.520 819	34.265 582	96
25	21.696 823	24.490 973	27.640 905	31.191 408	35.192 843	39.701 831	100
26	24.538 725	27.833 401	31.565 622	35.792 858	40.580 046	46.000 543	104
27	27.752 867	31.631 990	36.047 607	41.073 128	46.791 903	53.298 548	108
28	31.388 004	35.948 995	41.165 986	47.132 359	53.954 650	61.754 385	112
29	35.499 280	40.855 168	47.011 122	54.085 466	62.213 846	71.551 744	116
30	40.149 060	46.430 915	53.686 205	62.064 316	71.737 333	82.903 458	120

FUTURE VALUE OF $1

QTRS	15.50% ANNUAL RATE	16.00% ANNUAL RATE	16.50% ANNUAL RATE	17.00% ANNUAL RATE	17.50% ANNUAL RATE	18.00% ANNUAL RATE	QTRS
1	1.038 750	1.040 000	1.041 250	1.042 500	1.043 750	1.045 000	1
2	1.079 002	1.081 600	1.084 202	1.086 806	1.089 414	1.092 025	2
3	1.120 813	1.124 864	1.128 925	1.132 996	1.137 076	1.141 166	3
4	1.164 244	1.169 859	1.175 493	1.181 148	1.186 823	1.192 519	4
5	1.209 359	1.216 653	1.223 982	1.231 347	1.238 747	1.246 182	5
6	1.256 221	1.265 319	1.274 471	1.283 679	1.292 942	1.302 260	6
7	1.304 900	1.315 932	1.327 043	1.338 235	1.349 508	1.360 862	7
8	1.355 465	1.368 569	1.381 784	1.395 110	1.408 549	1.422 101	8
9	1.407 989	1.423 312	1.438 782	1.454 402	1.470 173	1.486 095	9
10	1.462 549	1.480 244	1.498 132	1.516 214	1.534 493	1.552 969	10
11	1.519 223	1.539 454	1.559 930	1.580 654	1.601 627	1.622 853	11
12	1.578 092	1.601 032	1.624 277	1.647 831	1.671 698	1.695 881	12
13	1.639 244	1.665 074	1.691 279	1.717 864	1.744 835	1.772 196	13
14	1.702 764	1.731 676	1.761 044	1.790 873	1.821 171	1.851 945	14
15	1.768 746	1.800 944	1.833 687	1.866 986	1.900 848	1.935 282	15
16	1.837 285	1.872 981	1.909 327	1.946 332	1.984 010	2.022 370	16
17	1.908 480	1.947 900	1.988 086	2.029 052	2.070 810	2.113 377	17
18	1.982 434	2.025 817	2.070 095	2.115 286	2.161 408	2.208 479	18
19	2.059 253	2.106 849	2.155 486	2.205 186	2.255 970	2.307 860	19
20	2.139 049	2.191 123	2.244 400	2.298 906	2.354 668	2.411 714	20
21	2.221 937	2.278 768	2.336 982	2.396 610	2.457 685	2.520 241	21
22	2.308 037	2.369 919	2.433 382	2.498 466	2.565 209	2.633 652	22
23	2.397 474	2.464 716	2.533 759	2.604 651	2.677 437	2.752 166	23
24	2.490 376	2.563 304	2.638 277	2.715 348	2.794 575	2.876 014	24
25	2.586 878	2.665 836	2.747 106	2.830 750	2.916 837	3.005 434	25
26	2.687 119	2.772 470	2.860 424	2.951 057	3.044 449	3.140 679	26
27	2.791 245	2.883 369	2.978 416	3.076 477	3.177 644	3.282 010	27
28	2.899 406	2.998 703	3.101 276	3.207 228	3.316 666	3.429 700	28
29	3.011 758	3.118 651	3.229 204	3.343 535	3.461 770	3.584 036	29
30	3.128 464	3.243 398	3.362 408	3.485 635	3.613 222	3.745 318	30
31	3.249 692	3.373 133	3.501 108	3.633 775	3.771 301	3.913 857	31
32	3.375 617	3.508 059	3.645 528	3.788 210	3.936 295	4.089 981	32
33	3.506 422	3.648 381	3.795 906	3.949 209	4.108 508	4.274 030	33
34	3.642 296	3.794 316	3.952 487	4.117 050	4.288 255	4.466 362	34
35	3.783 435	3.946 089	4.115 527	4.292 025	4.475 866	4.667 348	35
36	3.930 043	4.103 933	4.285 293	4.474 436	4.671 685	4.877 378	36
37	4.082 332	4.268 090	4.462 061	4.664 599	4.876 072	5.096 860	37
38	4.240 523	4.438 813	4.646 121	4.862 845	5.089 400	5.326 219	38
39	4.404 843	4.616 366	4.837 774	5.069 516	5.312 061	5.565 899	39
40	4.575 531	4.801 021	5.037 332	5.284 970	5.544 464	5.816 365	40
41	4.752 832	4.993 061	5.245 122	5.509 581	5.787 034	6.078 101	41
42	4.937 005	5.192 784	5.461 483	5.743 739	6.040 217	6.351 615	42
43	5.128 314	5.400 495	5.686 769	5.987 848	6.304 476	6.637 438	43
44	5.327 036	5.616 515	5.921 349	6.242 331	6.580 297	6.936 123	44
45	5.533 458	5.841 176	6.165 604	6.507 630	6.868 185	7.248 248	45
46	5.747 880	6.074 823	6.419 935	6.784 204	7.168 668	7.574 420	46
47	5.970 610	6.317 816	6.684 758	7.072 533	7.482 297	7.915 268	47
48	6.201 971	6.570 528	6.960 504	7.373 116	7.809 648	8.271 456	48
49	6.442 298	6.833 349	7.247 625	7.686 473	8.151 320	8.643 671	49
50	6.691 937	7.106 683	7.546 589	8.013 148	8.507 940	9.032 636	50
51	6.951 249	7.390 951	7.857 886	8.353 707	8.880 162	9.439 105	51
52	7.220 610	7.686 589	8.182 024	8.708 740	9.268 670	9.863 865	52
53	7.500 409	7.994 052	8.519 533	9.078 861	9.674 174	10.307 739	53
54	7.791 050	8.313 814	8.870 963	9.464 713	10.097 419	10.771 587	54
55	8.092 953	8.646 367	9.236 890	9.866 963	10.539 181	11.256 308	55

YRS							
14	8.406 555	8.992 222	9.617 912	10.286 309	11.000 270	11.762 842	56
15	9.787 284	10.519 627	11.305 789	12.149 651	13.055 374	14.027 408	60
16	11.394 791	12.306 476	13.289 876	14.350 534	15.494 418	16.727 945	64
17	13.266 321	14.396 836	15.622 156	16.950 102	18.389 131	19.948 385	68
18	15.445 240	16.842 262	18.363 736	20.020 577	21.824 644	23.788 821	72
19	17.982 033	19.703 065	21.586 444	23.647 261	25.901 990	28.368 611	76
20	20.935 481	23.049 799	25.374 714	27.930 910	30.741 077	33.830 096	80
21	24.374 016	26.965 005	29.827 799	32.990 534	36.484 217	40.343 019	84
22	28.377 311	31.545 242	35.062 370	38.966 698	43.300 308	48.109 801	88
23	33.038 124	36.903 471	41.215 571	46.025 430	51.389 802	57.371 832	92
24	38.464 450	43.171 841	48.448 617	54.362 837	60.990 599	68.416 977	96
25	44.782 020	50.504 948	56.951 011	64.210 546	72.385 045	81.588 518	100
26	52.137 215	59.083 646	66.945 517	75.842 147	85.908 236	97.295 825	104
27	60.700 459	69.119 509	78.693 988	89.580 787	101.957 871	116.027 081	108
28	70.670 168	80.860 049	92.504 235	105.808 152	121.005 946	138.364 453	112
29	82.277 345	94.594 821	108.738 083	124.975 068	143.612 640	165.002 184	116
30	95.790 936	110.662 561	127.820 858	147.614 030	170.442 784	196.768 173	120

SECTION 1

QTRS	18.50% ANNUAL RATE	19.00% ANNUAL RATE	19.50% ANNUAL RATE	20.00% ANNUAL RATE	20.50% ANNUAL RATE	21.00% ANNUAL RATE	QTRS
1	1.046 250	1.047 500	1.048 750	1.050 000	1.051 250	1.052 500	1
2	1.094 639	1.097 256	1.099 877	1.102 500	1.105 127	1.107 756	2
3	1.145 266	1.149 376	1.153 496	1.157 625	1.161 764	1.165 913	3
4	1.198 235	1.203 971	1.209 728	1.215 506	1.221 305	1.227 124	4
5	1.253 653	1.261 160	1.268 703	1.276 282	1.283 897	1.291 548	5
6	1.311 634	1.321 065	1.330 552	1.340 096	1.349 696	1.359 354	6
7	1.372 298	1.383 816	1.395 416	1.407 100	1.418 868	1.430 720	7
8	1.435 766	1.449 547	1.463 443	1.477 455	1.491 585	1.505 833	8
9	1.502 171	1.518 400	1.534 786	1.551 328	1.568 029	1.584 889	9
10	1.571 646	1.590 524	1.609 607	1.628 895	1.648 390	1.668 096	10
11	1.644 335	1.666 074	1.688 075	1.710 339	1.732 870	1.755 671	11
12	1.720 385	1.745 213	1.770 369	1.795 856	1.821 680	1.847 844	12
13	1.799 953	1.828 110	1.856 674	1.885 649	1.915 041	1.944 856	13
14	1.883 201	1.914 946	1.947 187	1.979 932	2.013 187	2.046 961	14
15	1.970 299	2.005 906	2.042 112	2.078 928	2.116 363	2.154 426	15
16	2.061 425	2.101 186	2.141 665	2.182 875	2.224 826	2.267 533	16
17	2.156 766	2.200 992	2.246 071	2.292 018	2.338 849	2.386 579	17
18	2.256 516	2.305 540	2.355 567	2.406 619	2.458 715	2.511 874	18
19	2.360 880	2.415 053	2.470 401	2.526 950	2.584 724	2.643 748	19
20	2.470 071	2.529 768	2.590 833	2.653 298	2.717 191	2.782 544	20
21	2.584 312	2.649 932	2.717 136	2.785 963	2.856 447	2.928 628	21
22	2.703 836	2.775 803	2.849 597	2.925 261	3.002 840	3.082 381	22
23	2.828 889	2.907 654	2.988 515	3.071 524	3.156 736	3.244 206	23
24	2.959 725	3.045 768	3.134 205	3.225 100	3.318 518	3.414 527	24
25	3.096 612	3.190 442	3.286 997	3.386 355	3.488 592	3.593 789	25
26	3.239 830	3.341 988	3.447 238	3.555 673	3.667 383	3.782 463	26
27	3.389 672	3.500 732	3.615 291	3.733 456	3.855 336	3.981 043	27
28	3.546 445	3.667 017	3.791 537	3.920 129	4.052 922	4.190 047	28
29	3.710 468	3.841 200	3.976 374	4.116 136	4.260 634	4.410 025	29
30	3.882 077	4.023 657	4.170 222	4.321 942	4.478 992	4.641 551	30
31	4.061 623	4.214 781	4.373 521	4.538 039	4.708 540	4.885 233	31
32	4.249 473	4.414 983	4.586 730	4.764 941	4.949 853	5.141 707	32
33	4.446 011	4.624 694	4.810 333	5.003 189	5.203 533	5.411 647	33
34	4.651 639	4.844 367	5.044 837	5.253 348	5.470 214	5.695 758	34
35	4.866 777	5.074 475	5.290 772	5.516 015	5.750 562	5.994 786	35
36	5.091 866	5.315 512	5.548 698	5.791 816	6.045 279	6.309 512	36
37	5.327 365	5.567 999	5.819 197	6.081 407	6.355 099	6.640 761	37
38	5.573 755	5.832 479	6.102 882	6.385 477	6.680 798	6.989 401	38
39	5.831 541	6.109 522	6.400 398	6.704 751	7.023 189	7.356 345	39
40	6.101 250	6.399 724	6.712 417	7.039 989	7.383 127	7.742 553	40
41	6.383 433	6.703 711	7.039 648	7.391 988	7.761 512	8.149 037	41
42	6.678 667	7.022 137	7.382 831	7.761 588	8.159 290	8.576 861	42
43	6.987 555	7.355 689	7.742 744	8.149 667	8.577 454	9.027 147	43
44	7.310 730	7.705 084	8.120 202	8.557 150	9.017 048	9.501 072	44
45	7.648 851	8.071 076	8.516 062	8.985 008	9.479 172	9.999 878	45
46	8.002 610	8.454 452	8.931 220	9.434 258	9.964 979	10.524 872	46
47	8.372 731	8.856 038	9.366 617	9.905 971	10.475 685	11.077 427	47
48	8.759 970	9.276 700	9.823 240	10.401 270	11.012 563	11.658 992	48
49	9.165 118	9.717 343	10.302 123	10.921 333	11.576 957	12.271 089	49
50	9.589 005	10.178 917	10.804 351	11.467 400	12.170 276	12.915 322	50
51	10.032 497	10.662 416	11.331 063	12.040 770	12.794 003	13.593 376	51
52	10.496 500	11.168 881	11.883 453	12.642 808	13.449 696	14.307 028	52
53	10.981 963	11.699 402	12.462 771	13.274 949	14.138 993	15.058 147	53
54	11.489 878	12.255 124	13.070 331	13.938 696	14.863 616	15.848 700	54
55	12.021 285	12.837 242	13.707 510	14.635 631	15.625 376	16.680 757	55

YRS							
14	12.577 270	13.447 011	14.375 751	15.367 412	16.426 177	17.556 496	56
15	15.070 521	16.189 815	17.390 755	18.679 186	20.061 367	21.543 997	60
16	18.058 021	19.492 073	21.038 091	22.704 667	24.501 042	26.437 153	64
17	21.637 746	23.467 896	25.450 377	27.597 665	29.923 239	32.441 663	68
18	25.927 098	28.254 673	30.788 045	33.545 134	36.545 393	39.809 940	72
19	31.066 748	34.017 814	37.245 174	40.774 320	44.633 061	48.851 729	76
20	37.225 255	40.956 471	45.056 547	49.561 441	54.510 568	59.947 125	80
21	44.604 591	49.310 415	54.506 187	60.242 241	66.574 013	73.562 551	84
22	53.446 768	59.368 323	65.937 685	73.224 821	81.307 157	90.270 365	88
23	64.041 771	71.477 756	79.766 694	89.005 227	99.300 814	110.772 923	92
24	76.737 071	86.057 165	96.496 039	108.186 410	121.276 553	135.932 102	96
25	91.949 019	103.610 356	116.734 004	131.501 258	148.115 627	166.805 532	100
26	110.176 503	124.743 892	141.216 447	159.840 601	180.894 314	204.691 057	104
27	132.017 307	150.188 063	170.833 553	194.287 249	220.927 079	251.181 290	108
28	158.187 715	180.822 114	206.662 210	236.157 366	269.819 284	308.230 567	112
29	189.546 005	217.704 632	250.005 156	287.050 754	329.531 565	378.237 098	116
30	227.120 597	262.110 124	302.438 350	348.911 986	402.458 456	464.143 787	120

FUTURE VALUE OF $1

QTRS	21.50% ANNUAL RATE	22.00% ANNUAL RATE	22.50% ANNUAL RATE	23.00% ANNUAL RATE	23.50% ANNUAL RATE	24.00% ANNUAL RATE	QTRS
1	1.053 750	1.055 000	1.056 250	1.057 500	1.058 750	1.060 000	1
2	1.110 389	1.113 025	1.115 664	1.118 306	1.120 952	1.123 600	2
3	1.170 072	1.174 241	1.178 420	1.182 609	1.186 807	1.191 016	3
4	1.232 964	1.238 825	1.244 706	1.250 609	1.256 532	1.262 477	4
5	1.299 236	1.306 960	1.314 721	1.322 519	1.330 354	1.338 226	5
6	1.369 070	1.378 843	1.388 674	1.398 564	1.408 512	1.418 519	6
7	1.442 657	1.454 679	1.466 787	1.478 981	1.491 262	1.503 630	7
8	1.520 200	1.534 687	1.549 294	1.564 023	1.578 874	1.593 848	8
9	1.601 911	1.619 094	1.636 442	1.653 954	1.671 633	1.689 479	9
10	1.688 013	1.708 144	1.728 491	1.749 056	1.769 841	1.790 848	10
11	1.778 744	1.802 092	1.825 719	1.849 627	1.873 819	1.898 299	11
12	1.874 352	1.901 207	1.928 416	1.955 980	1.983 906	2.012 196	12
13	1.975 098	2.005 774	2.036 889	2.068 449	2.100 460	2.132 928	13
14	2.081 259	2.116 091	2.151 464	2.187 385	2.223 862	2.260 904	14
15	2.193 127	2.232 476	2.272 484	2.313 160	2.354 514	2.396 558	15
16	2.311 008	2.355 263	2.400 311	2.446 167	2.492 842	2.540 352	16
17	2.435 224	2.484 802	2.535 329	2.586 821	2.639 297	2.692 773	17
18	2.566 118	2.621 466	2.677 941	2.735 563	2.794 355	2.854 339	18
19	2.704 047	2.765 647	2.828 575	2.892 858	2.958 524	3.025 600	19
20	2.849 389	2.917 757	2.987 682	3.059 198	3.132 337	3.207 135	20
21	3.002 544	3.078 234	3.155 740	3.235 101	3.316 362	3.399 564	21
22	3.163 930	3.247 537	3.333 250	3.421 120	3.511 198	3.603 537	22
23	3.333 992	3.426 152	3.520 745	3.617 834	3.717 481	3.819 750	23
24	3.513 194	3.614 590	3.718 787	3.825 860	3.935 883	4.048 935	24
25	3.702 028	3.813 392	3.927 969	4.045 846	4.167 116	4.291 871	25
26	3.901 012	4.023 129	4.148 917	4.278 483	4.411 934	4.549 383	26
27	4.110 691	4.244 401	4.382 294	4.524 495	4.671 135	4.822 346	27
28	4.331 641	4.477 843	4.628 798	4.784 654	4.945 564	5.111 687	28
29	4.564 467	4.724 124	4.889 168	5.059 772	5.236 116	5.418 388	29
30	4.809 807	4.983 951	5.164 183	5.350 708	5.543 738	5.743 491	30
31	5.068 334	5.258 069	5.454 669	5.658 374	5.869 433	6.088 101	31
32	5.340 757	5.547 262	5.761 494	5.983 731	6.214 262	6.453 387	32
33	5.627 823	5.852 362	6.085 578	6.327 795	6.579 350	6.840 590	33
34	5.930 318	6.174 242	6.427 892	6.691 643	6.965 886	7.251 025	34
35	6.249 073	6.513 825	6.789 461	7.076 413	7.375 132	7.686 087	35
36	6.584 960	6.872 085	7.171 368	7.483 307	7.808 421	8.147 252	36
37	6.938 902	7.250 050	7.574 757	7.913 597	8.267 166	8.636 087	37
38	7.311 868	7.648 803	8.000 837	8.368 629	8.752 862	9.154 252	38
39	7.704 881	8.069 487	8.450 884	8.849 825	9.267 093	9.703 507	39
40	8.119 018	8.513 309	8.926 247	9.358 690	9.811 534	10.285 718	40
41	8.555 415	8.981 541	9.428 348	9.896 814	10.387 962	10.902 861	41
42	9.015 269	9.475 525	9.958 692	10.465 881	10.998 255	11.557 033	42
43	9.499 840	9.996 679	10.518 869	11.067 669	11.644 402	12.250 455	43
44	10.010 456	10.546 497	11.110 555	11.704 060	12.328 511	12.985 482	44
45	10.548 518	11.126 554	11.735 524	12.377 044	13.052 811	13.764 611	45
46	11.115 501	11.738 515	12.395 647	13.088 724	13.819 664	14.590 487	46
47	11.712 959	12.384 133	13.092 902	13.841 325	14.631 569	15.465 917	47
48	12.342 530	13.065 260	13.829 378	14.637 201	15.491 174	16.393 872	48
49	13.005 941	13.783 849	14.607 281	15.478 841	16.401 280	17.377 504	49
50	13.705 011	14.541 961	15.428 940	16.368 874	17.364 855	18.420 154	50
51	14.441 655	15.341 769	16.296 818	17.310 084	18.385 040	19.525 364	51
52	15.217 894	16.185 566	17.213 514	18.305 414	19.465 162	20.696 885	52
53	16.035 856	17.075 773	18.181 774	19.357 975	20.608 740	21.938 698	53
54	16.897 783	18.014 940	19.204 499	20.471 059	21.819 503	23.255 020	54
55	17.806 039	19.005 762	20.284 752	21.648 145	23.101 399	24.650 322	55

YRS

YRS							QTRS
14	18.763 114	20.051 079	21.425 770	22.892 913	24.458 606	26.129 341	56
15	23.134 241	24.839 770	26.668 790	28.630 080	30.733 031	32.987 691	60
16	28.523 683	30.772 120	33.194 811	35.805 032	38.617 050	41.646 200	64
17	35.168 671	38.121 261	41.317 791	44.778 091	48.523 575	52.577 368	68
18	43.361 701	47.225 558	51.428 515	55.999 877	60.971 444	66.377 715	72
19	53.463 411	58.504 185	64.013 396	70.033 943	76.612 595	83.800 336	76
20	65.918 454	72.476 426	79.677 878	87.585 070	96.266 208	105.795 993	80
21	81.275 072	89.785 583	99.175 556	109.534 666	120.961 611	133.565 004	84
22	100.209 227	111.228 594	123.444 440	136.985 025	151.992 183	168.622 741	88
23	123.554 356	137.792 724	153.652 072	171.314 687	190.983 104	212.882 325	92
24	152.338 057	170.701 023	191.251 702	214.247 667	239.976 459	268.759 030	96
25	187.827 321	211.468 636	238.052 198	267.940 032	301.538 197	339.302 084	100
26	231.584 300	261.972 559	296.305 071	335.088 180	378.892 516	428.361 063	104
27	285.535 075	324.538 064	368.812 788	419.064 250	476.090 725	540.795 972	108
28	352.054 431	402.045 753	459.063 601	524.085 468	598.223 424	682.742 455	112
29	434.070 394	498.064 190	571.399 357	655.425 934	751.687 117	861.946 619	116
30	535.193 113	617.014 196	711.224 379	819.681 486	944.519 222	1088.187 748	120

SEMIANNUAL COMPOUNDING

SECTION 1

HALF YRS	7.00% ANNUAL RATE	8.00% ANNUAL RATE	9.00% ANNUAL RATE	10.00% ANNUAL RATE	10.50% ANNUAL RATE	11.00% ANNUAL RATE	HALF YRS
1	1.035 000	1.040 000	1.045 000	1.050 000	1.052 500	1.055 000	1
2	1.071 225	1.081 600	1.092 025	1.102 500	1.107 756	1.113 025	2
3	1.108 718	1.124 864	1.141 166	1.157 625	1.165 913	1.174 241	3
4	1.147 523	1.169 859	1.192 519	1.215 506	1.227 124	1.238 825	4
5	1.187 686	1.216 653	1.246 182	1.276 282	1.291 548	1.306 960	5
6	1.229 255	1.265 319	1.302 260	1.340 096	1.359 354	1.378 843	6
7	1.272 279	1.315 932	1.360 862	1.407 100	1.430 720	1.454 679	7
8	1.316 809	1.368 569	1.422 101	1.477 455	1.505 833	1.534 687	8
9	1.362 897	1.423 312	1.486 095	1.551 328	1.584 889	1.619 094	9
10	1.410 599	1.480 244	1.552 969	1.628 895	1.668 096	1.708 144	10
11	1.459 970	1.539 454	1.622 853	1.710 339	1.755 671	1.802 092	11
12	1.511 069	1.601 032	1.695 881	1.795 856	1.847 844	1.901 207	12
13	1.563 956	1.665 074	1.772 196	1.885 649	1.944 856	2.005 774	13
14	1.618 695	1.731 676	1.851 945	1.979 932	2.046 961	2.116 091	14
15	1.675 349	1.800 944	1.935 282	2.078 928	2.154 426	2.232 476	15
16	1.733 986	1.872 981	2.022 370	2.182 875	2.267 533	2.355 263	16
17	1.794 676	1.947 900	2.113 377	2.292 018	2.386 579	2.484 802	17
18	1.857 489	2.025 817	2.208 479	2.406 619	2.511 874	2.621 466	18
19	1.922 501	2.106 849	2.307 860	2.526 950	2.643 748	2.765 647	19
20	1.989 789	2.191 123	2.411 714	2.653 298	2.782 544	2.917 757	20
21	2.059 431	2.278 768	2.520 241	2.785 963	2.928 628	3.078 234	21
22	2.131 512	2.369 919	2.633 652	2.925 261	3.082 381	3.247 537	22
23	2.206 114	2.464 716	2.752 166	3.071 524	3.244 206	3.426 152	23
24	2.283 328	2.563 304	2.876 014	3.225 100	3.414 527	3.614 590	24
25	2.363 245	2.665 836	3.005 434	3.386 355	3.593 789	3.813 392	25
26	2.445 959	2.772 470	3.140 679	3.555 673	3.782 463	4.023 129	26
27	2.531 567	2.883 369	3.282 010	3.733 456	3.981 043	4.244 401	27
28	2.620 172	2.998 703	3.429 700	3.920 129	4.190 047	4.477 843	28
29	2.711 878	3.118 651	3.584 036	4.116 136	4.410 025	4.724 124	29
30	2.806 794	3.243 398	3.745 318	4.321 942	4.641 551	4.983 951	30
31	2.905 031	3.373 133	3.913 857	4.538 039	4.885 233	5.258 069	31
32	3.006 708	3.508 059	4.089 981	4.764 941	5.141 707	5.547 262	32
33	3.111 942	3.648 381	4.274 030	5.003 189	5.411 647	5.852 362	33
34	3.220 860	3.794 316	4.466 362	5.253 348	5.695 758	6.174 242	34
35	3.333 590	3.946 089	4.667 348	5.516 015	5.994 786	6.513 825	35
36	3.450 266	4.103 933	4.877 378	5.791 816	6.309 512	6.872 085	36
37	3.571 025	4.268 090	5.096 860	6.081 407	6.640 761	7.250 050	37
38	3.696 011	4.438 813	5.326 219	6.385 477	6.989 401	7.648 803	38
39	3.825 372	4.616 366	5.565 899	6.704 751	7.356 345	8.069 487	39
40	3.959 260	4.801 021	5.816 365	7.039 989	7.742 553	8.513 309	40
41	4.097 834	4.993 061	6.078 101	7.391 988	8.149 037	8.981 541	41
42	4.241 258	5.192 784	6.351 615	7.761 588	8.576 861	9.475 525	42
43	4.389 702	5.400 495	6.637 438	8.149 667	9.027 147	9.996 679	43
44	4.543 342	5.616 515	6.936 123	8.557 150	9.501 072	10.546 497	44
45	4.702 359	5.841 176	7.248 248	8.985 008	9.999 878	11.126 554	45
46	4.866 941	6.074 823	7.574 420	9.434 258	10.524 872	11.738 515	46
47	5.037 284	6.317 816	7.915 268	9.905 971	11.077 427	12.384 133	47
48	5.213 589	6.570 528	8.271 456	10.401 270	11.658 992	13.065 260	48
49	5.396 065	6.833 349	8.643 671	10.921 333	12.271 089	13.783 849	49
50	5.584 927	7.106 683	9.032 636	11.467 400	12.915 322	14.541 961	50
51	5.780 399	7.390 951	9.439 105	12.040 770	13.593 376	15.341 769	51
52	5.982 713	7.686 589	9.863 865	12.642 808	14.307 028	16.185 566	52
53	6.192 108	7.994 052	10.307 739	13.274 949	15.058 147	17.075 773	53
54	6.408 832	8.313 814	10.771 587	13.938 696	15.848 700	18.014 940	54
55	6.633 141	8.646 367	11.256 308	14.635 631	16.680 757	19.005 762	55
56	6.865 301	8.992 222	11.762 842	15.367 412	17.556 496	20.051 079	56
57	7.105 587	9.351 910	12.292 170	16.135 783	18.478 212	21.153 888	57
58	7.354 282	9.725 987	12.845 318	16.942 572	19.448 319	22.317 352	58
59	7.611 682	10.115 026	13.423 357	17.789 701	20.469 355	23.544 806	59
YRS							YRS
30	7.878 091	10.519 627	14.027 408	18.679 186	21.543 997	24.839 770	60
31	8.439 208	11.378 029	15.318 280	20.593 802	23.865 497	27.647 285	62
32	9.040 291	12.306 476	16.727 945	22.704 667	26.437 153	30.772 120	64
33	9.684 185	13.310 685	18.267 334	25.031 896	29.285 922	34.250 139	66
34	10.373 941	14.396 836	19.948 385	27.597 665	32.441 663	38.121 261	68
35	11.112 825	15.571 618	21.784 136	30.426 426	35.937 455	42.429 916	70
36	11.904 336	16.842 262	23.788 821	33.545 134	39.809 940	47.225 558	72
37	12.752 223	18.216 591	25.977 987	36.983 510	44.099 710	52.563 226	74
38	13.660 500	19.703 065	28.368 611	40.774 320	48.851 729	58.504 185	76
39	14.633 469	21.310 835	30.979 233	44.953 688	54.115 809	65.116 620	78
40	15.675 738	23.049 799	33.830 096	49.561 441	59.947 125	72.476 426	80

HALF YRS	11.50% ANNUAL RATE	12.00% ANNUAL RATE	12.50% ANNUAL RATE	13.00% ANNUAL RATE	13.50% ANNUAL RATE	14.00% ANNUAL RATE	HALF YRS
1	1.057 500	1.060 000	1.062 500	1.065 000	1.067 500	1.070 000	1
2	1.118 306	1.123 600	1.128 906	1.134 225	1.139 556	1.144 900	2
3	1.182 609	1.191 016	1.199 463	1.207 950	1.216 476	1.225 043	3
4	1.250 609	1.262 477	1.274 429	1.286 466	1.298 588	1.310 796	4
5	1.322 519	1.338 226	1.354 081	1.370 087	1.386 243	1.402 552	5
6	1.398 564	1.418 519	1.438 711	1.459 142	1.479 815	1.500 730	6
7	1.478 981	1.503 630	1.528 631	1.553 987	1.579 702	1.605 781	7
8	1.564 023	1.593 848	1.624 170	1.654 996	1.686 332	1.718 186	8
9	1.653 954	1.689 479	1.725 681	1.762 570	1.800 159	1.838 459	9
10	1.749 056	1.790 848	1.833 536	1.877 137	1.921 670	1.967 151	10
11	1.849 627	1.898 299	1.948 132	1.999 151	2.051 383	2.104 852	11
12	1.955 980	2.012 196	2.069 890	2.129 096	2.189 851	2.252 192	12
13	2.068 449	2.132 928	2.199 258	2.267 487	2.337 666	2.409 845	13
14	2.187 385	2.260 904	2.336 712	2.414 874	2.495 459	2.578 534	14
15	2.313 160	2.396 558	2.482 756	2.571 841	2.663 902	2.759 032	15
16	2.446 167	2.540 352	2.637 928	2.739 011	2.843 715	2.952 164	16
17	2.586 821	2.692 773	2.802 799	2.917 046	3.035 666	3.158 815	17
18	2.735 563	2.854 339	2.977 974	3.106 654	3.240 574	3.379 932	18
19	2.892 858	3.025 600	3.164 097	3.308 587	3.459 312	3.616 528	19
20	3.059 198	3.207 135	3.361 853	3.523 645	3.692 816	3.869 684	20
21	3.235 101	3.399 564	3.571 969	3.752 682	3.942 081	4.140 562	21
22	3.421 120	3.603 537	3.795 217	3.996 606	4.208 172	4.430 402	22
23	3.617 834	3.819 750	4.032 418	4.256 386	4.492 223	4.740 530	23
24	3.825 860	4.048 935	4.284 445	4.533 051	4.795 448	5.072 367	24
25	4.045 846	4.291 871	4.552 222	4.827 699	5.119 141	5.427 433	25
26	4.278 483	4.549 383	4.836 736	5.141 500	5.464 683	5.807 353	26
27	4.524 495	4.822 346	5.139 032	5.475 697	5.833 549	6.213 868	27
28	4.784 654	5.111 687	5.460 222	5.831 617	6.227 314	6.648 838	28
29	5.059 772	5.418 388	5.801 486	6.210 672	6.647 657	7.114 257	29
30	5.350 708	5.743 491	6.164 079	6.614 366	7.096 374	7.612 255	30
31	5.658 374	6.088 101	6.549 333	7.044 300	7.575 380	8.145 113	31
32	5.983 731	6.453 387	6.958 667	7.502 179	8.086 718	8.715 271	32
33	6.327 795	6.840 590	7.393 583	7.989 821	8.632 571	9.325 340	33
34	6.691 643	7.251 025	7.855 682	8.509 159	9.215 270	9.978 114	34
35	7.076 413	7.686 087	8.346 663	9.062 255	9.837 300	10.676 581	35
36	7.483 307	8.147 252	8.868 329	9.651 301	10.501 318	11.423 942	36
37	7.913 597	8.636 087	9.422 600	10.278 636	11.210 157	12.223 618	37
38	8.368 629	9.154 252	10.011 512	10.946 747	11.966 843	13.079 271	38
39	8.849 825	9.703 507	10.637 231	11.658 286	12.774 605	13.994 820	39
40	9.358 690	10.285 718	11.302 058	12.416 075	13.636 890	14.974 458	40
41	9.896 814	10.902 861	12.008 437	13.223 119	14.557 380	16.022 670	41
42	10.465 881	11.557 033	12.758 964	14.082 622	15.540 004	17.144 257	42
43	11.067 669	12.250 455	13.556 400	14.997 993	16.588 954	18.344 355	43
44	11.704 060	12.985 482	14.403 675	15.972 862	17.708 708	19.628 460	44
45	12.377 044	13.764 611	15.303 904	17.011 098	18.904 046	21.002 452	45
46	13.088 724	14.590 487	16.260 398	18.116 820	20.180 069	22.472 623	46
47	13.841 325	15.465 917	17.276 673	19.294 413	21.542 224	24.045 707	47
48	14.637 201	16.393 872	18.356 465	20.548 550	22.996 324	25.728 907	48
49	15.478 841	17.377 504	19.503 744	21.884 205	24.548 576	27.529 930	49
50	16.368 874	18.420 154	20.722 728	23.306 679	26.205 605	29.457 025	50
51	17.310 084	19.525 364	22.017 899	24.821 613	27.974 483	31.519 017	51
52	18.305 414	20.696 885	23.394 018	26.435 018	29.862 761	33.725 348	52
53	19.357 975	21.938 698	24.856 144	28.153 294	31.878 497	36.086 122	53
54	20.471 059	23.255 020	26.409 653	29.983 258	34.030 295	38.612 151	54
55	21.648 145	24.650 322	28.060 256	31.932 170	36.327 340	41.315 001	55
56	22.892 913	26.129 341	29.814 022	34.007 761	38.779 436	44.207 052	56
57	24.209 256	27.697 101	31.677 398	36.218 265	41.397 048	47.301 545	57
58	25.601 288	29.358 927	33.657 236	38.572 452	44.191 349	50.612 653	58
59	27.073 362	31.120 463	35.760 813	41.079 662	47.174 265	54.155 539	59

YRS

YRS	11.50%	12.00%	12.50%	13.00%	13.50%	14.00%	YRS
30	28.630 080	32.987 691	37.995 864	43.749 840	50.358 527	57.946 427	60
31	32.017 197	37.064 969	42.893 768	49.622 162	57.386 375	66.342 864	62
32	35.805 032	41.646 200	48.423 043	56.282 697	65.395 002	75.955 945	64
33	40.040 991	46.793 670	54.665 076	63.837 242	74.521 283	86.961 962	66
34	44.778 091	52.577 368	61.711 746	72.405 795	84.921 194	99.562 750	68
35	50.075 619	59.075 930	69.666 776	82.124 463	96.772 477	113.989 392	70
36	55.999 877	66.377 715	78.647 258	93.147 619	110.277 681	130.506 455	72
37	62.625 013	74.582 001	88.785 382	105.650 359	125.667 621	149.416 840	74
38	70.033 943	83.800 336	100.230 372	119.831 278	143.205 323	171.067 341	76
39	78.319 396	94.158 058	113.150 694	135.915 631	163.190 521	195.854 998	78
40	87.585 070	105.795 993	127.736 525	154.158 907	185.964 778	224.234 388	80

SECTION 1

HALF YRS	14.50% ANNUAL RATE	15.00% ANNUAL RATE	15.50% ANNUAL RATE	16.00% ANNUAL RATE	16.50% ANNUAL RATE	17.00% ANNUAL RATE	HALF YRS
1	1.072 500	1.075 000	1.077 500	1.080 000	1.082 500	1.085 000	1
2	1.150 256	1.155 625	1.161 006	1.166 400	1.171 806	1.177 225	2
3	1.233 650	1.242 297	1.250 984	1.259 712	1.268 480	1.277 289	3
4	1.323 089	1.335 469	1.347 936	1.360 489	1.373 130	1.385 859	4
5	1.419 013	1.435 629	1.452 401	1.469 328	1.486 413	1.503 657	5
6	1.521 892	1.543 302	1.564 962	1.586 874	1.609 042	1.631 468	6
7	1.632 229	1.659 049	1.686 246	1.713 824	1.741 788	1.770 142	7
8	1.750 566	1.783 478	1.816 930	1.850 930	1.885 486	1.920 604	8
9	1.877 482	1.917 239	1.957 742	1.999 005	2.041 038	2.083 856	9
10	2.013 599	2.061 032	2.109 467	2.158 925	2.209 424	2.260 983	10
11	2.159 585	2.215 609	2.272 951	2.331 639	2.391 701	2.453 167	11
12	2.316 155	2.381 780	2.449 105	2.518 170	2.589 017	2.661 686	12
13	2.484 076	2.560 413	2.638 910	2.719 624	2.802 611	2.887 930	13
14	2.664 172	2.752 444	2.843 426	2.937 194	3.033 826	3.133 404	14
15	2.857 324	2.958 877	3.063 791	3.172 169	3.284 117	3.399 743	15
16	3.064 480	3.180 793	3.301 235	3.425 943	3.555 056	3.688 721	16
17	3.286 655	3.419 353	3.557 081	3.700 018	3.848 348	4.002 262	17
18	3.524 937	3.675 804	3.832 755	3.996 019	4.165 837	4.342 455	18
19	3.780 495	3.951 489	4.129 793	4.315 701	4.509 519	4.711 563	19
20	4.054 581	4.247 851	4.449 852	4.660 957	4.881 554	5.112 046	20
21	4.348 538	4.566 440	4.794 716	5.033 834	5.284 282	5.546 570	21
22	4.663 808	4.908 923	5.166 306	5.436 540	5.720 236	6.018 028	22
23	5.001 934	5.277 092	5.566 695	5.871 464	6.192 155	6.529 561	23
24	5.364 574	5.672 874	5.998 114	6.341 181	6.703 008	7.084 574	24
25	5.753 505	6.098 340	6.462 967	6.848 475	7.256 006	7.686 762	25
26	6.170 634	6.555 715	6.963 847	7.396 353	7.854 626	8.340 137	26
27	6.618 005	7.047 394	7.503 546	7.988 061	8.502 633	9.049 049	27
28	7.097 811	7.575 948	8.085 070	8.627 106	9.204 100	9.818 218	28
29	7.612 402	8.144 144	8.711 663	9.317 275	9.963 439	10.652 766	29
30	8.164 301	8.754 955	9.386 817	10.062 657	10.785 422	11.558 252	30
31	8.756 213	9.411 577	10.114 296	10.867 669	11.675 220	12.540 703	31
32	9.391 039	10.117 445	10.898 154	11.737 083	12.638 425	13.606 663	32
33	10.071 889	10.876 253	11.742 760	12.676 050	13.681 095	14.763 229	33
34	10.802 101	11.691 972	12.652 824	13.690 134	14.809 786	16.018 104	34
35	11.585 253	12.568 870	13.633 418	14.785 344	16.031 593	17.379 642	35
36	12.425 184	13.511 536	14.690 008	15.968 172	17.354 199	18.856 912	36
37	13.326 010	14.524 901	15.828 484	17.245 626	18.785 921	20.459 750	37
38	14.292 146	15.614 268	17.055 191	18.625 276	20.335 759	22.198 828	38
39	15.328 326	16.785 339	18.376 969	20.115 298	22.013 459	24.085 729	39
40	16.439 630	18.044 239	19.801 184	21.724 521	23.829 570	26.133 016	40
41	17.631 503	19.397 557	21.335 775	23.462 483	25.795 509	28.354 322	41
42	18.909 787	20.852 374	22.989 298	25.339 482	27.923 639	30.764 439	42
43	20.280 747	22.416 302	24.770 969	27.366 640	30.227 339	33.379 417	43
44	21.751 101	24.097 524	26.690 719	29.555 972	32.721 094	36.216 667	44
45	23.328 055	25.904 839	28.759 249	31.920 449	35.420 285	39.295 084	45
46	25.019 339	27.847 702	30.988 091	34.474 085	38.342 783	42.635 166	46
47	26.833 242	29.936 279	33.389 668	37.232 012	41.506 063	46.259 155	47
48	28.778 652	32.181 500	35.977 368	40.210 573	44.930 313	50.191 183	48
49	30.865 104	34.595 113	38.765 614	43.427 419	48.637 064	54.457 434	49
50	33.102 824	37.189 746	41.769 949	46.901 613	52.649 621	59.086 316	50
51	35.502 779	39.978 977	45.007 120	50.653 742	56.993 215	64.108 652	51
52	38.076 730	42.977 400	48.495 171	54.706 041	61.695 155	69.557 888	52
53	40.837 293	46.200 705	52.253 547	59.082 524	66.785 006	75.470 308	53
54	43.797 997	49.665 758	56.303 197	63.809 126	72.294 768	81.885 284	54
55	46.973 351	53.390 690	60.666 695	68.913 856	78.259 087	88.845 534	55
56	50.378 919	57.394 992	65.368 364	74.426 965	84.715 462	96.397 404	56
57	54.031 391	61.699 616	70.434 412	80.381 122	91.704 487	104.591 183	57
58	57.948 667	66.327 087	75.893 079	86.811 612	99.270 107	113.481 434	58
59	62.149 945	71.301 619	81.774 793	93.756 540	107.459 891	123.127 356	59

YRS							
30	66.655 816	76.649 240	88.112 339	101.257 064	116.325 332	133.593 181	60
31	76.671 269	88.577 778	102.298 976	118.106 239	136.310 751	157.269 233	62
32	88.191 607	102.362 695	118.769 751	137.759 117	159.729 790	185.141 272	64
33	101.442 947	118.292 890	137.892 423	160.682 234	187.172 367	217.952 934	66
34	116.685 384	136.702 221	160.093 965	187.419 758	219.329 749	256.579 643	68
35	134.218 092	157.976 504	185.870 094	218.606 406	257.011 971	302.051 970	70
36	154.385 199	182.561 597	215.796 341	254.982 512	301.168 234	355.583 131	72
37	177.582 540	210.972 746	250.540 900	297.411 602	352.910 818	418.601 351	74
38	204.265 426	243.805 379	290.879 551	346.900 892	413.543 103	492.787 975	76
39	234.957 583	281.747 591	337.712 977	404.625 201	484.592 393	580.122 324	78
40	270.261 429	325.594 560	392.086 877	471.954 834	567.848 394	682.934 503	80

SECTION 1

HALF YRS	17.50% ANNUAL RATE	18.00% ANNUAL RATE	18.50% ANNUAL RATE	19.00% ANNUAL RATE	19.50% ANNUAL RATE	20.00% ANNUAL RATE	HALF YRS
1	1.087 500	1.090 000	1.092 500	1.095 000	1.097 500	1.100 000	1
2	1.182 656	1.188 100	1.193 556	1.199 025	1.204 506	1.210 000	2
3	1.286 139	1.295 029	1.303 960	1.312 932	1.321 946	1.331 000	3
4	1.398 676	1.411 582	1.424 577	1.437 661	1.450 835	1.464 100	4
5	1.521 060	1.538 624	1.556 350	1.574 239	1.592 292	1.610 510	5
6	1.654 153	1.677 100	1.700 312	1.723 791	1.747 540	1.771 561	6
7	1.798 891	1.828 039	1.857 591	1.887 552	1.917 925	1.948 717	7
8	1.956 294	1.992 563	2.029 418	2.066 869	2.104 923	2.143 589	8
9	2.127 470	2.171 893	2.217 139	2.263 222	2.310 153	2.357 948	9
10	2.313 623	2.367 364	2.422 225	2.478 228	2.535 393	2.593 742	10
11	2.516 065	2.580 426	2.646 281	2.713 659	2.782 594	2.853 117	11
12	2.736 221	2.812 665	2.891 062	2.971 457	3.053 897	3.138 428	12
13	2.975 640	3.065 805	3.158 485	3.253 745	3.351 652	3.452 271	13
14	3.236 009	3.341 727	3.450 645	3.562 851	3.678 438	3.797 498	14
15	3.519 160	3.642 482	3.769 829	3.901 322	4.037 085	4.177 248	15
16	3.827 086	3.970 306	4.118 539	4.271 948	4.430 701	4.594 973	16
17	4.161 956	4.327 633	4.499 503	4.677 783	4.862 695	5.054 470	17
18	4.526 127	4.717 120	4.915 707	5.122 172	5.336 807	5.559 917	18
19	4.922 164	5.141 661	5.370 410	5.608 778	5.857 146	6.115 909	19
20	5.352 853	5.604 411	5.867 173	6.141 612	6.428 218	6.727 500	20
21	5.821 228	6.108 808	6.409 887	6.725 065	7.054 969	7.400 250	21
22	6.330 585	6.658 600	7.002 801	7.363 946	7.742 828	8.140 275	22
23	6.884 511	7.257 874	7.650 560	8.063 521	8.497 754	8.954 302	23
24	7.486 906	7.911 083	8.358 237	8.829 556	9.326 285	9.849 733	24
25	8.142 010	8.623 081	9.131 374	9.668 364	10.235 598	10.834 706	25
26	8.854 436	9.399 158	9.976 026	10.586 858	11.233 569	11.918 177	26
27	9.629 199	10.245 082	10.898 809	11.592 610	12.328 842	13.109 994	27
28	10.471 754	11.167 140	11.906 949	12.693 908	13.530 904	14.420 994	28
29	11.388 033	12.172 182	13.008 341	13.899 829	14.850 167	15.863 093	29
30	12.384 485	13.267 678	14.211 613	15.220 313	16.298 058	17.449 402	30
31	13.468 128	14.461 770	15.526 187	16.666 242	17.887 119	19.194 342	31
32	14.646 589	15.763 329	16.962 359	18.249 535	19.631 113	21.113 777	32
33	15.928 166	17.182 028	18.531 378	19.983 241	21.545 147	23.225 154	33
34	17.321 880	18.728 411	20.245 530	21.881 649	23.645 798	25.547 670	34
35	18.837 545	20.413 968	22.118 242	23.960 406	25.951 264	28.102 437	35
36	20.485 830	22.251 225	24.164 179	26.236 644	28.481 512	30.912 681	36
37	22.278 340	24.253 835	26.399 365	28.729 126	31.258 459	34.003 949	37
38	24.227 695	26.436 680	28.841 307	31.458 393	34.306 159	37.404 343	38
39	26.347 618	28.815 982	31.509 128	34.446 940	37.651 010	41.144 778	39
40	28.653 035	31.409 420	34.423 722	37.719 399	41.321 983	45.259 256	40
41	31.160 175	34.236 268	37.607 916	41.302 742	45.350 877	49.785 181	41
42	33.886 691	37.317 532	41.086 649	45.226 503	49.772 587	54.763 699	42
43	36.851 776	40.676 110	44.887 164	49.523 020	54.625 414	60.240 069	43
44	40.076 306	44.336 960	49.039 226	54.227 707	59.951 392	66.264 076	44
45	43.582 983	48.327 286	53.575 355	59.379 340	65.796 653	72.890 484	45
46	47.396 494	52.676 742	58.531 075	65.020 377	72.211 827	80.179 532	46
47	51.543 687	57.417 649	63.945 199	71.197 313	79.252 480	88.197 485	47
48	56.053 760	62.585 237	69.860 130	77.961 057	86.979 596	97.017 234	48
49	60.958 464	68.217 908	76.322 192	85.367 358	95.460 107	106.718 957	49
50	66.292 330	74.357 520	83.381 995	93.477 257	104.767 467	117.390 853	50
51	72.092 909	81.049 697	91.094 830	102.357 596	114.982 295	129.129 938	51
52	78.401 038	88.344 170	99.521 101	112.081 568	126.193 069	142.042 932	52
53	85.261 129	96.295 145	108.726 803	122.729 317	138.496 894	156.247 225	53
54	92.721 478	104.961 708	118.784 033	134.388 602	152.000 341	171.871 948	54
55	100.834 607	114.408 262	129.771 556	147.155 519	166.820 374	189.059 142	55
56	109.657 635	124.705 005	141.775 424	161.135 293	183.085 360	207.965 057	56
57	119.252 678	135.928 456	154.889 651	176.443 146	200.936 183	228.761 562	57
58	129.687 287	148.162 017	169.216 944	193.205 245	220.527 461	251.637 719	58
59	141.034 925	161.496 598	184.869 511	211.559 743	242.028 888	276.801 490	59
YRS							
30	153.375 481	176.031 292	201.969 941	231.657 919	265.626 705	304.481 640	60
31	181.390 471	209.142 778	241.062 485	277.763 636	319.949 026	368.422 784	62
32	214.522 574	248.482 535	287.721 636	333.045 544	385.380 602	445.791 568	64
33	253.706 463	295.222 099	343.411 957	399.329 933	464.193 343	539.407 798	66
34	300.047 535	350.753 376	409.881 488	478.806 573	559.123 783	652.683 435	68
35	354.853 092	416.730 086	489.216 611	574.101 052	673.468 092	789.746 957	70
36	419.669 227	495.117 015	583.907 544	688.361 513	811.196 525	955.593 818	72
37	496.324 434	588.248 526	696.926 498	825.362 664	977.091 285	1156.268 519	74
38	586.981 194	698.898 074	831.820 978	989.630 468	1176.912 559	1399.084 909	76
39	694.196 978	830.360 801	992.825 127	1186.591 671	1417.598 534	1692.892 739	78
40	820.996 395	986.551 668	1184.992 636	1422.753 079	1707.506 294	2048.400 215	80

25

SECTION 1

YRS	7.00% ANNUAL RATE	8.00% ANNUAL RATE	9.00% ANNUAL RATE	10.00% ANNUAL RATE	10.25% ANNUAL RATE	10.50% ANNUAL RATE	YRS
1	1.070 000	1.080 000	1.090 000	1.100 000	1.102 500	1.105 000	1
2	1.144 900	1.166 400	1.188 100	1.210 000	1.215 506	1.221 025	2
3	1.225 043	1.259 712	1.295 029	1.331 000	1.340 096	1.349 233	3
4	1.310 796	1.360 489	1.411 582	1.464 100	1.477 455	1.490 902	4
5	1.402 552	1.469 328	1.538 624	1.610 510	1.628 895	1.647 447	5
6	1.500 730	1.586 874	1.677 100	1.771 561	1.795 856	1.820 429	6
7	1.605 781	1.713 824	1.828 039	1.948 717	1.979 932	2.011 574	7
8	1.718 186	1.850 930	1.992 563	2.143 589	2.182 875	2.222 789	8
9	1.838 459	1.999 005	2.171 893	2.357 948	2.406 619	2.456 182	9
10	1.967 151	2.158 925	2.367 364	2.593 742	2.653 298	2.714 081	10
11	2.104 852	2.331 639	2.580 426	2.853 117	2.925 261	2.999 059	11
12	2.252 192	2.518 170	2.812 665	3.138 428	3.225 100	3.313 961	12
13	2.409 845	2.719 624	3.065 805	3.452 271	3.555 673	3.661 926	13
14	2.578 534	2.937 194	3.341 727	3.797 498	3.920 129	4.046 429	14
15	2.759 032	3.172 169	3.642 482	4.177 248	4.321 942	4.471 304	15
16	2.952 164	3.425 943	3.970 306	4.594 973	4.764 941	4.940 791	16
17	3.158 815	3.700 018	4.327 633	5.054 470	5.253 348	5.459 574	17
18	3.379 932	3.996 019	4.717 120	5.559 917	5.791 816	6.032 829	18
19	3.616 528	4.315 701	5.141 661	6.115 909	6.385 477	6.666 276	19
20	3.869 684	4.660 957	5.604 411	6.727 500	7.039 989	7.366 235	20
21	4.140 562	5.033 834	6.108 808	7.400 250	7.761 588	8.139 690	21
22	4.430 402	5.436 540	6.658 600	8.140 275	8.557 150	8.994 357	22
23	4.740 530	5.871 464	7.257 874	8.954 302	9.434 258	9.938 764	23
24	5.072 367	6.341 181	7.911 083	9.849 733	10.401 270	10.982 335	24
25	5.427 433	6.848 475	8.623 081	10.834 706	11.467 400	12.135 480	25
26	5.807 353	7.396 353	9.399 158	11.918 177	12.642 808	13.409 705	26
27	6.213 868	7.988 061	10.245 082	13.109 994	13.938 696	14.817 724	27
28	6.648 838	8.627 106	11.167 140	14.420 994	15.367 412	16.373 585	28
29	7.114 257	9.317 275	12.172 182	15.863 093	16.942 572	18.092 812	29
30	7.612 255	10.062 657	13.267 678	17.449 402	18.679 186	19.992 557	30
31	8.145 113	10.867 669	14.461 770	19.194 342	20.593 802	22.091 775	31
32	8.715 271	11.737 083	15.763 329	21.113 777	22.704 667	24.411 412	32
33	9.325 340	12.676 050	17.182 028	23.225 154	25.031 896	26.974 610	33
34	9.978 114	13.690 134	18.728 411	25.547 670	27.597 665	29.806 944	34
35	10.676 581	14.785 344	20.413 968	28.102 437	30.426 426	32.936 673	35
36	11.423 942	15.968 172	22.251 225	30.912 681	33.545 134	36.395 024	36
37	12.223 618	17.245 626	24.253 835	34.003 949	36.983 510	40.216 501	37
38	13.079 271	18.625 276	26.436 680	37.404 343	40.774 320	44.439 234	38
39	13.994 820	20.115 298	28.815 982	41.144 778	44.953 688	49.105 354	39
40	14.974 458	21.724 521	31.409 420	45.259 256	49.561 441	54.261 416	40
41	16.022 670	23.462 483	34.236 268	49.785 181	54.641 489	59.958 864	41
42	17.144 257	25.339 482	37.317 532	54.763 699	60.242 241	66.254 545	42
43	18.344 355	27.366 640	40.676 110	60.240 069	66.417 071	73.211 272	43
44	19.628 460	29.555 972	44.336 960	66.264 076	73.224 821	80.898 456	44
45	21.002 452	31.920 449	48.327 286	72.890 484	80.730 365	89.392 794	45
46	22.472 623	34.474 085	52.676 742	80.179 532	89.005 227	98.779 037	46
47	24.045 707	37.232 012	57.417 649	88.197 485	98.128 263	109.150 836	47
48	25.728 907	40.210 573	62.585 237	97.017 234	108.186 410	120.611 674	48
49	27.529 930	43.427 419	68.217 908	106.718 957	119.275 517	133.275 900	49
50	29.457 025	46.901 613	74.357 520	117.390 853	131.501 258	147.269 869	50

FUTURE VALUE OF $1

YRS	10.75% ANNUAL RATE	11.00% ANNUAL RATE	11.25% ANNUAL RATE	11.50% ANNUAL RATE	11.75% ANNUAL RATE	12.00% ANNUAL RATE	YRS
1	1.107 500	1.110 000	1.112 500	1.115 000	1.117 500	1.120 000	1
2	1.226 556	1.232 100	1.237 656	1.243 225	1.248 806	1.254 400	2
3	1.358 411	1.367 631	1.376 893	1.386 196	1.395 541	1.404 928	3
4	1.504 440	1.518 070	1.531 793	1.545 608	1.559 517	1.573 519	4
5	1.666 168	1.685 058	1.704 120	1.723 353	1.742 760	1.762 342	5
6	1.845 281	1.870 415	1.895 833	1.921 539	1.947 535	1.973 823	6
7	2.043 648	2.076 160	2.109 114	2.142 516	2.176 370	2.210 681	7
8	2.263 340	2.304 538	2.346 390	2.388 905	2.432 093	2.475 963	8
9	2.506 650	2.558 037	2.610 359	2.663 629	2.717 864	2.773 079	9
10	2.776 114	2.839 421	2.904 024	2.969 947	3.037 213	3.105 848	10
11	3.074 547	3.151 757	3.230 727	3.311 491	3.394 086	3.478 550	11
12	3.405 060	3.498 451	3.594 183	3.692 312	3.792 891	3.895 976	12
13	3.771 104	3.883 280	3.998 529	4.116 928	4.238 556	4.363 493	13
14	4.176 498	4.310 441	4.448 364	4.590 375	4.736 586	4.887 112	14
15	4.625 472	4.784 589	4.948 804	5.118 268	5.293 135	5.473 566	15
16	5.122 710	5.310 894	5.505 545	5.706 869	5.915 078	6.130 394	16
17	5.673 401	5.895 093	6.124 919	6.363 159	6.610 100	6.866 041	17
18	6.283 292	6.543 553	6.813 972	7.094 922	7.386 787	7.689 966	18
19	6.958 746	7.263 344	7.580 544	7.910 838	8.254 734	8.612 762	19
20	7.706 811	8.062 312	8.433 355	8.820 584	9.224 666	9.646 293	20
21	8.535 293	8.949 166	9.382 108	9.834 951	10.308 564	10.803 848	21
22	9.452 837	9.933 574	10.437 595	10.965 971	11.519 820	12.100 310	22
23	10.469 017	11.026 267	11.611 824	12.227 057	12.873 399	13.552 347	23
24	11.594 436	12.239 157	12.918 154	13.633 169	14.386 023	15.178 629	24
25	12.840 838	13.585 464	14.371 447	15.200 983	16.076 381	17.000 064	25
26	14.221 228	15.079 865	15.988 235	16.949 096	17.965 356	19.040 072	26
27	15.750 010	16.738 650	17.786 911	18.898 243	20.076 285	21.324 881	27
28	17.443 136	18.579 901	19.787 938	21.071 540	22.435 249	23.883 866	28
29	19.318 274	20.623 691	22.014 081	23.494 768	25.071 391	26.749 930	29
30	21.394 988	22.892 297	24.490 666	26.196 666	28.017 279	29.959 922	30
31	23.694 949	25.410 449	27.245 866	29.209 282	31.309 309	33.555 113	31
32	26.242 156	28.205 599	30.311 025	32.568 350	34.988 153	37.581 726	32
33	29.063 188	31.308 214	33.721 016	36.313 710	39.099 261	42.091 533	33
34	32.187 481	34.752 118	37.514 630	40.489 787	43.693 424	47.142 517	34
35	35.647 635	38.574 851	41.735 026	45.146 112	48.827 402	52.799 620	35
36	39.479 756	42.818 085	46.430 216	50.337 915	54.564 621	59.135 574	36
37	43.723 829	47.528 074	51.653 616	56.126 776	60.975 964	66.231 843	37
38	48.424 141	52.756 162	57.464 647	62.581 355	68.140 640	74.179 664	38
39	53.629 736	58.559 340	63.929 420	69.778 211	76.147 165	83.081 224	39
40	59.394 933	65.000 867	71.121 480	77.802 705	85.094 457	93.050 970	40
41	65.779 888	72.150 963	79.122 647	86.750 016	95.093 056	104.217 087	41
42	72.851 226	80.087 569	88.023 944	96.726 268	106.266 490	116.723 137	42
43	80.682 733	88.897 201	97.926 638	107.849 788	118.752 803	130.729 914	43
44	89.356 127	98.675 893	108.943 385	120.252 514	132.706 257	146.417 503	44
45	98.961 910	109.530 242	121.199 516	134.081 553	148.299 242	163.987 604	45
46	109.600 316	121.578 568	134.834 461	149.500 932	165.724 403	183.666 116	46
47	121.382 350	134.952 211	150.003 338	166.693 539	185.197 020	205.706 050	47
48	134.430 952	149.796 954	166.878 714	185.863 296	206.957 670	230.390 776	48
49	148.882 280	166.274 619	185.652 569	207.237 575	231.275 196	258.037 669	49
50	164.887 125	184.564 827	206.538 483	231.069 896	258.450 032	289.002 190	50

SECTION 1

YRS	12.25% ANNUAL RATE	12.50% ANNUAL RATE	12.75% ANNUAL RATE	13.00% ANNUAL RATE	13.25% ANNUAL RATE	13.50% ANNUAL RATE	YRS
1	1.122 500	1.125 000	1.127 500	1.130 000	1.132 500	1.135 000	1
2	1.260 006	1.265 625	1.271 256	1.276 900	1.282 556	1.288 225	2
3	1.414 357	1.423 828	1.433 341	1.442 897	1.452 495	1.462 135	3
4	1.587 616	1.601 807	1.616 092	1.630 474	1.644 951	1.659 524	4
5	1.782 099	1.802 032	1.822 144	1.842 435	1.862 906	1.883 559	5
6	2.000 406	2.027 287	2.054 468	2.081 952	2.109 742	2.137 840	6
7	2.245 455	2.280 697	2.316 412	2.352 605	2.389 282	2.426 448	7
8	2.520 524	2.565 785	2.611 755	2.658 444	2.705 862	2.754 019	8
9	2.829 288	2.886 508	2.944 754	3.004 042	3.064 389	3.125 811	9
10	3.175 876	3.247 321	3.320 210	3.394 567	3.470 421	3.547 796	10
11	3.564 920	3.653 236	3.743 536	3.835 861	3.930 251	4.026 748	11
12	4.001 623	4.109 891	4.220 837	4.334 523	4.451 010	4.570 359	12
13	4.491 822	4.623 627	4.758 994	4.898 011	5.040 768	5.187 358	13
14	5.042 070	5.201 580	5.365 766	5.534 753	5.708 670	5.887 651	14
15	5.659 724	5.851 778	6.049 901	6.254 270	6.465 069	6.682 484	15
16	6.353 040	6.583 250	6.821 263	7.067 326	7.321 691	7.584 619	16
17	7.131 287	7.406 156	7.690 974	7.986 078	8.291 815	8.608 543	17
18	8.004 870	8.331 926	8.671 574	9.024 268	9.390 480	9.770 696	18
19	8.985 467	9.373 417	9.777 199	10.197 423	10.634 719	11.089 740	19
20	10.086 186	10.545 094	11.023 792	11.523 088	12.043 819	12.586 855	20
21	11.321 744	11.863 231	12.429 326	13.021 089	13.639 625	14.286 080	21
22	12.708 658	13.346 134	14.014 065	14.713 831	15.446 875	16.214 701	22
23	14.265 469	15.014 401	15.800 858	16.626 629	17.493 586	18.403 686	23
24	16.012 989	16.891 201	17.815 467	18.788 091	19.811 486	20.888 184	24
25	17.974 580	19.002 602	20.086 939	21.230 542	22.436 508	23.708 088	25
26	20.176 466	21.377 927	22.648 024	23.990 513	25.409 345	26.908 680	26
27	22.648 083	24.050 168	25.535 647	27.109 279	28.776 084	30.541 352	27
28	25.422 473	27.056 438	28.791 442	30.633 486	32.588 915	34.664 435	28
29	28.536 726	30.438 493	32.462 351	34.615 839	36.906 946	39.344 133	29
30	32.032 475	34.243 305	36.601 300	39.115 898	41.797 116	44.655 591	30
31	35.956 453	38.523 718	41.267 966	44.200 965	47.335 234	50.684 096	31
32	40.361 118	43.339 183	46.529 632	49.947 090	53.607 153	57.526 449	32
33	45.305 355	48.756 581	52.462 160	56.440 212	60.710 101	65.292 520	33
34	50.855 261	54.851 153	59.151 085	63.777 439	68.754 189	74.107 010	34
35	57.085 031	61.707 547	66.692 849	72.068 506	77.864 119	84.111 457	35
36	64.077 947	69.420 991	75.196 187	81.437 412	88.181 115	95.466 503	36
37	71.927 495	78.098 615	84.783 701	92.024 276	99.865 112	108.354 481	37
38	80.738 614	87.860 942	95.593 623	103.987 432	113.097 240	122.982 336	38
39	90.629 094	98.843 559	107.781 810	117.505 798	128.082 624	139.584 951	39
40	101.731 158	111.199 004	121.523 990	132.781 552	145.053 572	158.428 920	40
41	114.193 225	125.098 880	137.018 299	150.043 153	164.273 170	179.816 824	41
42	128.181 895	140.736 240	154.488 132	169.548 763	186.039 365	204.092 095	42
43	143.884 177	158.328 270	174.185 369	191.590 103	210.689 581	231.644 528	43
44	161.509 988	178.119 303	196.394 004	216.496 816	238.605 950	262.916 539	44
45	181.294 962	200.384 216	221.434 239	244.641 402	270.221 239	298.410 272	45
46	203.503 595	225.432 243	249.667 105	276.444 784	306.025 553	338.695 659	46
47	228.432 785	253.611 274	281.499 661	312.382 606	346.573 939	384.419 573	47
48	256.415 801	285.312 683	317.390 868	352.992 345	392.494 986	436.316 215	48
49	287.826 737	320.976 768	357.858 203	398.881 350	444.500 571	495.218 904	49
50	323.085 512	361.098 864	403.485 124	450.735 925	503.396 897	562.073 456	50

SECTION 1

YRS	13.75% ANNUAL RATE	14.00% ANNUAL RATE	14.25% ANNUAL RATE	14.50% ANNUAL RATE	14.75% ANNUAL RATE	15.00% ANNUAL RATE	YRS
1	1.137 500	1.140 000	1.142 500	1.145 000	1.147 500	1.150 000	1
2	1.293 906	1.299 600	1.305 306	1.311 025	1.316 756	1.322 500	2
3	1.471 818	1.481 544	1.491 312	1.501 124	1.510 978	1.520 875	3
4	1.674 193	1.688 960	1.703 824	1.718 787	1.733 847	1.749 006	4
5	1.904 395	1.925 415	1.946 619	1.968 011	1.989 589	2.011 357	5
6	2.166 249	2.194 973	2.224 013	2.253 372	2.283 054	2.313 061	6
7	2.464 109	2.502 269	2.540 934	2.580 111	2.619 804	2.660 020	7
8	2.802 923	2.852 586	2.903 018	2.954 227	3.006 225	3.059 023	8
9	3.188 325	3.251 949	3.316 698	3.382 590	3.449 644	3.517 876	9
10	3.626 720	3.707 221	3.789 327	3.873 066	3.958 466	4.045 558	10
11	4.125 394	4.226 232	4.329 306	4.434 660	4.542 340	4.652 391	11
12	4.692 636	4.817 905	4.946 232	5.077 686	5.212 335	5.350 250	12
13	5.337 873	5.492 411	5.651 070	5.813 950	5.981 155	6.152 788	13
14	6.071 831	6.261 349	6.456 348	6.656 973	6.863 375	7.075 706	14
15	6.906 708	7.137 938	7.376 377	7.622 234	7.875 723	8.137 062	15
16	7.856 380	8.137 249	8.427 511	8.727 458	9.037 392	9.357 621	16
17	8.936 632	9.276 464	9.628 432	9.992 940	10.370 407	10.761 264	17
18	10.165 419	10.575 169	11.000 483	11.441 916	11.900 042	12.375 454	18
19	11.563 164	12.055 693	12.568 052	13.100 994	13.655 298	14.231 772	19
20	13.153 100	13.743 490	14.358 999	15.000 638	15.669 455	16.366 537	20
21	14.961 651	15.667 578	16.405 157	17.175 731	17.980 699	18.821 518	21
22	17.018 878	17.861 039	18.742 892	19.666 212	20.632 852	21.644 746	22
23	19.358 973	20.361 585	21.413 754	22.517 812	23.676 198	24.891 458	23
24	22.020 832	23.212 207	24.465 213	25.782 895	27.168 437	28.625 176	24
25	25.048 697	26.461 916	27.951 506	29.521 415	31.175 782	32.918 953	25
26	28.492 892	30.166 584	31.934 596	33.802 020	35.774 210	37.856 796	26
27	32.410 665	34.389 906	36.485 276	38.703 313	41.050 906	43.535 315	27
28	36.867 132	39.204 493	41.684 428	44.315 293	47.105 914	50.065 612	28
29	41.936 362	44.693 122	47.624 459	50.741 011	54.054 037	57.575 454	29
30	47.702 612	50.950 159	54.410 944	58.098 457	62.027 007	66.211 772	30
31	54.261 721	58.083 181	62.164 504	66.522 734	71.175 991	76.143 538	31
32	61.722 708	66.214 826	71.022 946	76.168 530	81.674 449	87.565 068	32
33	70.209 580	75.484 902	81.143 715	87.212 967	93.721 431	100.699 829	33
34	79.863 397	86.052 788	92.706 695	99.858 847	107.545 342	115.804 803	34
35	90.844 615	98.100 178	105.917 399	114.338 380	123.408 279	133.175 523	35
36	103.335 749	111.834 203	121.010 628	130.917 445	141.611 001	153.151 852	36
37	117.544 415	127.490 992	138.254 642	149.900 474	162.498 623	176.124 630	37
38	133.706 772	145.339 731	157.955 929	171.636 043	186.467 170	202.543 324	38
39	152.091 453	165.687 293	180.464 649	196.523 269	213.971 078	232.924 823	39
40	173.004 027	188.883 514	206.180 861	225.019 143	245.531 812	267.863 546	40
41	196.792 081	215.327 206	235.561 634	257.646 919	281.747 754	308.043 078	41
42	223.850 992	245.473 015	269.129 167	295.005 722	323.305 548	354.249 540	42
43	254.630 504	279.839 237	307.480 073	337.781 552	370.993 116	407.386 971	43
44	289.642 198	319.016 730	351.295 984	386.759 877	425.714 601	468.495 017	44
45	329.468 000	363.679 072	401.355 661	442.840 059	488.507 504	538.769 269	45
46	374.769 850	414.594 142	458.548 843	507.051 868	560.562 361	619.584 659	46
47	426.300 705	472.637 322	523.892 053	580.574 389	643.245 309	712.522 358	47
48	484.917 051	538.806 547	598.546 671	664.757 675	738.123 992	819.400 712	48
49	551.593 146	614.239 464	683.839 572	761.147 538	846.997 281	942.310 819	49
50	627.437 204	700.232 988	781.286 710	871.513 931	971.929 380	1083.657 442	50

YRS	15.25% ANNUAL RATE	15.50% ANNUAL RATE	15.75% ANNUAL RATE	16.00% ANNUAL RATE	16.25% ANNUAL RATE	16.50% ANNUAL RATE	YRS
1	1.152 500	1.155 000	1.157 500	1.160 000	1.162 500	1.165 000	1
2	1.328 256	1.334 025	1.339 806	1.345 600	1.351 406	1.357 225	2
3	1.530 815	1.540 799	1.550 826	1.560 896	1.571 010	1.581 167	3
4	1.764 265	1.779 623	1.795 081	1.810 639	1.826 299	1.842 060	4
5	2.033 315	2.055 464	2.077 806	2.100 342	2.123 072	2.146 000	5
6	2.343 396	2.374 061	2.405 060	2.436 396	2.468 072	2.500 089	6
7	2.700 763	2.742 041	2.783 857	2.826 220	2.869 133	2.912 604	7
8	3.112 630	3.167 057	3.222 315	3.278 415	3.335 367	3.393 184	8
9	3.587 306	3.657 951	3.729 830	3.802 961	3.877 365	3.953 059	9
10	4.134 370	4.224 933	4.317 278	4.411 435	4.507 436	4.605 314	10
11	4.764 861	4.879 798	4.997 249	5.117 265	5.239 895	5.365 191	11
12	5.491 503	5.636 166	5.784 316	5.936 027	6.091 378	6.250 447	12
13	6.328 957	6.509 772	6.695 346	6.885 791	7.081 227	7.281 771	13
14	7.294 123	7.518 787	7.749 862	7.987 518	8.231 926	8.483 263	14
15	8.406 477	8.684 199	8.970 466	9.265 521	9.569 614	9.883 002	15
16	9.688 464	10.030 250	10.383 314	10.748 004	11.124 676	11.513 697	16
17	11.165 955	11.584 938	12.018 686	12.467 685	12.932 436	13.413 457	17
18	12.868 763	13.380 604	13.911 629	14.462 514	15.033 957	15.626 678	18
19	14.831 250	15.454 598	16.102 711	16.776 517	17.476 975	18.205 080	19
20	17.093 015	17.850 060	18.638 888	19.460 759	20.316 984	21.208 918	20
21	19.699 700	20.616 820	21.574 513	22.574 481	23.618 494	24.708 389	21
22	22.703 904	23.812 427	24.972 498	26.186 398	27.456 499	28.785 273	22
23	26.166 250	27.503 353	28.905 667	30.376 222	31.918 180	33.534 843	23
24	30.156 603	31.766 372	33.458 309	35.236 417	37.104 884	39.068 093	24
25	34.755 485	36.690 160	38.727 993	40.874 244	43.134 428	45.514 328	25
26	40.055 696	42.377 135	44.827 652	47.414 123	50.143 772	53.024 192	26
27	46.164 190	48.945 591	51.888 007	55.000 382	58.292 135	61.773 184	27
28	53.204 229	56.532 157	60.060 368	63.800 444	67.764 607	71.965 759	28
29	61.317 874	65.294 642	69.519 876	74.008 515	78.776 356	83.840 109	29
30	70.668 850	75.415 311	80.469 257	85.849 877	91.577 513	97.673 727	30
31	81.445 849	87.104 684	93.143 165	99.585 857	106.458 859	113.789 892	31
32	93.866 341	100.605 910	107.813 213	115.519 594	123.758 424	132.565 224	32
33	108.180 958	116.199 826	124.793 794	134.002 729	143.869 168	154.438 487	33
34	124.678 554	134.210 800	144.448 817	155.443 166	167.247 908	179.920 837	34
35	143.692 034	155.013 474	167.199 506	180.314 073	194.425 693	209.607 775	35
36	165.605 069	179.040 562	193.533 428	209.164 324	226.019 868	244.193 058	36
37	190.859 842	206.791 849	224.014 943	242.630 616	262.748 096	284.484 912	37
38	219.965 968	238.844 586	259.297 296	281.451 515	305.444 662	331.424 923	38
39	253.510 778	275.865 496	300.136 620	326.483 757	355.079 419	386.110 035	39
40	292.171 172	318.624 648	347.408 138	378.721 158	412.779 825	449.818 191	40
41	336.727 276	368.011 469	402.124 920	439.316 544	479.856 546	524.038 192	41
42	388.078 185	425.053 246	465.459 595	509.607 191	557.833 235	610.504 494	42
43	447.260 108	490.936 500	538.769 481	591.144 341	648.481 136	711.237 736	43
44	515.467 275	567.031 657	623.625 674	685.727 436	753.859 321	828.591 962	44
45	594.076 034	654.921 564	721.846 718	795.443 826	876.361 460	965.309 636	45
46	684.672 629	756.434 406	835.537 576	922.714 838	1018.770 197	1124.585 725	46
47	789.085 205	873.681 739	967.134 744	1070.349 212	1184.320 355	1310.142 370	47
48	909.420 699	1009.102 409	1119.458 466	1241.605 086	1376.772 412	1526.315 861	48
49	1048.107 356	1165.513 282	1295.773 175	1440.261 900	1600.497 929	1778.157 978	49
50	1207.943 728	1346.167 841	1499.857 450	1670.703 804	1860.578 843	2071.554 045	50

FUTURE VALUE OF $1

YRS	16.75% ANNUAL RATE	17.00% ANNUAL RATE	17.25% ANNUAL RATE	17.50% ANNUAL RATE	17.75% ANNUAL RATE	18.00% ANNUAL RATE	YRS
1	1.167 500	1.170 000	1.172 500	1.175 000	1.177 500	1.180 000	1
2	1.363 056	1.368 900	1.374 756	1.380 625	1.386 506	1.392 400	2
3	1.591 368	1.601 613	1.611 902	1.622 234	1.632 611	1.643 032	3
4	1.857 922	1.873 887	1.889 955	1.906 125	1.922 400	1.938 778	4
5	2.169 124	2.192 448	2.215 972	2.239 697	2.263 626	2.287 758	5
6	2.532 453	2.565 164	2.598 227	2.631 644	2.665 419	2.699 554	6
7	2.956 638	3.001 242	3.046 421	3.092 182	3.138 531	3.185 474	7
8	3.451 875	3.511 453	3.571 929	3.633 314	3.695 620	3.758 859	8
9	4.030 065	4.108 400	4.188 087	4.269 144	4.351 593	4.435 454	9
10	4.705 100	4.806 828	4.910 532	5.016 244	5.124 000	5.233 836	10
11	5.493 205	5.623 989	5.757 598	5.894 087	6.033 511	6.175 926	11
12	6.413 316	6.580 067	6.750 784	6.925 552	7.104 459	7.287 593	12
13	7.487 547	7.698 679	7.915 294	8.137 524	8.365 500	8.599 359	13
14	8.741 711	9.007 454	9.280 683	9.561 590	9.850 376	10.147 244	14
15	10.205 948	10.538 721	10.881 600	11.234 869	11.598 818	11.973 748	15
16	11.915 444	12.330 304	12.758 676	13.200 971	13.657 608	14.129 023	16
17	13.911 281	14.426 456	14.959 548	15.511 141	16.081 834	16.672 247	17
18	16.241 420	16.878 953	17.540 070	18.225 590	18.936 359	19.673 251	18
19	18.961 858	19.748 375	20.565 732	21.415 068	22.297 563	23.214 436	19
20	22.137 969	23.105 599	24.113 321	25.162 705	26.255 380	27.393 035	20
21	25.846 079	27.033 551	28.272 869	29.566 179	30.915 710	32.323 781	21
22	30.175 298	31.629 255	33.149 939	34.740 260	36.403 249	38.142 061	22
23	35.229 660	37.006 228	38.868 303	40.819 806	42.864 826	45.007 632	23
24	41.130 628	43.297 287	45.573 086	47.963 272	50.473 332	53.109 006	24
25	48.020 008	50.657 826	53.434 443	56.356 844	59.432 349	62.668 627	25
26	56.063 360	59.269 656	62.651 884	66.219 292	69.981 591	73.948 980	26
27	65.453 972	69.345 497	73.459 334	77.807 668	82.403 323	87.259 797	27
28	76.417 513	81.134 232	86.131 069	91.424 010	97.029 913	102.966 560	28
29	89.217 446	94.927 051	100.988 679	107.423 211	114.252 723	121.500 541	29
30	104.161 369	111.064 650	118.409 226	126.222 273	134.532 581	143.370 638	30
31	121.608 398	129.945 641	138.834 817	148.311 171	158.412 114	169.177 353	31
32	141.977 804	152.036 399	162.783 823	174.265 626	186.530 264	199.629 277	32
33	165.759 087	177.882 587	190.864 033	204.762 111	219.639 386	235.562 547	33
34	193.523 734	208.122 627	223.788 078	240.595 480	258.625 377	277.963 805	34
35	225.938 959	243.503 474	262.391 522	282.699 689	304.531 382	327.997 290	35
36	263.783 735	284.899 064	307.654 059	332.172 135	358.585 702	387.036 802	36
37	307.967 510	333.331 905	360.724 385	390.302 259	422.234 664	456.703 427	37
38	359.552 068	389.998 329	422.949 341	458.605 154	497.181 317	538.910 044	38
39	419.777 039	456.298 045	495.908 102	538.861 056	585.431 001	635.913 852	39
40	490.089 694	533.868 713	581.452 250	633.161 741	689.345 003	750.378 345	40
41	572.179 717	624.626 394	681.752 763	743.965 045	811.703 742	885.446 447	41
42	668.019 820	730.812 881	799.355 115	874.158 928	955.781 156	1044.826 807	42
43	779.913 140	855.051 071	937.243 872	1027.136 740	1125.432 311	1232.895 633	43
44	910.548 591	1000.409 753	1098.918 440	1206.885 670	1325.196 546	1454.816 847	44
45	1063.065 480	1170.479 411	1288.481 871	1418.090 662	1560.418 933	1716.683 879	45
46	1241.128 947	1369.460 910	1510.744 994	1666.256 528	1837.393 293	2025.686 977	46
47	1449.018 046	1602.269 265	1771.348 505	1957.851 421	2163.530 603	2390.310 633	47
48	1691.728 569	1874.655 040	2076.906 122	2300.475 419	2547.557 285	2820.566 547	48
49	1975.093 104	2193.346 397	2435.172 429	2703.058 618	2999.748 703	3328.268 525	49
50	2305.921 199	2566.215 284	2855.239 673	3176.093 876	3532.204 098	3927.356 860	50

FUTURE VALUE OF $1

YRS	18.25% ANNUAL RATE	18.50% ANNUAL RATE	18.75% ANNUAL RATE	19.00% ANNUAL RATE	19.25% ANNUAL RATE	19.50% ANNUAL RATE	YRS
1	1.182 500	1.185 000	1.187 500	1.190 000	1.192 500	1.195 000	1
2	1.398 306	1.404 225	1.410 156	1.416 100	1.422 056	1.428 025	2
3	1.653 497	1.664 007	1.674 561	1.685 159	1.695 802	1.706 490	3
4	1.955 260	1.971 848	1.988 541	2.005 339	2.022 244	2.039 255	4
5	2.312 095	2.336 640	2.361 392	2.386 354	2.411 526	2.436 910	5
6	2.734 053	2.768 918	2.804 153	2.839 761	2.875 745	2.912 108	6
7	3.233 017	3.281 168	3.329 932	3.379 315	3.429 326	3.479 969	7
8	3.823 043	3.888 184	3.954 294	4.021 385	4.089 471	4.158 563	8
9	4.520 748	4.607 498	4.695 724	4.785 449	4.876 694	4.969 482	9
10	5.345 785	5.459 885	5.576 172	5.694 684	5.815 457	5.938 531	10
11	6.321 391	6.469 964	6.621 705	6.776 674	6.934 933	7.096 545	11
12	7.475 045	7.666 907	7.863 274	8.064 242	8.269 908	8.480 371	12
13	8.839 240	9.085 285	9.337 638	9.596 448	9.861 865	10.134 044	13
14	10.452 402	10.766 063	11.088 445	11.419 773	11.760 274	12.110 182	14
15	12.359 965	12.757 784	13.167 529	13.589 530	14.024 126	14.471 668	15
16	14.615 659	15.117 974	15.636 440	16.171 540	16.723 771	17.293 643	16
17	17.283 016	17.914 800	18.568 273	19.244 133	19.943 097	20.665 903	17
18	20.437 167	21.229 038	22.049 824	22.900 518	23.782 143	24.695 754	18
19	24.166 950	25.156 410	26.184 166	27.251 616	28.360 205	29.511 426	19
20	28.577 418	29.810 345	31.093 697	32.429 423	33.819 545	35.266 154	20
21	33.792 797	35.325 259	36.923 766	38.591 014	40.329 807	42.143 055	21
22	39.959 982	41.860 432	43.846 972	45.923 307	48.093 295	50.360 950	22
23	47.252 679	49.604 612	52.068 279	54.648 735	57.351 254	60.181 336	23
24	55.876 293	58.781 465	61.831 081	65.031 994	68.391 370	71.916 696	24
25	66.073 716	69.656 036	73.424 409	77.388 073	81.556 709	85.940 452	25
26	78.132 170	82.542 403	87.191 485	92.091 807	97.256 376	102.698 840	26
27	92.391 291	97.812 748	103.539 889	109.589 251	115.978 228	122.725 114	27
28	109.252 701	115.908 106	122.953 618	130.411 208	138.304 037	146.656 511	28
29	129.191 319	137.351 106	146.007 421	155.189 338	164.927 564	175.254 530	29
30	152.768 735	162.761 060	173.383 813	184.675 312	196.676 120	209.429 164	30
31	180.649 029	192.871 856	205.893 278	219.763 621	234.536 273	250.267 851	31
32	213.617 477	228.553 150	244.498 267	261.518 710	279.684 505	299.070 082	32
33	252.602 666	270.835 483	290.341 692	311.207 264	333.523 773	357.388 747	33
34	298.702 653	320.940 047	344.780 760	370.336 645	397.727 099	427.079 553	34
35	353.215 887	380.313 956	409.427 152	440.700 607	474.289 565	510.360 066	35
36	417.677 787	450.672 037	486.194 743	524.433 722	565.590 307	609.880 279	36
37	493.903 983	534.046 364	577.356 257	624.076 130	674.466 441	728.806 933	37
38	584.041 459	632.844 942	685.610 556	742.650 594	804.301 230	870.924 285	38
39	690.629 026	749.921 256	814.162 535	883.754 207	959.129 217	1040.754 521	39
40	816.668 823	888.656 688	966.818 010	1051.667 507	1143.761 592	1243.701 652	40
41	965.710 883	1053.058 176	1148.096 387	1251.484 333	1363.935 698	1486.223 475	41
42	1141.953 119	1247.873 938	1363.364 459	1489.266 356	1626.493 320	1776.037 052	42
43	1350.359 564	1478.730 617	1618.995 295	1772.226 964	1939.593 284	2122.364 277	43
44	1596.800 184	1752.295 781	1922.556 913	2108.950 087	2312.964 991	2536.225 312	44
45	1888.216 218	2076.470 500	2283.036 335	2509.660 603	2758.210 752	3030.789 247	45
46	2232.815 678	2460.617 543	2711.105 647	2986.484 218	3289.166 321	3621.793 151	46
47	2640.304 539	2915.831 788	3219.437 956	3553.916 219	3922.330 838	4328.042 815	47
48	3122.160 117	3455.260 669	3823.082 573	4229.160 301	4677.379 525	5172.011 164	48
49	3691.954 338	4094.483 893	4539.910 555	5032.700 758	5577.775 083	6180.553 341	49
50	4365.736 005	4851.963 413	5391.143 785	5988.913 902	6651.496 787	7385.761 242	50

FUTURE VALUE OF $1

YRS	19.75% ANNUAL RATE	20.00% ANNUAL RATE	21.00% ANNUAL RATE	22.00% ANNUAL RATE	23.00% ANNUAL RATE	24.00% ANNUAL RATE	YRS
1	1.197 500	1.200 000	1.210 000	1.220 000	1.230 000	1.240 000	1
2	1.434 006	1.440 000	1.464 100	1.488 400	1.512 900	1.537 600	2
3	1.717 222	1.728 000	1.771 561	1.815 848	1.860 867	1.906 624	3
4	2.056 374	2.073 600	2.143 589	2.215 335	2.288 866	2.364 214	4
5	2.462 508	2.488 320	2.593 742	2.702 708	2.815 306	2.931 625	5
6	2.948 853	2.985 984	3.138 428	3.297 304	3.462 826	3.635 215	6
7	3.531 252	3.583 181	3.797 498	4.022 711	4.259 276	4.507 667	7
8	4.228 674	4.299 817	4.594 973	4.907 707	5.238 909	5.589 507	8
9	5.063 837	5.159 780	5.559 917	5.987 403	6.443 859	6.930 988	9
10	6.063 945	6.191 736	6.727 500	7.304 631	7.925 946	8.594 426	10
11	7.261 574	7.430 084	8.140 275	8.911 650	9.748 914	10.657 088	11
12	8.695 734	8.916 100	9.849 733	10.872 213	11.991 164	13.214 789	12
13	10.413 142	10.699 321	11.918 177	13.264 100	14.749 132	16.386 338	13
14	12.469 737	12.839 185	14.420 994	16.182 202	18.141 432	20.319 059	14
15	14.932 511	15.407 022	17.449 402	19.742 287	22.313 961	25.195 633	15
16	17.881 681	18.488 426	21.113 777	24.085 590	27.446 172	31.242 585	16
17	21.413 314	22.186 111	25.547 670	29.384 420	33.758 792	38.740 806	17
18	25.642 443	26.623 333	30.912 681	35.848 992	41.523 314	48.038 599	18
19	30.706 825	31.948 000	37.404 343	43.735 771	51.073 676	59.567 863	19
20	36.771 423	38.337 600	45.259 256	53.357 640	62.820 622	73.864 150	20
21	44.033 780	46.005 120	54.763 699	65.096 321	77.269 364	91.591 546	21
22	52.730 451	55.206 144	66.264 076	79.417 512	95.041 318	113.573 517	22
23	63.144 715	66.247 373	80.179 532	96.889 364	116.900 822	140.831 161	23
24	75.615 796	79.496 847	97.017 234	118.205 024	143.788 010	174.630 639	24
25	90.549 916	95.396 217	117.390 853	144.210 130	176.859 253	216.541 993	25
26	108.433 525	114.475 460	142.042 932	175.936 358	217.536 881	268.512 071	26
27	129.849 146	137.370 552	171.871 948	214.642 357	267.570 364	332.954 968	27
28	155.494 352	164.844 662	207.965 057	261.863 675	329.111 547	412.864 160	28
29	186.204 486	197.813 595	251.637 719	319.473 684	404.807 203	511.951 559	29
30	222.979 872	237.376 314	304.481 640	389.757 894	497.912 860	634.819 933	30
31	267.018 397	284.851 577	368.422 784	475.504 631	612.432 818	787.176 717	31
32	319.754 531	341.821 892	445.791 568	580.115 650	753.292 366	976.099 129	32
33	382.906 050	410.186 270	539.407 798	707.741 093	926.549 610	1210.362 920	33
34	458.529 995	492.223 524	652.683 435	863.444 133	1139.656 020	1500.850 021	34
35	549.089 670	590.668 229	789.746 957	1053.401 842	1401.776 905	1861.054 026	35
36	657.534 879	708.801 875	955.593 818	1285.150 248	1724.185 593	2307.706 992	36
37	787.398 018	850.562 250	1156.268 519	1567.883 302	2120.748 279	2861.556 670	37
38	942.909 126	1020.674 700	1399.084 909	1912.817 629	2608.520 383	3548.330 270	38
39	1129.133 679	1224.809 640	1692.892 739	2333.637 507	3208.480 071	4399.929 535	39
40	1352.137 580	1469.771 568	2048.400 215	2847.037 759	3946.430 488	5455.912 624	40
41	1619.184 753	1763.725 882	2478.564 260	3473.386 066	4854.109 500	6765.331 653	41
42	1938.973 741	2116.471 058	2999.062 754	4237.531 000	5970.554 685	8389.011 250	42
43	2321.921 055	2539.765 269	3628.865 933	5169.787 820	7343.782 263	10402.373 950	43
44	2780.500 464	3047.718 323	4390.927 778	6307.141 140	9032.852 183	12898.943 698	44
45	3329.649 305	3657.261 988	5313.022 612	7694.712 191	11110.408 185	15994.690 166	45
46	3987.255 043	4388.714 386	6428.757 360	9387.548 873	13665.802 068	19833.415 831	46
47	4774.737 914	5266.457 263	7778.796 406	11452.809 626	16808.936 543	24593.435 630	47
48	5717.748 652	6319.748 715	9412.343 651	13972.427 743	20674.991 948	30495.860 181	48
49	6847.004 010	7583.698 458	11388.935 818	17046.361 847	25430.240 096	37814.866 624	49
50	8199.287 303	9100.438 150	13780.612 340	20796.561 453	31279.195 318	46890.434 614	50

Section 2.   The Future Value of $1.00 per period:

These factors represent the growth of the investment of $1.00 per period. It is important to understand that each investment is made at the end of each period. Convention dictates this technique.

That is, if we begin an investment period at a particular time, then the first $1.00 investment is made at the end of the first period. An example: If the investment intervals are to be monthly, and the beginning period is January 1, then the first regular investment of $1.00 will be made at the end of January. All investments are made in equal amounts ($1) and at the exact same intervals (monthly, quarterly, annual and semiannual).

These factors are based on the assumption that no funds will be withdrawn at any point during the investment.

In this section the following four (4) periods are presented in detail: monthly, quarterly, semiannual, and annual.

Monthly:

The factors presented on pages 36 through 43 indicate the value of a $1 investment made at the end of each stated monthly interval. That is, the regular monthly investment, plus interest earned on the interest and on the investment.

Example C

If you invest $150 at the end of each month, what will be the value of your investment in 10 years? Assume an annual interest rate of 12.0% and monthly compounding of interest.

Turn to page 37 and locate the 12% column. Proceed down that column until you locate the point where the 10 year row intersects the 12.0% interest column. The number is 230.038689 for each $1 invested. So, to determine your answer, multiply 230.038689 by $150. The correct answer is $34,505.80. That is, the value of that monthly investment of $150 is $34,505.80 in 10 years.

Note: If your investment period is less than 4 years, we have provided all the monthly payment amounts for each monthly period; over 4 years, only the annual figures are provided.

Quarterly:

The factors presented on pages 44 through 49 indicate the value of a $1 investment, made at the end of each stated quarterly interval. That is, the regular quarterly interval, plus interest earned on the interest and on the investment.

Example D

If you deposit $500 in a savings account at the end of every quarter, what is the value of that account at the end of 30 years? Assume an interest rate of 7.0% and quarterly compounding.

Turn to page 44 and locate the 7.0% column. Proceed down that column until you locate the point where the 30 years row intersects the 7.0% interest column. The number is 401.096196 for each $1 invested. So, to determine your answer, multiply 401.096196 by $500. The correct answer is $200,548.10. That is, the value of that $500 per quarter investment is $200,548.10 in 30 years.

Note: For investments of 14 years and more, only the annual amounts are shown.

Semiannual:

The factors on pages 50 through 53 cover semiannual compounding, or the interest being compounded every 6 months. They are used the same way as the monthly or quarterly tables.

Annual:

The factors on pages 54 through 61 cover annual compounding (or the interest being compounded every year). They are used the same way as the monthly, quarterly, and semiannual tables.

For you formula buffs . . .

$$S_{\overline{n}|} = \frac{(1 + i)^n - 1}{i}$$

$S_{\overline{n}|}$ = The future value of $1.00 per period
i = Interest rate per period
n = number of compounding periods

FUTURE VALUE OF $1 PER PERIOD

MONTHLY COMPOUNDING

MOS	7.00% ANNUAL RATE	8.00% ANNUAL RATE	9.00% ANNUAL RATE	10.00% ANNUAL RATE	10.25% ANNUAL RATE	10.50% ANNUAL RATE	MOS
1	1.000 000	1.000 000	1.000 000	1.000 000	1.000 000	1.000 000	1
2	2.005 833	2.006 667	2.007 500	2.008 333	2.008 542	2.008 750	2
3	3.017 534	3.020 044	3.022 556	3.025 069	3.025 698	3.026 327	3
4	4.035 136	4.040 178	4.045 225	4.050 278	4.051 542	4.052 807	4
5	5.058 675	5.067 113	5.075 565	5.084 031	5.086 149	5.088 269	5
6	6.088 184	6.100 893	6.113 631	6.126 398	6.129 594	6.132 791	6
7	7.123 698	7.141 566	7.159 484	7.177 451	7.181 951	7.186 453	7
8	8.165 253	8.189 176	8.213 180	8.237 263	8.243 296	8.249 335	8
9	9.212 883	9.243 771	9.274 779	9.305 907	9.313 708	9.321 516	9
10	10.266 625	10.305 396	10.344 339	10.383 456	10.393 262	10.403 080	10
11	11.326 514	11.374 099	11.421 922	11.469 985	11.482 038	11.494 107	11
12	12.392 585	12.449 926	12.507 586	12.565 568	12.580 114	12.594 680	12
13	13.464 875	13.532 926	13.601 393	13.670 281	13.687 569	13.704 884	13
14	14.543 420	14.623 145	14.703 404	14.784 200	14.804 484	14.824 801	14
15	15.628 257	15.720 633	15.813 679	15.907 402	15.930 939	15.954 518	15
16	16.719 422	16.825 437	16.932 282	17.039 964	17.067 015	17.094 120	16
17	17.816 952	17.937 606	18.059 274	18.181 963	18.212 796	18.243 694	17
18	18.920 884	19.057 191	19.194 718	19.333 480	19.368 364	19.403 326	18
19	20.031 256	20.184 238	20.338 679	20.494 592	20.533 802	20.573 105	19
20	21.148 105	21.318 800	21.491 219	21.665 380	21.709 195	21.753 120	20
21	22.271 469	22.460 925	22.652 403	22.845 925	22.894 628	22.943 460	21
22	23.401 386	23.610 665	23.822 296	24.036 308	24.090 186	24.144 215	22
23	24.537 894	24.768 069	25.000 963	25.236 610	25.295 956	25.355 477	23
24	25.681 032	25.933 190	26.188 471	26.446 915	26.512 026	26.577 337	24
25	26.830 838	27.106 078	27.384 884	27.667 306	27.738 483	27.809 889	25
26	27.987 351	28.286 785	28.590 271	28.897 867	28.975 416	29.053 226	26
27	29.150 610	29.475 363	29.804 698	30.138 683	30.222 914	30.307 441	27
28	30.320 656	30.671 866	31.028 233	31.389 838	31.481 068	31.572 631	28
29	31.497 526	31.876 345	32.260 945	32.651 420	32.749 969	32.848 892	29
30	32.681 262	33.088 854	33.502 902	33.923 516	34.029 708	34.136 320	30
31	33.871 902	34.309 446	34.754 174	35.206 212	35.320 379	35.435 012	31
32	35.069 488	35.538 176	36.014 830	36.499 597	36.622 073	36.745 069	32
33	36.274 060	36.775 097	37.284 941	37.803 760	37.934 887	38.066 588	33
34	37.485 659	38.020 264	38.564 578	39.118 791	39.258 914	39.399 671	34
35	38.704 325	39.273 733	39.853 813	40.444 781	40.594 251	40.744 418	35
36	39.930 101	40.535 558	41.152 716	41.781 821	41.940 993	42.100 932	36
37	41.163 026	41.805 795	42.461 361	43.130 003	43.299 239	43.469 315	37
38	42.403 144	43.084 500	43.779 822	44.489 420	44.669 087	44.849 671	38
39	43.650 496	44.371 730	45.108 170	45.860 165	46.050 635	46.242 106	39
40	44.905 124	45.667 542	46.446 482	47.242 333	47.443 985	47.646 724	40
41	46.167 070	46.971 692	47.794 830	48.636 019	48.849 235	49.063 633	41
42	47.436 378	48.285 139	49.153 291	50.041 319	50.266 489	50.492 940	42
43	48.713 090	49.607 039	50.521 941	51.458 330	51.695 849	51.934 753	43
44	49.997 250	50.937 753	51.900 856	52.887 150	53.137 417	53.389 182	44
45	51.288 900	52.277 338	53.290 112	54.327 876	54.591 300	54.856 338	45
46	52.588 086	53.625 854	54.689 788	55.780 608	56.057 600	56.336 331	46
47	53.894 850	54.983 359	56.099 961	57.245 446	57.536 426	57.829 273	47

YRS							
4	55.209 236	56.349 915	57.520 711	58.722 492	59.027 882	59.335 280	48
5	71.592 902	73.476 856	75.424 137	77.437 072	77.950 846	78.468 912	60
6	89.160 944	92.025 325	95.007 028	98.111 314	98.907 179	99.711 137	72
7	107.998 981	112.113 308	116.426 928	120.950 418	122.115 378	123.294 329	84
8	128.198 821	133.868 583	139.856 164	146.181 076	147.817 417	149.476 469	96
9	149.858 909	157.429 535	165.483 223	174.053 713	176.281 272	178.543 972	108
10	173.084 807	182.946 035	193.514 277	204.844 979	207.803 714	210.814 814	120
11	197.989 707	210.580 392	224.174 837	238.860 493	242.713 406	246.642 013	132
12	224.694 985	240.508 387	257.711 570	276.437 876	281.374 322	286.417 494	144
13	253.330 789	272.920 390	294.394 279	317.950 102	324.189 554	330.576 371	156
14	284.036 677	308.022 674	334.518 079	363.809 201	371.605 502	379.601 707	168
15	316.962 297	346.038 222	378.405 769	414.470 346	424.116 537	434.029 805	180
16	352.268 112	387.209 149	426.410 427	470.436 376	482.270 153	494.456 068	192
17	390.126 188	431.797 244	478.918 252	532.262 780	546.672 673	561.541 512	204
18	430.721 027	480.086 128	536.351 674	600.563 216	617.995 576	636.020 005	216
19	474.240 470	532.382 966	599.172 747	676.015 601	696.982 491	718.706 284	228
20	520.926 660	589.020 416	667.886 870	759.368 836	784.456 956	810.504 876	240
21	570.977 075	650.358 746	743.046 852	851.450 244	881.331 002	912.419 990	252
22	624.645 640	716.788 127	825.257 358	953.173 779	988.614 662	1025.566 501	264
23	682.193 909	788.731 114	915.179 777	1065.549 097	1107.426 503	1151.182 148	276
24	743.902 347	866.645 333	1013.537 539	1189.691 580	1239.005 287	1290.641 073	288
25	810.071 693	951.026 395	1121.121 937	1326.833 403	1384.722 888	1445.468 853	300
26	881.024 427	1042.411 042	1238.798 495	1478.335 767	1546.098 594	1617.359 188	312
27	957.106 339	1141.380 571	1367.513 924	1645.702 407	1724.814 949	1808.192 431	324
28	1038.688 219	1248.564 521	1508.303 750	1830.594 523	1922.735 295	2020.056 156	336
29	1126.167 659	1364.644 687	1662.300 631	2034.847 258	2141.923 199	2255.267 995	348
30	1219.970 996	1490.359 449	1830.743 483	2260.487 925	2384.663 970	2516.400 990	360

FUTURE VALUE OF
$1 PER PERIOD

MONTHLY
COMPOUNDING

MOS	10.75% ANNUAL RATE	11.00% ANNUAL RATE	11.25% ANNUAL RATE	11.50% ANNUAL RATE	11.75% ANNUAL RATE	12.00% ANNUAL RATE	MOS
1	1.000 000	1.000 000	1.000 000	1.000 000	1.000 000	1.000 000	1
2	2.008 958	2.009 167	2.009 375	2.009 583	2.009 792	2.010 000	2
3	3.026 955	3.027 584	3.028 213	3.028 842	3.029 471	3.030 100	3
4	4.054 072	4.055 337	4.056 602	4.057 868	4.059 134	4.060 401	4
5	5.090 389	5.092 511	5.094 633	5.096 756	5.098 880	5.101 005	5
6	6.135 991	6.139 192	6.142 395	6.145 600	6.148 807	6.152 015	6
7	7.190 959	7.195 468	7.199 980	7.204 495	7.209 014	7.213 535	7
8	8.255 378	8.261 427	8.267 480	8.273 538	8.279 602	8.285 671	8
9	9.329 333	9.337 156	9.344 988	9.352 827	9.360 673	9.368 527	9
10	10.412 908	10.422 747	10.432 597	10.442 458	10.452 330	10.462 213	10
11	11.506 190	11.518 289	11.530 402	11.542 531	11.554 675	11.566 835	11
12	12.609 266	12.623 873	12.638 500	12.653 147	12.667 815	12.682 503	12
13	13.722 224	13.739 592	13.756 986	13.774 407	13.791 854	13.809 328	13
14	14.845 153	14.865 538	14.885 958	14.906 411	14.926 899	14.947 421	14
15	15.978 141	16.001 806	16.025 514	16.049 264	16.073 058	16.096 896	15
16	17.121 278	17.148 489	17.175 753	17.203 070	17.230 440	17.257 864	16
17	18.274 656	18.305 683	18.336 775	18.367 933	18.399 155	18.430 443	17
18	19.438 367	19.473 485	19.508 683	19.543 959	19.579 314	19.614 748	18
19	20.612 502	20.651 992	20.691 577	20.731 255	20.771 028	20.810 895	19
20	21.797 156	21.841 302	21.885 560	21.929 929	21.974 411	22.019 004	20
21	22.992 422	23.041 514	23.090 737	23.140 091	23.189 577	23.239 194	21
22	24.198 396	24.252 728	24.307 213	24.361 851	24.416 641	24.471 586	22
23	25.415 173	25.475 045	25.535 093	25.595 318	25.655 721	25.716 302	23
24	26.642 850	26.708 566	26.774 484	26.840 607	26.906 933	26.973 465	24
25	27.881 526	27.953 394	28.025 495	28.097 829	28.170 397	28.243 200	25
26	29.131 298	29.209 634	29.288 234	29.367 100	29.446 232	29.525 631	26
27	30.392 266	30.477 389	30.562 812	30.648 535	30.734 560	30.820 888	27
28	31.664 530	31.756 765	31.849 338	31.942 250	32.035 502	32.129 097	28
29	32.948 191	33.047 869	33.147 925	33.248 363	33.349 183	33.450 388	29
30	34.243 352	34.350 807	34.458 687	34.566 993	34.675 727	34.784 892	30
31	35.550 116	35.665 690	35.781 737	35.898 260	36.015 261	36.132 740	31
32	36.868 585	36.992 625	37.117 191	37.242 285	37.367 910	37.494 068	32
33	38.198 866	38.331 724	38.465 165	38.599 191	38.733 804	38.869 009	33
34	39.541 065	39.683 099	39.825 776	39.969 099	40.113 073	40.257 699	34
35	40.895 287	41.046 860	41.199 142	41.352 137	41.505 846	41.660 276	35
36	42.261 640	42.423 123	42.585 384	42.748 428	42.912 258	43.076 878	36
37	43.640 234	43.812 002	43.984 622	44.158 100	44.332 440	44.507 647	37
38	45.031 178	45.213 612	45.396 978	45.581 282	45.766 529	45.952 724	38
39	46.434 582	46.628 070	46.822 575	47.018 103	47.214 659	47.412 251	39
40	47.850 559	48.055 494	48.261 537	48.468 693	48.676 970	48.886 373	40
41	49.279 220	49.496 003	49.713 988	49.933 185	50.153 598	50.375 237	41
42	50.720 680	50.949 716	51.180 057	51.411 711	51.644 686	51.878 989	42
43	52.175 052	52.416 755	52.659 870	52.904 406	53.150 373	53.397 779	43
44	53.642 454	53.897 242	54.153 556	54.411 407	54.670 804	54.931 757	44
45	55.123 001	55.391 300	55.661 246	55.932 850	56.206 122	56.481 075	45
46	56.616 811	56.899 054	57.183 070	57.468 873	57.756 474	58.045 885	46
47	58.124 003	58.420 628	58.719 161	59.019 616	59.322 006	59.626 344	47

YRS							
4	59.644 698	59.956 151	60.269 654	60.585 221	60.902 867	61.222 608	48
5	78.991 310	79.518 080	80.049 260	80.584 891	81.125 014	81.669 670	60
6	100.523 278	101.343 692	102.172 472	103.009 708	103.855 497	104.709 931	72
7	124.487 454	125.694 940	126.916 973	128.153 744	129.405 446	130.672 274	84
8	151.158 576	152.864 085	154.593 349	156.346 728	158.124 586	159.927 293	96
9	180.842 414	183.177 212	185.548 987	187.958 374	190.406 019	192.892 579	108
10	213.879 280	216.998 139	220.172 433	223.403 228	226.691 611	230.038 689	120
11	250.647 925	254.732 784	258.898 270	263.146 100	267.478 031	271.895 856	132
12	291.569 882	296.834 038	302.212 574	307.708 167	313.323 559	319.061 559	144
13	337.114 303	343.807 200	350.659 014	357.673 800	364.855 722	372.209 054	156
14	387.803 331	396.216 042	404.845 676	413.698 232	422.779 884	432.096 982	168
15	444.218 090	454.689 575	465.452 695	476.516 149	487.888 901	499.580 198	180
16	507.005 349	519.929 596	533.240 794	546.951 324	561.073 978	575.621 974	192
17	576.884 931	592.719 117	609.060 830	625.927 421	643.336 860	661.307 751	204
18	654.657 972	673.931 757	693.864 473	714.480 107	735.803 550	757.860 630	216
19	741.216 102	764.542 228	788.716 155	813.770 632	839.739 717	866.658 830	228
20	837.551 665	865.638 038	894.806 428	925.101 060	956.568 025	989.255 365	240
21	944.769 102	978.432 537	1013.466 907	1049.931 340	1087.887 601	1127.400 210	252
22	1064.097 607	1104.279 485	1146.186 983	1189.898 456	1235.495 930	1283.065 279	264
23	1196.905 224	1244.689 295	1294.632 522	1346.837 891	1401.413 451	1458.472 574	276
24	1344.714 524	1401.347 165	1460.666 770	1522.807 696	1587.911 219	1656.125 905	288
25	1509.220 069	1576.133 301	1646.373 742	1720.115 481	1797.541 987	1878.846 626	300
26	1692.307 834	1771.145 485	1854.084 378	1941.348 676	2033.175 151	2129.813 909	312
27	1896.076 828	1988.724 252	2086.405 804	2189.408 459	2298.036 022	2412.610 125	324
28	2122.863 162	2231.480 981	2346.254 051	2467.547 806	2595.749 977	2731.271 980	336
29	2375.266 830	2502.329 236	2636.890 662	2779.414 142	2930.392 078	3090.348 134	348
30	2656.181 515	2804.519 736	2961.963 624	3129.097 181	3306.542 859	3494.964 133	360

FUTURE VALUE OF $1 PER PERIOD

MONTHLY COMPOUNDING

MOS	12.25% ANNUAL RATE	12.50% ANNUAL RATE	12.75% ANNUAL RATE	13.00% ANNUAL RATE	13.25% ANNUAL RATE	13.50% ANNUAL RATE	MOS
1	1.000 000	1.000 000	1.000 000	1.000 000	1.000 000	1.000 000	1
2	2.010 208	2.010 417	2.010 625	2.010 833	2.011 042	2.011 250	2
3	3.030 729	3.031 359	3.031 988	3.032 617	3.033 247	3.033 877	3
4	4.061 668	4.062 935	4.064 203	4.065 471	4.066 739	4.068 008	4
5	5.103 131	5.105 257	5.107 385	5.109 513	5.111 643	5.113 773	5
6	6.155 225	6.158 437	6.161 651	6.164 866	6.168 084	6.171 303	6
7	7.218 060	7.222 588	7.227 118	7.231 652	7.236 190	7.240 730	7
8	8.291 744	8.297 823	8.303 907	8.309 995	8.316 089	8.322 188	8
9	9.376 389	9.384 258	9.392 136	9.400 020	9.407 913	9.415 813	9
10	10.472 106	10.482 011	10.491 927	10.501 854	10.511 792	10.521 741	10
11	11.579 009	11.591 199	11.603 404	11.615 624	11.627 859	11.640 110	11
12	12.697 212	12.711 940	12.726 690	12.741 460	12.756 250	12.771 061	12
13	13.826 829	13.844 357	13.861 911	13.879 492	13.897 101	13.914 736	13
14	14.967 978	14.988 569	15.009 194	15.029 853	15.050 548	15.071 277	14
15	16.120 776	16.144 699	16.168 666	16.192 677	16.216 731	16.240 828	15
16	17.285 342	17.312 873	17.340 459	17.368 098	17.395 791	17.423 538	16
17	18.461 797	18.493 216	18.524 701	18.556 252	18.587 869	18.619 553	17
18	19.650 261	19.685 854	19.721 526	19.757 278	19.793 110	19.829 023	18
19	20.850 857	20.890 914	20.931 067	20.971 315	21.011 659	21.052 099	19
20	22.063 710	22.108 528	22.153 460	22.198 504	22.243 663	22.288 935	20
21	23.288 943	23.338 825	23.388 840	23.438 988	23.489 270	23.539 686	21
22	24.526 685	24.581 938	24.637 347	24.692 911	24.748 631	24.804 507	22
23	25.777 061	25.838 000	25.899 118	25.960 417	26.021 897	26.083 558	23
24	27.040 202	27.107 146	27.174 297	27.241 655	27.309 222	27.376 998	24
25	28.316 238	28.389 512	28.463 023	28.536 773	28.610 761	28.684 989	25
26	29.605 299	29.685 236	29.765 443	29.845 921	29.926 672	30.007 695	26
27	30.907 520	30.994 457	31.081 701	31.169 252	31.257 112	31.345 282	27
28	32.223 034	32.317 316	32.411 944	32.506 919	32.602 243	32.697 916	28
29	33.551 978	33.653 955	33.756 321	33.859 077	33.962 226	34.065 768	29
30	34.894 487	35.004 517	35.114 982	35.225 884	35.337 225	35.449 008	30
31	36.250 702	36.369 147	36.488 078	36.607 498	36.727 407	36.847 809	31
32	37.620 761	37.747 993	37.875 764	38.004 079	38.132 939	38.262 347	32
33	39.004 806	39.141 201	39.278 194	39.415 790	39.553 990	39.692 798	33
34	40.402 981	40.548 922	40.695 525	40.842 794	40.990 732	41.139 342	34
35	41.815 428	41.971 306	42.127 915	42.285 258	42.443 338	42.602 160	35
36	43.242 293	43.408 507	43.575 524	43.743 348	43.911 983	44.081 434	36
37	44.683 725	44.860 679	45.038 514	45.217 234	45.396 845	45.577 350	37
38	46.139 872	46.327 978	46.517 048	46.707 088	46.898 102	47.090 095	38
39	47.610 883	47.810 561	48.011 292	48.213 081	48.415 935	48.619 859	39
40	49.096 911	49.308 588	49.521 412	49.735 390	49.950 527	50.166 832	40
41	50.598 108	50.822 219	51.047 577	51.274 190	51.502 065	51.731 209	41
42	52.114 631	52.351 617	52.589 957	52.829 660	53.070 733	53.313 185	42
43	53.646 634	53.896 946	54.148 726	54.401 981	54.656 723	54.912 959	43
44	55.194 277	55.458 373	55.724 056	55.991 336	56.260 224	56.530 730	44
45	56.757 718	57.036 064	57.316 124	57.597 909	57.881 430	58.166 700	45
46	58.337 120	58.630 190	58.925 108	59.221 886	59.520 538	59.821 076	46
47	59.932 645	60.240 921	60.551 187	60.863 457	61.177 744	61.494 063	47

YRS	12.25% ANNUAL RATE	12.50% ANNUAL RATE	12.75% ANNUAL RATE	13.00% ANNUAL RATE	13.25% ANNUAL RATE	13.50% ANNUAL RATE	MOS
4	61.544 457	61.868 431	62.194 543	62.522 811	62.853 248	63.185 871	48
5	82.218 899	82.772 744	83.331 247	83.894 449	84.462 395	85.035 127	60
6	105.573 198	106.445 124	107.326 078	108.216 068	109.115 196	110.023 563	72
7	131.954 428	133.252 107	134.565 516	135.894 861	137.240 351	138.602 198	84
8	161.755 225	163.608 765	165.488 300	167.394 225	169.326 941	171.286 853	96
9	195.418 723	197.985 131	200.592 497	203.241 525	205.932 935	208.667 457	108
10	233.445 595	236.913 480	240.443 521	244.036 917	247.694 894	251.418 698	120
11	276.401 410	280.996 567	285.683 243	290.463 399	295.339 035	300.312 201	132
12	324.925 044	330.916 961	337.040 330	343.298 242	349.693 867	356.230 450	144
13	379.738 185	387.447 618	395.341 977	403.426 010	411.704 591	420.182 722	156
14	441.656 060	451.463 840	461.527 236	471.853 363	482.449 541	493.323 301	168
15	511.599 567	523.956 837	536.662 137	549.725 914	563.158 937	576.972 311	180
16	590.608 968	606.049 070	621.956 861	638.347 406	655.236 272	672.639 547	192
17	679.859 359	699.011 633	718.785 230	739.201 542	760.282 725	782.051 719	204
18	780.678 151	804.283 930	828.706 835	853.976 825	880.124 998	907.183 624	216
19	894.564 809	923.495 968	953.492 158	984.594 826	1016.847 086	1050.293 785	228
20	1023.213 156	1058.493 594	1095.151 087	1133.242 353	1172.826 517	1213.965 218	240
21	1168.536 564	1211.367 071	1255.965 290	1302.408 067	1350.775 692	1401.152 054	252
22	1332.696 408	1384.483 450	1438.524 963	1494.924 144	1553.789 056	1616.232 853	264
23	1518.134 220	1580.523 215	1645.770 552	1714.013 694	1785.396 905	1860.071 591	276
24	1727.607 992	1802.521 791	1881.040 113	1963.344 717	2049.626 781	2140.087 398	288
25	1964.233 204	2053.916 541	2148.123 079	2247.091 520	2351.073 504	2460.334 319	300
26	2231.529 152	2338.599 989	2451.321 292	2570.004 599	2694.979 079	2826.592 538	312
27	2533.471 198	2660.980 094	2795.518 294	2937.490 172	3087.323 844	3245.472 702	324
28	2874.550 389	3026.048 499	3186.257 987	3355.700 690	3534.930 473	3724.535 238	336
29	3259.839 255	3439.457 817	3629.833 924	3831.637 843	4045.582 614	4272.426 817	348
30	3695.068 249	3907.609 164	4133.390 677	4373.269 783	4628.160 244	4899.036 412	360

FUTURE VALUE OF
$1 PER PERIOD

MOS	13.75% ANNUAL RATE	14.00% ANNUAL RATE	14.25% ANNUAL RATE	14.50% ANNUAL RATE	14.75% ANNUAL RATE	15.00% ANNUAL RATE	MOS
1	1.000 000	1.000 000	1.000 000	1.000 000	1.000 000	1.000 000	1
2	2.011 458	2.011 667	2.011 875	2.012 083	2.012 292	2.012 500	2
3	3.034 506	3.035 136	3.035 875	3.036 396	3.037 026	3.037 656	3
4	4.069 277	4.070 546	4.071 816	4.073 086	4.074 356	4.075 627	4
5	5.115 904	5.118 036	5.120 169	5.122 302	5.124 437	5.126 572	5
6	6.174 524	6.177 746	6.180 971	6.184 197	6.187 425	6.190 654	6
7	7.245 273	7.249 820	7.254 370	7.258 922	7.263 478	7.268 038	7
8	8.328 292	8.334 401	8.340 515	8.346 634	8.352 759	8.358 888	8
9	9.423 720	9.431 636	9.439 559	9.447 490	9.455 428	9.463 374	9
10	10.531 701	10.541 672	10.551 654	10.561 647	10.571 651	10.581 666	10
11	11.652 376	11.664 658	11.676 954	11.689 267	11.701 594	11.713 937	11
12	12.785 893	12.800 745	12.815 618	12.830 512	12.845 426	12.860 361	12
13	13.932 398	13.950 087	13.967 804	13.985 547	14.003 318	14.021 116	13
14	15.092 040	15.112 838	15.133 671	15.154 539	15.175 442	15.196 380	14
15	16.264 970	16.289 155	16.313 384	16.337 657	16.361 974	16.386 335	15
16	17.451 339	17.479 195	17.507 105	17.535 070	17.563 090	17.591 164	16
17	18.651 302	18.683 119	18.715 002	18.746 952	18.778 969	18.811 053	17
18	19.865 015	19.901 089	19.937 243	19.973 478	20.009 794	20.046 192	18
19	21.092 635	21.133 268	21.173 998	21.214 824	21.255 748	21.296 769	19
20	22.334 322	22.379 823	22.425 439	22.471 170	22.517 016	22.562 979	20
21	23.590 236	23.640 921	23.691 741	23.742 696	23.793 788	23.845 016	21
22	24.860 541	24.916 731	24.973 080	25.029 587	25.086 253	25.143 078	22
23	26.145 401	26.207 427	26.269 636	26.332 028	26.394 605	26.457 367	23
24	27.444 984	27.513 180	27.581 587	27.650 207	27.719 039	27.788 084	24
25	28.759 457	28.834 167	28.909 119	28.984 314	29.059 752	29.135 435	25
26	30.088 993	30.170 566	30.252 415	30.334 541	30.416 945	30.499 628	26
27	31.433 763	31.522 556	31.611 662	31.701 083	31.790 820	31.880 873	27
28	32.793 941	32.890 319	32.987 051	33.084 138	33.181 582	33.279 384	28
29	34.169 705	34.274 039	34.378 772	34.483 904	34.589 439	34.695 377	29
30	35.561 233	35.673 903	35.787 020	35.900 585	36.014 601	36.129 069	30
31	36.968 705	37.090 099	37.211 991	37.334 384	37.457 280	37.580 682	31
32	38.392 305	38.522 816	38.653 883	38.785 507	38.917 693	39.050 441	32
33	39.832 217	39.972 249	40.112 898	40.254 166	40.396 056	40.538 571	33
34	41.288 628	41.438 592	41.589 238	41.740 570	41.892 591	42.045 303	34
35	42.761 727	42.922 042	43.083 111	43.244 935	43.407 520	43.570 870	35
36	44.251 705	44.422 800	44.594 723	44.767 478	44.941 071	45.115 505	36
37	45.758 756	45.941 065	46.124 285	46.308 419	46.493 472	46.679 449	37
38	47.283 075	47.477 045	47.672 011	47.867 979	48.064 954	48.262 942	38
39	48.824 860	49.030 943	49.238 116	49.446 384	49.655 753	49.866 229	39
40	50.384 311	50.602 971	50.822 819	51.043 861	51.266 105	51.489 557	40
41	51.961 632	52.193 339	52.426 340	52.660 641	52.896 250	53.133 177	41
42	53.557 025	53.802 261	54.048 902	54.296 957	54.546 433	54.797 341	42
43	55.170 700	55.429 954	55.690 733	55.953 045	56.216 900	56.482 308	43
44	56.802 864	57.076 637	57.352 060	57.629 144	57.907 899	58.188 337	44
45	58.453 730	58.742 531	59.033 116	59.325 496	59.619 684	59.915 691	45
46	60.123 512	60.427 861	60.734 134	61.042 346	61.352 509	61.664 637	46
47	61.812 428	62.132 853	62.455 352	62.779 941	63.106 634	63.435 445	47
YRS							
4	63.520 695	63.857 736	64.197 010	64.538 532	64.882 320	65.228 388	48
5	85.612 689	86.195 125	86.782 480	87.374 798	87.972 126	88.574 508	60
6	110.941 271	111.868 425	112.805 130	113.751 493	114.707 620	115.673 621	72
7	139.980 618	141.375 828	142.788 050	144.217 508	145.664 428	147.129 040	84
8	173.274 375	175.289 927	177.333 935	179.406 832	181.509 058	183.641 059	96
9	211.445 835	214.268 826	217.137 201	220.051 745	223.013 257	226.022 551	108
10	255.209 605	259.068 912	262.997 946	266.998 057	271.070 626	275.217 058	120
11	305.384 987	310.559 534	315.838 029	321.222 707	326.715 854	332.319 805	132
12	362.911 316	369.739 871	376.719 606	383.854 095	391.147 001	398.602 077	144
13	428.865 540	437.758 319	446.866 473	456.195 562	465.751 291	475.539 523	156
14	504.482 389	515.934 780	527.688 675	539.752 513	552.134 980	564.845 011	168
15	591.177 487	605.786 272	620.810 841	636.263 747	652.157 936	668.506 759	180
16	690.573 853	709.056 369	728.104 847	747.737 633	767.973 687	788.832 603	192
17	804.532 285	827.749 031	851.727 442	876.493 913	902.075 783	928.501 369	204
18	935.186 201	964.167 496	994.163 599	1025.211 968	1057.351 487	1090.622 520	216
19	1084.981 571	1120.958 972	1158.276 469	1196.986 579	1237.143 935	1278.805 378	228
20	1256.722 716	1301.166 005	1347.364 934	1395.392 327	1445.324 119	1497.239 481	240
21	1453.624 802	1508.285 522	1565.229 914	1624.557 981	1686.374 225	1750.787 854	252
22	1679.374 032	1746.336 688	1816.250 779	1889.252 413	1965.484 142	2045.095 272	264
23	1938.196 659	2019.938 898	2105.473 371	2194.983 839	2288.663 198	2386.713 938	276
24	2234.938 102	2334.401 417	2438.711 438	2548.114 445	2662.869 543	2783.249 347	288
25	2575.153 657	2695.826 407	2822.663 497	2955.992 779	3096.159 965	3243.529 615	300
26	2965.212 500	3111.227 338	3265.047 479	3427.106 674	3597.863 346	3777.802 015	312
27	3412.416 924	3588.665 088	3774.755 874	3971.259 878	4178.781 527	4397.961 118	324
28	3925.139 043	4137.404 359	4362.034 480	4599.776 067	4851.421 866	5117.813 598	336
29	4512.977 528	4768.093 467	5038.688 355	5325.734 484	5630.266 531	5953.385 616	348
30	5186.937 305	5492.970 967	5818.319 116	6164.242 121	6532.084 302	6923.279 611	360

FUTURE VALUE OF
$1 PER PERIOD

MONTHLY
COMPOUNDING

MOS	15.25% ANNUAL RATE	15.50% ANNUAL RATE	15.75% ANNUAL RATE	16.00% ANNUAL RATE	16.25% ANNUAL RATE	16.50% ANNUAL RATE	MOS
1	1.000 000	1.000 000	1.000 000	1.000 000	1.000 000	1.000 000	1
2	2.012 708	2.012 917	2.013 125	2.013 333	2.013 542	2.013 750	2
3	3.038 287	3.038 917	3.039 547	3.040 178	3.040 808	3.041 439	3
4	4.076 898	4.078 170	4.079 441	4.080 713	4.081 986	4.083 259	4
5	5.128 709	5.130 846	5.132 984	5.135 123	5.137 263	5.139 404	5
6	6.193 886	6.197 119	6.200 354	6.203 591	6.206 830	6.210 070	6
7	7.272 600	7.277 165	7.281 734	7.286 306	7.290 881	7.295 459	7
8	8.365 023	8.371 162	8.377 307	8.383 457	8.389 611	8.395 771	8
9	9.471 328	9.479 290	9.487 259	9.495 236	9.503 221	9.511 213	9
10	10.591 693	10.601 730	10.611 779	10.621 839	10.631 910	10.641 993	10
11	11.726 296	11.738 669	11.751 059	11.763 464	11.775 884	11.788 320	11
12	12.875 317	12.890 294	12.905 291	12.920 310	12.935 349	12.950 409	12
13	14.038 941	14.056 794	14.074 673	14.092 581	14.110 515	14.128 477	13
14	15.217 353	15.238 361	15.259 404	15.280 482	15.301 595	15.322 744	14
15	16.410 740	16.435 189	16.459 683	16.484 221	16.508 804	16.533 432	15
16	17.619 293	17.647 477	17.675 717	17.704 011	17.732 361	17.760 766	16
17	18.843 205	18.875 424	18.907 710	18.940 065	18.972 487	19.004 977	17
18	20.082 671	20.119 231	20.155 874	20.192 599	20.229 406	20.266 295	18
19	21.337 888	21.379 105	21.420 420	21.461 833	21.503 346	21.544 957	19
20	22.609 057	22.655 252	22.701 563	22.747 991	22.794 537	22.841 200	20
21	23.896 380	23.947 882	23.999 521	24.051 298	24.103 213	24.155 267	21
22	25.200 063	25.257 209	25.314 515	25.371 982	25.429 611	25.487 402	22
23	26.520 314	26.583 448	26.646 768	26.710 275	26.773 970	26.837 853	23
24	27.857 343	27.926 817	27.996 506	28.066 412	28.136 534	28.206 874	24
25	29.211 364	29.287 539	29.363 961	29.440 631	29.517 550	29.594 718	25
26	30.582 591	30.665 836	30.749 363	30.833 172	30.917 266	31.001 646	26
27	31.971 245	32.061 936	32.152 948	32.244 281	32.335 938	32.427 918	27
28	33.377 546	33.476 070	33.574 955	33.674 205	33.773 820	33.873 802	28
29	34.801 719	34.908 469	35.015 627	35.123 195	35.231 174	35.339 567	29
30	36.243 991	36.359 370	36.475 207	36.591 504	36.708 263	36.825 486	30
31	37.704 592	37.829 012	37.953 944	38.079 390	38.205 354	38.331 836	31
32	39.183 754	39.317 637	39.452 089	39.587 116	39.722 718	39.858 899	32
33	40.681 715	40.825 489	40.969 898	41.114 944	41.260 630	41.406 959	33
34	42.198 711	42.352 819	42.507 628	42.663 143	42.819 368	42.976 305	34
35	43.734 987	43.899 876	44.065 541	44.231 985	44.399 213	44.567 229	35
36	45.290 786	45.466 916	45.643 901	45.821 745	46.000 453	46.180 028	36
37	46.866 356	47.054 197	47.242 977	47.432 701	47.623 375	47.815 004	37
38	48.461 949	48.661 980	48.863 041	49.065 137	49.268 275	49.472 460	38
39	50.077 820	50.290 531	50.504 368	50.719 339	50.935 450	51.152 706	39
40	51.714 225	51.940 117	52.167 238	52.395 597	52.625 201	52.856 056	40
41	53.371 427	53.611 010	53.851 933	54.094 205	54.337 834	54.582 827	41
42	55.049 689	55.303 486	55.558 740	55.815 461	56.073 658	56.333 341	42
43	56.749 279	57.017 822	57.287 948	57.559 667	57.832 989	58.107 924	43
44	58.470 468	58.754 302	59.039 853	59.327 130	59.616 144	59.906 908	44
45	60.213 530	60.513 212	60.814 751	61.118 158	61.423 446	61.730 628	45
46	61.978 743	62.294 841	62.612 944	62.933 067	63.255 222	63.579 424	46
47	63.766 390	64.099 483	64.434 739	64.772 174	65.111 803	65.453 641	47

YRS

	15.25% ANNUAL RATE	15.50% ANNUAL RATE	15.75% ANNUAL RATE	16.00% ANNUAL RATE	16.25% ANNUAL RATE	16.50% ANNUAL RATE	MOS
4	65.576 754	65.927 435	66.280 445	66.635 803	66.993 526	67.353 629	48
5	89.181 991	89.794 622	90.412 448	91.035 516	91.663 875	92.297 573	60
6	116.649 607	117.635 687	118.631 976	119.638 587	120.655 636	121.683 238	72
7	148.611 579	150.112 280	151.631 383	153.169 132	154.725 772	156.301 554	84
8	185.803 291	187.996 213	190.220 294	192.476 010	194.763 845	197.084 288	96
9	229.080 453	232.187 807	235.345 470	238.554 316	241.815 234	245.129 128	108
10	279.438 790	283.737 285	288.114 037	292.570 569	297.108 435	301.729 222	120
11	338.036 951	343.869 732	349.820 646	355.892 244	362.087 136	368.407 990	132
12	406.223 167	414.014 209	421.979 241	430.122 395	438.447 908	446.960 120	144
13	485.566 272	495.837 716	506.360 199	517.140 233	528.184 505	539.499 881	156
14	577.891 799	591.284 807	605.033 769	619.148 703	633.639 919	648.518 025	168
15	685.323 983	702.623 803	720.420 860	738.730 255	757.567 556	776.948 825	180
16	810.334 631	832.500 700	855.352 443	878.912 215	903.203 125	928.249 057	192
17	955.799 999	984.002 053	1013.139 000	1043.243 434	1074.349 121	1106.491 039	204
18	1125.066 967	1160.728 325	1197.651 751	1235.884 123	1275.474 109	1316.472 236	216
19	1322.030 043	1366.879 457	1413.417 633	1461.711 177	1511.829 393	1563.844 393	228
20	1551.220 979	1607.354 675	1665.730 360	1726.441 638	1789.586 131	1855.265 646	240
21	1817.912 996	1887.868 929	1960.780 310	2036.777 427	2115.996 458	2198.579 736	252
22	2128.242 190	2215.088 702	2305.806 395	2400.575 011	2499.582 837	2603.027 124	264
23	2489.348 633	2596.790 447	2709.273 672	2827.044 294	2950.360 579	3079.493 701	276
24	2909.540 692	3042.045 391	3181.081 024	3326.981 781	3480.099 338	3640.803 789	288
25	3398.486 184	3561.435 118	3732.804 025	3913.043 898	4102.630 916	4302.065 315	300
26	3967.434 806	4167.303 044	4377.978 944	4600.067 404	4834.207 889	5081.076 442	312
27	4629.476 978	4874.047 755	5132.434 850	5405.444 997	5693.932 837	5998.804 623	324
28	5399.845 021	5698.465 199	6014.681 969	6349.565 632	6704.252 874	7079.950 943	336
29	6296.263 629	6660.147 843	7046.365 826	7456.330 682	7891.546 631	8353.614 965	348
30	7339.357 678	7781.950 293	8252.798 308	8753.759 030	9286.814 107	9854.077 955	360

FUTURE VALUE OF
$1 PER PERIOD

MONTHLY
COMPOUNDING

MOS	16.75% ANNUAL RATE	17.00% ANNUAL RATE	17.25% ANNUAL RATE	17.50% ANNUAL RATE	17.75% ANNUAL RATE	18.00% ANNUAL RATE	MOS
1	1.000 000	1.000 000	1.000 000	1.000 000	1.000 000	1.000 000	1
2	2.013 958	2.014 167	2.014 375	2.014 583	2.014 792	2.015 000	2
3	3.042 070	3.042 701	3.043 332	3.043 963	3.044 594	3.045 225	3
4	4.084 532	4.085 806	4.087 080	4.088 354	4.089 628	4.090 903	4
5	5.141 545	5.143 688	5.145 831	5.147 976	5.150 121	5.152 267	5
6	6.213 313	6.216 557	6.219 803	6.223 050	6.226 300	6.229 551	6
7	7.300 040	7.304 625	7.309 212	7.313 803	7.318 397	7.322 994	7
8	8.401 937	8.408 107	8.414 282	8.420 463	8.426 648	8.432 839	8
9	9.519 214	9.527 222	9.535 238	9.543 261	9.551 293	9.559 332	9
10	10.652 086	10.662 191	10.672 307	10.682 434	10.692 572	10.702 722	10
11	11.800 771	11.813 238	11.825 721	11.838 219	11.850 733	11.863 262	11
12	12.965 490	12.980 593	12.995 716	13.010 860	13.026 025	13.041 211	12
13	14.146 467	14.164 484	14.182 529	14.200 602	14.218 702	14.236 830	13
14	15.343 928	15.365 148	15.386 403	15.407 694	15.429 020	15.450 382	14
15	16.558 104	16.582 821	16.607 583	16.632 389	16.657 241	16.682 138	15
16	17.789 227	17.817 744	17.846 317	17.874 945	17.903 629	17.932 370	16
17	19.037 535	19.070 162	19.102 857	19.135 621	19.168 454	19.201 355	17
18	20.303 268	20.340 323	20.377 461	20.414 682	20.451 987	20.489 376	18
19	21.586 667	21.628 477	21.670 387	21.712 396	21.754 506	21.796 716	19
20	22.887 981	22.934 881	22.981 899	23.029 036	23.076 292	23.123 667	20
21	24.207 459	24.259 792	24.312 263	24.364 876	24.417 628	24.470 522	21
22	25.545 355	25.603 472	25.661 752	25.720 197	25.778 806	25.837 580	22
23	26.901 926	26.966 188	27.030 640	27.095 283	27.160 117	27.225 144	23
24	28.277 432	28.348 209	28.419 205	28.490 422	28.561 861	28.633 521	24
25	29.672 138	29.749 808	29.827 732	29.905 908	29.984 338	30.063 024	25
26	31.086 311	31.171 264	31.256 505	31.342 036	31.427 857	31.513 969	26
27	32.520 224	32.612 857	32.705 817	32.799 107	32.892 727	32.986 678	27
28	33.974 152	34.074 872	34.175 964	34.277 427	34.379 265	34.481 479	28
29	35.448 375	35.557 600	35.667 243	35.777 306	35.887 792	35.998 701	29
30	36.943 175	37.061 332	37.179 960	37.299 059	37.418 632	37.538 681	30
31	38.458 840	38.586 368	38.714 422	38.843 003	38.972 116	39.101 762	31
32	39.995 662	40.133 008	40.270 941	40.409 464	40.548 579	40.688 288	32
33	41.553 934	41.701 559	41.849 836	41.998 769	42.148 360	42.298 612	33
34	43.133 958	43.292 331	43.451 428	43.611 251	43.771 804	43.933 092	34
35	44.736 036	44.905 639	45.076 042	45.247 248	45.419 262	45.592 088	35
36	46.360 477	46.541 802	46.724 010	46.907 104	47.091 089	47.275 969	36
37	48.007 592	48.201 145	48.395 668	48.591 166	48.787 644	48.985 109	37
38	49.677 698	49.883 994	50.091 355	50.299 787	50.509 295	50.719 885	38
39	51.371 116	51.590 684	51.811 418	52.033 325	52.256 412	52.480 684	39
40	53.088 171	53.321 552	53.556 208	53.792 145	54.029 371	54.267 894	40
41	54.829 193	55.076 941	55.326 078	55.576 614	55.828 555	56.081 912	41
42	56.594 517	56.857 197	57.121 390	57.387 106	57.654 353	57.923 141	42
43	58.384 482	58.662 674	58.942 510	59.224 001	59.507 157	59.791 988	43
44	60.199 433	60.493 729	60.789 809	61.087 684	61.387 367	61.688 868	44
45	62.039 716	62.350 723	62.663 663	62.978 546	63.295 388	63.614 201	45
46	63.905 687	64.234 025	64.564 453	64.896 984	65.231 633	65.568 414	46
47	65.797 704	66.144 007	66.492 567	66.843 398	67.196 517	67.551 940	47
YRS							
4	67.716 130	68.081 048	68.448 397	68.818 198	69.190 466	69.565 219	48
5	92.936 659	93.581 182	94.231 192	94.886 740	95.547 876	96.214 652	60
6	122.721 513	123.770 579	124.830 558	125.901 571	126.983 743	128.077 197	72
7	157.896 730	159.511 558	161.146 296	162.801 210	164.476 566	166.172 636	84
8	199.437 840	201.825 006	204.246 302	206.702 250	209.193 381	211.720 235	96
9	248.496 920	251.919 548	255.397 966	258.933 147	262.526 080	266.177 771	108
10	306.434 548	311.226 062	316.105 448	321.074 424	326.134 743	331.288 191	120
11	374.857 532	381.438 553	388.153 901	395.006 493	401.999 308	409.135 393	132
12	455.663 479	464.562 540	473.661 972	482.966 559	492.481 202	502.210 922	144
13	551.093 414	562.972 341	575.144 098	587.616 318	600.396 841	613.493 716	156
14	663.793 937	679.478 890	695.584 446	712.122 501	729.105 301	746.545 446	168
15	796.890 622	817.410 030	838.524 666	860.252 699	882.612 872	905.624 513	180
16	954.074 698	980.705 566	1008.168 036	1036.489 374	1065.697 763	1095.822 335	192
17	1139.705 420	1174.029 800	1209.503 064	1246.165 497	1284.058 832	1323.226 308	204
18	1358.930 965	1402.904 761	1448.450 176	1495.625 924	1544.492 974	1595.114 630	216
19	1617.831 213	1673.867 935	1732.035 813	1792.419 399	1855.106 687	1920.189 249	228
20	1923.586 357	1994.658 995	2068.599 050	2145.526 975	2225.568 401	2308.854 370	240
21	2284.676 038	2374.440 878	2468.036 816	2565.633 784	2667.409 426	2773.549 452	252
22	2711.114 516	2824.061 507	2942.094 913	3065.452 376	3194.382 887	3329.147 335	264
23	3214.728 397	3356.363 651	3504.713 421	3660.107 401	3822.891 814	3993.430 261	276
24	3809.484 623	3986.551 756	4172.436 614	4367.593 285	4572.499 718	4787.658 998	288
25	4511.877 833	4732.626 240	4964.899 455	5209.318 748	5466.539 540	5737.253 308	300
26	5341.387 803	5615.897 651	5905.404 985	6210.754 636	6532.839 934	6872.605 521	312
27	6321.019 699	6661.595 368	7021.609 663	7402.204 679	7804.591 485	8230.053 258	324
28	7477.942 081	7899.588 246	8346.336 128	8819.722 487	9321.379 828	9853.042 439	336
29	8844.240 387	9365.237 774	9918.539 384	10506.202 542	11130.417 824	11793.517 795	348
30	10457.806 766	11100.408 126	11784.451 297	12512.678 200	13288.015 149	14113.585 393	360

FUTURE VALUE OF
$1 PER PERIOD

MONTHLY
COMPOUNDING

MOS	18.25% ANNUAL RATE	18.50% ANNUAL RATE	18.75% ANNUAL RATE	19.00% ANNUAL RATE	19.25% ANNUAL RATE	19.50% ANNUAL RATE	MOS
1	1.000 000	1.000 000	1.000 000	1.000 000	1.000 000	1.000 000	1
2	2.015 208	2.015 417	2.015 625	2.015 833	2.016 042	2.016 250	2
3	3.045 856	3.046 488	3.047 119	3.047 751	3.048 382	3.049 014	3
4	4.092 179	4.093 454	4.094 730	4.096 007	4.097 283	4.098 561	4
5	5.154 414	5.156 562	5.158 711	5.160 860	5.163 011	5.165 162	5
6	6.232 804	6.236 059	6.239 315	6.242 574	6.245 834	6.249 096	6
7	7.327 595	7.332 198	7.336 805	7.341 415	7.346 028	7.350 644	7
8	8.439 035	8.445 236	8.451 442	8.457 654	8.463 870	8.470 092	8
9	9.567 379	9.575 433	9.583 496	9.591 566	9.599 645	9.607 731	9
10	10.712 883	10.723 055	10.733 238	10.743 433	10.753 639	10.763 856	10
11	11.875 808	11.888 368	11.900 945	11.913 537	11.926 145	11.938 769	11
12	13.056 419	13.071 647	13.086 897	13.102 168	13.117 461	13.132 774	12
13	14.254 985	14.273 169	14.291 380	14.309 619	14.327 886	14.346 182	13
14	15.471 780	15.493 213	15.514 683	15.536 188	15.557 730	15.579 307	14
15	16.707 080	16.732 067	16.757 100	16.782 178	16.807 302	16.832 471	15
16	17.961 167	17.990 020	18.018 929	18.047 896	18.076 919	18.105 999	16
17	19.234 326	19.267 366	19.300 475	19.333 654	19.366 903	19.400 221	17
18	20.526 848	20.564 405	20.602 045	20.639 770	20.677 580	20.715 475	18
19	21.839 027	21.881 439	21.923 952	21.966 567	22.009 283	22.052 101	19
20	23.171 162	23.218 778	23.266 514	23.314 371	23.362 348	23.410 448	20
21	24.523 557	24.576 734	24.630 053	24.683 515	24.737 119	24.790 867	21
22	25.896 520	25.955 625	26.014 898	26.074 337	26.133 944	26.193 719	22
23	27.290 363	27.355 775	27.421 381	27.487 181	27.553 176	27.619 367	23
24	28.705 403	28.777 510	28.849 840	28.922 394	28.995 175	29.068 182	24
25	30.141 965	30.221 163	30.300 618	30.380 332	30.460 306	30.540 540	25
26	31.600 374	31.687 072	31.774 066	31.861 354	31.948 940	32.036 823	26
27	33.080 963	33.175 581	33.270 535	33.365 826	33.461 454	33.557 422	27
28	34.584 069	34.687 038	34.790 387	34.894 118	34.998 232	35.102 730	28
29	36.110 035	36.221 797	36.333 987	36.446 608	36.559 662	36.673 149	29
30	37.659 209	37.780 216	37.901 706	38.023 680	38.146 140	38.269 088	30
31	39.231 943	39.362 661	39.493 920	39.625 721	39.758 067	39.890 961	31
32	40.828 595	40.969 502	41.111 012	41.253 128	41.395 853	41.539 189	32
33	42.449 530	42.601 115	42.753 372	42.906 303	43.059 911	43.214 201	33
34	44.095 116	44.257 883	44.421 393	44.585 653	44.750 664	44.916 431	34
35	45.765 730	45.940 192	46.115 478	46.291 592	46.468 539	46.646 323	35
36	47.461 750	47.648 436	47.836 032	48.024 542	48.213 972	48.404 326	36
37	49.183 564	49.383 016	49.583 470	49.784 931	49.987 405	50.190 896	37
38	50.931 564	51.144 338	51.358 212	51.573 192	51.789 286	52.006 498	38
39	52.706 149	52.932 813	53.160 684	53.389 768	53.620 072	53.851 604	39
40	54.507 721	54.748 860	54.991 319	55.235 106	55.480 228	55.726 693	40
41	56.336 693	56.592 905	56.850 559	57.109 662	57.370 223	57.632 251	41
42	58.193 480	58.465 379	58.738 849	59.013 898	59.290 537	59.568 775	42
43	60.078 506	60.366 721	60.656 643	60.948 285	61.241 656	61.536 768	43
44	61.992 200	62.297 374	62.604 403	62.913 299	63.224 074	63.536 741	44
45	63.934 998	64.257 792	64.582 597	64.909 427	65.238 294	65.569 213	45
46	65.907 343	66.248 433	66.591 700	66.937 159	67.284 825	67.634 712	46
47	67.909 683	68.269 763	68.632 196	68.996 998	69.364 185	69.733 776	47

YRS							
4	69.942 477	70.322 255	70.704 574	71.089 450	71.476 903	71.866 950	48
5	96.887 119	97.565 330	98.249 338	98.939 196	99.634 957	100.336 676	60
6	129.182 062	130.298 463	131.426 532	132.566 399	133.718 196	134.882 057	72
7	167.889 694	169.628 018	171.387 891	173.169 599	174.973 432	176.799 685	84
8	214.283 360	216.883 312	219.520 659	222.195 973	224.909 840	227.662 852	96
9	269.889 247	273.661 552	277.495 748	281.392 918	285.354 163	289.380 604	108
10	336.536 595	341.881 813	347.325 745	352.870 328	358.517 538	364.269 392	120
11	416.417 864	423.849 905	431.434 773	439.175 798	447.076 385	455.140 015	132
12	512.160 866	522.336 307	532.742 648	543.385 424	554.270 310	565.403 117	144
13	626.915 210	640.669 811	654.766 237	669.213 441	684.020 615	699.197 202	156
14	764.455 906	782.850 028	801.741 549	821.144 606	841.073 750	861.543 958	168
15	929.307 560	953.682 578	978.770 779	1004.594 042	1031.174 936	1058.536 743	180
16	1126.893 208	1158.941 514	1191.999 436	1226.100 247	1261.278 342	1297.569 280	192
17	1363.712 721	1405.564 483	1448.829 680	1493.558 135	1539.801 470	1587.613 173	204
18	1647.556 626	1701.887 217	1758.177 284	1816.500 430	1876.933 087	1939.554 631	216
19	1987.762 384	2057.925 274	2130.781 143	2206.437 425	2285.005 937	2366.603 063	228
20	2395.521 565	2485.712 559	2579.576 071	2677.267 240	2778.947 897	2884.786 867	240
21	2884.248 007	2999.708 064	3120.141 830	3245.771 169	3376.828 052	3513.555 022	252
22	3470.019 084	3617.284 577	3771.243 971	3932.211 806	4100.517 696	4276.507 066	264
23	4172.104 598	4359.315 869	4555.485 283	4761.055 238	4976.490 405	5202.278 860	276
24	5013.600 685	5250.882 223	5500.090 431	5761.843 068	6036.790 486	6325.617 371	288
25	6022.189 595	6322.118 126	6637.851 055	6970.245 332	7320.205 198	7688.684 833	300
26	7231.050 344	7609.230 808	8008.264 125	8429.331 851	8873.683 644	9342.641 223	312
27	8679.950 185	9155.724 025	9658.903 054	10191.107 326	10754.054 236	11349.564 442	324
28	10416.552 809	11013.868 459	11647.069 205	12318.364 881	13030.103 558	13784.780 285	336
29	12497.986 313	13246.468 450	14041.781 078	14886.924 139	15785.092 675	16739.689 647	348
30	14992.722 513	15928.984 743	16926.170 269	17988.333 579	19119.802 939	20325.199 061	360

FUTURE VALUE OF
$1 PER PERIOD

MOS	19.75% ANNUAL RATE	20.00% ANNUAL RATE	21.00% ANNUAL RATE	22.00% ANNUAL RATE	23.00% ANNUAL RATE	24.00% ANNUAL RATE	MOS
1	1.000 000	1.000 000	1.000 000	1.000 000	1.000 000	1.000 000	1
2	2.016 458	2.016 667	2.017 500	2.018 333	2.019 167	2.020 000	2
3	3.049 646	3.050 278	3.052 806	3.055 336	3.057 867	3.060 400	3
4	4.099 838	4.101 116	4.106 230	4.111 351	4.116 476	4.121 608	4
5	5.167 314	5.169 468	5.178 089	5.186 725	5.195 376	5.204 040	5
6	6.252 360	6.255 625	6.268 706	6.281 815	6.294 954	6.308 121	6
7	7.355 263	7.359 886	7.378 408	7.396 982	7.415 607	7.434 283	7
8	8.476 319	8.482 551	8.507 530	8.532 593	8.557 739	8.582 969	8
9	9.615 825	9.623 926	9.656 412	9.689 024	9.721 763	9.754 628	9
10	10.774 085	10.784 325	10.825 399	10.866 656	10.908 097	10.949 721	10
11	11.951 409	11.964 064	12.014 844	12.065 878	12.117 168	12.168 715	11
12	13.148 109	13.163 465	13.225 104	13.287 086	13.349 414	13.412 090	12
13	14.364 505	14.382 856	14.456 543	14.530 683	14.605 278	14.680 332	13
14	15.600 921	15.622 570	15.709 533	15.797 078	15.885 212	15.973 938	14
15	16.857 686	16.882 947	16.984 449	17.086 692	17.189 679	17.293 417	15
16	18.135 135	18.164 329	18.281 677	18.399 948	18.519 148	18.639 285	16
17	19.433 609	19.467 068	19.601 607	19.737 280	19.874 098	20.012 071	17
18	20.753 454	20.791 519	20.944 635	21.099 130	21.255 018	21.412 312	18
19	22.095 021	22.138 044	22.311 166	22.485 948	22.662 406	22.840 559	19
20	23.458 669	23.507 012	23.701 611	23.898 190	24.096 769	24.297 370	20
21	24.844 759	24.898 795	25.116 389	25.336 323	25.558 624	25.783 317	21
22	26.253 663	26.313 775	26.555 926	26.800 823	27.048 497	27.298 984	22
23	27.685 754	27.752 338	28.020 655	28.292 171	28.566 927	28.844 963	23
24	29.141 415	29.214 877	29.511 016	29.810 861	30.114 460	30.421 862	24
25	30.621 035	30.701 792	31.027 459	31.357 393	31.691 653	32.030 300	25
26	32.125 006	32.213 488	32.570 440	32.932 279	33.299 077	33.670 906	26
27	33.653 730	33.750 380	34.140 422	34.536 037	34.937 309	35.344 324	27
28	35.207 614	35.312 886	35.737 880	36.169 198	36.606 941	37.051 210	28
29	36.787 073	36.901 434	37.363 293	37.832 300	38.308 574	38.792 235	29
30	38.392 527	38.516 458	39.017 150	39.525 892	40.042 822	40.568 079	30
31	40.024 404	40.158 399	40.699 950	41.250 533	41.810 309	42.379 441	31
32	41.683 139	41.827 706	42.412 200	43.006 793	43.611 673	44.227 030	32
33	43.369 174	43.524 834	44.154 413	44.795 251	45.447 564	46.111 570	33
34	45.082 958	45.250 248	45.927 115	46.616 497	47.318 642	48.033 802	34
35	46.824 948	47.004 419	47.730 840	48.471 133	49.225 583	49.994 478	35
36	48.595 609	48.787 826	49.566 129	50.359 771	51.169 073	51.994 367	36
37	50.395 412	50.600 956	51.433 537	52.283 033	53.149 813	54.034 255	37
38	52.224 836	52.444 305	53.333 624	54.241 555	55.168 518	56.114 940	38
39	54.084 370	54.318 377	55.266 962	56.235 984	57.225 915	58.237 238	39
40	55.974 509	56.223 683	57.234 134	58.266 977	59.322 745	60.401 983	40
41	57.895 756	58.160 745	59.235 731	60.335 205	61.459 764	62.610 023	41
42	59.848 623	60.130 091	61.272 357	62.441 350	63.637 743	64.862 223	42
43	61.833 632	62.132 259	63.344 623	64.586 108	65.857 466	67.159 468	43
44	63.851 310	64.167 796	65.453 154	66.770 187	68.119 734	69.502 657	44
45	65.902 197	66.237 260	67.598 584	68.994 307	70.425 363	71.892 710	45
46	67.986 837	68.341 214	69.781 559	71.259 203	72.775 182	74.330 564	46
47	70.105 787	70.480 234	72.002 736	73.565 621	75.170 040	76.817 176	47

YRS							
4	72.259 611	72.654 905	74.262 784	75.914 324	77.610 799	79.353 519	48
5	101.044 408	101.758 208	104.675 216	107.693 880	110.818 005	114.051 539	60
6	136.058 119	137.246 517	142.126 280	147.214 827	152.521 731	158.057 019	72
7	178.648 655	180.520 645	188.244 992	196.362 941	204.895 930	213.866 607	84
8	230.455 611	233.288 730	245.037 388	257.483 368	270.670 790	284.646 659	96
9	293.473 383	297.633 662	314.973 777	333.492 521	353.275 053	374.412 879	108
10	370.127 946	376.095 300	401.096 196	428.017 244	457.014 754	488.258 152	120
11	463.370 247	471.770 720	507.150 729	545.567 866	587.297 686	632.641 484	132
12	576.789 805	588.436 476	637.750 450	691.753 417	750.915 300	815.754 461	144
13	714.752 897	730.697 658	798.576 080	873.549 268	956.396 733	1047.985 991	156
14	882.570 645	904.169 675	996.623 085	1099.629 967	1214.453 422	1342.511 724	168
15	1086.703 475	1115.699 905	1240.505 953	1380.783 150	1538.537 467	1716.041 568	180
16	1335.009 825	1373.637 983	1540.832 905	1730.424 286	1945.542 878	2189.767 727	192
17	1637.048 666	1688.165 376	1910.667 320	2165.236 806	2456.686 228	2790.567 042	204
18	2004.447 491	2071.697 274	2366.095 959	2705.968 169	3098.612 642	3552.525 843	216
19	2451.349 938	2539.372 652	2926.928 691	3378.419 841	3904.784 769	4518.873 840	228
20	2994.960 268	3109.651 838	3617.560 166	4214.678 439	4917.227 136	5744.436 758	240
21	3656.205 678	3805.045 193	4468.030 916	5254.646 770	6188.716 824	7298.746 872	252
22	4460.541 922	4653.001 652	5515.334 034	6547.947 827	7785.534 657	9269.987 921	264
23	5438.933 280	5686.992 197	6805.024 269	8156.292 597	9790.920 321	11769.998 206	276
24	6629.044 574	6947.831 050	8393.199 527	10156.424 648	12309.411 522	14940.615 736	288
25	8076.691 143	8485.286 707	10348.940 980	12643.782 022	15472.293 377	18961.725 403	300
26	9837.602 581	10360.046 428	12757.317 895	15737.051 142	19444.442 108	24061.464 743	312
27	11979.568 138	12646.111 719	15723.087 912	19583.830 033	24432.919 789	30529.167 315	324
28	14585.046 388	15433.719 354	19375.253 711	24367.671 098	30697.768 177	38731.778 032	336
29	17754.339 603	18832.903 252	23872.674 261	30316.839 476	38565.564 293	49134.671 768	348
30	21609.455 063	22977.837 794	29410.974 741	37715.204 912	48446.444 386	62328.056 387	360

FUTURE VALUE OF $1 PER PERIOD

QUARTERLY COMPOUNDING

QTRS	6.50% ANNUAL RATE	7.00% ANNUAL RATE	7.50% ANNUAL RATE	8.00% ANNUAL RATE	8.50% ANNUAL RATE	9.00% ANNUAL RATE	QTRS
1	1.000 000	1.000 000	1.000 000	1.000 000	1.000 000	1.000 000	1
2	2.016 250	2.017 500	2.018 750	2.020 000	2.021 250	2.022 500	2
3	3.049 014	3.052 806	3.056 602	3.060 400	3.064 202	3.068 006	3
4	4.098 561	4.106 230	4.113 913	4.121 608	4.129 316	4.137 036	4
5	5.165 162	5.178 089	5.191 049	5.204 040	5.217 064	5.230 120	5
6	6.249 096	6.268 706	6.288 381	6.308 121	6.327 926	6.347 797	6
7	7.350 644	7.378 408	7.406 288	7.434 283	7.462 395	7.490 623	7
8	8.470 092	8.507 530	8.545 156	8.582 969	8.620 971	8.659 162	8
9	9.607 731	9.656 412	9.705 378	9.754 628	9.804 166	9.853 993	9
10	10.763 856	10.825 399	10.887 353	10.949 721	11.012 505	11.075 708	10
11	11.938 769	12.014 844	12.091 491	12.168 715	12.246 521	12.324 911	11
12	13.132 774	13.225 104	13.318 207	13.412 090	13.506 759	13.602 222	12
13	14.346 182	14.456 543	14.567 923	14.680 332	14.793 778	14.908 272	13
14	15.579 307	15.709 533	15.841 072	15.973 938	16.108 146	16.243 708	14
15	16.832 471	16.984 449	17.138 092	17.293 417	17.450 444	17.609 191	15
16	18.105 999	18.281 677	18.459 431	18.639 285	18.821 266	19.005 398	16
17	19.400 221	19.601 607	19.805 545	20.012 071	20.221 218	20.433 020	17
18	20.715 475	20.944 635	21.176 899	21.412 312	21.650 918	21.892 763	18
19	22.052 101	22.311 166	22.573 966	22.840 559	23.111 000	23.385 350	19
20	23.410 448	23.701 611	23.997 228	24.297 370	24.602 109	24.911 520	20
21	24.790 867	25.116 389	25.447 176	25.783 317	26.124 904	26.472 029	21
22	26.193 719	26.555 926	26.924 311	27.298 984	27.680 058	28.067 650	22
23	27.619 367	28.020 655	28.429 141	28.844 963	29.268 259	29.699 172	23
24	29.068 182	29.511 016	29.962 188	30.421 862	30.890 210	31.367 403	24
25	30.540 540	31.027 459	31.523 979	32.030 300	32.546 627	33.073 170	25
26	32.036 823	32.570 440	33.115 053	33.670 906	34.238 243	34.817 316	26
27	33.557 422	34.140 422	34.735 961	35.344 324	35.965 805	36.600 706	27
28	35.102 730	35.737 880	36.387 260	37.051 210	37.730 079	38.424 222	28
29	36.673 149	37.363 293	38.069 521	38.792 235	39.531 843	40.288 767	29
30	38.269 088	39.017 150	39.783 325	40.568 079	41.371 895	42.195 264	30
31	39.890 961	40.699 950	41.529 262	42.379 441	43.251 047	44.144 657	31
32	41.539 189	42.412 200	43.307 936	44.227 030	45.170 132	46.137 912	32
33	43.214 201	44.154 413	45.119 959	46.111 570	47.129 997	48.176 015	33
34	44.916 431	45.927 115	46.965 959	48.033 802	49.131 510	50.259 976	34
35	46.646 323	47.730 840	48.846 570	49.994 478	51.175 554	52.390 825	35
36	48.404 326	49.566 129	50.762 444	51.994 367	53.263 035	54.569 619	36
37	50.190 896	51.433 537	52.714 239	54.034 255	55.394 874	56.797 435	37
38	52.006 498	53.333 624	54.702 631	56.114 940	57.572 016	59.075 377	38
39	53.851 604	55.266 962	56.728 306	58.237 238	59.795 421	61.404 573	39
40	55.726 693	57.234 134	58.791 961	60.401 983	62.066 074	63.786 176	40
41	57.632 251	59.235 731	60.894 311	62.610 023	64.384 978	66.221 365	41
42	59.568 775	61.272 357	63.036 079	64.862 223	66.753 158	68.711 346	42
43	61.536 768	63.344 623	65.218 006	67.159 468	69.171 663	71.257 351	43
44	63.536 741	65.453 154	67.440 843	69.502 657	71.641 561	73.860 642	44
45	65.569 213	67.598 584	69.705 359	71.892 710	74.163 944	76.522 506	45
46	67.634 712	69.781 559	72.012 334	74.330 564	76.739 928	79.244 262	46
47	69.733 776	72.002 736	74.362 566	76.817 176	79.370 651	82.027 258	47
48	71.866 950	74.262 784	76.756 864	79.353 519	82.057 278	84.872 872	48
49	74.034 788	76.562 383	79.196 055	81.940 590	84.800 995	87.782 511	49
50	76.237 853	78.902 225	81.680 981	84.579 401	87.603 016	90.757 618	50
51	78.476 719	81.283 014	84.212 499	87.270 989	90.464 580	93.799 664	51
52	80.751 965	83.705 466	86.791 484	90.016 409	93.386 952	96.910 157	52
53	83.064 185	86.170 312	89.418 824	92.816 737	96.371 425	100.090 635	53
54	85.413 978	88.678 292	92.095 427	95.673 072	99.419 318	103.342 674	54
55	87.801 955	91.230 163	94.822 216	98.586 534	102.531 978	106.667 885	55
YRS							
14	90.228 737	93.826 690	97.600 133	101.558 264	105.710 783	110.067 912	56
15	100.336 676	104.675 216	109.242 516	114.051 539	119.116 005	124.450 435	60
16	111.117 821	116.303 306	121.782 945	127.574 662	133.697 507	140.171 731	64
17	122.617 007	128.766 979	135.290 691	142.212 525	149.558 507	157.356 417	68
18	134.882 057	142.126 280	149.840 369	158.057 019	166.811 276	176.140 711	72
19	147.963 980	156.445 567	165.512 348	175.207 608	185.577 942	196.673 509	76
20	161.917 180	171.793 824	182.393 199	193.771 958	205.991 344	219.117 569	80
21	176.799 685	188.244 992	200.576 169	213.866 607	228.195 980	243.650 796	84
22	192.673 389	205.878 326	220.161 699	235.617 701	252.349 028	270.467 657	88
23	209.604 307	224.778 773	241.257 975	259.161 785	278.621 457	299.780 720	92
24	227.662 852	245.037 388	263.981 530	284.646 659	307.199 238	331.822 341	96
25	246.924 124	266.751 768	288.457 887	312.232 306	338.284 660	366.846 502	100
26	267.468 229	290.026 522	314.822 249	342.091 897	372.097 766	405.130 828	104
27	289.380 604	314.973 777	343.220 248	374.412 879	408.877 902	446.978 787	108
28	312.752 378	341.713 718	373.808 752	409.398 150	448.885 420	492.722 092	112
29	337.680 750	370.375 165	406.756 727	447.267 331	492.403 517	542.723 336	116
30	364.269 392	401.096 196	442.246 172	488.258 152	539.740 238	597.378 862	120

FUTURE VALUE OF
$1 PER PERIOD

QUARTERLY COMPOUNDING

QTRS	9.50% ANNUAL RATE	10.00% ANNUAL RATE	10.50% ANNUAL RATE	11.00% ANNUAL RATE	11.50% ANNUAL RATE	12.00% ANNUAL RATE	QTRS
1	1.000 000	1.000 000	1.000 000	1.000 000	1.000 000	1.000 000	1
2	2.023 750	2.025 000	2.026 250	2.027 500	2.028 750	2.030 000	2
3	3.071 814	3.075 625	3.079 439	3.083 256	3.087 077	3.090 900	3
4	4.144 770	4.152 516	4.160 274	4.168 046	4.175 830	4.183 627	4
5	5.243 208	5.256 329	5.269 482	5.282 667	5.295 885	5.309 136	5
6	6.367 734	6.387 737	6.407 805	6.427 940	6.448 142	6.468 410	6
7	7.518 968	7.547 430	7.576 010	7.604 709	7.633 526	7.662 462	7
8	8.697 543	8.736 116	8.774 881	8.813 838	8.852 990	8.892 336	8
9	9.904 110	9.954 519	10.005 221	10.056 219	10.107 513	10.159 106	9
10	11.139 333	11.203 882	11.267 858	11.332 765	11.398 104	11.463 879	10
11	12.403 892	12.483 466	12.563 640	12.644 416	12.725 800	12.807 796	11
12	13.698 484	13.795 553	13.893 435	13.992 137	14.091 666	14.192 030	12
13	15.023 823	15.140 442	15.258 138	15.376 921	15.496 802	15.617 790	13
14	16.380 639	16.518 953	16.658 664	16.799 786	16.942 335	17.086 324	14
15	17.769 679	17.931 927	18.095 954	18.261 781	18.429 427	18.598 914	15
16	19.191 709	19.380 225	19.570 973	19.763 979	19.959 273	20.156 881	16
17	20.647 512	20.864 730	21.084 711	21.307 489	21.533 102	21.761 588	17
18	22.137 890	22.386 349	22.638 184	22.893 445	23.152 179	23.414 435	18
19	23.663 665	23.946 007	24.232 437	24.523 015	24.817 804	25.116 868	19
20	25.225 677	25.544 658	25.868 538	26.197 398	26.531 316	26.870 374	20
21	26.824 787	27.183 274	27.547 587	27.917 826	28.294 091	28.676 486	21
22	28.461 876	28.862 856	29.270 711	29.685 566	30.107 546	30.536 780	22
23	30.137 846	30.584 427	31.039 068	31.501 919	31.973 138	32.452 884	23
24	31.853 619	32.349 038	32.853 843	33.368 222	33.892 366	34.426 470	24
25	33.610 143	34.157 764	34.716 256	35.285 848	35.866 772	36.459 264	25
26	35.408 384	36.011 708	36.627 558	37.256 209	37.897 941	38.553 042	26
27	37.249 333	37.912 001	38.589 032	39.280 755	39.987 507	40.709 634	27
28	39.134 004	39.859 801	40.601 994	41.360 975	42.137 148	42.930 923	28
29	41.063 437	41.856 296	42.667 796	43.498 402	44.348 591	45.218 850	29
30	43.038 694	43.902 703	44.787 826	45.694 608	46.623 613	47.575 416	30
31	45.060 863	46.000 271	46.963 506	47.951 210	48.964 042	50.002 678	31
32	47.131 058	48.150 278	49.196 298	50.269 868	51.371 758	52.502 759	32
33	49.250 421	50.354 034	51.487 701	52.652 290	53.848 696	55.077 841	33
34	51.420 118	52.612 885	53.839 253	55.100 228	56.396 846	57.730 177	34
35	53.641 346	54.928 207	56.252 533	57.615 484	59.018 255	60.462 082	35
36	55.915 328	57.301 413	58.729 162	60.199 910	61.715 030	63.275 944	36
37	58.243 317	59.733 948	61.270 803	62.855 407	64.489 337	66.174 223	37
38	60.626 596	62.227 297	63.879 162	65.583 931	67.343 406	69.159 449	38
39	63.066 478	64.782 979	66.555 990	68.387 489	70.279 529	72.234 233	39
40	65.564 306	67.402 554	69.303 084	71.268 145	73.300 065	75.401 260	40
41	68.121 459	70.087 617	72.122 290	74.228 019	76.407 442	78.663 298	41
42	70.739 343	72.839 808	75.015 500	77.269 289	79.604 156	82.023 196	42
43	73.419 403	75.660 803	77.984 657	80.394 195	82.892 775	85.483 892	43
44	76.163 114	78.552 323	81.031 754	83.605 035	86.275 943	89.048 409	44
45	78.971 987	81.516 131	84.158 838	86.904 174	89.756 376	92.719 861	45
46	81.847 572	84.554 034	87.368 008	90.294 039	93.336 872	96.501 457	46
47	84.791 452	87.667 885	90.661 418	93.777 125	97.020 307	100.396 501	47
48	87.805 249	90.859 582	94.041 280	97.355 996	100.809 641	104.408 396	48
49	90.890 624	94.131 072	97.509 864	101.033 285	104.707 918	108.540 648	49
50	94.049 276	97.484 349	101.069 497	104.811 701	108.718 271	112.796 867	50
51	97.282 946	100.921 458	104.722 572	108.694 023	112.843 921	117.180 773	51
52	100.593 416	104.444 494	108.471 539	112.683 108	117.088 184	121.696 197	52
53	103.982 510	108.055 606	112.318 917	116.781 894	121.454 469	126.347 082	53
54	107.452 094	111.756 996	116.267 289	120.993 396	125.946 285	131.137 495	54
55	111.004 082	115.550 921	120.319 305	125.320 714	130.567 240	136.071 620	55

YRS							
14	114.640 429	119.439 694	124.477 687	129.767 034	135.321 049	141.153 768	56
15	130.070 205	135.991 590	142.231 821	148.809 140	155.742 862	163.053 437	60
16	147.018 862	154.261 786	161.924 834	170.033 877	178.616 419	187.701 707	64
17	165.635 915	174.428 663	183.768 467	193.691 420	204.236 064	215.443 551	68
18	186.085 599	196.689 122	207.997 581	220.060 621	232.931 477	246.667 242	72
19	208.548 315	221.260 504	234.872 689	249.452 292	265.071 922	281.809 781	76
20	233.222 222	248.382 713	264.682 753	282.212 873	301.070 990	321.363 019	80
21	260.324 986	278.320 556	297.748 290	318.728 514	341.391 934	365.880 536	84
22	290.095 699	311.366 333	334.424 821	359.429 624	386.553 611	415.985 393	88
23	322.796 990	347.842 687	375.106 694	404.795 946	437.137 178	472.378 852	92
24	358.717 340	388.105 758	420.231 321	455.362 213	493.793 562	535.850 186	96
25	398.173 627	432.548 654	470.283 882	511.724 449	557.251 834	607.287 733	100
26	441.513 923	481.605 296	525.802 543	574.546 995	628.328 595	687.691 320	104
27	489.120 564	535.754 649	587.384 241	644.570 941	707.938 486	778.186 267	108
28	541.413 520	595.525 404	655.691 105	722.619 851	797.105 951	880.039 126	112
29	598.854 105	661.501 133	731.457 570	809.615 495	896.978 426	994.675 416	116
30	661.949 042	734.325 993	815.498 278	906.582 688	1008.841 102	1123.699 571	120

FUTURE VALUE OF
$1 PER PERIOD

QTRS	12.50% ANNUAL RATE	13.00% ANNUAL RATE	13.50% ANNUAL RATE	14.00% ANNUAL RATE	14.50% ANNUAL RATE	15.00% ANNUAL RATE	QTRS
1	1.000 000	1.000 000	1.000 000	1.000 000	1.000 000	1.000 000	1
2	2.031 250	2.032 500	2.033 750	2.035 000	2.036 250	2.037 500	2
3	3.094 727	3.098 556	3.102 389	3.106 225	3.110 064	3.113 906	3
4	4.191 437	4.199 259	4.207 095	4.214 943	4.222 804	4.230 678	4
5	5.322 419	5.335 735	5.349 084	5.362 466	5.375 881	5.389 328	5
6	6.488 745	6.509 147	6.529 616	6.550 152	6.570 756	6.591 428	6
7	7.691 518	7.720 694	7.749 990	7.779 408	7.808 946	7.838 607	7
8	8.931 878	8.971 616	9.011 552	9.051 687	9.092 020	9.132 554	8
9	10.210 999	10.263 194	10.315 692	10.368 496	10.421 606	10.475 025	9
10	11.530 093	11.596 748	11.663 847	11.731 393	11.799 389	11.867 838	10
11	12.890 408	12.973 642	13.057 502	13.141 992	13.227 117	13.312 882	11
12	14.293 234	14.395 285	14.498 192	14.601 962	14.706 600	14.812 116	12
13	15.739 897	15.863 132	15.987 506	16.113 030	16.239 714	16.367 570	13
14	17.231 769	17.378 684	17.527 085	17.676 986	17.828 404	17.981 354	14
15	18.770 262	18.943 491	19.118 624	19.295 681	19.474 684	19.655 654	15
16	20.356 832	20.559 155	20.763 877	20.971 030	21.180 641	21.392 742	16
17	21.992 983	22.227 327	22.464 658	22.705 016	22.948 439	23.194 969	17
18	23.680 264	23.949 715	24.222 841	24.499 691	24.780 320	25.064 781	18
19	25.420 272	25.728 081	26.040 361	26.357 180	26.678 607	27.004 710	19
20	27.214 656	27.564 244	27.919 224	28.279 682	28.645 706	29.017 387	20
21	29.065 114	29.460 082	29.861 497	30.269 471	30.684 113	31.105 539	21
22	30.973 399	31.417 534	31.869 323	32.328 902	32.796 412	33.271 996	22
23	32.941 317	33.438 604	33.944 913	34.460 414	34.985 282	35.519 696	23
24	34.970 734	35.525 359	36.090 553	36.666 528	37.253 499	37.851 685	24
25	37.063 569	37.679 933	38.308 610	38.949 857	39.603 938	40.271 123	25
26	39.221 805	39.904 531	40.601 525	41.313 102	42.039 581	42.781 290	26
27	41.447 487	42.201 428	42.971 827	43.759 060	44.563 516	45.385 588	27
28	43.742 721	44.572 975	45.422 126	46.290 627	47.178 943	48.087 548	28
29	46.109 681	47.021 596	47.955 123	48.910 799	49.889 180	50.890 831	29
30	48.550 608	49.549 798	50.573 608	51.622 677	52.697 663	53.799 237	30
31	51.067 815	52.160 167	53.280 467	54.429 471	55.607 953	56.816 709	31
32	53.663 684	54.855 372	56.078 683	57.334 502	58.623 741	59.947 335	32
33	56.340 674	57.638 172	58.971 338	60.341 210	61.748 852	63.195 360	33
34	59.101 320	60.511 412	61.961 621	63.453 152	64.987 248	66.565 186	34
35	61.948 237	63.478 033	65.052 826	66.674 013	68.343 035	70.061 381	35
36	64.884 119	66.541 069	68.248 359	70.007 603	71.820 470	73.688 682	36
37	67.911 748	69.703 654	71.551 741	73.457 869	75.423 962	77.452 008	37
38	71.033 990	72.969 023	74.966 612	77.028 895	79.158 081	81.356 458	38
39	74.253 802	76.340 516	78.496 735	80.724 906	83.027 561	85.407 326	39
40	77.574 233	79.821 583	82.146 000	84.550 278	87.037 311	89.610 100	40
41	80.998 428	83.415 784	85.918 428	88.509 537	91.192 413	93.970 479	41
42	84.529 629	87.126 797	89.818 175	92.607 371	95.498 138	98.494 372	42
43	88.171 180	90.958 418	93.849 538	96.848 629	99.959 946	103.187 911	43
44	91.926 529	94.914 566	98.016 960	101.238 331	104.583 494	108.057 458	44
45	95.799 233	98.999 290	102.325 032	105.781 673	109.374 645	113.109 612	45
46	99.792 959	103.216 767	106.778 502	110.484 031	114.339 476	118.351 223	46
47	103.911 489	107.571 312	111.382 276	115.350 973	119.484 282	123.789 394	47
48	108.158 723	112.067 379	116.141 428	120.388 257	124.815 587	129.431 496	48
49	112.538 683	116.709 569	121.061 202	125.601 846	130.340 152	135.285 177	49
50	117.055 517	121.502 630	126.147 017	130.997 910	136.064 983	141.358 371	50
51	121.713 502	126.451 466	131.404 479	136.582 837	141.997 338	147.659 310	51
52	126.517 049	131.561 138	136.839 380	142.363 236	148.144 742	154.196 534	52
53	131.470 707	136.836 875	142.457 709	148.345 950	154.514 989	160.978 904	53
54	136.579 167	142.284 074	148.265 657	154.538 058	161.116 157	168.015 613	54
55	141.847 266	147.908 306	154.269 623	160.946 890	167.956 618	175.316 198	55
YRS							
14	147.279 993	153.715 326	160.476 223	167.580 031	175.045 045	182.890 556	56
15	170.762 516	178.893 027	187.469 247	196.516 883	206.063 157	216.136 896	60
16	197.320 837	207.506 879	218.294 996	229.722 586	241.829 416	254.657 782	64
17	227.357 830	240.025 832	253.497 677	267.826 894	283.070 655	299.290 023	68
18	261.329 141	276.982 839	293.698 766	311.552 464	330.624 964	351.003 187	72
19	299.750 096	318.983 589	339.607 986	361.728 561	385.458 727	410.920 666	76
20	343.203 519	366.716 429	392.035 830	419.306 787	448.686 258	480.344 078	80
21	392.348 576	420.963 654	451.907 875	485.379 125	521.592 447	560.781 543	84
22	447.930 771	482.614 318	520.281 119	561.198 653	605.658 870	653.980 445	88
23	510.793 254	552.678 815	598.362 641	648.203 305	702.593 899	761.965 392	92
24	581.889 617	632.305 428	687.530 915	748.043 145	814.367 417	887.082 195	96
25	662.298 352	722.799 158	789.360 144	862.611 657	943.250 850	1032.048 832	100
26	753.239 215	825.643 103	905.648 048	994.081 659	1091.863 525	1200.014 485	104
27	856.091 731	942.522 771	1038.447 607	1144.946 512	1263.224 899	1394.627 959	108
28	972.416 117	1075.353 700	1190.103 302	1318.067 399	1460.817 927	1620.116 941	112
29	1103.976 950	1226.312 854	1363.292 505	1516.727 600	1688.657 832	1881.379 844	116
30	1252.769 936	1397.874 298	1561.072 748	1744.694 750	1951.374 705	2184.092 215	120

FUTURE VALUE OF
$1 PER PERIOD

QTRS	15.50% ANNUAL RATE	16.00% ANNUAL RATE	16.50% ANNUAL RATE	17.00% ANNUAL RATE	17.50% ANNUAL RATE	18.00% ANNUAL RATE	QTRS
1	1.000 000	1.000 000	1.000 000	1.000 000	1.000 000	1.000 000	1
2	2.038 750	2.040 000	2.041 250	2.042 500	2.043 750	2.045 000	2
3	3.117 752	3.121 600	3.125 452	3.129 306	3.133 164	3.137 025	3
4	4.238 564	4.246 464	4.254 376	4.262 302	4.270 240	4.278 191	4
5	5.402 809	5.416 323	5.429 869	5.443 450	5.457 063	5.470 710	5
6	6.612 168	6.632 975	6.653 852	6.674 796	6.695 809	6.716 892	6
7	7.868 389	7.898 294	7.928 323	7.958 475	7.988 751	8.019 152	7
8	9.173 289	9.214 226	9.255 366	9.296 710	9.338 259	9.380 014	8
9	10.528 754	10.582 795	10.637 150	10.691 820	10.746 808	10.802 114	9
10	11.936 743	12.006 107	12.075 933	12.146 223	12.216 981	12.288 209	10
11	13.399 292	13.486 351	13.574 065	13.662 437	13.751 474	13.841 179	11
12	14.918 515	15.025 805	15.133 995	15.243 091	15.353 101	15.464 032	12
13	16.496 607	16.626 838	16.758 272	16.890 922	17.024 799	17.159 913	13
14	18.135 851	18.291 911	18.449 551	18.608 786	18.769 634	18.932 109	14
15	19.838 615	20.023 588	20.210 595	20.399 660	20.590 805	20.784 054	15
16	21.607 361	21.824 531	22.044 282	22.266 645	22.491 653	22.719 337	16
17	23.444 647	23.697 512	23.953 609	24.212 978	24.475 663	24.741 707	17
18	25.353 127	25.645 413	25.941 695	26.242 029	26.546 473	26.855 084	18
19	27.335 560	27.671 229	28.011 790	28.357 316	28.707 881	29.063 562	19
20	29.394 813	29.778 079	30.167 276	30.562 501	30.963 851	31.371 423	20
21	31.533 862	31.969 202	32.411 676	32.861 408	33.318 519	33.783 137	21
22	33.755 799	34.247 970	34.748 658	35.258 018	35.776 205	36.303 378	22
23	36.063 837	36.617 889	37.182 040	37.756 483	38.341 414	38.937 030	23
24	38.461 310	39.082 604	39.715 799	40.361 134	41.018 850	41.689 196	24
25	40.951 686	41.645 908	42.354 076	43.076 482	43.813 425	44.565 210	25
26	43.538 564	44.311 745	45.101 182	45.907 233	46.730 262	47.570 645	26
27	46.225 683	47.084 214	47.961 605	48.858 290	49.774 711	50.711 324	27
28	49.016 928	49.967 583	50.940 022	51.934 767	52.952 355	53.993 333	28
29	51.916 334	52.966 286	54.041 298	55.141 995	56.269 021	57.423 033	29
30	54.928 092	56.084 938	57.270 501	58.485 530	59.730 790	61.007 070	30
31	58.056 556	59.328 335	60.632 909	61.971 165	63.344 012	64.752 388	31
32	61.306 248	62.701 469	64.134 017	65.604 939	67.115 313	68.666 245	32
33	64.681 865	66.209 527	67.779 545	69.393 149	71.051 608	72.756 226	33
34	68.188 287	69.857 909	71.575 451	73.342 358	75.160 116	77.030 256	34
35	71.830 583	73.652 225	75.527 939	77.459 408	79.448 371	81.496 618	35
36	75.614 018	77.598 314	79.643 466	81.751 433	83.924 237	86.163 966	36
37	79.544 061	81.702 246	83.928 759	86.225 869	88.595 922	91.041 344	37
38	83.626 394	85.970 336	88.390 820	90.890 468	93.471 994	96.138 205	38
39	87.866 916	90.409 150	93.036 942	95.753 313	98.561 394	101.464 424	39
40	92.271 759	95.025 516	97.874 716	100.822 829	103.873 455	107.030 323	40
41	96.847 290	99.826 536	102.912 048	106.107 799	109.417 918	112.846 688	41
42	101.600 123	104.819 598	108.157 170	111.617 381	115.204 952	118.924 789	42
43	106.537 127	110.012 382	113.618 653	117.361 119	121.245 169	125.276 404	43
44	111.665 441	115.412 877	119.305 422	123.348 967	127.549 645	131.913 842	44
45	116.992 477	121.029 392	125.226 771	129.591 298	134.129 942	138.849 965	45
46	122.525 935	126.870 568	131.392 375	136.098 928	140.998 127	146.098 214	46
47	128.273 815	132.945 390	137.812 311	142.883 133	148.166 795	153.672 633	47
48	134.244 426	139.263 206	144.497 068	149.955 666	155.649 092	161.587 902	48
49	140.446 397	145.833 734	151.457 572	157.328 782	163.458 740	169.859 357	49
50	146.888 695	152.667 084	158.705 197	165.015 255	171.610 060	178.503 028	50
51	153.580 632	159.773 767	166.251 787	173.028 403	180.118 000	187.535 665	51
52	160.531 882	167.164 718	174.109 673	181.382 110	188.998 162	196.974 769	52
53	167.752 492	174.851 306	182.291 697	190.090 850	198.266 832	206.838 634	53
54	175.252 901	182.845 359	190.811 229	199.169 711	207.941 006	217.146 373	54
55	183.043 951	191.159 173	199.682 193	208.634 424	218.038 425	227.917 959	55

YRS							
14	191.136 904	199.805 540	208.919 083	218.501 387	228.577 606	239.174 268	56
15	226.768 629	237.990 685	249.837 302	262.344 740	275.551 400	289.497 954	60
16	268.252 665	282.661 904	297.936 383	314.130 221	331.300 979	349.509 886	64
17	316.550 220	334.920 912	354.476 518	375.296 529	397.465 862	421.075 231	68
18	372.780 376	396.056 560	420.939 052	447.542 980	475.991 866	506.418 237	72
19	438.246 019	467.576 621	499.065 297	532.876 720	569.188 335	608.191 358	76
20	514.464 026	551.244 977	590.902 154	633.668 480	679.796 047	729.557 699	80
21	603.200 411	649.125 119	698.855 738	752.718 449	811.067 823	874.289 317	84
22	706.511 248	763.631 041	825.754 424	893.334 060	966.864 187	1046.884 464	88
23	826.790 309	897.586 774	974.922 945	1059.421 884	1151.766 894	1252.707 387	92
24	966.824 528	1054.296 034	1150.269 502	1255.596 156	1371.213 680	1498.155 051	96
25	1129.858 580	1237.623 705	1356.388 156	1487.306 971	1631.658 173	1790.855 956	100
26	1319.670 057	1452.091 149	1598.679 197	1760.991 695	1940.759 687	2139.907 230	104
27	1540.657 001	1702.987 724	1883.490 627	2084.253 813	2307.608 473	2556.157 367	108
28	1797.939 807	1996.501 231	2218.284 477	2466.074 159	2742.993 050	3052.543 397	112
29	2097.479 865	2339.870 519	2611.832 314	2917.060 432	3259.717 480	3644.492 971	116
30	2446.217 693	2741.564 020	3074.445 052	3449.741 886	3872.977 917	4350.403 849	120

47

FUTURE VALUE OF
$1 PER PERIOD

QUARTERLY
COMPOUNDING

QTRS	18.50% ANNUAL RATE	19.00% ANNUAL RATE	19.50% ANNUAL RATE	20.00% ANNUAL RATE	20.50% ANNUAL RATE	21.00% ANNUAL RATE	QTRS
1	1.000 000	1.000 000	1.000 000	1.000 000	1.000 000	1.000 000	1
2	2.046 250	2.047 500	2.048 750	2.050 000	2.051 250	2.052 500	2
3	3.140 889	3.144 756	3.148 627	3.152 500	3.156 377	3.160 256	3
4	4.286 155	4.294 132	4.302 122	4.310 125	4.318 141	4.326 170	4
5	5.484 390	5.498 103	5.511 851	5.525 631	5.539 446	5.553 294	5
6	6.738 043	6.759 263	6.780 553	6.801 913	6.823 342	6.844 842	6
7	8.049 677	8.080 328	8.111 105	8.142 008	8.173 038	8.204 196	7
8	9.421 975	9.464 144	9.506 522	9.549 109	9.591 907	9.634 916	8
9	10.857 741	10.913 691	10.969 965	11.026 564	11.083 492	11.140 749	9
10	12.359 912	12.432 091	12.504 750	12.577 893	12.651 521	12.725 638	10
11	13.931 558	14.022 615	14.114 357	14.206 787	14.299 911	14.393 734	11
12	15.575 892	15.688 690	15.802 432	15.917 127	16.032 782	16.149 405	12
13	17.296 277	17.433 902	17.572 800	17.712 983	17.854 462	17.997 249	13
14	19.096 230	19.262 013	19.429 474	19.598 632	19.769 503	19.942 105	14
15	20.979 431	21.176 958	21.376 661	21.578 564	21.782 690	21.989 065	15
16	22.949 729	23.182 864	23.418 773	23.657 492	23.899 053	24.143 491	16
17	25.011 154	25.284 050	25.560 439	25.840 366	26.123 879	26.411 025	17
18	27.167 920	27.485 042	27.806 510	28.132 385	28.462 728	28.797 603	18
19	29.424 437	29.790 582	30.162 077	30.539 004	30.921 443	31.309 478	19
20	31.785 317	32.205 635	32.632 479	33.065 954	33.506 167	33.953 225	20
21	34.255 388	34.735 402	35.223 312	35.719 252	36.223 358	36.735 769	21
22	36.839 699	37.385 334	37.940 449	38.505 214	39.079 805	39.664 397	22
23	39.543 536	40.161 137	40.790 045	41.430 475	42.082 645	42.746 778	23
24	42.372 424	43.068 791	43.778 560	44.501 999	45.239 381	45.990 984	24
25	45.332 149	46.114 559	46.912 765	47.727 099	48.557 899	49.405 511	25
26	48.428 761	49.305 000	50.199 762	51.113 454	52.046 491	52.999 300	26
27	51.668 591	52.646 988	53.647 001	54.669 126	55.713 874	56.781 763	27
28	55.058 263	56.147 720	57.262 292	58.402 583	59.569 210	60.762 806	28
29	58.604 708	59.814 736	61.053 829	62.322 712	63.622 132	64.952 853	29
30	62.315 175	63.655 936	65.030 203	66.438 848	67.882 766	69.362 878	30
31	66.197 252	67.679 593	69.200 425	70.760 790	72.361 758	74.004 429	31
32	70.258 875	71.894 374	73.573 946	75.298 829	77.070 298	78.889 662	32
33	74.508 348	76.309 357	78.160 676	80.063 771	82.020 151	84.031 369	33
34	78.954 359	80.934 051	82.971 009	85.066 959	87.223 684	89.443 016	34
35	83.605 998	85.778 419	88.015 845	90.320 307	92.693 897	95.138 774	35
36	88.472 776	90.852 894	93.306 618	95.836 323	98.444 460	101.133 560	36
37	93.564 642	96.168 406	98.855 315	101.628 139	104.489 738	107.443 071	37
38	98.892 006	101.736 605	104.674 512	107.709 546	110.844 837	114.083 833	38
39	104.465 762	107.568 884	110.777 395	114.095 023	117.525 635	121.073 234	39
40	110.297 303	113.678 406	117.177 792	120.799 774	124.548 824	128.429 579	40
41	116.398 553	120.078 131	123.890 210	127.839 763	131.931 951	136.172 132	41
42	122.781 987	126.781 842	130.929 858	135.231 751	139.693 464	144.321 169	42
43	129.460 653	133.803 980	138.312 688	142.993 339	147.852 754	152.898 030	43
44	136.448 209	141.159 669	146.055 432	151.143 006	156.430 207	161.925 176	44
45	143.758 938	148.864 753	154.175 634	159.700 156	165.447 255	171.426 248	45
46	151.407 789	156.935 829	162.691 696	168.685 164	174.926 427	181.426 126	46
47	159.410 399	165.390 280	171.622 916	178.119 422	184.891 407	191.950 998	47
48	167.783 130	174.246 319	180.989 534	188.025 393	195.367 091	203.028 425	48
49	176.543 100	183.523 019	190.812 773	198.426 663	206.379 655	214.687 418	49
50	185.708 219	193.240 362	201.114 896	209.347 996	217.956 612	226.958 507	50
51	195.297 224	203.419 279	211.919 247	220.815 396	230.126 888	239.873 829	51
52	205.329 720	214.081 695	223.250 310	232.856 165	242.920 891	253.467 205	52
53	215.826 220	225.250 576	235.133 763	245.498 974	256.370 587	267.774 233	53
54	226.808 183	236.949 978	247.596 534	258.773 922	270.509 580	282.832 380	54
55	238.298 061	249.205 102	260.666 865	272.712 618	285.373 196	298.681 080	55

YRS							
14	250.319 346	262.042 344	274.374 375	287.348 249	300.998 572	315.361 837	56
15	304.227 476	319.785 589	336.220 610	353.583 718	371.929 117	391.314 220	60
16	368.822 067	389.306 796	411.037 760	434.093 344	458.556 927	484.517 205	64
17	446.221 546	473.008 333	501.546 196	531.953 298	564.355 880	598.888 816	68
18	538.964 285	573.782 579	611.036 826	650.902 683	693.568 640	739.236 955	72
19	650.091 851	695.111 877	743.490 756	795.486 404	851.376 794	911.461 512	76
20	783.248 754	841.188 868	903.724 044	971.228 821	1044.108 637	1122.802 384	80
21	942.801 973	1017.061 368	1097.562 811	1184.844 828	1279.492 946	1382.143 820	84
22	1133.984 173	1228.806 808	1332.055 084	1444.496 418	1566.968 914	1700.387 898	88
23	1363.065 315	1483.742 235	1615.727 057	1760.104 549	1918.064 671	2090.912 814	92
24	1637.558 283	1790.677 168	1958.893 115	2143.728 205	2346.859 575	2570.135 276	96
25	1966.465 276	2160.218 011	2374.030 860	2610.025 157	2870.548 814	3158.200 618	100
26	2360.573 040	2605.134 971	2876.234 801	3176.812 016	3510.132 954	3879.829 659	104
27	2832.806 630	3140.801 332	3483.765 197	3865.744 985	4291.260 083	4765.357 908	108
28	3398.653 292	3785.728 726	4218.712 004	4703.147 316	5245.254 331	5852.010 796	112
29	4076.670 386	4562.202 786	5107.798 067	5721.015 082	6410.372 009	7185.468 535	116
30	4889.093 979	5497.055 251	6183.350 775	6958.239 713	7833.335 727	8821.786 410	120

48

FUTURE VALUE OF
$1 PER PERIOD

QUARTERLY
COMPOUNDING

QTRS	21.50% ANNUAL RATE	22.00% ANNUAL RATE	22.50% ANNUAL RATE	23.00% ANNUAL RATE	23.50% ANNUAL RATE	24.00% ANNUAL RATE	QTRS
1	1.000 000	1.000 000	1.000 000	1.000 000	1.000 000	1.000 000	1
2	2.053 750	2.055 000	2.056 250	2.057 500	2.058 750	2.060 000	2
3	3.164 139	3.168 025	3.171 914	3.175 806	3.179 702	3.183 600	3
4	4.334 212	4.342 266	4.350 334	4.358 415	4.366 509	4.374 616	4
5	5.567 175	5.581 091	5.595 041	5.609 024	5.623 041	5.637 093	5
6	6.866 411	6.888 051	6.909 762	6.931 543	6.953 395	6.975 319	6
7	8.235 481	8.266 894	8.298 436	8.330 107	8.361 907	8.393 838	7
8	9.678 138	9.721 573	9.765 223	9.809 088	9.853 169	9.897 468	8
9	11.198 338	11.256 260	11.314 516	11.373 110	11.432 043	11.491 316	9
10	12.800 248	12.875 354	12.950 958	13.027 064	13.103 675	13.180 795	10
11	14.488 262	14.583 498	14.679 449	14.776 120	14.873 516	14.971 643	11
12	16.267 006	16.385 591	16.505 168	16.625 747	16.747 335	16.869 941	12
13	18.141 357	18.286 798	18.433 584	18.581 728	18.731 241	18.882 138	13
14	20.116 455	20.292 572	20.470 473	20.650 177	20.831 702	21.015 066	14
15	22.197 715	22.408 663	22.621 937	22.837 562	23.055 564	23.275 970	15
16	24.390 842	24.641 140	24.894 421	25.150 722	25.410 079	25.672 528	16
17	26.701 850	26.996 403	27.294 733	27.596 888	27.902 921	28.212 880	17
18	29.137 074	29.481 205	29.830 061	30.183 710	30.542 217	30.905 653	18
19	31.703 192	32.102 671	32.508 002	32.919 273	33.336 573	33.759 992	19
20	34.407 238	34.868 318	35.336 577	35.812 131	36.295 096	36.785 591	20
21	37.256 627	37.786 076	38.324 260	38.871 329	39.427 433	39.992 727	21
22	40.259 171	40.864 310	41.479 999	42.106 430	42.743 795	43.392 290	22
23	43.423 102	44.111 847	44.813 249	45.527 550	46.254 993	46.995 828	23
24	46.757 093	47.537 998	48.333 995	49.145 384	49.972 474	50.815 577	24
25	50.270 287	51.152 588	52.052 782	52.971 243	53.908 356	54.864 512	25
26	53.972 315	54.965 981	55.980 751	57.017 090	58.075 472	59.156 383	26
27	57.873 327	58.989 109	60.129 668	61.295 573	62.487 406	63.705 766	27
28	61.984 018	63.233 510	64.511 962	65.820 068	67.158 541	68.528 112	28
29	66.315 659	67.711 354	69.140 760	70.604 722	72.104 106	73.639 798	29
30	70.880 126	72.435 478	74.029 927	75.664 493	77.340 222	79.058 186	30
31	75.689 933	77.419 429	79.194 111	81.015 202	82.883 960	84.801 677	31
32	80.758 267	82.677 498	84.648 780	86.673 576	88.753 393	90.889 778	32
33	86.099 023	88.224 760	90.410 273	92.657 307	94.967 654	97.343 165	33
34	91.726 846	94.077 122	96.495 851	98.985 102	101.547 004	104.183 755	34
35	97.657 164	100.251 364	102.923 743	105.676 745	108.512 891	111.434 780	35
36	103.906 236	106.765 189	109.713 203	112.753 158	115.888 023	119.120 867	36
37	110.491 197	113.637 274	116.884 571	120.236 464	123.696 444	127.268 119	37
38	117.430 098	120.887 324	124.459 328	128.150 061	131.963 610	135.904 206	38
39	124.741 966	128.536 127	132.460 165	136.518 690	140.716 473	145.058 458	39
40	132.446 847	136.605 614	140.911 050	145.368 514	149.983 565	154.761 966	40
41	140.565 865	145.118 923	149.837 296	154.727 204	159.795 100	165.047 684	41
42	149.121 280	154.100 464	159.265 644	164.624 018	170.183 062	175.950 545	42
43	158.136 549	163.575 989	169.224 337	175.089 899	181.181 317	187.507 577	43
44	167.636 388	173.572 669	179.743 206	186.157 568	192.825 719	199.758 032	44
45	177.646 844	184.119 165	190.853 761	197.861 628	205.154 230	212.743 514	45
46	188.195 362	195.245 719	202.589 285	210.238 672	218.207 041	226.508 125	46
47	199.310 863	206.984 234	214.984 932	223.327 396	232.026 705	241.098 612	47
48	211.023 822	219.368 367	228.077 835	237.168 721	246.658 274	256.564 529	48
49	223.366 352	232.433 627	241.907 213	251.805 922	262.149 447	272.958 401	49
50	236.372 294	246.217 476	256.514 494	267.284 763	278.550 727	290.335 905	50
51	250.077 304	260.759 438	271.943 434	283.653 637	295.915 583	308.756 059	51
52	264.518 960	276.101 207	288.240 252	300.963 721	314.300 623	328.281 422	52
53	279.736 854	292.286 773	305.453 766	319.269 135	333.765 785	348.978 308	53
54	295.772 710	309.362 546	323.635 541	338.627 110	354.374 524	370.917 006	54
55	312.670 493	327.377 486	342.840 040	359.098 169	376.194 028	394.172 027	55
YRS							
14	330.476 532	346.383 247	363.124 792	380.746 314	399.295 427	418.822 348	56
15	411.799 835	433.450 372	456.334 051	480.523 132	506.094 152	533.128 181	60
16	512.068 530	541.311 272	572.352 202	605.304 906	640.290 212	677.436 661	64
17	635.696 208	674.932 013	716.760 727	761.358 098	808.911 909	859.622 792	68
18	788.124 668	840.464 682	896.506 926	956.519 605	1020.790 536	1089.628 586	72
19	976.063 452	1045.530 633	1120.238 154	1200.590 316	1287.022 896	1380.005 601	76
20	1207.785 183	1299.571 387	1398.717 822	1505.827 313	1621.552 485	1746.599 891	80
21	1493.489 706	1614.283 336	1745.343 220	1887.559 407	2041.899 753	2209.416 737	84
22	1845.753 059	2004.156 256	2176.790 036	2364.956 950	2570.079 718	2793.712 342	88
23	2280.081 046	2487.140 440	2713.814 607	2961.994 551	3233.754 959	3531.372 080	92
24	2815.591 763	3085.473 153	3382.252 474	3708.655 070	4067.684 406	4462.650 505	96
25	3475.857 128	3826.702 467	4214.261 298	4642.435 337	5115.543 781	5638.368 059	100
26	4289.940 468	4744.955 613	5249.867 923	5810.229 220	6432.213 041	7122.684 382	104
27	5293.675 813	5882.510 246	6538.894 014	7270.682 608	8086.650 634	8996.599 542	108
28	6531.245 229	7291.740 966	8143.352 910	9097.138 567	10165.505 082	11362.374 256	112
29	8057.123 606	9037.530 721	10140.433 008	11381.320 587	12777.653 063	14349.110 325	116
30	9938.476 515	11200.258 105	12626.211 187	14237.938 880	16059.901 649	18119.795 797	120

FUTURE VALUE OF
$1 PER PERIOD

SEMIANNUAL
COMPOUNDING

HALF YRS	7.00% ANNUAL RATE	8.00% ANNUAL RATE	9.00% ANNUAL RATE	10.00% ANNUAL RATE	10.50% ANNUAL RATE	11.00% ANNUAL RATE	HALF YRS
1	1.000 000	1.000 000	1.000 000	1.000 000	1.000 000	1.000 000	1
2	2.035 000	2.040 000	2.045 000	2.050 000	2.052 500	2.055 000	2
3	3.106 225	3.121 600	3.137 025	3.152 500	3.160 256	3.168 025	3
4	4.214 943	4.246 464	4.278 191	4.310 125	4.326 170	4.342 266	4
5	5.362 466	5.416 323	5.470 710	5.525 631	5.553 294	5.581 091	5
6	6.550 152	6.632 975	6.716 892	6.801 913	6.844 842	6.888 051	6
7	7.779 408	7.898 294	8.019 152	8.142 008	8.204 196	8.266 894	7
8	9.051 687	9.214 226	9.380 014	9.549 109	9.634 916	9.721 573	8
9	10.368 496	10.582 795	10.802 114	11.026 564	11.140 749	11.256 260	9
10	11.731 393	12.006 107	12.288 209	12.577 893	12.725 638	12.875 354	10
11	13.141 992	13.486 351	13.841 179	14.206 787	14.393 734	14.583 498	11
12	14.601 962	15.025 805	15.464 032	15.917 127	16.149 405	16.385 591	12
13	16.113 030	16.626 838	17.159 913	17.712 983	17.997 249	18.286 798	13
14	17.676 986	18.291 911	18.932 109	19.598 632	19.942 105	20.292 572	14
15	19.295 681	20.023 588	20.784 054	21.578 564	21.989 065	22.408 663	15
16	20.971 030	21.824 531	22.719 337	23.657 492	24.143 491	24.641 140	16
17	22.705 016	23.697 512	24.741 707	25.840 366	26.411 025	26.996 403	17
18	24.499 691	25.645 413	26.855 084	28.132 385	28.797 603	29.481 205	18
19	26.357 180	27.671 229	29.063 562	30.539 004	31.309 478	32.102 671	19
20	28.279 682	29.778 079	31.371 423	33.065 954	33.953 225	34.868 318	20
21	30.269 471	31.969 202	33.783 137	35.719 252	36.735 769	37.786 076	21
22	32.328 902	34.247 970	36.303 378	38.505 214	39.664 397	40.864 310	22
23	34.460 414	36.617 889	38.937 030	41.430 475	42.746 778	44.111 847	23
24	36.666 528	39.082 604	41.689 196	44.501 999	45.990 984	47.537 998	24
25	38.949 857	41.645 908	44.565 210	47.727 099	49.405 511	51.152 588	25
26	41.313 102	44.311 745	47.570 645	51.113 454	52.999 300	54.965 981	26
27	43.759 060	47.084 214	50.711 324	54.669 126	56.781 763	58.989 109	27
28	46.290 627	49.967 583	53.993 333	58.402 583	60.762 806	63.233 510	28
29	48.910 799	52.966 286	57.423 033	62.322 712	64.952 853	67.711 354	29
30	51.622 677	56.084 938	61.007 070	66.438 848	69.362 878	72.435 478	30
31	54.429 471	59.328 335	64.752 388	70.760 790	74.004 429	77.419 429	31
32	57.334 502	62.701 469	68.666 245	75.298 829	78.889 662	82.677 498	32
33	60.341 210	66.209 527	72.756 226	80.063 771	84.031 369	88.224 760	33
34	63.453 152	69.857 909	77.030 256	85.066 959	89.443 016	94.077 122	34
35	66.674 013	73.652 225	81.496 618	90.320 307	95.138 774	100.251 364	35
36	70.007 603	77.598 314	86.163 966	95.836 323	101.133 560	106.765 189	36
37	73.457 869	81.702 246	91.041 344	101.628 139	107.443 071	113.637 274	37
38	77.028 895	85.970 336	96.138 205	107.709 546	114.083 833	120.887 324	38
39	80.724 906	90.409 150	101.464 424	114.095 023	121.073 234	128.536 127	39
40	84.550 278	95.025 516	107.030 323	120.799 774	128.429 579	136.605 614	40
41	88.509 537	99.826 536	112.846 688	127.839 763	136.172 132	145.118 923	41
42	92.607 371	104.819 598	118.924 789	135.231 751	144.321 169	154.100 464	42
43	96.848 629	110.012 382	125.276 404	142.993 339	152.898 030	163.575 989	43
44	101.238 331	115.412 877	131.913 842	151.143 006	161.925 176	173.572 669	44
45	105.781 673	121.029 392	138.849 965	159.700 156	171.426 248	184.119 165	45
46	110.484 031	126.870 568	146.098 214	168.685 164	181.426 126	195.245 719	46
47	115.350 973	132.945 390	153.672 633	178.119 422	191.950 998	206.984 234	47
48	120.388 257	139.263 206	161.587 902	188.025 393	203.028 425	219.368 367	48
49	125.601 846	145.833 734	169.859 357	198.426 663	214.687 418	232.433 627	49
50	130.997 910	152.667 084	178.503 028	209.347 996	226.958 507	246.217 476	50
51	136.582 837	159.773 767	187.535 665	220.815 396	239.873 829	260.759 438	51
52	142.363 236	167.164 718	196.974 769	232.856 165	253.467 205	276.101 207	52
53	148.345 950	174.851 306	206.838 634	245.498 974	267.774 233	292.286 773	53
54	154.538 058	182.845 359	217.146 373	258.773 922	282.832 380	309.362 546	54
55	160.946 890	191.159 173	227.917 959	272.712 618	298.681 080	327.377 486	55
56	167.580 031	199.805 540	239.174 268	287.348 249	315.361 837	346.383 247	56
57	174.445 332	208.797 762	250.937 110	302.715 662	332.918 333	366.434 326	57
58	181.550 919	218.149 672	263.229 280	318.851 445	351.396 546	387.588 214	58
59	188.905 201	227.875 659	276.074 597	335.794 017	370.844 864	409.905 566	59

YRS							
30	196.516 883	237.990 685	289.497 954	353.583 718	391.314 220	433.450 372	60
31	212.548 798	259.450 725	318.184 003	391.876 049	435.533 273	484.496 100	62
32	229.722 586	282.661 904	349.509 886	434.093 344	484.517 205	541.311 272	64
33	248.119 577	307.767 116	383.718 533	480.637 912	538.779 462	604.547 978	66
34	267.826 894	334.920 912	421.075 231	531.953 298	598.888 816	674.932 013	68
35	288.937 865	364.290 459	461.869 680	588.528 511	665.475 329	753.271 204	70
36	311.552 464	396.056 560	506.418 237	650.902 683	739.236 955	840.464 582	72
37	335.777 788	430.414 776	555.066 375	719.670 208	820.946 857	937.513 203	74
38	361.728 561	467.576 621	608.191 358	795.486 404	911.461 512	1045.530 633	76
39	389.527 678	507.770 873	666.205 168	879.073 761	1011.729 687	1165.756 732	78
40	419.306 787	551.244 977	729.557 699	971.228 821	1122.802 384	1299.571 387	80

FUTURE VALUE OF
$1 PER PERIOD

SEMIANNUAL COMPOUNDING

HALF YRS	11.50% ANNUAL RATE	12.00% ANNUAL RATE	12.50% ANNUAL RATE	13.00% ANNUAL RATE	13.50% ANNUAL RATE	14.00% ANNUAL RATE	HALF YRS
1	1.000 000	1.000 000	1.000 000	1.000 000	1.000 000	1.000 000	1
2	2.057 500	2.060 000	2.062 500	2.065 000	2.067 500	2.070 000	2
3	3.175 806	3.183 600	3.191 406	3.199 225	3.207 056	3.214 900	3
4	4.358 415	4.374 616	4.390 869	4.407 175	4.423 533	4.439 943	4
5	5.609 024	5.637 093	5.665 298	5.693 641	5.722 121	5.750 739	5
6	6.931 543	6.975 319	7.019 380	7.063 728	7.108 364	7.153 291	6
7	8.330 107	8.393 838	8.458 091	8.522 870	8.588 179	8.654 021	7
8	9.809 088	9.897 468	9.986 722	10.076 856	10.167 881	10.259 803	8
9	11.373 110	11.491 316	11.610 892	11.731 852	11.854 213	11.977 989	9
10	13.027 064	13.180 795	13.336 572	13.494 423	13.654 372	13.816 448	10
11	14.776 120	14.971 643	15.170 108	15.371 560	15.576 042	15.783 599	11
12	16.625 747	16.869 941	17.118 240	17.370 711	17.627 425	17.888 451	12
13	18.581 728	18.882 138	19.188 130	19.499 808	19.817 276	20.140 643	13
14	20.650 177	21.015 066	21.387 388	21.767 295	22.154 942	22.550 488	14
15	22.837 562	23.275 970	23.724 100	24.182 169	24.650 401	25.129 022	15
16	25.150 722	25.672 528	26.206 856	26.754 010	27.314 303	27.888 054	16
17	27.596 888	28.212 880	28.844 784	29.493 021	30.158 019	30.840 217	17
18	30.183 710	30.905 653	31.647 583	32.410 067	33.193 685	33.999 033	18
19	32.919 273	33.759 992	34.625 557	35.516 722	36.434 259	37.378 965	19
20	35.812 131	36.785 591	37.789 655	38.825 309	39.893 571	40.995 492	20
21	38.871 329	39.992 727	41.151 508	42.348 954	43.586 387	44.865 177	21
22	42.106 430	43.392 290	44.723 477	46.101 636	47.528 468	49.005 739	22
23	45.527 550	46.995 828	48.518 695	50.098 242	51.736 640	53.436 141	23
24	49.145 384	50.815 577	52.551 113	54.354 628	56.228 863	58.176 671	24
25	52.971 243	54.864 512	56.835 558	58.887 679	61.024 311	63.249 038	25
26	57.017 090	59.156 383	61.387 780	63.715 378	66.143 452	68.676 470	26
27	61.295 573	63.705 766	66.224 516	68.856 877	71.608 135	74.483 823	27
28	65.820 068	68.528 112	71.363 549	74.332 574	77.441 684	80.697 691	28
29	70.604 722	73.639 798	76.823 771	80.164 192	83.668 998	87.346 529	29
30	75.664 493	79.058 186	82.625 256	86.374 864	90.316 655	94.460 786	30
31	81.015 202	84.801 677	88.789 335	92.989 230	97.413 030	102.073 041	31
32	86.673 576	90.889 778	95.338 668	100.033 530	104.988 409	110.218 154	32
33	92.657 307	97.343 165	102.297 335	107.535 710	113.075 127	118.933 425	33
34	98.985 102	104.183 755	109.690 918	115.525 531	121.707 698	128.258 765	34
35	105.676 745	111.434 780	117.546 601	124.034 690	130.922 967	138.236 878	35
36	112.753 158	119.120 867	125.893 263	133.096 945	140.760 268	148.913 460	36
37	120.236 464	127.268 119	134.761 592	142.748 247	151.261 586	160.337 402	37
38	128.150 061	135.904 206	144.184 192	153.026 883	162.471 743	172.561 020	38
39	136.518 690	145.058 458	154.195 704	163.973 630	174.438 586	185.640 292	39
40	145.368 514	154.761 966	164.832 935	175.631 916	187.213 190	199.635 112	40
41	154.727 204	165.047 684	176.134 994	188.047 990	200.850 080	214.609 570	41
42	164.624 018	175.950 545	188.143 431	201.271 110	215.407 461	230.632 240	42
43	175.089 899	187.507 577	200.902 395	215.353 732	230.947 464	247.776 496	43
44	186.157 568	199.758 032	214.458 795	230.351 725	247.536 418	266.120 851	44
45	197.861 628	212.743 514	228.862 470	246.324 587	265.245 127	285.749 311	45
46	210.238 672	226.508 125	244.166 374	263.335 685	284.149 173	306.751 763	46
47	223.327 396	241.098 612	260.426 772	281.452 504	304.329 242	329.224 386	47
48	237.168 721	256.564 529	277.703 445	300.746 917	325.871 466	353.270 093	48
49	251.805 922	272.958 401	296.059 911	321.295 467	348.867 789	378.999 000	49
50	267.284 763	290.335 905	315.563 655	343.179 672	373.416 365	406.528 929	50
51	283.653 637	308.756 059	336.286 384	366.486 351	399.621 970	435.985 955	51
52	300.963 721	328.281 422	358.304 283	391.307 963	427.596 453	467.504 971	52
53	319.269 135	348.978 308	381.698 300	417.742 981	457.459 213	501.230 319	53
54	338.627 110	370.917 006	406.554 444	445.896 275	489.337 710	537.316 442	54
55	359.098 169	394.172 027	432.964 097	475.879 533	523.368 006	575.928 593	55
56	380.746 314	418.822 348	461.024 353	507.811 702	559.695 346	617.243 594	56
57	403.639 227	444.951 689	490.838 375	541.819 463	598.474 782	661.450 646	57
58	427.848 482	472.648 790	522.515 773	578.037 728	639.871 830	708.752 191	58
59	453.449 770	502.007 718	556.173 009	616.610 180	684.063 178	759.364 844	59

YRS	11.50%	12.00%	12.50%	13.00%	13.50%	14.00%	HALF YRS
30	480.523 132	533.128 181	591.933 822	657.689 842	731.237 443	813.520 383	60
31	539.429 522	601.082 824	670.300 292	748.033 261	835.353 698	933.469 487	62
32	605.304 906	677.436 661	758.768 689	850.503 026	954.000 028	1070.799 216	64
33	678.973 759	763.227 832	858.641 215	966.726 794	1089.204 194	1228.028 022	66
34	761.358 098	859.622 792	971.387 934	1098.550 698	1243.276 947	1408.039 282	68
35	853.489 020	967.932 170	1098.668 410	1248.068 666	1418.851 516	1614.134 174	70
36	956.519 605	1089.628 586	1242.356 135	1417.655 682	1618.928 612	1850.092 216	72
37	1071.739 353	1226.366 679	1404.566 105	1610.005 516	1846.927 719	2120.240 578	74
38	1200.590 316	1380.005 601	1587.685 954	1828.173 507	2106.745 525	2429.533 438	76
39	1344.685 155	1552.634 293	1794.411 097	2075.625 096	2402.822 530	2783.642 833	78
40	1505.827 313	1746.599 891	2027.784 403	2356.290 874	2740.218 932	3189.062 680	80

FUTURE VALUE OF
$1 PER PERIOD

SEMIANNUAL
COMPOUNDING

HALF YRS	14.50% ANNUAL RATE	15.00% ANNUAL RATE	15.50% ANNUAL RATE	16.00% ANNUAL RATE	16.50% ANNUAL RATE	17.00% ANNUAL RATE	HALF YRS
1	1.000 000	1.000 000	1.000 000	1.000 000	1.000 000	1.000 000	1
2	2.072 500	2.075 000	2.077 500	2.080 000	2.082 500	2.085 000	2
3	3.222 756	3.230 625	3.238 506	3.246 400	3.254 306	3.262 225	3
4	4.456 406	4.472 922	4.489 490	4.506 112	4.522 787	4.539 514	4
5	5.779 496	5.808 391	5.837 426	5.866 601	5.895 916	5.925 373	5
6	7.198 509	7.244 020	7.289 827	7.335 929	7.382 330	7.429 030	6
7	8.720 401	8.787 322	8.854 788	8.922 803	8.991 372	9.060 497	7
8	10.352 630	10.446 371	10.541 034	10.636 628	10.733 160	10.830 639	8
9	12.103 196	12.229 849	12.357 964	12.487 558	12.618 646	12.751 244	9
10	13.980 677	14.147 087	14.315 707	14.486 562	14.659 684	14.835 099	10
11	15.994 276	16.208 119	16.425 174	16.645 487	16.869 108	17.096 083	11
12	18.153 861	18.423 728	18.698 125	18.977 126	19.260 809	19.549 250	12
13	20.470 016	20.805 508	21.147 229	21.495 297	21.849 826	22.210 936	13
14	22.954 093	23.365 921	23.786 140	24.214 920	24.652 436	25.098 866	14
15	25.618 264	26.118 365	26.629 566	27.152 114	27.686 262	28.232 269	15
16	28.475 588	29.077 242	29.693 357	30.324 283	30.970 379	31.632 012	16
17	31.540 069	32.258 035	32.994 592	33.750 226	34.525 435	35.320 733	17
18	34.826 724	35.677 388	36.551 673	37.450 244	38.373 784	39.322 995	18
19	38.351 661	39.353 192	40.384 428	41.446 263	42.539 621	43.665 450	19
20	42.132 156	43.304 681	44.514 221	45.761 964	47.049 140	48.377 013	20
21	46.186 738	47.552 532	48.964 073	50.422 921	51.930 694	53.489 059	21
22	50.535 276	52.118 972	53.758 788	55.456 755	57.214 976	59.035 629	22
23	55.199 284	57.027 895	58.925 095	60.893 296	62.935 212	65.053 658	23
24	60.201 017	62.304 987	64.491 789	66.764 759	69.127 366	71.583 219	24
25	65.565 591	67.977 862	70.489 903	73.105 940	75.830 374	78.667 792	25
26	71.319 096	74.076 201	76.952 870	79.954 415	83.086 380	86.354 555	26
27	77.489 731	80.631 916	83.916 718	87.350 768	90.941 006	94.694 692	27
28	84.107 736	87.679 310	91.420 264	95.338 830	99.443 639	103.743 741	28
29	91.205 547	95.255 258	99.505 334	103.965 936	108.647 740	113.561 959	29
30	98.817 949	103.399 403	108.216 997	113.283 211	118.611 178	124.214 725	30
31	106.982 251	112.154 358	117.603 815	123.345 868	129.396 600	135.772 977	31
32	115.738 464	121.565 935	127.718 110	134.213 537	141.071 820	148.313 680	32
33	125.129 503	131.683 380	138.616 264	145.950 620	153.710 245	161.920 343	33
34	135.201 392	142.559 633	150.359 024	158.626 670	167.391 340	176.683 572	34
35	146.003 492	154.251 606	163.011 849	172.316 804	182.201 126	192.701 675	35
36	157.588 746	166.820 476	176.645 267	187.102 148	198.232 719	210.081 318	36
37	170.013 930	180.332 012	191.335 275	203.070 320	215.586 918	228.938 230	37
38	183.339 940	194.856 913	207.163 759	220.315 945	234.372 839	249.397 979	38
39	197.632 085	210.471 181	224.218 950	238.941 221	254.708 598	271.596 808	39
40	212.960 411	227.256 520	242.595 919	259.056 519	276.722 058	295.682 536	40
41	229.400 041	245.300 759	262.397 103	280.781 040	300.551 627	321.815 552	41
42	247.031 544	264.698 315	283.732 878	304.243 523	326.347 137	350.169 874	42
43	265.941 331	285.550 689	306.722 176	329.583 005	354.270 775	380.934 313	43
44	286.222 078	307.966 991	331.493 145	356.949 646	384.498 114	414.313 730	44
45	307.973 178	332.064 515	358.183 864	386.505 617	417.219 209	450.530 397	45
46	331.301 234	357.969 354	386.943 113	418.426 067	452.639 793	489.825 480	46
47	356.320 573	385.817 055	417.931 204	452.900 152	490.982 576	532.460 646	47
48	383.153 815	415.753 334	451.320 873	490.132 164	532.488 639	578.719 801	48
49	411.932 466	447.934 835	487.298 240	530.342 737	577.418 952	628.910 984	49
50	442.797 570	482.529 947	526.063 854	573.770 156	626.056 015	683.368 418	50
51	475.900 394	519.719 693	567.833 803	620.671 769	678.705 636	742.454 733	51
52	511.403 173	559.698 670	612.840 922	671.325 510	735.698 851	806.563 386	52
53	549.479 903	602.676 070	661.336 094	726.031 551	797.394 007	876.121 273	53
54	590.317 195	648.876 776	713.589 641	785.114 075	864.179 012	951.591 582	54
55	634.115 192	698.542 534	769.892 838	848.923 201	936.473 781	1033.476 866	55
56	681.088 544	751.933 224	830.559 533	917.837 058	1014.732 868	1122.322 400	56
57	731.467 463	809.328 216	895.927 897	992.264 022	1099.448 329	1218.719 804	57
58	785.498 854	871.027 832	966.362 309	1072.645 144	1191.152 816	1323.310 987	58
59	843.447 521	937.354 919	1042.255 388	1159.456 755	1290.422 924	1436.792 421	59
YRS							
30	905.597 466	1008.656 538	1124.030 180	1253.213 296	1397.882 815	1559.919 777	60
31	1043.741 646	1167.703 712	1307.083 565	1463.827 988	1640.130 319	1838.461 559	62
32	1202.642 851	1351.502 602	1519.609 688	1709.488 966	1923.997 459	2166.367 909	64
33	1385.419 956	1563.905 195	1766.353 845	1996.027 929	2256.634 747	2552.387 462	66
34	1595.660 463	1809.362 940	2052.825 354	2330.246 977	2646.421 201	3006.819 330	68
35	1837.490 921	2093.020 048	2385.420 566	2720.080 074	3103.175 403	3541.787 885	70
36	2115.657 916	2420.821 293	2771.565 686	3174.781 398	3638.402 832	4171.566 243	72
37	2435.621 241	2799.636 607	3219.882 584	3705.145 023	4265.585 679	4912.957 071	74
38	2803.661 055	3237.405 054	3740.381 304	4323.761 154	5000.522 458	5785.740 887	76
39	3227.001 151	3743.301 215	4344.683 572	5045.315 011	5861.725 970	6813.203 816	78
40	3713.950 743	4327.927 467	5046.282 281	5886.935 428	6870.889 627	8022.758 863	80

FUTURE VALUE OF
$1 PER PERIOD

HALF YRS	17.50% ANNUAL RATE	18.00% ANNUAL RATE	18.50% ANNUAL RATE	19.00% ANNUAL RATE	19.50% ANNUAL RATE	20.00% ANNUAL RATE	HALF YRS
1	1.000 000	1.000 000	1.000 000	1.000 000	1.000 000	1.000 000	1
2	2.087 500	2.090 000	2.092 500	2.095 000	2.097 500	2.100 000	2
3	3.270 156	3.278 100	3.286 056	3.294 025	3.302 006	3.310 000	3
4	4.556 295	4.573 129	4.590 016	4.606 957	4.623 952	4.641 000	4
5	5.954 971	5.984 711	6.014 593	6.044 618	6.074 787	6.105 100	5
6	7.476 031	7.523 335	7.570 943	7.618 857	7.667 079	7.715 610	6
7	9.130 183	9.200 435	9.271 255	9.342 648	9.414 619	9.487 171	7
8	10.929 074	11.028 474	11.128 846	11.230 200	11.332 544	11.435 888	8
9	12.885 368	13.021 036	13.158 264	13.297 069	13.437 468	13.579 477	9
10	15.012 838	15.192 930	15.375 404	15.560 291	15.747 621	15.937 425	10
11	17.326 461	17.560 293	17.797 629	18.038 518	18.283 014	18.531 167	11
12	19.842 527	20.140 720	20.443 909	20.752 178	21.065 607	21.384 284	12
13	22.578 748	22.953 385	23.334 971	23.723 634	24.119 504	24.522 712	13
14	25.554 388	26.019 189	26.493 456	26.977 380	27.471 156	27.974 983	14
15	28.790 397	29.360 916	29.944 100	30.540 231	31.149 594	31.772 482	15
16	32.309 557	33.003 399	33.713 930	34.441 553	35.186 679	35.949 730	16
17	36.136 643	36.973 705	37.832 468	38.713 500	39.617 380	40.544 703	17
18	40.298 600	41.301 338	42.331 972	43.391 283	44.480 075	45.599 173	18
19	44.824 727	46.018 458	47.247 679	48.513 454	49.816 882	51.159 090	19
20	49.746 891	51.160 120	52.618 089	54.122 233	55.674 028	57.274 999	20
21	55.099 744	56.764 530	58.485 262	60.263 845	62.102 246	64.002 499	21
22	60.920 971	62.873 338	64.895 149	66.988 910	69.157 215	71.402 749	22
23	67.251 556	69.531 939	71.897 951	74.352 856	76.900 043	79.543 024	23
24	74.136 067	76.789 813	79.548 511	82.416 378	85.397 797	88.497 327	24
25	81.622 973	84.700 896	87.906 748	91.245 934	94.724 083	98.347 059	25
26	89.764 984	93.323 977	97.038 122	100.914 297	104.959 681	109.181 765	26
27	98.619 420	102.723 135	107.014 149	111.501 156	116.193 249	121.099 942	27
28	108.248 619	112.968 217	117.912 958	123.093 766	128.522 091	134.209 936	28
29	118.720 373	124.135 356	129.819 906	135.787 673	142.052 995	148.630 930	29
30	130.108 406	136.307 539	142.828 247	149.687 502	156.903 162	164.494 023	30
31	142.492 891	149.575 217	157.039 860	164.907 815	173.201 221	181.943 425	31
32	155.961 019	164.036 987	172.566 047	181.574 057	191.088 340	201.137 767	32
33	170.607 608	179.800 315	189.528 407	199.823 593	210.719 453	222.251 544	33
34	186.535 774	196.982 344	208.059 784	219.806 834	232.264 599	245.476 699	34
35	203.857 654	215.710 755	228.305 315	241.688 483	255.910 398	271.024 368	35
36	222.695 199	236.124 723	250.423 556	265.648 889	281.861 661	299.126 805	36
37	243.181 029	258.375 948	274.587 735	291.885 534	310.343 173	330.039 486	37
38	265.459 369	282.629 783	300.987 101	320.614 659	341.601 633	364.043 434	38
39	289.687 064	309.066 463	329.828 407	352.073 052	375.907 792	401.447 778	39
40	316.034 682	337.882 445	361.337 535	386.519 992	413.558 802	442.592 556	40
41	344.687 716	369.291 865	395.761 257	424.239 391	454.880 785	487.851 811	41
42	375.847 892	403.528 133	433.369 173	465.542 133	500.231 662	537.636 992	42
43	409.734 582	440.845 665	474.455 822	510.768 636	550.004 249	592.400 692	43
44	446.586 358	481.521 775	519.342 985	560.291 656	604.629 663	652.640 761	44
45	486.662 664	525.858 734	568.382 212	614.519 364	664.581 055	718.904 837	45
46	530.245 648	574.186 021	621.957 566	673.898 703	730.377 708	791.795 321	46
47	577.642 142	626.862 762	680.488 641	738.919 080	802.589 534	871.974 853	47
48	629.185 829	684.280 411	744.433 840	810.116 393	881.842 014	960.172 338	48
49	685.239 589	746.865 648	814.293 970	888.077 450	968.821 610	1057.189 572	49
50	746.198 053	815.083 556	890.616 163	973.444 808	1064.281 717	1163.908 529	50
51	812.490 383	889.441 076	973.998 158	1066.922 065	1169.049 185	1281.299 382	51
52	884.583 291	970.490 773	1065.092 987	1169.279 661	1284.031 480	1410.429 320	52
53	962.984 329	1058.834 943	1164.614 089	1281.361 229	1410.224 549	1552.472 252	53
54	1048.245 458	1155.130 088	1273.340 892	1404.090 545	1548.721 443	1708.719 477	54
55	1140.966 936	1260.091 796	1392.124 924	1538.479 147	1700.721 784	1880.591 425	55
56	1241.801 543	1374.500 057	1521.896 480	1685.634 666	1867.542 158	2069.650 567	56
57	1351.459 178	1499.205 063	1663.671 904	1846.769 959	2050.627 518	2277.615 624	57
58	1470.711 856	1635.133 518	1818.561 555	2023.213 106	2251.563 701	2506.377 186	58
59	1600.399 143	1783.295 535	1987.778 499	2216.418 351	2472.091 162	2758.014 905	59

YRS							
30	1741.434 068	1944.792 133	2172.648 011	2427.978 094	2714.120 050	3034.816 395	60
31	2061.605 385	2312.697 533	2595.270 112	2913.301 434	3271.272 064	3674.227 838	62
32	2440.257 993	2749.805 939	3099.693 363	3495.216 252	3942.365 146	4447.915 685	64
33	2888.073 867	3269.134 436	3701.750 886	4192.946 666	4750.700 958	5384.077 978	66
34	3417.686 109	3886.148 624	4420.340 406	5029.542 877	5724.346 496	6516.834 354	68
35	4044.035 338	4619.223 180	5278.017 419	6032.642 648	6897.108 632	7887.469 568	70
36	4784.791 168	5490.189 060	6301.703 178	7235.384 351	8309.707 954	9545.938 177	72
37	5660.850 679	6524.983 622	7523.529 713	8677.501 721	10011.192 666	11552.685 195	74
38	6696.927 936	7754.423 041	8981.848 411	10406.636 591	12060.641 636	13980.849 085	76
39	7922.251 179	9215.120 015	10722.433 808	12479.912 331	14529.215 729	16918.927 393	78
40	9371.387 371	10950.574 090	12799.920 387	14965.821 882	17502.628 654	20474.002 146	80

FUTURE VALUE OF
$1 PER PERIOD

ANNUAL
COMPOUNDING

YRS	7.00% ANNUAL RATE	8.00% ANNUAL RATE	9.00% ANNUAL RATE	10.00% ANNUAL RATE	10.25% ANNUAL RATE	10.50% ANNUAL RATE	YRS
1	1.000 000	1.000 000	1.000 000	1.000 000	1.000 000	1.000 000	1
2	2.070 000	2.080 000	2.090 000	2.100 000	2.102 500	2.105 000	2
3	3.214 900	3.246 400	3.278 100	3.310 000	3.318 006	3.326 025	3
4	4.439 943	4.506 112	4.573 129	4.641 000	4.658 102	4.675 258	4
5	5.750 739	5.866 601	5.984 711	6.105 100	6.135 557	6.166 160	5
6	7.153 291	7.335 929	7.523 335	7.715 610	7.764 452	7.813 606	6
7	8.654 021	8.922 803	9.200 435	9.487 171	9.560 308	9.634 035	7
8	10.259 803	10.636 628	11.028 474	11.435 888	11.540 240	11.645 609	8
9	11.977 989	12.487 558	13.021 036	13.579 477	13.723 114	13.868 398	9
10	13.816 448	14.486 562	15.192 930	15.937 425	16.129 734	16.324 579	10
11	15.783 599	16.645 487	17.560 293	18.531 167	18.783 031	19.038 660	11
12	17.888 451	18.977 126	20.140 720	21.384 284	21.708 292	22.037 720	12
13	20.140 643	21.495 297	22.953 385	24.522 712	24.933 392	25.351 680	13
14	22.550 488	24.214 920	26.019 189	27.974 983	28.489 065	29.013 607	14
15	25.129 022	27.152 114	29.360 916	31.772 482	32.409 194	33.060 035	15
16	27.888 054	30.324 283	33.003 399	35.949 730	36.731 136	37.531 339	16
17	30.840 217	33.750 226	36.973 705	40.544 703	41.496 078	42.472 130	17
18	33.999 033	37.450 244	41.301 338	45.599 173	46.749 426	47.931 703	18
19	37.378 965	41.446 263	46.018 458	51.159 090	52.541 242	53.964 532	19
20	40.995 492	45.761 964	51.160 120	57.274 999	58.926 719	60.630 808	20
21	44.865 177	50.422 921	56.764 530	64.002 499	65.966 708	67.997 043	21
22	49.005 739	55.456 755	62.873 338	71.402 749	73.728 295	76.136 732	22
23	53.436 141	60.893 296	69.531 939	79.543 024	82.285 446	85.131 089	23
24	58.176 671	66.764 759	76.789 813	88.497 327	91.719 704	95.069 854	24
25	63.249 038	73.105 940	84.700 896	98.347 059	102.120 974	106.052 188	25
26	68.676 470	79.954 415	93.323 977	109.181 765	113.588 373	118.187 668	26
27	74.483 823	87.350 768	102.723 135	121.099 942	126.231 182	131.597 373	27
28	80.697 691	95.338 830	112.968 217	134.209 936	140.169 878	146.415 097	28
29	87.346 529	103.965 936	124.135 356	148.630 930	155.537 290	162.788 683	29
30	94.460 786	113.283 211	136.307 539	164.494 023	172.479 862	180.881 494	30
31	102.073 041	123.345 868	149.575 217	181.943 425	191.159 048	200.874 051	31
32	110.218 154	134.213 537	164.036 987	201.137 767	211.752 851	222.965 827	32
33	118.933 425	145.950 620	179.800 315	222.251 544	234.457 518	247.377 238	33
34	128.258 765	158.626 670	196.982 344	245.476 699	259.489 414	274.351 848	34
35	138.236 878	172.316 804	215.710 755	271.024 368	287.087 078	304.158 792	35
36	148.913 460	187.102 148	236.124 723	299.126 805	317.513 504	337.095 466	36
37	160.337 402	203.070 320	258.375 948	330.039 486	351.058 638	373.490 489	37
38	172.561 020	220.315 945	282.629 783	364.043 434	388.042 148	413.706 991	38
39	185.640 292	238.941 221	309.066 463	401.447 778	428.816 469	458.146 225	39
40	199.635 112	259.056 519	337.882 445	442.592 556	473.770 157	507.251 579	40
41	214.609 570	280.781 040	369.291 865	487.851 811	523.331 598	561.512 994	41
42	230.632 240	304.243 523	403.528 133	537.636 992	577.973 087	621.471 859	42
43	247.776 496	329.583 005	440.845 665	592.400 692	638.215 328	687.726 404	43
44	266.120 851	356.949 646	481.521 775	652.640 761	704.632 399	760.937 676	44
45	285.749 311	386.505 617	525.858 734	718.904 837	777.857 220	841.836 132	45
46	306.751 763	418.426 067	574.186 021	791.795 321	858.587 585	931.228 926	46
47	329.224 386	452.900 152	626.862 762	871.974 853	947.592 813	1030.007 963	47
48	353.270 093	490.132 164	684.280 411	960.172 338	1045.721 076	1139.158 800	48
49	378.999 000	530.342 737	746.865 648	1057.189 572	1153.907 486	1259.770 473	49
50	406.528 929	573.770 156	815.083 556	1163.908 529	1273.183 003	1393.046 373	50

FUTURE VALUE OF
$1 PER PERIOD

YRS	10.75% ANNUAL RATE	11.00% ANNUAL RATE	11.25% ANNUAL RATE	11.50% ANNUAL RATE	11.75% ANNUAL RATE	12.00% ANNUAL RATE	YRS
1	1.000 000	1.000 000	1.000 000	1.000 000	1.000 000	1.000 000	1
2	2.107 500	2.110 000	2.112 500	2.115 000	2.117 500	2.120 000	2
3	3.334 056	3.342 100	3.350 156	3.358 225	3.366 306	3.374 400	3
4	4.692 467	4.709 731	4.727 049	4.744 421	4.761 847	4.779 328	4
5	6.196 908	6.227 801	6.258 842	6.290 029	6.321 364	6.352 847	5
6	7.863 075	7.912 860	7.962 962	8.013 383	8.064 125	8.115 189	6
7	9.708 356	9.783 274	9.858 795	9.934 922	10.011 659	10.089 012	7
8	11.752 004	11.859 434	11.967 909	12.077 438	12.188 029	12.299 693	8
9	14.015 344	14.163 972	14.314 299	14.466 343	14.620 123	14.775 656	9
10	16.521 994	16.722 009	16.924 657	17.129 972	17.337 987	17.548 735	10
11	19.298 108	19.561 430	19.828 681	20.099 919	20.375 200	20.654 583	11
12	22.372 655	22.713 187	23.059 408	23.411 410	23.769 287	24.133 133	12
13	25.777 715	26.211 638	26.653 592	27.103 722	27.562 178	28.029 109	13
14	29.548 820	30.094 918	30.652 121	31.220 650	31.800 734	32.392 602	14
15	33.725 318	34.405 359	35.100 484	35.811 025	36.537 320	37.279 715	15
16	38.350 789	39.189 948	40.049 289	40.929 293	41.830 455	42.753 280	16
17	43.473 499	44.500 843	45.554 834	46.636 161	47.745 533	48.883 674	17
18	49.146 900	50.395 936	51.679 752	52.999 320	54.355 634	55.749 715	18
19	55.430 192	56.939 488	58.493 725	60.094 242	61.742 420	63.439 681	19
20	62.388 938	64.202 832	66.074 269	68.005 080	69.997 155	72.052 442	20
21	70.095 749	72.265 144	74.507 624	76.825 664	79.221 821	81.698 736	21
22	78.631 042	81.214 309	83.889 731	86.660 615	89.530 384	92.502 584	22
23	88.083 879	91.147 884	94.327 326	97.626 586	101.050 205	104.602 894	23
24	98.552 895	102.174 151	105.939 150	109.853 643	113.923 604	118.155 241	24
25	110.147 332	114.413 307	118.857 305	123.486 812	128.309 627	133.333 870	25
26	122.988 170	127.998 771	133.228 752	138.687 796	144.386 008	150.333 934	26
27	137.209 398	143.078 636	149.216 986	155.636 892	162.351 364	169.374 007	27
28	152.959 408	159.817 286	167.003 897	174.535 135	182.427 650	190.698 887	28
29	170.402 545	178.397 187	186.791 836	195.606 675	204.862 898	214.582 754	29
30	189.720 818	199.020 878	208.805 917	219.101 443	229.934 289	241.332 684	30
31	211.115 806	221.913 174	233.296 583	245.298 109	257.951 568	271.292 606	31
32	234.810 756	247.323 624	260.542 448	274.507 391	289.260 877	304.847 719	32
33	261.052 912	275.529 222	290.853 474	307.075 741	324.249 030	342.429 446	33
34	290.116 100	306.837 437	324.574 489	343.389 451	363.348 291	384.520 979	34
35	322.303 581	341.589 555	362.089 120	383.879 238	407.041 715	431.663 496	35
36	357.951 215	380.164 406	403.824 145	429.025 351	455.869 117	484.463 116	36
37	397.430 971	422.982 490	450.254 362	479.363 266	510.433 738	543.598 690	37
38	441.154 801	470.510 564	501.907 978	535.490 042	571.409 702	609.830 533	38
39	489.578 942	523.266 726	559.372 625	598.071 396	639.550 343	684.010 197	39
40	543.208 678	581.826 066	623.302 045	667.849 607	715.697 508	767.091 420	40
41	602.603 611	646.826 934	694.423 525	745.652 312	800.791 965	860.142 391	41
42	668.383 499	718.977 896	773.546 172	832.402 327	895.885 021	964.359 478	42
43	741.234 725	799.065 465	861.570 116	929.128 595	1002.151 511	1081.082 615	43
44	821.917 458	887.962 666	959.496 755	1036.978 384	1120.904 313	1211.812 529	44
45	911.273 585	986.638 559	1068.440 139	1157.230 898	1253.610 570	1358.230 032	45
46	1010.235 495	1096.168 801	1189.639 655	1291.312 451	1401.909 812	1522.217 636	46
47	1119.835 811	1217.747 369	1324.474 116	1440.813 383	1567.634 215	1705.883 752	47
48	1241.218 160	1352.699 580	1474.477 454	1607.506 922	1752.831 235	1911.589 803	48
49	1375.649 113	1502.496 533	1641.356 168	1793.370 218	1959.788 905	2141.980 579	49
50	1524.531 392	1668.771 152	1827.008 737	2000.607 793	2191.064 102	2400.018 249	50

FUTURE VALUE OF
$1 PER PERIOD

ANNUAL
COMPOUNDING

YRS	12.25% ANNUAL RATE	12.50% ANNUAL RATE	12.75% ANNUAL RATE	13.00% ANNUAL RATE	13.25% ANNUAL RATE	13.50% ANNUAL RATE	YRS
1	1.000 000	1.000 000	1.000 000	1.000 000	1.000 000	1.000 000	1
2	2.122 500	2.125 000	2.127 500	2.130 000	2.132 500	2.135 000	2
3	3.382 506	3.390 625	3.398 756	3.406 900	3.415 056	3.423 225	3
4	4.796 863	4.814 453	4.832 098	4.849 797	4.867 551	4.885 360	4
5	6.384 479	6.416 260	6.448 190	6.480 271	6.512 502	6.544 884	5
6	8.166 578	8.218 292	8.270 334	8.322 706	8.375 408	8.428 443	6
7	10.166 983	10.245 579	10.324 802	10.404 658	10.485 150	10.566 283	7
8	12.412 439	12.526 276	12.641 214	12.757 263	12.874 432	12.992 731	8
9	14.932 963	15.092 061	15.252 969	15.415 707	15.580 294	15.746 750	9
10	17.762 251	17.978 568	18.197 723	18.419 749	18.644 683	18.872 561	10
11	20.938 126	21.225 889	21.517 932	21.814 317	22.115 104	22.420 357	11
12	24.503 047	24.879 125	25.261 469	25.650 178	26.045 355	26.447 106	12
13	28.504 670	28.989 016	29.482 306	29.984 701	30.496 365	31.017 465	13
14	32.996 492	33.612 643	34.241 300	34.882 712	35.537 133	36.204 823	14
15	38.038 562	38.814 223	39.607 066	40.417 464	41.245 803	42.092 474	15
16	43.698 286	44.666 001	45.656 966	46.671 735	47.710 872	48.774 957	16
17	50.051 326	51.249 252	52.478 230	53.739 060	55.032 563	56.359 577	17
18	57.182 614	58.655 408	60.169 204	61.725 138	63.324 377	64.968 120	18
19	65.187 484	66.987 334	68.840 777	70.749 406	72.714 857	74.738 816	19
20	74.172 951	76.360 751	78.617 977	80.946 829	83.349 576	85.828 556	20
21	84.259 137	86.905 845	89.641 769	92.469 917	95.393 395	98.415 411	21
22	95.580 882	98.769 075	102.071 094	105.491 006	109.033 020	112.701 491	22
23	108.289 540	112.115 210	116.085 159	120.204 837	124.479 895	128.916 193	23
24	122.555 008	127.129 611	131.886 016	136.831 465	141.973 481	147.319 879	24
25	138.567 997	144.020 812	149.701 483	155.619 556	161.784 967	168.208 062	25
26	156.542 576	163.023 414	169.788 423	176.850 098	184.221 475	191.916 151	26
27	176.719 042	184.401 340	192.436 446	200.840 611	209.630 821	218.824 831	27
28	199.367 125	208.451 508	217.972 093	227.949 890	238.406 904	249.366 183	28
29	224.789 597	235.507 946	246.763 535	258.583 376	270.995 819	284.030 618	29
30	253.326 323	265.946 440	279.225 886	293.199 215	307.902 765	323.374 752	30
31	285.358 798	300.189 745	315.827 187	332.315 113	349.699 882	368.030 343	31
32	321.315 250	338.713 463	357.095 153	376.516 078	397.035 116	418.714 439	32
33	361.676 369	382.052 645	403.624 785	426.463 168	450.642 269	476.240 889	33
34	406.981 724	430.809 226	456.086 945	482.903 380	511.352 369	541.533 409	34
35	457.836 985	485.660 379	515.238 030	546.680 819	580.106 558	615.640 419	35
36	514.922 016	547.367 927	581.930 879	618.749 325	657.970 677	699.751 875	36
37	578.999 963	616.788 918	657.127 066	700.186 738	746.151 792	795.218 378	37
38	650.927 458	694.887 532	741.910 767	792.211 014	846.016 904	903.572 859	38
39	731.666 072	782.748 474	837.504 390	896.198 445	959.114 144	1026.555 195	39
40	822.295 165	881.592 033	945.286 200	1013.704 243	1087.196 768	1166.140 147	40
41	924.026 323	992.791 037	1066.810 190	1146.485 795	1232.250 340	1324.569 067	41
42	1038.219 548	1117.889 917	1203.828 490	1296.528 948	1396.523 510	1504.385 891	42
43	1166.401 442	1258.626 157	1358.316 622	1466.077 712	1582.562 875	1708.477 986	43
44	1310.285 619	1416.954 426	1532.501 991	1657.667 814	1793.252 456	1940.122 514	44
45	1471.795 607	1595.073 729	1728.895 995	1874.164 630	2031.858 407	2203.039 053	45
46	1653.090 569	1795.457 946	1950.330 235	2118.806 032	2302.079 646	2501.449 326	46
47	1856.594 164	2020.890 189	2199.997 339	2395.250 816	2608.105 199	2840.144 984	47
48	2085.026 949	2274.501 462	2481.497 000	2707.633 422	2954.679 138	3224.564 557	48
49	2341.442 750	2559.814 145	2798.887 868	3060.625 767	3347.174 124	3660.880 773	49
50	2629.269 487	2880.790 913	3156.746 071	3459.507 117	3791.674 695	4156.099 677	50

FUTURE VALUE OF
$1 PER PERIOD

ANNUAL
COMPOUNDING

YRS	13.75% ANNUAL RATE	14.00% ANNUAL RATE	14.25% ANNUAL RATE	14.50% ANNUAL RATE	14.75% ANNUAL RATE	15.00% ANNUAL RATE	YRS
1	1.000 000	1.000 000	1.000 000	1.000 000	1.000 000	1.000 000	1
2	2.137 500	2.140 000	2.142 500	2.145 000	2.147 500	2.150 000	2
3	3.431 406	3.439 600	3.447 806	3.456 025	3.464 256	3.472 500	3
4	4.903 225	4.921 144	4.939 119	4.957 149	4.975 234	4.993 375	4
5	6.577 418	6.610 104	6.642 943	6.675 935	6.709 081	6.742 381	5
6	8.481 813	8.535 519	8.589 562	8.643 946	8.698 671	8.753 738	6
7	10.648 062	10.730 491	10.813 575	10.897 318	10.981 724	11.066 799	7
8	13.112 171	13.232 760	13.354 510	13.477 429	13.601 529	13.726 819	8
9	15.915 094	16.085 347	16.257 527	16.431 656	16.607 754	16.785 842	9
10	19.103 420	19.337 295	19.574 225	19.814 246	20.057 398	20.303 718	10
11	22.730 140	23.044 516	23.363 552	23.687 312	24.015 864	24.349 276	11
12	26.855 534	27.270 749	27.692 858	28.121 972	28.558 204	29.001 667	12
13	31.548 170	32.088 654	32.639 090	33.199 658	33.770 539	34.351 917	13
14	36.886 044	37.581 065	38.290 161	39.013 609	39.751 694	40.504 705	14
15	42.957 875	43.842 414	44.746 508	45.670 582	46.615 069	47.580 411	15
16	49.864 582	50.980 352	52.122 886	53.292 816	54.490 791	55.717 472	16
17	57.720 962	59.117 601	60.550 397	62.020 275	63.528 183	65.075 093	17
18	66.657 595	68.394 066	70.178 829	72.013 215	73.898 590	75.836 357	18
19	76.823 014	78.969 235	81.179 312	83.455 131	85.798 632	88.211 811	19
20	88.386 178	91.024 928	93.747 364	96.556 125	99.453 930	102.443 583	20
21	101.539 278	104.768 418	108.106 363	111.556 763	115.123 385	118.810 120	21
22	116.500 929	120.435 996	124.511 520	128.732 494	133.104 084	137.631 638	22
23	133.519 806	138.297 035	143.254 411	148.398 705	153.736 937	159.276 384	23
24	152.878 780	158.658 620	164.668 165	170.916 517	177.413 135	184.167 841	24
25	174.899 612	181.870 827	189.133 378	196.699 412	204.581 573	212.793 017	25
26	199.948 309	208.332 743	217.084 885	226.220 827	235.757 354	245.711 970	26
27	228.441 201	238.499 327	249.019 481	260.022 847	271.531 564	283.568 766	27
28	260.851 866	272.889 233	285.504 757	298.726 160	312.582 470	327.104 080	28
29	297.718 998	312.093 725	327.189 185	343.041 453	359.688 384	377.169 693	29
30	339.655 360	356.786 847	374.813 643	393.782 464	413.742 421	434.745 146	30
31	387.357 972	407.737 006	429.224 588	451.880 921	475.769 428	500.956 918	31
32	441.619 693	465.820 186	491.389 091	518.403 655	546.945 419	577.100 456	32
33	503.342 401	532.035 012	562.412 037	594.572 185	628.619 868	664.665 524	33
34	573.551 981	607.519 914	643.555 752	681.785 151	722.341 299	765.365 353	34
35	653.415 378	693.572 702	736.262 447	781.643 998	829.886 640	881.170 156	35
36	744.259 993	791.672 881	842.179 845	895.982 378	953.294 920	1014.345 680	36
37	847.595 742	903.507 084	963.190 473	1026.899 823	1094.905 920	1167.497 532	37
38	965.140 157	1030.998 076	1101.445 116	1176.800 297	1257.404 543	1343.622 161	38
39	1098.846 928	1176.337 806	1259.401 045	1348.436 340	1443.871 714	1546.165 485	39
40	1250.938 381	1342.025 099	1439.865 694	1544.959 609	1657.842 791	1779.090 308	40
41	1423.942 408	1530.908 613	1646.046 555	1769.978 753	1903.374 603	2046.953 854	41
42	1620.734 489	1746.235 819	1881.608 189	2027.625 672	2185.122 357	2354.996 933	42
43	1844.585 481	1991.708 833	2150.737 356	2322.631 394	2508.427 905	2709.246 473	43
44	2099.215 985	2271.548 070	2458.217 430	2660.412 947	2879.421 020	3116.633 443	44
45	2388.858 183	2590.564 800	2809.513 413	3047.172 824	3305.135 621	3585.128 460	45
46	2718.326 183	2954.243 872	3210.869 075	3490.012 883	3793.643 125	4123.897 729	46
47	3093.096 034	3368.838 014	3669.417 918	3997.064 751	4354.205 486	4743.482 388	47
48	3519.396 738	3841.475 336	4193.309 971	4577.639 140	4997.450 795	5456.004 746	48
49	4004.313 790	4380.281 883	4791.856 642	5242.396 816	5735.574 787	6275.405 458	49
50	4555.906 936	4994.521 346	5475.696 214	6003.544 354	6582.572 069	7217.716 277	50

FUTURE VALUE OF
$1 PER PERIOD

YRS	15.25% ANNUAL RATE	15.50% ANNUAL RATE	15.75% ANNUAL RATE	16.00% ANNUAL RATE	16.25% ANNUAL RATE	16.50% ANNUAL RATE	YRS
1	1.000 000	1.000 000	1.000 000	1.000 000	1.000 000	1.000 000	1
2	2.152 500	2.155 000	2.157 500	2.160 000	2.162 500	2.165 000	2
3	3.480 756	3.489 025	3.497 306	3.505 600	3.513 906	3.522 225	3
4	5.011 572	5.029 824	5.048 132	5.066 496	5.084 916	5.103 392	4
5	6.775 836	6.809 447	6.843 213	6.877 135	6.911 215	6.945 452	5
6	8.809 151	8.864 911	8.921 019	8.977 477	9.034 287	9.091 451	6
7	11.152 547	11.238 972	11.326 079	11.413 873	11.502 359	11.591 541	7
8	13.853 310	13.981 013	14.109 937	14.240 093	14.371 492	14.504 145	8
9	16.965 940	17.148 070	17.332 252	17.518 508	17.706 860	17.897 329	9
10	20.553 246	20.806 020	21.062 081	21.321 469	21.584 225	21.850 388	10
11	24.687 616	25.030 954	25.379 359	25.732 904	26.091 661	26.455 702	11
12	29.452 477	29.910 751	30.376 608	30.850 169	31.331 556	31.820 893	12
13	34.943 980	35.546 918	36.160 924	36.786 196	37.422 934	38.071 341	13
14	41.272 937	42.056 690	42.856 270	43.671 987	44.504 160	45.353 112	14
15	48.567 060	49.575 477	50.606 132	51.659 505	52.736 087	53.836 375	15
16	56.973 537	58.259 676	59.576 598	60.925 026	62.305 701	63.719 377	16
17	66.662 001	68.289 926	69.959 912	71.673 030	73.430 377	75.233 075	17
18	77.827 956	79.874 864	81.978 598	84.140 715	86.362 813	88.646 532	18
19	90.696 719	93.255 468	95.890 228	98.603 230	101.396 770	104.273 210	19
20	105.527 969	108.710 066	111.992 938	115.379 747	118.873 746	122.478 289	20
21	122.620 984	126.560 126	130.631 826	134.840 506	139.190 729	143.687 207	21
22	142.320 685	147.176 945	152.206 339	157.414 987	162.809 223	168.395 596	22
23	165.024 589	170.989 372	177.178 837	183.601 385	190.265 721	197.180 869	23
24	191.190 839	198.492 725	206.084 504	213.977 607	222.183 901	230.715 713	24
25	221.347 442	230.259 097	239.542 813	249.214 024	259.288 785	269.783 805	25
26	256.102 927	266.949 257	278.270 806	290.088 267	302.423 213	315.298 133	26
27	296.158 623	309.326 392	323.098 458	337.502 390	352.566 985	368.322 325	27
28	342.322 813	358.271 982	374.986 466	392.502 773	410.859 120	430.095 509	28
29	395.527 042	414.804 140	435.046 834	456.303 216	478.623 727	502.061 268	29
30	456.844 916	480.098 781	504.566 710	530.311 731	557.400 082	585.901 377	30
31	527.513 765	555.514 092	585.035 967	616.161 608	648.977 596	683.575 105	31
32	608.959 615	642.618 777	678.179 132	715.747 465	755.436 455	797.364 997	32
33	702.825 956	743.224 687	785.992 345	831.267 059	879.194 879	929.930 221	33
34	811.006 914	859.424 513	910.786 140	965.269 789	1023.064 047	1084.368 708	34
35	935.685 468	993.635 313	1055.234 957	1120.712 955	1190.311 954	1264.289 545	35
36	1079.377 502	1148.648 787	1222.434 462	1301.027 028	1384.737 647	1473.897 320	36
37	1244.982 571	1327.689 348	1415.967 890	1510.191 352	1610.757 515	1718.090 377	37
38	1435.842 414	1534.481 197	1639.982 833	1752.821 968	1873.505 611	2002.575 290	38
39	1655.808 382	1773.325 783	1899.280 129	2034.273 483	2178.950 272	2334.000 212	39
40	1909.319 160	2049.191 279	2199.416 750	2360.757 241	2534.029 692	2720.110 247	40
41	2201.490 332	2367.815 928	2546.824 888	2739.478 399	2946.809 517	3169.928 438	41
42	2538.217 607	2735.827 397	2948.949 807	3178.794 943	3426.666 063	3693.966 630	42
43	2926.295 792	3160.880 643	3414.409 402	3688.402 134	3984.499 298	4304.471 124	43
44	3373.555 901	3651.817 143	3953.178 883	4279.546 475	4632.980 434	5015.708 860	44
45	3889.023 176	4218.848 800	4576.804 557	4965.273 911	5386.839 755	5844.300 822	45
46	4483.099 210	4873.770 364	5298.651 275	5760.717 737	6263.201 215	6809.610 458	46
47	5167.771 839	5630.204 770	6134.188 850	6683.432 575	7281.971 412	7934.196 183	47
48	5956.857 045	6503.886 510	7101.323 594	7753.781 787	8466.291 767	9244.338 553	48
49	6866.277 744	7512.988 919	8220.782 060	8995.386 873	9843.064 179	10770.654 414	49
50	7914.385 100	8678.502 201	9516.555 235	10435.648 773	11443.562 108	12548.812 393	50

YRS	16.75% ANNUAL RATE	17.00% ANNUAL RATE	17.25% ANNUAL RATE	17.50% ANNUAL RATE	17.75% ANNUAL RATE	18.00% ANNUAL RATE	YRS
1	1.000 000	1.000 000	1.000 000	1.000 000	1.000 000	1.000 000	1
2	2.167 500	2.170 000	2.172 500	2.175 000	2.177 500	2.180 000	2
3	3.530 556	3.538 900	3.547 256	3.555 625	3.564 006	3.572 400	3
4	5.121 924	5.140 513	5.159 158	5.177 859	5.196 617	5.215 432	4
5	6.979 847	7.014 400	7.049 113	7.083 985	7.119 017	7.154 210	5
6	9.148 971	9.206 848	9.265 085	9.323 682	9.382 642	9.441 968	6
7	11.681 424	11.772 012	11.863 312	11.955 326	12.048 061	12.141 522	7
8	14.638 062	14.773 255	14.909 733	15.047 509	15.186 592	15.326 996	8
9	18.089 938	18.284 708	18.481 662	18.680 823	18.882 213	19.085 855	9
10	22.120 002	22.393 108	22.669 749	22.949 967	23.233 805	23.521 309	10
11	26.825 103	27.199 937	27.580 280	27.966 211	28.357 806	28.755 144	11
12	32.318 307	32.823 926	33.337 879	33.860 298	34.391 316	34.931 070	12
13	38.731 624	39.403 993	40.088 663	40.785 850	41.495 775	42.218 663	13
14	46.219 171	47.102 672	48.003 957	48.923 373	49.861 275	50.818 022	14
15	54.960 882	56.110 126	57.284 640	58.484 964	59.711 651	60.965 266	15
16	65.166 830	66.648 848	68.166 240	69.719 832	71.310 469	72.939 014	16
17	77.082 273	78.979 152	80.924 916	82.920 803	84.968 078	87.068 036	17
18	90.993 554	93.405 608	95.884 464	98.431 944	101.049 911	103.740 283	18
19	107.234 975	110.284 561	113.424 535	116.657 534	119.986 271	123.413 534	19
20	126.196 833	130.032 936	133.990 267	138.072 602	142.283 834	146.627 970	20
21	148.334 802	153.138 535	158.103 588	163.235 307	168.539 214	174.021 005	21
22	174.180 882	180.172 086	186.376 457	192.801 486	199.454 925	206.344 785	22
23	204.356 179	211.801 341	219.526 395	227.541 746	235.858 174	244.486 847	23
24	239.585 839	248.807 569	258.394 699	268.361 552	278.723 000	289.494 479	24
25	280.716 468	292.104 856	303.967 784	316.324 823	329.196 332	342.603 486	25
26	328.736 476	342.762 681	357.402 227	372.681 667	388.628 681	405.272 113	26
27	384.799 836	402.032 337	420.054 111	438.900 959	458.610 272	479.221 093	27
28	450.253 808	471.377 835	493.513 445	516.708 627	541.013 595	566.480 890	28
29	526.671 321	552.512 066	579.644 514	608.132 637	638.043 508	669.447 450	29
30	615.888 767	647.439 118	680.633 193	715.555 848	752.296 231	790.947 991	30
31	720.050 136	758.503 768	799.042 419	841.778 122	886.828 812	934.318 630	31
32	841.658 533	888.449 408	937.877 236	990.089 293	1045.240 926	1103.495 983	32
33	983.636 338	1040.485 808	1100.661 059	1164.354 919	1231.771 190	1303.125 260	33
34	1149.395 424	1218.368 395	1291.525 092	1369.117 030	1451.410 576	1538.687 807	34
35	1342.919 158	1426.491 022	1515.313 171	1609.712 511	1710.035 954	1816.651 612	35
36	1568.858 117	1669.994 496	1777.704 693	1892.412 200	2014.567 335	2144.648 902	36
37	1832.641 851	1954.893 560	2085.358 752	2224.584 335	2373.153 037	2531.685 705	37
38	2140.609 362	2288.225 465	2446.083 137	2614.886 594	2795.387 701	2988.389 132	38
39	2500.161 430	2678.223 794	2869.032 478	3073.491 747	3292.569 018	3527.299 175	39
40	2919.938 469	3134.521 839	3364.940 580	3612.352 803	3878.000 019	4163.213 027	40
41	3410.028 163	3668.390 552	3946.392 830	4245.514 544	4567.345 023	4913.591 372	41
42	3982.207 880	4293.016 946	4628.145 594	4989.479 589	5379.048 764	5799.037 819	42
43	4650.227 700	5023.829 827	5427.500 708	5863.638 517	6334.829 920	6843.864 626	43
44	5430.140 839	5878.880 897	6364.744 581	6890.775 258	7460.262 231	8076.760 259	44
45	6340.689 430	6879.290 650	7463.663 021	8097.660 928	8785.458 777	9531.577 105	45
46	7403.754 909	8049.770 061	8752.144 892	9515.751 590	10345.877 709	11248.260 984	46
47	8644.883 857	9419.230 971	10262.889 886	11182.008 118	12183.271 003	13273.947 961	47
48	10093.901 903	11021.500 236	12034.238 391	13139.859 539	14346.801 606	15664.258 594	48
49	11785.630 472	12896.155 276	14111.144 514	15440.334 958	16894.358 891	18484.825 141	49
50	13760.723 576	15089.501 673	16546.316 942	18143.393 576	19894.107 594	21813.093 666	50

FUTURE VALUE OF
$1 PER PERIOD

ANNUAL
COMPOUNDING

YRS	18.25% ANNUAL RATE	18.50% ANNUAL RATE	18.75% ANNUAL RATE	19.00% ANNUAL RATE	19.25% ANNUAL RATE	19.50% ANNUAL RATE	YRS
1	1.000 000	1.000 000	1.000 000	1.000 000	1.000 000	1.000 000	1
2	2.182 500	2.185 000	2.187 500	2.190 000	2.192 500	2.195 000	2
3	3.580 806	3.589 225	3.597 656	3.606 100	3.614 556	3.623 025	3
4	5.234 303	5.253 232	5.272 217	5.291 259	5.310 358	5.329 515	4
5	7.189 564	7.225 079	7.260 757	7.296 598	7.332 602	7.368 770	5
6	9.501 659	9.561 719	9.622 149	9.682 952	9.744 128	9.805 680	6
7	12.235 712	12.330 637	12.426 302	12.522 713	12.619 873	12.717 788	7
8	15.468 729	15.611 805	15.756 234	15.902 028	16.049 198	16.197 757	8
9	19.291 772	19.499 989	19.710 528	19.923 413	20.138 669	20.356 319	9
10	23.812 521	24.107 487	24.406 252	24.708 862	25.015 363	25.325 802	10
11	29.158 306	29.567 372	29.982 424	30.403 546	30.830 820	31.264 333	11
12	35.479 697	36.037 336	36.604 129	37.180 220	37.765 753	38.360 878	12
13	42.954 742	43.704 243	44.467 403	45.244 461	46.035 661	46.841 249	13
14	51.793 982	52.789 528	53.805 041	54.840 909	55.897 526	56.975 293	14
15	62.246 384	63.555 591	64.893 487	66.260 682	67.657 799	69.085 475	15
16	74.606 349	76.313 375	78.061 015	79.850 211	81.681 926	83.557 143	16
17	89.222 007	91.431 350	93.697 456	96.021 751	98.405 696	100.850 785	17
18	106.505 024	109.346 149	112.265 729	115.265 884	118.348 793	121.516 689	18
19	126.942 190	130.575 187	134.315 553	138.166 402	142.130 935	146.212 443	19
20	151.109 140	155.731 596	160.499 719	165.418 018	170.491 140	175.723 869	20
21	179.686 558	185.541 942	191.593 416	197.847 442	204.310 685	210.990 024	21
22	213.479 355	220.867 201	228.517 182	236.438 456	244.640 492	253.133 078	22
23	253.439 337	262.727 633	272.364 153	282.361 762	292.733 786	303.494 029	23
24	300.692 016	312.332 245	324.432 432	337.010 497	350.085 040	363.675 364	24
25	356.568 309	371.113 710	386.263 513	402.042 491	418.476 411	435.592 060	25
26	422.642 026	440.769 747	459.687 921	479.430 565	500.033 120	521.532 512	26
27	500.774 195	523.312 150	546.879 407	571.522 372	597.289 495	624.231 352	27
28	593.165 486	621.124 898	650.419 295	681.111 623	713.267 723	746.956 465	28
29	702.418 187	737.033 004	773.372 913	811.522 831	851.571 759	893.612 976	29
30	831.609 507	874.384 110	919.380 335	966.712 169	1016.499 323	1068.867 506	30
31	984.378 241	1037.145 170	1092.764 147	1151.387 481	1213.175 443	1278.296 670	31
32	1165.027 271	1230.017 026	1298.657 425	1371.151 103	1447.711 716	1528.564 521	32
33	1378.644 747	1458.570 176	1543.155 692	1632.669 812	1727.396 221	1827.634 602	33
34	1631.247 414	1729.405 659	1833.497 384	1943.877 077	2060.919 993	2185.023 350	34
35	1929.950 067	2050.345 706	2178.278 144	2314.213 721	2458.647 092	2612.102 903	35
36	2283.165 954	2430.659 662	2587.705 296	2754.914 328	2932.936 657	3122.462 969	36
37	2700.843 741	2881.331 699	3073.900 039	3279.348 051	3498.526 964	3732.343 248	37
38	3194.747 723	3415.378 063	3651.256 296	3903.424 180	4172.993 405	4461.150 181	38
39	3778.789 183	4048.223 005	4336.866 852	4646.074 775	4977.294 635	5332.074 466	39
40	4469.418 209	4798.144 261	5151.029 386	5529.828 982	5936.423 852	6372.828 987	40
41	5286.087 032	5686.800 949	6117.847 396	6581.496 488	7080.185 444	7616.530 640	41
42	6251.797 915	6739.859 125	7265.943 783	7832.980 821	8444.121 142	9102.754 114	42
43	7393.751 034	7987.733 063	8629.308 242	9322.247 177	10070.614 461	10878.791 167	43
44	8744.110 598	9466.463 679	10248.303 538	11094.474 141	12010.207 745	13001.155 444	44
45	10340.910 782	11218.759 460	12170.860 451	13203.424 228	14323.172 736	15537.380 756	45
46	12229.127 000	13295.229 960	14453.896 786	15713.074 831	17081.383 488	18568.170 003	46
47	14461.942 678	15755.847 503	17165.002 433	18699.559 049	20370.549 809	22189.963 154	47
48	17102.247 216	18671.679 291	20384.440 390	22253.475 268	24292.880 647	26518.005 968	48
49	20224.407 333	22126.939 959	24207.522 963	26482.635 569	28970.260 172	31690.017 132	49
50	23916.361 672	26221.423 852	28747.433 518	31515.336 327	34548.035 255	37870.570 473	50

FUTURE VALUE OF
$1 PER PERIOD

ANNUAL
COMPOUNDING

YRS	19.75% ANNUAL RATE	20.00% ANNUAL RATE	21.00% ANNUAL RATE	22.00% ANNUAL RATE	23.00% ANNUAL RATE	24.00% ANNUAL RATE	YRS
1	1.000 000	1.000 000	1.000 000	1.000 000	1.000 000	1.000 000	1
2	2.197 500	2.200 000	2.210 000	2.220 000	2.230 000	2.240 000	2
3	3.631 506	3.640 000	3.674 100	3.708 400	3.742 900	3.777 600	3
4	5.348 729	5.368 000	5.445 661	5.524 248	5.603 767	5.684 224	4
5	7.405 103	7.441 600	7.589 250	7.739 583	7.892 633	8.048 438	5
6	9.867 610	9.929 920	10.182 992	10.442 291	10.707 939	10.980 063	6
7	12.816 463	12.915 904	13.321 421	13.739 595	14.170 765	14.615 278	7
8	16.347 715	16.499 085	17.118 919	17.762 306	18.430 041	19.122 945	8
9	20.576 389	20.798 902	21.713 892	22.670 013	23.668 950	24.712 451	9
10	25.640 226	25.958 682	27.273 809	28.657 416	30.112 809	31.643 440	10
11	31.704 170	32.150 419	34.001 309	35.962 047	38.038 755	40.237 865	11
12	38.965 744	39.580 502	42.141 584	44.873 697	47.787 669	50.894 953	12
13	47.661 478	48.496 603	51.991 317	55.745 911	59.778 833	64.109 741	13
14	58.074 620	59.195 923	63.909 493	69.010 011	74.527 964	80.496 079	14
15	70.544 357	72.035 108	78.330 487	85.192 213	92.669 396	100.815 138	15
16	85.476 868	87.442 129	95.779 889	104.934 500	114.983 357	126.010 772	16
17	103.358 549	105.930 555	116.893 666	129.020 090	142.429 529	157.253 357	17
18	124.771 863	128.116 666	142.441 336	158.404 510	176.188 321	195.994 162	18
19	150.414 306	154.740 000	173.354 016	194.253 503	217.711 635	244.032 761	19
20	181.121 131	186.688 000	210.758 360	237.989 273	268.785 311	303.600 624	20
21	217.892 555	225.025 600	256.017 615	291.346 913	331.605 932	377.464 774	21
22	261.926 334	271.030 719	310.781 315	356.443 234	408.875 297	469.056 320	22
23	314.656 785	326.236 863	377.045 391	435.860 746	503.916 615	582.629 836	23
24	377.801 500	392.484 236	457.224 923	532.750 110	620.817 437	723.460 997	24
25	453.417 297	471.981 083	554.242 157	650.955 134	764.605 447	898.091 636	25
26	543.967 213	567.377 300	671.633 009	795.165 264	941.464 700	1114.633 629	26
27	652.400 737	681.852 760	813.675 941	971.101 622	1159.001 581	1383.145 700	27
28	782.249 883	819.223 312	985.547 889	1185.743 978	1426.571 945	1716.100 668	28
29	937.744 235	984.067 974	1193.512 946	1447.607 654	1755.683 492	2128.964 828	29
30	1123.948 721	1181.881 569	1445.150 664	1767.081 337	2160.490 695	2640.916 387	30
31	1346.928 593	1419.257 883	1749.632 304	2156.839 232	2658.403 555	3275.736 320	31
32	1613.946 991	1704.109 459	2118.055 088	2632.343 863	3270.836 373	4062.913 037	32
33	1933.701 521	2045.931 351	2563.846 656	3212.459 512	4024.128 738	5039.012 166	33
34	2316.607 572	2456.117 621	3103.254 454	3920.200 605	4950.678 348	6249.375 086	34
35	2775.137 567	2948.341 146	3755.937 890	4783.644 738	6090.334 368	7750.225 106	35
36	3324.227 237	3539.009 375	4545.684 846	5837.046 581	7492.111 273	9611.279 132	36
37	3981.762 116	4247.811 250	5501.278 664	7122.196 829	9216.296 866	11918.986 124	37
38	4769.160 134	5098.373 500	6657.547 183	8690.080 131	11337.045 145	14780.542 793	38
39	5712.069 260	6119.048 200	8056.632 092	10602.897 760	13945.565 528	18328.873 064	39
40	6841.202 939	7343.857 840	9749.524 831	12936.535 267	17154.045 599	22728.802 599	40
41	8193.340 519	8813.629 408	11797.925 046	15783.573 025	21100.476 087	28184.715 222	41
42	9812.525 272	10577.355 289	14276.489 306	19256.959 091	25954.585 587	34950.046 876	42
43	11751.499 013	12693.826 347	17275.552 060	23494.490 091	31925.140 272	43339.058 126	43
44	14073.420 068	15233.591 617	20904.417 992	28664.277 911	39268.922 535	53741.432 076	44
45	16853.920 532	18281.309 940	25295.345 771	34971.419 051	48301.774 718	66640.375 775	45
46	20183.569 837	21938.571 928	30608.368 383	42666.131 243	59412.182 903	82635.065 961	46
47	24170.824 880	26327.286 314	37037.125 743	52053.680 116	73077.984 971	102468.481 791	47
48	28945.562 794	31593.743 576	44815.922 149	63506.489 742	89886.921 514	127061.917 421	48
49	34663.311 445	37913.492 292	54228.265 800	77478.917 485	110561.913 462	157557.777 602	49
50	41510.315 456	45497.190 750	65617.201 618	94525.279 331	135992.153 559	195372.644 226	50

Section 3. Sinking Fund Factors

These factors represent the fixed amount of money that must be invested at a stated rate of interest for a specific interval, i.e., monthly, to accumulate $1. It is also assumed that the regular investment is made at the end of each interval (according to the dictates of convention). These factors are based on the assumption that no funds will be withdrawn at any point during the investment.

In this section, the following four (4) periods are presented in detail: monthly, quarterly, semiannual, and annual.

Monthly:

The factors presented on pages 64 through 71 will indicate the amount of the monthly investment necessary to accumulate $1 in the stated interval. Interest is being earned on each monthly investment, plus interest is being earned on the interest.

Example E

If you want $10,000 at the end of five (5) years, what will the monthly payment be? Assume the annual interest rate of 11.0% and monthly compounding.

Turn to page 65 and locate the 11.0% annual interest rate column. Proceed down that column until you locate the point where the 5 year row intersects the 11.0% interest column. The number is 0.012576. That means that your monthly deposit will be 0.012576 for each $1 you want to accumulate. So, to determine your answer, multiply 0.012576 by $10,000. The correct answer is $125.76. That is, you need to make a monthly payment of $125.76 to accumulate $10,000 in 5 years.

Note: If your investment period is less than 4 years, we have provided all the monthly payment amounts for each monthly period; over 4 years, only the annual figures are provided.

Quarterly:

The factors presented on pages 72 through 77 will indicate the amount of the quarterly investment necessary to accumulate $1 in the stated interval. Interest is being earned on each quarterly investment, plus interest is being earned on the interest.

Example F

If you want $15,000 in 25 years, what will the quarterly payment be? Assume an annual interest rate of 9.0% and quarterly compounding.

Turn to page 72 and locate the 9.0% column. Proceed down that column until you locate the point where the 25 year intersects the 9.0% interest column. The number is 0.002726. That means that your quarterly deposit will be 0.002726 for each $1 you want to accumulate. So, to detemine your answer, multiply 0.002726 by $15,000. The correct answer is $40.89. You will need to make a quarterly payment of $40.89 to accumulate $15,000 in 25 years.

Note: For investments of 14 years and more, only the annual amounts are shown.

Semiannual:

The factors on pages 78 through 81 cover semiannual compounding. The interest is being compounded every six months. They are used the same way as the monthly or quarterly tables.

Annual:

The factors on pages 82 through 89 cover annual compounding (or the interest being compounded every year). They are used the same way as the monthly, quarterly, and semiannual tables.

If you want to do it the hard way, here's the formula . . .

$$\frac{1}{S\overline{n}|} = \frac{i}{(1 + i)^n - 1}$$

$S\overline{n}|$ = Future value of $1 per period
i = interest rate per period
n = number of compounding periods

SINKING FUND FACTORS

MOS	7.00% ANNUAL RATE	8.00% ANNUAL RATE	9.00% ANNUAL RATE	10.00% ANNUAL RATE	10.25% ANNUAL RATE	10.50% ANNUAL RATE	MOS
1	1.000 000	1.000 000	1.000 000	1.000 000	1.000 000	1.000 000	1
2	0.498 546	0.498 339	0.498 132	0.497 925	0.497 874	0.497 822	2
3	0.331 396	0.331 121	0.330 846	0.330 571	0.330 502	0.330 434	3
4	0.247 823	0.247 514	0.247 205	0.246 897	0.246 820	0.246 743	4
5	0.197 680	0.197 351	0.197 022	0.196 694	0.196 612	0.196 530	5
6	0.164 253	0.163 910	0.163 569	0.163 228	0.163 143	0.163 058	6
7	0.140 377	0.140 025	0.139 675	0.139 325	0.139 238	0.139 151	7
8	0.122 470	0.122 112	0.121 756	0.121 400	0.121 311	0.121 222	8
9	0.108 544	0.108 181	0.107 819	0.107 459	0.107 369	0.107 279	9
10	0.097 403	0.097 037	0.096 671	0.096 307	0.096 216	0.096 125	10
11	0.088 288	0.087 919	0.087 551	0.087 184	0.087 093	0.087 001	11
12	0.080 693	0.080 322	0.079 951	0.079 583	0.079 491	0.079 399	12
13	0.074 267	0.073 894	0.073 522	0.073 151	0.073 059	0.072 967	13
14	0.068 760	0.068 385	0.068 011	0.067 640	0.067 547	0.067 455	14
15	0.063 987	0.063 611	0.063 236	0.062 864	0.062 771	0.062 678	15
16	0.059 811	0.059 434	0.059 059	0.058 686	0.058 593	0.058 500	16
17	0.056 126	0.055 749	0.055 373	0.055 000	0.054 906	0.054 813	17
18	0.052 852	0.052 474	0.052 098	0.051 724	0.051 631	0.051 538	18
19	0.049 922	0.049 544	0.049 167	0.048 793	0.048 700	0.048 607	19
20	0.047 286	0.046 907	0.046 531	0.046 157	0.046 063	0.045 970	20
21	0.044 900	0.044 522	0.044 145	0.043 771	0.043 678	0.043 585	21
22	0.042 733	0.042 354	0.041 977	0.041 604	0.041 511	0.041 418	22
23	0.040 753	0.040 375	0.039 998	0.039 625	0.039 532	0.039 439	23
24	0.038 939	0.038 561	0.038 185	0.037 812	0.037 719	0.037 626	24
25	0.037 271	0.036 892	0.036 516	0.036 144	0.036 051	0.035 958	25
26	0.035 730	0.035 352	0.034 977	0.034 605	0.034 512	0.034 420	26
27	0.034 305	0.033 927	0.033 552	0.033 180	0.033 087	0.032 995	27
28	0.032 981	0.032 603	0.032 229	0.031 857	0.031 765	0.031 673	28
29	0.031 749	0.031 371	0.030 997	0.030 627	0.030 534	0.030 442	29
30	0.030 599	0.030 222	0.029 848	0.029 478	0.029 386	0.029 294	30
31	0.029 523	0.029 146	0.028 774	0.028 404	0.028 312	0.028 221	31
32	0.028 515	0.028 139	0.027 766	0.027 398	0.027 306	0.027 215	32
33	0.027 568	0.027 192	0.026 820	0.026 452	0.026 361	0.026 270	33
34	0.026 677	0.026 302	0.025 931	0.025 563	0.025 472	0.025 381	34
35	0.025 837	0.025 462	0.025 092	0.024 725	0.024 634	0.024 543	35
36	0.025 044	0.024 670	0.024 300	0.023 934	0.023 843	0.023 752	36
37	0.024 294	0.023 920	0.023 551	0.023 186	0.023 095	0.023 005	37
38	0.023 583	0.023 210	0.022 842	0.022 477	0.022 387	0.022 297	38
39	0.022 909	0.022 537	0.022 169	0.021 805	0.021 715	0.021 625	39
40	0.022 269	0.021 897	0.021 530	0.021 167	0.021 077	0.020 988	40
41	0.021 660	0.021 289	0.020 923	0.020 561	0.020 471	0.020 382	41
42	0.021 081	0.020 710	0.020 345	0.019 983	0.019 894	0.019 805	42
43	0.020 528	0.020 158	0.019 793	0.019 433	0.019 344	0.019 255	43
44	0.020 001	0.019 632	0.019 268	0.018 908	0.018 819	0.018 730	44
45	0.019 497	0.019 129	0.018 765	0.018 407	0.018 318	0.018 229	45
46	0.019 016	0.018 648	0.018 285	0.017 927	0.017 839	0.017 751	46
47	0.018 555	0.018 187	0.017 825	0.017 469	0.017 380	0.017 292	47
YRS							
4	0.018 113	0.017 746	0.017 385	0.017 029	0.016 941	0.016 853	48
5	0.013 968	0.013 610	0.013 258	0.012 914	0.012 829	0.012 744	60
6	0.011 216	0.010 867	0.010 526	0.010 193	0.010 110	0.010 029	72
7	0.009 259	0.008 920	0.008 589	0.008 268	0.008 189	0.008 111	84
8	0.007 800	0.007 470	0.007 150	0.006 841	0.006 765	0.006 690	96
9	0.006 673	0.006 352	0.006 043	0.005 745	0.005 673	0.005 601	108
10	0.005 778	0.005 466	0.005 168	0.004 882	0.004 812	0.004 743	120
11	0.005 051	0.004 749	0.004 461	0.004 187	0.004 120	0.004 054	132
12	0.004 450	0.004 158	0.003 880	0.003 617	0.003 554	0.003 491	144
13	0.003 947	0.003 664	0.003 397	0.003 145	0.003 085	0.003 025	156
14	0.003 521	0.003 247	0.002 989	0.002 749	0.002 691	0.002 634	168
15	0.003 155	0.002 890	0.002 643	0.002 413	0.002 358	0.002 304	180
16	0.002 839	0.002 583	0.002 345	0.002 126	0.002 074	0.002 022	192
17	0.002 563	0.002 316	0.002 088	0.001 879	0.001 829	0.001 781	204
18	0.002 322	0.002 083	0.001 864	0.001 665	0.001 618	0.001 572	216
19	0.002 109	0.001 878	0.001 669	0.001 479	0.001 435	0.001 391	228
20	0.001 920	0.001 698	0.001 497	0.001 317	0.001 275	0.001 234	240
21	0.001 751	0.001 538	0.001 346	0.001 174	0.001 135	0.001 096	252
22	0.001 601	0.001 395	0.001 212	0.001 049	0.001 012	0.000 975	264
23	0.001 466	0.001 268	0.001 093	0.000 938	0.000 903	0.000 869	276
24	0.001 344	0.001 154	0.000 987	0.000 841	0.000 807	0.000 775	288
25	0.001 234	0.001 051	0.000 892	0.000 754	0.000 722	0.000 692	300
26	0.001 135	0.000 959	0.000 807	0.000 676	0.000 647	0.000 618	312
27	0.001 045	0.000 876	0.000 731	0.000 608	0.000 580	0.000 553	324
28	0.000 963	0.000 801	0.000 663	0.000 546	0.000 520	0.000 495	336
29	0.000 888	0.000 733	0.000 602	0.000 491	0.000 467	0.000 443	348
30	0.000 820	0.000 671	0.000 546	0.000 442	0.000 419	0.000 397	360

SINKING FUND FACTORS

MONTHLY COMPOUNDING

MOS	10.75% ANNUAL RATE	11.00% ANNUAL RATE	11.25% ANNUAL RATE	11.50% ANNUAL RATE	11.75% ANNUAL RATE	12.00% ANNUAL RATE	MOS
1	1.000 000	1.000 000	1.000 000	1.000 000	1.000 000	1.000 000	1
2	0.497 770	0.497 719	0.497 667	0.497 616	0.497 564	0.497 512	2
3	0.330 365	0.330 296	0.330 228	0.330 159	0.330 091	0.330 022	3
4	0.246 666	0.246 589	0.246 512	0.246 435	0.246 358	0.246 281	4
5	0.196 449	0.196 367	0.196 285	0.196 203	0.196 121	0.196 040	5
6	0.162 973	0.162 888	0.162 803	0.162 718	0.162 633	0.162 548	6
7	0.139 064	0.138 976	0.138 889	0.138 802	0.138 715	0.138 628	7
8	0.121 133	0.121 044	0.120 956	0.120 867	0.120 779	0.120 690	8
9	0.107 189	0.107 099	0.107 009	0.106 920	0.106 830	0.106 740	9
10	0.096 035	0.095 944	0.095 853	0.095 763	0.095 672	0.095 582	10
11	0.086 910	0.086 818	0.086 727	0.086 636	0.086 545	0.086 454	11
12	0.079 307	0.079 215	0.079 123	0.079 032	0.078 940	0.078 849	12
13	0.072 874	0.072 782	0.072 690	0.072 598	0.072 507	0.072 415	13
14	0.067 362	0.067 270	0.067 177	0.067 085	0.066 993	0.066 901	14
15	0.062 586	0.062 493	0.062 400	0.062 308	0.062 216	0.062 124	15
16	0.058 407	0.058 314	0.058 222	0.058 129	0.058 037	0.057 945	16
17	0.054 721	0.054 628	0.054 535	0.054 443	0.054 350	0.054 258	17
18	0.051 445	0.051 352	0.051 259	0.051 167	0.051 074	0.050 982	18
19	0.048 514	0.048 421	0.048 329	0.048 236	0.048 144	0.048 052	19
20	0.045 878	0.045 785	0.045 692	0.045 600	0.045 507	0.045 415	20
21	0.043 493	0.043 400	0.043 307	0.043 215	0.043 123	0.043 031	21
22	0.041 325	0.041 232	0.041 140	0.041 048	0.040 956	0.040 864	22
23	0.039 347	0.039 254	0.039 162	0.039 070	0.038 978	0.038 886	23
24	0.037 534	0.037 441	0.037 349	0.037 257	0.037 165	0.037 073	24
25	0.035 866	0.035 774	0.035 682	0.035 590	0.035 498	0.035 407	25
26	0.034 327	0.034 235	0.034 143	0.034 052	0.033 960	0.033 869	26
27	0.032 903	0.032 811	0.032 720	0.032 628	0.032 537	0.032 446	27
28	0.031 581	0.031 489	0.031 398	0.031 306	0.031 215	0.031 124	28
29	0.030 351	0.030 259	0.030 168	0.030 077	0.029 986	0.029 895	29
30	0.029 203	0.029 111	0.029 020	0.028 929	0.028 839	0.028 748	30
31	0.028 129	0.028 038	0.027 947	0.027 857	0.027 766	0.027 676	31
32	0.027 123	0.027 032	0.026 942	0.026 851	0.026 761	0.026 671	32
33	0.026 179	0.026 088	0.025 998	0.025 907	0.025 817	0.025 727	33
34	0.025 290	0.025 200	0.025 109	0.025 019	0.024 930	0.024 840	34
35	0.024 453	0.024 362	0.024 272	0.024 183	0.024 093	0.024 004	35
36	0.023 662	0.023 572	0.023 482	0.023 393	0.023 303	0.023 214	36
37	0.022 915	0.022 825	0.022 735	0.022 646	0.022 557	0.022 468	37
38	0.022 207	0.022 117	0.022 028	0.021 939	0.021 850	0.021 761	38
39	0.021 536	0.021 446	0.021 357	0.021 268	0.021 180	0.021 092	39
40	0.020 898	0.020 809	0.020 720	0.020 632	0.020 544	0.020 456	40
41	0.020 293	0.020 204	0.020 115	0.020 027	0.019 939	0.019 851	41
42	0.019 716	0.019 627	0.019 539	0.019 451	0.019 363	0.019 276	42
43	0.019 166	0.019 078	0.018 990	0.018 902	0.018 815	0.018 727	43
44	0.018 642	0.018 554	0.018 466	0.018 378	0.018 291	0.018 204	44
45	0.018 141	0.018 053	0.017 966	0.017 879	0.017 792	0.017 705	45
46	0.017 663	0.017 575	0.017 488	0.017 401	0.017 314	0.017 228	46
47	0.017 205	0.017 117	0.017 030	0.016 944	0.016 857	0.016 771	47

YRS							MOS
4	0.016 766	0.016 679	0.016 592	0.016 506	0.016 420	0.016 334	48
5	0.012 660	0.012 576	0.012 492	0.012 409	0.012 327	0.012 244	60
6	0.009 948	0.009 867	0.009 787	0.009 708	0.009 629	0.009 550	72
7	0.008 033	0.007 956	0.007 879	0.007 803	0.007 728	0.007 653	84
8	0.006 616	0.006 542	0.006 469	0.006 396	0.006 324	0.006 253	96
9	0.005 530	0.005 459	0.005 389	0.005 320	0.005 252	0.005 184	108
10	0.004 676	0.004 608	0.004 542	0.004 476	0.004 411	0.004 347	120
11	0.003 990	0.003 926	0.003 863	0.003 800	0.003 739	0.003 678	132
12	0.003 430	0.003 369	0.003 309	0.003 250	0.003 192	0.003 134	144
13	0.002 966	0.002 909	0.002 852	0.002 796	0.002 741	0.002 687	156
14	0.002 579	0.002 524	0.002 470	0.002 417	0.002 365	0.002 314	168
15	0.002 251	0.002 199	0.002 148	0.002 099	0.002 050	0.002 002	180
16	0.001 972	0.001 923	0.001 875	0.001 828	0.001 782	0.001 737	192
17	0.001 733	0.001 687	0.001 642	0.001 598	0.001 554	0.001 512	204
18	0.001 528	0.001 484	0.001 441	0.001 400	0.001 359	0.001 320	216
19	0.001 349	0.001 308	0.001 268	0.001 229	0.001 191	0.001 154	228
20	0.001 194	0.001 155	0.001 118	0.001 081	0.001 045	0.001 011	240
21	0.001 058	0.001 022	0.000 987	0.000 952	0.000 919	0.000 887	252
22	0.000 940	0.000 906	0.000 872	0.000 840	0.000 809	0.000 779	264
23	0.000 835	0.000 803	0.000 772	0.000 742	0.000 714	0.000 686	276
24	0.000 744	0.000 714	0.000 685	0.000 657	0.000 630	0.000 604	288
25	0.000 663	0.000 634	0.000 607	0.000 581	0.000 556	0.000 532	300
26	0.000 591	0.000 565	0.000 539	0.000 515	0.000 492	0.000 470	312
27	0.000 527	0.000 503	0.000 479	0.000 457	0.000 435	0.000 414	324
28	0.000 471	0.000 448	0.000 426	0.000 405	0.000 385	0.000 366	336
29	0.000 421	0.000 400	0.000 379	0.000 360	0.000 341	0.000 324	348
30	0.000 376	0.000 357	0.000 338	0.000 320	0.000 302	0.000 286	360

MOS	12.25% ANNUAL RATE	12.50% ANNUAL RATE	12.75% ANNUAL RATE	13.00% ANNUAL RATE	13.25% ANNUAL RATE	13.50% ANNUAL RATE	MOS
1	1.000 000	1.000 000	1.000 000	1.000 000	1.000 000	1.000 000	1
2	0.497 461	0.497 409	0.497 358	0.497 306	0.497 255	0.497 203	2
3	0.329 954	0.329 885	0.329 817	0.329 748	0.329 680	0.329 611	3
4	0.246 204	0.246 127	0.246 051	0.245 974	0.245 897	0.245 821	4
5	0.195 958	0.195 877	0.195 795	0.195 713	0.195 632	0.195 550	5
6	0.162 464	0.162 379	0.162 294	0.162 210	0.162 125	0.162 040	6
7	0.138 541	0.138 455	0.138 368	0.138 281	0.138 194	0.138 108	7
8	0.120 602	0.120 514	0.120 425	0.120 337	0.120 249	0.120 161	8
9	0.106 651	0.106 561	0.106 472	0.106 383	0.106 294	0.106 204	9
10	0.095 492	0.095 402	0.095 311	0.095 221	0.095 131	0.095 041	10
11	0.086 363	0.086 272	0.086 182	0.086 091	0.086 000	0.085 910	11
12	0.078 757	0.078 666	0.078 575	0.078 484	0.078 393	0.078 302	12
13	0.072 323	0.072 232	0.072 140	0.072 049	0.071 957	0.071 866	13
14	0.066 809	0.066 718	0.066 626	0.066 534	0.066 443	0.066 351	14
15	0.062 032	0.061 940	0.061 848	0.061 756	0.061 665	0.061 573	15
16	0.057 852	0.057 760	0.057 669	0.057 577	0.057 485	0.057 394	16
17	0.054 166	0.054 074	0.053 982	0.053 890	0.053 799	0.053 707	17
18	0.050 890	0.050 798	0.050 706	0.050 614	0.050 523	0.050 431	18
19	0.047 960	0.047 868	0.047 776	0.047 684	0.047 593	0.047 501	19
20	0.045 323	0.045 231	0.045 140	0.045 048	0.044 957	0.044 865	20
21	0.042 939	0.042 847	0.042 755	0.042 664	0.042 573	0.042 481	21
22	0.040 772	0.040 680	0.040 589	0.040 497	0.040 406	0.040 315	22
23	0.038 794	0.038 703	0.038 611	0.038 520	0.038 429	0.038 338	23
24	0.036 982	0.036 891	0.036 799	0.036 708	0.036 618	0.036 527	24
25	0.035 315	0.035 224	0.035 133	0.035 043	0.034 952	0.034 861	25
26	0.033 778	0.033 687	0.033 596	0.033 505	0.033 415	0.033 325	26
27	0.032 355	0.032 264	0.032 173	0.032 083	0.031 993	0.031 903	27
28	0.031 034	0.030 943	0.030 853	0.030 763	0.030 673	0.030 583	28
29	0.029 805	0.029 714	0.029 624	0.029 534	0.029 444	0.029 355	29
30	0.028 658	0.028 568	0.028 478	0.028 388	0.028 299	0.028 210	30
31	0.027 586	0.027 496	0.027 406	0.027 317	0.027 228	0.027 139	31
32	0.026 581	0.026 491	0.026 402	0.026 313	0.026 224	0.026 135	32
33	0.025 638	0.025 549	0.025 459	0.025 371	0.025 282	0.025 193	33
34	0.024 751	0.024 662	0.024 573	0.024 484	0.024 396	0.024 308	34
35	0.023 915	0.023 826	0.023 737	0.023 649	0.023 561	0.023 473	35
36	0.023 126	0.023 037	0.022 949	0.022 861	0.022 773	0.022 685	36
37	0.022 380	0.022 291	0.022 203	0.022 115	0.022 028	0.021 941	37
38	0.021 673	0.021 585	0.021 497	0.021 410	0.021 323	0.021 236	38
39	0.021 004	0.020 916	0.020 828	0.020 741	0.020 654	0.020 568	39
40	0.020 368	0.020 280	0.020 193	0.020 106	0.020 020	0.019 933	40
41	0.019 764	0.019 676	0.019 590	0.019 503	0.019 417	0.019 331	41
42	0.019 188	0.019 102	0.019 015	0.018 929	0.018 843	0.018 757	42
43	0.018 640	0.018 554	0.018 468	0.018 382	0.018 296	0.018 211	43
44	0.018 118	0.018 032	0.017 946	0.017 860	0.017 775	0.017 689	44
45	0.017 619	0.017 533	0.017 447	0.017 362	0.017 277	0.017 192	45
46	0.017 142	0.017 056	0.016 971	0.016 886	0.016 801	0.016 717	46
47	0.016 685	0.016 600	0.016 515	0.016 430	0.016 346	0.016 262	47

YRS							
4	0.016 248	0.016 163	0.016 079	0.015 994	0.015 910	0.015 826	48
5	0.012 163	0.012 081	0.012 000	0.011 920	0.011 840	0.011 760	60
6	0.009 472	0.009 395	0.009 317	0.009 241	0.009 165	0.009 089	72
7	0.007 578	0.007 505	0.007 431	0.007 359	0.007 286	0.007 215	84
8	0.006 182	0.006 112	0.006 043	0.005 974	0.005 906	0.005 838	96
9	0.005 117	0.005 051	0.004 985	0.004 920	0.004 856	0.004 792	108
10	0.004 284	0.004 221	0.004 159	0.004 098	0.004 037	0.003 977	120
11	0.003 618	0.003 559	0.003 500	0.003 443	0.003 386	0.003 330	132
12	0.003 078	0.003 022	0.002 967	0.002 913	0.002 860	0.002 807	144
13	0.002 633	0.002 581	0.002 529	0.002 479	0.002 429	0.002 380	156
14	0.002 264	0.002 215	0.002 167	0.002 119	0.002 073	0.002 027	168
15	0.001 955	0.001 909	0.001 863	0.001 819	0.001 776	0.001 733	180
16	0.001 693	0.001 650	0.001 608	0.001 567	0.001 526	0.001 487	192
17	0.001 471	0.001 431	0.001 391	0.001 353	0.001 315	0.001 279	204
18	0.001 281	0.001 243	0.001 207	0.001 171	0.001 136	0.001 102	216
19	0.001 118	0.001 083	0.001 049	0.001 016	0.000 983	0.000 952	228
20	0.000 977	0.000 945	0.000 913	0.000 882	0.000 853	0.000 824	240
21	0.000 856	0.000 826	0.000 796	0.000 768	0.000 740	0.000 714	252
22	0.000 750	0.000 722	0.000 695	0.000 669	0.000 644	0.000 619	264
23	0.000 659	0.000 633	0.000 608	0.000 583	0.000 560	0.000 538	276
24	0.000 579	0.000 555	0.000 532	0.000 509	0.000 488	0.000 467	288
25	0.000 509	0.000 487	0.000 466	0.000 445	0.000 425	0.000 406	300
26	0.000 448	0.000 428	0.000 408	0.000 389	0.000 371	0.000 354	312
27	0.000 395	0.000 376	0.000 358	0.000 340	0.000 324	0.000 308	324
28	0.000 348	0.000 330	0.000 314	0.000 298	0.000 283	0.000 268	336
29	0.000 307	0.000 291	0.000 275	0.000 261	0.000 247	0.000 234	348
30	0.000 271	0.000 256	0.000 242	0.000 229	0.000 216	0.000 204	360

MOS	13.75% ANNUAL RATE	14.00% ANNUAL RATE	14.25% ANNUAL RATE	14.50% ANNUAL RATE	14.75% ANNUAL RATE	15.00% ANNUAL RATE	MOS
1	1.000 000	1.000 000	1.000 000	1.000 000	1.000 000	1.000 000	1
2	0.497 152	0.497 100	0.497 049	0.496 997	0.496 946	0.496 894	2
3	0.329 543	0.329 475	0.329 406	0.329 338	0.329 269	0.329 201	3
4	0.245 744	0.245 667	0.245 591	0.245 514	0.245 438	0.245 361	4
5	0.195 469	0.195 387	0.195 306	0.195 225	0.195 143	0.195 062	5
6	0.161 956	0.161 871	0.161 787	0.161 702	0.161 618	0.161 534	6
7	0.138 021	0.137 934	0.137 848	0.137 761	0.137 675	0.137 589	7
8	0.120 073	0.119 985	0.119 897	0.119 809	0.119 721	0.119 633	8
9	0.106 115	0.106 026	0.105 937	0.105 848	0.105 759	0.105 671	9
10	0.094 951	0.094 862	0.094 772	0.094 682	0.094 593	0.094 503	10
11	0.085 819	0.085 729	0.085 639	0.085 549	0.085 458	0.085 368	11
12	0.078 211	0.078 120	0.078 030	0.077 939	0.077 849	0.077 758	12
13	0.071 775	0.071 684	0.071 593	0.071 502	0.071 412	0.071 321	13
14	0.066 260	0.066 169	0.066 078	0.065 987	0.065 896	0.065 805	14
15	0.061 482	0.061 391	0.061 299	0.061 208	0.061 117	0.061 026	15
16	0.057 302	0.057 211	0.057 120	0.057 029	0.056 938	0.056 847	16
17	0.053 616	0.053 524	0.053 433	0.053 342	0.053 251	0.053 160	17
18	0.050 340	0.050 249	0.050 157	0.050 066	0.049 976	0.049 885	18
19	0.047 410	0.047 319	0.047 228	0.047 137	0.047 046	0.046 955	19
20	0.044 774	0.044 683	0.044 592	0.044 501	0.044 411	0.044 320	20
21	0.042 390	0.042 300	0.042 209	0.042 118	0.042 028	0.041 937	21
22	0.040 224	0.040 134	0.040 043	0.039 953	0.039 862	0.039 772	22
23	0.038 248	0.038 157	0.038 067	0.037 977	0.037 887	0.037 797	23
24	0.036 437	0.036 346	0.036 256	0.036 166	0.036 076	0.035 987	24
25	0.034 771	0.034 681	0.034 591	0.034 501	0.034 412	0.034 322	25
26	0.033 235	0.033 145	0.033 055	0.032 966	0.032 876	0.032 787	26
27	0.031 813	0.031 723	0.031 634	0.031 545	0.031 456	0.031 367	27
28	0.030 493	0.030 404	0.030 315	0.030 226	0.030 137	0.030 049	28
29	0.029 266	0.029 177	0.029 088	0.028 999	0.028 911	0.028 822	29
30	0.028 121	0.028 032	0.027 943	0.027 855	0.027 767	0.027 679	30
31	0.027 050	0.026 961	0.026 873	0.026 785	0.026 697	0.026 609	31
32	0.026 047	0.025 959	0.025 871	0.025 783	0.025 695	0.025 608	32
33	0.025 105	0.025 017	0.024 930	0.024 842	0.024 755	0.024 668	33
34	0.024 220	0.024 132	0.024 045	0.023 958	0.023 871	0.023 784	34
35	0.023 385	0.023 298	0.023 211	0.023 124	0.023 037	0.022 951	35
36	0.022 598	0.022 511	0.022 424	0.022 338	0.022 251	0.022 165	36
37	0.021 854	0.021 767	0.021 681	0.021 594	0.021 508	0.021 423	37
38	0.021 149	0.021 063	0.020 977	0.020 891	0.020 805	0.020 720	38
39	0.020 481	0.020 395	0.020 309	0.020 224	0.020 139	0.020 054	39
40	0.019 847	0.019 762	0.019 676	0.019 591	0.019 506	0.019 421	40
41	0.019 245	0.019 160	0.019 074	0.018 990	0.018 905	0.018 821	41
42	0.018 672	0.018 587	0.018 502	0.018 417	0.018 333	0.018 249	42
43	0.018 126	0.018 041	0.017 956	0.017 872	0.017 788	0.017 705	43
44	0.017 605	0.017 520	0.017 436	0.017 352	0.017 269	0.017 186	44
45	0.017 108	0.017 023	0.016 940	0.016 856	0.016 773	0.016 690	45
46	0.016 632	0.016 549	0.016 465	0.016 382	0.016 299	0.016 217	46
47	0.016 178	0.016 095	0.016 011	0.015 929	0.015 846	0.015 764	47
YRS							
4	0.015 743	0.015 660	0.015 577	0.015 495	0.015 413	0.015 331	48
5	0.011 681	0.011 602	0.011 523	0.011 445	0.011 367	0.011 290	60
6	0.009 014	0.008 939	0.008 865	0.008 791	0.008 718	0.008 645	72
7	0.007 144	0.007 073	0.007 003	0.006 934	0.006 865	0.006 797	84
8	0.005 771	0.005 705	0.005 639	0.005 574	0.005 509	0.005 445	96
9	0.004 729	0.004 667	0.004 605	0.004 544	0.004 484	0.004 424	108
10	0.003 918	0.003 860	0.003 802	0.003 745	0.003 689	0.003 633	120
11	0.003 275	0.003 220	0.003 166	0.003 113	0.003 061	0.003 009	132
12	0.002 755	0.002 705	0.002 654	0.002 605	0.002 557	0.002 509	144
13	0.002 332	0.002 284	0.002 238	0.002 192	0.002 147	0.002 103	156
14	0.001 982	0.001 938	0.001 895	0.001 853	0.001 811	0.001 770	168
15	0.001 692	0.001 651	0.001 611	0.001 572	0.001 533	0.001 496	180
16	0.001 448	0.001 410	0.001 373	0.001 337	0.001 302	0.001 268	192
17	0.001 243	0.001 208	0.001 174	0.001 141	0.001 109	0.001 077	204
18	0.001 069	0.001 037	0.001 006	0.000 975	0.000 946	0.000 917	216
19	0.000 922	0.000 892	0.000 863	0.000 835	0.000 808	0.000 782	228
20	0.000 796	0.000 769	0.000 742	0.000 717	0.000 692	0.000 668	240
21	0.000 688	0.000 663	0.000 639	0.000 616	0.000 593	0.000 571	252
22	0.000 595	0.000 573	0.000 551	0.000 529	0.000 509	0.000 489	264
23	0.000 516	0.000 495	0.000 475	0.000 456	0.000 437	0.000 419	276
24	0.000 447	0.000 428	0.000 410	0.000 392	0.000 376	0.000 359	288
25	0.000 388	0.000 371	0.000 354	0.000 338	0.000 323	0.000 308	300
26	0.000 337	0.000 321	0.000 306	0.000 292	0.000 278	0.000 265	312
27	0.000 293	0.000 279	0.000 265	0.000 252	0.000 239	0.000 227	324
28	0.000 255	0.000 242	0.000 229	0.000 217	0.000 206	0.000 195	336
29	0.000 222	0.000 210	0.000 198	0.000 188	0.000 178	0.000 168	348
30	0.000 193	0.000 182	0.000 172	0.000 162	0.000 153	0.000 144	360

MOS	15.25% ANNUAL RATE	15.50% ANNUAL RATE	15.75% ANNUAL RATE	16.00% ANNUAL RATE	16.25% ANNUAL RATE	16.50% ANNUAL RATE	MOS
1	1.000 000	1.000 000	1.000 000	1.000 000	1.000 000	1.000 000	1
2	0.496 843	0.496 792	0.496 740	0.496 689	0.496 637	0.496 586	2
3	0.329 133	0.329 065	0.328 996	0.328 928	0.328 860	0.328 792	3
4	0.245 285	0.245 208	0.245 132	0.245 055	0.244 979	0.244 902	4
5	0.194 981	0.194 900	0.194 818	0.194 737	0.194 656	0.194 575	5
6	0.161 450	0.161 365	0.161 281	0.161 197	0.161 113	0.161 029	6
7	0.137 502	0.137 416	0.137 330	0.137 244	0.137 158	0.137 072	7
8	0.119 545	0.119 458	0.119 370	0.119 283	0.119 195	0.119 108	8
9	0.105 582	0.105 493	0.105 405	0.105 316	0.105 227	0.105 139	9
10	0.094 414	0.094 324	0.094 235	0.094 146	0.094 056	0.093 967	10
11	0.085 278	0.085 189	0.085 099	0.085 009	0.084 919	0.084 830	11
12	0.077 668	0.077 578	0.077 488	0.077 398	0.077 308	0.077 218	12
13	0.071 230	0.071 140	0.071 050	0.070 959	0.070 869	0.070 779	13
14	0.065 714	0.065 624	0.065 533	0.065 443	0.065 353	0.065 262	14
15	0.060 936	0.060 845	0.060 755	0.060 664	0.060 574	0.060 484	15
16	0.056 756	0.056 665	0.056 575	0.056 484	0.056 394	0.056 304	16
17	0.053 070	0.052 979	0.052 888	0.052 798	0.052 708	0.052 618	17
18	0.049 794	0.049 704	0.049 613	0.049 523	0.049 433	0.049 343	18
19	0.046 865	0.046 775	0.046 684	0.046 594	0.046 504	0.046 415	19
20	0.044 230	0.044 140	0.044 050	0.043 960	0.043 870	0.043 781	20
21	0.041 847	0.041 757	0.041 667	0.041 578	0.041 488	0.041 399	21
22	0.039 682	0.039 593	0.039 503	0.039 414	0.039 324	0.039 235	22
23	0.037 707	0.037 617	0.037 528	0.037 439	0.037 350	0.037 261	23
24	0.035 897	0.035 808	0.035 719	0.035 630	0.035 541	0.035 452	24
25	0.034 233	0.034 144	0.034 055	0.033 967	0.033 878	0.033 790	25
26	0.032 698	0.032 610	0.032 521	0.032 433	0.032 344	0.032 256	26
27	0.031 278	0.031 190	0.031 101	0.031 013	0.030 925	0.030 838	27
28	0.029 960	0.029 872	0.029 784	0.029 696	0.029 609	0.029 521	28
29	0.028 734	0.028 646	0.028 559	0.028 471	0.028 384	0.028 297	29
30	0.027 591	0.027 503	0.027 416	0.027 329	0.027 242	0.027 155	30
31	0.026 522	0.026 435	0.026 348	0.026 261	0.026 174	0.026 088	31
32	0.025 521	0.025 434	0.025 347	0.025 261	0.025 175	0.025 089	32
33	0.024 581	0.024 495	0.024 408	0.024 322	0.024 236	0.024 151	33
34	0.023 697	0.023 611	0.023 525	0.023 439	0.023 354	0.023 269	34
35	0.022 865	0.022 779	0.022 693	0.022 608	0.022 523	0.022 438	35
36	0.022 080	0.021 994	0.021 909	0.021 824	0.021 739	0.021 654	36
37	0.021 337	0.021 252	0.021 167	0.021 083	0.020 998	0.020 914	37
38	0.020 635	0.020 550	0.020 465	0.020 381	0.020 297	0.020 213	38
39	0.019 969	0.019 884	0.019 800	0.019 716	0.019 633	0.019 549	39
40	0.019 337	0.019 253	0.019 169	0.019 086	0.019 002	0.018 919	40
41	0.018 737	0.018 653	0.018 569	0.018 486	0.018 403	0.018 321	41
42	0.018 165	0.018 082	0.017 999	0.017 916	0.017 834	0.017 751	42
43	0.017 621	0.017 538	0.017 456	0.017 373	0.017 291	0.017 209	43
44	0.017 103	0.017 020	0.016 938	0.016 856	0.016 774	0.016 693	44
45	0.016 608	0.016 525	0.016 443	0.016 362	0.016 280	0.016 199	45
46	0.016 135	0.016 053	0.015 971	0.015 890	0.015 809	0.015 728	46
47	0.015 682	0.015 601	0.015 520	0.015 439	0.015 358	0.015 278	47

YRS							
4	0.015 249	0.015 168	0.015 087	0.015 007	0.014 927	0.014 847	48
5	0.011 213	0.011 137	0.011 060	0.010 985	0.010 909	0.010 835	60
6	0.008 573	0.008 501	0.008 429	0.008 359	0.008 288	0.008 218	72
7	0.006 729	0.006 662	0.006 595	0.006 529	0.006 463	0.006 398	84
8	0.005 382	0.005 319	0.005 257	0.005 195	0.005 134	0.005 074	96
9	0.004 365	0.004 307	0.004 249	0.004 192	0.004 135	0.004 079	108
10	0.003 579	0.003 524	0.003 471	0.003 418	0.003 366	0.003 314	120
11	0.002 958	0.002 908	0.002 859	0.002 810	0.002 762	0.002 714	132
12	0.002 462	0.002 415	0.002 370	0.002 325	0.002 281	0.002 237	144
13	0.002 059	0.002 017	0.001 975	0.001 934	0.001 893	0.001 854	156
14	0.001 730	0.001 691	0.001 653	0.001 615	0.001 578	0.001 542	168
15	0.001 459	0.001 423	0.001 388	0.001 354	0.001 320	0.001 287	180
16	0.001 234	0.001 201	0.001 169	0.001 138	0.001 107	0.001 077	192
17	0.001 046	0.001 016	0.000 987	0.000 959	0.000 931	0.000 904	204
18	0.000 889	0.000 862	0.000 835	0.000 809	0.000 784	0.000 760	216
19	0.000 756	0.000 732	0.000 708	0.000 684	0.000 661	0.000 639	228
20	0.000 645	0.000 622	0.000 600	0.000 579	0.000 559	0.000 539	240
21	0.000 550	0.000 530	0.000 510	0.000 491	0.000 473	0.000 455	252
22	0.000 470	0.000 451	0.000 434	0.000 417	0.000 400	0.000 384	264
23	0.000 402	0.000 385	0.000 369	0.000 354	0.000 339	0.000 325	276
24	0.000 344	0.000 329	0.000 314	0.000 301	0.000 287	0.000 275	288
25	0.000 294	0.000 281	0.000 268	0.000 256	0.000 244	0.000 232	300
26	0.000 252	0.000 240	0.000 228	0.000 217	0.000 207	0.000 197	312
27	0.000 216	0.000 205	0.000 195	0.000 185	0.000 176	0.000 167	324
28	0.000 185	0.000 175	0.000 166	0.000 157	0.000 149	0.000 141	336
29	0.000 159	0.000 150	0.000 142	0.000 134	0.000 127	0.000 120	348
30	0.000 136	0.000 129	0.000 121	0.000 114	0.000 108	0.000 101	360

MOS	16.75% ANNUAL RATE	17.00% ANNUAL RATE	17.25% ANNUAL RATE	17.50% ANNUAL RATE	17.75% ANNUAL RATE	18.00% ANNUAL RATE	MOS
1	1.000 000	1.000 000	1.000 000	1.000 000	1.000 000	1.000 000	1
2	0.496 535	0.496 483	0.496 432	0.496 381	0.496 329	0.496 278	2
3	0.328 724	0.328 655	0.328 587	0.328 519	0.328 451	0.328 383	3
4	0.244 826	0.244 750	0.244 673	0.244 597	0.244 521	0.244 445	4
5	0.194 494	0.194 413	0.194 332	0.194 251	0.194 170	0.194 089	5
6	0.160 945	0.160 861	0.160 777	0.160 693	0.160 609	0.160 525	6
7	0.136 986	0.136 900	0.136 814	0.136 728	0.136 642	0.136 556	7
8	0.119 020	0.118 933	0.118 846	0.118 758	0.118 671	0.118 584	8
9	0.105 051	0.104 962	0.104 874	0.104 786	0.104 698	0.104 610	9
10	0.093 878	0.093 789	0.093 700	0.093 612	0.093 523	0.093 434	10
11	0.084 740	0.084 651	0.084 561	0.084 472	0.084 383	0.084 294	11
12	0.077 128	0.077 038	0.076 948	0.076 859	0.076 769	0.076 680	12
13	0.070 689	0.070 599	0.070 509	0.070 420	0.070 330	0.070 240	13
14	0.065 172	0.065 082	0.064 992	0.064 903	0.064 813	0.064 723	14
15	0.060 393	0.060 303	0.060 213	0.060 124	0.060 034	0.059 944	15
16	0.056 214	0.056 124	0.056 034	0.055 944	0.055 855	0.055 765	16
17	0.052 528	0.052 438	0.052 348	0.052 259	0.052 169	0.052 080	17
18	0.049 253	0.049 163	0.049 074	0.048 984	0.048 895	0.048 806	18
19	0.046 325	0.046 235	0.046 146	0.046 057	0.045 967	0.045 878	19
20	0.043 691	0.043 602	0.043 513	0.043 423	0.043 335	0.043 246	20
21	0.041 310	0.041 220	0.041 132	0.041 043	0.040 954	0.040 865	21
22	0.039 146	0.039 057	0.038 969	0.038 880	0.038 792	0.038 703	22
23	0.037 172	0.037 083	0.036 995	0.036 907	0.036 819	0.036 731	23
24	0.035 364	0.035 276	0.035 187	0.035 100	0.035 012	0.034 924	24
25	0.033 702	0.033 614	0.033 526	0.033 438	0.033 351	0.033 263	25
26	0.032 169	0.032 081	0.031 993	0.031 906	0.031 819	0.031 732	26
27	0.030 750	0.030 663	0.030 576	0.030 489	0.030 402	0.030 315	27
28	0.029 434	0.029 347	0.029 260	0.029 174	0.029 087	0.029 001	28
29	0.028 210	0.028 123	0.028 037	0.027 951	0.027 865	0.027 779	29
30	0.027 069	0.026 982	0.026 896	0.026 810	0.026 725	0.026 639	30
31	0.026 002	0.025 916	0.025 830	0.025 745	0.025 659	0.025 574	31
32	0.025 003	0.024 917	0.024 832	0.024 747	0.024 662	0.024 577	32
33	0.024 065	0.023 980	0.023 895	0.023 810	0.023 726	0.023 641	33
34	0.023 184	0.023 099	0.023 014	0.022 930	0.022 846	0.022 762	34
35	0.022 353	0.022 269	0.022 185	0.022 101	0.022 017	0.021 934	35
36	0.021 570	0.021 486	0.021 402	0.021 319	0.021 235	0.021 152	36
37	0.020 830	0.020 746	0.020 663	0.020 580	0.020 497	0.020 414	37
38	0.020 130	0.020 047	0.019 964	0.019 881	0.019 798	0.019 716	38
39	0.019 466	0.019 383	0.019 301	0.019 218	0.019 136	0.019 055	39
40	0.018 837	0.018 754	0.018 672	0.018 590	0.018 508	0.018 427	40
41	0.018 238	0.018 156	0.018 075	0.017 993	0.017 912	0.017 831	41
42	0.017 670	0.017 588	0.017 507	0.017 426	0.017 345	0.017 264	42
43	0.017 128	0.017 047	0.016 966	0.016 885	0.016 805	0.016 725	43
44	0.016 611	0.016 531	0.016 450	0.016 370	0.016 290	0.016 210	44
45	0.016 119	0.016 038	0.015 958	0.015 878	0.015 799	0.015 720	45
46	0.015 648	0.015 568	0.015 488	0.015 409	0.015 330	0.015 251	46
47	0.015 198	0.015 119	0.015 039	0.014 960	0.014 882	0.014 803	47

YRS

YRS	16.75%	17.00%	17.25%	17.50%	17.75%	18.00%	MOS
4	0.014 768	0.014 688	0.014 610	0.014 531	0.014 453	0.014 375	48
5	0.010 760	0.010 686	0.010 612	0.010 539	0.010 466	0.010 393	60
6	0.008 149	0.008 079	0.008 011	0.007 943	0.007 875	0.007 808	72
7	0.006 333	0.006 269	0.006 206	0.006 142	0.006 080	0.006 018	84
8	0.005 014	0.004 955	0.004 896	0.004 838	0.004 780	0.004 723	96
9	0.004 024	0.003 970	0.003 915	0.003 862	0.003 809	0.003 757	108
10	0.003 263	0.003 213	0.003 164	0.003 115	0.003 066	0.003 019	120
11	0.002 668	0.002 622	0.002 576	0.002 532	0.002 488	0.002 444	132
12	0.002 195	0.002 153	0.002 111	0.002 071	0.002 031	0.001 991	144
13	0.001 815	0.001 776	0.001 739	0.001 702	0.001 666	0.001 630	156
14	0.001 506	0.001 472	0.001 438	0.001 404	0.001 372	0.001 340	168
15	0.001 255	0.001 223	0.001 193	0.001 162	0.001 133	0.001 104	180
16	0.001 048	0.001 020	0.000 992	0.000 965	0.000 938	0.000 913	192
17	0.000 877	0.000 852	0.000 827	0.000 802	0.000 779	0.000 756	204
18	0.000 736	0.000 713	0.000 690	0.000 669	0.000 647	0.000 627	216
19	0.000 618	0.000 597	0.000 577	0.000 558	0.000 539	0.000 521	228
20	0.000 520	0.000 501	0.000 483	0.000 466	0.000 449	0.000 433	240
21	0.000 438	0.000 421	0.000 405	0.000 390	0.000 375	0.000 361	252
22	0.000 369	0.000 354	0.000 340	0.000 326	0.000 313	0.000 300	264
23	0.000 311	0.000 298	0.000 285	0.000 273	0.000 262	0.000 250	276
24	0.000 263	0.000 251	0.000 240	0.000 229	0.000 219	0.000 209	288
25	0.000 222	0.000 211	0.000 201	0.000 192	0.000 183	0.000 174	300
26	0.000 187	0.000 178	0.000 169	0.000 161	0.000 153	0.000 146	312
27	0.000 158	0.000 150	0.000 142	0.000 135	0.000 128	0.000 122	324
28	0.000 134	0.000 127	0.000 120	0.000 113	0.000 107	0.000 101	336
29	0.000 113	0.000 107	0.000 101	0.000 095	0.000 090	0.000 085	348
30	0.000 096	0.000 090	0.000 085	0.000 080	0.000 075	0.000 071	360

MOS	18.25% ANNUAL RATE	18.50% ANNUAL RATE	18.75% ANNUAL RATE	19.00% ANNUAL RATE	19.25% ANNUAL RATE	19.50% ANNUAL RATE	MOS
1	1.000 000	1.000 000	1.000 000	1.000 000	1.000 000	1.000 000	1
2	0.496 227	0.496 175	0.496 124	0.496 073	0.496 021	0.495 970	2
3	0.328 315	0.328 247	0.328 179	0.328 111	0.328 043	0.327 975	3
4	0.244 369	0.244 292	0.244 216	0.244 140	0.244 064	0.243 988	4
5	0.194 008	0.193 928	0.193 847	0.193 766	0.193 685	0.193 605	5
6	0.160 441	0.160 358	0.160 274	0.160 190	0.160 107	0.160 023	6
7	0.136 470	0.136 385	0.136 299	0.136 214	0.136 128	0.136 043	7
8	0.118 497	0.118 410	0.118 323	0.118 236	0.118 149	0.118 062	8
9	0.104 522	0.104 434	0.104 346	0.104 258	0.104 171	0.104 083	9
10	0.093 346	0.093 257	0.093 169	0.093 080	0.092 992	0.092 904	10
11	0.084 205	0.084 116	0.084 027	0.083 938	0.083 849	0.083 761	11
12	0.076 591	0.076 501	0.076 412	0.076 323	0.076 234	0.076 145	12
13	0.070 151	0.070 062	0.069 972	0.069 883	0.069 794	0.069 705	13
14	0.064 634	0.064 544	0.064 455	0.064 366	0.064 277	0.064 188	14
15	0.059 855	0.059 765	0.059 676	0.059 587	0.059 498	0.059 409	15
16	0.055 676	0.055 586	0.055 497	0.055 408	0.055 319	0.055 230	16
17	0.051 990	0.051 901	0.051 812	0.051 723	0.051 634	0.051 546	17
18	0.048 717	0.048 628	0.048 539	0.048 450	0.048 362	0.048 273	18
19	0.045 790	0.045 701	0.045 612	0.045 524	0.045 435	0.045 347	19
20	0.043 157	0.043 069	0.042 980	0.042 892	0.042 804	0.042 716	20
21	0.040 777	0.040 689	0.040 601	0.040 513	0.040 425	0.040 337	21
22	0.038 615	0.038 527	0.038 440	0.038 352	0.038 264	0.038 177	22
23	0.036 643	0.036 555	0.036 468	0.036 381	0.036 293	0.036 206	23
24	0.034 837	0.034 749	0.034 662	0.034 575	0.034 488	0.034 402	24
25	0.033 176	0.033 089	0.033 003	0.032 916	0.032 830	0.032 743	25
26	0.031 645	0.031 559	0.031 472	0.031 386	0.031 300	0.031 214	26
27	0.030 229	0.030 143	0.030 057	0.029 971	0.029 885	0.029 800	27
28	0.028 915	0.028 829	0.028 744	0.028 658	0.028 573	0.028 488	28
29	0.027 693	0.027 608	0.027 522	0.027 437	0.027 353	0.027 268	29
30	0.026 554	0.026 469	0.026 384	0.026 299	0.026 215	0.026 131	30
31	0.025 489	0.025 405	0.025 320	0.025 236	0.025 152	0.025 068	31
32	0.024 493	0.024 408	0.024 324	0.024 241	0.024 157	0.024 074	32
33	0.023 557	0.023 474	0.023 390	0.023 307	0.023 223	0.023 141	33
34	0.022 678	0.022 595	0.022 512	0.022 429	0.022 346	0.022 264	34
35	0.021 850	0.021 767	0.021 685	0.021 602	0.021 520	0.021 438	35
36	0.021 070	0.020 987	0.020 905	0.020 823	0.020 741	0.020 659	36
37	0.020 332	0.020 250	0.020 168	0.020 086	0.020 005	0.019 924	37
38	0.019 634	0.019 553	0.019 471	0.019 390	0.019 309	0.019 228	38
39	0.018 973	0.018 892	0.018 811	0.018 730	0.018 650	0.018 570	39
40	0.018 346	0.018 265	0.018 185	0.018 104	0.018 024	0.017 945	40
41	0.017 750	0.017 670	0.017 590	0.017 510	0.017 431	0.017 351	41
42	0.017 184	0.017 104	0.017 025	0.016 945	0.016 866	0.016 787	42
43	0.016 645	0.016 565	0.016 486	0.016 407	0.016 329	0.016 250	43
44	0.016 131	0.016 052	0.015 973	0.015 895	0.015 817	0.015 739	44
45	0.015 641	0.015 562	0.015 484	0.015 406	0.015 328	0.015 251	45
46	0.015 173	0.015 095	0.015 017	0.014 939	0.014 862	0.014 785	46
47	0.014 725	0.014 648	0.014 570	0.014 493	0.014 417	0.014 340	47

YRS

YRS							
4	0.014 297	0.014 220	0.014 143	0.014 067	0.013 991	0.013 915	48
5	0.010 321	0.010 250	0.010 178	0.010 107	0.010 037	0.009 966	60
6	0.007 741	0.007 675	0.007 609	0.007 543	0.007 478	0.007 414	72
7	0.005 956	0.005 895	0.005 835	0.005 775	0.005 715	0.005 656	84
8	0.004 667	0.004 611	0.004 555	0.004 501	0.004 446	0.004 392	96
9	0.003 705	0.003 654	0.003 604	0.003 554	0.003 504	0.003 456	108
10	0.002 971	0.002 925	0.002 879	0.002 834	0.002 789	0.002 745	120
11	0.002 401	0.002 359	0.002 318	0.002 277	0.002 237	0.002 197	132
12	0.001 953	0.001 914	0.001 877	0.001 840	0.001 804	0.001 769	144
13	0.001 595	0.001 561	0.001 527	0.001 494	0.001 462	0.001 430	156
14	0.001 308	0.001 277	0.001 247	0.001 218	0.001 189	0.001 161	168
15	0.001 076	0.001 049	0.001 022	0.000 995	0.000 970	0.000 945	180
16	0.000 887	0.000 863	0.000 839	0.000 816	0.000 793	0.000 771	192
17	0.000 733	0.000 711	0.000 690	0.000 670	0.000 649	0.000 630	204
18	0.000 607	0.000 588	0.000 569	0.000 551	0.000 533	0.000 516	216
19	0.000 503	0.000 486	0.000 469	0.000 453	0.000 438	0.000 423	228
20	0.000 417	0.000 402	0.000 388	0.000 374	0.000 360	0.000 347	240
21	0.000 347	0.000 333	0.000 320	0.000 308	0.000 296	0.000 285	252
22	0.000 288	0.000 276	0.000 265	0.000 254	0.000 244	0.000 234	264
23	0.000 240	0.000 229	0.000 220	0.000 210	0.000 201	0.000 192	276
24	0.000 199	0.000 190	0.000 182	0.000 174	0.000 166	0.000 158	288
25	0.000 166	0.000 158	0.000 151	0.000 143	0.000 137	0.000 130	300
26	0.000 138	0.000 131	0.000 125	0.000 119	0.000 113	0.000 107	312
27	0.000 115	0.000 109	0.000 104	0.000 098	0.000 093	0.000 088	324
28	0.000 096	0.000 091	0.000 086	0.000 081	0.000 077	0.000 073	336
29	0.000 080	0.000 075	0.000 071	0.000 067	0.000 063	0.000 060	348
30	0.000 067	0.000 063	0.000 059	0.000 056	0.000 052	0.000 049	360

SINKING FUND FACTORS

MONTHLY COMPOUNDING

MOS	19.75% ANNUAL RATE	20.00% ANNUAL RATE	21.00% ANNUAL RATE	22.00% ANNUAL RATE	23.00% ANNUAL RATE	24.00% ANNUAL RATE	MOS
1	1.000 000	1.000 000	1.000 000	1.000 000	1.000 000	1.000 000	1
2	0.495 919	0.495 868	0.495 663	0.495 458	0.495 254	0.495 050	2
3	0.327 907	0.327 839	0.327 567	0.327 296	0.327 025	0.326 755	3
4	0.243 912	0.243 836	0.243 532	0.243 229	0.242 926	0.242 624	4
5	0.193 524	0.193 444	0.193 121	0.192 800	0.192 479	0.192 158	5
6	0.159 940	0.159 856	0.159 523	0.159 190	0.158 857	0.158 526	6
7	0.135 957	0.135 872	0.135 531	0.135 190	0.134 851	0.134 512	7
8	0.117 976	0.117 889	0.117 543	0.117 198	0.116 853	0.116 510	8
9	0.103 995	0.103 908	0.103 558	0.103 210	0.102 862	0.102 515	9
10	0.092 815	0.092 727	0.092 375	0.092 025	0.091 675	0.091 327	10
11	0.083 672	0.083 584	0.083 230	0.082 878	0.082 528	0.082 178	11
12	0.076 057	0.075 968	0.075 614	0.075 261	0.074 910	0.074 560	12
13	0.069 616	0.069 527	0.069 173	0.068 820	0.068 468	0.068 118	13
14	0.064 099	0.064 010	0.063 656	0.063 303	0.062 952	0.062 602	14
15	0.059 320	0.059 231	0.058 877	0.058 525	0.058 174	0.057 825	15
16	0.055 142	0.055 053	0.054 700	0.054 348	0.053 998	0.053 650	16
17	0.051 457	0.051 369	0.051 016	0.050 666	0.050 317	0.049 970	17
18	0.048 185	0.048 097	0.047 745	0.047 395	0.047 048	0.046 702	18
19	0.045 259	0.045 171	0.044 821	0.044 472	0.044 126	0.043 782	19
20	0.042 628	0.042 540	0.042 191	0.041 844	0.041 499	0.041 157	20
21	0.040 250	0.040 163	0.039 815	0.039 469	0.039 126	0.038 785	21
22	0.038 090	0.038 003	0.037 656	0.037 312	0.036 971	0.036 631	22
23	0.036 120	0.036 033	0.035 688	0.035 345	0.035 006	0.034 668	23
24	0.034 315	0.034 229	0.033 886	0.033 545	0.033 207	0.032 871	24
25	0.032 657	0.032 571	0.032 230	0.031 890	0.031 554	0.031 220	25
26	0.031 128	0.031 043	0.030 703	0.030 365	0.030 031	0.029 699	26
27	0.029 714	0.029 629	0.029 291	0.028 955	0.028 623	0.028 293	27
28	0.028 403	0.028 318	0.027 982	0.027 648	0.027 317	0.026 990	28
29	0.027 183	0.027 099	0.026 764	0.026 432	0.026 104	0.025 778	29
30	0.026 047	0.025 963	0.025 630	0.025 300	0.024 973	0.024 650	30
31	0.024 985	0.024 901	0.024 570	0.024 242	0.023 918	0.023 596	31
32	0.023 991	0.023 908	0.023 578	0.023 252	0.022 930	0.022 611	32
33	0.023 058	0.022 975	0.022 648	0.022 324	0.022 003	0.021 687	33
34	0.022 181	0.022 099	0.021 774	0.021 452	0.021 133	0.020 819	34
35	0.021 356	0.021 275	0.020 951	0.020 631	0.020 315	0.020 002	35
36	0.020 578	0.020 497	0.020 175	0.019 857	0.019 543	0.019 233	36
37	0.019 843	0.019 762	0.019 443	0.019 127	0.018 815	0.018 507	37
38	0.019 148	0.019 068	0.018 750	0.018 436	0.018 126	0.017 821	38
39	0.018 490	0.018 410	0.018 094	0.017 782	0.017 475	0.017 171	39
40	0.017 865	0.017 786	0.017 472	0.017 162	0.016 857	0.016 556	40
41	0.017 272	0.017 194	0.016 882	0.016 574	0.016 271	0.015 972	41
42	0.016 709	0.016 631	0.016 321	0.016 015	0.015 714	0.015 417	42
43	0.016 172	0.016 095	0.015 787	0.015 483	0.015 184	0.014 890	43
44	0.015 661	0.015 584	0.015 278	0.014 977	0.014 680	0.014 388	44
45	0.015 174	0.015 097	0.014 793	0.014 494	0.014 199	0.013 910	45
46	0.014 709	0.014 632	0.014 330	0.014 033	0.013 741	0.013 453	46
47	0.014 264	0.014 188	0.013 888	0.013 593	0.013 303	0.013 018	47

YRS	19.75%	20.00%	21.00%	22.00%	23.00%	24.00%	
4	0.013 839	0.013 764	0.013 466	0.013 173	0.012 885	0.012 602	48
5	0.009 897	0.009 827	0.009 553	0.009 286	0.009 024	0.008 768	60
6	0.007 350	0.007 286	0.007 036	0.006 793	0.006 556	0.006 327	72
7	0.005 598	0.005 540	0.005 312	0.005 093	0.004 881	0.004 676	84
8	0.004 339	0.004 287	0.004 081	0.003 884	0.003 695	0.003 513	96
9	0.003 407	0.003 360	0.003 175	0.002 999	0.002 831	0.002 671	108
10	0.002 702	0.002 659	0.002 493	0.002 336	0.002 188	0.002 048	120
11	0.002 158	0.002 120	0.001 972	0.001 833	0.001 703	0.001 581	132
12	0.001 734	0.001 699	0.001 568	0.001 446	0.001 332	0.001 226	144
13	0.001 399	0.001 369	0.001 252	0.001 145	0.001 046	0.000 954	156
14	0.001 133	0.001 106	0.001 003	0.000 909	0.000 823	0.000 745	168
15	0.000 920	0.000 896	0.000 806	0.000 724	0.000 650	0.000 583	180
16	0.000 749	0.000 728	0.000 649	0.000 578	0.000 514	0.000 457	192
17	0.000 611	0.000 592	0.000 523	0.000 462	0.000 407	0.000 358	204
18	0.000 499	0.000 483	0.000 423	0.000 370	0.000 323	0.000 281	216
19	0.000 408	0.000 394	0.000 342	0.000 296	0.000 256	0.000 221	228
20	0.000 334	0.000 322	0.000 276	0.000 237	0.000 203	0.000 174	240
21	0.000 274	0.000 263	0.000 224	0.000 190	0.000 162	0.000 137	252
22	0.000 224	0.000 215	0.000 181	0.000 153	0.000 128	0.000 108	264
23	0.000 184	0.000 176	0.000 147	0.000 123	0.000 102	0.000 085	276
24	0.000 151	0.000 144	0.000 119	0.000 098	0.000 081	0.000 067	288
25	0.000 124	0.000 118	0.000 097	0.000 079	0.000 065	0.000 053	300
26	0.000 102	0.000 097	0.000 078	0.000 064	0.000 051	0.000 042	312
27	0.000 083	0.000 079	0.000 064	0.000 051	0.000 041	0.000 033	324
28	0.000 069	0.000 065	0.000 052	0.000 041	0.000 033	0.000 026	336
29	0.000 056	0.000 053	0.000 042	0.000 033	0.000 026	0.000 020	348
30	0.000 046	0.000 044	0.000 034	0.000 027	0.000 021	0.000 016	360

SINKING FUND FACTORS

QUARTERLY COMPOUNDING

QTRS	6.50% ANNUAL RATE	7.00% ANNUAL RATE	7.50% ANNUAL RATE	8.00% ANNUAL RATE	8.50% ANNUAL RATE	9.00% ANNUAL RATE	QTRS
1	1.000 000	1.000 000	1.000 000	1.000 000	1.000 000	1.000 000	1
2	0.495 970	0.495 663	0.495 356	0.495 050	0.494 743	0.494 438	2
3	0.327 975	0.327 567	0.327 161	0.326 755	0.326 349	0.325 945	3
4	0.243 988	0.243 532	0.243 078	0.242 624	0.242 171	0.241 719.	4
5	0.193 605	0.193 121	0.192 639	0.192 158	0.191 679	0.191 200	5
6	0.160 023	0.159 523	0.159 023	0.158 526	0.158 030	0.157 535	6
7	0.136 043	0.135 531	0.135 020	0.134 512	0.134 005	0.133 500	7
8	0.118 062	0.117 543	0.117 025	0.116 510	0.115 996	0.115 485	8
9	0.104 083	0.103 558	0.103 036	0.102 515	0.101 997	0.101 482	9
10	0.092 904	0.092 375	0.091 850	0.091 327	0.090 806	0.090 288	10
11	0.083 761	0.083 230	0.082 703	0.082 178	0.081 656	0.081 136	11
12	0.076 145	0.075 614	0.075 085	0.074 560	0.074 037	0.073 517	12
13	0.069 705	0.069 173	0.068 644	0.068 118	0.067 596	0.067 077	13
14	0.064 188	0.063 656	0.063 127	0.062 602	0.062 080	0.061 562	14
15	0.059 409	0.058 877	0.058 350	0.057 825	0.057 305	0.056 789	15
16	0.055 230	0.054 700	0.054 173	0.053 650	0.053 131	0.052 617	16
17	0.051 546	0.051 016	0.050 491	0.049 970	0.049 453	0.048 940	17
18	0.048 273	0.047 745	0.047 221	0.046 702	0.046 187	0.045 677	18
19	0.045 347	0.044 821	0.044 299	0.043 782	0.043 269	0.042 762	19
20	0.042 716	0.042 191	0.041 671	0.041 157	0.040 647	0.040 142	20
21	0.040 337	0.039 815	0.039 297	0.038 785	0.038 278	0.037 776	21
22	0.038 177	0.037 656	0.037 141	0.036 631	0.036 127	0.035 628	22
23	0.036 206	0.035 688	0.035 175	0.034 668	0.034 167	0.033 671	23
24	0.034 402	0.033 886	0.033 375	0.032 871	0.032 373	0.031 880	24
25	0.032 743	0.032 230	0.031 722	0.031 220	0.030 725	0.030 236	25
26	0.031 214	0.030 703	0.030 198	0.029 699	0.029 207	0.028 721	26
27	0.029 800	0.029 291	0.028 789	0.028 293	0.027 804	0.027 322	27
28	0.028 488	0.027 982	0.027 482	0.026 990	0.026 504	0.026 025	28
29	0.027 268	0.026 764	0.026 268	0.025 778	0.025 296	0.024 821	29
30	0.026 131	0.025 630	0.025 136	0.024 650	0.024 171	0.023 699	30
31	0.025 068	0.024 570	0.024 079	0.023 596	0.023 121	0.022 653	31
32	0.024 074	0.023 578	0.023 090	0.022 611	0.022 139	0.021 674	32
33	0.023 141	0.022 648	0.022 163	0.021 687	0.021 218	0.020 757	33
34	0.022 264	0.021 774	0.021 292	0.020 819	0.020 354	0.019 897	34
35	0.021 438	0.020 951	0.020 472	0.020 002	0.019 541	0.019 087	35
36	0.020 659	0.020 175	0.019 700	0.019 233	0.018 775	0.018 325	36
37	0.019 924	0.019 443	0.018 970	0.018 507	0.018 052	0.017 606	37
38	0.019 228	0.018 750	0.018 281	0.017 821	0.017 370	0.016 928	38
39	0.018 570	0.018 094	0.017 628	0.017 171	0.016 724	0.016 285	39
40	0.017 945	0.017 472	0.017 009	0.016 556	0.016 112	0.015 677	40
41	0.017 351	0.016 882	0.016 422	0.015 972	0.015 532	0.015 101	41
42	0.016 787	0.016 321	0.015 864	0.015 417	0.014 981	0.014 554	42
43	0.016 250	0.015 787	0.015 333	0.014 890	0.014 457	0.014 034	43
44	0.015 739	0.015 278	0.014 828	0.014 388	0.013 958	0.013 539	44
45	0.015 251	0.014 793	0.014 346	0.013 910	0.013 484	0.013 068	45
46	0.014 785	0.014 330	0.013 887	0.013 453	0.013 031	0.012 619	46
47	0.014 340	0.013 888	0.013 448	0.013 018	0.012 599	0.012 191	47
48	0.013 915	0.013 466	0.013 028	0.012 602	0.012 187	0.011 782	48
49	0.013 507	0.013 061	0.012 627	0.012 204	0.011 792	0.011 392	49
50	0.013 117	0.012 674	0.012 243	0.011 823	0.011 415	0.011 018	50
51	0.012 743	0.012 303	0.011 875	0.011 459	0.011 054	0.010 661	51
52	0.012 384	0.011 947	0.011 522	0.011 109	0.010 708	0.010 319	52
53	0.012 039	0.011 605	0.011 183	0.010 774	0.010 377	0.009 991	53
54	0.011 708	0.011 277	0.010 858	0.010 452	0.010 058	0.009 677	54
55	0.011 389	0.010 961	0.010 546	0.010 143	0.009 753	0.009 375	55
YRS							
14	0.011 083	0.010 658	0.010 246	0.009 847	0.009 460	0.009 085	56
15	0.009 966	0.009 553	0.009 154	0.008 768	0.008 395	0.008 035	60
16	0.008 999	0.008 598	0.008 211	0.007 839	0.007 480	0.007 134	64
17	0.008 155	0.007 766	0.007 391	0.007 032	0.006 686	0.006 355	68
18	0.007 414	0.007 036	0.006 674	0.006 327	0.005 995	0.005 677	72
19	0.006 758	0.006 392	0.006 042	0.005 708	0.005 389	0.005 085	76
20	0.006 176	0.005 821	0.005 483	0.005 161	0.004 855	0.004 564	80
21	0.005 656	0.005 312	0.004 986	0.004 676	0.004 382	0.004 104	84
22	0.005 190	0.004 857	0.004 542	0.004 244	0.003 963	0.003 697	88
23	0.004 771	0.004 449	0.004 145	0.003 859	0.003 589	0.003 336	92
24	0.004 392	0.004 081	0.003 788	0.003 513	0.003 255	0.003 014	96
25	0.004 050	0.003 749	0.003 467	0.003 203	0.002 956	0.002 726	100
26	0.003 739	0.003 448	0.003 176	0.002 923	0.002 687	0.002 468	104
27	0.003 456	0.003 175	0.002 914	0.002 671	0.002 446	0.002 237	108
28	0.003 197	0.002 926	0.002 675	0.002 443	0.002 228	0.002 030	112
29	0.002 961	0.002 700	0.002 458	0.002 236	0.002 031	0.001 843	116
30	0.002 745	0.002 493	0.002 261	0.002 048	0.001 853	0.001 674	120

SINKING FUND FACTORS

QTRS	9.50% ANNUAL RATE	10.00% ANNUAL RATE	10.50% ANNUAL RATE	11.00% ANNUAL RATE	11.50% ANNUAL RATE	12.00% ANNUAL RATE	QTRS
1	1.000 000	1.000 000	1.000 000	1.000 000	1.000 000	1.000 000	1
2	0.494 132	0.493 827	0.493 523	0.493 218	0.492 914	0.492 611	2
3	0.325 541	0.325 137	0.324 734	0.324 332	0.323 931	0.323 530	3
4	0.241 268	0.240 818	0.240 369	0.239 921	0.239 473	0.239 027	4
5	0.190 723	0.190 247	0.189 772	0.189 298	0.188 826	0.188 355	5
6	0.157 042	0.156 550	0.156 060	0.155 571	0.155 083	0.154 598	6
7	0.132 997	0.132 495	0.131 996	0.131 497	0.131 001	0.130 506	7
8	0.114 975	0.114 467	0.113 962	0.113 458	0.112 956	0.112 456	8
9	0.100 968	0.100 457	0.099 948	0.099 441	0.098 936	0.098 434	9
10	0.089 772	0.089 259	0.088 748	0.088 240	0.087 734	0.087 231	10
11	0.080 620	0.080 106	0.079 595	0.079 086	0.078 581	0.078 077	11
12	0.073 001	0.072 487	0.071 976	0.071 469	0.070 964	0.070 462	12
13	0.066 561	0.066 048	0.065 539	0.065 033	0.064 529	0.064 030	13
14	0.061 048	0.060 537	0.060 029	0.059 525	0.059 024	0.058 526	14
15	0.056 276	0.055 766	0.055 261	0.054 759	0.054 261	0.053 767	15
16	0.052 106	0.051 599	0.051 096	0.050 597	0.050 102	0.049 611	16
17	0.048 432	0.047 928	0.047 428	0.046 932	0.046 440	0.045 953	17
18	0.045 171	0.044 670	0.044 173	0.043 681	0.043 192	0.042 709	18
19	0.042 259	0.041 761	0.041 267	0.040 778	0.040 294	0.039 814	19
20	0.039 642	0.039 147	0.038 657	0.038 172	0.037 691	0.037 216	20
21	0.037 279	0.036 787	0.036 301	0.035 819	0.035 343	0.034 872	21
22	0.035 135	0.034 647	0.034 164	0.033 686	0.033 214	0.032 747	22
23	0.033 181	0.032 696	0.032 217	0.031 744	0.031 276	0.030 814	23
24	0.031 394	0.030 913	0.030 438	0.029 969	0.029 505	0.029 047	24
25	0.029 753	0.029 276	0.028 805	0.028 340	0.027 881	0.027 428	25
26	0.028 242	0.027 769	0.027 302	0.026 841	0.026 387	0.025 938	26
27	0.026 846	0.026 377	0.025 914	0.025 458	0.025 008	0.024 564	27
28	0.025 553	0.025 088	0.024 629	0.024 177	0.023 732	0.023 293	28
29	0.024 353	0.023 891	0.023 437	0.022 989	0.022 549	0.022 115	29
30	0.023 235	0.022 778	0.022 327	0.021 884	0.021 448	0.021 019	30
31	0.022 192	0.021 739	0.021 293	0.020 855	0.020 423	0.019 999	31
32	0.021 217	0.020 768	0.020 327	0.019 893	0.019 466	0.019 047	32
33	0.020 304	0.019 859	0.019 422	0.018 993	0.018 571	0.018 156	33
34	0.019 448	0.019 007	0.018 574	0.018 149	0.017 731	0.017 322	34
35	0.018 642	0.018 206	0.017 777	0.017 356	0.016 944	0.016 539	35
36	0.017 884	0.017 452	0.017 027	0.016 611	0.016 204	0.015 804	36
37	0.017 169	0.016 741	0.016 321	0.015 910	0.015 506	0.015 112	37
38	0.016 494	0.016 070	0.015 655	0.015 248	0.014 849	0.014 459	38
39	0.015 856	0.015 436	0.015 025	0.014 623	0.014 229	0.013 844	39
40	0.015 252	0.014 836	0.014 429	0.014 032	0.013 643	0.013 262	40
41	0.014 680	0.014 268	0.013 865	0.013 472	0.013 088	0.012 712	41
42	0.014 136	0.013 729	0.013 331	0.012 942	0.012 562	0.012 192	42
43	0.013 620	0.013 217	0.012 823	0.012 439	0.012 064	0.011 698	43
44	0.013 130	0.012 730	0.012 341	0.011 961	0.011 591	0.011 230	44
45	0.012 663	0.012 268	0.011 882	0.011 507	0.011 141	0.010 785	45
46	0.012 218	0.011 827	0.011 446	0.011 075	0.010 714	0.010 363	46
47	0.011 794	0.011 407	0.011 030	0.010 664	0.010 307	0.009 961	47
48	0.011 389	0.011 006	0.010 634	0.010 272	0.009 920	0.009 578	48
49	0.011 002	0.010 623	0.010 255	0.009 898	0.009 550	0.009 213	49
50	0.010 633	0.010 258	0.009 894	0.009 541	0.009 198	0.008 865	50
51	0.010 279	0.009 909	0.009 549	0.009 200	0.008 862	0.008 534	51
52	0.009 941	0.009 574	0.009 219	0.008 874	0.008 541	0.008 217	52
53	0.009 617	0.009 254	0.008 903	0.008 563	0.008 234	0.007 915	53
54	0.009 306	0.008 948	0.008 601	0.008 265	0.007 940	0.007 626	54
55	0.009 009	0.008 654	0.008 311	0.007 980	0.007 659	0.007 349	55

YRS

YRS	9.50% ANNUAL RATE	10.00% ANNUAL RATE	10.50% ANNUAL RATE	11.00% ANNUAL RATE	11.50% ANNUAL RATE	12.00% ANNUAL RATE	QTRS
14	0.008 723	0.008 372	0.008 034	0.007 706	0.007 390	0.007 084	56
15	0.007 688	0.007 353	0.007 031	0.006 720	0.006 421	0.006 133	60
16	0.006 802	0.006 482	0.006 176	0.005 881	0.005 599	0.005 328	64
17	0.006 037	0.005 733	0.005 442	0.005 163	0.004 896	0.004 642	68
18	0.005 374	0.005 084	0.004 808	0.004 544	0.004 293	0.004 054	72
19	0.004 795	0.004 520	0.004 258	0.004 009	0.003 773	0.003 548	76
20	0.004 288	0.004 026	0.003 778	0.003 543	0.003 321	0.003 112	80
21	0.003 841	0.003 593	0.003 359	0.003 137	0.002 929	0.002 733	84
22	0.003 447	0.003 212	0.002 990	0.002 782	0.002 587	0.002 404	88
23	0.003 098	0.002 875	0.002 666	0.002 470	0.002 288	0.002 117	92
24	0.002 788	0.002 577	0.002 380	0.002 196	0.002 025	0.001 866	96
25	0.002 511	0.002 312	0.002 126	0.001 954	0.001 795	0.001 647	100
26	0.002 265	0.002 076	0.001 902	0.001 741	0.001 592	0.001 454	104
27	0.002 044	0.001 867	0.001 702	0.001 551	0.001 413	0.001 285	108
28	0.001 847	0.001 679	0.001 525	0.001 384	0.001 255	0.001 136	112
29	0.001 670	0.001 512	0.001 367	0.001 235	0.001 115	0.001 005	116
30	0.001 511	0.001 362	0.001 226	0.001 103	0.000 991	0.000 890	120

QTRS	12.50% ANNUAL RATE	13.00% ANNUAL RATE	13.50% ANNUAL RATE	14.00% ANNUAL RATE	14.50% ANNUAL RATE	15.00% ANNUAL RATE	QTRS
1	1.000 000	1.000 000	1.000 000	1.000 000	1.000 000	1.000 000	1
2	0.492 308	0.492 005	0.491 703	0.491 400	0.491 099	0.490 798	2
3	0.323 130	0.322 731	0.322 332	0.321 934	0.321 537	0.321 140	3
4	0.238 582	0.238 137	0.237 694	0.237 251	0.236 809	0.236 369	4
5	0.187 884	0.187 416	0.186 948	0.186 481	0.186 016	0.185 552	5
6	0.154 113	0.153 630	0.153 148	0.152 668	0.152 189	0.151 712	6
7	0.130 013	0.129 522	0.129 032	0.128 544	0.128 058	0.127 574	7
8	0.111 959	0.111 463	0.110 969	0.110 477	0.109 987	0.109 498	8
9	0.097 934	0.097 436	0.096 940	0.096 446	0.095 954	0.095 465	9
10	0.086 730	0.086 231	0.085 735	0.085 241	0.084 750	0.084 261	10
11	0.077 577	0.077 079	0.076 584	0.076 092	0.075 602	0.075 115	11
12	0.069 963	0.069 467	0.068 974	0.068 484	0.067 997	0.067 512	12
13	0.063 533	0.063 039	0.062 549	0.062 062	0.061 577	0.061 096	13
14	0.058 032	0.057 542	0.057 055	0.056 571	0.056 090	0.055 613	14
15	0.053 276	0.052 789	0.052 305	0.051 825	0.051 349	0.050 876	15
16	0.049 124	0.048 640	0.048 161	0.047 685	0.047 213	0.046 745	16
17	0.045 469	0.044 990	0.044 514	0.044 043	0.043 576	0.043 113	17
18	0.042 229	0.041 754	0.041 283	0.040 817	0.040 355	0.039 897	18
19	0.039 339	0.038 868	0.038 402	0.037 940	0.037 483	0.037 031	19
20	0.036 745	0.036 279	0.035 818	0.035 361	0.034 909	0.034 462	20
21	0.034 406	0.033 944	0.033 488	0.033 037	0.032 590	0.032 149	21
22	0.032 286	0.031 829	0.031 378	0.030 932	0.030 491	0.030 055	22
23	0.030 357	0.029 906	0.029 459	0.029 019	0.028 583	0.028 153	23
24	0.028 595	0.028 149	0.027 708	0.027 273	0.026 843	0.026 419	24
25	0.026 981	0.026 539	0.026 104	0.025 674	0.025 250	0.024 832	25
26	0.025 496	0.025 060	0.024 630	0.024 205	0.023 787	0.023 375	26
27	0.024 127	0.023 696	0.023 271	0.022 852	0.022 440	0.022 033	27
28	0.022 861	0.022 435	0.022 016	0.021 603	0.021 196	0.020 795	28
29	0.021 687	0.021 267	0.020 853	0.020 445	0.020 044	0.019 650	29
30	0.020 597	0.020 182	0.019 773	0.019 371	0.018 976	0.018 588	30
31	0.019 582	0.019 172	0.018 769	0.018 372	0.017 983	0.017 600	31
32	0.018 635	0.018 230	0.017 832	0.017 442	0.017 058	0.016 681	32
33	0.017 749	0.017 350	0.016 957	0.016 572	0.016 195	0.015 824	33
34	0.016 920	0.016 526	0.016 139	0.015 760	0.015 388	0.015 023	34
35	0.016 143	0.015 753	0.015 372	0.014 998	0.014 632	0.014 273	35
36	0.015 412	0.015 028	0.014 652	0.014 284	0.013 924	0.013 571	36
37	0.014 725	0.014 346	0.013 976	0.013 613	0.013 258	0.012 911	37
38	0.014 078	0.013 704	0.013 339	0.012 982	0.012 633	0.012 292	38
39	0.013 467	0.013 099	0.012 739	0.012 388	0.012 044	0.011 709	39
40	0.012 891	0.012 528	0.012 173	0.011 827	0.011 489	0.011 159	40
41	0.012 346	0.011 988	0.011 639	0.011 298	0.010 966	0.010 642	41
42	0.011 830	0.011 478	0.011 134	0.010 798	0.010 471	0.010 153	42
43	0.011 342	0.010 994	0.010 655	0.010 325	0.010 004	0.009 691	43
44	0.010 878	0.010 536	0.010 202	0.009 878	0.009 562	0.009 254	44
45	0.010 438	0.010 101	0.009 773	0.009 453	0.009 143	0.008 841	45
46	0.010 021	0.009 688	0.009 365	0.009 051	0.008 746	0.008 449	46
47	0.009 624	0.009 296	0.008 978	0.008 669	0.008 369	0.008 078	47
48	0.009 246	0.008 923	0.008 610	0.008 306	0.008 012	0.007 726	48
49	0.008 886	0.008 568	0.008 260	0.007 962	0.007 672	0.007 392	49
50	0.008 543	0.008 230	0.007 927	0.007 634	0.007 349	0.007 074	50
51	0.008 216	0.007 908	0.007 610	0.007 322	0.007 042	0.006 772	51
52	0.007 904	0.007 601	0.007 308	0.007 024	0.006 750	0.006 485	52
53	0.007 606	0.007 308	0.007 020	0.006 741	0.006 472	0.006 212	53
54	0.007 322	0.007 028	0.006 745	0.006 471	0.006 207	0.005 952	54
55	0.007 050	0.006 761	0.006 482	0.006 213	0.005 954	0.005 704	55
YRS							
14	0.006 790	0.006 506	0.006 231	0.005 967	0.005 713	0.005 468	56
15	0.005 856	0.005 590	0.005 334	0.005 089	0.004 853	0.004 627	60
16	0.005 068	0.004 819	0.004 581	0.004 353	0.004 135	0.003 927	64
17	0.004 398	0.004 166	0.003 945	0.003 734	0.003 533	0.003 341	68
18	0.003 827	0.003 610	0.003 405	0.003 210	0.003 025	0.002 849	72
19	0.003 336	0.003 135	0.002 945	0.002 765	0.002 594	0.002 434	76
20	0.002 914	0.002 727	0.002 551	0.002 385	0.002 229	0.002 082	80
21	0.002 549	0.002 376	0.002 213	0.002 060	0.001 917	0.001 783	84
22	0.002 232	0.002 072	0.001 922	0.001 782	0.001 651	0.001 529	88
23	0.001 958	0.001 809	0.001 671	0.001 543	0.001 423	0.001 312	92
24	0.001 719	0.001 582	0.001 454	0.001 337	0.001 228	0.001 127	96
25	0.001 510	0.001 384	0.001 267	0.001 159	0.001 060	0.000 969	100
26	0.001 328	0.001 211	0.001 104	0.001 006	0.000 916	0.000 833	104
27	0.001 168	0.001 061	0.000 963	0.000 873	0.000 792	0.000 717	108
28	0.001 028	0.000 930	0.000 840	0.000 759	0.000 685	0.000 617	112
29	0.000 906	0.000 815	0.000 734	0.000 659	0.000 592	0.000 532	116
30	0.000 798	0.000 715	0.000 641	0.000 573	0.000 512	0.000 458	120

SINKING FUND FACTORS

QUARTERLY COMPOUNDING

QTRS	15.50% ANNUAL RATE	16.00% ANNUAL RATE	16.50% ANNUAL RATE	17.00% ANNUAL RATE	17.50% ANNUAL RATE	18.00% ANNUAL RATE	QTRS
1	1.000 000	1.000 000	1.000 000	1.000 000	1.000 000	1.000 000	1
2	0.490 497	0.490 196	0.489 896	0.489 596	0.489 297	0.488 998	2
3	0.320 744	0.320 349	0.319 954	0.319 560	0.319 166	0.318 773	3
4	0.235 929	0.235 490	0.235 052	0.234 615	0.234 179	0.233 744	4
5	0.185 089	0.184 627	0.184 166	0.183 707	0.183 249	0.182 792	5
6	0.151 236	0.150 762	0.150 289	0.149 817	0.149 347	0.148 878	6
7	0.127 091	0.126 610	0.126 130	0.125 652	0.125 176	0.124 701	7
8	0.109 012	0.108 528	0.108 045	0.107 565	0.107 086	0.106 610	8
9	0.094 978	0.094 493	0.094 010	0.093 529	0.093 051	0.092 574	9
10	0.083 775	0.083 291	0.082 809	0.082 330	0.081 853	0.081 379	10
11	0.074 631	0.074 149	0.073 670	0.073 193	0.072 719	0.072 248	11
12	0.067 031	0.066 552	0.066 076	0.065 603	0.065 133	0.064 666	12
13	0.060 619	0.060 144	0.059 672	0.059 203	0.058 738	0.058 275	13
14	0.055 139	0.054 669	0.054 202	0.053 738	0.053 278	0.052 820	14
15	0.050 407	0.049 941	0.049 479	0.049 020	0.048 565	0.048 114	15
16	0.046 281	0.045 820	0.045 363	0.044 910	0.044 461	0.044 015	16
17	0.042 654	0.042 199	0.041 747	0.041 300	0.040 857	0.040 418	17
18	0.039 443	0.038 993	0.038 548	0.038 107	0.037 670	0.037 237	18
19	0.036 582	0.036 139	0.035 699	0.035 264	0.034 834	0.034 407	19
20	0.034 020	0.033 582	0.033 149	0.032 720	0.032 296	0.031 876	20
21	0.031 712	0.031 280	0.030 853	0.030 431	0.030 013	0.029 601	21
22	0.029 625	0.029 199	0.028 778	0.028 362	0.027 952	0.027 546	22
23	0.027 729	0.027 309	0.026 895	0.026 486	0.026 081	0.025 682	23
24	0.026 000	0.025 587	0.025 179	0.024 776	0.024 379	0.023 987	24
25	0.024 419	0.024 012	0.023 610	0.023 215	0.022 824	0.022 439	25
26	0.022 968	0.022 567	0.022 172	0.021 783	0.021 399	0.021 021	26
27	0.021 633	0.021 239	0.020 850	0.020 467	0.020 091	0.019 719	27
28	0.020 401	0.020 013	0.019 631	0.019 255	0.018 885	0.018 521	28
29	0.019 262	0.018 880	0.018 504	0.018 135	0.017 772	0.017 415	29
30	0.018 206	0.017 830	0.017 461	0.017 098	0.016 742	0.016 392	30
31	0.017 225	0.016 855	0.016 493	0.016 137	0.015 787	0.015 443	31
32	0.016 312	0.015 949	0.015 592	0.015 243	0.014 900	0.014 563	32
33	0.015 460	0.015 104	0.014 754	0.014 411	0.014 074	0.013 745	33
34	0.014 665	0.014 315	0.013 971	0.013 635	0.013 305	0.012 982	34
35	0.013 922	0.013 577	0.013 240	0.012 910	0.012 587	0.012 270	35
36	0.013 225	0.012 887	0.012 556	0.012 232	0.011 916	0.011 606	36
37	0.012 572	0.012 240	0.011 915	0.011 597	0.011 287	0.010 984	37
38	0.011 958	0.011 632	0.011 313	0.011 002	0.010 698	0.010 402	38
39	0.011 381	0.011 061	0.010 748	0.010 444	0.010 146	0.009 856	39
40	0.010 838	0.010 523	0.010 217	0.009 918	0.009 627	0.009 343	40
41	0.010 326	0.010 017	0.009 717	0.009 424	0.009 139	0.008 862	41
42	0.009 843	0.009 540	0.009 246	0.008 959	0.008 680	0.008 409	42
43	0.009 386	0.009 090	0.008 801	0.008 521	0.008 248	0.007 982	43
44	0.008 955	0.008 665	0.008 382	0.008 107	0.007 840	0.007 581	44
45	0.008 548	0.008 262	0.007 986	0.007 717	0.007 455	0.007 202	45
46	0.008 162	0.007 882	0.007 611	0.007 348	0.007 092	0.006 845	46
47	0.007 796	0.007 522	0.007 256	0.006 999	0.006 749	0.006 507	47
48	0.007 449	0.007 181	0.006 921	0.006 669	0.006 425	0.006 189	48
49	0.007 120	0.006 857	0.006 603	0.006 356	0.006 118	0.005 887	49
50	0.006 808	0.006 550	0.006 301	0.006 060	0.005 827	0.005 602	50
51	0.006 511	0.006 259	0.006 015	0.005 779	0.005 552	0.005 332	51
52	0.006 229	0.005 982	0.005 744	0.005 513	0.005 291	0.005 077	52
53	0.005 961	0.005 719	0.005 486	0.005 261	0.005 044	0.004 835	53
54	0.005 706	0.005 469	0.005 241	0.005 021	0.004 809	0.004 605	54
55	0.005 463	0.005 231	0.005 008	0.004 793	0.004 586	0.004 388	55

YRS							
14	0.005 232	0.005 005	0.004 787	0.004 577	0.004 375	0.004 181	56
15	0.004 410	0.004 202	0.004 003	0.003 812	0.003 629	0.003 454	60
16	0.003 728	0.003 538	0.003 356	0.003 183	0.003 018	0.002 861	64
17	0.003 159	0.002 986	0.002 821	0.002 665	0.002 516	0.002 375	68
18	0.002 683	0.002 525	0.002 376	0.002 234	0.002 101	0.001 975	72
19	0.002 282	0.002 139	0.002 004	0.001 877	0.001 757	0.001 644	76
20	0.001 944	0.001 814	0.001 692	0.001 578	0.001 471	0.001 371	80
21	0.001 658	0.001 541	0.001 431	0.001 329	0.001 233	0.001 144	84
22	0.001 415	0.001 310	0.001 211	0.001 119	0.001 034	0.000 955	88
23	0.001 209	0.001 114	0.001 026	0.000 944	0.000 868	0.000 798	92
24	0.001 034	0.000 949	0.000 869	0.000 796	0.000 729	0.000 667	96
25	0.000 885	0.000 808	0.000 737	0.000 672	0.000 613	0.000 558	100
26	0.000 758	0.000 689	0.000 626	0.000 568	0.000 515	0.000 467	104
27	0.000 649	0.000 587	0.000 531	0.000 480	0.000 433	0.000 391	108
28	0.000 556	0.000 501	0.000 451	0.000 406	0.000 365	0.000 328	112
29	0.000 477	0.000 427	0.000 383	0.000 343	0.000 307	0.000 274	116
30	0.000 409	0.000 365	0.000 325	0.000 290	0.000 258	0.000 230	120

SINKING FUND FACTORS

QUARTERLY COMPOUNDING

QTRS	18.50% ANNUAL RATE	19.00% ANNUAL RATE	19.50% ANNUAL RATE	20.00% ANNUAL RATE	20.50% ANNUAL RATE	21.00% ANNUAL RATE	QTRS
1	1.000 000	1.000 000	1.000 000	1.000 000	1.000 000	1.000 000	1
2	0.488 699	0.488 400	0.488 103	0.487 805	0.487 508	0.487 211	2
3	0.318 381	0.317 990	0.317 599	0.317 209	0.316 819	0.316 430	3
4	0.233 309	0.232 876	0.232 443	0.232 012	0.231 581	0.231 151	4
5	0.182 336	0.181 881	0.181 427	0.180 975	0.180 523	0.180 073	5
6	0.148 411	0.147 945	0.147 481	0.147 017	0.146 556	0.146 095	6
7	0.124 229	0.123 757	0.123 288	0.122 820	0.122 354	0.121 889	7
8	0.106 135	0.105 662	0.105 191	0.104 722	0.104 255	0.103 789	8
9	0.092 100	0.091 628	0.091 158	0.090 690	0.090 224	0.089 761	9
10	0.080 907	0.080 437	0.079 970	0.079 505	0.079 042	0.078 582	10
11	0.071 779	0.071 313	0.070 850	0.070 389	0.069 931	0.069 475	11
12	0.064 202	0.063 740	0.063 281	0.062 825	0.062 372	0.061 922	12
13	0.057 816	0.057 360	0.056 906	0.056 456	0.056 008	0.055 564	13
14	0.052 366	0.051 916	0.051 468	0.051 024	0.050 583	0.050 145	14
15	0.047 666	0.047 221	0.046 780	0.046 342	0.045 908	0.045 477	15
16	0.043 573	0.043 135	0.042 701	0.042 270	0.041 843	0.041 419	16
17	0.039 982	0.039 551	0.039 123	0.038 699	0.038 279	0.037 863	17
18	0.036 808	0.036 383	0.035 963	0.035 546	0.035 134	0.034 725	18
19	0.033 985	0.033 568	0.033 154	0.032 745	0.032 340	0.031 939	19
20	0.031 461	0.031 050	0.030 644	0.030 243	0.029 845	0.029 452	20
21	0.029 192	0.028 789	0.028 390	0.027 996	0.027 606	0.027 221	21
22	0.027 145	0.026 748	0.026 357	0.025 971	0.025 589	0.025 212	22
23	0.025 289	0.024 900	0.024 516	0.024 137	0.023 763	0.023 394	23
24	0.023 600	0.023 219	0.022 842	0.022 471	0.022 105	0.021 743	24
25	0.022 059	0.021 685	0.021 316	0.020 952	0.020 594	0.020 241	25
26	0.020 649	0.020 282	0.019 920	0.019 564	0.019 214	0.018 868	26
27	0.019 354	0.018 994	0.018 640	0.018 292	0.017 949	0.017 611	27
28	0.018 163	0.017 810	0.017 463	0.017 123	0.016 787	0.016 457	28
29	0.017 063	0.016 718	0.016 379	0.016 046	0.015 718	0.015 396	29
30	0.016 047	0.015 709	0.015 377	0.015 051	0.014 731	0.014 417	30
31	0.015 106	0.014 776	0.014 451	0.014 132	0.013 819	0.013 513	31
32	0.014 233	0.013 909	0.013 592	0.013 280	0.012 975	0.012 676	32
33	0.013 421	0.013 105	0.012 794	0.012 490	0.012 192	0.011 900	33
34	0.012 666	0.012 356	0.012 052	0.011 755	0.011 465	0.011 180	34
35	0.011 961	0.011 658	0.011 362	0.011 072	0.010 788	0.010 511	35
36	0.011 303	0.011 007	0.010 717	0.010 434	0.010 158	0.009 888	36
37	0.010 688	0.010 398	0.010 116	0.009 840	0.009 570	0.009 307	37
38	0.010 112	0.009 829	0.009 553	0.009 284	0.009 022	0.008 765	38
39	0.009 573	0.009 296	0.009 027	0.008 765	0.008 509	0.008 259	39
40	0.009 066	0.008 797	0.008 534	0.008 278	0.008 029	0.007 786	40
41	0.008 591	0.008 328	0.008 072	0.007 822	0.007 580	0.007 344	41
42	0.008 145	0.007 888	0.007 638	0.007 395	0.007 159	0.006 929	42
43	0.007 724	0.007 474	0.007 230	0.006 993	0.006 763	0.006 540	43
44	0.007 329	0.007 084	0.006 847	0.006 616	0.006 393	0.006 176	44
45	0.006 956	0.006 718	0.006 486	0.006 262	0.006 044	0.005 833	45
46	0.006 605	0.006 372	0.006 147	0.005 928	0.005 717	0.005 512	46
47	0.006 273	0.006 046	0.005 827	0.005 614	0.005 409	0.005 210	47
48	0.005 960	0.005 739	0.005 525	0.005 318	0.005 119	0.004 925	48
49	0.005 664	0.005 449	0.005 241	0.005 040	0.004 845	0.004 658	49
50	0.005 385	0.005 175	0.004 972	0.004 777	0.004 588	0.004 406	50
51	0.005 120	0.004 916	0.004 719	0.004 529	0.004 345	0.004 169	51
52	0.004 870	0.004 671	0.004 479	0.004 294	0.004 117	0.003 945	52
53	0.004 633	0.004 440	0.004 253	0.004 073	0.003 901	0.003 734	53
54	0.004 409	0.004 220	0.004 039	0.003 864	0.003 697	0.003 536	54
55	0.004 196	0.004 013	0.003 836	0.003 667	0.003 504	0.003 348	55

YRS							
14	0.003 995	0.003 816	0.003 645	0.003 480	0.003 322	0.003 171	56
15	0.003 287	0.003 127	0.002 974	0.002 828	0.002 689	0.002 555	60
16	0.002 711	0.002 569	0.002 433	0.002 304	0.002 181	0.002 064	64
17	0.002 241	0.002 114	0.001 994	0.001 880	0.001 772	0.001 670	68
18	0.001 855	0.001 743	0.001 637	0.001 536	0.001 442	0.001 353	72
19	0.001 538	0.001 439	0.001 345	0.001 257	0.001 175	0.001 097	76
20	0.001 277	0.001 189	0.001 107	0.001 030	0.000 958	0.000 891	80
21	0.001 061	0.000 983	0.000 911	0.000 844	0.000 782	0.000 724	84
22	0.000 882	0.000 814	0.000 751	0.000 692	0.000 638	0.000 588	88
23	0.000 734	0.000 674	0.000 619	0.000 568	0.000 521	0.000 478	92
24	0.000 611	0.000 558	0.000 510	0.000 466	0.000 426	0.000 389	96
25	0.000 509	0.000 463	0.000 421	0.000 383	0.000 348	0.000 317	100
26	0.000 424	0.000 384	0.000 348	0.000 315	0.000 285	0.000 258	104
27	0.000 353	0.000 318	0.000 287	0.000 259	0.000 233	0.000 210	108
28	0.000 294	0.000 264	0.000 237	0.000 213	0.000 191	0.000 171	112
29	0.000 245	0.000 219	0.000 196	0.000 175	0.000 156	0.000 139	116
30	0.000 205	0.000 182	0.000 162	0.000 144	0.000 128	0.000 113	120

QTRS	21.50% ANNUAL RATE	22.00% ANNUAL RATE	22.50% ANNUAL RATE	23.00% ANNUAL RATE	23.50% ANNUAL RATE	24.00% ANNUAL RATE	QTRS
1	1.000 000	1.000 000	1.000 000	1.000 000	1.000 000	1.000 000	1
2	0.486 914	0.486 618	0.486 322	0.486 027	0.485 732	0.485 437	2
3	0.316 042	0.315 654	0.315 267	0.314 881	0.314 495	0.314 110	3
4	0.230 722	0.230 294	0.229 867	0.229 441	0.229 016	0.228 591	4
5	0.179 624	0.179 176	0.178 730	0.178 284	0.177 840	0.177 396	5
6	0.145 636	0.145 179	0.144 723	0.144 268	0.143 815	0.143 363	6
7	0.121 426	0.120 964	0.120 505	0.120 046	0.119 590	0.119 135	7
8	0.103 326	0.102 864	0.102 404	0.101 946	0.101 490	0.101 036	8
9	0.089 299	0.088 839	0.088 382	0.087 927	0.087 473	0.087 022	9
10	0.078 123	0.077 668	0.077 214	0.076 763	0.076 314	0.075 868	10
11	0.069 021	0.068 571	0.068 122	0.067 677	0.067 234	0.066 793	11
12	0.061 474	0.061 029	0.060 587	0.060 148	0.059 711	0.059 277	12
13	0.055 123	0.054 684	0.054 249	0.053 816	0.053 387	0.052 960	13
14	0.049 711	0.049 279	0.048 851	0.048 426	0.048 004	0.047 585	14
15	0.045 050	0.044 626	0.044 205	0.043 788	0.043 373	0.042 963	15
16	0.040 999	0.040 583	0.040 170	0.039 760	0.039 354	0.038 952	16
17	0.037 451	0.037 042	0.036 637	0.036 236	0.035 839	0.035 445	17
18	0.034 321	0.033 920	0.033 523	0.033 130	0.032 742	0.032 357	18
19	0.031 543	0.031 150	0.030 762	0.030 377	0.029 997	0.029 621	19
20	0.029 064	0.028 679	0.028 299	0.027 923	0.027 552	0.027 185	20
21	0.026 841	0.026 465	0.026 093	0.025 726	0.025 363	0.025 005	21
22	0.024 839	0.024 471	0.024 108	0.023 749	0.023 395	0.023 046	22
23	0.023 029	0.022 670	0.022 315	0.021 965	0.021 619	0.021 278	23
24	0.021 387	0.021 036	0.020 689	0.020 348	0.020 011	0.019 679	24
25	0.019 892	0.019 549	0.019 211	0.018 878	0.018 550	0.018 227	25
26	0.018 528	0.018 193	0.017 863	0.017 539	0.017 219	0.016 904	26
27	0.017 279	0.016 952	0.016 631	0.016 314	0.016 003	0.015 697	27
28	0.016 133	0.015 814	0.015 501	0.015 193	0.014 890	0.014 593	28
29	0.015 079	0.014 769	0.014 463	0.014 163	0.013 869	0.013 580	29
30	0.014 108	0.013 805	0.013 508	0.013 216	0.012 930	0.012 649	30
31	0.013 212	0.012 917	0.012 627	0.012 343	0.012 065	0.011 792	31
32	0.012 383	0.012 095	0.011 814	0.011 538	0.011 267	0.011 002	32
33	0.011 615	0.011 335	0.011 061	0.010 792	0.010 530	0.010 273	33
34	0.010 902	0.010 630	0.010 363	0.010 103	0.009 848	0.009 598	34
35	0.010 240	0.009 975	0.009 716	0.009 463	0.009 215	0.008 974	35
36	0.009 624	0.009 366	0.009 115	0.008 869	0.008 629	0.008 395	36
37	0.009 050	0.008 800	0.008 555	0.008 317	0.008 084	0.007 857	37
38	0.008 516	0.008 272	0.008 035	0.007 803	0.007 578	0.007 358	38
39	0.008 017	0.007 780	0.007 549	0.007 325	0.007 106	0.006 894	39
40	0.007 550	0.007 320	0.007 097	0.006 879	0.006 667	0.006 462	40
41	0.007 114	0.006 891	0.006 674	0.006 463	0.006 258	0.006 059	41
42	0.006 706	0.006 489	0.006 279	0.006 074	0.005 876	0.005 683	42
43	0.006 324	0.006 113	0.005 909	0.005 711	0.005 519	0.005 333	43
44	0.005 965	0.005 761	0.005 563	0.005 372	0.005 186	0.005 006	44
45	0.005 629	0.005 431	0.005 240	0.005 054	0.004 874	0.004 700	45
46	0.005 314	0.005 122	0.004 936	0.004 756	0.004 583	0.004 415	46
47	0.005 017	0.004 831	0.004 651	0.004 478	0.004 310	0.004 148	47
48	0.004 739	0.004 559	0.004 384	0.004 216	0.004 054	0.003 898	48
49	0.004 477	0.004 302	0.004 134	0.003 971	0.003 815	0.003 664	49
50	0.004 231	0.004 061	0.003 898	0.003 741	0.003 590	0.003 444	50
51	0.003 999	0.003 835	0.003 677	0.003 525	0.003 379	0.003 239	51
52	0.003 780	0.003 622	0.003 469	0.003 323	0.003 182	0.003 046	52
53	0.003 575	0.003 421	0.003 274	0.003 132	0.002 996	0.002 866	53
54	0.003 381	0.003 232	0.003 090	0.002 953	0.002 822	0.002 696	54
55	0.003 198	0.003 055	0.002 917	0.002 785	0.002 658	0.002 537	55
YRS							
14	0.003 026	0.002 887	0.002 754	0.002 626	0.002 504	0.002 388	56
15	0.002 428	0.002 307	0.002 191	0.002 081	0.001 976	0.001 876	60
16	0.001 953	0.001 847	0.001 747	0.001 652	0.001 562	0.001 476	64
17	0.001 573	0.001 482	0.001 395	0.001 313	0.001 236	0.001 163	68
18	0.001 269	0.001 190	0.001 115	0.001 045	0.000 980	0.000 918	72
19	0.001 025	0.000 956	0.000 893	0.000 833	0.000 777	0.000 725	76
20	0.000 828	0.000 769	0.000 715	0.000 664	0.000 617	0.000 573	80
21	0.000 670	0.000 619	0.000 573	0.000 530	0.000 490	0.000 453	84
22	0.000 542	0.000 499	0.000 459	0.000 423	0.000 389	0.000 358	88
23	0.000 439	0.000 402	0.000 368	0.000 338	0.000 309	0.000 283	92
24	0.000 355	0.000 324	0.000 296	0.000 270	0.000 246	0.000 224	96
25	0.000 288	0.000 261	0.000 237	0.000 215	0.000 195	0.000 177	100
26	0.000 233	0.000 211	0.000 190	0.000 172	0.000 155	0.000 140	104
27	0.000 189	0.000 170	0.000 153	0.000 138	0.000 124	0.000 111	108
28	0.000 153	0.000 137	0.000 123	0.000 110	0.000 098	0.000 088	112
29	0.000 124	0.000 111	0.000 099	0.000 088	0.000 078	0.000 070	116
30	0.000 101	0.000 089	0.000 079	0.000 070	0.000 062	0.000 055	120

HALF YRS	7.00% ANNUAL RATE	8.00% ANNUAL RATE	9.00% ANNUAL RATE	10.00% ANNUAL RATE	10.50% ANNUAL RATE	11.00% ANNUAL RATE	HALF YRS
1	1.000 000	1.000 000	1.000 000	1.000 000	1.000 000	1.000 000	1
2	0.491 400	0.490 196	0.488 998	0.487 805	0.487 211	0.486 618	2
3	0.321 934	0.320 349	0.318 773	0.317 209	0.316 430	0.315 654	3
4	0.237 251	0.235 490	0.233 744	0.232 012	0.231 151	0.230 294	4
5	0.186 481	0.184 627	0.182 792	0.180 975	0.180 073	0.179 176	5
6	0.152 668	0.150 762	0.148 878	0.147 017	0.146 095	0.145 179	6
7	0.128 544	0.126 610	0.124 701	0.122 820	0.121 889	0.120 964	7
8	0.110 477	0.108 528	0.106 610	0.104 722	0.103 789	0.102 864	8
9	0.096 446	0.094 493	0.092 574	0.090 690	0.089 761	0.088 839	9
10	0.085 241	0.083 291	0.081 379	0.079 505	0.078 582	0.077 668	10
11	0.076 092	0.074 149	0.072 248	0.070 389	0.069 475	0.068 571	11
12	0.068 484	0.066 552	0.064 666	0.062 825	0.061 922	0.061 029	12
13	0.062 062	0.060 144	0.058 275	0.056 456	0.055 564	0.054 684	13
14	0.056 571	0.054 669	0.052 820	0.051 024	0.050 145	0.049 279	14
15	0.051 825	0.049 941	0.048 114	0.046 342	0.045 477	0.044 626	15
16	0.047 685	0.045 820	0.044 015	0.042 270	0.041 419	0.040 583	16
17	0.044 043	0.042 199	0.040 418	0.038 699	0.037 863	0.037 042	17
18	0.040 817	0.038 993	0.037 237	0.035 546	0.034 725	0.033 920	18
19	0.037 940	0.036 139	0.034 407	0.032 745	0.031 939	0.031 150	19
20	0.035 361	0.033 582	0.031 876	0.030 243	0.029 452	0.028 679	20
21	0.033 037	0.031 280	0.029 601	0.027 996	0.027 221	0.026 465	21
22	0.030 932	0.029 199	0.027 546	0.025 971	0.025 212	0.024 471	22
23	0.029 019	0.027 309	0.025 682	0.024 137	0.023 394	0.022 670	23
24	0.027 273	0.025 587	0.023 987	0.022 471	0.021 743	0.021 036	24
25	0.025 674	0.024 012	0.022 439	0.020 952	0.020 241	0.019 549	25
26	0.024 205	0.022 567	0.021 021	0.019 564	0.018 868	0.018 193	26
27	0.022 852	0.021 239	0.019 719	0.018 292	0.017 611	0.016 952	27
28	0.021 603	0.020 013	0.018 521	0.017 123	0.016 457	0.015 814	28
29	0.020 445	0.018 880	0.017 415	0.016 046	0.015 396	0.014 769	29
30	0.019 371	0.017 830	0.016 392	0.015 051	0.014 417	0.013 805	30
31	0.018 372	0.016 855	0.015 443	0.014 132	0.013 513	0.012 917	31
32	0.017 442	0.015 949	0.014 563	0.013 280	0.012 676	0.012 095	32
33	0.016 572	0.015 104	0.013 745	0.012 490	0.011 900	0.011 335	33
34	0.015 760	0.014 315	0.012 982	0.011 755	0.011 180	0.010 630	34
35	0.014 998	0.013 577	0.012 270	0.011 072	0.010 511	0.009 975	35
36	0.014 284	0.012 887	0.011 606	0.010 434	0.009 888	0.009 366	36
37	0.013 613	0.012 240	0.010 984	0.009 840	0.009 307	0.008 800	37
38	0.012 982	0.011 632	0.010 402	0.009 284	0.008 765	0.008 272	38
39	0.012 388	0.011 061	0.009 856	0.008 765	0.008 259	0.007 780	39
40	0.011 827	0.010 523	0.009 343	0.008 278	0.007 786	0.007 320	40
41	0.011 298	0.010 017	0.008 862	0.007 822	0.007 344	0.006 891	41
42	0.010 798	0.009 540	0.008 409	0.007 395	0.006 929	0.006 489	42
43	0.010 325	0.009 090	0.007 982	0.006 993	0.006 540	0.006 113	43
44	0.009 878	0.008 665	0.007 581	0.006 616	0.006 176	0.005 761	44
45	0.009 453	0.008 262	0.007 202	0.006 262	0.005 833	0.005 431	45
46	0.009 051	0.007 882	0.006 845	0.005 928	0.005 512	0.005 122	46
47	0.008 669	0.007 522	0.006 507	0.005 614	0.005 210	0.004 831	47
48	0.008 306	0.007 181	0.006 189	0.005 318	0.004 925	0.004 559	48
49	0.007 962	0.006 857	0.005 887	0.005 040	0.004 658	0.004 302	49
50	0.007 634	0.006 550	0.005 602	0.004 777	0.004 406	0.004 061	50
51	0.007 322	0.006 259	0.005 332	0.004 529	0.004 169	0.003 835	51
52	0.007 024	0.005 982	0.005 077	0.004 294	0.003 945	0.003 622	52
53	0.006 741	0.005 719	0.004 835	0.004 073	0.003 734	0.003 421	53
54	0.006 471	0.005 469	0.004 605	0.003 864	0.003 536	0.003 232	54
55	0.006 213	0.005 231	0.004 388	0.003 667	0.003 348	0.003 055	55
56	0.005 967	0.005 005	0.004 181	0.003 480	0.003 171	0.002 887	56
57	0.005 732	0.004 789	0.003 985	0.003 303	0.003 004	0.002 729	57
58	0.005 508	0.004 584	0.003 799	0.003 136	0.002 846	0.002 580	58
59	0.005 294	0.004 388	0.003 622	0.002 978	0.002 697	0.002 440	59

YRS							
30	0.005 089	0.004 202	0.003 454	0.002 828	0.002 555	0.002 307	60
31	0.004 705	0.003 854	0.003 143	0.002 552	0.002 296	0.002 064	62
32	0.004 353	0.003 538	0.002 861	0.002 304	0.002 064	0.001 847	64
33	0.004 030	0.003 249	0.002 606	0.002 081	0.001 856	0.001 654	66
34	0.003 734	0.002 986	0.002 375	0.001 880	0.001 670	0.001 482	68
35	0.003 461	0.002 745	0.002 165	0.001 699	0.001 503	0.001 328	70
36	0.003 210	0.002 525	0.001 975	0.001 536	0.001 353	0.001 190	72
37	0.002 978	0.002 323	0.001 802	0.001 390	0.001 218	0.001 067	74
38	0.002 765	0.002 139	0.001 644	0.001 257	0.001 097	0.000 956	76
39	0.002 567	0.001 969	0.001 501	0.001 138	0.000 988	0.000 858	78
40	0.002 385	0.001 814	0.001 371	0.001 030	0.000 891	0.000 769	80

SINKING FUND FACTORS

SEMIANNUAL COMPOUNDING

HALF YRS	11.50% ANNUAL RATE	12.00% ANNUAL RATE	12.50% ANNUAL RATE	13.00% ANNUAL RATE	13.50% ANNUAL RATE	14.00% ANNUAL RATE	HALF YRS
1	1.000 000	1.000 000	1.000 000	1.000 000	1.000 000	1.000 000	1
2	0.486 027	0.485 437	0.484 848	0.484 262	0.483 676	0.483 092	2
3	0.314 881	0.314 110	0.313 341	0.312 576	0.311 812	0.311 052	3
4	0.229 441	0.228 591	0.227 745	0.226 903	0.226 064	0.225 228	4
5	0.178 284	0.177 396	0.176 513	0.175 635	0.174 760	0.173 891	5
6	0.144 268	0.143 363	0.142 463	0.141 568	0.140 679	0.139 796	6
7	0.120 046	0.119 135	0.118 230	0.117 331	0.116 439	0.115 553	7
8	0.101 946	0.101 036	0.100 133	0.099 237	0.098 349	0.097 468	8
9	0.087 927	0.087 022	0.086 126	0.085 238	0.084 358	0.083 486	9
10	0.076 763	0.075 868	0.074 982	0.074 105	0.073 237	0.072 378	10
11	0.067 677	0.066 793	0.065 919	0.065 055	0.064 201	0.063 357	11
12	0.060 148	0.059 277	0.058 417	0.057 568	0.056 730	0.055 902	12
13	0.053 816	0.052 960	0.052 116	0.051 283	0.050 461	0.049 651	13
14	0.048 426	0.047 585	0.046 757	0.045 940	0.045 137	0.044 345	14
15	0.043 788	0.042 963	0.042 151	0.041 353	0.040 567	0.039 795	15
16	0.039 760	0.038 952	0.038 158	0.037 378	0.036 611	0.035 858	16
17	0.036 236	0.035 445	0.034 668	0.033 906	0.033 159	0.032 425	17
18	0.033 130	0.032 357	0.031 598	0.030 855	0.030 126	0.029 413	18
19	0.030 377	0.029 621	0.028 880	0.028 156	0.027 447	0.026 753	19
20	0.027 923	0.027 185	0.026 462	0.025 756	0.025 067	0.024 393	20
21	0.025 726	0.025 005	0.024 300	0.023 613	0.022 943	0.022 289	21
22	0.023 749	0.023 046	0.022 360	0.021 691	0.021 040	0.020 406	22
23	0.021 965	0.021 278	0.020 611	0.019 961	0.019 329	0.018 714	23
24	0.020 348	0.019 679	0.019 029	0.018 398	0.017 784	0.017 189	24
25	0.018 878	0.018 227	0.017 595	0.016 981	0.016 387	0.015 811	25
26	0.017 539	0.016 904	0.016 290	0.015 695	0.015 119	0.014 561	26
27	0.016 314	0.015 697	0.015 100	0.014 523	0.013 965	0.013 426	27
28	0.015 193	0.014 593	0.014 013	0.013 453	0.012 913	0.012 392	28
29	0.014 163	0.013 580	0.013 017	0.012 474	0.011 952	0.011 449	29
30	0.013 216	0.012 649	0.012 103	0.011 577	0.011 072	0.010 586	30
31	0.012 343	0.011 792	0.011 263	0.010 754	0.010 266	0.009 797	31
32	0.011 538	0.011 002	0.010 489	0.009 997	0.009 525	0.009 073	32
33	0.010 792	0.010 273	0.009 775	0.009 299	0.008 844	0.008 408	33
34	0.010 103	0.009 598	0.009 117	0.008 656	0.008 216	0.007 797	34
35	0.009 463	0.008 974	0.008 507	0.008 062	0.007 638	0.007 234	35
36	0.008 869	0.008 395	0.007 943	0.007 513	0.007 104	0.006 715	36
37	0.008 317	0.007 857	0.007 421	0.007 005	0.006 611	0.006 237	37
38	0.007 803	0.007 358	0.006 936	0.006 535	0.006 155	0.005 795	38
39	0.007 325	0.006 894	0.006 485	0.006 099	0.005 733	0.005 387	39
40	0.006 879	0.006 462	0.006 067	0.005 694	0.005 342	0.005 009	40
41	0.006 463	0.006 059	0.005 677	0.005 318	0.004 979	0.004 660	41
42	0.006 074	0.005 683	0.005 315	0.004 968	0.004 642	0.004 336	42
43	0.005 711	0.005 333	0.004 978	0.004 644	0.004 330	0.004 036	43
44	0.005 372	0.005 006	0.004 663	0.004 341	0.004 040	0.003 758	44
45	0.005 054	0.004 700	0.004 369	0.004 060	0.003 770	0.003 500	45
46	0.004 756	0.004 415	0.004 096	0.003 797	0.003 519	0.003 260	46
47	0.004 478	0.004 148	0.003 840	0.003 553	0.003 286	0.003 037	47
48	0.004 216	0.003 898	0.003 601	0.003 325	0.003 069	0.002 831	48
49	0.003 971	0.003 664	0.003 378	0.003 112	0.002 866	0.002 639	49
50	0.003 741	0.003 444	0.003 169	0.002 914	0.002 678	0.002 460	50
51	0.003 525	0.003 239	0.002 974	0.002 729	0.002 502	0.002 294	51
52	0.003 323	0.003 046	0.002 791	0.002 556	0.002 339	0.002 139	52
53	0.003 132	0.002 866	0.002 620	0.002 394	0.002 186	0.001 995	53
54	0.002 953	0.002 696	0.002 460	0.002 243	0.002 044	0.001 861	54
55	0.002 785	0.002 537	0.002 310	0.002 101	0.001 911	0.001 736	55
56	0.002 626	0.002 388	0.002 169	0.001 969	0.001 787	0.001 620	56
57	0.002 477	0.002 247	0.002 037	0.001 846	0.001 671	0.001 512	57
58	0.002 337	0.002 116	0.001 914	0.001 730	0.001 563	0.001 411	58
59	0.002 205	0.001 992	0.001 798	0.001 622	0.001 462	0.001 317	59
YRS							
30	0.002 081	0.001 876	0.001 689	0.001 520	0.001 368	0.001 229	60
31	0.001 854	0.001 664	0.001 492	0.001 337	0.001 197	0.001 071	62
32	0.001 652	0.001 476	0.001 318	0.001 176	0.001 048	0.000 934	64
33	0.001 473	0.001 310	0.001 165	0.001 034	0.000 918	0.000 814	66
34	0.001 313	0.001 163	0.001 029	0.000 910	0.000 804	0.000 710	68
35	0.001 172	0.001 033	0.000 910	0.000 801	0.000 705	0.000 620	70
36	0.001 045	0.000 918	0.000 805	0.000 705	0.000 618	0.000 541	72
37	0.000 933	0.000 815	0.000 712	0.000 621	0.000 541	0.000 472	74
38	0.000 833	0.000 725	0.000 630	0.000 547	0.000 475	0.000 412	76
39	0.000 744	0.000 644	0.000 557	0.000 482	0.000 416	0.000 359	78
40	0.000 664	0.000 573	0.000 493	0.000 424	0.000 365	0.000 314	80

SINKING FUND FACTORS

HALF YRS	14.50% ANNUAL RATE	15.00% ANNUAL RATE	15.50% ANNUAL RATE	16.00% ANNUAL RATE	16.50% ANNUAL RATE	17.00% ANNUAL RATE	HALF YRS
1	1.000 000	1.000 000	1.000 000	1.000 000	1.000 000	1.000 000	1
2	0.482 509	0.481 928	0.481 348	0.480 769	0.480 192	0.479 616	2
3	0.310 293	0.309 538	0.308 784	0.308 034	0.307 285	0.306 539	3
4	0.224 396	0.223 568	0.222 742	0.221 921	0.221 103	0.220 288	4
5	0.173 025	0.172 165	0.171 308	0.170 456	0.169 609	0.168 766	5
6	0.138 918	0.138 045	0.137 177	0.136 315	0.135 459	0.134 607	6
7	0.114 674	0.113 800	0.112 933	0.112 072	0.111 218	0.110 369	7
8	0.096 594	0.095 727	0.094 867	0.094 015	0.093 169	0.092 331	8
9	0.082 623	0.081 767	0.080 919	0.080 080	0.079 248	0.078 424	9
10	0.071 527	0.070 686	0.069 853	0.069 029	0.068 214	0.067 408	10
11	0.062 522	0.061 697	0.060 882	0.060 076	0.059 280	0.058 493	11
12	0.055 085	0.054 278	0.053 481	0.052 695	0.051 919	0.051 153	12
13	0.048 852	0.048 064	0.047 288	0.046 522	0.045 767	0.045 023	13
14	0.043 565	0.042 797	0.042 041	0.041 297	0.040 564	0.039 842	14
15	0.039 035	0.038 287	0.037 552	0.036 830	0.036 119	0.035 420	15
16	0.035 118	0.034 391	0.033 678	0.032 977	0.032 289	0.031 614	16
17	0.031 706	0.031 000	0.030 308	0.029 629	0.028 964	0.028 312	17
18	0.028 714	0.028 029	0.027 359	0.026 702	0.026 059	0.025 430	18
19	0.026 074	0.025 411	0.024 762	0.024 128	0.023 507	0.022 901	19
20	0.023 735	0.023 092	0.022 465	0.021 852	0.021 254	0.020 671	20
21	0.021 651	0.021 029	0.020 423	0.019 832	0.019 256	0.018 695	21
22	0.019 788	0.019 187	0.018 602	0.018 032	0.017 478	0.016 939	22
23	0.018 116	0.017 535	0.016 971	0.016 422	0.015 889	0.015 372	23
24	0.016 611	0.016 050	0.015 506	0.014 978	0.014 466	0.013 970	24
25	0.015 252	0.014 711	0.014 186	0.013 679	0.013 187	0.012 712	25
26	0.014 021	0.013 500	0.012 995	0.012 507	0.012 036	0.011 580	26
27	0.012 905	0.012 402	0.011 917	0.011 448	0.010 996	0.010 560	27
28	0.011 890	0.011 405	0.010 938	0.010 489	0.010 056	0.009 639	28
29	0.010 964	0.010 498	0.010 050	0.009 619	0.009 204	0.008 806	29
30	0.010 120	0.009 671	0.009 241	0.008 827	0.008 431	0.008 051	30
31	0.009 347	0.008 916	0.008 503	0.008 107	0.007 728	0.007 365	31
32	0.008 640	0.008 226	0.007 830	0.007 451	0.007 089	0.006 742	32
33	0.007 992	0.007 594	0.007 214	0.006 852	0.006 506	0.006 176	33
34	0.007 396	0.007 015	0.006 651	0.006 304	0.005 974	0.005 660	34
35	0.006 849	0.006 483	0.006 135	0.005 803	0.005 488	0.005 189	35
36	0.006 346	0.005 994	0.005 661	0.005 345	0.005 045	0.004 760	36
37	0.005 882	0.005 545	0.005 226	0.004 924	0.004 639	0.004 368	37
38	0.005 454	0.005 132	0.004 827	0.004 539	0.004 267	0.004 010	38
39	0.005 060	0.004 751	0.004 460	0.004 185	0.003 926	0.003 682	39
40	0.004 696	0.004 400	0.004 122	0.003 860	0.003 614	0.003 382	40
41	0.004 359	0.004 077	0.003 811	0.003 561	0.003 327	0.003 107	41
42	0.004 048	0.003 778	0.003 524	0.003 287	0.003 064	0.002 856	42
43	0.003 760	0.003 502	0.003 260	0.003 034	0.002 823	0.002 625	43
44	0.003 494	0.003 247	0.003 017	0.002 802	0.002 601	0.002 414	44
45	0.003 247	0.003 011	0.002 792	0.002 587	0.002 397	0.002 220	45
46	0.003 018	0.002 794	0.002 584	0.002 390	0.002 209	0.002 042	46
47	0.002 806	0.002 592	0.002 393	0.002 208	0.002 037	0.001 878	47
48	0.002 610	0.002 405	0.002 216	0.002 040	0.001 878	0.001 728	48
49	0.002 428	0.002 232	0.002 052	0.001 886	0.001 732	0.001 590	49
50	0.002 258	0.002 072	0.001 901	0.001 743	0.001 597	0.001 463	50
51	0.002 101	0.001 924	0.001 761	0.001 611	0.001 473	0.001 347	51
52	0.001 955	0.001 787	0.001 632	0.001 490	0.001 359	0.001 240	52
53	0.001 820	0.001 659	0.001 512	0.001 377	0.001 254	0.001 141	53
54	0.001 694	0.001 541	0.001 401	0.001 274	0.001 157	0.001 051	54
55	0.001 577	0.001 432	0.001 299	0.001 178	0.001 068	0.000 968	55
56	0.001 468	0.001 330	0.001 204	0.001 090	0.000 985	0.000 891	56
57	0.001 367	0.001 236	0.001 116	0.001 008	0.000 910	0.000 821	57
58	0.001 273	0.001 148	0.001 035	0.000 932	0.000 840	0.000 756	58
59	0.001 186	0.001 067	0.000 959	0.000 862	0.000 775	0.000 696	59
YRS							
30	0.001 104	0.000 991	0.000 890	0.000 798	0.000 715	0.000 641	60
31	0.000 958	0.000 856	0.000 765	0.000 683	0.000 610	0.000 544	62
32	0.000 832	0.000 740	0.000 658	0.000 585	0.000 520	0.000 462	64
33	0.000 722	0.000 639	0.000 566	0.000 501	0.000 443	0.000 392	66
34	0.000 627	0.000 553	0.000 487	0.000 429	0.000 378	0.000 333	68
35	0.000 544	0.000 478	0.000 419	0.000 368	0.000 322	0.000 282	70
36	0.000 473	0.000 413	0.000 361	0.000 315	0.000 275	0.000 240	72
37	0.000 411	0.000 357	0.000 311	0.000 270	0.000 234	0.000 204	74
38	0.000 357	0.000 309	0.000 267	0.000 231	0.000 200	0.000 173	76
39	0.000 310	0.000 267	0.000 230	0.000 198	0.000 171	0.000 147	78
40	0.000 269	0.000 231	0.000 198	0.000 170	0.000 146	0.000 125	80

SINKING FUND FACTORS

HALF YRS	17.50% ANNUAL RATE	18.00% ANNUAL RATE	18.50% ANNUAL RATE	19.00% ANNUAL RATE	19.50% ANNUAL RATE	20.00% ANNUAL RATE	HALF YRS
1	1.000 000	1.000 000	1.000 000	1.000 000	1.000 000	1.000 000	1
2	0.479 042	0.478 469	0.477 897	0.477 327	0.476 758	0.476 190	2
3	0.305 796	0.305 055	0.304 316	0.303 580	0.302 846	0.302 115	3
4	0.219 477	0.218 669	0.217 864	0.217 063	0.216 265	0.215 471	4
5	0.167 927	0.167 092	0.166 262	0.165 436	0.164 615	0.163 797	5
6	0.133 761	0.132 920	0.132 084	0.131 253	0.130 428	0.129 607	6
7	0.109 527	0.108 691	0.107 860	0.107 036	0.106 218	0.105 405	7
8	0.091 499	0.090 674	0.089 857	0.089 046	0.088 241	0.087 444	8
9	0.077 607	0.076 799	0.075 998	0.075 205	0.074 419	0.073 641	9
10	0.066 610	0.065 820	0.065 039	0.064 266	0.063 502	0.062 745	10
11	0.057 715	0.056 947	0.056 187	0.055 437	0.054 696	0.053 963	11
12	0.050 397	0.049 651	0.048 914	0.048 188	0.047 471	0.046 763	12
13	0.044 289	0.043 567	0.042 854	0.042 152	0.041 460	0.040 779	13
14	0.039 132	0.038 433	0.037 745	0.037 068	0.036 402	0.035 746	14
15	0.034 734	0.034 059	0.033 396	0.032 744	0.032 103	0.031 474	15
16	0.030 951	0.030 300	0.029 661	0.029 035	0.028 420	0.027 817	16
17	0.027 673	0.027 046	0.026 432	0.025 831	0.025 241	0.024 664	17
18	0.024 815	0.024 212	0.023 623	0.023 046	0.022 482	0.021 930	18
19	0.022 309	0.021 730	0.021 165	0.020 613	0.020 074	0.019 547	19
20	0.020 102	0.019 546	0.019 005	0.018 477	0.017 962	0.017 460	20
21	0.018 149	0.017 617	0.017 098	0.016 594	0.016 102	0.015 624	21
22	0.016 415	0.015 905	0.015 409	0.014 928	0.014 460	0.014 005	22
23	0.014 870	0.014 382	0.013 909	0.013 449	0.013 004	0.012 572	23
24	0.013 489	0.013 023	0.012 571	0.012 134	0.011 710	0.011 300	24
25	0.012 251	0.011 806	0.011 376	0.010 959	0.010 557	0.010 168	25
26	0.011 140	0.010 715	0.010 305	0.009 909	0.009 527	0.009 159	26
27	0.010 140	0.009 735	0.009 345	0.008 969	0.008 606	0.008 258	27
28	0.009 238	0.008 852	0.008 481	0.008 124	0.007 781	0.007 451	28
29	0.008 423	0.008 056	0.007 703	0.007 364	0.007 040	0.006 728	29
30	0.007 686	0.007 336	0.007 001	0.006 681	0.006 373	0.006 079	30
31	0.007 018	0.006 686	0.006 368	0.006 064	0.005 774	0.005 496	31
32	0.006 412	0.006 096	0.005 795	0.005 507	0.005 233	0.004 972	32
33	0.005 861	0.005 562	0.005 276	0.005 004	0.004 746	0.004 499	33
34	0.005 361	0.005 077	0.004 806	0.004 549	0.004 305	0.004 074	34
35	0.004 905	0.004 636	0.004 380	0.004 138	0.003 908	0.003 690	35
36	0.004 490	0.004 235	0.003 993	0.003 764	0.003 548	0.003 343	36
37	0.004 112	0.003 870	0.003 642	0.003 426	0.003 222	0.003 030	37
38	0.003 767	0.003 538	0.003 322	0.003 119	0.002 927	0.002 747	38
39	0.003 452	0.003 236	0.003 032	0.002 840	0.002 660	0.002 491	39
40	0.003 164	0.002 960	0.002 767	0.002 587	0.002 418	0.002 259	40
41	0.002 901	0.002 708	0.002 527	0.002 357	0.002 198	0.002 050	41
42	0.002 661	0.002 478	0.002 308	0.002 148	0.001 999	0.001 860	42
43	0.002 441	0.002 268	0.002 108	0.001 958	0.001 818	0.001 688	43
44	0.002 239	0.002 077	0.001 926	0.001 785	0.001 654	0.001 532	44
45	0.002 055	0.001 902	0.001 759	0.001 627	0.001 505	0.001 391	45
46	0.001 886	0.001 742	0.001 608	0.001 484	0.001 369	0.001 263	46
47	0.001 731	0.001 595	0.001 470	0.001 353	0.001 246	0.001 147	47
48	0.001 589	0.001 461	0.001 343	0.001 234	0.001 134	0.001 041	48
49	0.001 459	0.001 339	0.001 228	0.001 126	0.001 032	0.000 946	49
50	0.001 340	0.001 227	0.001 123	0.001 027	0.000 940	0.000 859	50
51	0.001 231	0.001 124	0.001 027	0.000 937	0.000 855	0.000 780	51
52	0.001 130	0.001 030	0.000 939	0.000 855	0.000 779	0.000 709	52
53	0.001 038	0.000 944	0.000 859	0.000 780	0.000 709	0.000 644	53
54	0.000 954	0.000 866	0.000 785	0.000 712	0.000 646	0.000 585	54
55	0.000 876	0.000 794	0.000 718	0.000 650	0.000 588	0.000 532	55
56	0.000 805	0.000 728	0.000 657	0.000 593	0.000 535	0.000 483	56
57	0.000 740	0.000 667	0.000 601	0.000 541	0.000 488	0.000 439	57
58	0.000 680	0.000 612	0.000 550	0.000 494	0.000 444	0.000 399	58
59	0.000 625	0.000 561	0.000 503	0.000 451	0.000 405	0.000 363	59

YRS

							YRS
30	0.000 574	0.000 514	0.000 460	0.000 412	0.000 368	0.000 330	60
31	0.000 485	0.000 432	0.000 385	0.000 343	0.000 306	0.000 272	62
32	0.000 410	0.000 364	0.000 323	0.000 286	0.000 254	0.000 225	64
33	0.000 346	0.000 306	0.000 270	0.000 238	0.000 210	0.000 186	66
34	0.000 293	0.000 257	0.000 226	0.000 199	0.000 175	0.000 153	68
35	0.000 247	0.000 216	0.000 189	0.000 166	0.000 145	0.000 127	70
36	0.000 209	0.000 182	0.000 159	0.000 138	0.000 120	0.000 105	72
37	0.000 177	0.000 153	0.000 133	0.000 115	0.000 100	0.000 087	74
38	0.000 149	0.000 129	0.000 111	0.000 096	0.000 083	0.000 072	76
39	0.000 126	0.000 109	0.000 093	0.000 080	0.000 069	0.000 059	78
40	0.000 107	0.000 091	0.000 078	0.000 067	0.000 057	0.000 049	80

YRS	7.00% ANNUAL RATE	8.00% ANNUAL RATE	9.00% ANNUAL RATE	10.00% ANNUAL RATE	10.25% ANNUAL RATE	10.50% ANNUAL RATE	YRS
1	1.000 000	1.000 000	1.000 000	1.000 000	1.000 000	1.000 000	1
2	0.483 092	0.480 769	0.478 469	0.476 190	0.475 624	0.475 059	2
3	0.311 052	0.308 034	0.305 055	0.302 115	0.301 386	0.300 659	3
4	0.225 228	0.221 921	0.218 669	0.215 471	0.214 680	0.213 892	4
5	0.173 891	0.170 456	0.167 092	0.163 797	0.162 984	0.162 175	5
6	0.139 796	0.136 315	0.132 920	0.129 607	0.128 792	0.127 982	6
7	0.115 553	0.112 072	0.108 691	0.105 405	0.104 599	0.103 799	7
8	0.097 468	0.094 015	0.090 674	0.087 444	0.086 653	0.085 869	8
9	0.083 486	0.080 080	0.076 799	0.073 641	0.072 870	0.072 106	9
10	0.072 378	0.069 029	0.065 820	0.062 745	0.061 997	0.061 257	10
11	0.063 357	0.060 076	0.056 947	0.053 963	0.053 240	0.052 525	11
12	0.055 902	0.052 695	0.049 651	0.046 763	0.046 065	0.045 377	12
13	0.049 651	0.046 522	0.043 567	0.040 779	0.040 107	0.039 445	13
14	0.044 345	0.041 297	0.038 433	0.035 746	0.035 101	0.034 467	14
15	0.039 795	0.036 830	0.034 059	0.031 474	0.030 855	0.030 248	15
16	0.035 858	0.032 977	0.030 300	0.027 817	0.027 225	0.026 644	16
17	0.032 425	0.029 629	0.027 046	0.024 664	0.024 099	0.023 545	17
18	0.029 413	0.026 702	0.024 212	0.021 930	0.021 391	0.020 863	18
19	0.026 753	0.024 128	0.021 730	0.019 547	0.019 033	0.018 531	19
20	0.024 393	0.021 852	0.019 546	0.017 460	0.016 970	0.016 493	20
21	0.022 289	0.019 832	0.017 617	0.015 624	0.015 159	0.014 707	21
22	0.020 406	0.018 032	0.015 905	0.014 005	0.013 563	0.013 134	22
23	0.018 714	0.016 422	0.014 382	0.012 572	0.012 153	0.011 747	23
24	0.017 189	0.014 978	0.013 023	0.011 300	0.010 903	0.010 519	24
25	0.015 811	0.013 679	0.011 806	0.010 168	0.009 792	0.009 429	25
26	0.014 561	0.012 507	0.010 715	0.009 159	0.008 804	0.008 461	26
27	0.013 426	0.011 448	0.009 735	0.008 258	0.007 922	0.007 599	27
28	0.012 392	0.010 489	0.008 852	0.007 451	0.007 134	0.006 830	28
29	0.011 449	0.009 619	0.008 056	0.006 728	0.006 429	0.006 143	29
30	0.010 586	0.008 827	0.007 336	0.006 079	0.005 798	0.005 528	30
31	0.009 797	0.008 107	0.006 686	0.005 496	0.005 231	0.004 978	31
32	0.009 073	0.007 451	0.006 096	0.004 972	0.004 722	0.004 485	32
33	0.008 408	0.006 852	0.005 562	0.004 499	0.004 265	0.004 042	33
34	0.007 797	0.006 304	0.005 077	0.004 074	0.003 854	0.003 645	34
35	0.007 234	0.005 803	0.004 636	0.003 690	0.003 483	0.003 288	35
36	0.006 715	0.005 345	0.004 235	0.003 343	0.003 149	0.002 967	36
37	0.006 237	0.004 924	0.003 870	0.003 030	0.002 849	0.002 677	37
38	0.005 795	0.004 539	0.003 538	0.002 747	0.002 577	0.002 417	38
39	0.005 387	0.004 185	0.003 236	0.002 491	0.002 332	0.002 183	39
40	0.005 009	0.003 860	0.002 960	0.002 259	0.002 111	0.001 971	40
41	0.004 660	0.003 561	0.002 708	0.002 050	0.001 911	0.001 781	41
42	0.004 336	0.003 287	0.002 478	0.001 860	0.001 730	0.001 609	42
43	0.004 036	0.003 034	0.002 268	0.001 688	0.001 567	0.001 454	43
44	0.003 758	0.002 802	0.002 077	0.001 532	0.001 419	0.001 314	44
45	0.003 500	0.002 587	0.001 902	0.001 391	0.001 286	0.001 188	45
46	0.003 260	0.002 390	0.001 742	0.001 263	0.001 165	0.001 074	46
47	0.003 037	0.002 208	0.001 595	0.001 147	0.001 055	0.000 971	47
48	0.002 831	0.002 040	0.001 461	0.001 041	0.000 956	0.000 878	48
49	0.002 639	0.001 886	0.001 339	0.000 946	0.000 867	0.000 794	49
50	0.002 460	0.001 743	0.001 227	0.000 859	0.000 785	0.000 718	50

YRS	10.75% ANNUAL RATE	11.00% ANNUAL RATE	11.25% ANNUAL RATE	11.50% ANNUAL RATE	11.75% ANNUAL RATE	12.00% ANNUAL RATE	YRS
1	1.000 000	1.000 000	1.000 000	1.000 000	1.000 000	1.000 000	1
2	0.474 496	0.473 934	0.473 373	0.472 813	0.472 255	0.471 698	2
3	0.299 935	0.299 213	0.298 494	0.297 776	0.297 062	0.296 349	3
4	0.213 108	0.212 326	0.211 548	0.210 774	0.210 003	0.209 234	4
5	0.161 371	0.160 570	0.159 774	0.158 982	0.158 194	0.157 410	5
6	0.127 177	0.126 377	0.125 581	0.124 791	0.124 006	0.123 226	6
7	0.103 004	0.102 215	0.101 432	0.100 655	0.099 884	0.099 118	7
8	0.085 092	0.084 321	0.083 557	0.082 799	0.082 048	0.081 303	8
9	0.071 350	0.070 602	0.069 860	0.069 126	0.068 399	0.067 679	9
10	0.060 525	0.059 801	0.059 085	0.058 377	0.057 677	0.056 984	10
11	0.051 819	0.051 121	0.050 432	0.049 751	0.049 079	0.048 415	11
12	0.044 697	0.044 027	0.043 366	0.042 714	0.042 071	0.041 437	12
13	0.038 793	0.038 151	0.037 518	0.036 895	0.036 282	0.035 677	13
14	0.033 842	0.033 228	0.032 624	0.032 030	0.031 446	0.030 871	14
15	0.029 651	0.029 065	0.028 490	0.027 924	0.027 369	0.026 824	15
16	0.026 075	0.025 517	0.024 969	0.024 432	0.023 906	0.023 390	16
17	0.023 003	0.022 471	0.021 952	0.021 443	0.020 944	0.020 457	17
18	0.020 347	0.019 843	0.019 350	0.018 868	0.018 397	0.017 937	18
19	0.018 041	0.017 563	0.017 096	0.016 641	0.016 196	0.015 763	19
20	0.016 028	0.015 576	0.015 134	0.014 705	0.014 286	0.013 879	20
21	0.014 266	0.013 838	0.013 421	0.013 016	0.012 623	0.012 240	21
22	0.012 718	0.012 313	0.011 920	0.011 539	0.011 169	0.010 811	22
23	0.011 353	0.010 971	0.010 601	0.010 243	0.009 896	0.009 560	23
24	0.010 147	0.009 787	0.009 439	0.009 103	0.008 778	0.008 463	24
25	0.009 079	0.008 740	0.008 413	0.008 098	0.007 794	0.007 500	25
26	0.008 131	0.007 813	0.007 506	0.007 210	0.006 926	0.006 652	26
27	0.007 288	0.006 989	0.006 702	0.006 425	0.006 159	0.005 904	27
28	0.006 538	0.006 257	0.005 988	0.005 730	0.005 482	0.005 244	28
29	0.005 868	0.005 605	0.005 354	0.005 112	0.004 881	0.004 660	29
30	0.005 271	0.005 025	0.004 789	0.004 564	0.004 349	0.004 144	30
31	0.004 737	0.004 506	0.004 286	0.004 077	0.003 877	0.003 686	31
32	0.004 259	0.004 043	0.003 838	0.003 643	0.003 457	0.003 280	32
33	0.003 831	0.003 629	0.003 438	0.003 257	0.003 084	0.002 920	33
34	0.003 447	0.003 259	0.003 081	0.002 912	0.002 752	0.002 601	34
35	0.003 103	0.002 927	0.002 762	0.002 605	0.002 457	0.002 317	35
36	0.002 794	0.002 630	0.002 476	0.002 331	0.002 194	0.002 064	36
37	0.002 516	0.002 364	0.002 221	0.002 086	0.001 959	0.001 840	37
38	0.002 267	0.002 125	0.001 992	0.001 867	0.001 750	0.001 640	38
39	0.002 043	0.001 911	0.001 788	0.001 672	0.001 564	0.001 462	39
40	0.001 841	0.001 719	0.001 604	0.001 497	0.001 397	0.001 304	40
41	0.001 659	0.001 546	0.001 440	0.001 341	0.001 249	0.001 163	41
42	0.001 496	0.001 391	0.001 293	0.001 201	0.001 116	0.001 037	42
43	0.001 349	0.001 251	0.001 161	0.001 076	0.000 998	0.000 925	43
44	0.001 217	0.001 126	0.001 042	0.000 964	0.000 892	0.000 825	44
45	0.001 097	0.001 014	0.000 936	0.000 864	0.000 798	0.000 736	45
46	0.000 990	0.000 912	0.000 841	0.000 774	0.000 713	0.000 657	46
47	0.000 893	0.000 821	0.000 755	0.000 694	0.000 638	0.000 586	47
48	0.000 806	0.000 739	0.000 678	0.000 622	0.000 571	0.000 523	48
49	0.000 727	0.000 666	0.000 609	0.000 558	0.000 510	0.000 467	49
50	0.000 656	0.000 599	0.000 547	0.000 500	0.000 456	0.000 417	50

SINKING FUND FACTORS

YRS	12.25% ANNUAL RATE	12.50% ANNUAL RATE	12.75% ANNUAL RATE	13.00% ANNUAL RATE	13.25% ANNUAL RATE	13.50% ANNUAL RATE	YRS
1	1.000 000	1.000 000	1.000 000	1.000 000	1.000 000	1.000 000	1
2	0.471 143	0.470 588	0.470 035	0.469 484	0.468 933	0.468 384	2
3	0.295 639	0.294 931	0.294 225	0.293 522	0.292 821	0.292 122	3
4	0.208 470	0.207 708	0.206 949	0.206 194	0.205 442	0.204 693	4
5	0.156 630	0.155 854	0.155 082	0.154 315	0.153 551	0.152 791	5
6	0.122 450	0.121 680	0.120 914	0.120 153	0.119 397	0.118 646	6
7	0.098 358	0.097 603	0.096 854	0.096 111	0.095 373	0.094 641	7
8	0.080 564	0.079 832	0.079 106	0.078 387	0.077 673	0.076 966	8
9	0.066 966	0.066 260	0.065 561	0.064 869	0.064 184	0.063 505	9
10	0.056 299	0.055 622	0.054 952	0.054 290	0.053 635	0.052 987	10
11	0.047 760	0.047 112	0.046 473	0.045 841	0.045 218	0.044 602	11
12	0.040 811	0.040 194	0.039 586	0.038 986	0.038 395	0.037 811	12
13	0.035 082	0.034 496	0.033 919	0.033 350	0.032 791	0.032 240	13
14	0.030 306	0.029 751	0.029 204	0.028 667	0.028 140	0.027 621	14
15	0.026 289	0.025 764	0.025 248	0.024 742	0.024 245	0.023 757	15
16	0.022 884	0.022 388	0.021 902	0.021 426	0.020 960	0.020 502	16
17	0.019 979	0.019 512	0.019 056	0.018 608	0.018 171	0.017 743	17
18	0.017 488	0.017 049	0.016 620	0.016 201	0.015 792	0.015 392	18
19	0.015 340	0.014 928	0.014 526	0.014 134	0.013 752	0.013 380	19
20	0.013 482	0.013 096	0.012 720	0.012 354	0.011 998	0.011 651	20
21	0.011 868	0.011 507	0.011 156	0.010 814	0.010 483	0.010 161	21
22	0.010 462	0.010 125	0.009 797	0.009 479	0.009 172	0.008 873	22
23	0.009 235	0.008 919	0.008 614	0.008 319	0.008 033	0.007 757	23
24	0.008 160	0.007 866	0.007 582	0.007 308	0.007 044	0.006 788	24
25	0.007 217	0.006 943	0.006 680	0.006 426	0.006 181	0.005 945	25
26	0.006 388	0.006 134	0.005 890	0.005 655	0.005 428	0.005 211	26
27	0.005 659	0.005 423	0.005 197	0.004 979	0.004 770	0.004 570	27
28	0.005 016	0.004 797	0.004 588	0.004 387	0.004 195	0.004 010	28
29	0.004 449	0.004 246	0.004 052	0.003 867	0.003 690	0.003 521	29
30	0.003 947	0.003 760	0.003 581	0.003 411	0.003 248	0.003 092	30
31	0.003 504	0.003 331	0.003 166	0.003 009	0.002 860	0.002 717	31
32	0.003 112	0.002 952	0.002 800	0.002 656	0.002 519	0.002 388	32
33	0.002 765	0.002 617	0.002 478	0.002 345	0.002 219	0.002 100	33
34	0.002 457	0.002 321	0.002 193	0.002 071	0.001 956	0.001 847	34
35	0.002 184	0.002 059	0.001 941	0.001 829	0.001 724	0.001 624	35
36	0.001 942	0.001 827	0.001 718	0.001 616	0.001 520	0.001 429	36
37	0.001 727	0.001 621	0.001 522	0.001 428	0.001 340	0.001 258	37
38	0.001 536	0.001 439	0.001 348	0.001 262	0.001 182	0.001 107	38
39	0.001 367	0.001 278	0.001 194	0.001 116	0.001 043	0.000 974	39
40	0.001 216	0.001 134	0.001 058	0.000 986	0.000 920	0.000 858	40
41	0.001 082	0.001 007	0.000 937	0.000 872	0.000 812	0.000 755	41
42	0.000 963	0.000 895	0.000 831	0.000 771	0.000 716	0.000 665	42
43	0.000 857	0.000 795	0.000 736	0.000 682	0.000 632	0.000 585	43
44	0.000 763	0.000 706	0.000 653	0.000 603	0.000 558	0.000 515	44
45	0.000 679	0.000 627	0.000 578	0.000 534	0.000 492	0.000 454	45
46	0.000 605	0.000 557	0.000 513	0.000 472	0.000 434	0.000 400	46
47	0.000 539	0.000 495	0.000 455	0.000 417	0.000 383	0.000 352	47
48	0.000 480	0.000 440	0.000 403	0.000 369	0.000 338	0.000 310	48
49	0.000 427	0.000 391	0.000 357	0.000 327	0.000 299	0.000 273	49
50	0.000 380	0.000 347	0.000 317	0.000 289	0.000 264	0.000 241	50

SINKING FUND FACTORS

YRS	13.75% ANNUAL RATE	14.00% ANNUAL RATE	14.25% ANNUAL RATE	14.50% ANNUAL RATE	14.75% ANNUAL RATE	15.00% ANNUAL RATE	YRS
1	1.000 000	1.000 000	1.000 000	1.000 000	1.000 000	1.000 000	1
2	0.467 836	0.467 290	0.466 744	0.466 200	0.465 658	0.465 116	2
3	0.291 426	0.290 731	0.290 039	0.289 350	0.288 662	0.287 977	3
4	0.203 947	0.203 205	0.202 465	0.201 729	0.200 996	0.200 265	4
5	0.152 035	0.151 284	0.150 536	0.149 792	0.149 052	0.148 316	5
6	0.117 899	0.117 157	0.116 420	0.115 688	0.114 960	0.114 237	6
7	0.093 914	0.093 192	0.092 476	0.091 766	0.091 060	0.090 360	7
8	0.076 265	0.075 570	0.074 881	0.074 198	0.073 521	0.072 850	8
9	0.062 833	0.062 168	0.061 510	0.060 858	0.060 213	0.059 574	9
10	0.052 347	0.051 714	0.051 088	0.050 469	0.049 857	0.049 252	10
11	0.043 994	0.043 394	0.042 802	0.042 217	0.041 639	0.041 069	11
12	0.037 236	0.036 669	0.036 110	0.035 559	0.035 016	0.034 481	12
13	0.031 698	0.031 164	0.030 638	0.030 121	0.029 612	0.029 110	13
14	0.027 111	0.026 609	0.026 116	0.025 632	0.025 156	0.024 688	14
15	0.023 279	0.022 809	0.022 348	0.021 896	0.021 452	0.021 017	15
16	0.020 054	0.019 615	0.019 185	0.018 764	0.018 352	0.017 948	16
17	0.017 325	0.016 915	0.016 515	0.016 124	0.015 741	0.015 367	17
18	0.015 002	0.014 621	0.014 249	0.013 886	0.013 532	0.013 186	18
19	0.013 017	0.012 663	0.012 318	0.011 982	0.011 655	0.011 336	19
20	0.011 314	0.010 986	0.010 667	0.010 357	0.010 055	0.009 761	20
21	0.009 848	0.009 545	0.009 250	0.008 964	0.008 686	0.008 417	21
22	0.008 584	0.008 303	0.008 031	0.007 768	0.007 513	0.007 266	22
23	0.007 490	0.007 231	0.006 981	0.006 739	0.006 505	0.006 278	23
24	0.006 541	0.006 303	0.006 073	0.005 851	0.005 637	0.005 430	24
25	0.005 718	0.005 498	0.005 287	0.005 084	0.004 888	0.004 699	25
26	0.005 001	0.004 800	0.004 606	0.004 420	0.004 242	0.004 070	26
27	0.004 377	0.004 193	0.004 016	0.003 846	0.003 683	0.003 526	27
28	0.003 834	0.003 664	0.003 503	0.003 348	0.003 199	0.003 057	28
29	0.003 359	0.003 204	0.003 056	0.002 915	0.002 780	0.002 651	29
30	0.002 944	0.002 803	0.002 668	0.002 539	0.002 417	0.002 300	30
31	0.002 582	0.002 453	0.002 330	0.002 213	0.002 102	0.001 996	31
32	0.002 264	0.002 147	0.002 035	0.001 929	0.001 828	0.001 733	32
33	0.001 987	0.001 880	0.001 778	0.001 682	0.001 591	0.001 505	33
34	0.001 744	0.001 646	0.001 554	0.001 467	0.001 384	0.001 307	34
35	0.001 530	0.001 442	0.001 358	0.001 279	0.001 205	0.001 135	35
36	0.001 344	0.001 263	0.001 187	0.001 116	0.001 049	0.000 986	36
37	0.001 180	0.001 107	0.001 038	0.000 974	0.000 913	0.000 857	37
38	0.001 036	0.000 970	0.000 908	0.000 850	0.000 795	0.000 744	38
39	0.000 910	0.000 850	0.000 794	0.000 742	0.000 693	0.000 647	39
40	0.000 799	0.000 745	0.000 695	0.000 647	0.000 603	0.000 562	40
41	0.000 702	0.000 653	0.000 608	0.000 565	0.000 525	0.000 489	41
42	0.000 617	0.000 573	0.000 531	0.000 493	0.000 458	0.000 425	42
43	0.000 542	0.000 502	0.000 465	0.000 431	0.000 399	0.000 369	43
44	0.000 476	0.000 440	0.000 407	0.000 376	0.000 347	0.000 321	44
45	0.000 419	0.000 386	0.000 356	0.000 328	0.000 303	0.000 279	45
46	0.000 368	0.000 338	0.000 311	0.000 287	0.000 264	0.000 242	46
47	0.000 323	0.000 297	0.000 273	0.000 250	0.000 230	0.000 211	47
48	0.000 284	0.000 260	0.000 238	0.000 218	0.000 200	0.000 183	48
49	0.000 250	0.000 228	0.000 209	0.000 191	0.000 174	0.000 159	49
50	0.000 219	0.000 200	0.000 183	0.000 167	0.000 152	0.000 139	50

SINKING FUND FACTORS

YRS	15.25% ANNUAL RATE	15.50% ANNUAL RATE	15.75% ANNUAL RATE	16.00% ANNUAL RATE	16.25% ANNUAL RATE	16.50% ANNUAL RATE	YRS
1	1.000 000	1.000 000	1.000 000	1.000 000	1.000 000	1.000 000	1
2	0.464 576	0.464 037	0.463 499	0.462 963	0.462 428	0.461 894	2
3	0.287 294	0.286 613	0.285 934	0.285 258	0.284 584	0.283 911	3
4	0.199 538	0.198 814	0.198 093	0.197 375	0.196 660	0.195 948	4
5	0.147 583	0.146 855	0.146 130	0.145 409	0.144 692	0.143 979	5
6	0.113 518	0.112 804	0.112 095	0.111 390	0.110 689	0.109 993	6
7	0.089 666	0.088 976	0.088 292	0.087 613	0.086 939	0.086 270	7
8	0.072 185	0.071 526	0.070 872	0.070 224	0.069 582	0.068 946	8
9	0.058 942	0.058 316	0.057 696	0.057 082	0.056 475	0.055 874	9
10	0.048 654	0.048 063	0.047 479	0.046 901	0.046 330	0.045 766	10
11	0.040 506	0.039 951	0.039 402	0.038 861	0.038 326	0.037 799	11
12	0.033 953	0.033 433	0.032 920	0.032 415	0.031 917	0.031 426	12
13	0.028 617	0.028 132	0.027 654	0.027 184	0.026 722	0.026 266	13
14	0.024 229	0.023 777	0.023 334	0.022 898	0.022 470	0.022 049	14
15	0.020 590	0.020 171	0.019 760	0.019 358	0.018 962	0.018 575	15
16	0.017 552	0.017 165	0.016 785	0.016 414	0.016 050	0.015 694	16
17	0.015 001	0.014 643	0.014 294	0.013 952	0.013 618	0.013 292	17
18	0.012 849	0.012 520	0.012 198	0.011 885	0.011 579	0.011 281	18
19	0.011 026	0.010 723	0.010 429	0.010 142	0.009 862	0.009 590	19
20	0.009 476	0.009 199	0.008 929	0.008 667	0.008 412	0.008 165	20
21	0.008 155	0.007 901	0.007 655	0.007 416	0.007 184	0.006 960	21
22	0.007 026	0.006 795	0.006 570	0.006 353	0.006 142	0.005 938	22
23	0.006 060	0.005 848	0.005 644	0.005 447	0.005 256	0.005 071	23
24	0.005 230	0.005 038	0.004 852	0.004 673	0.004 501	0.004 334	24
25	0.004 518	0.004 343	0.004 175	0.004 013	0.003 857	0.003 707	25
26	0.003 905	0.003 746	0.003 594	0.003 447	0.003 307	0.003 172	26
27	0.003 377	0.003 233	0.003 095	0.002 963	0.002 836	0.002 715	27
28	0.002 921	0.002 791	0.002 667	0.002 548	0.002 434	0.002 325	28
29	0.002 528	0.002 411	0.002 299	0.002 192	0.002 089	0.001 992	29
30	0.002 189	0.002 083	0.001 982	0.001 886	0.001 794	0.001 707	30
31	0.001 896	0.001 800	0.001 709	0.001 623	0.001 541	0.001 463	31
32	0.001 642	0.001 556	0.001 475	0.001 397	0.001 324	0.001 254	32
33	0.001 423	0.001 345	0.001 272	0.001 203	0.001 137	0.001 075	33
34	0.001 233	0.001 164	0.001 098	0.001 036	0.000 977	0.000 922	34
35	0.001 069	0.001 006	0.000 948	0.000 892	0.000 840	0.000 791	35
36	0.000 926	0.000 871	0.000 818	0.000 769	0.000 722	0.000 678	36
37	0.000 803	0.000 753	0.000 706	0.000 662	0.000 621	0.000 582	37
38	0.000 696	0.000 652	0.000 610	0.000 571	0.000 534	0.000 499	38
39	0.000 604	0.000 564	0.000 527	0.000 492	0.000 459	0.000 428	39
40	0.000 524	0.000 488	0.000 455	0.000 424	0.000 395	0.000 368	40
41	0.000 454	0.000 422	0.000 393	0.000 365	0.000 339	0.000 315	41
42	0.000 394	0.000 366	0.000 339	0.000 315	0.000 292	0.000 271	42
43	0.000 342	0.000 316	0.000 293	0.000 271	0.000 251	0.000 232	43
44	0.000 296	0.000 274	0.000 253	0.000 234	0.000 216	0.000 199	44
45	0.000 257	0.000 237	0.000 218	0.000 201	0.000 186	0.000 171	45
46	0.000 223	0.000 205	0.000 189	0.000 174	0.000 160	0.000 147	46
47	0.000 194	0.000 178	0.000 163	0.000 150	0.000 137	0.000 126	47
48	0.000 168	0.000 154	0.000 141	0.000 129	0.000 118	0.000 108	48
49	0.000 146	0.000 133	0.000 122	0.000 111	0.000 102	0.000 093	49
50	0.000 126	0.000 115	0.000 105	0.000 096	0.000 087	0.000 080	50

SINKING FUND FACTORS

ANNUAL COMPOUNDING

YRS	16.75% ANNUAL RATE	17.00% ANNUAL RATE	17.25% ANNUAL RATE	17.50% ANNUAL RATE	17.75% ANNUAL RATE	18.00% ANNUAL RATE	YRS
1	1.000 000	1.000 000	1.000 000	1.000 000	1.000 000	1.000 000	1
2	0.461 361	0.460 829	0.460 299	0.459 770	0.459 242	0.458 716	2
3	0.283 241	0.282 574	0.281 908	0.281 245	0.280 583	0.279 924	3
4	0.195 239	0.194 533	0.193 830	0.193 130	0.192 433	0.191 739	4
5	0.143 270	0.142 564	0.141 862	0.141 163	0.140 469	0.139 778	5
6	0.109 302	0.108 615	0.107 932	0.107 254	0.106 580	0.105 910	6
7	0.085 606	0.084 947	0.084 293	0.083 645	0.083 001	0.082 362	7
8	0.068 315	0.067 690	0.067 070	0.066 456	0.065 848	0.065 244	8
9	0.055 279	0.054 691	0.054 108	0.053 531	0.052 960	0.052 395	9
10	0.045 208	0.044 657	0.044 112	0.043 573	0.043 041	0.042 515	10
11	0.037 279	0.036 765	0.036 258	0.035 757	0.035 264	0.034 776	11
12	0.030 942	0.030 466	0.029 996	0.029 533	0.029 077	0.028 628	12
13	0.025 819	0.025 378	0.024 945	0.024 518	0.024 099	0.023 686	13
14	0.021 636	0.021 230	0.020 832	0.020 440	0.020 056	0.019 678	14
15	0.018 195	0.017 822	0.017 457	0.017 098	0.016 747	0.016 403	15
16	0.015 345	0.015 004	0.014 670	0.014 343	0.014 023	0.013 710	16
17	0.012 973	0.012 662	0.012 357	0.012 060	0.011 769	0.011 485	17
18	0.010 990	0.010 706	0.010 429	0.010 159	0.009 896	0.009 639	18
19	0.009 325	0.009 067	0.008 816	0.008 572	0.008 334	0.008 103	19
20	0.007 924	0.007 690	0.007 463	0.007 243	0.007 028	0.006 820	20
21	0.006 742	0.006 530	0.006 325	0.006 126	0.005 933	0.005 746	21
22	0.005 741	0.005 550	0.005 365	0.005 187	0.005 014	0.004 846	22
23	0.004 893	0.004 721	0.004 555	0.004 395	0.004 240	0.004 090	23
24	0.004 174	0.004 019	0.003 870	0.003 726	0.003 588	0.003 454	24
25	0.003 562	0.003 423	0.003 290	0.003 161	0.003 038	0.002 919	25
26	0.003 042	0.002 917	0.002 798	0.002 683	0.002 573	0.002 467	26
27	0.002 599	0.002 487	0.002 381	0.002 278	0.002 181	0.002 087	27
28	0.002 221	0.002 121	0.002 026	0.001 935	0.001 848	0.001 765	28
29	0.001 899	0.001 810	0.001 725	0.001 644	0.001 567	0.001 494	29
30	0.001 624	0.001 545	0.001 469	0.001 398	0.001 329	0.001 264	30
31	0.001 389	0.001 318	0.001 251	0.001 188	0.001 128	0.001 070	31
32	0.001 188	0.001 126	0.001 066	0.001 010	0.000 957	0.000 906	32
33	0.001 017	0.000 961	0.000 909	0.000 859	0.000 812	0.000 767	33
34	0.000 870	0.000 821	0.000 774	0.000 730	0.000 689	0.000 650	34
35	0.000 745	0.000 701	0.000 660	0.000 621	0.000 585	0.000 550	35
36	0.000 637	0.000 599	0.000 563	0.000 528	0.000 496	0.000 466	36
37	0.000 546	0.000 512	0.000 480	0.000 450	0.000 421	0.000 395	37
38	0.000 467	0.000 437	0.000 409	0.000 382	0.000 358	0.000 335	38
39	0.000 400	0.000 373	0.000 349	0.000 325	0.000 304	0.000 284	39
40	0.000 342	0.000 319	0.000 297	0.000 277	0.000 258	0.000 240	40
41	0.000 293	0.000 273	0.000 253	0.000 236	0.000 219	0.000 204	41
42	0.000 251	0.000 233	0.000 216	0.000 200	0.000 186	0.000 172	42
43	0.000 215	0.000 199	0.000 184	0.000 171	0.000 158	0.000 146	43
44	0.000 184	0.000 170	0.000 157	0.000 145	0.000 134	0.000 124	44
45	0.000 158	0.000 145	0.000 134	0.000 123	0.000 114	0.000 105	45
46	0.000 135	0.000 124	0.000 114	0.000 105	0.000 097	0.000 089	46
47	0.000 116	0.000 106	0.000 097	0.000 089	0.000 082	0.000 075	47
48	0.000 099	0.000 091	0.000 083	0.000 076	0.000 070	0.000 064	48
49	0.000 085	0.000 078	0.000 071	0.000 065	0.000 059	0.000 054	49
50	0.000 073	0.000 066	0.000 060	0.000 055	0.000 050	0.000 046	50

SINKING FUND FACTORS

YRS	18.25% ANNUAL RATE	18.50% ANNUAL RATE	18.75% ANNUAL RATE	19.00% ANNUAL RATE	19.25% ANNUAL RATE	19.50% ANNUAL RATE	YRS
1	1.000 000	1.000 000	1.000 000	1.000 000	1.000 000	1.000 000	1
2	0.458 190	0.457 666	0.457 143	0.456 621	0.456 100	0.455 581	2
3	0.279 267	0.278 612	0.277 959	0.277 308	0.276 659	0.276 012	3
4	0.191 047	0.190 359	0.189 674	0.188 991	0.188 311	0.187 634	4
5	0.139 090	0.138 407	0.137 727	0.137 050	0.136 377	0.135 708	5
6	0.105 245	0.104 584	0.103 927	0.103 274	0.102 626	0.101 982	6
7	0.081 728	0.081 099	0.080 474	0.079 855	0.079 240	0.078 630	7
8	0.064 647	0.064 054	0.063 467	0.062 885	0.062 308	0.061 737	8
9	0.051 836	0.051 282	0.050 734	0.050 192	0.049 656	0.049 125	9
10	0.041 995	0.041 481	0.040 973	0.040 471	0.039 975	0.039 485	10
11	0.034 296	0.033 821	0.033 353	0.032 891	0.032 435	0.031 985	11
12	0.028 185	0.027 749	0.027 319	0.026 896	0.026 479	0.026 068	12
13	0.023 280	0.022 881	0.022 488	0.022 102	0.021 722	0.021 349	13
14	0.019 307	0.018 943	0.018 586	0.018 235	0.017 890	0.017 551	14
15	0.016 065	0.015 734	0.015 410	0.015 092	0.014 780	0.014 475	15
16	0.013 404	0.013 104	0.012 810	0.012 523	0.012 243	0.011 968	16
17	0.011 208	0.010 937	0.010 673	0.010 414	0.010 162	0.009 916	17
18	0.009 389	0.009 145	0.008 907	0.008 676	0.008 450	0.008 229	18
19	0.007 878	0.007 658	0.007 445	0.007 238	0.007 036	0.006 839	19
20	0.006 618	0.006 421	0.006 231	0.006 045	0.005 865	0.005 691	20
21	0.005 565	0.005 390	0.005 219	0.005 054	0.004 895	0.004 740	21
22	0.004 684	0.004 528	0.004 376	0.004 229	0.004 088	0.003 950	22
23	0.003 946	0.003 806	0.003 672	0.003 542	0.003 416	0.003 295	23
24	0.003 326	0.003 202	0.003 082	0.002 967	0.002 856	0.002 750	24
25	0.002 805	0.002 695	0.002 589	0.002 487	0.002 390	0.002 296	25
26	0.002 366	0.002 269	0.002 175	0.002 086	0.002 000	0.001 917	26
27	0.001 997	0.001 911	0.001 829	0.001 750	0.001 674	0.001 602	27
28	0.001 686	0.001 610	0.001 537	0.001 468	0.001 402	0.001 339	28
29	0.001 424	0.001 357	0.001 293	0.001 232	0.001 174	0.001 119	29
30	0.001 202	0.001 144	0.001 088	0.001 034	0.000 984	0.000 936	30
31	0.001 016	0.000 964	0.000 915	0.000 869	0.000 824	0.000 782	31
32	0.000 858	0.000 813	0.000 770	0.000 729	0.000 691	0.000 654	32
33	0.000 725	0.000 686	0.000 648	0.000 612	0.000 579	0.000 547	33
34	0.000 613	0.000 578	0.000 545	0.000 514	0.000 485	0.000 458	34
35	0.000 518	0.000 488	0.000 459	0.000 432	0.000 407	0.000 383	35
36	0.000 438	0.000 411	0.000 386	0.000 363	0.000 341	0.000 320	36
37	0.000 370	0.000 347	0.000 325	0.000 305	0.000 286	0.000 268	37
38	0.000 313	0.000 293	0.000 274	0.000 256	0.000 240	0.000 224	38
39	0.000 265	0.000 247	0.000 231	0.000 215	0.000 201	0.000 188	39
40	0.000 224	0.000 208	0.000 194	0.000 181	0.000 168	0.000 157	40
41	0.000 189	0.000 176	0.000 163	0.000 152	0.000 141	0.000 131	41
42	0.000 160	0.000 148	0.000 138	0.000 128	0.000 118	0.000 110	42
43	0.000 135	0.000 125	0.000 116	0.000 107	0.000 099	0.000 092	43
44	0.000 114	0.000 106	0.000 098	0.000 090	0.000 083	0.000 077	44
45	0.000 097	0.000 089	0.000 082	0.000 076	0.000 070	0.000 064	45
46	0.000 082	0.000 075	0.000 069	0.000 064	0.000 059	0.000 054	46
47	0.000 069	0.000 063	0.000 058	0.000 053	0.000 049	0.000 045	47
48	0.000 058	0.000 054	0.000 049	0.000 045	0.000 041	0.000 038	48
49	0.000 049	0.000 045	0.000 041	0.000 038	0.000 035	0.000 032	49
50	0.000 042	0.000 038	0.000 035	0.000 032	0.000 029	0.000 026	50

SINKING FUND FACTORS

YRS	19.75% ANNUAL RATE	20.00% ANNUAL RATE	21.00% ANNUAL RATE	22.00% ANNUAL RATE	23.00% ANNUAL RATE	24.00% ANNUAL RATE	YRS
1	1.000 000	1.000 000	1.000 000	1.000 000	1.000 000	1.000 000	1
2	0.455 063	0.454 545	0.452 489	0.450 450	0.448 430	0.446 429	2
3	0.275 368	0.274 725	0.272 175	0.269 658	0.267 173	0.264 718	3
4	0.186 960	0.186 289	0.183 632	0.181 020	0.178 451	0.175 926	4
5	0.135 042	0.134 380	0.131 765	0.129 206	0.126 700	0.124 248	5
6	0.101 342	0.100 706	0.098 203	0.095 764	0.093 389	0.091 074	6
7	0.078 025	0.077 424	0.075 067	0.072 782	0.070 568	0.068 422	7
8	0.061 171	0.060 609	0.058 415	0.056 299	0.054 259	0.052 293	8
9	0.048 599	0.048 079	0.046 053	0.044 111	0.042 249	0.040 465	9
10	0.039 001	0.038 523	0.036 665	0.034 895	0.033 208	0.031 602	10
11	0.031 542	0.031 104	0.029 411	0.027 807	0.026 289	0.024 852	11
12	0.025 664	0.025 265	0.023 730	0.022 285	0.020 926	0.019 648	12
13	0.020 981	0.020 620	0.019 234	0.017 939	0.016 728	0.015 598	13
14	0.017 219	0.016 893	0.015 647	0.014 491	0.013 418	0.012 423	14
15	0.014 175	0.013 882	0.012 766	0.011 738	0.010 791	0.009 919	15
16	0.011 699	0.011 436	0.010 441	0.009 530	0.008 697	0.007 936	16
17	0.009 675	0.009 440	0.008 555	0.007 751	0.007 021	0.006 359	17
18	0.008 015	0.007 805	0.007 020	0.006 313	0.005 676	0.005 102	18
19	0.006 648	0.006 462	0.005 769	0.005 148	0.004 593	0.004 098	19
20	0.005 521	0.005 357	0.004 745	0.004 202	0.003 720	0.003 294	20
21	0.004 589	0.004 444	0.003 906	0.003 432	0.003 016	0.002 649	21
22	0.003 818	0.003 690	0.003 218	0.002 805	0.002 446	0.002 132	22
23	0.003 178	0.003 065	0.002 652	0.002 294	0.001 984	0.001 716	23
24	0.002 647	0.002 548	0.002 187	0.001 877	0.001 611	0.001 382	24
25	0.002 205	0.002 119	0.001 804	0.001 536	0.001 308	0.001 113	25
26	0.001 838	0.001 762	0.001 489	0.001 258	0.001 062	0.000 897	26
27	0.001 533	0.001 467	0.001 229	0.001 030	0.000 863	0.000 723	27
28	0.001 278	0.001 221	0.001 015	0.000 843	0.000 701	0.000 583	28
29	0.001 066	0.001 016	0.000 838	0.000 691	0.000 570	0.000 470	29
30	0.000 890	0.000 846	0.000 692	0.000 566	0.000 463	0.000 379	30
31	0.000 742	0.000 705	0.000 572	0.000 464	0.000 376	0.000 305	31
32	0.000 620	0.000 587	0.000 472	0.000 380	0.000 306	0.000 246	32
33	0.000 517	0.000 489	0.000 390	0.000 311	0.000 249	0.000 198	33
34	0.000 432	0.000 407	0.000 322	0.000 255	0.000 202	0.000 160	34
35	0.000 360	0.000 339	0.000 266	0.000 209	0.000 164	0.000 129	35
36	0.000 301	0.000 283	0.000 220	0.000 171	0.000 133	0.000 104	36
37	0.000 251	0.000 235	0.000 182	0.000 140	0.000 109	0.000 084	37
38	0.000 210	0.000 196	0.000 150	0.000 115	0.000 088	0.000 068	38
39	0.000 175	0.000 163	0.000 124	0.000 094	0.000 072	0.000 055	39
40	0.000 146	0.000 136	0.000 103	0.000 077	0.000 058	0.000 044	40
41	0.000 122	0.000 113	0.000 085	0.000 063	0.000 047	0.000 035	41
42	0.000 102	0.000 095	0.000 070	0.000 052	0.000 039	0.000 029	42
43	0.000 085	0.000 079	0.000 058	0.000 043	0.000 031	0.000 023	43
44	0.000 071	0.000 066	0.000 048	0.000 035	0.000 025	0.000 019	44
45	0.000 059	0.000 055	0.000 040	0.000 029	0.000 021	0.000 015	45
46	0.000 050	0.000 046	0.000 033	0.000 023	0.000 017	0.000 012	46
47	0.000 041	0.000 038	0.000 027	0.000 019	0.000 014	0.000 010	47
48	0.000 035	0.000 032	0.000 022	0.000 016	0.000 011	0.000 008	48
49	0.000 029	0.000 026	0.000 018	0.000 013	0.000 009	0.000 006	49
50	0.000 024	0.000 022	0.000 015	0.000 011	0.000 007	0.000 005	50

Section 4.   Present Value of $1.00

These tables indicate what amount of money must be invested today in order to accumulate $1 at a given time in the future. In this section it is important to understand that investment of the initial amount of money will begin the investment period. The factors are also based on the fact that no additional investments may be made, and that the future growth of this fund depends upon the interest paid. No funds may be withdrawn at any point in the duration of the investment.

In this section the following four (4) periods are presented in detail: monthly, quarterly, semiannual, and annual.

Monthly:

The factors presented on pages 92 through 99 will indicate the amount of money needed to invest today to receive $1 at the end of the stated period. These factors are based on the condition that interest is earned at the end of each monthly period during the term of the investment. Therefore, the interest is compounding monthly. This is interest earned on interest.

Example G

You will need $1,000.00 in 1 year, and you should estimate how much money to invest now to achieve your monetary goal. You can predict an annual interest rate of 7.0%, and interest will compound at the end of each monthly period.

Turn to page 92 and locate the 7.0% column. Proceed down that column until you locate the point where the 12 month (or 1 year) row intersects with the 7.0% column. The number is 0.932583 for each $1 you need to accumulate. So, to determine your answer, multiply 0.932583 by $1,000.00. The correct answer is $932.58. That is, you will need to invest $932.58 today to accumulate $1,000.00 in 12 months or 1 year.

Note: If your investment is less than 4 years, we have provided all the $1 amounts for each monthly period. For 4 years and over, the annual figures are provided.

Quarterly:

The factors presented on pages 100 through 105, will indicate the amount of money needed to invest today to receive $1 at the end of the stated period. These factors are based on the condition that interest is earned at the end of each quarterly period during the term of the investment. Therefore, the interest is compounding quarterly, i.e., interest earned on interest.

Example H

You need to open a savings account today that will produce $10,000.00 in 10 years. Your credit union compounds interest at the end of every quarter, and pays 8.0% annual interest. How much do you deposit today?

Turn to page 100 and locate the 8.0% column. Proceed down that column until you locate the point where the 40 quarters row intersects the 8% interest column. The answer is 0.452890 for every $1 you need to accumulate. So, to determine your answer, multiply 0.452890 by $10,000. The correct answer is $4528.90. Just deposit this $4528.90 today and you will have $10,000.00 in ten (10) years.

Note: For investment of 14 years and more, only the annual amounts are shown.

Semiannual:

The factors on pages 106 through 109 cover semiannual compounding (or the interest being compounded every six (6) months).

Annual:

The factors on pages 110 through 117 cover annual compounding (or the interest being compounded every year).

Both the semiannual and annual tables are used the same way as the monthly and quarterly tables.

Just in case you need to know, here is the formula.

$$V^n = \frac{1}{(1 + i)^n}$$

V^n = Present value of $1
i = interest rate per period
n = number of compounding periods

91

MOS	7.00% ANNUAL RATE	8.00% ANNUAL RATE	9.00% ANNUAL RATE	10.00% ANNUAL RATE	10.25% ANNUAL RATE	10.50% ANNUAL RATE	MOS
1	0.994 200	0.993 377	0.992 556	0.991 736	0.991 531	0.991 326	1
2	0.988 435	0.986 799	0.985 167	0.983 539	0.983 133	0.982 727	2
3	0.982 702	0.980 264	0.977 833	0.975 411	0.974 807	0.974 203	3
4	0.977 003	0.973 772	0.970 554	0.967 350	0.966 551	0.965 752	4
5	0.971 337	0.967 323	0.963 329	0.959 355	0.958 365	0.957 375	5
6	0.965 704	0.960 917	0.956 158	0.951 427	0.950 248	0.949 071	6
7	0.960 103	0.954 553	0.949 040	0.943 563	0.942 200	0.940 839	7
8	0.954 535	0.948 232	0.941 975	0.935 765	0.934 220	0.932 678	8
9	0.948 999	0.941 952	0.934 963	0.928 032	0.926 308	0.924 588	9
10	0.943 495	0.935 714	0.928 003	0.920 362	0.918 463	0.916 568	10
11	0.938 024	0.929 517	0.921 095	0.912 756	0.910 684	0.908 617	11
12	0.932 583	0.923 361	0.914 238	0.905 212	0.902 971	0.900 736	12
13	0.927 175	0.917 246	0.907 432	0.897 731	0.895 324	0.892 923	13
14	0.921 798	0.911 172	0.900 677	0.890 312	0.887 741	0.885 177	14
15	0.916 452	0.905 138	0.893 973	0.882 954	0.880 222	0.877 499	15
16	0.911 137	0.899 143	0.887 318	0.875 657	0.872 767	0.869 888	16
17	0.905 853	0.893 189	0.880 712	0.868 420	0.865 376	0.862 342	17
18	0.900 599	0.887 274	0.874 156	0.861 243	0.858 046	0.854 862	18
19	0.895 376	0.881 398	0.867 649	0.854 125	0.850 779	0.847 447	19
20	0.890 183	0.875 561	0.861 190	0.847 067	0.843 574	0.840 096	20
21	0.885 021	0.869 762	0.854 779	0.840 066	0.836 429	0.832 809	21
22	0.879 888	0.864 002	0.848 416	0.833 123	0.829 345	0.825 585	22
23	0.874 785	0.858 280	0.842 100	0.826 238	0.822 321	0.818 424	23
24	0.869 712	0.852 596	0.835 831	0.819 410	0.815 357	0.811 325	24
25	0.864 668	0.846 950	0.829 609	0.812 638	0.808 451	0.804 287	25
26	0.859 653	0.841 341	0.823 434	0.805 922	0.801 604	0.797 311	26
27	0.854 668	0.835 769	0.817 304	0.799 261	0.794 815	0.790 395	27
28	0.849 711	0.830 234	0.811 220	0.792 656	0.788 084	0.783 539	28
29	0.844 783	0.824 736	0.805 181	0.786 105	0.781 409	0.776 743	29
30	0.839 884	0.819 274	0.799 187	0.779 608	0.774 791	0.770 005	30
31	0.835 013	0.813 849	0.793 238	0.773 165	0.768 229	0.763 326	31
32	0.830 170	0.808 459	0.787 333	0.766 775	0.761 723	0.756 705	32
33	0.825 356	0.803 105	0.781 472	0.760 438	0.755 272	0.750 141	33
34	0.820 569	0.797 786	0.775 654	0.754 154	0.748 875	0.743 634	34
35	0.815 810	0.792 503	0.769 880	0.747 921	0.742 532	0.737 184	35
36	0.811 079	0.787 255	0.764 149	0.741 740	0.736 244	0.730 789	36
37	0.806 375	0.782 041	0.758 461	0.735 610	0.730 008	0.724 451	37
38	0.801 699	0.776 862	0.752 814	0.729 530	0.723 826	0.718 167	38
39	0.797 049	0.771 717	0.747 210	0.723 501	0.717 695	0.711 937	39
40	0.792 427	0.766 606	0.741 648	0.717 522	0.711 617	0.705 762	40
41	0.787 831	0.761 530	0.736 127	0.711 592	0.705 590	0.699 640	41
42	0.783 262	0.756 486	0.730 647	0.705 711	0.699 614	0.693 571	42
43	0.778 719	0.751 477	0.725 208	0.699 879	0.693 689	0.687 555	43
44	0.774 203	0.746 500	0.719 810	0.694 094	0.687 814	0.681 591	44
45	0.769 713	0.741 556	0.714 451	0.688 358	0.681 988	0.675 679	45
46	0.765 249	0.736 645	0.709 133	0.682 669	0.676 212	0.669 818	46
47	0.760 811	0.731 767	0.703 854	0.677 027	0.670 485	0.664 008	47
YRS							
4	0.756 399	0.726 921	0.698 614	0.671 432	0.664 807	0.658 248	48
5	0.705 405	0.671 210	0.638 700	0.607 789	0.600 301	0.592 908	60
6	0.657 849	0.619 770	0.583 924	0.550 178	0.542 055	0.534 053	72
7	0.613 499	0.572 272	0.533 845	0.498 028	0.489 460	0.481 041	84
8	0.572 139	0.528 414	0.488 062	0.450 821	0.441 968	0.433 291	96
9	0.533 568	0.487 917	0.446 205	0.408 089	0.399 084	0.390 280	108
10	0.497 596	0.450 523	0.407 937	0.369 407	0.360 362	0.351 540	120
11	0.464 050	0.415 996	0.372 952	0.334 392	0.325 396	0.316 644	132
12	0.432 765	0.384 115	0.340 967	0.302 696	0.293 823	0.285 213	144
13	0.403 590	0.354 677	0.311 725	0.274 004	0.265 314	0.256 901	156
14	0.376 381	0.327 495	0.284 991	0.248 032	0.239 571	0.231 400	168
15	0.351 007	0.302 396	0.260 549	0.224 521	0.216 326	0.208 431	180
16	0.327 343	0.279 221	0.238 204	0.203 240	0.195 336	0.187 741	192
17	0.305 275	0.257 822	0.217 775	0.183 975	0.176 383	0.169 105	204
18	0.284 694	0.238 063	0.199 099	0.166 536	0.159 268	0.152 319	216
19	0.265 501	0.219 818	0.182 024	0.150 751	0.143 815	0.137 199	228
20	0.247 602	0.202 971	0.166 413	0.136 462	0.129 861	0.123 580	240
21	0.230 910	0.187 416	0.152 141	0.123 527	0.117 260	0.111 313	252
22	0.215 342	0.173 053	0.139 093	0.111 818	0.105 883	0.100 264	264
23	0.200 825	0.159 790	0.127 164	0.101 219	0.095 609	0.090 311	276
24	0.187 286	0.147 544	0.116 258	0.091 625	0.086 332	0.081 346	288
25	0.174 660	0.136 237	0.106 288	0.082 940	0.077 955	0.073 272	300
26	0.162 885	0.125 796	0.097 172	0.075 078	0.070 392	0.065 998	312
27	0.151 904	0.116 155	0.088 839	0.067 962	0.063 561	0.059 447	324
28	0.141 663	0.107 253	0.081 220	0.061 520	0.057 394	0.053 546	336
29	0.132 112	0.099 033	0.074 254	0.055 688	0.051 825	0.048 231	348
30	0.123 206	0.091 443	0.067 886	0.050 410	0.046 797	0.043 443	360

MONTHLY COMPOUNDING

SECTION 4

MOS	10.75% ANNUAL RATE	11.00% ANNUAL RATE	11.25% ANNUAL RATE	11.50% ANNUAL RATE	11.75% ANNUAL RATE	12.00% ANNUAL RATE	MOS
1	0.991 121	0.990 917	0.990 712	0.990 508	0.990 303	0.990 099	1
2	0.982 321	0.981 916	0.981 510	0.981 105	0.980 701	0.980 296	2
3	0.973 599	0.972 997	0.972 394	0.971 792	0.971 191	0.970 590	3
4	0.964 955	0.964 158	0.963 363	0.962 568	0.961 774	0.960 980	4
5	0.956 387	0.955 401	0.954 415	0.953 431	0.952 448	0.951 466	5
6	0.947 896	0.946 722	0.945 551	0.944 380	0.943 212	0.942 045	6
7	0.939 480	0.938 123	0.936 768	0.935 416	0.934 066	0.932 718	7
8	0.931 138	0.929 602	0.928 068	0.926 537	0.925 009	0.923 483	8
9	0.922 871	0.921 158	0.919 448	0.917 742	0.916 039	0.914 340	9
10	0.914 677	0.912 790	0.910 908	0.909 030	0.907 156	0.905 287	10
11	0.906 556	0.904 499	0.902 448	0.900 401	0.898 360	0.896 324	11
12	0.898 506	0.896 283	0.894 066	0.891 854	0.889 649	0.887 449	12
13	0.890 529	0.888 142	0.885 762	0.883 389	0.881 022	0.878 663	13
14	0.882 622	0.880 075	0.877 535	0.875 003	0.872 479	0.869 963	14
15	0.874 785	0.872 080	0.869 384	0.866 697	0.864 019	0.861 349	15
16	0.867 018	0.864 159	0.861 310	0.858 470	0.855 641	0.852 821	16
17	0.859 320	0.856 309	0.853 310	0.850 321	0.847 344	0.844 377	17
18	0.851 691	0.848 531	0.845 384	0.842 250	0.839 127	0.836 017	18
19	0.844 129	0.840 824	0.837 532	0.834 255	0.830 991	0.827 740	19
20	0.836 634	0.833 186	0.829 754	0.826 336	0.822 933	0.819 544	20
21	0.829 205	0.825 618	0.822 047	0.818 492	0.814 953	0.811 430	21
22	0.821 843	0.818 119	0.814 412	0.810 722	0.807 051	0.803 396	22
23	0.814 546	0.810 687	0.806 848	0.803 027	0.799 225	0.795 442	23
24	0.807 314	0.803 323	0.799 354	0.795 404	0.791 475	0.787 566	24
25	0.800 146	0.796 027	0.791 929	0.787 854	0.783 800	0.779 768	25
26	0.793 042	0.788 796	0.784 574	0.780 375	0.776 200	0.772 048	26
27	0.786 000	0.781 631	0.777 287	0.772 968	0.768 673	0.764 404	27
28	0.779 022	0.774 531	0.770 067	0.765 630	0.761 220	0.756 836	28
29	0.772 105	0.767 496	0.762 915	0.758 363	0.753 838	0.749 342	29
30	0.765 249	0.760 524	0.755 829	0.751 164	0.746 529	0.741 923	30
31	0.758 455	0.753 616	0.748 809	0.744 034	0.739 290	0.734 577	31
32	0.751 721	0.746 771	0.741 854	0.736 971	0.732 121	0.727 304	32
33	0.745 046	0.739 988	0.734 964	0.729 976	0.725 022	0.720 103	33
34	0.738 431	0.733 266	0.728 138	0.723 046	0.717 992	0.712 973	34
35	0.731 875	0.726 605	0.721 375	0.716 183	0.711 029	0.705 914	35
36	0.725 377	0.720 005	0.714 675	0.709 385	0.704 135	0.698 925	36
37	0.718 936	0.713 465	0.708 037	0.702 651	0.697 307	0.692 005	37
38	0.712 553	0.706 985	0.701 461	0.695 981	0.690 545	0.685 153	38
39	0.706 226	0.700 563	0.694 946	0.689 375	0.683 849	0.678 370	39
40	0.699 956	0.694 199	0.688 491	0.682 831	0.677 218	0.671 653	40
41	0.693 741	0.687 894	0.682 096	0.676 349	0.670 652	0.665 003	41
42	0.687 582	0.681 645	0.675 761	0.669 929	0.664 148	0.658 419	42
43	0.681 477	0.675 453	0.669 485	0.663 570	0.657 708	0.651 900	43
44	0.675 426	0.669 318	0.663 267	0.657 271	0.651 331	0.645 445	44
45	0.669 429	0.663 238	0.657 106	0.651 032	0.645 015	0.639 055	45
46	0.663 485	0.657 214	0.651 003	0.644 852	0.638 760	0.632 728	46
47	0.657 594	0.651 244	0.644 957	0.638 731	0.632 567	0.626 463	47

YRS							
4	0.651 756	0.645 329	0.638 966	0.632 668	0.626 433	0.620 260	48
5	0.585 607	0.578 397	0.571 278	0.564 248	0.557 305	0.550 450	60
6	0.526 171	0.518 408	0.510 760	0.503 227	0.495 806	0.488 496	72
7	0.472 769	0.464 640	0.456 653	0.448 805	0.441 093	0.433 515	84
8	0.424 786	0.416 449	0.408 278	0.400 269	0.392 418	0.384 723	96
9	0.381 673	0.373 256	0.365 027	0.356 981	0.349 114	0.341 422	108
10	0.342 935	0.334 543	0.326 358	0.318 375	0.310 589	0.302 995	120
11	0.308 130	0.299 846	0.291 786	0.283 944	0.276 315	0.268 892	132
12	0.276 856	0.268 747	0.260 876	0.253 237	0.245 823	0.238 628	144
13	0.248 757	0.240 873	0.233 240	0.225 851	0.218 697	0.211 771	156
14	0.223 510	0.215 890	0.208 532	0.201 426	0.194 563	0.187 936	168
15	0.200 825	0.193 499	0.186 441	0.179 642	0.173 093	0.166 783	180
16	0.180 443	0.173 430	0.166 691	0.160 215	0.153 992	0.148 012	192
17	0.162 129	0.155 442	0.149 033	0.142 888	0.136 999	0.131 353	204
18	0.145 674	0.139 320	0.133 245	0.127 436	0.121 881	0.116 569	216
19	0.130 889	0.124 870	0.119 130	0.113 654	0.108 431	0.103 449	228
20	0.117 605	0.111 919	0.106 510	0.101 363	0.096 466	0.091 806	240
21	0.105 669	0.100 311	0.095 227	0.090 401	0.085 820	0.081 473	252
22	0.094 944	0.089 907	0.085 139	0.080 624	0.076 350	0.072 303	264
23	0.085 308	0.080 582	0.076 120	0.071 905	0.067 925	0.064 165	276
24	0.076 649	0.072 225	0.068 056	0.064 129	0.060 429	0.056 944	288
25	0.068 870	0.064 734	0.060 847	0.057 194	0.053 761	0.050 534	300
26	0.061 880	0.058 020	0.054 401	0.051 008	0.047 828	0.044 847	312
27	0.055 600	0.052 002	0.048 638	0.045 492	0.042 550	0.039 799	324
28	0.049 957	0.046 609	0.043 486	0.040 572	0.037 855	0.035 320	336
29	0.044 886	0.041 775	0.038 879	0.036 185	0.033 677	0.031 345	348
30	0.040 331	0.037 442	0.034 760	0.032 271	0.029 961	0.027 817	360

PRESENT VALUE OF $1

MOS	12.25% ANNUAL RATE	12.50% ANNUAL RATE	12.75% ANNUAL RATE	13.00% ANNUAL RATE	13.25% ANNUAL RATE	13.50% ANNUAL RATE	MOS
1	0.989 895	0.989 691	0.989 487	0.989 283	0.989 079	0.988 875	1
2	0.979 892	0.979 488	0.979 084	0.978 680	0.978 277	0.977 874	2
3	0.969 990	0.969 390	0.968 791	0.968 192	0.967 593	0.966 995	3
4	0.960 188	0.959 396	0.958 605	0.957 815	0.957 026	0.956 238	4
5	0.950 485	0.949 506	0.948 527	0.947 550	0.946 574	0.945 600	5
6	0.940 880	0.939 717	0.938 555	0.937 395	0.936 237	0.935 080	6
7	0.931 372	0.930 029	0.928 688	0.927 349	0.926 012	0.924 677	7
8	0.921 961	0.920 441	0.918 924	0.917 410	0.915 899	0.914 391	8
9	0.912 644	0.910 952	0.909 263	0.907 578	0.905 896	0.904 218	9
10	0.903 422	0.901 561	0.899 704	0.897 851	0.896 003	0.894 159	10
11	0.894 292	0.892 266	0.890 245	0.888 229	0.886 218	0.884 211	11
12	0.885 256	0.883 068	0.880 886	0.878 710	0.876 539	0.874 375	12
13	0.876 310	0.873 964	0.871 625	0.869 292	0.866 966	0.864 647	13
14	0.867 455	0.864 954	0.862 461	0.859 976	0.857 498	0.855 028	14
15	0.858 689	0.856 037	0.853 394	0.850 759	0.848 133	0.845 516	15
16	0.850 012	0.847 212	0.844 422	0.841 641	0.838 871	0.836 110	16
17	0.841 422	0.838 478	0.835 544	0.832 621	0.829 710	0.826 808	17
18	0.832 919	0.829 834	0.826 760	0.823 698	0.820 648	0.817 610	18
19	0.824 503	0.821 279	0.818 068	0.814 870	0.811 686	0.808 515	19
20	0.816 171	0.812 812	0.809 467	0.806 137	0.802 821	0.799 520	20
21	0.807 923	0.804 432	0.800 957	0.797 498	0.794 054	0.790 625	21
22	0.799 759	0.796 139	0.792 536	0.788 951	0.785 382	0.781 830	22
23	0.791 677	0.787 932	0.784 204	0.780 495	0.776 805	0.773 132	23
24	0.783 677	0.779 809	0.775 960	0.772 130	0.768 321	0.764 531	24
25	0.775 758	0.771 769	0.767 802	0.763 855	0.759 930	0.756 026	25
26	0.767 919	0.763 813	0.759 730	0.755 669	0.751 631	0.747 615	26
27	0.760 159	0.755 939	0.751 742	0.747 570	0.743 422	0.739 298	27
28	0.752 477	0.748 145	0.743 839	0.739 558	0.735 303	0.731 073	28
29	0.744 874	0.740 432	0.736 019	0.731 632	0.727 273	0.722 940	29
30	0.737 346	0.732 799	0.728 281	0.723 791	0.719 330	0.714 898	30
31	0.729 895	0.725 245	0.720 624	0.716 034	0.711 474	0.706 945	31
32	0.722 520	0.717 768	0.713 048	0.708 360	0.703 704	0.699 080	32
33	0.715 219	0.710 368	0.705 552	0.700 769	0.696 019	0.691 303	33
34	0.707 991	0.703 045	0.698 134	0.693 258	0.688 418	0.683 612	34
35	0.700 837	0.695 797	0.690 794	0.685 829	0.680 900	0.676 007	35
36	0.693 755	0.688 624	0.683 532	0.678 478	0.673 463	0.668 487	36
37	0.686 744	0.681 524	0.676 346	0.671 207	0.666 109	0.661 050	37
38	0.679 804	0.674 498	0.669 235	0.664 014	0.658 834	0.653 696	38
39	0.672 935	0.667 545	0.662 199	0.656 897	0.651 639	0.646 424	39
40	0.666 135	0.660 663	0.655 237	0.649 857	0.644 522	0.639 232	40
41	0.659 403	0.653 852	0.648 348	0.642 892	0.637 483	0.632 121	41
42	0.652 740	0.647 111	0.641 532	0.636 002	0.630 521	0.625 089	42
43	0.646 144	0.640 440	0.634 788	0.629 186	0.623 635	0.618 135	43
44	0.639 615	0.633 838	0.628 114	0.622 443	0.616 825	0.611 258	44
45	0.633 151	0.627 303	0.621 510	0.615 772	0.610 088	0.604 458	45
46	0.626 753	0.620 836	0.614 976	0.609 173	0.603 425	0.597 733	46
47	0.620 420	0.614 436	0.608 511	0.602 644	0.596 835	0.591 084	47
YRS							
4	0.614 150	0.608 101	0.602 113	0.596 185	0.590 317	0.584 508	48
5	0.543 680	0.536 995	0.530 393	0.523 874	0.517 436	0.511 079	60
6	0.481 296	0.474 203	0.467 216	0.460 333	0.453 553	0.446 874	72
7	0.426 070	0.418 753	0.411 564	0.404 499	0.397 557	0.390 736	84
8	0.377 180	0.369 787	0.362 540	0.355 437	0.348 474	0.341 649	96
9	0.333 901	0.326 547	0.319 357	0.312 326	0.305 451	0.298 730	108
10	0.295 588	0.288 363	0.281 317	0.274 444	0.267 740	0.261 202	120
11	0.261 671	0.254 644	0.247 808	0.241 156	0.234 685	0.228 388	132
12	0.231 645	0.224 868	0.218 290	0.211 906	0.205 710	0.199 697	144
13	0.205 065	0.198 574	0.192 289	0.186 204	0.180 313	0.174 610	156
14	0.181 535	0.175 354	0.169 385	0.163 619	0.158 052	0.152 674	168
15	0.160 705	0.154 849	0.149 208	0.143 774	0.138 538	0.133 495	180
16	0.142 265	0.136 743	0.131 436	0.126 336	0.121 434	0.116 724	192
17	0.125 941	0.120 753	0.115 780	0.111 012	0.106 442	0.102 061	204
18	0.111 490	0.106 633	0.101 989	0.097 548	0.093 301	0.089 239	216
19	0.098 697	0.094 164	0.089 840	0.085 716	0.081 782	0.078 029	228
20	0.087 372	0.083 153	0.079 139	0.075 319	0.071 685	0.068 226	240
21	0.077 347	0.073 430	0.069 712	0.066 184	0.062 835	0.059 655	252
22	0.068 472	0.064 844	0.061 409	0.058 156	0.055 077	0.052 161	264
23	0.060 615	0.057 261	0.054 094	0.051 103	0.048 277	0.045 608	276
24	0.053 660	0.050 566	0.047 651	0.044 904	0.042 317	0.039 879	288
25	0.047 502	0.044 653	0.041 975	0.039 458	0.037 092	0.034 869	300
26	0.042 052	0.039 432	0.036 975	0.034 672	0.032 513	0.030 489	312
27	0.037 227	0.034 821	0.032 571	0.030 467	0.028 499	0.026 658	324
28	0.032 955	0.030 749	0.028 691	0.026 771	0.024 980	0.023 309	336
29	0.029 174	0.027 153	0.025 274	0.023 524	0.021 896	0.020 381	348
30	0.025 826	0.023 978	0.022 263	0.020 671	0.019 193	0.017 821	360

MOS	13.75% ANNUAL RATE	14.00% ANNUAL RATE	14.25% ANNUAL RATE	14.50% ANNUAL RATE	14.75% ANNUAL RATE	15.00% ANNUAL RATE	MOS
1	0.988 671	0.988 468	0.988 264	0.988 061	0.987 858	0.987 654	1
2	0.977 471	0.977 069	0.976 666	0.976 264	0.975 863	0.975 461	2
3	0.966 398	0.965 801	0.965 205	0.964 609	0.964 013	0.963 418	3
4	0.955 450	0.954 663	0.953 877	0.953 092	0.952 308	0.951 524	4
5	0.944 626	0.943 654	0.942 683	0.941 713	0.940 745	0.939 777	5
6	0.933 925	0.932 772	0.931 620	0.930 470	0.929 322	0.928 175	6
7	0.923 345	0.922 015	0.920 687	0.919 361	0.918 037	0.916 716	7
8	0.912 885	0.911 382	0.909 882	0.908 385	0.906 890	0.905 398	8
9	0.902 543	0.900 872	0.899 204	0.897 539	0.895 878	0.894 221	9
10	0.892 319	0.890 483	0.888 651	0.886 824	0.885 000	0.883 181	10
11	0.882 210	0.880 214	0.878 222	0.876 236	0.874 254	0.872 277	11
12	0.872 216	0.870 063	0.867 916	0.865 774	0.863 639	0.861 509	12
13	0.862 335	0.860 029	0.857 730	0.855 438	0.853 152	0.850 873	13
14	0.852 566	0.850 111	0.847 664	0.845 225	0.842 793	0.840 368	14
15	0.842 908	0.840 308	0.837 716	0.835 133	0.832 559	0.829 993	15
16	0.833 359	0.830 617	0.827 885	0.825 163	0.822 450	0.819 746	16
17	0.823 918	0.821 038	0.818 169	0.815 311	0.812 463	0.809 626	17
18	0.814 584	0.811 570	0.808 568	0.805 577	0.802 598	0.799 631	18
19	0.805 356	0.802 211	0.799 079	0.795 959	0.792 853	0.789 759	19
20	0.796 233	0.792 960	0.789 701	0.786 456	0.783 225	0.780 009	20
21	0.787 213	0.783 815	0.780 433	0.777 067	0.773 715	0.770 379	21
22	0.778 295	0.774 776	0.771 274	0.767 789	0.764 320	0.760 868	22
23	0.769 478	0.765 841	0.762 223	0.758 622	0.755 040	0.751 475	23
24	0.760 761	0.757 010	0.753 278	0.749 565	0.745 872	0.742 197	24
25	0.752 142	0.748 280	0.744 438	0.740 616	0.736 815	0.733 034	25
26	0.743 622	0.739 650	0.735 701	0.731 774	0.727 868	0.723 984	26
27	0.735 198	0.731 121	0.727 067	0.723 037	0.719 030	0.715 046	27
28	0.726 869	0.722 689	0.718 535	0.714 405	0.710 299	0.706 219	28
29	0.718 635	0.714 355	0.710 102	0.705 875	0.701 675	0.697 500	29
30	0.710 493	0.706 117	0.701 769	0.697 448	0.693 155	0.688 889	30
31	0.702 445	0.697 974	0.693 533	0.689 121	0.684 738	0.680 384	31
32	0.694 487	0.689 925	0.685 394	0.680 894	0.676 424	0.671 984	32
33	0.686 619	0.681 969	0.677 350	0.672 764	0.668 210	0.663 688	33
34	0.678 841	0.674 104	0.669 401	0.664 732	0.660 097	0.655 494	34
35	0.671 151	0.666 330	0.661 545	0.656 796	0.652 081	0.647 402	35
36	0.663 548	0.658 646	0.653 782	0.648 954	0.644 164	0.639 409	36
37	0.656 031	0.651 051	0.646 109	0.641 206	0.636 342	0.631 515	37
38	0.648 599	0.643 543	0.638 527	0.633 551	0.628 615	0.623 719	38
39	0.641 251	0.636 121	0.631 033	0.625 987	0.620 982	0.616 019	39
40	0.633 987	0.628 785	0.623 628	0.618 513	0.613 442	0.608 413	40
41	0.626 805	0.621 534	0.616 309	0.611 129	0.605 993	0.600 902	41
42	0.619 704	0.614 366	0.609 076	0.603 833	0.598 635	0.593 484	42
43	0.612 683	0.607 281	0.601 928	0.596 623	0.591 366	0.586 157	43
44	0.605 743	0.600 278	0.594 864	0.589 500	0.584 186	0.578 920	44
45	0.598 880	0.593 356	0.587 883	0.582 462	0.577 092	0.571 773	45
46	0.592 096	0.586 513	0.580 984	0.575 508	0.570 085	0.564 714	46
47	0.585 388	0.579 749	0.574 166	0.568 637	0.563 163	0.557 742	47

YRS							
4	0.578 757	0.573 064	0.567 428	0.561 848	0.556 325	0.550 856	48
5	0.504 801	0.498 601	0.492 479	0.486 434	0.480 463	0.474 568	60
6	0.440 295	0.433 815	0.427 431	0.421 142	0.414 947	0.408 844	72
7	0.384 033	0.377 446	0.370 974	0.364 614	0.358 364	0.352 223	84
8	0.334 960	0.328 402	0.321 974	0.315 673	0.309 497	0.303 443	96
9	0.292 157	0.285 730	0.279 446	0.273 302	0.267 294	0.261 419	108
10	0.254 824	0.248 603	0.242 536	0.236 618	0.230 845	0.225 214	120
11	0.222 262	0.216 301	0.210 501	0.204 858	0.199 367	0.194 024	132
12	0.193 860	0.188 195	0.182 697	0.177 360	0.172 181	0.167 153	144
13	0.169 088	0.163 742	0.158 566	0.153 554	0.148 702	0.144 004	156
14	0.147 481	0.142 466	0.137 622	0.132 943	0.128 425	0.124 061	168
15	0.128 635	0.123 954	0.119 444	0.115 099	0.110 913	0.106 879	180
16	0.112 198	0.107 848	0.103 667	0.099 650	0.095 788	0.092 078	192
17	0.097 861	0.093 834	0.089 974	0.086 274	0.082 727	0.079 326	204
18	0.085 356	0.081 642	0.078 090	0.074 694	0.071 446	0.068 340	216
19	0.074 449	0.071 034	0.067 776	0.064 668	0.061 703	0.058 875	228
20	0.064 935	0.061 804	0.058 824	0.055 988	0.053 289	0.050 722	240
21	0.056 638	0.053 773	0.051 054	0.048 473	0.046 023	0.043 697	252
22	0.049 400	0.046 786	0.044 311	0.041 967	0.039 747	0.037 645	264
23	0.043 088	0.040 707	0.038 458	0.036 334	0.034 327	0.032 432	276
24	0.037 582	0.035 417	0.033 378	0.031 457	0.029 646	0.027 940	288
25	0.032 779	0.030 815	0.028 969	0.027 234	0.025 604	0.024 071	300
26	0.028 591	0.026 811	0.025 143	0.023 579	0.022 112	0.020 737	312
27	0.024 937	0.023 328	0.021 822	0.020 414	0.019 097	0.017 865	324
28	0.021 751	0.020 296	0.018 940	0.017 674	0.016 493	0.015 391	336
29	0.018 971	0.017 659	0.016 438	0.015 302	0.014 244	0.013 260	348
30	0.016 547	0.015 365	0.014 267	0.013 248	0.012 302	0.011 423	360

PRESENT VALUE OF $1

MONTHLY COMPOUNDING

MOS	15.25% ANNUAL RATE	15.50% ANNUAL RATE	15.75% ANNUAL RATE	16.00% ANNUAL RATE	16.25% ANNUAL RATE	16.50% ANNUAL RATE	MOS
1	0.987 451	0.987 248	0.987 045	0.986 842	0.986 639	0.986 436	1
2	0.975 060	0.974 659	0.974 258	0.973 857	0.973 457	0.973 057	2
3	0.962 824	0.962 230	0.961 636	0.961 043	0.960 451	0.959 859	3
4	0.950 742	0.949 960	0.949 178	0.948 398	0.947 619	0.946 840	4
5	0.938 811	0.937 846	0.936 882	0.935 919	0.934 958	0.933 997	5
6	0.927 030	0.925 886	0.924 745	0.923 604	0.922 466	0.921 329	6
7	0.915 397	0.914 080	0.912 765	0.911 452	0.910 141	0.908 833	7
8	0.903 909	0.902 423	0.900 940	0.899 459	0.897 981	0.896 506	8
9	0.892 566	0.890 916	0.889 268	0.887 624	0.885 983	0.884 346	9
10	0.881 366	0.879 555	0.877 748	0.875 945	0.874 146	0.872 351	10
11	0.870 306	0.868 339	0.866 376	0.864 419	0.862 467	0.860 519	11
12	0.859 384	0.857 266	0.855 153	0.853 045	0.850 943	0.848 847	12
13	0.848 600	0.846 334	0.844 074	0.841 821	0.839 574	0.837 334	13
14	0.837 951	0.835 541	0.833 139	0.830 744	0.828 357	0.825 977	14
15	0.827 436	0.824 887	0.822 346	0.819 814	0.817 289	0.814 774	15
16	0.817 052	0.814 368	0.811 692	0.809 026	0.806 370	0.803 722	16
17	0.806 799	0.803 983	0.801 177	0.798 381	0.795 596	0.792 821	17
18	0.796 675	0.793 731	0.790 798	0.787 876	0.784 966	0.782 068	18
19	0.786 677	0.783 609	0.780 553	0.777 510	0.774 479	0.771 460	19
20	0.776 806	0.773 616	0.770 441	0.767 279	0.764 131	0.760 996	20
21	0.767 058	0.763 751	0.760 460	0.757 183	0.753 922	0.750 675	21
22	0.757 432	0.754 012	0.750 608	0.747 220	0.743 849	0.740 493	22
23	0.747 927	0.744 397	0.740 884	0.737 389	0.733 910	0.730 449	23
24	0.738 541	0.734 904	0.731 286	0.727 686	0.724 105	0.720 542	24
25	0.729 273	0.725 533	0.721 812	0.718 111	0.714 430	0.710 769	25
26	0.720 122	0.716 281	0.712 461	0.708 662	0.704 885	0.701 128	26
27	0.711 085	0.707 147	0.703 231	0.699 338	0.695 467	0.691 618	27
28	0.702 162	0.698 129	0.694 121	0.690 136	0.686 175	0.682 238	28
29	0.693 351	0.689 227	0.685 129	0.681 055	0.677 007	0.672 984	29
30	0.684 650	0.680 438	0.676 253	0.672 094	0.667 962	0.663 856	30
31	0.676 058	0.671 761	0.667 492	0.663 251	0.659 038	0.654 852	31
32	0.667 574	0.663 195	0.658 845	0.654 524	0.650 232	0.645 970	32
33	0.659 197	0.654 738	0.650 309	0.645 912	0.641 545	0.637 208	33
34	0.650 925	0.646 388	0.641 885	0.637 413	0.632 973	0.628 565	34
35	0.642 757	0.638 146	0.633 569	0.629 026	0.624 516	0.620 040	35
36	0.634 691	0.630 008	0.625 361	0.620 749	0.616 172	0.611 630	36
37	0.626 726	0.621 974	0.617 260	0.612 581	0.607 940	0.603 334	37
38	0.618 861	0.614 043	0.609 263	0.604 521	0.599 817	0.595 151	38
39	0.611 095	0.606 213	0.601 370	0.596 567	0.591 803	0.587 079	39
40	0.603 427	0.598 482	0.593 579	0.588 717	0.583 896	0.579 116	40
41	0.595 855	0.590 850	0.585 889	0.580 971	0.576 095	0.571 261	41
42	0.588 377	0.583 316	0.578 299	0.573 327	0.568 398	0.563 513	42
43	0.580 994	0.575 878	0.570 807	0.565 783	0.560 804	0.555 869	43
44	0.573 703	0.568 534	0.563 413	0.558 338	0.553 311	0.548 330	44
45	0.566 504	0.561 284	0.556 114	0.550 992	0.545 918	0.540 893	45
46	0.559 395	0.554 127	0.548 909	0.543 742	0.538 624	0.533 556	46
47	0.552 375	0.547 060	0.541 798	0.536 587	0.531 428	0.526 319	47

YRS							
4	0.545 443	0.540 084	0.534 779	0.529 527	0.524 328	0.519 181	48
5	0.468 745	0.462 996	0.457 318	0.451 711	0.446 173	0.440 705	60
6	0.402 832	0.396 910	0.391 076	0.385 330	0.379 668	0.374 091	72
7	0.346 188	0.340 258	0.334 430	0.328 704	0.323 076	0.317 546	84
8	0.297 508	0.291 691	0.285 989	0.280 399	0.274 920	0.269 548	96
9	0.255 674	0.250 057	0.244 564	0.239 193	0.233 941	0.228 805	108
10	0.219 722	0.214 365	0.209 140	0.204 042	0.199 071	0.194 221	120
11	0.188 826	0.183 768	0.178 846	0.174 057	0.169 398	0.164 864	132
12	0.162 274	0.157 538	0.152 941	0.148 479	0.144 148	0.139 944	144
13	0.139 456	0.135 052	0.130 788	0.126 659	0.122 662	0.118 791	156
14	0.119 846	0.115 775	0.111 843	0.108 046	0.104 378	0.100 836	168
15	0.102 994	0.099 250	0.095 643	0.092 168	0.088 820	0.085 594	180
16	0.088 511	0.085 084	0.081 790	0.078 624	0.075 581	0.072 656	192
17	0.076 065	0.072 939	0.069 943	0.067 069	0.064 315	0.061 674	204
18	0.065 369	0.062 528	0.059 812	0.057 213	0.054 728	0.052 352	216
19	0.056 177	0.053 603	0.051 148	0.048 806	0.046 571	0.044 439	228
20	0.048 278	0.045 952	0.043 739	0.041 633	0.039 629	0.037 722	240
21	0.041 489	0.039 393	0.037 404	0.035 515	0.033 722	0.032 020	252
22	0.035 655	0.033 771	0.031 986	0.030 296	0.028 696	0.027 180	264
23	0.030 642	0.028 950	0.027 353	0.025 844	0.024 418	0.023 072	276
24	0.026 333	0.024 818	0.023 391	0.022 046	0.020 779	0.019 584	288
25	0.022 630	0.021 276	0.020 003	0.018 806	0.017 681	0.016 624	300
26	0.019 448	0.018 239	0.017 105	0.016 043	0.015 046	0.014 111	312
27	0.016 713	0.015 636	0.014 628	0.013 685	0.012 803	0.011 978	324
28	0.014 363	0.013 404	0.012 509	0.011 674	0.010 895	0.010 168	336
29	0.012 343	0.011 491	0.010 697	0.009 958	0.009 271	0.008 631	348
30	0.010 608	0.009 851	0.009 148	0.008 495	0.007 889	0.007 326	360

SECTION 4

MOS	16.75% ANNUAL RATE	17.00% ANNUAL RATE	17.25% ANNUAL RATE	17.50% ANNUAL RATE	17.75% ANNUAL RATE	18.00% ANNUAL RATE	MOS
1	0.986 234	0.986 031	0.985 829	0.985 626	0.985 424	0.985 222	1
2	0.972 657	0.972 258	0.971 858	0.971 459	0.971 060	0.970 662	2
3	0.959 267	0.958 676	0.958 086	0.957 496	0.956 906	0.956 317	3
4	0.946 062	0.945 285	0.944 508	0.943 733	0.942 958	0.942 184	4
5	0.933 038	0.932 080	0.931 124	0.930 168	0.929 214	0.928 260	5
6	0.920 194	0.919 060	0.917 928	0.916 798	0.915 669	0.914 542	6
7	0.907 526	0.906 222	0.904 920	0.903 620	0.902 322	0.901 027	7
8	0.895 033	0.893 563	0.892 096	0.890 632	0.889 170	0.887 711	8
9	0.882 712	0.881 081	0.879 454	0.877 830	0.876 210	0.874 592	9
10	0.870 560	0.868 774	0.866 991	0.865 212	0.863 438	0.861 667	10
11	0.858 576	0.856 638	0.854 705	0.852 776	0.850 852	0.848 933	11
12	0.846 757	0.844 672	0.842 592	0.840 519	0.838 450	0.836 387	12
13	0.835 100	0.832 873	0.830 652	0.828 437	0.826 229	0.824 027	13
14	0.823 604	0.821 239	0.818 880	0.816 529	0.814 186	0.811 849	14
15	0.812 266	0.809 767	0.807 276	0.804 793	0.802 318	0.799 852	15
16	0.801 084	0.798 455	0.795 836	0.793 225	0.790 624	0.788 031	16
17	0.790 056	0.787 302	0.784 558	0.781 823	0.779 099	0.776 385	17
18	0.779 180	0.776 304	0.773 439	0.770 586	0.767 743	0.764 912	18
19	0.768 454	0.765 460	0.762 479	0.759 510	0.756 552	0.753 607	19
20	0.757 875	0.754 768	0.751 674	0.748 593	0.745 525	0.742 470	20
21	0.747 442	0.744 225	0.741 021	0.737 833	0.734 658	0.731 498	21
22	0.737 153	0.733 829	0.730 520	0.727 227	0.723 950	0.720 688	22
23	0.727 005	0.723 578	0.720 168	0.716 774	0.713 397	0.710 037	23
24	0.716 997	0.713 471	0.709 962	0.706 471	0.702 999	0.699 544	24
25	0.707 127	0.703 504	0.699 901	0.696 317	0.692 752	0.689 206	25
26	0.697 392	0.693 677	0.689 982	0.686 308	0.682 654	0.679 021	26
27	0.687 792	0.683 987	0.680 204	0.676 443	0.672 704	0.668 986	27
28	0.678 324	0.674 433	0.670 565	0.666 720	0.662 898	0.659 099	28
29	0.668 986	0.665 012	0.661 062	0.657 137	0.653 236	0.649 359	29
30	0.659 776	0.655 722	0.651 694	0.647 692	0.643 714	0.639 762	30
31	0.650 694	0.646 563	0.642 459	0.638 382	0.634 332	0.630 308	31
32	0.641 736	0.637 531	0.633 354	0.629 206	0.625 086	0.620 993	32
33	0.632 902	0.628 626	0.624 379	0.620 162	0.615 974	0.611 816	33
34	0.624 189	0.619 844	0.615 531	0.611 248	0.606 996	0.602 774	34
35	0.615 597	0.611 186	0.606 808	0.602 462	0.598 148	0.593 866	35
36	0.607 122	0.602 648	0.598 209	0.593 802	0.589 430	0.585 090	36
37	0.598 764	0.594 230	0.589 731	0.585 267	0.580 838	0.576 443	37
38	0.590 522	0.585 930	0.581 374	0.576 855	0.572 372	0.567 924	38
39	0.582 392	0.577 745	0.573 135	0.568 563	0.564 029	0.559 531	39
40	0.574 375	0.569 674	0.565 013	0.560 391	0.555 807	0.551 262	40
41	0.566 468	0.561 717	0.557 006	0.552 336	0.547 706	0.543 116	41
42	0.558 670	0.553 870	0.549 113	0.544 397	0.539 723	0.535 089	42
43	0.550 979	0.546 133	0.541 331	0.536 572	0.531 855	0.527 182	43
44	0.543 394	0.538 505	0.533 660	0.528 859	0.524 103	0.519 391	44
45	0.535 914	0.530 982	0.526 097	0.521 258	0.516 464	0.511 715	45
46	0.528 537	0.523 565	0.518 642	0.513 765	0.508 936	0.504 153	46
47	0.521 261	0.516 252	0.511 292	0.506 381	0.501 517	0.496 702	47

YRS

	16.75%	17.00%	17.25%	17.50%	17.75%	18.00%	
4	0.514 085	0.509 040	0.504 046	0.499 102	0.494 207	0.489 362	48
5	0.435 305	0.429 972	0.424 705	0.419 504	0.414 368	0.409 296	60
6	0.368 597	0.363 185	0.357 854	0.352 601	0.347 427	0.342 330	72
7	0.312 112	0.306 772	0.301 525	0.296 368	0.291 300	0.286 321	84
8	0.264 283	0.259 122	0.254 062	0.249 103	0.244 241	0.239 475	96
9	0.223 784	0.218 873	0.214 071	0.209 375	0.204 784	0.200 294	108
10	0.189 490	0.184 876	0.180 375	0.175 984	0.171 701	0.167 523	120
11	0.160 452	0.156 159	0.151 982	0.147 918	0.143 963	0.140 114	132
12	0.135 864	0.131 903	0.128 059	0.124 328	0.120 706	0.117 190	144
13	0.115 044	0.111 415	0.107 902	0.104 500	0.101 206	0.098 016	156
14	0.097 414	0.094 109	0.090 917	0.087 834	0.084 856	0.081 979	168
15	0.082 486	0.079 491	0.076 606	0.073 826	0.071 147	0.068 567	180
16	0.069 846	0.067 144	0.064 548	0.062 052	0.059 654	0.057 348	192
17	0.059 142	0.056 715	0.054 387	0.052 156	0.050 017	0.047 965	204
18	0.050 079	0.047 905	0.045 826	0.043 838	0.041 936	0.040 118	216
19	0.042 405	0.040 464	0.038 613	0.036 847	0.035 162	0.033 554	228
20	0.035 907	0.034 179	0.032 535	0.030 970	0.029 481	0.028 064	240
21	0.030 404	0.028 870	0.027 414	0.026 031	0.024 719	0.023 472	252
22	0.025 745	0.024 386	0.023 099	0.021 880	0.020 725	0.019 632	264
23	0.021 800	0.020 598	0.019 463	0.018 390	0.017 377	0.016 420	276
24	0.018 459	0.017 399	0.016 399	0.015 457	0.014 570	0.013 733	288
25	0.015 630	0.014 696	0.013 818	0.012 992	0.012 216	0.011 486	300
26	0.013 235	0.012 413	0.011 643	0.010 920	0.010 243	0.009 607	312
27	0.011 207	0.010 485	0.009 810	0.009 179	0.008 588	0.008 035	324
28	0.009 490	0.008 857	0.008 266	0.007 715	0.007 201	0.006 721	336
29	0.008 035	0.007 481	0.006 965	0.006 484	0.006 037	0.005 621	348
30	0.006 804	0.006 319	0.005 868	0.005 450	0.005 062	0.004 701	360

PRESENT VALUE OF $1

MONTHLY COMPOUNDING

MOS	18.25% ANNUAL RATE	18.50% ANNUAL RATE	18.75% ANNUAL RATE	19.00% ANNUAL RATE	19.25% ANNUAL RATE	19.50% ANNUAL RATE	MOS
1	0.985 019	0.984 817	0.984 615	0.984 413	0.984 212	0.984 010	1
2	0.970 263	0.969 865	0.969 467	0.969 070	0.968 672	0.968 275	2
3	0.955 728	0.955 140	0.954 553	0.953 965	0.953 379	0.952 792	3
4	0.941 411	0.940 639	0.939 867	0.939 096	0.938 326	0.937 557	4
5	0.927 308	0.926 357	0.925 408	0.924 459	0.923 512	0.922 565	5
6	0.913 417	0.912 293	0.911 171	0.910 050	0.908 931	0.907 814	6
7	0.899 733	0.898 442	0.897 153	0.895 865	0.894 580	0.893 297	7
8	0.886 255	0.884 801	0.883 350	0.881 902	0.880 456	0.879 013	8
9	0.872 978	0.871 368	0.869 760	0.868 156	0.866 555	0.864 958	9
10	0.859 901	0.858 138	0.856 379	0.854 625	0.852 874	0.851 127	10
11	0.847 019	0.845 109	0.843 204	0.841 304	0.839 408	0.837 517	11
12	0.834 330	0.832 278	0.830 232	0.828 191	0.826 155	0.824 125	12
13	0.821 831	0.819 642	0.817 459	0.815 282	0.813 112	0.810 947	13
14	0.809 520	0.807 198	0.804 883	0.802 575	0.800 274	0.797 980	14
15	0.797 393	0.794 942	0.792 500	0.790 066	0.787 639	0.785 220	15
16	0.785 448	0.782 873	0.780 308	0.777 751	0.775 203	0.772 665	16
17	0.773 681	0.770 987	0.768 303	0.765 629	0.762 964	0.760 310	17
18	0.762 091	0.759 282	0.756 483	0.753 695	0.750 918	0.748 152	18
19	0.750 675	0.747 754	0.744 845	0.741 948	0.739 062	0.736 189	19
20	0.739 429	0.736 401	0.733 386	0.730 383	0.727 394	0.724 417	20
21	0.728 352	0.725 220	0.722 103	0.718 999	0.715 909	0.712 834	21
22	0.717 441	0.714 210	0.710 993	0.707 792	0.704 606	0.701 435	22
23	0.706 693	0.703 366	0.700 055	0.696 760	0.693 482	0.690 219	23
24	0.696 107	0.692 687	0.689 285	0.685 900	0.682 533	0.679 183	24
25	0.685 679	0.682 170	0.678 681	0.675 209	0.671 757	0.668 322	25
26	0.675 407	0.671 813	0.668 239	0.664 685	0.661 151	0.657 636	26
27	0.665 289	0.661 613	0.657 959	0.654 325	0.650 712	0.647 120	27
28	0.655 323	0.651 568	0.647 836	0.644 126	0.640 439	0.636 773	28
29	0.645 506	0.641 676	0.637 870	0.634 087	0.630 327	0.626 590	29
30	0.635 836	0.631 933	0.628 056	0.624 204	0.620 375	0.616 571	30
31	0.626 310	0.622 339	0.618 394	0.614 474	0.610 581	0.606 712	31
32	0.616 928	0.612 890	0.608 880	0.604 897	0.600 940	0.597 011	32
33	0.607 686	0.603 585	0.599 513	0.595 469	0.591 453	0.587 464	33
34	0.598 583	0.594 421	0.590 289	0.586 187	0.582 114	0.578 071	34
35	0.589 616	0.585 396	0.581 208	0.577 051	0.572 924	0.568 827	35
36	0.580 783	0.576 508	0.572 266	0.568 056	0.563 878	0.559 732	36
37	0.572 082	0.567 756	0.563 462	0.559 202	0.554 976	0.550 781	37
38	0.563 512	0.559 136	0.554 794	0.550 486	0.546 213	0.541 974	38
39	0.555 071	0.550 646	0.546 258	0.541 906	0.537 590	0.533 308	39
40	0.546 755	0.542 286	0.537 854	0.533 460	0.529 102	0.524 780	40
41	0.538 565	0.534 053	0.529 580	0.525 145	0.520 748	0.516 389	41
42	0.530 497	0.525 945	0.521 432	0.516 960	0.512 526	0.508 132	42
43	0.522 550	0.517 959	0.513 410	0.508 902	0.504 434	0.500 007	43
44	0.514 722	0.510 095	0.505 512	0.500 970	0.496 470	0.492 012	44
45	0.507 011	0.502 351	0.497 735	0.493 162	0.488 632	0.484 144	45
46	0.499 415	0.494 724	0.490 077	0.485 475	0.480 917	0.476 403	46
47	0.491 934	0.487 213	0.482 537	0.477 908	0.473 324	0.468 785	47

YRS							
4	0.484 565	0.479 815	0.475 114	0.470 459	0.465 851	0.461 289	48
5	0.404 287	0.399 340	0.394 455	0.389 630	0.384 865	0.380 160	60
6	0.337 309	0.332 362	0.327 489	0.322 688	0.317 959	0.313 300	72
7	0.281 427	0.276 618	0.271 892	0.267 247	0.262 683	0.258 198	84
8	0.234 803	0.230 223	0.225 733	0.221 332	0.217 017	0.212 788	96
9	0.195 903	0.191 609	0.187 411	0.183 305	0.179 290	0.175 364	108
10	0.163 448	0.159 472	0.155 594	0.151 812	0.148 121	0.144 522	120
11	0.136 369	0.132 725	0.129 179	0.125 729	0.122 371	0.119 104	132
12	0.113 777	0.110 464	0.107 249	0.104 128	0.101 098	0.098 157	144
13	0.094 928	0.091 937	0.089 041	0.086 238	0.083 522	0.080 893	156
14	0.079 201	0.076 517	0.073 925	0.071 421	0.069 003	0.066 666	168
15	0.066 080	0.063 684	0.061 375	0.059 150	0.057 007	0.054 941	180
16	0.055 132	0.053 003	0.050 955	0.048 988	0.047 096	0.045 279	192
17	0.045 999	0.044 113	0.042 305	0.040 571	0.038 909	0.037 315	204
18	0.038 378	0.036 714	0.035 123	0.033 601	0.032 145	0.030 752	216
19	0.032 020	0.030 556	0.029 160	0.027 828	0.026 557	0.025 344	228
20	0.026 715	0.025 431	0.024 210	0.023 047	0.021 940	0.020 887	240
21	0.022 289	0.021 166	0.020 100	0.019 087	0.018 126	0.017 213	252
22	0.018 597	0.017 616	0.016 687	0.015 808	0.014 975	0.014 186	264
23	0.015 516	0.014 661	0.013 854	0.013 092	0.012 371	0.011 691	276
24	0.012 945	0.012 202	0.011 502	0.010 843	0.010 221	0.009 635	288
25	0.010 801	0.010 156	0.009 550	0.008 980	0.008 444	0.007 940	300
26	0.009 011	0.008 452	0.007 928	0.007 437	0.006 976	0.006 544	312
27	0.007 518	0.007 035	0.006 582	0.006 159	0.005 763	0.005 393	324
28	0.006 273	0.005 855	0.005 465	0.005 101	0.004 761	0.004 444	336
29	0.005 234	0.004 873	0.004 537	0.004 225	0.003 934	0.003 663	348
30	0.004 367	0.004 056	0.003 767	0.003 499	0.003 250	0.003 019	360

PRESENT VALUE OF $1

MOS	19.75% ANNUAL RATE	20.00% ANNUAL RATE	21.00% ANNUAL RATE	22.00% ANNUAL RATE	23.00% ANNUAL RATE	24.00% ANNUAL RATE	MOS
1	0.983 808	0.983 607	0.982 801	0.981 997	0.981 194	0.980 392	1
2	0.967 878	0.967 482	0.965 898	0.964 318	0.962 741	0.961 169	2
3	0.952 207	0.951 622	0.949 285	0.946 957	0.944 636	0.942 322	3
4	0.936 789	0.936 021	0.932 959	0.929 908	0.926 871	0.923 845	4
5	0.921 620	0.920 677	0.916 913	0.913 167	0.909 440	0.905 731	5
6	0.906 698	0.905 583	0.901 143	0.896 727	0.892 337	0.887 971	6
7	0.892 017	0.890 738	0.885 644	0.880 583	0.875 555	0.870 560	7
8	0.877 573	0.876 136	0.870 412	0.864 730	0.859 089	0.853 490	8
9	0.863 364	0.861 773	0.855 441	0.849 162	0.842 933	0.836 755	9
10	0.849 384	0.847 645	0.840 729	0.833 874	0.827 081	0.820 348	10
11	0.835 631	0.833 749	0.826 269	0.818 861	0.811 526	0.804 263	11
12	0.822 101	0.820 081	0.812 058	0.804 119	0.796 265	0.788 493	12
13	0.808 789	0.806 637	0.798 091	0.789 643	0.781 290	0.773 033	13
14	0.795 694	0.793 414	0.784 365	0.775 426	0.766 597	0.757 875	14
15	0.782 810	0.780 407	0.770 875	0.761 466	0.752 180	0.743 015	15
16	0.770 135	0.767 614	0.757 616	0.747 757	0.738 034	0.728 446	16
17	0.757 665	0.755 030	0.744 586	0.734 295	0.724 155	0.714 163	17
18	0.745 397	0.742 652	0.731 780	0.721 075	0.710 536	0.700 159	18
19	0.733 327	0.730 478	0.719 194	0.708 094	0.697 174	0.686 431	19
20	0.721 454	0.718 503	0.706 825	0.695 346	0.684 062	0.672 971	20
21	0.709 772	0.706 724	0.694 668	0.682 827	0.671 198	0.659 776	21
22	0.698 279	0.695 138	0.682 720	0.670 534	0.658 575	0.646 839	22
23	0.686 973	0.683 742	0.670 978	0.658 462	0.646 190	0.634 156	23
24	0.675 850	0.672 534	0.659 438	0.646 608	0.634 037	0.621 721	24
25	0.664 906	0.661 508	0.648 096	0.634 967	0.622 114	0.609 531	25
26	0.654 140	0.650 664	0.636 950	0.623 535	0.610 414	0.597 579	26
27	0.643 549	0.639 997	0.625 995	0.612 310	0.598 934	0.585 862	27
28	0.633 128	0.629 506	0.615 228	0.601 286	0.587 671	0.574 375	28
29	0.622 877	0.619 186	0.604 647	0.590 461	0.576 619	0.563 112	29
30	0.612 791	0.609 035	0.594 248	0.579 831	0.565 775	0.552 071	30
31	0.602 869	0.599 051	0.584 027	0.569 392	0.555 135	0.541 246	31
32	0.593 108	0.589 231	0.573 982	0.559 141	0.544 695	0.530 633	32
33	0.583 504	0.579 571	0.564 111	0.549 075	0.534 451	0.520 229	33
34	0.574 056	0.570 070	0.554 408	0.539 189	0.524 400	0.510 028	34
35	0.564 761	0.560 725	0.544 873	0.529 482	0.514 538	0.500 028	35
36	0.555 616	0.551 532	0.535 502	0.519 950	0.504 862	0.490 223	36
37	0.546 620	0.542 491	0.526 292	0.510 589	0.495 367	0.480 611	37
38	0.537 769	0.533 597	0.517 240	0.501 397	0.486 051	0.471 187	38
39	0.529 062	0.524 850	0.508 344	0.492 370	0.476 910	0.461 948	39
40	0.520 495	0.516 246	0.499 601	0.483 506	0.467 941	0.452 890	40
41	0.512 067	0.507 783	0.491 008	0.474 801	0.459 141	0.444 010	41
42	0.503 776	0.499 459	0.482 563	0.466 253	0.450 507	0.435 304	42
43	0.495 619	0.491 271	0.474 264	0.457 859	0.442 034	0.426 769	43
44	0.487 594	0.483 217	0.466 107	0.449 616	0.433 721	0.418 401	44
45	0.479 699	0.475 295	0.458 090	0.441 521	0.425 565	0.410 197	45
46	0.471 932	0.467 504	0.450 212	0.433 573	0.417 561	0.402 154	46
47	0.464 290	0.459 840	0.442 469	0.425 767	0.409 709	0.394 268	47

YRS

	19.75%	20.00%	21.00%	22.00%	23.00%	24.00%	
4	0.456 773	0.452 301	0.434 858	0.418 102	0.402 004	0.386 538	48
5	0.375 513	0.370 924	0.353 130	0.336 204	0.320 101	0.304 782	60
6	0.308 710	0.304 188	0.286 762	0.270 348	0.254 885	0.240 319	72
7	0.253 790	0.249 459	0.232 868	0.217 392	0.202 956	0.189 490	84
8	0.208 641	0.204 577	0.189 102	0.174 809	0.161 607	0.149 411	96
9	0.171 524	0.167 769	0.153 562	0.140 567	0.128 682	0.117 810	108
10	0.141 010	0.137 585	0.124 701	0.113 033	0.102 465	0.092 892	120
11	0.115 925	0.112 831	0.101 264	0.090 892	0.081 589	0.073 245	132
12	0.095 302	0.092 530	0.082 233	0.073 088	0.064 967	0.057 753	144
13	0.078 348	0.075 882	0.066 778	0.058 771	0.051 731	0.045 538	156
14	0.064 410	0.062 230	0.054 227	0.047 259	0.041 191	0.035 906	168
15	0.052 951	0.051 033	0.044 036	0.038 002	0.032 799	0.028 312	180
16	0.043 531	0.041 852	0.035 760	0.030 558	0.026 117	0.022 324	192
17	0.035 787	0.034 322	0.029 039	0.024 572	0.020 796	0.017 602	204
18	0.029 421	0.028 147	0.023 581	0.019 759	0.016 559	0.013 879	216
19	0.024 187	0.023 082	0.019 149	0.015 889	0.013 185	0.010 944	228
20	0.019 884	0.018 930	0.015 550	0.012 776	0.010 499	0.008 629	240
21	0.016 347	0.015 524	0.012 628	0.010 274	0.008 360	0.006 804	252
22	0.013 438	0.012 731	0.010 254	0.008 261	0.006 657	0.005 365	264
23	0.011 048	0.010 440	0.008 327	0.006 643	0.005 301	0.004 230	276
24	0.009 082	0.008 562	0.006 762	0.005 342	0.004 221	0.003 335	288
25	0.007 467	0.007 021	0.005 491	0.004 295	0.003 361	0.002 630	300
26	0.006 138	0.005 758	0.004 459	0.003 454	0.002 676	0.002 074	312
27	0.005 046	0.004 722	0.003 621	0.002 777	0.002 131	0.001 635	324
28	0.004 149	0.003 873	0.002 941	0.002 233	0.001 697	0.001 289	336
29	0.003 411	0.003 176	0.002 388	0.001 796	0.001 351	0.001 017	348
30	0.002 804	0.002 604	0.001 939	0.001 444	0.001 076	0.000 802	360

PRESENT VALUE OF $1

QTRS	6.50% ANNUAL RATE	7.00% ANNUAL RATE	7.50% ANNUAL RATE	8.00% ANNUAL RATE	8.50% ANNUAL RATE	9.00% ANNUAL RATE	QTRS
1	0.984 010	0.982 801	0.981 595	0.980 392	0.979 192	0.977 995	1
2	0.968 275	0.965 898	0.963 529	0.961 169	0.958 817	0.956 474	2
3	0.952 792	0.949 285	0.945 795	0.942 322	0.938 866	0.935 427	3
4	0.937 557	0.932 959	0.928 388	0.923 845	0.919 331	0.914 843	4
5	0.922 565	0.916 913	0.911 301	0.905 731	0.900 201	0.894 712	5
6	0.907 814	0.901 143	0.894 529	0.887 971	0.881 470	0.875 024	6
7	0.893 297	0.885 644	0.878 065	0.870 560	0.863 129	0.855 769	7
8	0.879 013	0.870 412	0.861 904	0.853 490	0.845 169	0.836 938	8
9	0.864 958	0.855 441	0.846 041	0.836 755	0.827 583	0.818 522	9
10	0.851 127	0.840 729	0.830 470	0.820 348	0.810 362	0.800 510	10
11	0.837 517	0.826 269	0.815 185	0.804 263	0.793 501	0.782 895	11
12	0.824 125	0.812 058	0.800 182	0.788 493	0.776 990	0.765 667	12
13	0.810 947	0.798 091	0.785 454	0.773 033	0.760 822	0.748 819	13
14	0.797 980	0.784 365	0.770 998	0.757 875	0.744 991	0.732 341	14
15	0.785 220	0.770 875	0.756 808	0.743 015	0.729 489	0.716 226	15
16	0.772 665	0.757 616	0.742 879	0.728 446	0.714 310	0.700 466	16
17	0.760 310	0.744 586	0.729 206	0.714 163	0.699 447	0.685 052	17
18	0.748 152	0.731 780	0.715 785	0.700 159	0.684 893	0.669 978	18
19	0.736 189	0.719 194	0.702 611	0.686 431	0.670 642	0.655 235	19
20	0.724 417	0.706 825	0.689 680	0.672 971	0.656 687	0.640 816	20
21	0.712 834	0.694 668	0.676 986	0.659 776	0.643 023	0.626 715	21
22	0.701 435	0.682 720	0.664 527	0.646 839	0.629 643	0.612 925	22
23	0.690 219	0.670 978	0.652 296	0.634 156	0.616 542	0.599 437	23
24	0.679 183	0.659 438	0.640 291	0.621 721	0.603 713	0.586 247	24
25	0.668 322	0.648 096	0.628 506	0.609 531	0.591 151	0.573 346	25
26	0.657 636	0.636 950	0.616 938	0.597 579	0.578 850	0.560 730	26
27	0.647 120	0.625 995	0.605 584	0.585 862	0.566 806	0.548 391	27
28	0.636 773	0.615 228	0.594 438	0.574 375	0.555 012	0.536 324	28
29	0.626 590	0.604 647	0.583 497	0.563 112	0.543 463	0.524 522	29
30	0.616 571	0.594 248	0.572 758	0.552 071	0.532 155	0.512 980	30
31	0.603 712	0.584 027	0.562 217	0.541 246	0.521 082	0.501 692	31
32	0.597 011	0.573 982	0.551 869	0.530 633	0.510 239	0.490 652	32
33	0.587 464	0.564 111	0.541 712	0.520 229	0.499 622	0.479 856	33
34	0.578 071	0.554 408	0.531 742	0.510 028	0.489 226	0.469 296	34
35	0.568 827	0.544 873	0.521 955	0.500 028	0.479 046	0.458 970	35
36	0.559 732	0.535 502	0.512 349	0.490 223	0.469 078	0.448 870	36
37	0.550 781	0.526 292	0.502 919	0.480 611	0.459 318	0.438 993	37
38	0.541 974	0.517 240	0.493 663	0.471 187	0.449 761	0.429 333	38
39	0.533 308	0.508 344	0.484 577	0.461 948	0.440 402	0.419 885	39
40	0.524 780	0.499 601	0.475 658	0.452 890	0.431 238	0.410 646	40
41	0.516 389	0.491 008	0.466 904	0.444 010	0.422 265	0.401 610	41
42	0.508 132	0.482 563	0.458 311	0.435 304	0.413 479	0.392 772	42
43	0.500 007	0.474 264	0.449 875	0.426 769	0.404 875	0.384 129	43
44	0.492 012	0.466 107	0.441 596	0.418 401	0.396 450	0.375 677	44
45	0.484 144	0.458 090	0.433 468	0.410 197	0.388 201	0.367 410	45
46	0.476 403	0.450 212	0.425 490	0.402 154	0.380 124	0.359 325	46
47	0.468 785	0.442 469	0.417 659	0.394 268	0.372 214	0.351 418	47
48	0.461 289	0.434 858	0.409 972	0.386 538	0.364 469	0.343 685	48
49	0.453 913	0.427 379	0.402 426	0.378 958	0.356 885	0.336 122	49
50	0.446 655	0.420 029	0.395 020	0.371 528	0.349 459	0.328 726	50
51	0.439 513	0.412 805	0.387 750	0.364 243	0.342 188	0.321 493	51
52	0.432 485	0.405 705	0.380 613	0.357 101	0.335 068	0.314 418	52
53	0.425 569	0.398 727	0.373 608	0.350 099	0.328 096	0.307 499	53
54	0.418 764	0.391 869	0.366 732	0.343 234	0.321 269	0.300 733	54
55	0.412 068	0.385 130	0.359 982	0.336 504	0.314 584	0.294 115	55

YRS

YRS	6.50% ANNUAL RATE	7.00% ANNUAL RATE	7.50% ANNUAL RATE	8.00% ANNUAL RATE	8.50% ANNUAL RATE	9.00% ANNUAL RATE	QTRS
14	0.405 479	0.378 506	0.353 357	0.329 906	0.308 038	0.287 643	56
15	0.380 160	0.353 130	0.328 052	0.304 782	0.283 189	0.263 149	60
16	0.356 422	0.329 456	0.304 560	0.281 572	0.260 344	0.240 740	64
17	0.334 166	0.307 369	0.282 749	0.260 129	0.239 342	0.220 239	68
18	0.313 300	0.286 762	0.262 501	0.240 319	0.220 035	0.201 484	72
19	0.293 736	0.267 537	0.243 703	0.222 017	0.202 285	0.184 327	76
20	0.275 395	0.249 601	0.226 251	0.205 110	0.185 966	0.168 630	80
21	0.258 198	0.232 868	0.210 049	0.189 490	0.170 965	0.154 270	84
22	0.242 076	0.217 256	0.195 007	0.175 059	0.157 173	0.141 133	88
23	0.226 960	0.202 691	0.181 042	0.161 728	0.144 494	0.129 114	92
24	0.212 788	0.189 102	0.168 077	0.149 411	0.132 838	0.118 119	96
25	0.199 501	0.176 424	0.156 041	0.138 033	0.122 122	0.108 061	100
26	0.187 043	0.164 596	0.144 866	0.127 521	0.112 270	0.098 859	104
27	0.175 364	0.153 562	0.134 492	0.117 810	0.103 213	0.090 440	108
28	0.164 413	0.143 267	0.124 861	0.108 838	0.094 887	0.082 739	112
29	0.154 147	0.133 662	0.115 919	0.100 550	0.087 233	0.075 693	116
30	0.144 522	0.124 701	0.107 618	0.092 892	0.080 196	0.069 247	120

QTRS	9.50% ANNUAL RATE	10.00% ANNUAL RATE	10.50% ANNUAL RATE	11.00% ANNUAL RATE	11.50% ANNUAL RATE	12.00% ANNUAL RATE	QTRS
1	0.976 801	0.975 610	0.974 421	0.973 236	0.972 053	0.970 874	1
2	0.954 140	0.951 814	0.949 497	0.947 188	0.944 888	0.942 596	2
3	0.932 005	0.928 599	0.925 210	0.921 838	0.918 482	0.915 142	3
4	0.910 383	0.905 951	0.901 545	0.897 166	0.892 813	0.888 487	4
5	0.889 263	0.883 854	0.878 485	0.873 154	0.867 862	0.862 609	5
6	0.868 633	0.862 297	0.856 014	0.849 785	0.843 608	0.837 484	6
7	0.848 482	0.841 265	0.834 119	0.827 041	0.820 032	0.813 092	7
8	0.828 798	0.820 747	0.812 783	0.804 906	0.797 115	0.789 409	8
9	0.809 571	0.800 728	0.791 993	0.783 364	0.774 839	0.766 417	9
10	0.790 789	0.781 198	0.771 735	0.762 398	0.753 185	0.744 094	10
11	0.772 444	0.762 145	0.751 995	0.741 993	0.732 136	0.722 421	11
12	0.754 524	0.743 556	0.732 760	0.722 134	0.711 675	0.701 380	12
13	0.737 020	0.725 420	0.714 017	0.702 807	0.691 786	0.680 951	13
14	0.719 922	0.707 727	0.695 754	0.683 997	0.672 453	0.661 118	14
15	0.703 220	0.690 466	0.677 957	0.665 691	0.653 661	0.641 862	15
16	0.686 906	0.673 625	0.660 616	0.647 874	0.635 393	0.623 167	16
17	0.670 971	0.657 195	0.643 719	0.630 535	0.617 636	0.605 016	17
18	0.655 405	0.641 166	0.627 253	0.613 659	0.600 375	0.587 395	18
19	0.640 200	0.625 528	0.611 209	0.597 235	0.583 597	0.570 286	19
20	0.625 348	0.610 271	0.595 575	0.581 251	0.567 287	0.553 676	20
21	0.610 840	0.595 386	0.580 341	0.565 694	0.551 434	0.537 549	21
22	0.596 670	0.580 865	0.565 497	0.550 554	0.536 023	0.521 893	22
23	0.582 827	0.566 697	0.551 032	0.535 819	0.521 043	0.506 692	23
24	0.569 306	0.552 875	0.536 938	0.521 478	0.506 482	0.491 934	24
25	0.556 099	0.539 391	0.523 204	0.507 521	0.492 327	0.477 606	25
26	0.543 198	0.526 235	0.509 821	0.493 938	0.478 568	0.463 695	26
27	0.530 596	0.513 400	0.496 780	0.480 718	0.465 194	0.450 189	27
28	0.518 287	0.500 878	0.484 073	0.467 852	0.452 193	0.437 077	28
29	0.506 263	0.488 661	0.471 692	0.455 331	0.439 556	0.424 346	29
30	0.494 519	0.476 743	0.459 626	0.443 144	0.427 272	0.411 987	30
31	0.483 046	0.465 115	0.447 870	0.431 284	0.415 331	0.399 987	31
32	0.471 840	0.453 771	0.436 414	0.419 741	0.403 724	0.388 337	32
33	0.460 894	0.442 703	0.425 251	0.408 507	0.392 442	0.377 026	33
34	0.450 201	0.431 905	0.414 374	0.397 574	0.381 474	0.366 045	34
35	0.439 757	0.421 371	0.403 775	0.386 933	0.370 813	0.355 383	35
36	0.429 555	0.411 094	0.393 447	0.376 577	0.360 450	0.345 032	36
37	0.419 590	0.401 067	0.383 383	0.366 499	0.350 377	0.334 983	37
38	0.409 856	0.391 285	0.373 576	0.356 690	0.340 585	0.325 226	38
39	0.400 348	0.381 741	0.364 021	0.347 143	0.331 067	0.315 754	39
40	0.391 060	0.372 431	0.354 710	0.337 852	0.321 815	0.306 557	40
41	0.381 988	0.363 347	0.345 637	0.328 810	0.312 821	0.297 628	41
42	0.373 126	0.354 485	0.336 796	0.320 010	0.304 079	0.288 959	42
43	0.364 470	0.345 839	0.328 181	0.311 445	0.295 581	0.280 543	43
44	0.356 015	0.337 404	0.319 787	0.303 109	0.287 321	0.272 372	44
45	0.347 755	0.329 174	0.311 607	0.294 997	0.279 291	0.264 439	45
46	0.339 688	0.321 146	0.303 637	0.287 102	0.271 486	0.256 737	46
47	0.331 807	0.313 313	0.295 870	0.279 418	0.263 899	0.249 259	47
48	0.324 110	0.305 671	0.288 302	0.271 939	0.256 524	0.241 999	48
49	0.316 591	0.298 216	0.280 928	0.264 661	0.249 355	0.234 950	49
50	0.309 246	0.290 942	0.273 742	0.257 578	0.242 386	0.228 107	50
51	0.302 072	0.283 846	0.266 740	0.250 684	0.235 612	0.221 463	51
52	0.295 064	0.276 923	0.259 917	0.243 975	0.229 028	0.215 013	52
53	0.288 219	0.270 169	0.253 269	0.237 445	0.222 627	0.208 750	53
54	0.281 533	0.263 579	0.246 791	0.231 090	0.216 405	0.202 670	54
55	0.275 001	0.257 151	0.240 478	0.224 905	0.210 358	0.196 767	55
YRS							
14	0.268 622	0.250 879	0.234 327	0.218 886	0.204 479	0.191 036	56
15	0.244 549	0.227 284	0.211 256	0.196 377	0.182 561	0.169 733	60
16	0.222 633	0.205 908	0.190 457	0.176 183	0.162 993	0.150 806	64
17	0.202 681	0.186 542	0.171 706	0.158 065	0.145 523	0.133 989	68
18	0.184 518	0.168 998	0.154 800	0.141 810	0.129 924	0.119 047	72
19	0.167 982	0.153 104	0.139 559	0.127 227	0.115 998	0.105 772	76
20	0.152 928	0.138 705	0.125 819	0.114 144	0.103 565	0.093 977	80
21	0.139 223	0.125 659	0.113 432	0.102 406	0.092 464	0.083 497	84
22	0.126 746	0.113 841	0.102 264	0.091 875	0.082 553	0.074 186	88
23	0.115 388	0.103 135	0.092 195	0.082 427	0.073 704	0.065 914	92
24	0.105 047	0.093 435	0.083 118	0.073 951	0.065 804	0.058 563	96
25	0.095 633	0.084 647	0.074 935	0.066 346	0.058 751	0.052 033	100
26	0.087 063	0.076 686	0.067 557	0.059 524	0.052 454	0.046 231	104
27	0.079 261	0.069 474	0.060 906	0.053 403	0.046 831	0.041 075	108
28	0.072 158	0.062 940	0.054 909	0.047 911	0.041 812	0.036 495	112
29	0.065 691	0.057 021	0.049 503	0.042 984	0.037 330	0.032 425	116
30	0.059 804	0.051 658	0.044 629	0.038 564	0.033 329	0.028 809	120

QTRS	12.50% ANNUAL RATE	13.00% ANNUAL RATE	13.50% ANNUAL RATE	14.00% ANNUAL RATE	14.50% ANNUAL RATE	15.00% ANNUAL RATE	QTRS
1	0.969 697	0.968 523	0.967 352	0.966 184	0.965 018	0.963 855	1
2	0.940 312	0.938 037	0.935 770	0.933 511	0.931 260	0.929 017	2
3	0.911 818	0.908 510	0.905 219	0.901 943	0.898 683	0.895 438	3
4	0.884 187	0.879 913	0.875 665	0.871 442	0.867 245	0.863 073	4
5	0.857 394	0.852 216	0.847 076	0.841 973	0.836 907	0.831 878	5
6	0.831 412	0.825 391	0.819 421	0.813 501	0.807 631	0.801 810	6
7	0.806 218	0.799 410	0.792 668	0.785 991	0.779 378	0.772 829	7
8	0.781 787	0.774 247	0.766 789	0.759 412	0.752 114	0.744 895	8
9	0.758 096	0.749 876	0.741 755	0.733 731	0.725 804	0.717 971	9
10	0.735 124	0.726 272	0.717 538	0.708 919	0.700 414	0.692 020	10
11	0.712 847	0.703 411	0.694 112	0.684 946	0.675 912	0.667 008	11
12	0.691 246	0.681 270	0.671 450	0.661 783	0.652 267	0.642 899	12
13	0.670 299	0.659 826	0.649 528	0.639 404	0.629 450	0.619 662	13
14	0.649 987	0.639 056	0.628 323	0.617 782	0.607 430	0.597 264	14
15	0.630 290	0.618 941	0.607 809	0.596 891	0.586 181	0.575 676	15
16	0.611 191	0.599 458	0.587 965	0.576 706	0.565 675	0.554 869	16
17	0.592 670	0.580 589	0.568 769	0.557 204	0.545 887	0.534 813	17
18	0.574 710	0.562 314	0.550 200	0.538 361	0.526 791	0.515 483	18
19	0.557 294	0.544 614	0.532 237	0.520 156	0.508 363	0.496 851	19
20	0.540 407	0.527 471	0.514 860	0.502 566	0.490 579	0.478 892	20
21	0.524 031	0.510 868	0.498 051	0.485 571	0.473 418	0.461 583	21
22	0.508 151	0.494 787	0.481 791	0.469 151	0.456 857	0.444 899	22
23	0.492 753	0.479 213	0.466 061	0.453 286	0.440 875	0.428 819	23
24	0.477 821	0.464 129	0.450 845	0.437 957	0.425 452	0.413 319	24
25	0.463 341	0.449 519	0.436 126	0.423 147	0.410 569	0.398 380	25
26	0.449 301	0.435 370	0.421 887	0.408 838	0.396 207	0.383 981	26
27	0.435 685	0.421 666	0.408 113	0.395 012	0.382 347	0.370 102	27
28	0.422 483	0.408 393	0.394 789	0.381 654	0.368 971	0.356 725	28
29	0.409 680	0.395 538	0.381 900	0.368 748	0.356 064	0.343 831	29
30	0.397 266	0.383 088	0.369 432	0.356 278	0.343 608	0.331 403	30
31	0.385 227	0.371 029	0.357 371	0.344 230	0.331 588	0.319 425	31
32	0.373 554	0.359 350	0.345 703	0.332 590	0.319 989	0.307 879	32
33	0.362 234	0.348 039	0.334 417	0.321 343	0.308 795	0.296 751	33
34	0.351 257	0.337 084	0.323 498	0.310 476	0.297 993	0.286 025	34
35	0.340 613	0.326 473	0.312 937	0.299 977	0.287 568	0.275 687	35
36	0.330 291	0.316 197	0.302 720	0.289 833	0.277 509	0.265 722	36
37	0.320 283	0.306 244	0.292 837	0.280 032	0.267 801	0.256 118	37
38	0.310 577	0.296 604	0.283 276	0.270 562	0.258 433	0.246 861	38
39	0.301 166	0.287 268	0.274 028	0.261 413	0.249 392	0.237 938	39
40	0.292 039	0.278 226	0.265 081	0.252 572	0.240 668	0.229 338	40
41	0.283 190	0.269 468	0.256 427	0.244 031	0.232 249	0.221 049	41
42	0.274 608	0.260 986	0.248 055	0.235 779	0.224 124	0.213 059	42
43	0.266 287	0.252 771	0.239 957	0.227 806	0.216 284	0.205 358	43
44	0.258 218	0.244 815	0.232 122	0.220 102	0.208 718	0.197 935	44
45	0.250 393	0.237 109	0.224 544	0.212 659	0.201 417	0.190 781	45
46	0.242 805	0.229 645	0.217 213	0.205 468	0.194 371	0.183 885	46
47	0.235 447	0.222 417	0.210 121	0.198 520	0.187 571	0.177 239	47
48	0.228 313	0.215 416	0.203 261	0.191 806	0.181 010	0.170 833	48
49	0.221 394	0.208 635	0.196 625	0.185 320	0.174 678	0.164 658	49
50	0.214 685	0.202 068	0.190 206	0.179 053	0.168 567	0.158 707	50
51	0.208 179	0.195 707	0.183 996	0.172 998	0.162 670	0.152 970	51
52	0.201 871	0.189 547	0.177 989	0.167 148	0.156 980	0.147 441	52
53	0.195 754	0.183 581	0.172 178	0.161 496	0.151 488	0.142 112	53
54	0.189 822	0.177 802	0.166 557	0.156 035	0.146 189	0.136 975	54
55	0.184 070	0.172 205	0.161 119	0.150 758	0.141 075	0.132 024	55

YRS

YRS	12.50%	13.00%	13.50%	14.00%	14.50%	15.00%	QTRS
14	0.178 492	0.166 785	0.155 859	0.145 660	0.136 140	0.127 252	56
15	0.157 820	0.146 756	0.136 480	0.126 934	0.118 067	0.109 828	60
16	0.139 542	0.129 133	0.119 511	0.110 616	0.102 393	0.094 790	64
17	0.123 382	0.113 626	0.104 651	0.096 395	0.088 800	0.081 810	68
18	0.109 092	0.099 981	0.091 639	0.084 003	0.077 011	0.070 608	72
19	0.096 458	0.087 974	0.080 245	0.073 204	0.066 787	0.060 940	76
20	0.085 287	0.077 410	0.070 268	0.063 793	0.057 921	0.052 596	80
21	0.075 410	0.068 114	0.061 531	0.055 592	0.050 232	0.045 394	84
22	0.066 676	0.059 934	0.053 881	0.048 445	0.043 563	0.039 178	88
23	0.058 954	0.052 737	0.047 182	0.042 217	0.037 780	0.033 814	92
24	0.052 127	0.046 404	0.041 315	0.036 790	0.032 765	0.029 184	96
25	0.046 090	0.040 831	0.036 178	0.032 060	0.028 415	0.025 188	100
26	0.040 752	0.035 928	0.031 680	0.027 939	0.024 643	0.021 739	104
27	0.036 032	0.031 614	0.027 741	0.024 347	0.021 371	0.018 762	108
28	0.031 859	0.027 817	0.024 292	0.021 217	0.018 534	0.016 193	112
29	0.028 170	0.024 477	0.021 272	0.018 489	0.016 074	0.013 976	116
30	0.024 907	0.021 537	0.018 627	0.016 112	0.013 940	0.012 062	120

PRESENT VALUE OF $1

QTRS	15.50% ANNUAL RATE	16.00% ANNUAL RATE	16.50% ANNUAL RATE	17.00% ANNUAL RATE	17.50% ANNUAL RATE	18.00% ANNUAL RATE	QTRS
1	0.962 696	0.961 538	0.960 384	0.959 233	0.958 084	0.956 938	1
2	0.926 783	0.924 556	0.922 338	0.920 127	0.917 925	0.915 730	2
3	0.892 210	0.888 996	0.885 799	0.882 616	0.879 449	0.876 297	3
4	0.858 926	0.854 804	0.850 707	0.846 634	0.842 586	0.838 561	4
5	0.826 884	0.821 927	0.817 005	0.812 119	0.807 268	0.802 451	5
6	0.796 038	0.790 315	0.784 639	0.779 011	0.773 430	0.767 896	6
7	0.766 342	0.759 918	0.753 555	0.747 253	0.741 011	0.734 828	7
8	0.737 754	0.730 690	0.723 702	0.716 789	0.709 951	0.703 185	8
9	0.710 233	0.702 587	0.695 032	0.687 568	0.680 192	0.672 904	9
10	0.683 738	0.675 564	0.667 498	0.659 537	0.651 681	0.643 928	10
11	0.658 231	0.649 581	0.641 054	0.632 650	0.624 365	0.616 199	11
12	0.633 676	0.624 597	0.615 658	0.606 858	0.598 194	0.589 664	12
13	0.610 037	0.600 574	0.591 269	0.582 118	0.573 120	0.564 272	13
14	0.587 280	0.577 475	0.567 845	0.558 387	0.549 097	0.539 973	14
15	0.565 372	0.555 265	0.545 349	0.535 623	0.526 081	0.516 720	15
16	0.544 281	0.533 908	0.523 745	0.513 787	0.504 030	0.494 469	16
17	0.523 977	0.513 373	0.502 996	0.492 841	0.482 903	0.473 176	17
18	0.504 430	0.493 628	0.483 070	0.472 749	0.462 661	0.452 800	18
19	0.485 613	0.474 642	0.463 932	0.453 477	0.443 268	0.433 302	19
20	0.467 497	0.456 387	0.445 553	0.434 989	0.424 688	0.414 643	20
21	0.450 058	0.438 834	0.427 902	0.417 256	0.406 887	0.396 787	21
22	0.433 269	0.421 955	0.410 951	0.400 246	0.389 832	0.379 701	22
23	0.417 106	0.405 726	0.394 671	0.383 929	0.373 492	0.363 350	23
24	0.401 546	0.390 121	0.379 035	0.368 277	0.357 836	0.347 703	24
25	0.386 566	0.375 117	0.364 019	0.353 263	0.342 837	0.332 731	25
26	0.372 146	0.360 689	0.349 599	0.338 862	0.328 467	0.318 402	26
27	0.358 263	0.346 817	0.335 749	0.325 047	0.314 699	0.304 691	27
28	0.344 898	0.333 477	0.322 448	0.311 796	0.301 508	0.291 571	28
29	0.332 032	0.320 651	0.309 674	0.299 085	0.288 870	0.279 015	29
30	0.319 646	0.308 319	0.297 406	0.286 892	0.276 761	0.267 000	30
31	0.307 722	0.296 460	0.285 624	0.275 196	0.265 161	0.255 502	31
32	0.296 242	0.285 058	0.274 309	0.263 977	0.254 046	0.244 500	32
33	0.285 191	0.274 094	0.263 442	0.253 215	0.243 397	0.233 971	33
34	0.274 552	0.263 552	0.253 005	0.242 892	0.233 195	0.223 896	34
35	0.264 310	0.253 415	0.242 982	0.232 990	0.223 420	0.214 254	35
36	0.254 450	0.243 669	0.233 356	0.223 492	0.214 056	0.205 028	36
37	0.244 958	0.234 297	0.224 112	0.214 381	0.205 083	0.196 199	37
38	0.235 820	0.225 285	0.215 233	0.205 641	0.196 487	0.187 750	38
39	0.227 023	0.216 621	0.206 707	0.197 257	0.188 251	0.179 665	39
40	0.218 554	0.208 289	0.198 518	0.189 216	0.180 360	0.171 929	40
41	0.210 401	0.200 278	0.190 653	0.181 502	0.172 800	0.164 525	41
42	0.202 552	0.192 575	0.183 100	0.174 103	0.165 557	0.157 440	42
43	0.194 996	0.185 168	0.175 847	0.167 005	0.158 617	0.150 661	43
44	0.187 722	0.178 046	0.168 880	0.160 197	0.151 969	0.144 173	44
45	0.180 719	0.171 198	0.162 190	0.153 666	0.145 599	0.137 964	45
46	0.173 977	0.164 614	0.155 765	0.147 401	0.139 496	0.132 023	46
47	0.167 487	0.158 283	0.149 594	0.141 392	0.133 649	0.126 338	47
48	0.161 239	0.152 195	0.143 668	0.135 628	0.128 047	0.120 898	48
49	0.155 224	0.146 341	0.137 976	0.130 099	0.122 680	0.115 692	49
50	0.149 434	0.140 713	0.132 510	0.124 795	0.117 537	0.110 710	50
51	0.143 859	0.135 301	0.127 261	0.119 707	0.112 611	0.105 942	51
52	0.138 492	0.130 097	0.122 219	0.114 827	0.107 890	0.101 380	52
53	0.133 326	0.125 093	0.117 377	0.110 146	0.103 368	0.097 014	53
54	0.128 352	0.120 282	0.112 727	0.105 656	0.099 035	0.092 837	54
55	0.123 564	0.115 656	0.108 262	0.101 348	0.094 884	0.088 839	55

YRS

YRS	15.50%	16.00%	16.50%	17.00%	17.50%	18.00%	QTRS
14	0.118 955	0.111 207	0.103 973	0.097 217	0.090 907	0.085 013	56
15	0.102 173	0.095 060	0.088 450	0.082 307	0.076 597	0.071 289	60
16	0.087 759	0.081 258	0.075 245	0.069 684	0.064 539	0.059 780	64
17	0.075 379	0.069 460	0.064 012	0.058 997	0.054 380	0.050 129	68
18	0.064 745	0.059 374	0.054 455	0.049 949	0.045 820	0.042 037	72
19	0.055 611	0.050 754	0.046 325	0.042 288	0.038 607	0.035 250	76
20	0.047 766	0.043 384	0.039 409	0.035 803	0.032 530	0.029 559	80
21	0.041 027	0.037 085	0.033 526	0.030 312	0.027 409	0.024 787	84
22	0.035 239	0.031 701	0.028 521	0.025 663	0.023 095	0.020 786	88
23	0.030 268	0.027 098	0.024 263	0.021 727	0.019 459	0.017 430	92
24	0.025 998	0.023 163	0.020 640	0.018 395	0.016 396	0.014 616	96
25	0.022 330	0.019 800	0.017 559	0.015 574	0.013 815	0.012 257	100
26	0.019 180	0.016 925	0.014 938	0.013 185	0.011 640	0.010 278	104
27	0.016 474	0.014 468	0.012 707	0.011 163	0.009 808	0.008 619	108
28	0.014 150	0.012 367	0.010 810	0.009 451	0.008 264	0.007 227	112
29	0.012 154	0.010 571	0.009 196	0.008 002	0.006 963	0.006 061	116
30	0.010 439	0.009 036	0.007 823	0.006 774	0.005 867	0.005 082	120

QTRS	18.50% ANNUAL RATE	19.00% ANNUAL RATE	19.50% ANNUAL RATE	20.00% ANNUAL RATE	20.50% ANNUAL RATE	21.00% ANNUAL RATE	QTRS
1	0.955 795	0.954 654	0.953 516	0.952 381	0.951 249	0.950 119	1
2	0.913 543	0.911 364	0.909 193	0.907 029	0.904 874	0.902 726	2
3	0.873 160	0.870 037	0.866 930	0.863 838	0.860 760	0.857 697	3
4	0.834 561	0.830 585	0.826 632	0.822 702	0.818 796	0.814 914	4
5	0.797 669	0.792 921	0.788 207	0.783 526	0.778 879	0.774 265	5
6	0.762 408	0.756 965	0.751 568	0.746 215	0.740 907	0.735 643	6
7	0.728 705	0.722 640	0.716 632	0.710 681	0.704 787	0.698 949	7
8	0.696 492	0.689 871	0.683 320	0.676 839	0.670 428	0.664 084	8
9	0.665 703	0.658 588	0.651 557	0.644 609	0.637 743	0.630 959	9
10	0.636 276	0.628 723	0.621 270	0.613 913	0.606 652	0.599 486	10
11	0.608 149	0.600 213	0.592 391	0.584 679	0.577 077	0.569 583	11
12	0.581 265	0.572 996	0.564 854	0.556 837	0.548 944	0.541 171	12
13	0.555 570	0.547 013	0.538 598	0.530 321	0.522 182	0.514 177	13
14	0.531 011	0.522 208	0.513 561	0.505 068	0.496 725	0.488 529	14
15	0.507 537	0.498 528	0.489 689	0.481 017	0.472 509	0.464 161	15
16	0.485 101	0.475 922	0.466 926	0.458 112	0.449 473	0.441 008	16
17	0.463 657	0.454 341	0.445 222	0.436 297	0.427 561	0.419 010	17
18	0.443 161	0.433 738	0.424 526	0.415 521	0.406 717	0.398 109	18
19	0.423 571	0.414 070	0.404 793	0.395 734	0.386 889	0.378 251	19
20	0.404 847	0.395 293	0.385 976	0.376 889	0.368 027	0.359 383	20
21	0.386 950	0.377 368	0.368 035	0.358 942	0.350 085	0.341 457	21
22	0.369 845	0.360 256	0.350 927	0.341 850	0.333 018	0.324 425	22
23	0.353 496	0.343 920	0.334 614	0.325 571	0.316 783	0.308 242	23
24	0.337 869	0.328 324	0.319 060	0.310 068	0.301 339	0.292 866	24
25	0.322 934	0.313 436	0.304 229	0.295 303	0.286 649	0.278 258	25
26	0.308 658	0.299 223	0.290 087	0.281 241	0.272 674	0.264 378	26
27	0.295 014	0.285 655	0.276 603	0.267 848	0.259 381	0.251 190	27
28	0.281 973	0.272 701	0.263 745	0.255 094	0.246 736	0.238 661	28
29	0.269 508	0.260 335	0.251 485	0.242 946	0.234 707	0.226 756	29
30	0.257 594	0.248 530	0.239 795	0.231 377	0.223 265	0.215 445	30
31	0.246 207	0.237 260	0.228 649	0.220 359	0.212 380	0.204 699	31
32	0.235 323	0.226 501	0.218 020	0.209 866	0.202 026	0.194 488	32
33	0.224 921	0.216 231	0.207 886	0.199 873	0.192 177	0.184 787	33
34	0.214 978	0.206 425	0.198 222	0.190 355	0.182 808	0.175 569	34
35	0.205 475	0.197 065	0.189 008	0.181 290	0.173 896	0.166 812	35
36	0.196 392	0.188 129	0.180 222	0.172 657	0.165 418	0.158 491	36
37	0.187 710	0.179 598	0.171 845	0.164 436	0.157 354	0.150 585	37
38	0.179 412	0.171 454	0.163 857	0.156 605	0.149 683	0.143 074	38
39	0.171 481	0.163 679	0.156 240	0.149 148	0.142 385	0.135 937	39
40	0.163 901	0.156 257	0.148 978	0.142 046	0.135 444	0.129 156	40
41	0.156 656	0.149 171	0.142 053	0.135 282	0.128 841	0.122 714	41
42	0.149 730	0.142 407	0.135 449	0.128 840	0.122 560	0.116 593	42
43	0.143 112	0.135 949	0.129 153	0.122 704	0.116 585	0.110 777	43
44	0.136 785	0.129 784	0.123 150	0.116 861	0.110 901	0.105 251	44
45	0.130 739	0.123 899	0.117 425	0.111 297	0.105 494	0.100 001	45
46	0.124 959	0.118 281	0.111 967	0.105 997	0.100 351	0.095 013	46
47	0.119 435	0.112 917	0.106 762	0.100 949	0.095 459	0.090 274	47
48	0.114 156	0.107 797	0.101 799	0.096 142	0.090 805	0.085 771	48
49	0.109 109	0.102 909	0.097 067	0.091 564	0.086 378	0.081 492	49
50	0.104 286	0.098 242	0.092 555	0.087 204	0.082 167	0.077 427	50
51	0.099 676	0.093 787	0.088 253	0.083 051	0.078 162	0.073 565	51
52	0.095 270	0.089 534	0.084 151	0.079 096	0.074 351	0.069 896	52
53	0.091 058	0.085 474	0.080 239	0.075 330	0.070 726	0.066 409	53
54	0.087 033	0.081 599	0.076 509	0.071 743	0.067 278	0.063 097	54
55	0.083 186	0.077 898	0.072 953	0.068 326	0.063 998	0.059 949	55

YRS							
14	0.079 509	0.074 366	0.069 562	0.065 073	0.060 878	0.056 959	56
15	0.066 355	0.061 767	0.057 502	0.053 536	0.049 847	0.046 417	60
16	0.055 377	0.051 303	0.047 533	0.044 044	0.040 815	0.037 826	64
17	0.046 216	0.042 611	0.039 292	0.036 235	0.033 419	0.030 825	68
18	0.038 570	0.035 392	0.032 480	0.029 811	0.027 363	0.025 119	72
19	0.032 189	0.029 396	0.026 849	0.024 525	0.022 405	0.020 470	76
20	0.026 863	0.024 416	0.022 194	0.020 177	0.018 345	0.016 681	80
21	0.022 419	0.020 280	0.018 347	0.016 600	0.015 021	0.013 594	84
22	0.018 710	0.016 844	0.015 166	0.013 657	0.012 299	0.011 078	88
23	0.015 615	0.013 990	0.012 537	0.011 235	0.010 070	0.009 027	92
24	0.013 032	0.011 620	0.010 363	0.009 243	0.008 246	0.007 357	96
25	0.010 876	0.009 652	0.008 566	0.007 604	0.006 751	0.005 995	100
26	0.009 076	0.008 016	0.007 081	0.006 256	0.005 528	0.004 885	104
27	0.007 575	0.006 658	0.005 854	0.005 147	0.004 526	0.003 981	108
28	0.006 322	0.005 530	0.004 839	0.004 234	0.003 706	0.003 244	112
29	0.005 276	0.004 593	0.004 000	0.003 484	0.003 035	0.002 644	116
30	0.004 403	0.003 815	0.003 306	0.002 866	0.002 485	0.002 155	120

QUARTERLY COMPOUNDING

SECTION 4

QTRS	21.50% ANNUAL RATE	22.00% ANNUAL RATE	22.50% ANNUAL RATE	23.00% ANNUAL RATE	23.50% ANNUAL RATE	24.00% ANNUAL RATE	QTRS
1	0.948 992	0.947 867	0.946 746	0.945 626	0.944 510	0.943 396	1
2	0.900 585	0.898 452	0.896 327	0.894 209	0.892 099	0.889 996	2
3	0.854 648	0.851 614	0.848 594	0.845 588	0.842 597	0.839 619	3
4	0.811 054	0.807 217	0.803 402	0.799 611	0.795 841	0.792 094	4
5	0.769 683	0.765 134	0.760 618	0.756 133	0.751 680	0.747 258	5
6	0.730 423	0.725 246	0.720 111	0.715 019	0.709 969	0.704 961	6
7	0.693 165	0.687 437	0.681 762	0.676 141	0.670 573	0.665 057	7
8	0.657 808	0.651 599	0.645 455	0.639 377	0.633 363	0.627 412	8
9	0.624 255	0.617 629	0.611 082	0.604 612	0.598 218	0.591 898	9
10	0.592 412	0.585 431	0.578 539	0.571 737	0.565 023	0.558 395	10
11	0.562 194	0.554 911	0.547 729	0.540 650	0.533 669	0.526 788	11
12	0.533 518	0.525 982	0.518 560	0.511 253	0.504 056	0.496 969	12
13	0.506 304	0.498 561	0.490 945	0.483 454	0.476 086	0.468 839	13
14	0.480 478	0.472 569	0.464 800	0.457 167	0.449 668	0.442 301	14
15	0.455 970	0.447 933	0.440 047	0.432 309	0.424 716	0.417 265	15
16	0.432 712	0.424 581	0.416 613	0.408 803	0.401 149	0.393 646	16
17	0.410 640	0.402 447	0.394 426	0.386 575	0.378 889	0.371 364	17
18	0.389 694	0.381 466	0.373 421	0.365 555	0.357 864	0.350 344	18
19	0.369 816	0.361 579	0.353 535	0.345 679	0.338 006	0.330 513	19
20	0.350 952	0.342 729	0.334 708	0.326 883	0.319 250	0.311 805	20
21	0.333 051	0.324 862	0.316 883	0.309 109	0.301 535	0.294 155	21
22	0.316 063	0.307 926	0.300 008	0.292 302	0.284 803	0.277 505	22
23	0.299 941	0.291 873	0.284 031	0.276 408	0.268 999	0.261 797	23
24	0.284 641	0.276 657	0.268 905	0.261 379	0.254 073	0.246 979	24
25	0.270 122	0.262 234	0.254 584	0.247 167	0.239 974	0.232 999	25
26	0.256 344	0.248 563	0.241 027	0.233 728	0.226 658	0.219 810	26
27	0.243 268	0.235 605	0.228 191	0.221 019	0.214 081	0.207 368	27
28	0.230 859	0.223 322	0.216 039	0.209 002	0.202 201	0.195 630	28
29	0.219 084	0.211 679	0.204 534	0.197 637	0.190 981	0.184 557	29
30	0.207 909	0.200 644	0.193 641	0.186 891	0.180 384	0.174 110	30
31	0.197 303	0.190 184	0.183 329	0.176 729	0.170 374	0.164 255	31
32	0.187 239	0.180 269	0.173 566	0.167 120	0.160 920	0.154 957	32
33	0.177 689	0.170 871	0.164 323	0.158 033	0.151 991	0.146 186	33
34	0.168 625	0.161 963	0.155 572	0.149 440	0.143 557	0.137 912	34
35	0.160 024	0.153 520	0.147 287	0.141 315	0.135 591	0.130 105	35
36	0.151 861	0.145 516	0.139 443	0.133 631	0.128 067	0.122 741	36
37	0.144 115	0.137 930	0.132 017	0.126 365	0.120 960	0.115 793	37
38	0.136 764	0.130 739	0.124 987	0.119 494	0.114 248	0.109 239	38
39	0.129 788	0.123 924	0.118 331	0.112 997	0.107 909	0.103 056	39
40	0.123 168	0.117 463	0.112 029	0.106 853	0.101 921	0.097 222	40
41	0.116 885	0.111 339	0.106 063	0.101 043	0.096 265	0.091 719	41
42	0.110 923	0.105 535	0.100 415	0.095 549	0.090 924	0.086 527	42
43	0.105 265	0.100 033	0.095 067	0.090 353	0.085 878	0.081 630	43
44	0.099 896	0.094 818	0.090 005	0.085 440	0.081 113	0.077 009	44
45	0.094 800	0.089 875	0.085 211	0.080 795	0.076 612	0.072 650	45
46	0.089 964	0.085 190	0.080 673	0.076 402	0.072 361	0.068 538	46
47	0.085 376	0.080 748	0.076 377	0.072 247	0.068 345	0.064 658	47
48	0.081 021	0.076 539	0.072 310	0.068 319	0.064 553	0.060 998	48
49	0.076 888	0.072 549	0.068 459	0.064 604	0.060 971	0.057 546	49
50	0.072 966	0.068 767	0.064 813	0.061 092	0.057 588	0.054 288	50
51	0.069 244	0.065 182	0.061 362	0.057 770	0.054 392	0.051 215	51
52	0.065 712	0.061 783	0.058 094	0.054 629	0.051 374	0.048 316	52
53	0.062 360	0.058 563	0.055 000	0.051 658	0.048 523	0.045 582	53
54	0.059 179	0.055 509	0.052 071	0.048 849	0.045 831	0.043 001	54
55	0.056 161	0.052 616	0.049 298	0.046 193	0.043 287	0.040 567	55

YRS	21.50%	22.00%	22.50%	23.00%	23.50%	24.00%	
14	0.053 296	0.049 873	0.046 673	0.043 682	0.040 885	0.038 271	56
15	0.043 226	0.040 258	0.037 497	0.034 928	0.032 538	0.030 314	60
16	0.035 059	0.032 497	0.030 125	0.027 929	0.025 895	0.024 012	64
17	0.028 434	0.026 232	0.024 203	0.022 332	0.020 609	0.019 020	68
18	0.023 062	0.021 175	0.019 444	0.017 857	0.016 401	0.015 065	72
19	0.018 704	0.017 093	0.015 622	0.014 279	0.013 053	0.011 933	76
20	0.015 170	0.013 798	0.012 551	0.011 417	0.010 388	0.009 452	80
21	0.012 304	0.011 138	0.010 083	0.009 130	0.008 267	0.007 487	84
22	0.009 979	0.008 990	0.008 101	0.007 300	0.006 579	0.005 930	88
23	0.008 094	0.007 257	0.006 508	0.005 837	0.005 236	0.004 697	92
24	0.006 564	0.005 858	0.005 229	0.004 667	0.004 167	0.003 721	96
25	0.005 324	0.004 729	0.004 201	0.003 732	0.003 316	0.002 947	100
26	0.004 318	0.003 817	0.003 375	0.002 984	0.002 639	0.002 334	104
27	0.003 502	0.003 081	0.002 711	0.002 386	0.002 100	0.001 849	108
28	0.002 840	0.002 487	0.002 178	0.001 908	0.001 672	0.001 465	112
29	0.002 304	0.002 008	0.001 750	0.001 526	0.001 330	0.001 160	116
30	0.001 868	0.001 621	0.001 406	0.001 220	0.001 059	0.000 919	120

HALF YRS	7.00% ANNUAL RATE	8.00% ANNUAL RATE	9.00% ANNUAL RATE	10.00% ANNUAL RATE	10.50% ANNUAL RATE	11.00% ANNUAL RATE	HALF YRS
1	0.966 184	0.961 538	0.956 938	0.952 381	0.950 119	0.947 867	1
2	0.933 511	0.924 556	0.915 730	0.907 029	0.902 726	0.898 452	2
3	0.901 943	0.888 996	0.876 297	0.863 838	0.857 697	0.851 614	3
4	0.871 442	0.854 804	0.838 561	0.822 702	0.814 914	0.807 217	4
5	0.841 973	0.821 927	0.802 451	0.783 526	0.774 265	0.765 134	5
6	0.813 501	0.790 315	0.767 896	0.746 215	0.735 643	0.725 246	6
7	0.785 991	0.759 918	0.734 828	0.710 681	0.698 949	0.687 437	7
8	0.759 412	0.730 690	0.703 185	0.676 839	0.664 084	0.651 599	8
9	0.733 731	0.702 587	0.672 904	0.644 609	0.630 959	0.617 629	9
10	0.708 919	0.675 564	0.643 928	0.613 913	0.599 486	0.585 431	10
11	0.684 946	0.649 581	0.616 199	0.584 679	0.569 583	0.554 911	11
12	0.661 783	0.624 597	0.589 664	0.556 837	0.541 171	0.525 982	12
13	0.639 404	0.600 574	0.564 272	0.530 321	0.514 177	0.498 561	13
14	0.617 782	0.577 475	0.539 973	0.505 068	0.488 529	0.472 569	14
15	0.596 891	0.555 265	0.516 720	0.481 017	0.464 161	0.447 933	15
16	0.576 706	0.533 908	0.494 469	0.458 112	0.441 008	0.424 581	16
17	0.557 204	0.513 373	0.473 176	0.436 297	0.419 010	0.402 447	17
18	0.538 361	0.493 628	0.452 800	0.415 521	0.398 109	0.381 466	18
19	0.520 156	0.474 642	0.433 302	0.395 734	0.378 251	0.361 579	19
20	0.502 566	0.456 387	0.414 643	0.376 889	0.359 383	0.342 729	20
21	0.485 571	0.438 834	0.396 787	0.358 942	0.341 457	0.324 862	21
22	0.469 151	0.421 955	0.379 701	0.341 850	0.324 425	0.307 926	22
23	0.453 286	0.405 726	0.363 350	0.325 571	0.308 242	0.291 873	23
24	0.437 957	0.390 121	0.347 703	0.310 068	0.292 866	0.276 657	24
25	0.423 147	0.375 117	0.332 731	0.295 303	0.278 258	0.262 234	25
26	0.408 838	0.360 689	0.318 402	0.281 241	0.264 378	0.248 563	26
27	0.395 012	0.346 817	0.304 691	0.267 848	0.251 190	0.235 605	27
28	0.381 654	0.333 477	0.291 571	0.255 094	0.238 661	0.223 322	28
29	0.368 748	0.320 651	0.279 015	0.242 946	0.226 756	0.211 679	29
30	0.356 278	0.308 319	0.267 000	0.231 377	0.215 445	0.200 644	30
31	0.344 230	0.296 460	0.255 502	0.220 359	0.204 699	0.190 184	31
32	0.332 590	0.285 058	0.244 500	0.209 866	0.194 488	0.180 269	32
33	0.321 343	0.274 094	0.233 971	0.199 873	0.184 787	0.170 871	33
34	0.310 476	0.263 552	0.223 896	0.190 355	0.175 569	0.161 963	34
35	0.299 977	0.253 415	0.214 254	0.181 290	0.166 812	0.153 520	35
36	0.289 833	0.243 669	0.205 028	0.172 657	0.158 491	0.145 516	36
37	0.280 032	0.234 297	0.196 199	0.164 436	0.150 585	0.137 930	37
38	0.270 562	0.225 285	0.187 750	0.156 605	0.143 074	0.130 739	38
39	0.261 413	0.216 621	0.179 665	0.149 148	0.135 937	0.123 924	39
40	0.252 572	0.208 289	0.171 929	0.142 046	0.129 156	0.117 463	40
41	0.244 031	0.200 278	0.164 525	0.135 282	0.122 714	0.111 339	41
42	0.235 779	0.192 575	0.157 440	0.128 840	0.116 593	0.105 535	42
43	0.227 806	0.185 168	0.150 661	0.122 704	0.110 777	0.100 033	43
44	0.220 102	0.178 046	0.144 173	0.116 861	0.105 251	0.094 818	44
45	0.212 659	0.171 198	0.137 964	0.111 297	0.100 001	0.089 875	45
46	0.205 468	0.164 614	0.132 023	0.105 997	0.095 013	0.085 190	46
47	0.198 520	0.158 283	0.126 338	0.100 949	0.090 274	0.080 748	47
48	0.191 806	0.152 195	0.120 898	0.096 142	0.085 771	0.076 539	48
49	0.185 320	0.146 341	0.115 692	0.091 564	0.081 492	0.072 549	49
50	0.179 053	0.140 713	0.110 710	0.087 204	0.077 427	0.068 767	50
51	0.172 998	0.135 301	0.105 942	0.083 051	0.073 565	0.065 182	51
52	0.167 148	0.130 097	0.101 380	0.079 096	0.069 896	0.061 783	52
53	0.161 496	0.125 093	0.097 014	0.075 330	0.066 409	0.058 563	53
54	0.156 035	0.120 282	0.092 837	0.071 743	0.063 097	0.055 509	54
55	0.150 758	0.115 656	0.088 839	0.068 326	0.059 949	0.052 616	55
56	0.145 660	0.111 207	0.085 013	0.065 073	0.056 959	0.049 873	56
57	0.140 734	0.106 930	0.081 353	0.061 974	0.054 118	0.047 273	57
58	0.135 975	0.102 817	0.077 849	0.059 023	0.051 418	0.044 808	58
59	0.131 377	0.098 863	0.074 497	0.056 212	0.048 854	0.042 472	59
YRS							
30	0.126 934	0.095 060	0.071 289	0.053 536	0.046 417	0.040 258	60
31	0.118 495	0.087 889	0.065 281	0.048 558	0.041 901	0.036 170	62
32	0.110 616	0.081 258	0.059 780	0.044 044	0.037 826	0.032 497	64
33	0.103 261	0.075 128	0.054 743	0.039 949	0.034 146	0.029 197	66
34	0.096 395	0.069 460	0.050 129	0.036 235	0.030 825	0.026 232	68
35	0.089 986	0.064 219	0.045 905	0.032 866	0.027 826	0.023 568	70
36	0.084 003	0.059 374	0.042 037	0.029 811	0.025 119	0.021 175	72
37	0.078 418	0.054 895	0.038 494	0.027 039	0.022 676	0.019 025	74
38	0.073 204	0.050 754	0.035 250	0.024 525	0.020 470	0.017 093	76
39	0.068 336	0.046 924	0.032 280	0.022 245	0.018 479	0.015 357	78
40	0.063 793	0.043 384	0.029 559	0.020 177	0.016 681	0.013 798	80

SECTION 4

HALF YRS	11.50% ANNUAL RATE	12.00% ANNUAL RATE	12.50% ANNUAL RATE	13.00% ANNUAL RATE	13.50% ANNUAL RATE	14.00% ANNUAL RATE	HALF YRS
1	0.945 626	0.943 396	0.941 176	0.938 967	0.936 768	0.934 579	1
2	0.894 209	0.889 996	0.885 813	0.881 659	0.877 535	0.873 439	2
3	0.845 588	0.839 619	0.833 706	0.827 849	0.822 046	0.816 298	3
4	0.799 611	0.792 094	0.784 665	0.777 323	0.770 067	0.762 895	4
5	0.756 133	0.747 258	0.738 508	0.729 881	0.721 374	0.712 986	5
6	0.715 019	0.704 961	0.695 067	0.685 334	0.675 760	0.666 342	6
7	0.676 141	0.665 057	0.654 180	0.643 506	0.633 031	0.622 750	7
8	0.639 377	0.627 412	0.615 699	0.604 231	0.593 003	0.582 009	8
9	0.604 612	0.591 898	0.579 481	0.567 353	0.555 506	0.543 934	9
10	0.571 737	0.558 395	0.545 394	0.532 726	0.520 381	0.508 349	10
11	0.540 650	0.526 788	0.513 312	0.500 212	0.487 476	0.475 093	11
12	0.511 253	0.496 969	0.483 117	0.469 683	0.456 652	0.444 012	12
13	0.483 454	0.468 839	0.454 699	0.441 017	0.427 777	0.414 964	13
14	0.457 167	0.442 301	0.427 952	0.414 100	0.400 728	0.387 817	14
15	0.432 309	0.417 265	0.402 778	0.388 827	0.375 389	0.362 446	15
16	0.408 803	0.393 646	0.379 085	0.365 095	0.351 653	0.338 735	16
17	0.386 575	0.371 364	0.356 786	0.342 813	0.329 417	0.316 574	17
18	0.365 555	0.350 344	0.335 799	0.321 890	0.308 587	0.295 864	18
19	0.345 679	0.330 513	0.316 046	0.302 244	0.289 075	0.276 508	19
20	0.326 883	0.311 805	0.297 455	0.283 797	0.270 796	0.258 419	20
21	0.309 109	0.294 155	0.279 958	0.266 476	0.253 673	0.241 513	21
22	0.292 302	0.277 505	0.263 490	0.250 212	0.237 633	0.225 713	22
23	0.276 408	0.261 797	0.247 990	0.234 941	0.222 607	0.210 947	23
24	0.261 379	0.246 979	0.233 402	0.220 602	0.208 531	0.197 147	24
25	0.247 167	0.232 999	0.219 673	0.207 138	0.195 345	0.184 249	25
26	0.233 728	0.219 810	0.206 751	0.194 496	0.182 993	0.172 195	26
27	0.221 019	0.207 368	0.194 589	0.182 625	0.171 422	0.160 930	27
28	0.209 002	0.195 630	0.183 143	0.171 479	0.160 583	0.150 402	28
29	0.197 637	0.184 557	0.172 370	0.161 013	0.150 429	0.140 563	29
30	0.186 891	0.174 110	0.162 230	0.151 186	0.140 917	0.131 367	30
31	0.176 729	0.164 255	0.152 687	0.141 959	0.132 007	0.122 773	31
32	0.167 120	0.154 957	0.143 706	0.133 295	0.123 660	0.114 741	32
33	0.158 033	0.146 186	0.135 252	0.125 159	0.115 840	0.107 235	33
34	0.149 440	0.137 912	0.127 296	0.117 520	0.108 516	0.100 219	34
35	0.141 315	0.130 105	0.119 808	0.110 348	0.101 654	0.093 663	35
36	0.133 631	0.122 741	0.112 761	0.103 613	0.095 226	0.087 535	36
37	0.126 365	0.115 793	0.106 128	0.097 289	0.089 205	0.081 809	37
38	0.119 494	0.109 239	0.099 885	0.091 351	0.083 564	0.076 457	38
39	0.112 997	0.103 056	0.094 009	0.085 776	0.078 280	0.071 455	39
40	0.106 853	0.097 222	0.088 479	0.080 541	0.073 331	0.066 780	40
41	0.101 043	0.091 719	0.083 275	0.075 625	0.068 694	0.062 412	41
42	0.095 549	0.086 527	0.078 376	0.071 010	0.064 350	0.058 329	42
43	0.090 353	0.081 630	0.073 766	0.066 676	0.060 281	0.054 513	43
44	0.085 440	0.077 009	0.069 427	0.062 606	0.056 469	0.050 946	44
45	0.080 795	0.072 650	0.065 343	0.058 785	0.052 899	0.047 613	45
46	0.076 402	0.068 538	0.061 499	0.055 197	0.049 554	0.044 499	46
47	0.072 247	0.064 658	0.057 882	0.051 828	0.046 420	0.041 587	47
48	0.068 319	0.060 998	0.054 477	0.048 665	0.043 485	0.038 867	48
49	0.064 604	0.057 546	0.051 272	0.045 695	0.040 736	0.036 324	49
50	0.061 092	0.054 288	0.048 256	0.042 906	0.038 160	0.033 948	50
51	0.057 770	0.051 215	0.045 418	0.040 287	0.035 747	0.031 727	51
52	0.054 629	0.048 316	0.042 746	0.037 829	0.033 487	0.029 651	52
53	0.051 658	0.045 582	0.040 232	0.035 520	0.031 369	0.027 711	53
54	0.048 849	0.043 001	0.037 865	0.033 352	0.029 386	0.025 899	54
55	0.046 193	0.040 567	0.035 638	0.031 316	0.027 527	0.024 204	55
56	0.043 682	0.038 271	0.033 541	0.029 405	0.025 787	0.022 621	56
57	0.041 307	0.036 105	0.031 568	0.027 610	0.024 156	0.021 141	57
58	0.039 061	0.034 061	0.029 711	0.025 925	0.022 629	0.019 758	58
59	0.036 937	0.032 133	0.027 964	0.024 343	0.021 198	0.018 465	59

YRS

HALF YRS	11.50%	12.00%	12.50%	13.00%	13.50%	14.00%	HALF YRS
30	0.034 928	0.030 314	0.026 319	0.022 857	0.019 858	0.017 257	60
31	0.031 233	0.026 980	0.023 313	0.020 152	0.017 426	0.015 073	62
32	0.027 929	0.024 012	0.020 651	0.017 767	0.015 292	0.013 166	64
33	0.024 974	0.021 370	0.018 293	0.015 665	0.013 419	0.011 499	66
34	0.022 332	0.019 020	0.016 204	0.013 811	0.011 776	0.010 044	68
35	0.019 970	0.016 927	0.014 354	0.012 177	0.010 334	0.008 773	70
36	0.017 857	0.015 065	0.012 715	0.010 736	0.009 068	0.007 662	72
37	0.015 968	0.013 408	0.011 263	0.009 465	0.007 957	0.006 693	74
38	0.014 279	0.011 933	0.009 977	0.008 345	0.006 983	0.005 846	76
39	0.012 768	0.010 620	0.008 838	0.007 358	0.006 128	0.005 106	78
40	0.011 417	0.009 452	0.007 829	0.006 487	0.005 377	0.004 460	80

PRESENT VALUE OF $1

HALF YRS	14.50% ANNUAL RATE	15.00% ANNUAL RATE	15.50% ANNUAL RATE	16.00% ANNUAL RATE	16.50% ANNUAL RATE	17.00% ANNUAL RATE	HALF YRS
1	0.932 401	0.930 233	0.928 074	0.925 926	0.923 788	0.921 659	1
2	0.869 371	0.865 333	0.861 322	0.857 339	0.853 383	0.849 455	2
3	0.810 603	0.804 961	0.799 371	0.793 832	0.788 345	0.782 908	3
4	0.755 807	0.748 801	0.741 875	0.735 030	0.728 263	0.721 574	4
5	0.704 715	0.696 559	0.688 515	0.680 583	0.672 760	0.665 045	5
6	0.657 077	0.647 962	0.638 993	0.630 170	0.621 488	0.612 945	6
7	0.612 659	0.602 755	0.593 033	0.583 490	0.574 123	0.564 926	7
8	0.571 244	0.560 702	0.550 379	0.540 269	0.530 367	0.520 669	8
9	0.532 628	0.521 583	0.510 792	0.500 249	0.489 947	0.479 880	9
10	0.496 623	0.485 194	0.474 053	0.463 193	0.452 607	0.442 285	10
11	0.463 052	0.451 343	0.439 957	0.428 883	0.418 112	0.407 636	11
12	0.431 750	0.419 854	0.408 312	0.397 114	0.386 247	0.375 702	12
13	0.402 564	0.390 562	0.378 944	0.367 698	0.356 810	0.346 269	13
14	0.375 351	0.363 313	0.351 688	0.340 461	0.329 617	0.319 142	14
15	0.349 978	0.337 966	0.326 393	0.315 242	0.304 496	0.294 140	15
16	0.326 320	0.314 387	0.302 917	0.291 890	0.281 289	0.271 097	16
17	0.304 261	0.292 453	0.281 129	0.270 269	0.259 852	0.249 859	17
18	0.283 693	0.272 049	0.260 909	0.250 249	0.240 048	0.230 285	18
19	0.264 516	0.253 069	0.242 143	0.231 712	0.221 753	0.212 244	19
20	0.246 635	0.235 413	0.224 727	0.214 548	0.204 853	0.195 616	20
21	0.229 962	0.218 989	0.208 563	0.198 656	0.189 240	0.180 292	21
22	0.214 417	0.203 711	0.193 562	0.183 941	0.174 818	0.166 167	22
23	0.199 923	0.189 498	0.179 640	0.170 315	0.161 495	0.153 150	23
24	0.186 408	0.176 277	0.166 719	0.157 699	0.149 187	0.141 152	24
25	0.173 807	0.163 979	0.154 728	0.146 018	0.137 817	0.130 094	25
26	0.162 058	0.152 539	0.143 599	0.135 202	0.127 314	0.119 902	26
27	0.151 103	0.141 896	0.133 270	0.125 187	0.117 611	0.110 509	27
28	0.140 889	0.131 997	0.123 685	0.115 914	0.108 647	0.101 851	28
29	0.131 365	0.122 788	0.114 789	0.107 328	0.100 367	0.093 872	29
30	0.122 484	0.114 221	0.106 532	0.099 377	0.092 718	0.086 518	30
31	0.114 205	0.106 252	0.098 870	0.092 016	0.085 651	0.079 740	31
32	0.106 484	0.098 839	0.091 759	0.085 200	0.079 124	0.073 493	32
33	0.099 286	0.091 943	0.085 159	0.078 889	0.073 094	0.067 736	33
34	0.092 575	0.085 529	0.079 034	0.073 045	0.067 523	0.062 429	34
35	0.086 317	0.079 562	0.073 349	0.067 635	0.062 377	0.057 539	35
36	0.080 482	0.074 011	0.068 073	0.062 625	0.057 623	0.053 031	36
37	0.075 041	0.068 847	0.063 177	0.057 986	0.053 231	0.048 876	37
38	0.069 969	0.064 044	0.058 633	0.053 690	0.049 174	0.045 047	38
39	0.065 239	0.059 576	0.054 416	0.049 713	0.045 427	0.041 518	39
40	0.060 829	0.055 419	0.050 502	0.046 031	0.041 965	0.038 266	40
41	0.056 717	0.051 553	0.046 870	0.042 621	0.038 766	0.035 268	41
42	0.052 883	0.047 956	0.043 499	0.039 464	0.035 812	0.032 505	42
43	0.049 308	0.044 610	0.040 370	0.036 541	0.033 083	0.029 959	43
44	0.045 975	0.041 498	0.037 466	0.033 834	0.030 561	0.027 612	44
45	0.042 867	0.038 603	0.034 771	0.031 328	0.028 232	0.025 448	45
46	0.039 969	0.035 910	0.032 270	0.029 007	0.026 081	0.023 455	46
47	0.037 267	0.033 404	0.029 949	0.026 859	0.024 093	0.021 617	47
48	0.034 748	0.031 074	0.027 795	0.024 869	0.022 257	0.019 924	48
49	0.032 399	0.028 906	0.025 796	0.023 027	0.020 560	0.018 363	49
50	0.030 209	0.026 889	0.023 941	0.021 321	0.018 993	0.016 924	50
51	0.028 167	0.025 013	0.022 219	0.019 742	0.017 546	0.015 599	51
52	0.026 263	0.023 268	0.020 621	0.018 280	0.016 209	0.014 377	52
53	0.024 487	0.021 645	0.019 137	0.016 925	0.014 973	0.013 250	53
54	0.022 832	0.020 135	0.017 761	0.015 672	0.013 832	0.012 212	54
55	0.021 289	0.018 730	0.016 484	0.014 511	0.012 778	0.011 255	55
56	0.019 850	0.017 423	0.015 298	0.013 436	0.011 804	0.010 374	56
57	0.018 508	0.016 208	0.014 198	0.012 441	0.010 905	0.009 561	57
58	0.017 257	0.015 077	0.013 176	0.011 519	0.010 074	0.008 812	58
59	0.016 090	0.014 025	0.012 229	0.010 666	0.009 306	0.008 122	59
YRS							
30	0.015 002	0.013 046	0.011 349	0.009 876	0.008 597	0.007 485	60
31	0.013 043	0.011 290	0.009 775	0.008 467	0.007 336	0.006 359	62
32	0.011 339	0.009 769	0.008 420	0.007 259	0.006 261	0.005 401	64
33	0.009 858	0.008 454	0.007 252	0.006 223	0.005 343	0.004 588	66
34	0.008 570	0.007 315	0.006 246	0.005 336	0.004 559	0.003 897	68
35	0.007 451	0.006 330	0.005 380	0.004 574	0.003 891	0.003 311	70
36	0.006 477	0.005 478	0.004 634	0.003 922	0.003 320	0.002 812	72
37	0.005 631	0.004 740	0.003 991	0.003 362	0.002 834	0.002 389	74
38	0.004 896	0.004 102	0.003 438	0.002 883	0.002 418	0.002 029	76
39	0.004 256	0.003 549	0.002 961	0.002 471	0.002 064	0.001 724	78
40	0.003 700	0.003 071	0.002 550	0.002 119	0.001 761	0.001 464	80

PRESENT VALUE OF $1

	17.50% ANNUAL RATE	18.00% ANNUAL RATE	18.50% ANNUAL RATE	19.00% ANNUAL RATE	19.50% ANNUAL RATE	20.00% ANNUAL RATE	
HALF YRS							**HALF YRS**
1	0.919 540	0.917 431	0.915 332	0.913 242	0.911 162	0.909 091	1
2	0.845 554	0.841 680	0.837 832	0.834 011	0.830 216	0.826 446	2
3	0.777 521	0.772 183	0.766 895	0.761 654	0.756 461	0.751 315	3
4	0.714 962	0.708 425	0.701 963	0.695 574	0.689 258	0.683 013	4
5	0.657 436	0.649 931	0.642 529	0.635 228	0.628 026	0.620 921	5
6	0.604 539	0.596 267	0.588 127	0.580 117	0.572 233	0.564 474	6
7	0.555 898	0.547 034	0.538 332	0.529 787	0.521 397	0.513 158	7
8	0.511 171	0.501 866	0.492 752	0.483 824	0.475 077	0.466 507	8
9	0.470 042	0.460 428	0.451 032	0.441 848	0.432 872	0.424 098	9
10	0.432 222	0.422 411	0.412 844	0.403 514	0.394 416	0.385 543	10
11	0.397 446	0.387 533	0.377 889	0.368 506	0.359 377	0.350 494	11
12	0.365 468	0.355 535	0.345 894	0.336 535	0.327 450	0.318 631	12
13	0.336 062	0.326 179	0.316 608	0.307 338	0.298 360	0.289 664	13
14	0.309 023	0.299 246	0.289 801	0.280 674	0.271 855	0.263 331	14
15	0.284 159	0.274 538	0.265 264	0.256 323	0.247 703	0.239 392	15
16	0.261 295	0.251 870	0.242 805	0.234 085	0.225 698	0.217 629	16
17	0.240 272	0.231 073	0.222 247	0.213 777	0.205 647	0.197 845	17
18	0.220 939	0.211 994	0.203 430	0.195 230	0.187 378	0.179 859	18
19	0.203 163	0.194 490	0.186 206	0.178 292	0.170 732	0.163 508	19
20	0.186 816	0.178 431	0.170 440	0.162 824	0.155 564	0.148 644	20
21	0.171 785	0.163 698	0.156 009	0.148 697	0.141 744	0.135 131	21
22	0.157 963	0.150 182	0.142 800	0.135 797	0.129 152	0.122 846	22
23	0.145 254	0.137 781	0.130 709	0.124 015	0.117 678	0.111 678	23
24	0.133 567	0.126 405	0.119 642	0.113 256	0.107 224	0.101 526	24
25	0.122 820	0.115 968	0.109 513	0.103 430	0.097 698	0.092 295	25
26	0.112 938	0.106 393	0.100 240	0.094 457	0.089 019	0.083 905	26
27	0.103 851	0.097 608	0.091 753	0.086 262	0.081 111	0.076 278	27
28	0.095 495	0.089 548	0.083 985	0.078 778	0.073 905	0.069 343	28
29	0.087 811	0.082 155	0.076 874	0.071 943	0.067 339	0.063 039	29
30	0.080 746	0.075 371	0.070 365	0.065 702	0.061 357	0.057 309	30
31	0.074 249	0.069 148	0.064 407	0.060 002	0.055 906	0.052 099	31
32	0.068 275	0.063 438	0.058 954	0.054 796	0.050 940	0.047 362	32
33	0.062 782	0.058 200	0.053 963	0.050 042	0.046 414	0.043 057	33
34	0.057 730	0.053 395	0.049 394	0.045 700	0.042 291	0.039 143	34
35	0.053 085	0.048 986	0.045 212	0.041 736	0.038 534	0.035 584	35
36	0.048 814	0.044 941	0.041 384	0.038 115	0.035 110	0.032 349	36
37	0.044 887	0.041 231	0.037 880	0.034 808	0.031 991	0.029 408	37
38	0.041 275	0.037 826	0.034 672	0.031 788	0.029 149	0.026 735	38
39	0.037 954	0.034 703	0.031 737	0.029 030	0.026 560	0.024 304	39
40	0.034 900	0.031 838	0.029 050	0.026 512	0.024 200	0.022 095	40
41	0.032 092	0.029 209	0.026 590	0.024 211	0.022 050	0.020 086	41
42	0.029 510	0.026 797	0.024 339	0.022 111	0.020 091	0.018 260	42
43	0.027 136	0.024 584	0.022 278	0.020 193	0.018 306	0.016 600	43
44	0.024 952	0.022 555	0.020 392	0.018 441	0.016 680	0.015 091	44
45	0.022 945	0.020 692	0.018 665	0.016 841	0.015 198	0.013 719	45
46	0.021 099	0.018 984	0.017 085	0.015 380	0.013 848	0.012 472	46
47	0.019 401	0.017 416	0.015 638	0.014 045	0.012 618	0.011 338	47
48	0.017 840	0.015 978	0.014 314	0.012 827	0.011 497	0.010 307	48
49	0.016 405	0.014 659	0.013 102	0.011 714	0.010 476	0.009 370	49
50	0.015 085	0.013 449	0.011 993	0.010 698	0.009 545	0.008 519	50
51	0.013 871	0.012 338	0.010 978	0.009 770	0.008 697	0.007 744	51
52	0.012 755	0.011 319	0.010 048	0.008 922	0.007 924	0.007 040	52
53	0.011 729	0.010 385	0.009 197	0.008 148	0.007 220	0.006 400	53
54	0.010 785	0.009 527	0.008 419	0.007 441	0.006 579	0.005 818	54
55	0.009 917	0.008 741	0.007 706	0.006 796	0.005 994	0.005 289	55
56	0.009 119	0.008 019	0.007 053	0.006 206	0.005 462	0.004 809	56
57	0.008 386	0.007 357	0.006 456	0.005 668	0.004 977	0.004 371	57
58	0.007 711	0.006 749	0.005 910	0.005 176	0.004 535	0.003 974	58
59	0.007 090	0.006 192	0.005 409	0.004 727	0.004 132	0.003 613	59
YRS							
30	0.006 520	0.005 681	0.004 951	0.004 317	0.003 765	0.003 284	60
31	0.005 513	0.004 781	0.004 148	0.003 600	0.003 125	0.002 714	62
32	0.004 662	0.004 024	0.003 476	0.003 003	0.002 595	0.002 243	64
33	0.003 942	0.003 387	0.002 912	0.002 504	0.002 154	0.001 854	66
34	0.003 333	0.002 851	0.002 440	0.002 089	0.001 789	0.001 532	68
35	0.002 818	0.002 400	0.002 044	0.001 742	0.001 485	0.001 266	70
36	0.002 383	0.002 020	0.001 713	0.001 453	0.001 233	0.001 046	72
37	0.002 015	0.001 700	0.001 435	0.001 212	0.001 023	0.000 865	74
38	0.001 704	0.001 431	0.001 202	0.001 010	0.000 850	0.000 715	76
39	0.001 441	0.001 204	0.001 007	0.000 843	0.000 705	0.000 591	78
40	0.001 218	0.001 014	0.000 844	0.000 703	0.000 586	0.000 488	80

ANNUAL COMPOUNDING

SECTION 4

YRS	7.00% ANNUAL RATE	8.00% ANNUAL RATE	9.00% ANNUAL RATE	10.00% ANNUAL RATE	10.25% ANNUAL RATE	10.50% ANNUAL RATE	YRS
1	0.934 579	0.925 926	0.917 431	0.909 091	0.907 029	0.904 977	1
2	0.873 439	0.857 339	0.841 680	0.826 446	0.822 702	0.818 984	2
3	0.816 298	0.793 832	0.772 183	0.751 315	0.746 215	0.741 162	3
4	0.762 895	0.735 030	0.708 425	0.683 013	0.676 839	0.670 735	4
5	0.712 986	0.680 583	0.649 931	0.620 921	0.613 913	0.607 000	5
6	0.666 342	0.630 170	0.596 267	0.564 474	0.556 837	0.549 321	6
7	0.622 750	0.583 490	0.547 034	0.513 158	0.505 068	0.497 123	7
8	0.582 009	0.540 269	0.501 866	0.466 507	0.458 112	0.449 885	8
9	0.543 934	0.500 249	0.460 428	0.424 098	0.415 521	0.407 136	9
10	0.508 349	0.463 193	0.422 411	0.385 543	0.376 889	0.368 449	10
11	0.475 093	0.428 883	0.387 533	0.350 494	0.341 850	0.333 438	11
12	0.444 012	0.397 114	0.355 535	0.318 631	0.310 068	0.301 754	12
13	0.414 964	0.367 698	0.326 179	0.289 664	0.281 241	0.273 080	13
14	0.387 817	0.340 461	0.299 246	0.263 331	0.255 094	0.247 132	14
15	0.362 446	0.315 242	0.274 538	0.239 392	0.231 377	0.223 648	15
16	0.338 735	0.291 890	0.251 870	0.217 629	0.209 866	0.202 397	16
17	0.316 574	0.270 269	0.231 073	0.197 845	0.190 355	0.183 164	17
18	0.295 864	0.250 249	0.211 994	0.179 859	0.172 657	0.165 760	18
19	0.276 508	0.231 712	0.194 490	0.163 508	0.156 605	0.150 009	19
20	0.258 419	0.214 548	0.178 431	0.148 644	0.142 046	0.135 755	20
21	0.241 513	0.198 656	0.163 698	0.135 131	0.128 840	0.122 855	21
22	0.225 713	0.183 941	0.150 182	0.122 846	0.116 861	0.111 181	22
23	0.210 947	0.170 315	0.137 781	0.111 678	0.105 997	0.100 616	23
24	0.197 147	0.157 699	0.126 405	0.101 526	0.096 142	0.091 055	24
25	0.184 249	0.146 018	0.115 968	0.092 296	0.087 204	0.082 403	25
26	0.172 195	0.135 202	0.106 393	0.083 905	0.079 096	0.074 573	26
27	0.160 930	0.125 187	0.097 608	0.076 278	0.071 743	0.067 487	27
28	0.150 402	0.115 914	0.089 548	0.069 343	0.065 073	0.061 074	28
29	0.140 563	0.107 328	0.082 155	0.063 039	0.059 023	0.055 271	29
30	0.131 367	0.099 377	0.075 371	0.057 309	0.053 536	0.050 019	30
31	0.122 773	0.092 016	0.069 148	0.052 099	0.048 558	0.045 266	31
32	0.114 741	0.085 200	0.063 438	0.047 362	0.044 044	0.040 964	32
33	0.107 235	0.078 889	0.058 200	0.043 057	0.039 949	0.037 072	33
34	0.100 219	0.073 045	0.053 395	0.039 143	0.036 235	0.033 549	34
35	0.093 663	0.067 635	0.048 986	0.035 584	0.032 866	0.030 361	35
36	0.087 535	0.062 625	0.044 941	0.032 349	0.029 811	0.027 476	36
37	0.081 809	0.057 986	0.041 231	0.029 408	0.027 039	0.024 865	37
38	0.076 457	0.053 690	0.037 826	0.026 735	0.024 525	0.022 503	38
39	0.071 455	0.049 713	0.034 703	0.024 304	0.022 245	0.020 364	39
40	0.066 780	0.046 031	0.031 838	0.022 095	0.020 177	0.018 429	40
41	0.062 412	0.042 621	0.029 209	0.020 086	0.018 301	0.016 678	41
42	0.058 329	0.039 464	0.026 797	0.018 260	0.016 600	0.015 093	42
43	0.054 513	0.036 541	0.024 584	0.016 600	0.015 056	0.013 659	43
44	0.050 946	0.033 834	0.022 555	0.015 091	0.013 657	0.012 361	44
45	0.047 613	0.031 328	0.020 692	0.013 719	0.012 387	0.011 187	45
46	0.044 499	0.029 007	0.018 984	0.012 472	0.011 235	0.010 124	46
47	0.041 587	0.026 859	0.017 416	0.011 338	0.010 191	0.009 162	47
48	0.038 867	0.024 869	0.015 978	0.010 307	0.009 243	0.008 291	48
49	0.036 324	0.023 027	0.014 659	0.009 370	0.008 384	0.007 503	49
50	0.033 948	0.021 321	0.013 449	0.008 519	0.007 604	0.006 790	50

SECTION 4

YRS	10.75% ANNUAL RATE	11.00% ANNUAL RATE	11.25% ANNUAL RATE	11.50% ANNUAL RATE	11.75% ANNUAL RATE	12.00% ANNUAL RATE	YRS
1	0.902 935	0.900 901	0.898 876	0.896 861	0.894 855	0.892 857	1
2	0.815 291	0.811 622	0.807 979	0.804 360	0.800 765	0.797 194	2
3	0.736 154	0.731 191	0.726 273	0.721 399	0.716 568	0.711 780	3
4	0.664 699	0.658 731	0.652 830	0.646 994	0.641 224	0.635 518	4
5	0.600 180	0.593 451	0.586 813	0.580 264	0.573 802	0.567 427	5
6	0.541 923	0.534 641	0.527 473	0.520 416	0.513 470	0.506 631	6
7	0.489 321	0.481 658	0.474 133	0.466 741	0.459 481	0.452 349	7
8	0.441 825	0.433 926	0.426 187	0.418 602	0.411 168	0.403 883	8
9	0.398 939	0.390 925	0.383 089	0.375 428	0.367 936	0.360 610	9
10	0.360 216	0.352 184	0.344 350	0.336 706	0.329 249	0.321 973	10
11	0.325 251	0.317 283	0.309 528	0.301 979	0.294 630	0.287 476	11
12	0.293 681	0.285 841	0.278 227	0.270 833	0.263 651	0.256 675	12
13	0.265 174	0.257 514	0.250 092	0.242 900	0.235 929	0.229 174	13
14	0.239 435	0.231 995	0.224 802	0.217 847	0.211 123	0.204 620	14
15	0.216 194	0.209 004	0.202 069	0.195 379	0.188 924	0.182 696	15
16	0.195 209	0.188 292	0.181 635	0.175 227	0.169 059	0.163 122	16
17	0.176 261	0.169 633	0.163 267	0.157 155	0.151 284	0.145 644	17
18	0.159 152	0.152 822	0.146 757	0.140 946	0.135 377	0.130 040	18
19	0.143 704	0.137 678	0.131 917	0.126 409	0.121 143	0.116 107	19
20	0.129 755	0.124 034	0.118 577	0.113 371	0.108 405	0.103 667	20
21	0.117 161	0.111 742	0.106 586	0.101 678	0.097 007	0.092 560	21
22	0.105 788	0.100 669	0.095 808	0.091 191	0.086 807	0.082 643	22
23	0.095 520	0.090 693	0.086 119	0.081 786	0.077 680	0.073 788	23
24	0.086 248	0.081 705	0.077 410	0.073 351	0.069 512	0.065 882	24
25	0.077 877	0.073 608	0.069 582	0.065 785	0.062 203	0.058 823	25
26	0.070 317	0.066 314	0.062 546	0.059 000	0.055 663	0.052 521	26
27	0.063 492	0.059 742	0.056 221	0.052 915	0.049 810	0.046 894	27
28	0.057 329	0.053 822	0.050 536	0.047 457	0.044 573	0.041 869	28
29	0.051 764	0.048 488	0.045 425	0.042 563	0.039 886	0.037 383	29
30	0.046 740	0.043 683	0.040 832	0.038 173	0.035 692	0.033 378	30
31	0.042 203	0.039 354	0.036 703	0.034 236	0.031 939	0.029 802	31
32	0.038 107	0.035 454	0.032 991	0.030 705	0.028 581	0.026 609	32
33	0.034 408	0.031 940	0.029 655	0.027 538	0.025 576	0.023 758	33
34	0.031 068	0.028 775	0.026 656	0.024 698	0.022 887	0.021 212	34
35	0.028 052	0.025 924	0.023 961	0.022 150	0.020 480	0.018 940	35
36	0.025 329	0.023 355	0.021 538	0.019 866	0.018 327	0.016 910	36
37	0.022 871	0.021 040	0.019 360	0.017 817	0.016 400	0.015 098	37
38	0.020 651	0.018 955	0.017 402	0.015 979	0.014 676	0.013 481	38
39	0.018 646	0.017 077	0.015 642	0.014 331	0.013 132	0.012 036	39
40	0.016 836	0.015 384	0.014 060	0.012 853	0.011 752	0.010 747	40
41	0.015 202	0.013 860	0.012 639	0.011 527	0.010 516	0.009 595	41
42	0.013 727	0.012 486	0.011 361	0.010 338	0.009 410	0.008 567	42
43	0.012 394	0.011 249	0.010 212	0.009 272	0.008 421	0.007 649	43
44	0.011 191	0.010 134	0.009 179	0.008 316	0.007 535	0.006 830	44
45	0.010 105	0.009 130	0.008 251	0.007 458	0.006 743	0.006 098	45
46	0.009 124	0.008 225	0.007 417	0.006 689	0.006 034	0.005 445	46
47	0.008 238	0.007 410	0.006 667	0.005 999	0.005 400	0.004 861	47
48	0.007 439	0.006 676	0.005 992	0.005 380	0.004 832	0.004 340	48
49	0.006 717	0.006 014	0.005 386	0.004 825	0.004 324	0.003 875	49
50	0.006 065	0.005 418	0.004 842	0.004 328	0.003 869	0.003 460	50

PRESENT VALUE OF $1

YRS	12.25% ANNUAL RATE	12.50% ANNUAL RATE	12.75% ANNUAL RATE	13.00% ANNUAL RATE	13.25% ANNUAL RATE	13.50% ANNUAL RATE	YRS
1	0.890 869	0.888 889	0.886 918	0.884 956	0.883 002	0.881 057	1
2	0.793 647	0.790 123	0.786 623	0.783 147	0.779 693	0.776 262	2
3	0.707 035	0.702 332	0.697 670	0.693 050	0.688 471	0.683 931	3
4	0.629 875	0.624 295	0.618 776	0.613 319	0.607 921	0.602 583	4
5	0.561 136	0.554 929	0.548 804	0.542 760	0.536 796	0.530 910	5
6	0.499 899	0.493 270	0.486 744	0.480 319	0.473 992	0.467 762	6
7	0.445 344	0.438 462	0.431 702	0.425 061	0.418 536	0.412 125	7
8	0.396 743	0.389 744	0.382 884	0.376 160	0.369 568	0.363 106	8
9	0.353 446	0.346 439	0.339 587	0.332 885	0.326 329	0.319 917	9
10	0.314 874	0.307 946	0.301 186	0.294 588	0.288 150	0.281 865	10
11	0.280 511	0.273 730	0.267 127	0.260 698	0.254 437	0.248 339	11
12	0.249 899	0.243 315	0.236 920	0.230 706	0.224 668	0.218 801	12
13	0.222 627	0.216 280	0.210 128	0.204 165	0.198 382	0.192 776	13
14	0.198 331	0.192 249	0.186 367	0.180 677	0.175 172	0.169 847	14
15	0.176 687	0.170 888	0.165 292	0.159 891	0.154 677	0.149 645	15
16	0.157 405	0.151 901	0.146 600	0.141 496	0.136 580	0.131 846	16
17	0.140 227	0.135 023	0.130 023	0.125 218	0.120 601	0.116 164	17
18	0.124 924	0.120 020	0.115 319	0.110 812	0.106 491	0.102 347	18
19	0.111 291	0.106 685	0.102 279	0.098 064	0.094 032	0.090 173	19
20	0.099 145	0.094 831	0.090 713	0.086 782	0.083 030	0.079 448	20
21	0.088 326	0.084 294	0.080 455	0.076 798	0.073 316	0.069 998	21
22	0.078 687	0.074 928	0.071 357	0.067 963	0.064 738	0.061 672	22
23	0.070 099	0.066 603	0.063 288	0.060 144	0.057 164	0.054 337	23
24	0.062 449	0.059 202	0.056 131	0.053 225	0.050 476	0.047 874	24
25	0.055 634	0.052 624	0.049 784	0.047 102	0.044 570	0.042 180	25
26	0.049 563	0.046 777	0.044 154	0.041 683	0.039 356	0.037 163	26
27	0.044 154	0.041 580	0.039 161	0.036 888	0.034 751	0.032 742	27
28	0.039 335	0.036 960	0.034 733	0.032 644	0.030 685	0.028 848	28
29	0.035 043	0.032 853	0.030 805	0.028 889	0.027 095	0.025 417	29
30	0.031 218	0.029 203	0.027 321	0.025 565	0.023 925	0.022 394	30
31	0.027 811	0.025 958	0.024 232	0.022 624	0.021 126	0.019 730	31
32	0.024 776	0.023 074	0.021 492	0.020 021	0.018 654	0.017 383	32
33	0.022 072	0.020 510	0.019 061	0.017 718	0.016 472	0.015 316	33
34	0.019 664	0.018 231	0.016 906	0.015 680	0.014 545	0.013 494	34
35	0.017 518	0.016 205	0.014 994	0.013 876	0.012 843	0.011 889	35
36	0.015 606	0.014 405	0.013 299	0.012 279	0.011 340	0.010 475	36
37	0.013 903	0.012 804	0.011 795	0.010 867	0.010 014	0.009 229	37
38	0.012 386	0.011 382	0.010 461	0.009 617	0.008 842	0.008 131	38
39	0.011 034	0.010 117	0.009 278	0.008 510	0.007 807	0.007 164	39
40	0.009 830	0.008 993	0.008 229	0.007 531	0.006 894	0.006 312	40
41	0.008 757	0.007 994	0.007 298	0.006 665	0.006 087	0.005 561	41
42	0.007 801	0.007 105	0.006 473	0.005 898	0.005 375	0.004 900	42
43	0.006 950	0.006 316	0.005 741	0.005 219	0.004 746	0.004 317	43
44	0.006 192	0.005 614	0.005 092	0.004 619	0.004 191	0.003 803	44
45	0.005 516	0.004 990	0.004 516	0.004 088	0.003 701	0.003 351	45
46	0.004 914	0.004 436	0.004 005	0.003 617	0.003 268	0.002 953	46
47	0.004 378	0.003 943	0.003 552	0.003 201	0.002 885	0.002 601	47
48	0.003 900	0.003 505	0.003 151	0.002 833	0.002 548	0.002 292	48
49	0.003 474	0.003 115	0.002 794	0.002 507	0.002 250	0.002 019	49
50	0.003 095	0.002 769	0.002 478	0.002 219	0.001 987	0.001 779	50

YRS	13.75% ANNUAL RATE	14.00% ANNUAL RATE	14.25% ANNUAL RATE	14.50% ANNUAL RATE	14.75% ANNUAL RATE	15.00% ANNUAL RATE	YRS
1	0.879 121	0.877 193	0.875 274	0.873 362	0.871 460	0.869 565	1
2	0.772 854	0.769 468	0.766 104	0.762 762	0.759 442	0.756 144	2
3	0.679 432	0.674 972	0.670 550	0.666 168	0.661 823	0.657 516	3
4	0.597 303	0.592 080	0.586 915	0.581 806	0.576 752	0.571 753	4
5	0.525 101	0.519 369	0.513 711	0.508 127	0.502 616	0.497 177	5
6	0.461 627	0.455 587	0.449 638	0.443 779	0.438 010	0.432 328	6
7	0.405 826	0.399 637	0.393 556	0.387 580	0.381 708	0.375 937	7
8	0.356 770	0.350 559	0.344 469	0.338 498	0.332 643	0.326 902	8
9	0.313 644	0.307 508	0.301 505	0.295 631	0.289 885	0.284 262	9
10	0.275 731	0.269 744	0.263 899	0.258 193	0.252 623	0.247 185	10
11	0.242 401	0.236 617	0.230 984	0.225 496	0.220 151	0.214 943	11
12	0.213 100	0.207 559	0.202 174	0.196 940	0.191 853	0.186 907	12
13	0.187 341	0.182 069	0.176 958	0.172 000	0.167 192	0.162 528	13
14	0.164 695	0.159 710	0.154 886	0.150 218	0.145 701	0.141 329	14
15	0.144 787	0.140 096	0.135 568	0.131 195	0.126 972	0.122 894	15
16	0.127 285	0.122 892	0.118 659	0.114 581	0.110 651	0.106 865	16
17	0.111 899	0.107 800	0.103 859	0.100 071	0.096 428	0.092 926	17
18	0.098 373	0.094 561	0.090 905	0.087 398	0.084 033	0.080 805	18
19	0.086 482	0.082 948	0.079 567	0.076 330	0.073 232	0.070 265	19
20	0.076 028	0.072 762	0.069 643	0.066 664	0.063 818	0.061 100	20
21	0.066 838	0.063 826	0.060 956	0.058 222	0.055 615	0.053 131	21
22	0.058 758	0.055 988	0.053 354	0.050 849	0.048 466	0.046 201	22
23	0.051 656	0.049 112	0.046 699	0.044 409	0.042 237	0.040 174	23
24	0.045 412	0.043 081	0.040 874	0.038 785	0.036 807	0.034 934	24
25	0.039 922	0.037 790	0.035 776	0.033 874	0.032 076	0.030 378	25
26	0.035 096	0.033 149	0.031 314	0.029 584	0.027 953	0.026 415	26
27	0.030 854	0.029 078	0.027 408	0.025 838	0.024 360	0.022 970	27
28	0.027 124	0.025 507	0.023 990	0.022 566	0.021 229	0.019 974	28
29	0.023 846	0.022 375	0.020 998	0.019 708	0.018 500	0.017 369	29
30	0.020 963	0.019 627	0.018 379	0.017 212	0.016 122	0.015 103	30
31	0.018 429	0.017 217	0.016 086	0.015 032	0.014 050	0.013 133	31
32	0.016 201	0.015 102	0.014 080	0.013 129	0.012 244	0.011 420	32
33	0.014 243	0.013 248	0.012 324	0.011 466	0.010 670	0.009 931	33
34	0.012 521	0.011 621	0.010 787	0.010 014	0.009 298	0.008 635	34
35	0.011 008	0.010 194	0.009 441	0.008 746	0.008 103	0.007 509	35
36	0.009 677	0.008 942	0.008 264	0.007 638	0.007 062	0.006 529	36
37	0.008 507	0.007 844	0.007 233	0.006 671	0.006 154	0.005 678	37
38	0.007 479	0.006 880	0.006 331	0.005 826	0.005 363	0.004 937	38
39	0.006 575	0.006 035	0.005 541	0.005 088	0.004 674	0.004 293	39
40	0.005 780	0.005 294	0.004 850	0.004 444	0.004 073	0.003 733	40
41	0.005 082	0.004 644	0.004 245	0.003 881	0.003 549	0.003 246	41
42	0.004 467	0.004 074	0.003 716	0.003 390	0.003 093	0.002 823	42
43	0.003 927	0.003 573	0.003 252	0.002 960	0.002 695	0.002 455	43
44	0.003 453	0.003 135	0.002 847	0.002 586	0.002 349	0.002 134	44
45	0.003 035	0.002 750	0.002 492	0.002 258	0.002 047	0.001 856	45
46	0.002 668	0.002 412	0.002 181	0.001 972	0.001 784	0.001 614	46
47	0.002 346	0.002 116	0.001 909	0.001 722	0.001 555	0.001 403	47
48	0.002 062	0.001 856	0.001 671	0.001 504	0.001 355	0.001 220	48
49	0.001 813	0.001 628	0.001 462	0.001 314	0.001 181	0.001 061	49
50	0.001 594	0.001 428	0.001 280	0.001 147	0.001 029	0.000 923	50

YRS	15.25% ANNUAL RATE	15.50% ANNUAL RATE	15.75% ANNUAL RATE	16.00% ANNUAL RATE	16.25% ANNUAL RATE	16.50% ANNUAL RATE	YRS
1	0.867 679	0.865 801	0.863 931	0.862 069	0.860 215	0.858 369	1
2	0.752 867	0.749 611	0.746 377	0.743 163	0.739 970	0.736 798	2
3	0.653 247	0.649 014	0.644 818	0.640 658	0.636 533	0.632 444	3
4	0.566 808	0.561 917	0.557 078	0.552 291	0.547 556	0.542 871	4
5	0.491 808	0.486 508	0.481 277	0.476 113	0.471 015	0.465 983	5
6	0.426 731	0.421 219	0.415 790	0.410 442	0.405 175	0.399 986	6
7	0.370 266	0.364 692	0.359 214	0.353 830	0.348 537	0.343 335	7
8	0.321 272	0.315 751	0.310 336	0.305 025	0.299 817	0.294 708	8
9	0.278 761	0.273 377	0.268 109	0.262 953	0.257 907	0.252 969	9
10	0.241 875	0.236 690	0.231 627	0.226 684	0.221 856	0.217 140	10
11	0.209 870	0.204 927	0.200 110	0.195 417	0.190 844	0.186 387	11
12	0.182 100	0.177 426	0.172 881	0.168 463	0.164 166	0.159 989	12
13	0.158 004	0.153 615	0.149 357	0.145 227	0.141 218	0.137 329	13
14	0.137 097	0.133 000	0.129 035	0.125 195	0.121 478	0.117 879	14
15	0.118 956	0.115 152	0.111 477	0.107 927	0.104 497	0.101 184	15
16	0.103 216	0.099 698	0.096 308	0.093 041	0.089 890	0.086 853	16
17	0.089 558	0.086 319	0.083 204	0.080 207	0.077 325	0.074 552	17
18	0.077 708	0.074 735	0.071 882	0.069 144	0.066 516	0.063 993	18
19	0.067 425	0.064 706	0.062 101	0.059 607	0.057 218	0.054 930	19
20	0.058 503	0.056 022	0.053 651	0.051 385	0.049 220	0.047 150	20
21	0.050 762	0.048 504	0.046 351	0.044 298	0.042 340	0.040 472	21
22	0.044 045	0.041 995	0.040 044	0.038 188	0.036 421	0.034 740	22
23	0.038 217	0.036 359	0.034 595	0.032 920	0.031 330	0.029 820	23
24	0.033 160	0.031 480	0.029 888	0.028 380	0.026 951	0.025 596	24
25	0.028 772	0.027 255	0.025 821	0.024 465	0.023 183	0.021 971	25
26	0.024 965	0.023 598	0.022 308	0.021 091	0.019 943	0.018 859	26
27	0.021 662	0.020 431	0.019 272	0.018 182	0.017 155	0.016 188	27
28	0.018 795	0.017 689	0.016 650	0.015 674	0.014 757	0.013 895	28
29	0.016 308	0.015 315	0.014 384	0.013 512	0.012 694	0.011 927	29
30	0.014 151	0.013 260	0.012 427	0.011 648	0.010 920	0.010 238	30
31	0.012 278	0.011 480	0.010 736	0.010 042	0.009 393	0.008 788	31
32	0.010 653	0.009 940	0.009 275	0.008 657	0.008 080	0.007 543	32
33	0.009 244	0.008 606	0.008 013	0.007 463	0.006 951	0.006 475	33
34	0.008 021	0.007 451	0.006 923	0.006 433	0.005 979	0.005 558	34
35	0.006 959	0.006 451	0.005 98?	0.005 546	0.005 143	0.004 771	35
36	0.006 038	0.005 585	0.005 167	0.004 781	0.004 424	0.004 095	36
37	0.005 239	0.004 836	0.004 464	0.004 121	0.003 806	0.003 515	37
38	0.004 546	0.004 187	0.003 857	0.003 553	0.003 274	0.003 017	38
39	0.003 945	0.003 625	0.003 332	0.003 063	0.002 816	0.002 590	39
40	0.003 423	0.003 138	0.002 878	0.002 640	0.002 423	0.002 223	40
41	0.002 970	0.002 717	0.002 487	0.002 276	0.002 084	0.001 908	41
42	0.002 577	0.002 353	0.002 148	0.001 962	0.001 793	0.001 638	42
43	0.002 236	0.002 037	0.001 856	0.001 692	0.001 542	0.001 406	43
44	0.001 940	0.001 764	0.001 604	0.001 458	0.001 327	0.001 207	44
45	0.001 683	0.001 527	0.001 385	0.001 257	0.001 141	0.001 036	45
46	0.001 461	0.001 322	0.001 197	0.001 084	0.000 982	0.000 889	46
47	0.001 267	0.001 145	0.001 034	0.000 934	0.000 844	0.000 763	47
48	0.001 100	0.000 991	0.000 893	0.000 805	0.000 726	0.000 655	48
49	0.000 954	0.000 858	0.000 772	0.000 694	0.000 625	0.000 562	49
50	0.000 828	0.000 743	0.000 667	0.000 599	0.000 537	0.000 483	50

PRESENT VALUE OF $1

YRS	16.75% ANNUAL RATE	17.00% ANNUAL RATE	17.25% ANNUAL RATE	17.50% ANNUAL RATE	17.75% ANNUAL RATE	18.00% ANNUAL RATE	YRS
1	0.856 531	0.854 701	0.852 878	0.851 064	0.849 257	0.847 458	1
2	0.733 645	0.730 514	0.727 402	0.724 310	0.721 237	0.718 184	2
3	0.628 390	0.624 371	0.620 385	0.616 434	0.612 516	0.608 631	3
4	0.538 236	0.533 650	0.529 113	0.524 624	0.520 183	0.515 789	4
5	0.461 016	0.456 111	0.451 269	0.446 489	0.441 769	0.437 109	5
6	0.394 874	0.389 839	0.384 878	0.379 991	0.375 176	0.370 432	6
7	0.338 222	0.333 195	0.328 254	0.323 396	0.318 620	0.313 925	7
8	0.289 698	0.284 782	0.279 961	0.275 231	0.270 591	0.266 038	8
9	0.248 135	0.243 404	0.238 773	0.234 239	0.229 801	0.225 456	9
10	0.212 535	0.208 037	0.203 644	0.199 352	0.195 160	0.191 064	10
11	0.182 043	0.177 810	0.173 684	0.169 662	0.165 741	0.161 919	11
12	0.155 926	0.151 974	0.148 131	0.144 393	0.140 757	0.137 220	12
13	0.133 555	0.129 892	0.126 338	0.122 888	0.119 539	0.116 288	13
14	0.114 394	0.111 019	0.107 751	0.104 585	0.101 519	0.098 549	14
15	0.097 982	0.094 888	0.091 898	0.089 009	0.086 216	0.083 516	15
16	0.083 925	0.081 101	0.078 378	0.075 752	0.073 219	0.070 776	16
17	0.071 884	0.069 317	0.066 847	0.064 470	0.062 182	0.059 980	17
18	0.061 571	0.059 245	0.057 012	0.054 868	0.052 808	0.050 830	18
19	0.052 737	0.050 637	0.048 625	0.046 696	0.044 848	0.043 077	19
20	0.045 171	0.043 280	0.041 471	0.039 741	0.038 087	0.036 506	20
21	0.038 691	0.036 991	0.035 370	0.033 822	0.032 346	0.030 937	21
22	0.033 140	0.031 616	0.030 166	0.028 785	0.027 470	0.026 218	22
23	0.028 385	0.027 022	0.025 728	0.024 498	0.023 329	0.022 218	23
24	0.024 313	0.023 096	0.021 943	0.020 849	0.019 812	0.018 829	24
25	0.020 825	0.019 740	0.018 715	0.017 744	0.016 826	0.015 957	25
26	0.017 837	0.016 872	0.015 961	0.015 101	0.014 289	0.013 523	26
27	0.015 278	0.014 421	0.013 613	0.012 852	0.012 135	0.011 460	27
28	0.013 086	0.012 325	0.011 610	0.010 938	0.010 306	0.009 712	28
29	0.011 209	0.010 534	0.009 902	0.009 309	0.008 753	0.008 230	29
30	0.009 600	0.009 004	0.008 445	0.007 923	0.007 433	0.006 975	30
31	0.008 223	0.007 696	0.007 203	0.006 743	0.006 313	0.005 911	31
32	0.007 043	0.006 577	0.006 143	0.005 738	0.005 361	0.005 009	32
33	0.006 033	0.005 622	0.005 239	0.004 884	0.004 553	0.004 245	33
34	0.005 167	0.004 805	0.004 469	0.004 156	0.003 867	0.003 598	34
35	0.004 426	0.004 107	0.003 811	0.003 537	0.003 284	0.003 049	35
36	0.003 791	0.003 510	0.003 250	0.003 010	0.002 789	0.002 584	36
37	0.003 247	0.003 000	0.002 772	0.002 562	0.002 368	0.002 190	37
38	0.002 781	0.002 564	0.002 364	0.002 181	0.002 011	0.001 856	38
39	0.002 382	0.002 192	0.002 017	0.001 856	0.001 708	0.001 573	39
40	0.002 040	0.001 873	0.001 720	0.001 579	0.001 451	0.001 333	40
41	0.001 748	0.001 601	0.001 467	0.001 344	0.001 232	0.001 129	41
42	0.001 497	0.001 368	0.001 251	0.001 144	0.001 046	0.000 957	42
43	0.001 282	0.001 170	0.001 067	0.000 974	0.000 889	0.000 811	43
44	0.001 098	0.001 000	0.000 910	0.000 829	0.000 755	0.000 687	44
45	0.000 941	0.000 854	0.000 776	0.000 705	0.000 641	0.000 583	45
46	0.000 806	0.000 730	0.000 662	0.000 600	0.000 544	0.000 494	46
47	0.000 690	0.000 624	0.000 565	0.000 511	0.000 462	0.000 418	47
48	0.000 591	0.000 533	0.000 481	0.000 435	0.000 393	0.000 355	48
49	0.000 506	0.000 456	0.000 411	0.000 370	0.000 333	0.000 300	49
50	0.000 434	0.000 390	0.000 350	0.000 315	0.000 283	0.000 255	50

YRS	18.25% ANNUAL RATE	18.50% ANNUAL RATE	18.75% ANNUAL RATE	19.00% ANNUAL RATE	19.25% ANNUAL RATE	19.50% ANNUAL RATE	YRS
1	0.845 666	0.843 882	0.842 105	0.840 336	0.838 574	0.836 820	1
2	0.715 151	0.712 137	0.709 141	0.706 165	0.703 207	0.700 268	2
3	0.604 779	0.600 959	0.597 172	0.593 416	0.589 691	0.585 998	3
4	0.511 441	0.507 139	0.502 881	0.498 669	0.494 500	0.490 375	4
5	0.432 508	0.427 965	0.423 479	0.419 049	0.414 675	0.410 356	5
6	0.365 757	0.361 152	0.356 614	0.352 142	0.347 736	0.343 394	6
7	0.309 309	0.304 770	0.300 306	0.295 918	0.291 603	0.287 359	7
8	0.261 572	0.257 189	0.252 890	0.248 671	0.244 530	0.240 468	8
9	0.221 202	0.217 038	0.212 960	0.208 967	0.205 057	0.201 228	9
10	0.187 063	0.183 154	0.179 334	0.175 602	0.171 956	0.168 392	10
11	0.158 193	0.154 560	0.151 019	0.147 565	0.144 198	0.140 914	11
12	0.133 778	0.130 431	0.127 173	0.124 004	0.120 920	0.117 919	12
13	0.113 132	0.110 068	0.107 093	0.104 205	0.101 401	0.098 677	13
14	0.095 672	0.092 884	0.090 184	0.087 567	0.085 032	0.082 575	14
15	0.080 906	0.078 384	0.075 944	0.073 586	0.071 306	0.069 101	15
16	0.068 420	0.066 146	0.063 953	0.061 837	0.059 795	0.057 825	16
17	0.057 860	0.055 820	0.053 855	0.051 964	0.050 143	0.048 389	17
18	0.048 930	0.047 105	0.045 352	0.043 667	0.042 048	0.040 493	18
19	0.041 379	0.039 751	0.038 191	0.036 695	0.035 261	0.033 885	19
20	0.034 993	0.033 545	0.032 161	0.030 836	0.029 569	0.028 356	20
21	0.029 592	0.028 308	0.027 083	0.025 913	0.024 796	0.023 729	21
22	0.025 025	0.023 889	0.022 807	0.021 775	0.020 793	0.019 857	22
23	0.021 163	0.020 159	0.019 206	0.018 299	0.017 436	0.016 616	23
24	0.017 897	0.017 012	0.016 173	0.015 377	0.014 622	0.013 905	24
25	0.015 135	0.014 356	0.013 619	0.012 922	0.012 261	0.011 636	25
26	0.012 799	0.012 115	0.011 469	0.010 859	0.010 282	0.009 737	26
27	0.010 824	0.010 224	0.009 658	0.009 125	0.008 622	0.008 148	27
28	0.009 153	0.008 628	0.008 133	0.007 668	0.007 230	0.006 819	28
29	0.007 740	0.007 281	0.006 849	0.006 444	0.006 063	0.005 706	29
30	0.006 546	0.006 144	0.005 768	0.005 415	0.005 085	0.004 775	30
31	0.005 536	0.005 185	0.004 857	0.004 550	0.004 264	0.003 996	31
32	0.004 681	0.004 375	0.004 090	0.003 824	0.003 575	0.003 344	32
33	0.003 959	0.003 692	0.003 444	0.003 213	0.002 998	0.002 798	33
34	0.003 348	0.003 116	0.002 900	0.002 700	0.002 514	0.002 341	34
35	0.002 831	0.002 629	0.002 442	0.002 269	0.002 108	0.001 959	35
36	0.002 394	0.002 219	0.002 057	0.001 907	0.001 768	0.001 640	36
37	0.002 025	0.001 872	0.001 732	0.001 602	0.001 483	0.001 372	37
38	0.001 712	0.001 580	0.001 459	0.001 347	0.001 243	0.001 148	38
39	0.001 448	0.001 333	0.001 228	0.001 132	0.001 043	0.000 961	39
40	0.001 224	0.001 125	0.001 034	0.000 951	0.000 874	0.000 804	40
41	0.001 036	0.000 950	0.000 871	0.000 799	0.000 733	0.000 673	41
42	0.000 876	0.000 801	0.000 733	0.000 671	0.000 615	0.000 563	42
43	0.000 741	0.000 676	0.000 618	0.000 564	0.000 516	0.000 471	43
44	0.000 626	0.000 571	0.000 520	0.000 474	0.000 432	0.000 394	44
45	0.000 530	0.000 482	0.000 438	0.000 398	0.000 363	0.000 330	45
46	0.000 448	0.000 406	0.000 369	0.000 335	0.000 304	0.000 276	46
47	0.000 379	0.000 343	0.000 311	0.000 281	0.000 255	0.000 231	47
48	0.000 320	0.000 289	0.000 262	0.000 236	0.000 214	0.000 193	48
49	0.000 271	0.000 244	0.000 220	0.000 199	0.000 179	0.000 162	49
50	0.000 229	0.000 206	0.000 185	0.000 167	0.000 150	0.000 135	50

SECTION 4

YRS	19.75% ANNUAL RATE	20.00% ANNUAL RATE	21.00% ANNUAL RATE	22.00% ANNUAL RATE	23.00% ANNUAL RATE	24.00% ANNUAL RATE	YRS
1	0.835 073	0.833 333	0.826 446	0.819 672	0.813 008	0.806 452	1
2	0.697 347	0.694 444	0.683 013	0.671 862	0.660 982	0.650 364	2
3	0.582 336	0.578 704	0.564 474	0.550 707	0.537 384	0.524 487	3
4	0.486 293	0.482 253	0.466 507	0.451 399	0.436 897	0.422 974	4
5	0.406 090	0.401 878	0.385 543	0.369 999	0.355 201	0.341 108	5
6	0.339 115	0.334 898	0.318 631	0.303 278	0.288 781	0.275 087	6
7	0.283 186	0.279 082	0.263 331	0.248 589	0.234 782	0.221 844	7
8	0.236 481	0.232 568	0.217 629	0.203 761	0.190 879	0.178 907	8
9	0.197 479	0.193 807	0.179 859	0.167 017	0.155 187	0.144 280	9
10	0.164 909	0.161 506	0.148 644	0.136 899	0.126 168	0.116 354	10
11	0.137 711	0.134 588	0.122 846	0.112 213	0.102 576	0.093 834	11
12	0.114 999	0.112 157	0.101 526	0.091 978	0.083 395	0.075 673	12
13	0.096 032	0.093 464	0.083 905	0.075 391	0.067 801	0.061 026	13
14	0.080 194	0.077 887	0.069 343	0.061 796	0.055 122	0.049 215	14
15	0.066 968	0.064 905	0.057 309	0.050 653	0.044 815	0.039 689	15
16	0.055 923	0.054 088	0.047 362	0.041 519	0.036 435	0.032 008	16
17	0.046 700	0.045 073	0.039 143	0.034 032	0.029 622	0.025 813	17
18	0.038 998	0.037 561	0.032 349	0.027 895	0.024 083	0.020 817	18
19	0.032 566	0.031 301	0.026 735	0.022 865	0.019 580	0.016 788	19
20	0.027 195	0.026 084	0.022 095	0.018 741	0.015 918	0.013 538	20
21	0.022 710	0.021 737	0.018 260	0.015 362	0.012 942	0.010 918	21
22	0.018 964	0.018 114	0.015 091	0.012 592	0.010 522	0.008 805	22
23	0.015 837	0.015 095	0.012 472	0.010 321	0.008 554	0.007 101	23
24	0.013 225	0.012 579	0.010 307	0.008 460	0.006 955	0.005 726	24
25	0.011 044	0.010 483	0.008 519	0.006 934	0.005 654	0.004 618	25
26	0.009 222	0.008 735	0.007 040	0.005 684	0.004 597	0.003 724	26
27	0.007 701	0.007 280	0.005 818	0.004 659	0.003 737	0.003 003	27
28	0.006 431	0.006 066	0.004 809	0.003 819	0.003 038	0.002 422	28
29	0.005 370	0.005 055	0.003 974	0.003 130	0.002 470	0.001 953	29
30	0.004 485	0.004 213	0.003 284	0.002 566	0.002 008	0.001 575	30
31	0.003 745	0.003 511	0.002 714	0.002 103	0.001 633	0.001 270	31
32	0.003 127	0.002 926	0.002 243	0.001 724	0.001 328	0.001 024	32
33	0.002 612	0.002 438	0.001 854	0.001 413	0.001 079	0.000 826	33
34	0.002 181	0.002 032	0.001 532	0.001 158	0.000 877	0.000 666	34
35	0.001 821	0.001 693	0.001 266	0.000 949	0.000 713	0.000 537	35
36	0.001 521	0.001 411	0.001 046	0.000 778	0.000 580	0.000 433	36
37	0.001 270	0.001 176	0.000 865	0.000 638	0.000 472	0.000 349	37
38	0.001 061	0.000 980	0.000 715	0.000 523	0.000 383	0.000 282	38
39	0.000 886	0.000 816	0.000 591	0.000 429	0.000 312	0.000 227	39
40	0.000 740	0.000 680	0.000 488	0.000 351	0.000 253	0.000 183	40
41	0.000 618	0.000 567	0.000 403	0.000 288	0.000 206	0.000 148	41
42	0.000 516	0.000 472	0.000 333	0.000 236	0.000 167	0.000 119	42
43	0.000 431	0.000 394	0.000 276	0.000 193	0.000 136	0.000 096	43
44	0.000 360	0.000 328	0.000 228	0.000 159	0.000 111	0.000 078	44
45	0.000 300	0.000 273	0.000 188	0.000 130	0.000 090	0.000 063	45
46	0.000 251	0.000 228	0.000 156	0.000 107	0.000 073	0.000 050	46
47	0.000 209	0.000 190	0.000 129	0.000 087	0.000 059	0.000 041	47
48	0.000 175	0.000 158	0.000 106	0.000 072	0.000 048	0.000 033	48
49	0.000 146	0.000 132	0.000 088	0.000 059	0.000 039	0.000 026	49
50	0.000 122	0.000 110	0.000 073	0.000 048	0.000 032	0.000 021	50

Section 5.   Present Value of $1.00 Per Period:

These tables indicate the amount of money you must invest today to receive an income of $1 per period for a specific term. The initial investment will begin the investment period. These factors depend upon the same equal income per period. No additional withdrawals or investments can be made during the stated period.

In this section the following four (4) periods are presented in detail: monthly, quarterly, semiannual, and annual.

Monthly:

The factors presented on pages 120 through 127 indicate the amount of money you will need to invest today to receive a monthly income at the end of each month for a stated period of time. These factors are based on the condition that interest is earned at the end of each monthly period for the stated period of months. Therefore, the interest is compounded monthly. This is interest earned on interest.

Example I

You would like to establish a monthly retirement income for yourself. The desired income is $1,000.00 per month, and you want that income for 10 years, or 120 months. The interest is compounded monthly and the annual interest rate is 8.0%.

Turn to page 120 and locate the 8.0% column. Proceed down that column until you locate the part where the 10 years row intersects the 8.0% column. The answer is 82.421481 for every monthly income of $1 needed. So, to determine your answer, multiply 82.421481 by $1,000.00. The correct answer is $82,421.48. That means you must deposit or invest $82,421.48 today to receive a monthly income of $1,000.00 for 120 months.

Note: If your investment period is less than 4 years, we have provided all the factors for each monthly period. The annual figures are provided for 4 years and over.

Quarterly:

The factors presented on pages 128 through 133 indicate the amount of money you need to invest today to receive an income of $1 at the end of each quarter for a stated period of time. The interest is earned at the end of each quarter and is also compounded quarterly. This is interest earned on interest.

Example J

You are offered a choice of investments: $12,000.00 cash today or $1,000.00 at the end of each quarterly period over five (5) years or twenty (20) quarters. In order to evaluate these two options you will need to know today's value of the $1,000.00 per quarter, stream of income.

Let's assume an interest rate of 10.0% and quarterly compounding. Turn to page 129 and locate the 10.0% column. Proceed down that column until you locate the point where the five (5) years or twenty (20) quarter row intersects the 10.0% interest column. The number is 15.589162 for every $1 of quarterly income. So, to determine your answer, multiply 15.589162 by $1,000.00 and you arrive at the solution of $15,589.16. This means today's value of that stream of income is $15,589.16, which is $3,589.16 greater than the $12,000.00 cash. Therefore, unless you need the money, the $1,000.00 per quarter is a better investment.

Note: For investments of 14 years and more, only the annual amounts are shown.

Semiannual:

The factors on pages 134 through 137 cover semiannual compounding (or the interest being compounded every 6 months).

Annual:

The factors on pages 138 through 145 cover annual compounding (or the interest being compounded every year).

Both the semiannual and annual tables are used the same way as the monthly and quarterly tables.

Just in case you want to do it the hard way, here's the formula . . .

$$a_{\overline{n}|} = \frac{1 - V^n}{i}$$

V^n = Present value of $1
i = interest rate per period
$a_{\overline{n}|}$ = Present value of $1 per period

119

PRESENT VALUE OF
$1 PER PERIOD

MOS	7.00% ANNUAL RATE	8.00% ANNUAL RATE	9.00% ANNUAL RATE	10.00% ANNUAL RATE	10.25% ANNUAL RATE	10.50% ANNUAL RATE	MOS
1	0.994 200	0.993 377	0.992 556	0.991 736	0.991 531	0.991 326	1
2	1.982 635	1.980 176	1.977 723	1.975 275	1.974 664	1.974 053	2
3	2.965 337	2.960 440	2.955 556	2.950 686	2.949 470	2.948 256	3
4	3.942 340	3.934 212	3.926 110	3.918 036	3.916 021	3.914 008	4
5	4.913 677	4.901 535	4.889 440	4.877 391	4.874 386	4.871 384	5
6	5.879 381	5.862 452	5.845 598	5.828 817	5.824 634	5.820 455	6
7	6.839 484	6.817 005	6.794 638	6.772 381	6.766 834	6.761 293	7
8	7.794 019	7.765 237	7.736 613	7.708 146	7.701 054	7.693 971	8
9	8.743 018	8.707 189	8.671 576	8.636 178	8.627 362	8.618 559	9
10	9.686 513	9.642 903	9.599 580	9.556 540	9.545 824	9.535 126	10
11	10.624 537	10.572 420	10.520 675	10.469 296	10.456 508	10.443 743	11
12	11.557 120	11.495 782	11.434 913	11.374 508	11.359 479	11.344 479	12
13	12.484 295	12.413 028	12.342 345	12.272 240	12.254 803	12.237 402	13
14	13.406 093	13.324 200	13.243 022	13.162 552	13.142 544	13.122 579	14
15	14.322 545	14.229 338	14.136 995	14.045 506	14.022 766	14.000 079	15
16	15.233 682	15.128 481	15.024 313	14.921 163	14.895 533	14.869 967	16
17	16.139 534	16.021 670	15.905 025	15.789 583	15.760 909	15.732 309	17
18	17.040 133	16.908 944	16.779 181	16.650 826	16.618 955	16.587 171	18
19	17.935 510	17.790 342	17.646 830	17.504 952	17.469 735	17.434 618	19
20	18.825 693	18.665 902	18.508 020	18.352 018	18.313 309	18.274 714	20
21	19.710 714	19.535 665	19.362 799	19.192 084	19.149 738	19.107 524	21
22	20.590 602	20.399 667	20.211 215	20.025 207	19.979 083	19.933 109	22
23	21.465 387	21.257 947	21.053 315	20.851 445	20.801 405	20.751 533	23
24	22.335 099	22.110 544	21.889 146	21.670 855	21.616 761	21.562 858	24
25	23.199 767	22.957 494	22.718 755	22.483 492	22.425 213	22.367 145	25
26	24.059 421	23.798 835	23.542 189	23.289 414	23.226 817	23.164 456	26
27	24.914 089	24.634 604	24.359 493	24.088 675	24.021 632	23.954 852	27
28	25.763 800	25.464 838	25.170 713	24.881 331	24.809 716	24.738 391	28
29	26.608 583	26.289 575	25.975 893	25.667 435	25.591 125	25.515 133	29
30	27.448 467	27.108 849	26.775 080	26.447 043	26.365 916	26.285 138	30
31	28.283 480	27.922 698	27.568 318	27.220 208	27.134 145	27.048 464	31
32	29.113 650	28.731 157	28.355 650	27.986 983	27.895 868	27.805 169	32
33	29.939 006	29.534 262	29.137 122	28.747 421	28.651 140	28.555 310	33
34	30.759 575	30.332 048	29.912 776	29.501 575	29.400 014	29.298 944	34
35	31.575 385	31.124 551	30.682 656	30.249 496	30.142 547	30.036 128	35
36	32.386 464	31.911 806	31.446 805	30.991 236	30.878 791	30.766 918	36
37	33.192 840	32.693 847	32.205 266	31.726 845	31.608 799	31.491 368	37
38	33.994 538	33.470 708	32.958 080	32.456 375	32.332 624	32.209 535	38
39	34.791 587	34.242 426	33.705 290	33.179 876	33.050 319	32.921 472	39
40	35.584 014	35.009 032	34.446 938	33.897 398	33.761 936	33.627 233	40
41	36.371 845	35.770 562	35.183 065	34.608 990	34.467 526	34.326 873	41
42	37.155 107	36.527 048	35.913 713	35.314 701	35.167 140	35.020 444	42
43	37.933 826	37.278 525	36.638 921	36.014 579	35.860 829	35.707 999	43
44	38.708 029	38.025 024	37.358 730	36.708 674	36.548 643	36.389 591	44
45	39.477 742	38.766 580	38.073 181	37.397 032	37.230 631	37.065 269	45
46	40.242 991	39.503 226	38.782 314	38.079 701	37.906 843	37.735 087	46
47	41.003 803	40.234 992	39.486 168	38.756 728	38.577 329	38.399 095	47
YRS							
4	41.760 201	40.961 913	40.184 782	39.428 160	39.242 135	39.057 344	48
5	50.501 994	49.318 433	48.173 374	47.065 369	46.793 994	46.524 827	60
6	58.654 444	57.034 522	55.476 849	53.978 665	53.613 104	53.251 057	72
7	66.257 285	64.159 261	62.153 965	60.236 667	59.770 564	59.309 613	84
8	73.347 569	70.737 970	68.258 439	65.901 488	65.330 572	64.766 771	96
9	79.959 850	76.812 497	73.839 382	71.029 355	70.351 099	69.682 229	108
10	86.126 354	82.421 481	78.941 693	75.671 163	74.884 490	74.109 758	120
11	91.877 134	87.600 600	83.606 420	79.872 986	78.978 010	78.097 702	132
12	97.240 216	92.382 800	87.871 092	83.676 528	82.674 341	81.689 957	144
13	102.241 738	96.798 498	91.770 018	87.119 542	86.012 022	84.925 549	156
14	106.906 074	100.875 784	95.334 564	90.236 201	89.025 850	87.839 962	168
15	111.255 958	104.640 592	98.593 409	93.057 439	91.747 251	90.465 078	180
16	115.312 587	108.116 871	101.572 769	95.611 259	94.204 596	92.829 614	192
17	119.095 732	111.326 733	104.296 613	97.923 008	96.423 509	94.959 437	204
18	122.623 831	114.290 596	106.786 856	100.015 633	98.427 122	96.877 844	216
19	125.914 077	117.027 313	109.063 531	101.909 902	100.236 328	98.605 822	228
20	128.982 506	119.554 292	111.144 954	103.624 619	101.869 988	100.162 274	240
21	131.844 073	121.887 606	113.047 870	105.176 801	103.345 136	101.564 226	252
22	134.512 723	124.042 099	114.787 589	106.581 856	104.677 152	102.827 014	264
23	137.001 461	126.031 475	116.378 106	107.853 730	105.879 924	103.964 453	276
24	139.322 418	127.868 388	117.832 218	109.005 045	106.965 992	104.988 985	288
25	141.486 903	129.564 523	119.161 622	110.047 230	107.946 680	105.911 817	300
26	143.505 467	131.130 668	120.377 014	110.990 629	108.832 214	106.743 045	312
27	145.387 946	132.576 786	121.488 172	111.844 605	109.631 824	107.491 762	324
28	147.143 515	133.912 076	122.504 035	112.617 635	110.353 850	108.166 158	336
29	148.780 729	135.145 031	123.432 776	113.317 392	111.005 818	108.773 611	348
30	150.307 568	136.283 494	124.281 866	113.950 820	111.594 527	109.320 766	360

MOS	10.75% ANNUAL RATE	11.00% ANNUAL RATE	11.25% ANNUAL RATE	11.50% ANNUAL RATE	11.75% ANNUAL RATE	12.00% ANNUAL RATE	MOS
1	0.991 121	0.990 917	0.990 712	0.990 508	0.990 303	0.990 099	1
2	1.973 442	1.972 832	1.972 222	1.971 613	1.971 004	1.970 395	2
3	2.947 042	2.945 829	2.944 617	2.943 405	2.942 195	2.940 985	3
4	3.911 997	3.909 987	3.907 979	3.905 973	3.903 969	3.901 966	4
5	4.868 384	4.865 388	4.862 394	4.859 404	4.856 416	4.853 431	5
6	5.816 280	5.812 110	5.807 945	5.803 784	5.799 628	5.795 476	6
7	6.755 760	6.750 233	6.744 713	6.739 200	6.733 694	6.728 195	7
8	7.686 898	7.679 835	7.672 781	7.665 737	7.658 703	7.651 678	8
9	8.609 769	8.600 992	8.592 229	8.583 479	8.574 742	8.566 018	9
10	9.524 446	9.513 783	9.503 137	9.492 509	9.481 898	9.471 305	10
11	10.431 001	10.418 282	10.405 585	10.392 910	10.380 258	10.367 628	11
12	11.329 508	11.314 565	11.299 650	11.284 764	11.269 907	11.255 077	12
13	12.220 037	12.202 707	12.185 412	12.168 153	12.150 929	12.133 740	13
14	13.102 659	13.082 781	13.062 947	13.043 156	13.023 408	13.003 703	14
15	13.977 444	13.954 862	13.932 331	13.909 853	13.887 427	13.865 053	15
16	14.844 462	14.819 021	14.793 641	14.768 323	14.743 068	14.717 874	16
17	15.703 783	15.675 330	15.646 951	15.618 645	15.590 412	15.562 251	17
18	16.555 473	16.523 861	16.492 335	16.460 895	16.429 539	16.398 269	18
19	17.399 602	17.364 685	17.329 868	17.295 149	17.260 530	17.226 008	19
20	18.236 235	18.197 871	18.159 621	18.121 485	18.083 462	18.045 553	20
21	19.065 441	19.023 489	18.981 668	18.939 977	18.898 416	18.856 983	21
22	19.887 284	19.841 608	19.796 080	19.750 699	19.705 466	19.660 379	22
23	20.701 830	20.652 295	20.602 927	20.553 726	20.504 691	20.455 821	23
24	21.509 144	21.455 619	21.402 281	21.349 130	21.296 166	21.243 387	24
25	22.309 290	22.251 645	22.194 210	22.136 984	22.079 966	22.023 156	25
26	23.102 332	23.040 441	22.978 784	22.917 360	22.856 166	22.795 204	26
27	23.888 332	23.822 072	23.756 071	23.690 327	23.624 840	23.559 608	27
28	24.667 354	24.596 603	24.526 138	24.455 958	24.386 060	24.316 443	28
29	25.439 458	25.364 099	25.289 054	25.214 320	25.139 898	25.065 785	29
30	26.204 708	26.124 623	26.044 883	25.965 485	25.886 427	25.807 708	30
31	26.963 163	26.878 239	26.793 692	26.709 518	26.625 717	26.542 285	31
32	27.714 884	27.625 010	27.535 546	27.446 490	27.357 838	27.269 589	32
33	28.459 930	28.364 998	28.270 510	28.176 465	28.082 860	27.989 693	33
34	29.198 362	29.098 264	28.998 648	28.899 511	28.800 852	28.702 666	34
35	29.930 236	29.824 869	29.720 023	29.615 694	29.511 881	29.408 580	35
36	30.655 613	30.544 874	30.434 697	30.325 079	30.216 016	30.107 505	36
37	31.374 550	31.258 340	31.142 734	31.027 730	30.913 323	30.799 510	37
38	32.087 103	31.965 324	31.844 195	31.723 711	31.603 868	31.484 663	38
39	32.793 329	32.665 887	32.539 140	32.413 086	32.287 718	32.163 033	39
40	33.493 285	33.360 086	33.227 631	33.095 916	32.964 936	32.834 686	40
41	34.187 026	34.047 980	33.909 728	33.772 266	33.635 588	33.499 689	41
42	34.874 608	34.729 625	34.585 489	34.442 195	34.299 736	34.158 108	42
43	35.556 085	35.405 078	35.254 973	35.105 764	34.957 445	34.810 008	43
44	36.231 511	36.074 396	35.918 240	35.763 035	35.608 775	35.455 454	44
45	36.900 940	36.737 634	36.575 346	36.414 067	36.253 790	36.094 508	45
46	37.564 425	37.394 848	37.226 349	37.058 919	36.892 551	36.727 236	46
47	38.222 020	38.046 093	37.871 305	37.697 650	37.525 117	37.353 699	47
YRS							
4	38.873 775	38.691 421	38.510 272	38.330 318	38.151 550	37.973 959	48
5	46.257 847	45.993 034	45.730 366	45.469 825	45.211 389	44.955 038	60
6	52.892 484	52.537 346	52.185 606	51.837 225	51.492 166	51.150 391	72
7	58.853 748	58.402 903	57.957 015	57.516 018	57.079 852	56.648 453	84
8	64.209 982	63.660 103	63.117 034	62.580 675	62.050 930	61.527 703	96
9	69.022 594	68.372 043	67.730 430	67.097 611	66.473 444	65.857 790	108
10	73.346 757	72.595 275	71.855 110	71.126 060	70.407 928	69.700 522	120
11	77.232 045	76.380 487	75.542 845	74.718 850	73.908 238	73.110 752	132
12	80.723 001	79.773 109	78.839 923	77.923 095	77.022 284	76.137 157	144
13	83.859 649	82.813 859	81.787 728	80.780 815	79.792 692	78.822 939	156
14	86.677 947	85.539 231	84.423 259	83.329 485	82.257 381	81.206 434	168
15	89.210 206	87.981 937	86.779 597	85.602 527	84.450 090	83.321 664	180
16	91.485 457	90.171 293	88.886 318	87.629 750	86.400 830	85.198 824	192
17	93.529 785	92.133 576	90.769 865	89.437 737	88.136 304	86.864 707	204
18	95.366 626	93.892 337	92.453 881	91.050 199	89.680 267	88.343 095	216
19	97.017 041	95.468 685	93.959 501	92.488 279	91.053 851	89.655 089	228
20	98.499 949	96.881 539	95.305 625	93.770 838	92.275 859	90.819 416	240
21	99.832 351	98.147 856	96.509 148	94.914 693	93.363 017	91.852 698	252
22	101.029 524	99.282 835	97.585 177	95.934 846	94.330 205	92.769 683	264
23	102.105 191	100.300 098	98.547 217	96.844 673	95.190 663	93.583 461	276
24	103.071 685	101.211 853	99.407 345	97.656 106	95.956 169	94.305 647	288
25	103.940 086	102.029 044	100.176 355	98.379 787	96.637 200	94.946 551	300
26	104.720 350	102.761 478	100.863 902	99.025 204	97.243 079	95.515 321	312
27	105.421 422	103.417 947	101.478 613	99.600 823	97.782 098	96.020 075	324
28	106.051 340	104.006 328	102.028 205	100.114 191	98.261 636	96.468 019	336
29	106.617 325	104.533 685	102.519 577	100.572 040	98.688 256	96.865 546	348
30	107.125 867	105.006 346	102.958 896	100.980 375	99.067 798	97.218 331	360

PRESENT VALUE OF
$1 PER PERIOD

MONTHLY
COMPOUNDING

MOS	12.25% ANNUAL RATE	12.50% ANNUAL RATE	12.75% ANNUAL RATE	13.00% ANNUAL RATE	13.25% ANNUAL RATE	13.50% ANNUAL RATE	MOS
1	0.989 895	0.989 691	0.989 487	0.989 283	0.989 079	0.988 875	1
2	1.969 787	1.969 178	1.968 571	1.967 963	1.967 356	1.966 749	2
3	2.939 776	2.938 568	2.937 361	2.936 155	2.934 949	2.933 745	3
4	3.899 964	3.897 965	3.895 967	3.893 970	3.891 975	3.889 982	4
5	4.850 449	4.847 470	4.844 494	4.841 520	4.838 550	4.835 582	5
6	5.791 329	5.787 187	5.783 049	5.778 915	5.774 786	5.770 662	6
7	6.722 702	6.717 216	6.711 737	6.706 264	6.700 798	6.695 339	7
8	7.644 663	7.637 657	7.630 661	7.623 674	7.616 697	7.609 730	8
9	8.557 307	8.548 609	8.539 924	8.531 253	8.522 594	8.513 948	9
10	9.460 728	9.450 170	9.439 628	9.429 104	9.418 597	9.408 107	10
11	10.355 021	10.342 436	10.329 873	10.317 333	10.304 814	10.292 318	11
12	11.240 276	11.225 504	11.210 759	11.196 042	11.181 354	11.166 693	12
13	12.116 586	12.099 468	12.082 384	12.065 335	12.048 320	12.031 340	13
14	12.984 041	12.964 421	12.944 845	12.925 310	12.905 818	12.886 369	14
15	13.842 730	13.820 458	13.798 238	13.776 070	13.753 952	13.731 885	15
16	14.692 741	14.667 670	14.642 660	14.617 711	14.592 823	14.567 995	16
17	15.534 163	15.506 148	15.478 204	15.450 332	15.422 532	15.394 804	17
18	16.367 083	16.335 981	16.304 964	16.274 030	16.243 181	16.212 414	18
19	17.191 585	17.157 260	17.123 032	17.088 901	17.054 866	17.020 928	19
20	18.007 756	17.970 072	17.932 499	17.895 038	17.857 688	17.820 448	20
21	18.815 679	18.774 504	18.733 456	18.692 535	18.651 741	18.611 074	21
22	19.615 438	19.570 643	19.525 992	19.481 486	19.437 123	19.392 904	22
23	20.407 116	20.358 574	20.310 196	20.261 981	20.213 928	20.166 036	23
24	21.190 793	21.138 383	21.086 156	21.034 112	20.982 249	20.930 567	24
25	21.966 551	21.910 152	21.853 958	21.797 967	21.742 179	21.686 593	25
26	22.734 470	22.673 965	22.613 687	22.553 636	22.493 810	22.434 208	26
27	23.494 629	23.429 904	23.365 430	23.301 206	23.237 232	23.173 506	27
28	24.247 107	24.178 049	24.109 269	24.040 765	23.972 535	23.904 579	28
29	24.991 980	24.918 481	24.845 287	24.772 397	24.699 808	24.627 520	29
30	25.729 327	25.651 281	25.573 568	25.496 188	25.419 139	25.342 418	30
31	26.459 222	26.376 525	26.294 193	26.212 222	26.130 613	26.049 362	31
32	27.181 742	27.094 293	27.007 241	26.920 583	26.834 317	26.748 442	32
33	27.896 960	27.804 661	27.712 792	27.621 351	27.530 337	27.439 745	33
34	28.604 951	28.507 706	28.410 926	28.314 610	28.218 755	28.123 357	34
35	29.305 788	29.203 503	29.101 720	29.000 438	28.899 654	28.799 365	35
36	29.999 543	29.892 126	29.785 252	29.678 917	29.573 118	29.467 851	36
37	30.686 287	30.573 651	30.461 598	30.350 124	30.239 226	30.128 901	37
38	31.366 092	31.248 149	31.130 832	31.014 137	30.898 060	30.782 597	38
39	32.039 026	31.915 694	31.793 031	31.671 034	31.549 699	31.429 020	39
40	32.705 161	32.576 357	32.448 269	32.320 891	32.194 221	32.068 253	40
41	33.364 565	33.230 209	33.096 617	32.963 784	32.831 704	32.700 373	41
42	34.017 305	33.877 320	33.738 149	33.599 786	33.462 226	33.325 462	42
43	34.663 449	34.517 760	34.372 937	34.228 972	34.085 861	33.943 596	43
44	35.303 063	35.151 598	35.001 051	34.851 415	34.702 685	34.554 854	44
45	35.936 214	35.778 901	35.622 561	35.467 187	35.312 773	35.159 312	45
46	36.562 967	36.399 737	36.237 537	36.076 360	35.916 199	35.757 045	46
47	37.183 387	37.014 173	36.846 048	36.679 004	36.513 034	36.348 129	47
YRS							
4	37.797 537	37.622 274	37.448 161	37.275 190	37.103 351	36.932 637	48
5	44.700 755	44.448 517	44.198 308	43.950 107	43.703 896	43.459 656	60
6	50.811 866	50.476 552	50.144 416	49.815 421	49.489 533	49.166 717	72
7	56.221 761	55.799 715	55.382 257	54.969 328	54.560 870	54.156 827	84
8	61.010 900	60.500 428	59.996 197	59.498 115	59.006 096	58.520 052	96
9	65.250 512	64.651 476	64.060 550	63.477 604	62.902 511	62.335 146	108
10	69.003 652	68.317 132	67.640 780	66.974 419	66.317 872	65.670 968	120
11	72.326 139	71.554 154	70.794 564	70.047 103	69.311 569	68.587 726	132
12	75.267 390	74.412 664	73.572 668	72.747 100	71.935 663	71.138 066	144
13	77.871 148	76.936 921	76.019 869	75.119 613	74.235 783	73.368 018	156
14	80.176 140	79.166 011	78.175 574	77.204 363	76.251 929	75.317 832	168
15	82.216 646	81.134 449	80.074 503	79.036 253	78.019 160	77.022 700	180
16	84.023 015	82.872 712	81.747 242	80.645 952	79.568 208	78.513 394	192
17	85.622 114	84.407 717	83.220 735	82.060 410	80.926 008	79.816 818	204
18	87.037 725	85.763 229	84.518 713	83.303 307	82.116 174	80.956 500	216
19	88.290 902	86.960 239	85.662 083	84.395 453	83.159 401	81.953 009	228
20	89.400 284	88.017 279	86.669 262	85.355 132	84.073 830	82.824 331	240
21	90.382 370	88.950 717	87.556 471	86.198 412	84.875 363	83.586 193	252
22	91.251 768	89.775 006	88.338 001	86.939 409	85.577 938	84.252 345	264
23	92.021 407	90.502 909	89.026 440	87.590 531	86.193 773	84.834 813	276
24	92.702 734	91.145 697	89.632 875	88.162 677	86.733 576	85.344 107	288
25	93.305 883	91.713 322	90.167 076	88.665 428	87.206 735	85.789 421	300
26	93.839 823	92.214 573	90.637 645	89.107 200	87.621 477	86.178 793	312
27	94.312 497	92.657 212	91.052 163	89.495 389	87.985 015	86.519 249	324
28	94.730 934	93.048 092	91.417 306	89.836 495	88.303 670	86.816 936	336
29	95.101 358	93.393 265	91.738 956	90.136 227	88.582 983	87.077 226	348
30	95.429 278	93.698 077	92.022 292	90.399 605	88.827 813	87.304 817	360

PRESENT VALUE OF $1 PER PERIOD

MONTHLY COMPOUNDING

MOS	13.75% ANNUAL RATE	14.00% ANNUAL RATE	14.25% ANNUAL RATE	14.50% ANNUAL RATE	14.75% ANNUAL RATE	15.00% ANNUAL RATE	MOS
1	0.988 671	0.988 468	0.988 264	0.988 061	0.987 858	0.987 654	1
2	1.966 143	1.965 537	1.964 931	1.964 325	1.963 720	1.963 115	2
3	2.932 541	2.931 338	2.930 135	2.928 934	2.927 733	2.926 534	3
4	3.887 991	3.886 001	3.884 013	3.882 026	3.880 041	3.878 058	4
5	4.832 617	4.829 655	4.826 696	4.823 739	4.820 786	4.817 835	5
6	5.766 542	5.762 427	5.758 316	5.754 209	5.750 107	5.746 010	6
7	6.689 887	6.684 442	6.679 003	6.673 570	6.668 145	6.662 726	7
8	7.602 772	7.595 824	7.588 885	7.581 955	7.575 035	7.568 124	8
9	8.505 315	8.496 696	8.488 089	8.479 495	8.470 913	8.462 345	9
10	9.397 634	9.387 178	9.376 740	9.366 318	9.355 914	9.345 526	10
11	10.279 844	10.267 392	10.254 962	10.242 554	10.230 168	10.217 803	11
12	11.152 060	11.137 455	11.122 878	11.108 328	11.093 806	11.079 312	12
13	12.014 395	11.997 485	11.980 608	11.963 766	11.946 958	11.930 185	13
14	12.866 961	12.847 596	12.828 272	12.808 991	12.789 751	12.770 553	14
15	13.709 869	13.687 904	13.665 989	13.644 124	13.622 310	13.600 546	15
16	14.543 228	14.518 521	14.493 874	14.469 287	14.444 760	14.420 292	16
17	15.367 146	15.339 559	15.312 044	15.284 598	15.257 223	15.229 918	17
18	16.181 730	16.151 130	16.120 611	16.090 175	16.059 821	16.029 549	18
19	16.987 087	16.953 341	16.919 690	16.886 135	16.852 674	16.819 308	19
20	17.783 319	17.746 300	17.709 391	17.672 591	17.635 899	17.599 316	20
21	18.570 532	18.530 116	18.489 824	18.449 657	18.409 614	18.369 695	21
22	19.348 827	19.304 892	19.261 099	19.217 447	19.173 935	19.130 563	22
23	20.118 305	20.070 733	20.023 322	19.976 069	19.928 974	19.882 037	23
24	20.879 065	20.827 743	20.776 600	20.725 634	20.674 846	20.624 235	24
25	21.631 208	21.576 023	21.521 037	21.466 250	21.411 661	21.357 269	25
26	22.374 829	22.315 673	22.256 739	22.198 024	22.139 529	22.081 253	26
27	23.110 027	23.046 794	22.983 806	22.921 061	22.858 560	22.796 299	27
28	23.836 896	23.769 483	23.702 341	23.635 466	23.568 859	23.502 518	28
29	24.555 531	24.483 839	24.412 443	24.341 342	24.270 534	24.200 018	29
30	25.266 024	25.189 956	25.114 212	25.038 790	24.963 688	24.888 906	30
31	25.968 469	25.887 930	25.807 745	25.727 911	25.648 426	25.569 290	31
32	26.662 956	26.577 855	26.493 139	26.408 804	26.324 850	26.241 274	32
33	27.349 575	27.259 824	27.170 489	27.081 569	26.993 061	26.904 962	33
34	28.028 416	27.933 928	27.839 890	27.746 301	27.653 157	27.560 456	34
35	28.699 567	28.600 258	28.501 436	28.403 097	28.305 239	28.207 858	35
36	29.363 115	29.258 904	29.155 218	29.052 051	28.949 402	28.847 267	36
37	30.019 145	29.909 955	29.801 327	29.693 258	29.585 744	29.478 783	37
38	30.667 744	30.553 497	30.439 854	30.326 809	30.214 359	30.102 501	38
39	31.308 995	31.189 619	31.070 887	30.952 796	30.835 341	30.718 520	39
40	31.942 982	31.818 404	31.694 514	31.571 309	31.448 784	31.326 933	40
41	32.569 786	32.439 938	32.310 823	32.182 438	32.054 777	31.927 835	41
42	33.189 490	33.054 304	32.919 900	32.786 271	32.653 412	32.521 319	42
43	33.802 173	33.661 586	33.521 828	33.382 894	33.244 778	33.107 475	43
44	34.407 916	34.261 864	34.116 692	33.972 394	33.828 964	33.686 395	44
45	35.006 797	34.855 220	34.704 575	34.554 856	34.406 056	34.258 168	45
46	35.598 893	35.441 733	35.285 559	35.130 364	34.976 141	34.822 882	46
47	36.184 281	36.021 482	35.859 725	35.699 002	35.539 304	35.380 624	47

YRS	13.75%	14.00%	14.25%	14.50%	14.75%	15.00%	MOS
4	36.763 038	36.594 546	36.427 153	36.260 850	36.095 628	35.931 481	48
5	43.217 369	42.977 016	42.738 580	42.502 042	42.267 385	42.034 592	60
6	48.846 940	48.530 168	48.216 368	47.905 507	47.597 553	47.292 474	72
7	53.757 142	53.361 760	52.970 627	52.583 688	52.200 892	51.822 185	84
8	58.039 898	57.565 549	57.096 923	56.633 938	56.176 513	55.724 570	96
9	61.775 387	61.223 111	60.678 201	60.140 540	59.610 013	59.086 509	108
10	65.033 539	64.405 420	63.786 449	63.176 466	62.575 317	61.982 847	120
11	67.875 352	67.174 230	66.484 146	65.804 893	65.136 267	64.478 068	132
12	70.354 027	69.583 269	68.825 521	68.080 518	67.348 003	66.627 722	144
13	72.515 967	71.679 284	70.857 636	70.050 696	69.258 143	68.479 668	156
14	74.401 645	73.502 950	72.621 342	71.756 425	70.907 814	70.075 134	168
15	76.046 363	75.089 654	74.152 090	73.233 202	72.332 534	71.449 643	180
16	77.480 913	76.470 187	75.480 650	74.511 757	73.562 977	72.633 794	192
17	78.732 151	77.671 337	76.633 729	75.618 698	74.625 635	73.653 950	204
18	79.823 500	78.716 413	77.634 504	76.577 058	75.543 388	74.532 823	216
19	80.775 392	79.625 696	78.503 092	77.406 782	76.335 994	75.289 980	228
20	81.605 648	80.416 829	79.256 954	78.125 136	77.020 520	75.942 278	240
21	82.329 810	81.105 164	79.911 242	78.747 069	77.611 703	76.504 237	252
22	82.961 436	81.704 060	80.479 110	79.285 522	78.122 271	76.988 370	264
23	83.512 350	82.225 136	80.971 971	79.751 701	78.563 217	77.405 455	276
24	83.992 866	82.678 506	81.399 733	80.155 306	78.944 036	77.764 777	288
25	84.411 980	83.072 966	81.770 994	80.504 738	79.272 925	78.074 336	300
26	84.777 538	83.416 171	82.093 218	80.807 267	79.556 967	78.341 024	312
27	85.096 383	83.714 781	82.372 881	81.069 189	79.802 276	78.570 778	324
28	85.374 485	83.974 591	82.615 605	81.295 954	80.014 135	78.768 713	336
29	85.617 050	84.200 641	82.826 269	81.492 281	80.197 104	78.939 236	348
30	85.828 619	84.397 320	83.009 107	81.662 256	80.355 124	79.086 142	360

PRESENT VALUE OF
$1 PER PERIOD

MONTHLY
COMPOUNDING

MOS	15.25% ANNUAL RATE	15.50% ANNUAL RATE	15.75% ANNUAL RATE	16.00% ANNUAL RATE	16.25% ANNUAL RATE	16.50% ANNUAL RATE	MOS
1	0.987 451	0.987 248	0.987 045	0.986 842	0.986 639	0.986 436	1
2	1.962 511	1.961 907	1.961 303	1.960 699	1.960 096	1.959 493	2
3	2.925 335	2.924 137	2.922 939	2.921 743	2.920 547	2.919 352	3
4	3.876 076	3.874 096	3.872 118	3.870 141	3.868 166	3.866 192	4
5	4.814 887	4.811 942	4.809 000	4.806 060	4.803 124	4.800 190	5
6	5.741 917	5.737 828	5.733 744	5.729 665	5.725 589	5.721 519	6
7	6.657 314	6.651 908	6.646 509	6.641 116	6.635 731	6.630 351	7
8	7.561 223	7.554 331	7.547 449	7.540 575	7.533 712	7.526 857	8
9	8.453 789	8.445 247	8.436 717	8.428 199	8.419 695	8.411 203	9
10	9.335 155	9.324 801	9.314 464	9.304 144	9.293 841	9.283 554	10
11	10.205 461	10.193 140	10.180 841	10.168 563	10.156 307	10.144 073	11
12	11.064 845	11.050 406	11.035 993	11.021 609	11.007 251	10.992 921	12
13	11.913 445	11.896 739	11.880 068	11.863 430	11.846 825	11.830 255	13
14	12.751 396	12.732 281	12.713 207	12.694 174	12.675 182	12.656 231	14
15	13.578 832	13.557 167	13.535 553	13.513 987	13.492 472	13.471 005	15
16	14.395 884	14.371 535	14.347 245	14.323 014	14.298 841	14.274 728	16
17	15.202 683	15.175 518	15.148 422	15.121 395	15.094 438	15.067 549	17
18	15.999 358	15.969 248	15.939 220	15.909 272	15.879 404	15.849 617	18
19	16.786 036	16.752 857	16.719 773	16.686 781	16.653 883	16.621 077	19
20	17.562 841	17.526 474	17.490 214	17.454 060	17.418 014	17.382 073	20
21	18.329 899	18.290 225	18.250 674	18.211 244	18.171 935	18.132 748	21
22	19.087 330	19.044 237	19.001 282	18.958 464	18.915 784	18.873 241	22
23	19.835 257	19.788 634	19.742 166	19.695 853	19.649 695	19.603 690	23
24	20.573 799	20.523 538	20.473 452	20.423 539	20.373 799	20.324 232	24
25	21.303 072	21.249 071	21.195 264	21.141 650	21.088 230	21.035 001	25
26	22.023 194	21.965 352	21.907 725	21.850 313	21.793 115	21.736 129	26
27	22.734 279	22.672 499	22.610 956	22.549 651	22.488 582	22.427 747	27
28	23.436 441	23.370 628	23.305 077	23.239 787	23.174 757	23.109 985	28
29	24.129 792	24.059 855	23.990 206	23.920 842	23.851 764	23.782 969	29
30	24.814 442	24.740 293	24.666 458	24.592 937	24.519 726	24.446 825	30
31	25.490 500	25.412 054	25.333 950	25.256 187	25.178 764	25.101 677	31
32	26.158 074	26.075 248	25.992 795	25.910 711	25.828 996	25.747 647	32
33	26.817 271	26.729 986	26.643 104	26.556 623	26.470 541	26.384 855	33
34	27.468 196	27.376 375	27.284 989	27.194 036	27.103 514	27.013 421	34
35	28.110 953	28.014 520	27.918 558	27.823 062	27.728 030	27.633 461	35
36	28.745 644	28.644 529	28.543 919	28.443 811	28.344 203	28.245 091	36
37	29.372 370	29.266 503	29.161 178	29.056 392	28.952 142	28.848 425	37
38	29.991 231	29.880 546	29.770 441	29.660 914	29.551 960	29.443 576	38
39	30.602 327	30.486 759	30.371 811	30.257 480	30.144 763	30.030 654	39
40	31.205 754	31.085 241	30.965 390	30.846 198	30.727 659	30.609 770	40
41	31.801 608	31.676 091	31.551 280	31.427 169	31.303 754	31.181 031	41
42	32.389 986	32.259 407	32.129 579	32.000 496	31.872 152	31.744 543	42
43	32.970 979	32.835 285	32.700 386	32.566 279	32.432 956	32.300 413	43
44	33.544 682	33.403 819	33.263 799	33.124 617	32.986 267	32.848 742	44
45	34.111 186	33.965 103	33.819 913	33.675 609	33.532 185	33.389 635	45
46	34.670 581	34.519 230	34.368 822	34.219 351	34.070 809	33.923 191	46
47	35.222 956	35.066 290	34.910 620	34.755 938	34.602 238	34.449 510	47
YRS							
4	35.768 399	35.606 374	35.445 399	35.285 465	35.126 565	34.968 691	48
5	41.803 644	41.574 525	41.347 218	41.121 706	40.897 973	40.676 001	60
6	46.990 239	46.690 816	46.394 174	46.100 283	45.809 114	45.520 636	72
7	51.447 517	51.076 835	50.710 091	50.347 235	49.988 218	49.632 991	84
8	55.278 031	54.836 819	54.400 859	53.970 077	53.544 399	53.123 753	96
9	58.569 915	58.060 124	57.557 029	57.060 524	56.570 508	56.086 877	108
10	61.398 908	60.823 352	60.256 035	59.696 816	59.145 555	58.602 117	120
11	63.830 100	63.192 173	62.564 098	61.945 692	61.336 776	60.737 172	132
12	65.919 429	65.222 881	64.537 844	63.864 085	63.201 380	62.549 508	144
13	67.714 965	66.963 738	66.225 697	65.500 561	64.788 053	64.087 904	156
14	69.258 020	68.456 114	67.669 070	66.896 549	66.138 222	65.393 761	168
15	70.584 097	69.735 477	68.903 373	68.087 390	67.287 140	66.502 246	180
16	71.723 707	70.832 231	69.958 891	69.103 231	68.264 803	67.443 176	192
17	72.703 070	71.772 440	70.861 520	69.969 789	69.096 740	68.241 881	204
18	73.544 719	72.578 449	71.633 406	70.709 003	69.804 671	68.919 860	216
19	74.268 019	73.269 413	72.293 486	71.339 585	70.407 081	69.495 360	228
20	74.889 612	73.861 752	72.857 955	71.877 501	70.919 697	69.983 873	240
21	75.423 799	74.369 545	73.340 662	72.336 367	71.355 904	70.398 545	252
22	75.882 871	74.804 857	73.753 450	72.727 801	71.727 092	70.750 538	264
23	76.277 390	75.178 036	74.106 447	73.061 711	72.042 952	71.049 327	276
24	76.616 433	75.497 949	74.408 313	73.346 552	72.311 731	71.302 953	288
25	76.907 802	75.772 200	74.666 455	73.589 534	72.540 447	71.518 243	300
26	77.158 200	76.007 306	74.887 205	73.796 809	72.735 071	71.700 991	312
27	77.373 387	76.208 854	75.075 981	73.973 623	72.900 685	71.856 116	324
28	77.558 316	76.381 634	75.237 413	74.124 454	73.041 613	71.987 794	336
29	77.717 241	76.529 752	75.375 461	74.253 120	73.161 535	72.099 568	348
30	77.853 819	76.656 729	75.493 514	74.362 878	73.263 582	72.194 447	360

MOS	16.75% ANNUAL RATE	17.00% ANNUAL RATE	17.25% ANNUAL RATE	17.50% ANNUAL RATE	17.75% ANNUAL RATE	18.00% ANNUAL RATE	MOS
1	0.986 234	0.986 031	0.985 829	0.985 626	0.985 424	0.985 222	1
2	1.958 891	1.958 289	1.957 687	1.957 085	1.956 484	1.955 883	2
3	2.918 158	2.916 965	2.915 773	2.914 581	2.913 390	2.912 200	3
4	3.864 220	3.862 250	3.860 281	3.858 314	3.856 349	3.854 385	4
5	4.797 259	4.794 330	4.791 405	4.788 482	4.785 562	4.782 645	5
6	5.717 452	5.713 391	5.709 333	5.705 280	5.701 231	5.697 187	6
7	6.624 979	6.619 613	6.614 253	6.608 900	6.603 554	6.598 214	7
8	7.520 012	7.513 176	7.506 349	7.499 532	7.492 724	7.485 925	8
9	8.402 724	8.394 257	8.385 803	8.377 362	8.368 933	8.360 517	9
10	9.273 284	9.263 031	9.252 795	9.242 575	9.232 371	9.222 185	10
11	10.131 860	10.119 669	10.107 499	10.095 351	10.083 224	10.071 118	11
12	10.978 617	10.964 341	10.950 092	10.935 869	10.921 674	10.907 505	12
13	11.813 717	11.797 214	11.780 744	11.764 307	11.747 903	11.731 532	13
14	12.637 321	12.618 452	12.599 624	12.580 836	12.562 089	12.543 382	14
15	13.449 588	13.428 219	13.406 900	13.385 629	13.364 407	13.343 233	15
16	14.250 672	14.226 675	14.202 735	14.178 854	14.155 030	14.131 264	16
17	15.040 729	15.013 977	14.987 293	14.960 677	14.934 130	14.907 649	17
18	15.819 909	15.790 281	15.760 733	15.731 263	15.701 873	15.672 561	18
19	16.588 363	16.555 741	16.523 211	16.490 773	16.458 425	16.426 168	19
20	17.346 238	17.310 509	17.274 885	17.239 365	17.203 950	17.168 639	20
21	18.093 681	18.054 734	18.015 906	17.977 198	17.938 608	17.900 137	21
22	18.830 834	18.788 562	18.746 426	18.704 425	18.662 558	18.620 824	22
23	19.557 839	19.512 140	19.466 594	19.421 199	19.375 955	19.330 861	23
24	20.274 836	20.225 611	20.176 556	20.127 671	20.078 954	20.030 405	24
25	20.981 963	20.929 115	20.876 457	20.823 988	20.771 706	20.719 611	25
26	21.679 355	21.622 792	21.566 439	21.510 296	21.454 360	21.398 632	26
27	22.367 147	22.306 780	22.246 644	22.186 739	22.127 064	22.067 617	27
28	23.045 471	22.981 212	22.917 209	22.853 459	22.789 962	22.726 717	28
29	23.714 456	23.646 224	23.578 271	23.510 597	23.443 198	23.376 076	29
30	24.374 233	24.301 947	24.229 966	24.158 288	24.086 913	24.015 838	30
31	25.024 926	24.948 509	24.872 425	24.796 670	24.721 244	24.646 146	31
32	25.666 663	25.586 041	25.505 779	25.425 876	25.346 330	25.267 139	32
33	26.299 565	26.214 666	26.130 158	26.046 038	25.962 304	25.878 954	33
34	26.923 754	26.834 511	26.745 689	26.657 286	26.569 300	26.481 728	34
35	27.539 350	27.445 697	27.352 497	27.259 748	27.167 448	27.075 595	35
36	28.146 473	28.048 345	27.950 705	27.853 550	27.756 878	27.660 684	36
37	28.745 237	28.642 575	28.540 436	28.438 818	28.337 716	28.237 127	37
38	29.335 759	29.228 505	29.121 810	29.015 672	28.910 087	28.805 052	38
39	29.918 151	29.806 249	29.694 946	29.584 236	29.474 116	29.364 583	39
40	30.492 526	30.375 924	30.259 959	30.144 626	30.029 923	29.915 845	40
41	31.058 994	30.937 641	30.816 965	30.696 962	30.577 629	30.458 961	41
42	31.617 665	31.491 511	31.366 077	31.241 359	31.117 352	30.994 050	42
43	32.168 644	32.037 644	31.907 408	31.777 931	31.649 207	31.521 232	43
44	32.712 038	32.576 149	32.441 068	32.306 790	32.173 310	32.040 622	44
45	33.247 952	33.107 131	32.967 165	32.828 048	32.689 774	32.552 337	45
46	33.776 489	33.630 696	33.485 807	33.341 813	33.198 710	33.056 490	46
47	34.297 749	34.146 948	33.997 098	33.848 194	33.700 227	33.553 192	47
YRS							
4	34.811 834	34.655 988	34.501 144	34.347 296	34.194 435	34.042 554	48
5	40.455 775	40.237 278	40.020 495	39.805 409	39.592 006	39.380 269	60
6	45.234 820	44.951 636	44.671 058	44.393 055	44.117 601	43.844 667	72
7	49.281 508	48.933 722	48.589 587	48.249 057	47.912 087	47.578 633	84
8	52.708 070	52.297 278	51.891 310	51.490 098	51.093 575	50.701 675	96
9	55.609 534	55.138 379	54.673 317	54.214 253	53.761 094	53.313 749	108
10	58.066 368	57.538 177	57.017 415	56.503 956	55.997 676	55.498 454	120
11	60.146 709	59.565 218	58.992 534	58.428 493	57.872 939	57.325 714	132
12	61.908 252	61.277 403	60.656 754	60.046 103	59.445 253	58.854 011	144
13	63.399 851	62.723 638	62.059 014	61.405 734	60.763 561	60.132 260	156
14	64.662 872	63.945 231	63.240 547	62.548 529	61.868 896	61.201 371	168
15	65.732 344	64.977 077	64.236 098	63.509 070	62.795 665	62.095 562	180
16	66.637 927	65.848 648	65.074 942	64.316 422	63.572 714	62.843 452	192
17	67.404 735	66.584 839	65.781 745	64.995 017	64.224 231	63.468 978	204
18	68.054 035	67.206 679	66.377 292	65.565 388	64.770 496	63.992 160	216
19	68.603 834	67.731 930	66.879 096	66.044 796	65.228 512	64.429 743	228
20	69.069 380	68.175 595	67.301 912	66.447 747	65.612 535	64.795 732	240
21	69.463 585	68.550 346	67.658 173	66.786 434	65.934 520	65.101 841	252
22	69.797 380	68.866 887	67.958 356	67.071 108	66.204 488	65.357 866	264
23	70.080 024	69.134 261	68.211 288	67.310 381	66.430 843	65.572 002	276
24	70.319 354	69.360 104	68.424 407	67.511 495	66.620 630	65.751 103	288
25	70.522 008	69.550 868	68.603 979	67.680 535	66.779 757	65.900 901	300
26	70.693 607	69.712 000	68.755 285	67.822 616	66.913 177	66.026 190	312
27	70.838 910	69.848 104	68.882 775	67.942 037	67.025 043	66.130 980	324
28	70.961 946	69.963 067	68.990 196	68.042 414	67.118 838	66.218 625	336
29	71.066 128	70.060 174	69.080 709	68.126 782	67.197 479	66.291 930	348
30	71.154 344	70.142 196	69.156 974	68.197 695	67.263 417	66.353 242	360

PRESENT VALUE OF
$1 PER PERIOD

MONTHLY
COMPOUNDING

MOS	18.25% ANNUAL RATE	18.50% ANNUAL RATE	18.75% ANNUAL RATE	19.00% ANNUAL RATE	19.25% ANNUAL RATE	19.50% ANNUAL RATE	MOS
1	0.985 019	0.984 817	0.984 615	0.984 413	0.984 212	0.984 010	1
2	1.955 283	1.954 683	1.954 083	1.953 483	1.952 884	1.952 285*	2
3	2.911 011	2.909 823	2.908 635	2.907 449	2.906 263	2.905 078	3
4	3.852 422	3.850 462	3.848 503	3.846 545	3.844 589	3.842 635	4
5	4.779 731	4.776 819	4.773 910	4.771 004	4.768 101	4.765 200	5
6	5.693 147	5.689 112	5.685 081	5.681 054	5.677 032	5.673 014	6
7	6.592 881	6.587 554	6.582 233	6.576 920	6.571 612	6.566 311	7
8	7.479 135	7.472 355	7.465 584	7.458 822	7.452 069	7.445 325	8
9	8.352 114	8.343 723	8.335 344	8.326 978	8.318 624	8.310 283	9
10	9.212 014	9.201 861	9.191 723	9.181 602	9.171 498	9.161 410	10
11	10.059 033	10.046 970	10.034 928	10.022 906	10.010 906	9.998 927	11
12	10.893 363	10.879 248	10.865 159	10.851 097	10.837 062	10.823 053	12
13	11.715 195	11.698 890	11.682 618	11.666 380	11.650 174	11.634 000	13
14	12.524 715	12.506 088	12.487 501	12.468 955	12.450 448	12.431 980	14
15	13.322 108	13.301 030	13.280 001	13.259 020	13.238 087	13.217 201	15
16	14.107 555	14.083 904	14.060 309	14.036 771	14.013 290	13.989 866	16
17	14.881 236	14.854 891	14.828 612	14.802 400	14.776 254	14.750 175	17
18	15.643 327	15.614 172	15.585 095	15.556 095	15.527 173	15.498 327	18
19	16.394 002	16.361 926	16.329 939	16.298 043	16.266 235	16.234 517	19
20	17.133 431	17.098 327	17.063 325	17.028 426	16.993 629	16.958 934	20
21	17.861 783	17.823 547	17.785 428	17.747 425	17.709 538	17.671 768	21
22	18.579 224	18.537 757	18.496 421	18.455 217	18.414 145	18.373 203	22
23	19.285 917	19.241 123	19.196 476	19.151 978	19.107 627	19.063 422	23
24	19.982 024	19.933 810	19.885 761	19.837 878	19.790 160	19.742 605	24
25	20.667 703	20.615 980	20.564 442	20.513 087	20.461 916	20.410 928	25
26	21.343 110	21.287 793	21.232 681	21.177 773	21.123 067	21.068 563	26
27	22.008 399	21.949 406	21.890 640	21.832 098	21.773 779	21.715 684	27
28	22.663 721	22.600 975	22.538 476	22.476 224	22.414 218	22.352 456	28
29	23.309 227	23.242 651	23.176 346	23.110 311	23.044 545	22.979 047	29
30	23.945 062	23.874 584	23.804 402	23.734 515	23.664 920	23.595 618	30
31	24.571 373	24.496 923	24.422 796	24.348 989	24.275 501	24.202 330	31
32	25.188 301	25.109 814	25.031 676	24.953 886	24.876 441	24.799 341	32
33	25.795 987	25.713 399	25.631 189	25.549 354	25.467 894	25.386 805	33
34	26.394 569	26.307 820	26.221 478	26.135 542	26.050 008	25.964 876	34
35	26.984 185	26.893 216	26.802 686	26.712 592	26.622 932	26.533 703	35
36	27.564 967	27.469 724	27.374 952	27.280 649	27.186 810	27.093 435	36
37	28.137 050	28.037 480	27.938 415	27.839 851	27.741 786	27.644 216	37
38	28.700 562	28.596 615	28.493 208	28.390 337	28.287 999	28.186 191	38
39	29.255 633	29.147 262	29.039 467	28.932 243	28.825 589	28.719 499	39
40	29.802 388	29.689 548	29.577 321	29.465 703	29.354 691	29.244 279	40
41	30.340 953	30.223 601	30.106 901	29.990 848	29.875 439	29.760 669	41
42	30.871 449	30.749 545	30.628 333	30.507 808	30.387 965	30.268 801	42
43	31.393 999	31.267 505	31.141 743	31.016 710	30.892 400	30.768 807	43
44	31.908 721	31.777 600	31.647 255	31.517 680	31.388 870	31.260 819	44
45	32.415 731	32.279 951	32.144 989	32.010 842	31.877 501	31.744 963	45
46	32.915 147	32.774 674	32.635 066	32.496 317	32.358 419	32.221 366	46
47	33.407 081	33.261 887	33.117 604	32.974 225	32.831 743	32.690 151	47

YRS	18.25%	18.50%	18.75%	19.00%	19.25%	19.50%	MOS
4	33.891 645	33.741 702	33.592 718	33.444 684	33.297 594	33.151 440	48
5	39.170 183	38.961 733	38.754 905	38.549 682	38.346 051	38.143 997	60
6	43.574 226	43.306 252	43.040 717	42.777 596	42.516 861	42.258 489	72
7	47.248 652	46.922 100	46.598 935	46.279 115	45.962 599	45.649 346	84
8	50.314 336	49.931 492	49.553 081	49.179 042	48.809 314	48.443 838	96
9	52.872 128	52.436 143	52.005 707	51.580 735	51.161 144	50.746 850	108
10	55.006 171	54.520 710	54.041 956	53.569 796	53.104 120	52.644 820	120
11	56.786 667	56.255 650	55.732 514	55.217 118	54.709 321	54.208 986	132
12	58.272 189	57.699 602	57.136 070	56.581 415	56.035 467	55.498 055	144
13	59.511 605	58.901 372	58.301 346	57.711 314	57.131 069	56.560 409	156
14	60.545 686	59.901 580	59.268 796	58.647 086	58.036 207	57.435 922	168
15	61.408 452	60.734 031	60.072 003	59.422 084	58.783 991	58.157 454	180
16	62.128 283	61.426 861	60.738 852	60.063 930	59.401 778	58.752 088	192
17	62.728 860	62.003 489	61.292 491	60.595 501	59.912 165	59.242 140	204
18	63.229 939	62.483 404	61.752 140	61.035 743	60.333 824	59.646 005	216
19	63.648 005	62.882 827	62.133 755	61.400 348	60.682 181	59.978 840	228
20	63.996 810	63.215 258	62.450 584	61.702 310	60.969 977	60.253 138	240
21	64.287 828	63.491 933	62.713 625	61.952 393	61.207 742	60.479 194	252
22	64.530 633	63.722 203	62.932 011	62.159 509	61.404 172	60.665 492	264
23	64.733 213	63.913 852	63.113 321	62.331 041	61.566 454	60.819 025	276
24	64.902 231	64.073 358	63.263 851	62.473 102	61.700 525	60.945 556	288
25	65.043 248	64.206 111	63.388 826	62.590 755	61.811 288	61.049 833	300
26	65.160 903	64.316 598	63.492 584	62.688 195	61.902 795	61.135 770	312
27	65.259 066	64.408 554	63.578 727	62.768 894	61.978 394	61.206 593	324
28	65.340 966	64.485 088	63.650 245	62.835 728	62.040 851	61.264 961	336
29	65.409 298	64.548 785	63.709 623	62.891 079	62.092 450	61.313 062	348
30	65.466 310	64.601 798	63.758 919	62.936 920	62.135 079	61.352 704	360

PRESENT VALUE OF
$1 PER PERIOD

MONTHLY
COMPOUNDING

MOS	19.75% ANNUAL RATE	20.00% ANNUAL RATE	21.00% ANNUAL RATE	22.00% ANNUAL RATE	23.00% ANNUAL RATE	24.00% ANNUAL RATE	MOS
1	0.983 808	0.983 607	0.982 801	0.981 997	0.981 194	0.980 392	1
2	1.951 687	1.951 088	1.948 699	1.946 314	1.943 935	1.941 561	2
3	2.903 893	2.902 710	2.897 984	2.893 271	2.888 571	2.883 883	3
4	3.840 682	3.838 731	3.830 943	3.823 179	3.815 441	3.807 729	4
5	4.762 303	4.759 408	4.747 855	4.736 346	4.724 881	4.713 460	5
6	5.669 000	5.664 991	5.648 998	5.633 073	5.617 218	5.601 431	6
7	6.561 017	6.555 729	6.534 641	6.513 656	6.492 773	6.471 991	7
8	7.438 590	7.431 865	7.405 053	7.378 386	7.351 862	7.325 481	8
9	8.301 954	8.293 637	8.260 494	8.227 548	8.194 795	8.162 237	9
10	9.151 338	9.141 283	9.101 223	9.061 421	9.021 876	8.982 585	10
11	9.986 969	9.975 032	9.927 492	9.880 283	9.833 403	9.786 848	11
12	10.809 070	10.795 113	10.739 550	10.684 402	10.629 667	10.575 341	12
13	11.617 859	11.601 751	11.537 641	11.474 045	11.410 957	11.348 374	13
14	12.413 553	12.395 165	12.322 006	12.249 471	12.177 554	12.106 249	14
15	13.196 363	13.175 572	13.092 880	13.010 937	12.929 734	12.849 264	15
16	13.966 497	13.943 186	13.850 497	13.758 695	13.667 769	13.577 709	16
17	14.724 162	14.698 215	14.595 083	14.492 990	14.391 924	14.291 872	17
18	15.469 559	15.440 868	15.326 863	15.214 065	15.102 460	14.992 031	18
19	16.202 887	16.171 345	16.046 057	15.922 159	15.799 633	15.678 462	19
20	16.924 340	16.889 848	16.752 881	16.617 505	16.483 696	16.351 433	20
21	17.634 112	17.596 571	17.447 549	17.300 332	17.154 894	17.011 209	21
22	18.332 391	18.291 710	18.130 269	17.970 866	17.813 469	17.658 048	22
23	19.019 364	18.975 452	18.801 248	18.629 328	18.459 659	18.292 204	23
24	19.695 014	19.647 986	19.460 686	19.275 936	19.093 696	18.913 926	24
25	20.360 120	20.309 494	20.108 782	19.910 903	19.715 810	19.523 456	25
26	21.014 261	20.960 158	20.745 732	20.534 438	20.326 224	20.121 036	26
27	21.657 809	21.600 156	21.371 726	21.146 748	20.925 158	20.706 898	27
28	22.290 938	22.229 661	21.986 955	21.748 034	21.512 829	21.281 272	28
29	22.913 814	22.848 847	22.591 602	22.338 495	22.089 448	21.844 385	29
30	23.526 606	23.457 882	23.185 849	22.918 326	22.655 223	22.396 456	30
31	24.129 475	24.056 933	23.769 877	23.487 717	23.210 358	22.937 702	31
32	24.722 582	24.646 164	24.343 859	24.046 858	23.755 053	23.468 335	32
33	25.306 086	25.225 735	24.907 970	24.595 933	24.289 504	23.988 564	33
34	25.880 142	25.795 805	25.462 378	25.135 122	24.813 904	24.498 592	34
35	26.444 903	26.356 530	26.007 251	25.664 605	25.328 442	24.998 619	35
36	27.000 520	26.908 062	26.542 753	26.184 554	25.833 304	25.488 842	36
37	27.547 140	27.450 553	27.069 045	26.695 143	26.328 671	25.969 453	37
38	28.084 909	27.984 150	27.586 285	27.196 540	26.814 722	26.440 641	38
39	28.613 971	28.509 000	28.094 629	27.688 910	27.291 633	26.902 589	39
40	29.134 466	29.025 246	28.594 230	28.172 416	27.759 574	27.355 479	40
41	29.646 533	29.533 029	29.085 238	28.647 217	28.218 715	27.799 489	41
42	30.150 309	30.032 487	29.567 801	29.113 470	28.669 222	28.234 794	42
43	30.645 929	30.523 758	30.042 065	29.571 329	29.111 256	28.661 562	43
44	31.133 523	31.006 975	30.508 172	30.020 945	29.544 977	29.079 963	44
45	31.613 222	31.482 271	30.966 263	30.462 466	29.970 542	29.490 160	45
46	32.085 154	31.949 774	31.416 474	30.896 039	30.388 103	29.892 314	46
47	32.549 444	32.409 614	31.858 943	31.321 806	30.797 812	30.286 582	47
YRS							
4	33.006 217	32.861 916	32.293 801	31.739 908	31.199 816	30.673 120	48
5	37.943 505	37.744 561	36.963 986	36.207 074	35.472 979	34.760 887	60
6	42.002 452	41.748 727	40.756 445	39.799 209	38.875 549	37.984 063	72
7	45.339 316	45.032 470	43.836 142	42.687 714	41.584 895	40.525 516	84
8	48.082 555	47.725 406	46.337 035	45.010 417	43.742 252	42.529 434	96
9	50.337 773	49.933 833	48.367 904	46.878 147	45.460 079	44.109 510	108
10	52.191 790	51.744 924	50.017 087	48.380 024	46.827 924	45.355 389	120
11	53.715 978	53.230 165	51.356 319	49.587 713	47.917 090	46.337 756	132
12	54.969 014	54.448 184	52.443 854	50.558 839	48.784 355	47.112 345	144
13	55.999 136	55.447 059	53.326 994	51.339 740	49.474 928	47.723 104	156
14	56.846 000	56.266 217	54.044 156	51.967 678	50.024 806	48.204 683	168
15	57.542 208	56.937 994	54.626 532	52.472 614	50.462 655	48.584 405	180
16	58.114 561	57.488 906	55.099 456	52.878 644	50.811 299	48.883 813	192
17	58.585 092	57.940 698	55.483 497	53.205 140	51.088 911	49.119 894	204
18	58.971 917	58.311 205	55.795 361	53.467 682	51.309 965	49.306 042	216
19	59.289 925	58.615 050	56.048 612	53.678 797	51.485 981	49.452 819	228
20	59.551 361	58.864 229	56.254 267	53.848 558	51.626 137	49.568 552	240
21	59.766 287	59.068 575	56.421 270	53.985 067	51.737 739	49.659 806	252
22	59.942 977	59.236 156	56.556 887	54.094 836	51.826 603	49.731 759	264
23	60.088 235	59.373 585	56.667 015	54.183 103	51.897 362	49.788 494	276
24	60.207 651	59.486 289	56.756 446	54.254 081	51.953 705	49.833 229	288
25	60.305 824	59.578 715	56.829 069	54.311 155	51.998 569	49.868 502	300
26	60.386 531	59.654 512	56.888 043	54.357 050	52.034 293	49.896 315	312
27	60.452 881	59.716 672	56.935 933	54.393 955	52.062 739	49.918 245	324
28	60.507 427	59.767 648	56.974 823	54.423 631	52.085 389	49.935 537	336
29	60.552 270	59.809 452	57.006 404	54.447 494	52.103 424	49.949 171	348
30	60.589 135	59.843 735	57.032 049	54.466 682	52.117 785	49.959 922	360

127

PRESENT VALUE OF
$1 PER PERIOD

QUARTERLY COMPOUNDING

QTRS	6.50% ANNUAL RATE	7.00% ANNUAL RATE	7.50% ANNUAL RATE	8.00% ANNUAL RATE	8.50% ANNUAL RATE	9.00% ANNUAL RATE	QTRS
1	0.984 010	0.982 801	0.981 595	0.980 392	0.979 192	0.977 995	1
2	1.952 285	1.948 699	1.945 124	1.941 561	1.938 009	1.934 470	2
3	2.905 078	2.897 984	2.890 919	2.883 883	2.876 876	2.869 897	3
4	3.842 635	3.830 943	3.819 307	3.807 729	3.796 206	3.784 740	4
5	4.765 200	4.747 855	4.730 608	4.713 460	4.696 408	4.679 453	5
6	5.673 014	5.648 998	5.625 137	5.601 431	5.577 878	5.554 477	6
7	6.566 311	6.534 641	6.503 202	6.471 991	6.441 007	6.410 246	7
8	7.445 325	7.405 053	7.365 106	7.325 481	7.286 175	7.247 185	8
9	8.310 283	8.260 494	8.211 147	8.162 237	8.113 758	8.065 706	9
10	9.161 410	9.101 223	9.041 617	8.982 585	8.924 120	8.866 216	10
11	9.998 927	9.927 492	9.856 802	9.786 848	9.717 621	9.649 111	11
12	10.823 053	10.739 550	10.656 983	10.575 341	10.494 610	10.414 779	12
13	11.634 000	11.537 641	11.442 438	11.348 374	11.255 433	11.163 598	13
14	12.431 980	12.322 006	12.213 436	12.106 249	12.000 424	11.895 939	14
15	13.217 201	13.092 880	12.970 244	12.849 264	12.729 913	12.612 166	15
16	13.989 866	13.850 497	13.713 123	13.577 709	13.444 223	13.312 631	16
17	14.750 175	14.595 083	14.442 329	14.291 872	14.143 670	13.997 683	17
18	15.498 327	15.326 863	15.158 114	14.992 031	14.828 563	14.667 661	18
19	16.234 517	16.046 057	15.860 726	15.678 462	15.499 205	15.322 896	19
20	16.958 934	16.752 881	16.550 406	16.351 433	16.155 892	15.963 712	20
21	17.671 768	17.447 549	17.227 392	17.011 209	16.798 915	16.590 428	21
22	18.373 203	18.130 269	17.891 919	17.658 048	17.428 559	17.203 352	22
23	19.063 422	18.801 248	18.544 215	18.292 204	18.045 100	17.802 790	23
24	19.742 605	19.460 686	19.184 505	18.913 926	18.648 813	18.389 036	24
25	20.410 928	20.108 782	19.813 011	19.523 456	19.239 964	18.962 383	25
26	21.068 563	20.745 732	20.429 950	20.121 036	19.818 814	19.523 113	26
27	21.715 684	21.371 726	21.035 533	20.706 898	20.385 619	20.071 504	27
28	22.352 456	21.986 955	21.629 971	21.281 272	20.940 631	20.607 828	28
29	22.979 047	22.591 602	22.213 469	21.844 385	21.484 094	21.132 350	29
30	23.595 618	23.185 849	22.786 227	22.396 456	22.016 249	21.645 330	30
31	24.202 330	23.769 877	23.348 444	22.937 702	22.537 330	22.147 022	31
32	24.799 341	24.343 859	23.900 313	23.468 335	23.047 570	22.637 674	32
33	25.386 805	24.907 970	24.442 025	23.988 564	23.547 192	23.117 530	33
34	25.964 876	25.462 378	24.973 767	24.498 592	24.036 418	23.586 826	34
35	26.533 703	26.007 251	25.495 722	24.998 619	24.515 464	24.045 796	35
36	27.093 435	26.542 753	26.008 071	25.488 842	24.984 543	24.494 666	36
37	27.644 216	27.069 045	26.510 990	25.969 453	25.443 861	24.933 658	37
38	28.186 191	27.586 285	27.004 652	26.440 641	25.893 621	25.362 991	38
39	28.719 499	28.094 629	27.489 229	26.902 589	26.334 023	25.782 876	39
40	29.244 279	28.594 230	27.964 888	27.355 479	26.765 261	26.193 522	40
41	29.760 669	29.085 238	28.431 792	27.799 489	27.187 527	26.595 132	41
42	30.268 801	29.567 801	28.890 102	28.234 794	27.601 005	26.987 904	42
43	30.768 807	30.042 065	29.339 978	28.661 562	28.005 880	27.372 033	43
44	31.260 819	30.508 172	29.781 573	29.079 963	28.402 331	27.747 710	44
45	31.744 963	30.966 263	30.215 041	29.490 160	28.790 532	28.115 120	45
46	32.221 366	31.416 474	30.640 531	29.892 314	29.170 655	28.474 444	46
47	32.690 151	31.858 943	31.058 190	30.286 582	29.542 869	28.825 863	47
48	33.151 440	32.293 801	31.468 162	30.673 120	29.907 339	29.169 548	48
49	33.605 353	32.721 181	31.870 589	31.052 078	30.264 224	29.505 670	49
50	34.052 008	33.141 209	32.265 608	31.423 606	30.613 683	29.834 396	50
51	34.491 521	33.554 014	32.653 358	31.787 849	30.955 871	30.155 889	51
52	34.924 006	33.959 719	33.033 971	32.144 950	31.290 938	30.470 307	52
53	35.349 575	34.358 446	33.407 579	32.495 049	31.619 034	30.777 806	53
54	35.768 340	34.750 316	33.774 311	32.838 283	31.940 302	31.078 539	54
55	36.180 408	35.135 445	34.134 293	33.174 788	32.254 886	31.372 654	55

YRS	6.50%	7.00%	7.50%	8.00%	8.50%	9.00%	QTRS
14	36.585 887	35.513 951	34.487 649	33.504 694	32.562 924	31.660 298	56
15	38.143 997	36.963 986	35.837 226	34.760 887	33.732 299	32.748 953	60
16	39.604 813	38.316 807	37.090 158	35.921 415	34.807 342	33.744 902	64
17	40.974 412	39.578 934	38.253 364	36.993 564	35.795 661	34.656 039	68
18	42.258 489	40.756 445	39.333 271	37.984 063	36.704 254	35.489 587	72
19	43.462 385	41.855 015	40.335 844	38.899 132	37.539 551	36.252 153	76
20	44.591 106	42.879 935	41.266 620	39.744 514	38.307 464	36.949 781	80
21	45.649 346	43.836 142	42.130 742	40.525 516	39.013 431	37.588 001	84
22	46.641 508	44.728 244	42.932 982	41.247 041	39.662 448	38.171 873	88
23	47.571 715	45.560 539	43.677 772	41.913 619	40.259 109	38.706 024	92
24	48.443 838	46.337 035	44.369 226	42.529 434	40.807 638	39.194 689	96
25	49.261 503	47.061 473	45.011 164	43.098 352	41.311 917	39.641 741	100
26	50.028 111	47.737 344	45.607 131	43.623 944	41.775 517	40.050 723	104
27	50.746 850	48.367 904	46.160 420	44.109 510	42.201 718	40.424 877	108
28	51.420 709	48.956 190	46.674 087	44.558 097	42.593 538	40.767 170	112
29	52.052 490	49.505 036	47.150 969	44.972 523	42.953 749	41.080 315	116
30	52.644 820	50.017 087	47.593 700	45.355 389	43.284 903	41.366 793	120

PRESENT VALUE OF
$1 PER PERIOD

QTRS	9.50% ANNUAL RATE	10.00% ANNUAL RATE	10.50% ANNUAL RATE	11.00% ANNUAL RATE	11.50% ANNUAL RATE	12.00% ANNUAL RATE	QTRS
1	0.976 801	0.975 610	0.974 421	0.973 236	0.972 053	0.970 874	1
2	1.930 941	1.927 424	1.923 919	1.920 424	1.916 941	1.913 470	2
3	2.862 946	2.856 024	2.849 129	2.842 262	2.835 423	2.828 611	3
4	3.773 330	3.761 974	3.750 674	3.739 428	3.728 236	3.717 098	4
5	4.662 593	4.645 828	4.629 158	4.612 582	4.596 098	4.579 707	5
6	5.531 226	5.508 125	5.485 173	5.462 367	5.439 707	5.417 191	6
7	6.379 708	6.349 391	6.319 291	6.289 408	6.259 739	6.230 283	7
8	7.208 506	7.170 137	7.132 074	7.094 314	7.056 855	7.019 692	8
9	8.018 077	7.970 866	7.924 067	7.877 678	7.831 694	7.786 109	9
10	8.808 866	8.752 064	8.695 803	8.640 076	8.584 878	8.530 203	10
11	9.581 310	9.514 209	9.447 798	9.382 069	9.317 014	9.252 624	11
12	10.335 834	10.257 765	10.180 558	10.104 204	10.028 689	9.954 004	12
13	11.072 854	10.983 185	10.894 576	10.807 011	10.720 476	10.634 955	13
14	11.792 775	11.690 912	11.590 330	11.491 008	11.392 929	11.296 073	14
15	12.495 996	12.381 378	12.268 287	12.156 699	12.046 589	11.937 935	15
16	13.182 902	13.055 003	12.928 903	12.804 573	12.681 982	12.561 102	16
17	13.853 872	13.712 198	13.572 622	13.435 108	13.299 618	13.166 118	17
18	14.509 277	14.353 364	14.199 875	14.048 767	13.899 994	13.753 513	18
19	15.149 477	14.978 891	14.811 084	14.646 002	14.483 590	14.323 799	19
20	15.774 825	15.589 162	15.406 659	15.227 252	15.050 878	14.877 475	20
21	16.385 665	16.184 549	15.987 001	15.792 946	15.602 311	15.415 024	21
22	16.982 335	16.765 413	16.552 498	16.343 500	16.138 334	15.936 917	22
23	17.565 162	17.332 110	17.103 530	16.879 319	16.659 377	16.443 608	23
24	18.134 469	17.884 986	17.640 468	17.400 797	17.165 859	16.935 542	24
25	18.690 568	18.424 376	18.163 671	17.908 318	17.658 186	17.413 148	25
26	19.233 766	18.950 611	18.673 492	18.402 256	18.136 754	17.876 842	26
27	19.764 362	19.464 011	19.170 272	18.882 974	18.601 948	18.327 031	27
28	20.282 649	19.964 889	19.654 346	19.350 826	19.054 142	18.764 108	28
29	20.788 912	20.453 550	20.126 037	19.806 157	19.493 698	19.188 455	29
30	21.283 431	20.930 293	20.585 664	20.249 301	19.920 970	19.600 441	30
31	21.766 477	21.395 407	21.033 534	20.680 585	20.336 301	20.000 428	31
32	22.238 317	21.849 178	21.469 947	21.100 326	20.740 025	20.388 766	32
33	22.699 211	22.291 881	21.895 198	21.508 833	21.132 467	20.765 792	33
34	23.149 412	22.723 786	22.309 572	21.906 407	21.513 941	21.131 837	34
35	23.589 169	23.145 157	22.713 347	22.293 340	21.884 754	21.487 220	35
36	24.018 725	23.556 251	23.106 793	22.669 918	22.245 205	21.832 252	36
37	24.438 315	23.957 318	23.490 176	23.036 416	22.595 582	22.167 235	37
38	24.848 171	24.348 603	23.863 753	23.393 106	22.936 167	22.492 462	38
39	25.248 518	24.730 344	24.227 774	23.740 249	23.267 234	22.808 215	39
40	25.639 578	25.102 775	24.582 484	24.078 101	23.589 049	23.114 772	40
41	26.021 566	25.466 122	24.928 120	24.406 911	23.901 870	23.412 400	41
42	26.394 692	25.820 607	25.264 916	24.726 921	24.205 949	23.701 359	42
43	26.759 162	26.166 446	25.593 098	25.038 366	24.501 530	23.981 902	43
44	27.115 177	26.503 849	25.912 884	25.341 475	24.788 851	24.254 274	44
45	27.462 932	26.833 024	26.224 491	25.636 472	25.068 142	24.518 713	45
46	27.802 620	27.154 170	26.528 128	25.923 574	25.339 627	24.775 449	46
47	28.134 447	27.467 483	26.823 998	26.202 992	25.603 526	25.024 708	47
48	28.458 537	27.773 154	27.112 300	26.474 931	25.860 050	25.266 707	48
49	28.775 128	28.071 369	27.393 228	26.739 592	26.109 404	25.501 657	49
50	29.084 374	28.362 312	27.666 970	26.997 170	26.351 790	25.729 764	50
51	29.386 446	28.646 158	27.933 710	27.247 854	26.587 402	25.951 227	51
52	29.681 510	28.923 081	28.193 627	27.491 829	26.816 430	26.166 240	52
53	29.969 729	29.193 249	28.446 896	27.729 274	27.039 057	26.374 990	53
54	30.251 261	29.456 829	28.693 687	27.960 364	27.255 463	26.577 660	54
55	30.526 263	29.713 979	28.934 165	28.185 269	27.465 820	26.774 428	55

YRS							
14	30.794 884	29.964 858	29.168 492	28.404 155	27.670 299	26.965 464	56
15	31.808 482	30.908 656	30.047 377	29.222 662	28.432 645	27.675 564	60
16	32.731 244	31.763 691	30.839 730	29.956 999	29.113 277	28.306 478	64
17	33.571 311	32.538 311	31.554 073	30.615 821	29.720 954	28.867 038	68
18	34.336 095	33.240 078	32.198 084	31.206 893	30.263 497	29.365 088	72
19	35.032 341	33.875 844	32.778 690	31.737 183	30.747 886	29.807 598	76
20	35.666 192	34.451 817	33.302 132	32.212 941	31.180 355	30.200 763	80
21	36.243 240	34.973 620	33.774 038	32.639 775	31.566 469	30.550 086	84
22	36.768 574	35.446 348	34.199 482	33.022 715	31.911 197	30.860 454	88
23	37.246 830	35.874 616	34.583 040	33.366 276	32.218 974	31.136 212	92
24	37.682 226	36.262 606	34.928 834	33.674 508	32.493 762	31.381 219	96
25	38.078 604	36.614 105	35.240 583	33.951 042	32.739 096	31.598 905	100
26	38.439 459	36.932 546	35.521 638	34.199 140	32.958 134	31.792 317	104
27	38.767 976	37.221 039	35.775 023	34.421 724	33.153 693	31.964 160	108
28	39.067 052	37.482 398	36.003 460	34.621 419	33.328 291	32.116 840	112
29	39.339 326	37.719 177	36.209 406	34.800 579	33.484 175	32.252 495	116
30	39.587 200	37.933 687	36.395 076	34.961 315	33.623 350	32.373 023	120

PRESENT VALUE OF
$1 PER PERIOD

QUARTERLY
COMPOUNDING

QTRS	12.50% ANNUAL RATE	13.00% ANNUAL RATE	13.50% ANNUAL RATE	14.00% ANNUAL RATE	14.50% ANNUAL RATE	15.00% ANNUAL RATE	QTRS
1	0.969 697	0.968 523	0.967 352	0.966 184	0.965 018	0.963 855	1
2	1.910 009	1.906 560	1.903 122	1.899 694	1.896 278	1.892 873	2
3	2.821 827	2.815 070	2.808 340	2.801 637	2.794 961	2.788 311	3
4	3.706 014	3.694 983	3.684 005	3.673 079	3.662 206	3.651 384	4
5	4.563 408	4.547 199	4.531 081	4.515 052	4.499 113	4.483 262	5
6	5.394 820	5.372 590	5.350 501	5.328 553	5.306 743	5.285 072	6
7	6.201 037	6.172 000	6.143 170	6.114 544	6.086 122	6.057 900	7
8	6.982 824	6.946 247	6.909 958	6.873 956	6.838 235	6.802 796	8
9	7.740 920	7.696 123	7.651 713	7.607 687	7.564 039	7.520 767	9
10	8.476 044	8.422 395	8.369 251	8.316 605	8.264 453	8.212 787	10
11	9.188 891	9.125 806	9.063 362	9.001 551	8.940 364	8.879 795	11
12	9.880 137	9.807 076	9.734 812	9.663 334	9.592 632	9.522 694	12
13	10.550 436	10.466 902	10.384 341	10.302 738	10.222 081	10.142 356	13
14	11.200 422	11.105 958	11.012 664	10.920 520	10.829 511	10.739 620	14
15	11.830 713	11.724 899	11.620 473	11.517 411	11.415 692	11.315 296	15
16	12.441 903	12.324 358	12.208 438	12.094 117	11.981 368	11.870 165	16
17	13.034 573	12.904 947	12.777 207	12.651 321	12.527 255	12.404 978	17
18	13.609 283	13.467 261	13.327 407	13.189 682	13.054 046	12.920 461	18
19	14.166 577	14.011 875	13.859 644	13.709 837	13.562 408	13.417 312	19
20	14.706 984	14.539 346	14.374 505	14.212 403	14.052 988	13.896 204	20
21	15.231 015	15.050 214	14.872 556	14.697 974	14.526 405	14.357 787	21
22	15.739 166	15.545 002	15.354 347	15.167 125	14.983 262	14.802 686	22
23	16.231 918	16.024 215	15.820 408	15.620 410	15.424 137	15.231 505	23
24	16.709 739	16.488 343	16.271 253	16.058 368	15.849 590	15.644 824	24
25	17.173 080	16.937 863	16.707 379	16.481 515	16.260 159	16.043 204	25
26	17.622 381	17.373 233	17.129 266	16.890 352	16.656 366	16.427 185	26
27	18.058 066	17.794 899	17.537 380	17.285 365	17.038 712	16.797 286	27
28	18.480 549	18.203 292	17.932 169	17.667 019	17.407 684	17.154 011	28
29	18.890 229	18.598 830	18.314 069	18.035 767	17.763 748	17.497 842	29
30	19.287 495	18.981 917	18.683 501	18.392 045	18.107 356	17.829 245	30
31	19.672 723	19.352 947	19.040 872	18.736 276	18.438 944	18.148 670	31
32	20.046 276	19.712 297	19.386 575	19.068 865	18.758 933	18.456 549	32
33	20.408 510	20.060 336	19.720 991	19.390 208	19.067 728	18.753 301	33
34	20.759 768	20.397 420	20.044 490	19.700 684	19.365 721	19.039 326	34
35	21.100 381	20.723 893	20.357 427	20.000 661	19.653 289	19.315 013	35
36	21.430 672	21.040 090	20.660 147	20.290 494	19.930 797	19.580 735	36
37	21.750 955	21.346 335	20.952 983	20.570 525	20.198 598	19.836 853	37
38	22.061 532	21.642 939	21.236 260	20.841 087	20.457 031	20.083 714	38
39	22.362 698	21.930 207	21.510 287	21.102 500	20.706 423	20.321 652	39
40	22.654 737	22.208 433	21.775 369	21.355 072	20.947 091	20.550 990	40
41	22.937 927	22.477 901	22.031 796	21.599 104	21.179 340	20.772 039	41
42	23.212 535	22.738 888	22.279 851	21.834 883	21.403 464	20.985 097	42
43	23.478 822	22.991 659	22.519 807	22.062 689	21.619 749	21.190 455	43
44	23.737 040	23.236 473	22.751 930	22.282 791	21.828 467	21.388 391	44
45	23.987 432	23.473 582	22.976 474	22.495 450	22.029 883	21.579 172	45
46	24.230 237	23.703 227	23.193 687	22.700 918	22.224 254	21.763 057	46
47	24.465 685	23.925 644	23.403 808	22.899 438	22.411 825	21.940 296	47
48	24.693 997	24.141 059	23.607 070	23.091 244	22.592 835	22.111 129	48
49	24.915 391	24.349 694	23.803 695	23.276 564	22.767 513	22.275 787	49
50	25.130 077	24.551 762	23.993 901	23.455 618	22.936 080	22.434 493	50
51	25.338 256	24.747 469	24.177 897	23.628 616	23.098 750	22.587 463	51
52	25.540 127	24.937 016	24.355 886	23.795 765	23.255 730	22.734 904	52
53	25.735 881	25.120 597	24.528 063	23.957 260	23.407 218	22.877 016	53
54	25.925 703	25.298 399	24.694 620	24.113 295	23.553 407	23.013 992	54
55	26.109 772	25.470 604	24.855 739	24.264 053	23.694 482	23.146 016	55

YRS

	12.50% ANNUAL RATE	13.00% ANNUAL RATE	13.50% ANNUAL RATE	14.00% ANNUAL RATE	14.50% ANNUAL RATE	15.00% ANNUAL RATE	
14	26.288 264	25.637 389	25.011 597	24.409 713	23.830 622	23.273 268	56
15	26.949 757	26.253 656	25.585 781	24.944 734	24.329 195	23.737 916	60
16	27.534 640	26.795 918	26.088 574	25.410 974	24.761 579	24.138 941	64
17	28.051 787	27.273 061	26.528 852	25.817 275	25.136 563	24.485 054	68
18	28.509 041	27.692 905	26.914 387	26.171 343	25.461 765	24.783 776	72
19	28.913 339	28.062 332	27.251 987	26.479 892	25.743 795	25.041 594	76
20	29.270 815	28.387 395	27.547 612	26.748 776	25.988 384	25.264 110	80
21	29.586 890	28.673 422	27.806 480	26.983 092	26.200 503	25.456 158	84
22	29.866 359	28.925 102	28.033 162	27.187 285	26.384 462	25.621 909	88
23	30.113 462	29.146 557	28.231 659	27.365 227	26.544 000	25.764 965	92
24	30.331 948	29.341 419	28.405 476	27.520 294	26.682 358	25.888 432	96
25	30.525 130	29.512 881	28.557 681	27.655 425	26.802 348	25.994 993	100
26	30.695 939	29.663 752	28.690 962	27.773 185	26.906 410	26.086 963	104
27	30.846 966	29.796 506	28.807 671	27.875 805	26.996 656	26.166 340	108
28	30.980 502	29.913 317	28.909 870	27.965 233	27.074 922	26.234 848	112
29	31.098 573	30.016 101	28.999 361	28.043 164	27.142 797	26.293 976	116
30	31.202 970	30.106 542	29.077 726	28.111 077	27.201 662	26.345 007	120

PRESENT VALUE OF
$1 PER PERIOD

QUARTERLY COMPOUNDING

QTRS	15.50% ANNUAL RATE	16.00% ANNUAL RATE	16.50% ANNUAL RATE	17.00% ANNUAL RATE	17.50% ANNUAL RATE	18.00% ANNUAL RATE	QTRS
1	0.962 696	0.961 538	0.960 384	0.959 233	0.958 084	0.956 938	1
2	1.889 478	1.886 095	1.882 722	1.879 360	1.876 008	1.872 668	2
3	2.781 688	2.775 091	2.768 520	2.761 976	2.755 457	2.748 964	3
4	3.640 614	3.629 895	3.619 227	3.608 610	3.598 043	3.587 526	4
5	4.467 498	4.451 822	4.436 233	4.420 729	4.405 311	4.389 977	5
6	5.263 536	5.242 137	5.220 872	5.199 740	5.178 741	5.157 872	6
7	6.029 879	6.002 055	5.974 427	5.946 993	5.919 751	5.892 701	7
8	6.767 633	6.732 745	6.698 129	6.663 782	6.629 702	6.595 886	8
9	7.477 866	7.435 332	7.393 161	7.351 350	7.309 894	7.268 790	9
10	8.161 603	8.110 896	8.060 659	8.010 887	7.961 575	7.912 718	10
11	8.819 835	8.760 477	8.701 713	8.643 537	8.585 940	8.528 917	11
12	9.453 511	9.385 074	9.317 372	9.250 395	9.184 134	9.118 581	12
13	10.063 549	9.985 648	9.908 640	9.832 513	9.757 255	9.682 852	13
14	10.650 829	10.563 123	10.476 485	10.390 900	10.306 352	10.222 825	14
15	11.216 201	11.118 387	11.021 834	10.926 523	10.832 433	10.739 546	15
16	11.760 483	11.652 296	11.545 579	11.440 309	11.336 463	11.234 015	16
17	12.284 460	12.165 669	12.048 576	11.933 151	11.819 365	11.707 191	17
18	12.788 890	12.659 297	12.531 645	12.405 900	12.282 027	12.159 992	18
19	13.274 503	13.133 939	12.995 578	12.859 376	12.725 295	12.593 294	19
20	13.742 001	13.590 326	13.441 131	13.294 366	13.149 983	13.007 936	20
21	14.192 059	14.029 160	13.869 033	13.711 622	13.556 870	13.404 724	21
22	14.625 327	14.451 115	14.279 984	14.111 868	13.946 702	13.784 425	22
23	15.042 433	14.856 842	14.674 654	14.495 796	14.320 193	14.147 775	23
24	15.443 979	15.246 963	15.053 690	14.864 073	14.678 030	14.495 478	24
25	15.830 545	15.622 080	15.417 709	15.217 336	15.020 867	14.828 209	25
26	16.202 691	15.982 769	15.767 308	15.556 198	15.349 333	15.146 611	26
27	16.560 954	16.329 586	16.103 057	15.881 245	15.664 032	15.451 303	27
28	16.905 852	16.663 063	16.425 505	16.193 041	15.965 540	15.742 874	28
29	17.237 884	16.983 715	16.735 179	16.492 125	16.254 409	16.021 889	29
30	17.557 530	17.292 033	17.032 584	16.779 017	16.531 171	16.288 889	30
31	17.865 251	17.588 494	17.318 208	17.054 213	16.796 331	16.544 391	31
32	18.161 493	17.873 551	17.592 517	17.318 190	17.050 377	16.788 891	32
33	18.446 684	18.147 646	17.855 959	17.571 405	17.293 774	17.022 862	33
34	18.721 236	18.411 198	18.108 964	17.814 298	17.526 970	17.246 758	34
35	18.985 547	18.664 613	18.351 946	18.047 288	17.750 390	17.461 012	35
36	19.239 997	18.908 282	18.585 302	18.270 780	17.964 445	17.666 041	36
37	19.484 955	19.142 579	18.809 414	18.485 160	18.169 529	17.862 240	37
38	19.720 775	19.367 864	19.024 647	18.690 801	18.366 015	18.049 990	38
39	19.947 798	19.584 485	19.231 354	18.888 059	18.554 266	18.229 656	39
40	20.166 351	19.792 774	19.429 872	19.077 275	18.734 626	18.401 584	40
41	20.376 752	19.993 052	19.620 525	19.258 777	18.907 426	18.566 109	41
42	20.579 304	20.185 627	19.803 626	19.432 879	19.072 983	18.723 550	42
43	20.774 300	20.370 795	19.979 472	19.599 884	19.231 601	18.874 210	43
44	20.962 022	20.548 841	20.148 353	19.760 081	19.383 570	19.018 383	44
45	21.142 741	20.720 040	20.310 543	19.913 747	19.529 169	19.156 347	45
46	21.316 718	20.884 654	20.466 308	20.061 148	19.668 665	19.288 371	46
47	21.484 205	21.042 936	20.615 902	20.202 540	19.802 313	19.414 709	47
48	21.645 444	21.195 131	20.759 570	20.338 168	19.930 360	19.535 607	48
49	21.800 668	21.341 472	20.897 546	20.468 266	20.053 040	19.651 298	49
50	21.950 102	21.482 185	21.030 056	20.593 061	20.170 577	19.762 008	50
51	22.093 961	21.617 485	21.157 317	20.712 769	20.283 187	19.867 950	51
52	22.232 453	21.747 582	21.279 536	20.827 596	20.391 078	19.969 330	52
53	22.365 779	21.872 675	21.396 913	20.937 742	20.494 446	20.066 345	53
54	22.494 131	21.992 957	21.509 640	21.043 397	20.593 481	20.159 181	54
55	22.617 696	22.108 612	21.617 902	21.144 746	20.688 365	20.248 021	55

YRS							
14	22.736 651	22.219 819	21.721 875	21.241 962	20.779 272	20.333 034	56
15	23.169 719	22.623 490	22.098 175	21.592 779	21.106 359	20.638 022	60
16	23.541 693	22.968 549	22.418 297	21.889 793	21.381 957	20.893 773	64
17	23.861 191	23.263 507	22.690 627	22.141 254	21.614 173	21.108 236	68
18	24.135 616	23.515 639	22.922 299	22.354 150	21.809 834	21.288 077	72
19	24.371 327	23.731 162	23.119 385	22.534 395	21.974 695	21.438 884	76
20	24.573 786	23.915 392	23.287 047	22.686 997	22.113 605	21.565 345	80
21	24.747 683	24.072 872	23.429 678	22.816 195	22.230 649	21.671 390	84
22	24.897 047	24.207 487	23.551 016	22.925 578	22.329 268	21.760 316	88
23	25.025 340	24.322 557	23.654 238	23.018 185	22.412 363	21.834 885	92
24	25.135 535	24.420 919	23.742 050	23.096 590	22.482 378	21.897 417	96
25	25.230 183	24.504 999	23.816 753	23.162 970	22.541 371	21.949 853	100
26	25.311 480	24.576 871	23.880 303	23.219 170	22.591 078	21.993 824	104
27	25.381 307	24.638 308	23.934 365	23.266 750	22.632 961	22.030 696	108
28	25.441 284	24.690 824	23.980 356	23.307 034	22.668 250	22.061 616	112
29	25.492 800	24.735 715	24.019 481	23.341 139	22.697 985	22.087 544	116
30	25.537 048	24.774 088	24.052 765	23.370 014	22.723 038	22.109 286	120

PRESENT VALUE OF $1 PER PERIOD

QTRS	18.50% ANNUAL RATE	19.00% ANNUAL RATE	19.50% ANNUAL RATE	20.00% ANNUAL RATE	20.50% ANNUAL RATE	21.00% ANNUAL RATE	QTRS
1	0.955 795	0.954 654	0.953 516	0.952 381	0.951 249	0.950 119	1
2	1.869 338	1.866 018	1.862 709	1.859 410	1.856 122	1.852 844	2
3	2.742 497	2.736 055	2.729 639	2.723 248	2.716 882	2.710 541	3
4	3.577 058	3.566 640	3.556 271	3.545 951	3.535 679	3.525 455	4
5	4.374 727	4.359 561	4.344 478	4.329 477	4.314 557	4.299 719	5
6	5.137 135	5.116 526	5.096 045	5.075 692	5.055 465	5.035 363	6
7	5.865 840	5.839 166	5.812 677	5.786 373	5.760 252	5.734 311	7
8	6.562 332	6.529 036	6.495 998	6.463 213	6.430 680	6.398 396	8
9	7.228 035	7.187 624	7.147 554	7.107 822	7.068 423	7.029 355	9
10	7.864 311	7.816 348	7.768 824	7.721 735	7.675 075	7.628 840	10
11	8.472 459	8.416 561	8.361 215	8.306 414	8.252 153	8.198 423	11
12	9.053 725	8.989 557	8.926 069	8.863 252	8.801 096	8.739 595	12
13	9.609 295	9.536 570	9.464 666	9.393 573	9.323 278	9.253 772	13
14	10.140 306	10.058 778	9.978 228	9.898 641	9.820 003	9.742 301	14
15	10.647 843	10.557 306	10.467 917	10.379 658	10.292 512	10.206 462	15
16	11.132 944	11.033 228	10.934 843	10.837 770	10.741 985	10.647 469	16
17	11.596 601	11.487 568	11.380 065	11.274 066	11.169 546	11.066 479	17
18	12.039 762	11.921 306	11.804 591	11.689 587	11.576 263	11.464 588	18
19	12.463 333	12.335 376	12.209 384	12.085 321	11.963 151	11.842 839	19
20	12.868 180	12.730 669	12.595 360	12.462 210	12.331 178	12.202 223	20
21	13.255 130	13.108 037	12.963 395	12.821 153	12.681 263	12.543 679	21
22	13.624 975	13.468 293	13.314 321	13.163 003	13.014 281	12.868 104	22
23	13.978 471	13.812 213	13.648 936	13.488 574	13.331 064	13.176 346	23
24	14.316 340	14.140 538	13.967 996	13.798 642	13.632 404	13.469 212	24
25	14.639 274	14.453 974	14.272 225	14.093 945	13.919 052	13.747 470	25
26	14.947 932	14.753 197	14.562 312	14.375 185	14.191 726	14.011 848	26
27	15.242 946	15.038 852	14.838 915	14.643 034	14.451 107	14.263 038	27
28	15.524 918	15.311 553	15.102 660	14.898 127	14.697 843	14.501 699	28
29	15.794 426	15.571 888	15.354 146	15.141 074	14.932 549	14.728 455	29
30	16.052 020	15.820 418	15.593 941	15.372 451	15.155 814	14.943 901	30
31	16.298 227	16.057 679	15.822 590	15.592 811	15.368 194	15.148 599	31
32	16.533 550	16.284 180	16.040 610	15.802 677	15.570 220	15.343 087	32
33	16.758 471	16.500 410	16.248 496	16.002 549	15.762 397	15.527 874	33
34	16.973 449	16.706 836	16.446 719	16.192 904	15.945 206	15.703 443	34
35	17.178 924	16.903 901	16.635 727	16.374 194	16.119 102	15.870 255	35
36	17.375 315	17.092 029	16.815 949	16.546 852	16.284 520	16.028 745	36
37	17.563 026	17.271 627	16.987 794	16.711 287	16.441 874	16.179 331	37
38	17.742 438	17.443 081	17.151 651	16.867 893	16.591 557	16.322 404	38
39	17.913 919	17.606 759	17.307 892	17.017 041	16.733 942	16.458 341	39
40	18.077 820	17.763 016	17.456 869	17.159 086	16.869 386	16.587 498	40
41	18.234 475	17.912 187	17.598 922	17.294 368	16.998 227	16.710 212	41
42	18.384 206	18.054 594	17.734 371	17.423 208	17.120 787	16.826 804	42
43	18.527 317	18.190 543	17.863 524	17.545 912	17.237 371	16.937 581	43
44	18.664 103	18.320 328	17.986 674	17.662 773	17.348 272	17.042 833	44
45	18.794 841	18.444 227	18.104 099	17.774 070	17.453 767	17.142 834	45
46	18.919 800	18.562 508	18.216 066	17.880 066	17.554 118	17.237 847	46
47	19.039 236	18.675 425	18.322 828	17.981 016	17.649 577	17.328 121	47
48	19.153 391	18.783 222	18.424 628	18.077 158	17.740 383	17.413 891	48
49	19.262 501	18.886 131	18.521 695	18.168 722	17.826 761	17.495 384	49
50	19.366 787	18.984 373	18.614 250	18.255 925	17.908 929	17.572 811	50
51	19.466 463	19.078 160	18.702 503	18.338 977	17.987 090	17.646 376	51
52	19.561 733	19.167 695	18.786 654	18.418 073	18.061 441	17.716 272	52
53	19.652 791	19.253 169	18.866 893	18.493 403	18.132 168	17.782 681	53
54	19.739 824	19.334 768	18.943 402	18.565 146	18.199 446	17.845 778	54
55	19.823 010	19.412 666	19.016 355	18.633 472	18.263 445	17.905 727	55

YRS							
14	19.902 519	19.487 032	19.085 916	18.698 545	18.324 323	17.962 686	56
15	20.186 925	19.752 269	19.333 296	18.929 290	18.539 570	18.163 493	60
16	20.424 280	19.972 570	19.537 788	19.119 124	18.715 813	18.327 132	64
17	20.622 367	20.155 549	19.706 828	19.275 301	18.860 120	18.460 485	68
18	20.787 682	20.307 529	19.846 561	19.403 788	18.978 278	18.569 155	72
19	20.925 649	20.433 761	19.962 069	19.509 495	19.075 026	18.657 712	76
20	21.040 790	20.538 607	20.057 552	19.596 460	19.154 243	18.729 879	80
21	21.136 882	20.625 691	20.136 481	19.668 007	19.219 105	18.788 688	84
22	21.217 077	20.698 021	20.201 726	19.726 869	19.272 214	18.836 613	88
23	21.284 004	20.758 098	20.255 660	19.775 294	19.315 699	18.875 667	92
24	21.339 859	20.807 996	20.300 244	19.815 134	19.351 305	18.907 493	96
25	21.386 474	20.849 441	20.337 098	19.847 910	19.380 459	18.933 428	100
26	21.425 376	20.883 865	20.367 562	19.874 875	19.404 330	18.954 564	104
27	21.457 843	20.912 456	20.392 746	19.897 060	19.423 876	18.971 787	108
28	21.484 938	20.936 204	20.413 563	19.915 311	19.439 879	18.985 822	112
29	21.507 551	20.955 929	20.430 771	19.930 326	19.452 983	18.997 260	116
30	21.526 423	20.972 312	20.444 996	19.942 679	19.463 713	19.006 581	120

PRESENT VALUE OF
$1 PER PERIOD

QUARTERLY
COMPOUNDING

QTRS	21.50% ANNUAL RATE	22.00% ANNUAL RATE	22.50% ANNUAL RATE	23.00% ANNUAL RATE	23.50% ANNUAL RATE	24.00% ANNUAL RATE	QTRS
1	0.948 992	0.947 867	0.946 746	0.945 626	0.944 510	0.943 396	1
2	1.849 577	1.846 320	1.843 073	1.839 836	1.836 609	1.833 393	2
3	2.704 225	2.697 933	2.691 666	2.685 424	2.679 206	2.673 012	3
4	3.515 279	3.505 150	3.495 069	3.485 035	3.475 047	3.465 106	4
5	4.284 962	4.270 284	4.255 686	4.241 167	4.226 727	4.212 364	5
6	5.015 385	4.995 530	4.975 798	4.956 187	4.936 696	4.917 324	6
7	5.708 550	5.682 967	5.657 560	5.632 328	5.607 269	5.582 381	7
8	6.366 359	6.334 566	6.303 015	6.271 705	6.240 632	6.209 794	8
9	6.990 613	6.952 195	6.914 098	6.876 317	6.838 849	6.801 692	9
10	7.583 026	7.537 626	7.492 637	7.448 054	7.403 872	7.360 087	10
11	8.145 220	8.092 536	8.040 366	7.988 703	7.937 541	7.886 875	11
12	8.678 738	8.618 518	8.558 926	8.499 956	8.441 597	8.383 844	12
13	9.185 042	9.117 079	9.049 871	8.983 410	8.917 684	8.852 683	13
14	9.665 520	9.589 648	9.514 671	9.440 576	9.367 352	9.294 984	14
15	10.121 490	10.037 581	9.954 718	9.872 886	9.792 068	9.712 249	15
16	10.554 202	10.462 162	10.371 331	10.281 688	10.193 216	10.105 895	16
17	10.964 841	10.864 609	10.765 757	10.668 263	10.572 105	10.477 260	17
18	11.354 535	11.246 074	11.139 178	11.033 819	10.929 969	10.827 603	18
19	11.724 351	11.607 654	11.492 713	11.379 498	11.267 976	11.158 116	19
20	12.075 304	11.950 382	11.827 421	11.706 381	11.587 226	11.469 921	20
21	12.408 355	12.275 244	12.144 304	12.015 490	11.888 761	11.764 077	21
22	12.724 417	12.583 170	12.444 311	12.307 792	12.173 565	12.041 582	22
23	13.024 358	12.875 042	12.728 342	12.584 200	12.442 564	12.303 379	23
24	13.308 999	13.151 699	12.997 247	12.845 580	12.696 637	12.550 358	24
25	13.579 122	13.413 933	13.251 831	13.092 747	12.936 611	12.783 356	25
26	13.835 465	13.662 495	13.492 858	13.326 474	13.163 269	13.003 166	26
27	14.078 733	13.898 100	13.721 049	13.547 494	13.377 349	13.210 534	27
28	14.309 593	14.121 422	13.937 088	13.756 495	13.579 551	13.406 164	28
29	14.528 676	14.333 101	14.141 622	13.954 132	13.770 532	13.590 721	29
30	14.736 585	14.533 745	14.335 263	14.141 024	13.950 916	13.764 831	30
31	14.933 888	14.723 929	14.518 592	14.317 753	14.121 290	13.929 086	31
32	15.121 128	14.904 198	14.692 158	14.484 873	14.282 210	14.084 043	32
33	15.298 816	15.075 069	14.856 481	14.642 906	14.434 201	14.230 230	33
34	15.467 441	15.237 033	15.012 053	14.792 346	14.577 758	14.368 141	34
35	15.627 465	15.390 552	15.159 340	14.933 660	14.713 348	14.498 246	35
36	15.779 326	15.536 068	15.298 784	15.067 291	14.841 415	14.620 987	36
37	15.923 441	15.673 999	15.430 801	15.193 656	14.962 376	14.736 780	37
38	16.060 205	15.804 738	15.555 788	15.313 150	15.076 624	14.846 019	38
39	16.189 993	15.928 662	15.674 119	15.426 146	15.184 533	14.949 075	39
40	16.313 161	16.046 125	15.786 148	15.532 999	15.286 453	15.046 297	40
41	16.430 046	16.157 464	15.892 211	15.634 041	15.382 719	15.138 016	41
42	16.540 969	16.262 999	15.992 626	15.729 590	15.473 642	15.224 543	42
43	16.646 234	16.363 032	16.087 693	15.819 943	15.559 520	15.306 173	43
44	16.746 129	16.457 851	16.177 698	15.905 384	15.640 633	15.383 182	44
45	16.840 929	16.547 726	16.262 909	15.986 178	15.717 245	15.455 832	45
46	16.930 894	16.632 915	16.343 583	16.062 580	15.789 606	15.524 370	46
47	17.016 269	16.713 664	16.419 960	16.134 828	15.857 951	15.589 028	47
48	17.097 290	16.790 203	16.492 270	16.203 147	15.922 504	15.650 027	48
49	17.174 178	16.862 751	16.560 729	16.267 751	15.983 475	15.707 572	49
50	17.247 144	16.931 518	16.625 542	16.328 842	16.041 062	15.761 861	50
51	17.316 388	16.996 699	16.686 904	16.386 612	16.095 455	15.813 076	51
52	17.382 100	17.058 483	16.744 998	16.441 241	16.146 828	15.861 393	52
53	17.444 460	17.117 045	16.799 998	16.492 899	16.195 351	15.906 974	53
54	17.503 640	17.172 555	16.852 069	16.541 749	16.241 182	15.949 976	54
55	17.559 801	17.225 170	16.901 367	16.587 942	16.284 469	15.990 543	55

YRS							
14	17.613 097	17.275 043	16.948 040	16.631 624	16.325 355	16.028 814	56
15	17.800 447	17.449 854	17.111 164	16.783 856	16.467 434	16.161 428	60
16	17.952 398	17.590 965	17.242 219	16.905 582	16.580 506	16.266 470	64
17	18.075 639	17.704 871	17.347 508	17.002 916	16.670 493	16.349 673	68
18	18.175 594	17.796 819	17.432 098	17.080 745	16.742 109	16.415 578	72
19	18.256 663	17.871 040	17.500 058	17.142 978	16.799 103	16.467 781	76
20	18.322 414	17.930 953	17.554 657	17.192 740	16.844 462	16.509 131	80
21	18.375 741	17.979 316	17.598 522	17.232 530	16.880 560	16.541 883	84
22	18.418 993	18.018 355	17.633 763	17.264 347	16.909 289	16.567 827	88
23	18.454 072	18.049 868	17.662 076	17.289 788	16.932 152	16.588 376	92
24	18.482 524	18.075 306	17.684 823	17.310 131	16.950 348	16.604 653	96
25	18.505 599	18.095 839	17.703 098	17.326 397	16.964 828	16.617 546	100
26	18.524 315	18.112 415	17.717 780	17.339 404	16.976 353	16.627 759	104
27	18.539 494	18.125 794	17.729 575	17.349 804	16.985 524	16.635 848	108
28	18.551 805	18.136 595	17.739 052	17.358 120	16.992 824	16.642 255	112
29	18.561 790	18.145 313	17.746 665	17.364 770	16.998 632	16.647 331	116
30	18.569 889	18.152 351	17.752 782	17.370 087	17.003 255	16.651 351	120

133

PRESENT VALUE OF
$1 PER PERIOD

SEMIANNUAL
COMPOUNDING

HALF YRS	7.00% ANNUAL RATE	8.00% ANNUAL RATE	9.00% ANNUAL RATE	10.00% ANNUAL RATE	10.50% ANNUAL RATE	11.00% ANNUAL RATE	HALF YRS
1	0.966 184	0.961 538	0.956 938	0.952 381	0.950 119	0.947 867	1
2	1.899 694	1.886 095	1.872 668	1.859 410	1.852 844	1.846 320	2
3	2.801 637	2.775 091	2.748 964	2.723 248	2.710 541	2.697 933	3
4	3.673 079	3.629 895	3.587 526	3.545 951	3.525 455	3.505 150	4
5	4.515 052	4.451 822	4.389 977	4.329 477	4.299 719	4.270 284	5
6	5.328 553	5.242 137	5.157 872	5.075 692	5.035 363	4.995 530	6
7	6.114 544	6.002 055	5.892 701	5.786 373	5.734 311	5.682 967	7
8	6.873 956	6.732 745	6.595 886	6.463 213	6.398 396	6.334 566	8
9	7.607 687	7.435 332	7.268 790	7.107 822	7.029 355	6.952 195	9
10	8.316 605	8.110 896	7.912 718	7.721 735	7.628 840	7.537 626	10
11	9.001 551	8.760 477	8.528 917	8.306 414	8.198 423	8.092 536	11
12	9.663 334	9.385 074	9.118 581	8.863 252	8.739 595	8.618 518	12
13	10.302 738	9.985 648	9.682 852	9.393 573	9.253 772	9.117 079	13
14	10.920 520	10.563 123	10.222 825	9.898 641	9.742 301	9.589 648	14
15	11.517 411	11.118 387	10.739 546	10.379 658	10.206 462	10.037 581	15
16	12.094 117	11.652 296	11.234 015	10.837 770	10.647 469	10.462 162	16
17	12.651 321	12.165 669	11.707 191	11.274 066	11.066 479	10.864 609	17
18	13.189 682	12.659 297	12.159 992	11.689 587	11.464 588	11.246 074	18
19	13.709 837	13.133 939	12.593 294	12.085 321	11.842 839	11.607 654	19
20	14.212 403	13.590 326	13.007 936	12.462 210	12.202 223	11.950 382	20
21	14.697 974	14.029 160	13.404 724	12.821 153	12.543 679	12.275 244	21
22	15.167 125	14.451 115	13.784 425	13.163 003	12.868 104	12.583 170	22
23	15.620 410	14.856 842	14.147 775	13.488 574	13.176 346	12.875 042	23
24	16.058 368	15.246 963	14.495 478	13.798 642	13.469 212	13.151 699	24
25	16.481 515	15.622 080	14.828 209	14.093 945	13.747 470	13.413 933	25
26	16.890 352	15.982 769	15.146 611	14.375 185	14.011 848	13.662 495	26
27	17.285 365	16.329 586	15.451 303	14.643 034	14.263 038	13.898 100	27
28	17.667 019	16.663 063	15.742 874	14.898 127	14.501 699	14.121 422	28
29	18.035 767	16.983 715	16.021 889	15.141 074	14.728 455	14.333 101	29
30	18.392 045	17.292 033	16.288 889	15.372 451	14.943 901	14.533 745	30
31	18.736 276	17.588 494	16.544 391	15.592 811	15.148 599	14.723 929	31
32	19.068 865	17.873 551	16.788 891	15.802 677	15.343 087	14.904 198	32
33	19.390 208	18.147 646	17.022 862	16.002 549	15.527 874	15.075 069	33
34	19.700 684	18.411 198	17.246 758	16.192 904	15.703 443	15.237 033	34
35	20.000 661	18.664 613	17.461 012	16.374 194	15.870 255	15.390 552	35
36	20.290 494	18.908 282	17.666 041	16.546 852	16.028 745	15.536 068	36
37	20.570 525	19.142 579	17.862 240	16.711 287	16.179 331	15.673 999	37
38	20.841 087	19.367 864	18.049 990	16.867 893	16.322 404	15.804 738	38
39	21.102 500	19.584 485	18.229 656	17.017 041	16.458 341	15.928 662	39
40	21.355 072	19.792 774	18.401 584	17.159 086	16.587 498	16.046 125	40
41	21.599 104	19.993 052	18.566 109	17.294 368	16.710 212	16.157 464	41
42	21.834 883	20.185 627	18.723 550	17.423 208	16.826 804	16.262 999	42
43	22.062 689	20.370 795	18.874 210	17.545 912	16.937 581	16.363 032	43
44	22.282 791	20.548 841	19.018 383	17.662 773	17.042 833	16.457 851	44
45	22.495 450	20.720 040	19.156 347	17.774 070	17.142 834	16.547 726	45
46	22.700 918	20.884 654	19.288 371	17.880 066	17.237 847	16.632 915	46
47	22.899 534	21.042 936	19.414 709	17.981 016	17.328 121	16.713 664	47
48	23.091 244	21.195 131	19.535 607	18.077 158	17.413 891	16.790 203	48
49	23.276 564	21.341 472	19.651 298	18.168 722	17.495 384	16.862 751	49
50	23.455 618	21.482 185	19.762 008	18.255 925	17.572 811	16.931 518	50
51	23.628 616	21.617 485	19.867 950	18.338 977	17.646 376	16.996 699	51
52	23.795 765	21.747 582	19.969 330	18.418 073	17.716 272	17.058 483	52
53	23.957 260	21.872 675	20.066 345	18.493 403	17.782 681	17.117 045	53
54	24.113 295	21.992 957	20.159 181	18.565 146	17.845 778	17.172 555	54
55	24.264 053	22.108 612	20.248 021	18.633 472	17.905 727	17.225 170	55
56	24.409 713	22.219 819	20.333 034	18.698 545	17.962 686	17.275 043	56
57	24.550 448	22.326 749	20.414 387	18.760 519	18.016 804	17.322 316	57
58	24.686 423	22.429 567	20.492 236	18.819 542	18.068 222	17.367 124	58
59	24.817 800	22.528 430	20.566 733	18.875 754	18.117 076	17.409 596	59

YRS

HALF YRS	7.00% ANNUAL RATE	8.00% ANNUAL RATE	9.00% ANNUAL RATE	10.00% ANNUAL RATE	10.50% ANNUAL RATE	11.00% ANNUAL RATE	HALF YRS
30	24.944 734	22.623 490	20.638 022	18.929 290	18.163 493	17.449 854	60
31	25.185 870	22.802 783	20.771 523	19.028 834	18.249 495	17.524 183	62
32	25.410 974	22.968 549	20.893 773	19.119 124	18.327 132	17.590 965	64
33	25.621 110	23.121 810	21.005 722	19.201 019	18.397 217	17.650 964	66
34	25.817 275	23.263 507	21.108 236	19.275 301	18.460 485	17.704 871	68
35	26.000 397	23.394 515	21.202 112	19.342 677	18.517 598	17.753 304	70
36	26.171 343	23.515 639	21.288 077	19.403 788	18.569 155	17.796 819	72
37	26.330 923	23.627 625	21.366 797	19.459 218	18.615 697	17.835 914	74
38	26.479 892	23.731 162	21.438 884	19.509 495	18.657 712	17.871 040	76
39	26.618 957	23.826 888	21.504 896	19.555 098	18.695 640	17.902 599	78
40	26.748 776	23.915 392	21.565 345	19.596 460	18.729 879	17.930 953	80

PRESENT VALUE OF $1 PER PERIOD — SEMIANNUAL COMPOUNDING

HALF YRS	11.50% ANNUAL RATE	12.00% ANNUAL RATE	12.50% ANNUAL RATE	13.00% ANNUAL RATE	13.50% ANNUAL RATE	14.00% ANNUAL RATE	HALF YRS
1	0.945 626	0.943 396	0.941 176	0.938 967	0.936 768	0.934 579	1
2	1.839 836	1.833 393	1.826 990	1.820 626	1.814 303	1.808 018	2
3	2.685 424	2.673 012	2.660 696	2.648 476	2.636 349	2.624 316	3
4	3.485 035	3.465 106	3.445 361	3.425 799	3.406 416	3.387 211	4
5	4.241 167	4.212 364	4.183 869	4.155 679	4.127 790	4.100 197	5
6	4.956 187	4.917 324	4.878 936	4.841 014	4.803 551	4.766 540	6
7	5.632 328	5.582 381	5.533 116	5.484 520	5.436 581	5.389 289	7
8	6.271 705	6.209 794	6.148 815	6.088 751	6.029 584	5.971 299	8
9	6.876 317	6.801 692	6.728 297	6.656 104	6.585 091	6.515 232	9
10	7.448 054	7.360 087	7.273 691	7.188 830	7.105 471	7.023 582	10
11	7.988 703	7.886 875	7.787 003	7.689 042	7.592 947	7.498 674	11
12	8.499 956	8.383 844	8.270 121	8.158 725	8.049 600	7.942 686	12
13	8.983 410	8.852 683	8.724 819	8.599 742	8.477 377	8.357 651	13
14	9.440 576	9.294 984	9.152 771	9.013 842	8.878 105	8.745 468	14
15	9.872 886	9.712 249	9.555 549	9.402 669	9.253 494	9.107 914	15
16	10.281 688	10.105 895	9.934 635	9.767 764	9.605 146	9.446 649	16
17	10.668 263	10.477 260	10.291 421	10.110 577	9.934 563	9.763 223	17
18	11.033 819	10.827 603	10.627 220	10.432 466	10.243 151	10.059 087	18
19	11.379 498	11.158 116	10.943 266	10.734 710	10.532 225	10.335 595	19
20	11.706 381	11.469 921	11.240 721	11.018 507	10.803 021	10.594 014	20
21	12.015 490	11.764 077	11.520 678	11.284 983	11.056 695	10.835 527	21
22	12.307 792	12.041 582	11.784 168	11.535 196	11.294 327	11.061 240	22
23	12.584 200	12.303 379	12.032 158	11.770 137	11.516 934	11.272 187	23
24	12.845 580	12.550 358	12.265 560	11.990 739	11.725 465	11.469 334	24
25	13.092 747	12.783 356	12.485 233	12.197 877	11.920 811	11.653 583	25
26	13.326 474	13.003 166	12.691 984	12.392 373	12.103 804	11.825 779	26
27	13.547 494	13.210 534	12.886 573	12.574 998	12.275 226	11.986 709	27
28	13.756 495	13.406 164	13.069 716	12.746 477	12.435 809	12.137 111	28
29	13.954 132	13.590 721	13.242 086	12.907 490	12.586 238	12.277 674	29
30	14.141 024	13.764 831	13.404 316	13.058 676	12.727 155	12.409 041	30
31	14.317 753	13.929 086	13.557 003	13.200 635	12.859 162	12.531 814	31
32	14.484 873	14.084 043	13.700 709	13.333 929	12.982 821	12.646 555	32
33	14.642 906	14.230 230	13.835 961	13.459 088	13.098 662	12.753 790	33
34	14.792 346	14.368 141	13.963 258	13.576 609	13.207 177	12.854 009	34
35	14.933 660	14.498 246	14.083 066	13.686 957	13.308 831	12.947 672	35
36	15.067 291	14.620 987	14.195 827	13.790 570	13.404 057	13.035 208	36
37	15.193 656	14.736 780	14.301 955	13.887 859	13.493 262	13.117 017	37
38	15.313 150	14.846 019	14.401 840	13.979 210	13.576 826	13.193 473	38
39	15.426 146	14.949 075	14.495 849	14.064 986	13.655 107	13.264 928	39
40	15.532 999	15.046 297	14.584 329	14.145 527	13.728 437	13.331 709	40
41	15.634 041	15.138 016	14.667 603	14.221 152	13.797 131	13.394 120	41
42	15.729 590	15.224 543	14.745 980	14.292 161	13.861 481	13.452 449	42
43	15.819 943	15.306 173	14.819 746	14.358 837	13.921 762	13.506 962	43
44	15.905 384	15.383 182	14.889 172	14.421 443	13.978 231	13.557 908	44
45	15.986 178	15.455 832	14.954 515	14.480 228	14.031 130	13.605 522	45
46	16.062 580	15.524 370	15.016 014	14.535 426	14.080 684	13.650 020	46
47	16.134 828	15.589 028	15.073 896	14.587 254	14.127 104	13.691 608	47
48	16.203 147	15.650 027	15.128 372	14.635 919	14.170 589	13.730 474	48
49	16.267 751	15.707 572	15.179 645	14.681 615	14.211 325	13.766 799	49
50	16.328 842	15.761 861	15.227 901	14.724 521	14.249 485	13.800 746	50
51	16.386 612	15.813 076	15.273 318	14.764 808	14.285 232	13.832 473	51
52	16.441 241	15.861 393	15.316 064	14.802 637	14.318 718	13.862 124	52
53	16.492 899	15.906 974	15.356 296	14.838 157	14.350 087	13.889 836	53
54	16.541 749	15.949 976	15.394 161	14.871 509	14.379 473	13.915 735	54
55	16.587 942	15.990 543	15.429 799	14.902 825	14.407 000	13.939 939	55
56	16.631 624	16.028 814	15.463 340	14.932 230	14.432 787	13.962 560	56
57	16.672 930	16.064 919	15.494 908	14.959 840	14.456 944	13.983 701	57
58	16.711 991	16.098 980	15.524 619	14.985 766	14.479 572	14.003 458	58
59	16.748 927	16.131 113	15.552 583	15.010 109	14.500 770	14.021 924	59

YRS							YRS
30	16.783 856	16.161 428	15.578 902	15.032 966	14.520 628	14.039 181	60
31	16.848 118	16.217 006	15.626 985	15.074 580	14.556 656	14.070 383	62
32	16.905 582	16.266 470	15.669 579	15.111 270	14.588 271	14.097 635	64
33	16.956 967	16.310 493	15.707 309	15.143 618	14.616 015	14.121 439	66
34	17.002 916	16.349 673	15.740 730	15.172 138	14.640 361	14.142 230	68
35	17.044 004	16.384 544	15.770 335	15.197 282	14.661 726	14.160 389	70
36	17.080 745	16.415 578	15.796 560	15.219 452	14.680 474	14.176 251	72
37	17.113 599	16.443 159	15.819 790	15.238 997	14.696 926	14.190 104	74
38	17.142 978	16.467 781	15.840 368	15.256 230	14.711 363	14.202 205	76
39	17.169 248	16.489 659	15.858 596	15.271 423	14.724 032	14.212 774	78
40	17.192 740	16.509 131	15.874 742	15.284 818	14.735 150	14.222 005	80

HALF YRS	14.50% ANNUAL RATE	15.00% ANNUAL RATE	15.50% ANNUAL RATE	16.00% ANNUAL RATE	16.50% ANNUAL RATE	17.00% ANNUAL RATE	HALF YRS
1	0.932 401	0.930 233	0.928 074	0.925 926	0.923 788	0.921 659	1
2	1.801 772	1.795 565	1.789 396	1.783 265	1.777 171	1.771 114	2
3	2.612 375	2.600 526	2.588 767	2.577 097	2.565 516	2.554 022	3
4	3.368 182	3.349 326	3.330 642	3.312 127	3.293 779	3.275 597	4
5	4.072 897	4.045 885	4.019 157	3.992 710	3.966 540	3.940 642	5
6	4.729 974	4.693 846	4.658 151	4.622 880	4.588 027	4.553 587	6
7	5.342 633	5.296 601	5.251 184	5.206 370	5.162 150	5.118 514	7
8	5.913 877	5.857 304	5.801 563	5.746 639	5.692 517	5.639 183	8
9	6.446 505	6.378 887	6.312 355	6.246 888	6.182 464	6.119 063	9
10	6.943 128	6.864 081	6.786 409	6.710 081	6.635 071	6.561 348	10
11	7.406 180	7.315 424	7.226 365	7.138 964	7.053 183	6.968 984	11
12	7.837 930	7.735 278	7.634 678	7.536 078	7.439 430	7.344 686	12
13	8.240 495	8.125 840	8.013 622	7.903 776	7.796 240	7.690 955	13
14	8.615 846	8.489 154	8.365 310	8.244 237	8.125 857	8.010 097	14
15	8.965 824	8.827 120	8.691 703	8.559 479	8.430 353	8.304 237	15
16	9.292 143	9.141 507	8.994 620	8.851 369	8.711 642	8.575 333	16
17	9.596 404	9.433 960	9.275 750	9.121 638	8.971 494	8.825 192	17
18	9.880 097	9.706 009	9.536 659	9.371 887	9.211 542	9.055 476	18
19	10.144 612	9.959 078	9.778 802	9.603 599	9.433 295	9.267 720	19
20	10.391 247	10.194 491	10.003 528	9.818 147	9.638 148	9.463 337	20
21	10.621 209	10.413 480	10.212 091	10.016 803	9.827 388	9.643 628	21
22	10.835 626	10.617 191	10.405 653	10.200 744	10.002 206	9.809 796	22
23	11.035 549	10.806 689	10.585 293	10.371 059	10.163 701	9.962 945	23
24	11.221 957	10.982 967	10.752 012	10.528 758	10.312 888	10.104 097	24
25	11.395 764	11.146 946	10.906 740	10.674 776	10.450 705	10.234 191	25
26	11.557 822	11.299 485	11.050 338	10.809 978	10.578 018	10.354 093	26
27	11.708 925	11.441 381	11.183 609	10.935 165	10.695 629	10.464 602	27
28	11.849 814	11.573 378	11.307 293	11.051 078	10.804 276	10.566 453	28
29	11.981 178	11.696 165	11.422 082	11.158 406	10.904 643	10.660 326	29
30	12.103 663	11.810 386	11.528 614	11.257 783	10.997 361	10.746 844	30
31	12.217 867	11.916 638	11.627 484	11.349 799	11.083 012	10.826 584	31
32	12.324 352	12.015 478	11.719 243	11.434 999	11.162 136	10.900 078	32
33	12.423 638	12.107 421	11.804 402	11.513 888	11.235 230	10.967 813	33
34	12.516 213	12.192 950	11.883 436	11.586 934	11.302 752	11.030 243	34
35	12.602 529	12.272 511	11.956 785	11.654 568	11.365 129	11.087 781	35
36	12.683 011	12.346 522	12.024 858	11.717 193	11.422 752	11.140 812	36
37	12.758 052	12.415 370	12.088 036	11.775 179	11.475 984	11.189 689	37
38	12.828 021	12.479 414	12.146 669	11.828 869	11.525 158	11.234 736	38
39	12.893 259	12.538 989	12.201 085	11.878 582	11.570 585	11.276 255	39
40	12.954 088	12.594 409	12.251 587	11.924 613	11.612 549	11.314 520	40
41	13.010 805	12.645 962	12.298 456	11.967 235	11.651 316	11.349 788	41
42	13.063 687	12.693 918	12.341 955	12.006 699	11.687 128	11.382 293	42
43	13.112 995	12.738 528	12.382 325	12.043 240	11.720 210	11.412 252	43
44	13.158 970	12.780 026	12.419 791	12.077 074	11.750 772	11.439 864	44
45	13.201 837	12.818 629	12.454 562	12.108 402	11.779 004	11.465 312	45
46	13.241 806	12.854 539	12.486 833	12.137 409	11.805 085	11.488 767	46
47	13.279 073	12.887 943	12.516 782	12.164 267	11.829 177	11.510 384	47
48	13.313 821	12.919 017	12.544 577	12.189 136	11.851 434	11.530 308	48
49	13.346 220	12.947 922	12.570 373	12.212 163	11.871 995	11.548 671	49
50	13.376 429	12.974 812	12.594 314	12.233 485	11.890 988	11.565 595	50
51	13.404 596	12.999 825	12.616 533	12.253 227	11.908 534	11.581 194	51
52	13.430 858	13.023 093	12.637 153	12.271 506	11.924 743	11.595 570	52
53	13.455 346	13.044 737	12.656 291	12.288 432	11.939 716	11.608 821	53
54	13.478 178	13.064 872	12.674 052	12.304 103	11.953 548	11.621 033	54
55	13.499 467	13.083 602	12.690 535	12.318 614	11.966 326	11.632 288	55
56	13.519 316	13.101 025	12.705 833	12.332 050	11.978 131	11.642 662	56
57	13.537 824	13.117 233	12.720 031	12.344 491	11.989 035	11.652 223	57
58	13.555 081	13.132 309	12.733 207	12.356 010	11.999 109	11.661 035	58
59	13.571 171	13.146 334	12.745 436	12.366 676	12.008 415	11.669 157	59

YRS							YRS
30	13.586 173	13.159 381	12.756 785	12.376 552	12.017 011	11.676 642	60
31	13.613 204	13.182 806	12.777 093	12.394 163	12.032 289	11.689 900	62
32	13.636 704	13.203 078	12.794 585	12.409 262	12.045 326	11.701 161	64
33	13.657 134	13.220 619	12.809 651	12.422 207	12.056 452	11.710 728	66
34	13.674 896	13.235 798	12.822 628	12.433 305	12.065 947	11.718 854	68
35	13.690 337	13.248 933	12.833 805	12.442 820	12.074 050	11.725 757	70
36	13.703 761	13.260 299	12.843 432	12.450 977	12.080 965	11.731 620	72
37	13.715 432	13.270 134	12.851 724	12.457 971	12.086 866	11.736 601	74
38	13.725 578	13.278 645	12.858 866	12.463 967	12.091 901	11.740 832	76
39	13.734 399	13.286 010	12.865 018	12.469 107	12.096 199	11.744 426	78
40	13.742 067	13.292 383	12.870 317	12.473 514	12.099 866	11.747 479	80

PRESENT VALUE OF
$1 PER PERIOD

SEMIANNUAL
COMPOUNDING

HALF YRS	17.50% ANNUAL RATE	18.00% ANNUAL RATE	18.50% ANNUAL RATE	19.00% ANNUAL RATE	19.50% ANNUAL RATE	20.00% ANNUAL RATE	HALF YRS
1	0.919 540	0.917 431	0.915 332	0.913 242	0.911 162	0.909 091	1
2	1.765 094	1.759 111	1.753 164	1.747 253	1.741 377	1.735 537	2
3	2.542 616	2.531 295	2.520 059	2.508 907	2.497 838	2.486 852	3
4	3.257 578	3.239 720	3.222 022	3.204 481	3.187 096	3.169 865	4
5	3.915 014	3.889 651	3.864 551	3.839 709	3.815 122	3.790 787	5
6	4.519 553	4.485 919	4.452 678	4.419 825	4.387 355	4.355 261	6
7	5.075 451	5.032 953	4.991 010	4.949 612	4.908 752	4.868 419	7
8	5.586 622	5.534 819	5.483 762	5.433 436	5.383 828	5.334 926	8
9	6.056 664	5.995 247	5.934 793	5.875 284	5.816 700	5.759 024	9
10	6.488 886	6.417 658	6.347 637	6.278 798	6.211 116	6.144 567	10
11	6.886 332	6.805 191	6.725 526	6.647 304	6.570 493	6.495 061	11
12	7.251 800	7.160 725	7.071 419	6.983 839	6.897 944	6.813 692	12
13	7.587 862	7.486 904	7.388 027	7.291 178	7.196 304	7.103 356	13
14	7.896 884	7.786 150	7.677 828	7.571 852	7.468 159	7.366 687	14
15	8.181 043	8.060 688	7.943 092	7.828 175	7.715 862	7.606 080	15
16	8.442 338	8.312 558	8.185 896	8.062 260	7.941 560	7.823 709	16
17	8.682 610	8.543 631	8.408 143	8.276 037	8.147 207	8.021 553	17
18	8.903 549	8.755 625	8.611 573	8.471 266	8.334 585	8.201 412	18
19	9.106 712	8.950 115	8.797 778	8.649 558	8.505 317	8.364 920	19
20	9.293 528	9.128 546	8.968 218	8.812 382	8.660 881	8.513 564	20
21	9.465 313	9.292 244	9.124 227	8.961 080	8.802 625	8.648 694	21
22	9.623 277	9.442 425	9.267 027	9.096 876	8.931 777	8.771 540	22
23	9.768 530	9.580 207	9.397 736	9.220 892	9.049 455	8.883 218	23
24	9.902 097	9.706 612	9.517 379	9.334 148	9.156 679	8.984 744	24
25	10.024 917	9.822 580	9.626 891	9.437 578	9.254 377	9.077 040	25
26	10.137 854	9.928 972	9.727 132	9.532 034	9.343 396	9.160 945	26
27	10.241 705	10.026 580	9.818 885	9.618 296	9.424 506	9.237 223	27
28	10.337 200	10.116 128	9.902 869	9.697 074	9.498 411	9.306 567	28
29	10.425 012	10.198 283	9.979 743	9.769 018	9.565 751	9.369 606	29
30	10.505 758	10.273 654	10.050 108	9.834 719	9.627 108	9.426 914	30
31	10.580 007	10.342 802	10.114 516	9.894 721	9.683 014	9.479 013	31
32	10.648 282	10.406 240	10.173 470	9.949 517	9.733 953	9.526 376	32
33	10.711 064	10.464 441	10.227 432	9.999 559	9.780 368	9.569 432	33
34	10.768 795	10.517 835	10.276 826	10.045 259	9.822 658	9.608 575	34
35	10.821 880	10.566 821	10.322 037	10.086 995	9.861 192	9.644 159	35
36	10.870 695	10.611 763	10.363 421	10.125 109	9.896 303	9.676 508	36
37	10.915 581	10.652 993	10.401 301	10.159 917	9.928 294	9.705 917	37
38	10.956 856	10.690 820	10.435 973	10.191 705	9.957 443	9.732 651	38
39	10.994 810	10.725 523	10.467 710	10.220 735	9.984 003	9.756 956	39
40	11.029 711	10.757 360	10.496 760	10.247 247	10.008 203	9.779 051	40
41	11.061 803	10.786 569	10.523 350	10.271 458	10.030 253	9.799 137	41
42	11.091 313	10.813 366	10.547 689	10.293 569	10.050 345	9.817 397	42
43	11.118 449	10.837 950	10.569 967	10.313 762	10.068 651	9.833 998	43
44	11.143 401	10.860 505	10.590 358	10.332 203	10.085 331	9.849 089	44
45	11.166 346	10.881 197	10.609 024	10.349 043	10.100 530	9.862 808	45
46	11.187 444	10.900 181	10.626 109	10.364 423	10.114 378	9.875 280	46
47	11.206 846	10.917 597	10.641 747	10.378 469	10.126 996	9.886 618	47
48	11.224 686	10.933 575	10.656 061	10.391 296	10.138 493	9.896 926	48
49	11.241 090	10.948 234	10.669 164	10.403 010	10.148 968	9.906 296	49
50	11.256 175	10.961 683	10.681 157	10.413 707	10.158 513	9.914 814	50
51	11.270 046	10.974 021	10.692 134	10.423 477	10.167 210	9.922 559	51
52	11.282 801	10.985 340	10.702 182	10.432 399	10.175 135	9.929 599	52
53	11.294 529	10.995 725	10.711 380	10.440 547	10.182 355	9.935 999	53
54	11.305 314	11.005 252	10.719 798	10.447 988	10.188 934	9.941 817	54
55	11.315 232	11.013 993	10.727 504	10.454 784	10.194 928	9.947 106	55
56	11.324 351	11.022 012	10.734 558	10.460 990	10.200 390	9.951 915	56
57	11.332 737	11.029 369	10.741 014	10.466 657	10.205 367	9.956 286	57
58	11.340 447	11.036 118	10.746 924	10.471 833	10.209 902	9.960 260	58
59	11.347 538	11.042 310	10.752 333	10.476 560	10.214 033	9.963 873	59

YRS

YRS							
30	11.354 058	11.047 991	10.757 284	10.480 877	10.217 798	9.967 157	60
31	11.365 566	11.057 984	10.765 964	10.488 419	10.224 354	9.972 857	62
32	11.375 297	11.066 395	10.773 237	10.494 710	10.229 797	9.977 568	64
33	11.383 525	11.073 475	10.779 330	10.499 956	10.234 315	9.981 461	66
34	11.390 482	11.079 433	10.784 435	10.504 331	10.238 067	9.984 679	68
35	11.396 365	11.084 449	10.788 713	10.507 980	10.241 181	9.987 338	70
36	11.401 339	11.088 670	10.792 296	10.511 024	10.243 767	9.989 535	72
37	11.405 545	11.092 223	10.795 299	10.513 562	10.245 913	9.991 351	74
38	11.409 101	11.095 213	10.797 814	10.515 679	10.247 696	9.992 852	76
39	11.412 108	11.097 730	10.799 922	10.517 445	10.249 175	9.994 093	78
40	11.414 651	11.099 849	10.801 688	10.518 917	10.250 404	9.995 118	80

YRS	7.00% ANNUAL RATE	8.00% ANNUAL RATE	9.00% ANNUAL RATE	10.00% ANNUAL RATE	10.25% ANNUAL RATE	10.50% ANNUAL RATE	YRS
1	0.934 579	0.925 926	0.917 431	0.909 091	0.907 029	0.904 977	1
2	1.808 018	1.783 265	1.759 111	1.735 537	1.729 732	1.723 961	2
3	2.624 316	2.577 097	2.531 295	2.486 852	2.475 947	2.465 123	3
4	3.387 211	3.312 127	3.239 720	3.169 865	3.152 787	3.135 858	4
5	4.100 197	3.992 710	3.889 651	3.790 787	3.766 700	3.742 858	5
6	4.766 540	4.622 880	4.485 919	4.355 261	4.323 537	4.292 179	6
7	5.389 289	5.206 370	5.032 953	4.868 419	4.828 605	4.789 303	7
8	5.971 299	5.746 639	5.534 819	5.334 926	5.286 717	5.239 188	8
9	6.515 232	6.246 888	5.995 247	5.759 024	5.702 238	5.646 324	9
10	7.023 582	6.710 081	6.417 658	6.144 567	6.079 127	6.014 773	10
11	7.498 674	7.138 964	6.805 191	6.495 061	6.420 977	6.348 211	11
12	7.942 686	7.536 078	7.160 725	6.813 692	6.731 045	6.649 964	12
13	8.357 651	7.903 776	7.486 904	7.103 356	7.012 286	6.923 045	13
14	8.745 468	8.244 237	7.786 150	7.366 687	7.267 379	7.170 176	14
15	9.107 914	8.559 479	8.060 688	7.606 080	7.498 757	7.393 825	15
16	9.446 649	8.851 369	8.312 558	7.823 709	7.708 623	7.596 221	16
17	9.763 223	9.121 638	8.543 631	8.021 553	7.898 978	7.779 386	17
18	10.059 087	9.371 887	8.755 625	8.201 412	8.071 635	7.945 146	18
19	10.335 595	9.603 599	8.950 115	8.364 920	8.228 240	8.095 154	19
20	10.594 014	9.818 147	9.128 546	8.513 564	8.370 286	8.230 909	20
21	10.835 527	10.016 803	9.292 244	8.648 694	8.499 126	8.353 764	21
22	11.061 240	10.200 744	9.442 425	8.771 540	8.615 987	8.464 945	22
23	11.272 187	10.371 059	9.580 207	8.883 218	8.721 984	8.565 561	23
24	11.469 334	10.528 758	9.706 612	8.984 744	8.818 126	8.656 616	24
25	11.653 583	10.674 776	9.822 580	9.077 040	8.905 329	8.739 019	25
26	11.825 779	10.809 978	9.928 972	9.160 945	8.984 426	8.813 592	26
27	11.986 709	10.935 165	10.026 580	9.237 223	9.056 169	8.881 079	27
28	12.137 111	11.051 078	10.116 128	9.306 567	9.121 241	8.942 153	28
29	12.277 674	11.158 406	10.198 283	9.369 606	9.180 264	8.997 423	29
30	12.409 041	11.257 783	10.273 654	9.426 914	9.233 800	9.047 442	30
31	12.531 814	11.349 799	10.342 802	9.479 013	9.282 358	9.092 707	31
32	12.646 555	11.434 999	10.406 240	9.526 376	9.326 402	9.133 672	32
33	12.753 790	11.513 888	10.464 441	9.569 432	9.366 351	9.170 744	33
34	12.854 009	11.586 934	10.517 835	9.608 575	9.402 586	9.204 293	34
35	12.947 672	11.654 568	10.566 821	9.644 159	9.435 452	9.234 654	35
36	13.035 208	11.717 193	10.611 763	9.676 508	9.465 263	9.262 131	36
37	13.117 017	11.775 179	10.652 993	9.705 917	9.492 302	9.286 996	37
38	13.193 473	11.828 869	10.690 820	9.732 651	9.516 827	9.309 499	38
39	13.264 928	11.878 582	10.725 523	9.756 956	9.539 072	9.329 863	39
40	13.331 709	11.924 613	10.757 360	9.779 051	9.559 249	9.348 292	40
41	13.394 120	11.967 235	10.786 569	9.799 137	9.577 550	9.364 970	41
42	13.452 449	12.006 699	10.813 366	9.817 397	9.594 150	9.380 064	42
43	13.506 962	12.043 240	10.837 950	9.833 998	9.609 206	9.393 723	43
44	13.557 908	12.077 074	10.860 505	9.849 089	9.622 863	9.406 084	44
45	13.605 522	12.108 402	10.881 197	9.862 808	9.635 250	9.417 271	45
46	13.650 020	12.137 409	10.900 181	9.875 280	9.646 485	9.427 394	46
47	13.691 608	12.164 267	10.917 597	9.886 618	9.656 676	9.436 556	47
48	13.730 474	12.189 136	10.933 575	9.896 926	9.665 919	9.444 847	48
49	13.766 799	12.212 163	10.948 234	9.906 296	9.674 303	9.452 350	49
50	13.800 746	12.233 485	10.961 683	9.914 814	9.681 907	9.459 140	50

PRESENT VALUE OF
$1 PER PERIOD

ANNUAL
COMPOUNDING

YRS	10.75% ANNUAL RATE	11.00% ANNUAL RATE	11.25% ANNUAL RATE	11.50% ANNUAL RATE	11.75% ANNUAL RATE	12.00% ANNUAL RATE	YRS
1	0.902 935	0.900 901	0.898 876	0.896 861	0.894 855	0.892 857	1
2	1.718 225	1.712 523	1.706 855	1.701 221	1.695 619	1.690 051	2
3	2.454 380	2.443 715	2.433 128	2.422 619	2.412 187	2.401 831	3
4	3.119 079	3.102 446	3.085 958	3.069 614	3.053 411	3.037 349	4
5	3.719 258	3.695 897	3.672 771	3.649 878	3.627 214	3.604 776	5
6	4.261 181	4.230 538	4.200 244	4.170 294	4.140 684	4.111 407	6
7	4.750 502	4.712 196	4.674 376	4.637 035	4.600 164	4.563 757	7
8	5.192 327	5.146 123	5.100 563	5.055 637	5.011 333	4.967 640	8
9	5.591 266	5.537 048	5.483 652	5.431 064	5.379 269	5.328 250	9
10	5.951 482	5.889 232	5.828 002	5.767 771	5.708 518	5.650 223	10
11	6.276 733	6.206 515	6.137 530	6.069 750	6.003 148	5.937 699	11
12	6.570 414	6.492 356	6.415 757	6.340 583	6.266 799	6.194 374	12
13	6.835 588	6.749 870	6.665 849	6.583 482	6.502 728	6.423 548	13
14	7.075 023	6.981 865	6.890 651	6.801 329	6.713 851	6.628 168	14
15	7.291 217	7.190 870	7.092 720	6.996 708	6.902 775	6.810 864	15
16	7.486 426	7.379 162	7.274 355	7.171 935	7.071 834	6.973 986	16
17	7.662 687	7.548 794	7.437 622	7.329 090	7.223 118	7.119 630	17
18	7.821 840	7.701 617	7.584 380	7.470 036	7.358 495	7.249 670	18
19	7.965 544	7.839 294	7.716 296	7.596 445	7.479 637	7.365 777	19
20	8.095 299	7.963 328	7.834 873	7.709 816	7.588 042	7.469 444	20
21	8.212 460	8.075 070	7.941 459	7.811 494	7.685 049	7.562 003	21
22	8.318 248	8.175 739	8.037 267	7.902 685	7.771 856	7.644 646	22
23	8.413 768	8.266 432	8.123 386	7.984 471	7.849 536	7.718 434	23
24	8.500 016	8.348 137	8.200 796	8.057 822	7.919 048	7.784 316	24
25	8.577 893	8.421 745	8.270 379	8.123 607	7.981 251	7.843 139	25
26	8.648 210	8.488 058	8.332 925	8.182 607	8.036 913	7.895 660	26
27	8.711 702	8.547 800	8.389 146	8.235 522	8.086 723	7.942 554	27
28	8.769 031	8.601 622	8.439 681	8.282 979	8.131 296	7.984 423	28
29	8.820 796	8.650 110	8.485 107	8.325 542	8.171 182	8.021 806	29
30	8.867 536	8.693 793	8.525 939	8.363 715	8.206 874	8.055 184	30
31	8.909 739	8.733 146	8.562 642	8.397 951	8.238 814	8.084 986	31
32	8.947 845	8.768 600	8.595 633	8.428 655	8.267 395	8.111 594	32
33	8.982 253	8.800 541	8.625 288	8.456 193	8.292 971	8.135 352	33
34	9.013 321	8.829 316	8.651 944	8.480 891	8.315 858	8.156 564	34
35	9.041 373	8.855 240	8.675 905	8.503 041	8.336 338	8.175 504	35
36	9.066 703	8.878 594	8.697 443	8.522 907	8.354 665	8.192 414	36
37	9.089 574	8.899 635	8.716 802	8.540 723	8.371 065	8.207 513	37
38	9.110 225	8.918 590	8.734 204	8.556 703	8.385 740	8.220 993	38
39	9.128 871	8.935 666	8.749 847	8.571 034	8.398 873	8.233 030	39
40	9.145 707	8.951 051	8.763 907	8.583 887	8.410 624	8.243 777	40
41	9.160 910	8.964 911	8.776 546	8.595 414	8.421 140	8.253 372	41
42	9.174 636	8.977 397	8.787 906	8.605 753	8.430 551	8.261 939	42
43	9.187 030	8.988 646	8.798 118	8.615 025	8.438 971	8.269 589	43
44	9.198 222	8.998 780	8.807 297	8.623 341	8.446 507	8.276 418	44
45	9.208 327	9.007 910	8.815 548	8.630 799	8.453 250	8.282 516	45
46	9.217 451	9.016 135	8.822 964	8.637 488	8.459 284	8.287 961	46
47	9.225 689	9.023 545	8.829 631	8.643 487	8.464 684	8.292 822	47
48	9.233 128	9.030 221	8.835 623	8.648 867	8.469 516	8.297 163	48
49	9.239 845	9.036 235	8.841 010	8.653 692	8.473 840	8.301 038	49
50	9.245 909	9.041 653	8.845 851	8.658 020	8.477 709	8.304 498	50

PRESENT VALUE OF
$1 PER PERIOD

ANNUAL
COMPOUNDING

YRS	12.25% ANNUAL RATE	12.50% ANNUAL RATE	12.75% ANNUAL RATE	13.00% ANNUAL RATE	13.25% ANNUAL RATE	13.50% ANNUAL RATE	YRS
1	0.890 869	0.888 889	0.886 918	0.884 956	0.883 002	0.881 057	1
2	1.684 515	1.679 012	1.673 541	1.668 102	1.662 695	1.657 319	2
3	2.391 551	2.381 344	2.371 212	2.361 153	2.351 166	2.341 250	3
4	3.021 426	3.005 639	2.989 988	2.974 471	2.959 087	2.943 833	4
5	3.582 562	3.560 568	3.538 792	3.517 231	3.495 882	3.474 743	5
6	4.082 461	4.053 839	4.025 536	3.997 550	3.969 874	3.942 505	6
7	4.527 805	4.492 301	4.457 239	4.422 610	4.388 410	4.354 630	7
8	4.924 547	4.882 045	4.840 123	4.798 770	4.757 978	4.717 735	8
9	5.277 993	5.228 485	5.179 710	5.131 655	5.084 307	5.037 652	9
10	5.592 867	5.536 431	5.480 896	5.426 243	5.372 456	5.319 517	10
11	5.873 378	5.810 161	5.748 023	5.686 941	5.626 893	5.567 857	11
12	6.123 277	6.053 476	5.984 943	5.917 647	5.851 561	5.786 658	12
13	6.345 904	6.269 757	6.195 071	6.121 812	6.049 944	5.979 434	13
14	6.544 235	6.462 006	6.381 438	6.302 488	6.225 116	6.149 281	14
15	6.720 922	6.632 894	6.546 730	6.462 379	6.379 793	6.298 926	15
16	6.878 327	6.784 795	6.693 330	6.603 875	6.516 374	6.430 772	16
17	7.018 554	6.919 818	6.823 353	6.729 093	6.636 975	6.546 936	17
18	7.143 478	7.039 838	6.938 672	6.839 905	6.743 465	6.649 283	18
19	7.254 769	7.146 523	7.040 951	6.937 969	6.837 497	6.739 456	19
20	7.353 914	7.241 353	7.131 664	7.024 752	6.920 527	6.818 904	20
21	7.442 240	7.325 647	7.212 119	7.101 550	6.993 843	6.888 902	21
22	7.520 926	7.400 575	7.283 475	7.169 513	7.058 581	6.950 575	22
23	7.591 026	7.467 178	7.346 763	7.229 658	7.115 745	7.004 912	23
24	7.653 475	7.526 381	7.402 894	7.282 883	7.166 221	7.052 786	24
25	7.709 109	7.579 005	7.452 678	7.329 985	7.210 791	7.094 965	25
26	7.758 672	7.625 782	7.496 832	7.371 668	7.250 146	7.132 128	26
27	7.802 826	7.667 362	7.535 993	7.408 556	7.284 898	7.164 870	27
28	7.842 161	7.704 322	7.570 725	7.441 200	7.315 583	7.193 718	28
29	7.877 204	7.737 175	7.601 530	7.470 088	7.342 678	7.219 135	29
30	7.908 422	7.766 378	7.628 852	7.495 653	7.366 603	7.241 529	30
31	7.936 233	7.792 336	7.653 083	7.518 277	7.387 729	7.261 259	31
32	7.961 010	7.815 410	7.674 575	7.538 299	7.406 383	7.278 642	32
33	7.983 082	7.835 920	7.693 636	7.556 016	7.422 855	7.293 958	33
34	8.002 746	7.854 151	7.710 542	7.571 696	7.437 399	7.307 452	34
35	8.020 263	7.870 356	7.725 536	7.585 572	7.450 242	7.319 341	35
36	8.035 869	7.884 761	7.738 835	7.597 851	7.461 583	7.329 816	36
37	8.049 772	7.897 565	7.750 630	7.608 718	7.471 596	7.339 045	37
38	8.062 158	7.908 947	7.761 091	7.618 334	7.480 438	7.347 176	38
39	8.073 192	7.919 064	7.770 369	7.626 844	7.488 246	7.354 340	39
40	8.083 022	7.928 057	7.778 597	7.634 376	7.495 140	7.360 652	40
41	8.091 779	7.936 051	7.785 896	7.641 040	7.501 227	7.366 213	41
42	8.099 580	7.943 156	7.792 369	7.646 938	7.506 602	7.371 113	42
43	8.106 530	7.949 472	7.798 110	7.652 158	7.511 349	7.375 430	43
44	8.112 722	7.955 086	7.803 202	7.656 777	7.515 540	7.379 233	44
45	8.118 238	7.960 077	7.807 718	7.660 864	7.519 240	7.382 585	45
46	8.123 152	7.964 513	7.811 723	7.664 482	7.522 508	7.385 537	46
47	8.127 529	7.968 456	7.815 275	7.667 683	7.525 393	7.388 138	47
48	8.131 429	7.971 961	7.818 426	7.670 516	7.527 941	7.390 430	48
49	8.134 904	7.975 076	7.821 220	7.673 023	7.530 191	7.392 450	49
50	8.137 999	7.977 845	7.823 699	7.675 242	7.532 177	7.394 229	50

PRESENT VALUE OF
$1 PER PERIOD

ANNUAL
COMPOUNDING

YRS	13.75% ANNUAL RATE	14.00% ANNUAL RATE	14.25% ANNUAL RATE	14.50% ANNUAL RATE	14.75% ANNUAL RATE	15.00% ANNUAL RATE	YRS
1	0.879 121	0.877 193	0.875 274	0.873 362	0.871 460	0.869 565	1
2	1.651 974	1.646 661	1.641 377	1.636 124	1.630 902	1.625 709	2
3	2.331 406	2.321 632	2.311 928	2.302 292	2.292 725	2.283 225	3
4	2.928 709	2.913 712	2.898 843	2.884 098	2.869 477	2.854 978	4
5	3.453 810	3.433 081	3.412 554	3.392 225	3.372 093	3.352 155	5
6	3.915 437	3.888 668	3.862 191	3.836 005	3.810 103	3.784 483	6
7	4.321 263	4.288 305	4.255 747	4.223 585	4.191 811	4.160 420	7
8	4.678 034	4.638 864	4.600 217	4.562 083	4.524 454	4.487 322	8
9	4.991 678	4.946 372	4.901 721	4.857 714	4.814 339	4.771 584	9
10	5.267 409	5.216 116	5.165 620	5.115 908	5.066 962	5.018 769	10
11	5.509 810	5.452 733	5.396 604	5.341 404	5.287 113	5.233 712	11
12	5.722 910	5.660 292	5.598 778	5.538 344	5.478 965	5.420 619	12
13	5.910 251	5.842 362	5.775 736	5.710 344	5.646 157	5.583 147	13
14	6.074 946	6.002 072	5.930 622	5.860 563	5.791 858	5.724 476	14
15	6.219 732	6.142 168	6.066 190	5.991 758	5.918 831	5.847 370	15
16	6.347 018	6.265 060	6.184 849	6.106 339	6.029 482	5.954 235	16
17	6.458 917	6.372 859	6.288 708	6.206 409	6.125 910	6.047 161	17
18	6.557 289	6.467 420	6.379 613	6.293 807	6.209 944	6.127 966	18
19	6.643 771	6.550 369	6.459 180	6.370 137	6.283 175	6.198 231	19
20	6.719 798	6.623 131	6.528 823	6.436 801	6.346 994	6.259 331	20
21	6.786 636	6.686 957	6.589 779	6.495 023	6.402 609	6.312 462	21
22	6.845 394	6.742 944	6.643 133	6.545 871	6.451 075	6.358 663	22
23	6.897 050	6.792 056	6.689 832	6.590 281	6.493 312	6.398 837	23
24	6.942 461	6.835 137	6.730 706	6.629 066	6.530 119	6.433 771	24
25	6.982 384	6.872 927	6.766 482	6.662 940	6.562 195	6.464 149	25
26	7.017 480	6.906 077	6.797 796	6.692 524	6.590 148	6.490 564	26
27	7.048 334	6.935 155	6.825 205	6.718 362	6.614 508	6.513 534	27
28	7.075 459	6.960 662	6.849 195	6.740 927	6.635 737	6.533 508	28
29	7.099 304	6.983 037	6.870 192	6.760 635	6.654 237	6.550 877	29
30	7.120 268	7.002 664	6.888 571	6.777 847	6.670 359	6.565 980	30
31	7.138 697	7.019 881	6.904 657	6.792 880	6.684 409	6.579 113	31
32	7.154 898	7.034 983	6.918 737	6.806 008	6.696 653	6.590 533	32
33	7.169 141	7.048 231	6.931 061	6.817 475	6.707 323	6.600 463	33
34	7.181 663	7.059 852	6.941 848	6.827 489	6.716 621	6.609 099	34
35	7.192 670	7.070 045	6.951 289	6.836 235	6.724 724	6.616 607	35
36	7.202 348	7.078 987	6.959 553	6.843 873	6.731 786	6.623 137	36
37	7.210 855	7.086 831	6.966 786	6.850 544	6.737 940	6.628 815	37
38	7.218 334	7.093 711	6.973 117	6.856 370	6.743 303	6.633 752	38
39	7.224 909	7.099 747	6.978 658	6.861 459	6.747 976	6.638 045	39
40	7.230 689	7.105 041	6.983 508	6.865 903	6.752 049	6.641 778	40
41	7.235 771	7.109 685	6.987 753	6.869 784	6.755 598	6.645 025	41
42	7.240 238	7.113 759	6.991 469	6.873 174	6.758 691	6.647 848	42
43	7.244 165	7.117 332	6.994 721	6.876 135	6.761 387	6.650 302	43
44	7.247 618	7.120 467	6.997 568	6.878 720	6.763 736	6.652 437	44
45	7.250 653	7.123 217	7.000 059	6.880 978	6.765 783	6.654 293	45
46	7.253 321	7.125 629	7.002 240	6.882 950	6.767 567	6.655 907	46
47	7.255 667	7.127 744	7.004 149	6.884 673	6.769 121	6.657 310	47
48	7.257 729	7.129 600	7.005 820	6.886 177	6.770 476	6.658 531	48
49	7.259 542	7.131 228	7.007 282	6.887 491	6.771 657	6.659 592	49
50	7.261 136	7.132 656	7.008 562	6.888 638	6.772 686	6.660 515	50

PRESENT VALUE OF
$1 PER PERIOD

ANNUAL
COMPOUNDING

YRS	15.25% ANNUAL RATE	15.50% ANNUAL RATE	15.75% ANNUAL RATE	16.00% ANNUAL RATE	16.25% ANNUAL RATE	16.50% ANNUAL RATE	YRS
1	0.867 679	0.865 801	0.863 931	0.862 069	0.860 215	0.858 369	1
2	1.620 546	1.615 412	1.610 307	1.605 232	1.600 185	1.595 167	2
3	2.273 792	2.264 426	2.255 125	2.245 890	2.236 718	2.227 611	3
4	2.840 601	2.826 343	2.812 203	2.798 181	2.784 274	2.770 481	4
5	3.332 408	3.312 851	3.293 480	3.274 294	3.255 289	3.236 465	5
6	3.759 140	3.734 070	3.709 270	3.684 736	3.660 464	3.636 450	6
7	4.129 405	4.098 762	4.068 484	4.038 565	4.009 001	3.979 786	7
8	4.450 677	4.414 513	4.378 820	4.343 591	4.308 818	4.274 494	8
9	4.729 438	4.687 890	4.646 929	4.606 544	4.566 725	4.527 463	9
10	4.971 313	4.924 580	4.878 556	4.833 227	4.788 581	4.744 603	10
11	5.181 182	5.129 506	5.078 666	5.028 644	4.979 424	4.930 990	11
12	5.363 282	5.306 932	5.251 547	5.197 107	5.143 591	5.090 978	12
13	5.521 286	5.460 547	5.400 905	5.342 334	5.284 809	5.228 308	13
14	5.658 382	5.593 547	5.529 939	5.467 529	5.406 288	5.346 187	14
15	5.777 338	5.708 699	5.641 416	5.575 456	5.510 785	5.447 371	15
16	5.880 554	5.808 397	5.737 725	5.668 497	5.600 675	5.534 224	16
17	5.970 112	5.894 716	5.820 928	5.748 704	5.678 000	5.608 776	17
18	6.047 819	5.969 451	5.892 811	5.817 848	5.744 516	5.672 769	18
19	6.115 245	6.034 157	5.954 912	5.877 455	5.801 735	5.727 699	19
20	6.173 748	6.090 179	6.008 563	5.928 841	5.850 954	5.774 849	20
21	6.224 510	6.138 683	6.054 914	5.973 139	5.893 294	5.815 321	21
22	6.268 555	6.180 678	6.094 958	6.011 326	5.929 715	5.850 061	22
23	6.306 773	6.217 037	6.129 554	6.044 247	5.961 045	5.879 880	23
24	6.339 933	6.248 517	6.159 442	6.072 627	5.987 996	5.905 477	24
25	6.368 705	6.275 772	6.185 263	6.097 092	6.011 179	5.927 448	25
26	6.393 671	6.299 370	6.207 570	6.118 183	6.031 122	5.946 307	26
27	6.415 332	6.319 801	6.226 843	6.136 364	6.048 277	5.962 495	27
28	6.434 128	6.337 490	6.243 493	6.152 038	6.063 034	5.976 391	28
29	6.450 436	6.352 805	6.257 877	6.165 550	6.075 728	5.988 318	29
30	6.464 587	6.366 065	6.270 304	6.177 198	6.086 648	5.998 557	30
31	6.476 865	6.377 546	6.281 040	6.187 240	6.096 041	6.007 345	31
32	6.487 518	6.387 485	6.290 316	6.195 897	6.104 121	6.014 888	32
33	6.496 762	6.396 091	6.298 329	6.203 359	6.111 072	6.021 363	33
34	6.504 783	6.403 542	6.305 252	6.209 792	6.117 051	6.026 921	34
35	6.511 742	6.409 993	6.311 233	6.215 338	6.122 195	6.031 692	35
36	6.517 781	6.415 579	6.316 400	6.220 119	6.126 619	6.035 787	36
37	6.523 020	6.420 414	6.320 864	6.224 241	6.130 425	6.039 302	37
38	6.527 566	6.424 601	6.324 720	6.227 794	6.133 699	6.042 320	38
39	6.531 511	6.428 226	6.328 052	6.230 857	6.136 515	6.044 909	39
40	6.534 933	6.431 365	6.330 930	6.233 497	6.138 938	6.047 133	40
41	6.537 903	6.434 082	6.333 417	6.235 773	6.141 022	6.049 041	41
42	6.540 480	6.436 435	6.335 566	6.237 736	6.142 814	6.050 679	42
43	6.542 716	6.438 471	6.337 422	6.239 427	6.144 357	6.052 085	43
44	6.544 656	6.440 235	6.339 025	6.240 886	6.145 683	6.053 292	44
45	6.546 339	6.441 762	6.340 411	6.242 143	6.146 824	6.054 328	45
46	6.547 800	6.443 084	6.341 607	6.243 227	6.147 806	6.055 217	46
47	6.549 067	6.444 229	6.342 641	6.244 161	6.148 650	6.055 980	47
48	6.550 167	6.445 219	6.343 535	6.244 966	6.149 376	6.056 635	48
49	6.551 121	6.446 077	6.344 306	6.245 661	6.150 001	6.057 198	49
50	6.551 949	6.446 820	6.344 973	6.246 259	6.150 539	6.057 680	50

PRESENT VALUE OF
$1 PER PERIOD

YRS	16.75% ANNUAL RATE	17.00% ANNUAL RATE	17.25% ANNUAL RATE	17.50% ANNUAL RATE	17.75% ANNUAL RATE	18.00% ANNUAL RATE	YRS
1	0.856 531	0.854 701	0.852 878	0.851 064	0.849 257	0.847 458	1
2	1.590 176	1.585 214	1.580 280	1.575 373	1.570 494	1.565 642	2
3	2.218 567	2.209 585	2.200 665	2.191 807	2.183 010	2.174 273	3
4	2.756 802	2.743 235	2.729 779	2.716 432	2.703 193	2.690 062	4
5	3.217 818	3.199 346	3.181 048	3.162 921	3.144 962	3.127 171	5
6	3.612 692	3.589 185	3.565 926	3.542 911	3.520 138	3.497 603	6
7	3.950 914	3.922 380	3.894 180	3.866 307	3.838 758	3.811 528	7
8	4.240 611	4.207 163	4.174 140	4.141 538	4.109 349	4.077 566	8
9	4.488 746	4.450 566	4.412 913	4.375 777	4.339 150	4.303 022	9
10	4.701 282	4.658 604	4.616 557	4.575 129	4.534 310	4.494 086	10
11	4.883 325	4.836 413	4.790 240	4.744 791	4.700 051	4.656 005	11
12	5.039 250	4.988 387	4.938 371	4.889 184	4.840 807	4.793 225	12
13	5.172 805	5.118 280	5.064 709	5.012 071	4.960 346	4.909 513	13
14	5.287 200	5.229 299	5.172 460	5.116 657	5.061 865	5.008 062	14
15	5.385 182	5.324 187	5.264 358	5.205 665	5.148 081	5.091 578	15
16	5.469 106	5.405 288	5.342 736	5.281 417	5.221 300	5.162 354	16
17	5.540 990	5.474 605	5.409 583	5.345 887	5.283 482	5.222 334	17
18	5.602 561	5.533 851	5.466 595	5.400 755	5.336 290	5.273 164	18
19	5.655 299	5.584 488	5.515 220	5.447 451	5.381 138	5.316 241	19
20	5.700 470	5.627 767	5.556 691	5.487 192	5.419 226	5.352 746	20
21	5.739 161	5.664 758	5.592 060	5.521 015	5.451 572	5.383 683	21
22	5.772 300	5.696 375	5.622 226	5.549 800	5.479 042	5.409 901	22
23	5.800 686	5.723 397	5.647 954	5.574 298	5.502 371	5.432 120	23
24	5.824 998	5.746 493	5.669 897	5.595 147	5.522 183	5.450 949	24
25	5.845 823	5.766 234	5.688 611	5.612 891	5.539 009	5.466 906	25
26	5.863 660	5.783 106	5.704 573	5.627 992	5.553 299	5.480 429	26
27	5.878 938	5.797 526	5.718 186	5.640 845	5.565 434	5.491 889	27
28	5.892 024	5.809 851	5.729 796	5.651 783	5.575 740	5.501 601	28
29	5.903 232	5.820 386	5.739 698	5.661 092	5.584 493	5.509 831	29
30	5.912 833	5.829 390	5.748 143	5.669 014	5.591 926	5.516 806	30
31	5.921 056	5.837 085	5.755 346	5.675 757	5.598 239	5.522 717	31
32	5.928 099	5.843 663	5.761 489	5.681 495	5.603 600	5.527 726	32
33	5.934 132	5.849 284	5.766 729	5.686 379	5.608 153	5.531 971	33
34	5.939 300	5.854 089	5.771 197	5.690 535	5.612 019	5.535 569	34
35	5.943 726	5.858 196	5.775 008	5.694 072	5.615 303	5.538 618	35
36	5.947 517	5.861 706	5.778 259	5.697 083	5.618 092	5.541 201	36
37	5.950 764	5.864 706	5.781 031	5.699 645	5.620 460	5.543 391	37
38	5.953 545	5.867 270	5.783 395	5.701 826	5.622 471	5.545 247	38
39	5.955 927	5.869 461	5.785 412	5.703 681	5.624 179	5.546 819	39
40	5.957 968	5.871 335	5.787 131	5.705 261	5.625 630	5.548 152	40
41	5.959 715	5.872 936	5.788 598	5.706 605	5.626 862	5.549 281	41
42	5.961 212	5.874 304	5.789 849	5.707 749	5.627 908	5.550 238	42
43	5.962 494	5.875 473	5.790 916	5.708 722	5.628 797	5.551 049	43
44	5.963 593	5.876 473	5.791 826	5.709 551	5.629 552	5.551 737	44
45	5.964 533	5.877 327	5.792 602	5.710 256	5.630 192	5.552 319	45
46	5.965 339	5.878 058	5.793 264	5.710 856	5.630 737	5.552 813	46
47	5.966 029	5.878 682	5.793 829	5.711 367	5.631 199	5.553 231	47
48	5.966 620	5.879 215	5.794 310	5.711 802	5.631 591	5.553 586	48
49	5.967 127	5.879 671	5.794 721	5.712 172	5.631 925	5.553 886	49
50	5.967 560	5.880 061	5.795 071	5.712 487	5.632 208	5.554 141	50

PRESENT VALUE OF
$1 PER PERIOD

ANNUAL
COMPOUNDING

YRS	18.25% ANNUAL RATE	18.50% ANNUAL RATE	18.75% ANNUAL RATE	19.00% ANNUAL RATE	19.25% ANNUAL RATE	19.50% ANNUAL RATE	YRS
1	0.845 666	0.843 882	0.842 105	0.840 336	0.838 574	0.836 820	1
2	1.560 817	1.556 018	1.551 247	1.546 501	1.541 781	1.537 088	2
3	2.165 596	2.156 978	2.148 418	2.139 917	2.131 473	2.123 086	3
4	2.677 037	2.664 116	2.651 299	2.638 586	2.625 973	2.613 461	4
5	3.109 545	3.092 081	3.074 779	3.057 635	3.040 648	3.023 817	5
6	3.475 302	3.453 233	3.431 392	3.409 777	3.388 384	3.367 211	6
7	3.784 611	3.758 003	3.731 699	3.705 695	3.679 987	3.654 570	7
8	4.046 182	4.015 192	3.984 589	3.954 366	3.924 517	3.895 037	8
9	4.267 385	4.232 230	4.197 548	4.163 332	4.129 574	4.096 266	9
10	4.454 448	4.415 384	4.376 883	4.338 935	4.301 530	4.264 657	10
11	4.612 641	4.569 944	4.527 901	4.486 500	4.445 727	4.405 571	11
12	4.746 419	4.700 375	4.655 075	4.610 504	4.566 648	4.523 490	12
13	4.859 551	4.810 443	4.762 168	4.714 709	4.668 048	4.622 168	13
14	4.955 223	4.903 327	4.852 352	4.802 277	4.753 080	4.704 743	14
15	5.036 129	4.981 711	4.928 297	4.875 863	4.824 386	4.773 843	15
16	5.104 549	5.047 857	4.992 250	4.937 700	4.884 181	4.831 668	16
17	5.162 409	5.103 677	5.046 105	4.989 664	4.934 324	4.880 057	17
18	5.211 340	5.150 782	5.091 457	5.033 331	4.976 372	4.920 550	18
19	5.252 719	5.190 534	5.129 648	5.070 026	5.011 633	4.954 435	19
20	5.287 711	5.224 079	5.161 809	5.100 862	5.041 202	4.982 791	20
21	5.317 304	5.252 387	5.188 892	5.126 775	5.065 997	5.006 519	21
22	5.342 329	5.276 276	5.211 698	5.148 550	5.086 790	5.026 376	22
23	5.363 491	5.296 436	5.230 904	5.166 849	5.104 226	5.042 993	23
24	5.381 388	5.313 448	5.247 077	5.182 226	5.118 848	5.056 898	24
25	5.396 523	5.327 804	5.260 696	5.195 148	5.131 110	5.068 534	25
26	5.409 322	5.339 919	5.272 165	5.206 007	5.141 392	5.078 271	26
27	5.420 145	5.350 143	5.281 823	5.215 132	5.150 014	5.086 419	27
28	5.429 298	5.358 770	5.289 957	5.222 800	5.157 244	5.093 238	28
29	5.437 039	5.366 051	5.296 806	5.229 243	5.163 308	5.098 944	29
30	5.443 584	5.372 195	5.302 573	5.234 658	5.168 392	5.103 719	30
31	5.449 120	5.377 380	5.307 430	5.239 209	5.172 656	5.107 714	31
32	5.453 801	5.381 755	5.311 520	5.243 033	5.176 231	5.111 058	32
33	5.457 760	5.385 447	5.314 964	5.246 246	5.179 230	5.113 856	33
34	5.461 108	5.388 563	5.317 865	5.248 946	5.181 744	5.116 198	34
35	5.463 939	5.391 192	5.320 307	5.251 215	5.183 852	5.118 157	35
36	5.466 333	5.393 411	5.322 364	5.253 122	5.185 620	5.119 797	36
37	5.468 358	5.395 284	5.324 096	5.254 724	5.187 103	5.121 169	37
38	5.470 070	5.396 864	5.325 554	5.256 071	5.188 346	5.122 317	38
39	5.471 518	5.398 197	5.326 783	5.257 202	5.189 389	5.123 278	39
40	5.472 743	5.399 323	5.327 817	5.258 153	5.190 263	5.124 082	40
41	5.473 778	5.400 272	5.328 688	5.258 952	5.190 997	5.124 755	41
42	5.474 654	5.401 074	5.329 421	5.259 624	5.191 611	5.125 318	42
43	5.475 394	5.401 750	5.330 039	5.260 188	5.192 127	5.125 789	43
44	5.476 021	5.402 321	5.330 559	5.260 662	5.192 559	5.126 183	44
45	5.476 550	5.402 802	5.330 997	5.261 061	5.192 922	5.126 513	45
46	5.476 998	5.403 209	5.331 366	5.261 396	5.193 226	5.126 789	46
47	5.477 377	5.403 552	5.331 677	5.261 677	5.193 481	5.127 020	47
48	5.477 697	5.403 841	5.331 938	5.261 913	5.193 695	5.127 214	48
49	5.477 968	5.404 085	5.332 159	5.262 112	5.193 874	5.127 375	49
50	5.478 197	5.404 291	5.332 344	5.262 279	5.194 024	5.127 511	50

PRESENT VALUE OF
$1 PER PERIOD

YRS	19.75% ANNUAL RATE	20.00% ANNUAL RATE	21.00% ANNUAL RATE	22.00% ANNUAL RATE	23.00% ANNUAL RATE	24.00% ANNUAL RATE	YRS
1	0.835 073	0.833 333	0.826 446	0.819 672	0.813 008	0.806 452	1
2	1.532 420	1.527 778	1.509 460	1.491 535	1.473 990	1.456 816	2
3	2.114 756	2.106 481	2.073 934	2.042 241	2.011 374	1.981 303	3
4	2.601 049	2.588 735	2.540 441	2.493 641	2.448 272	2.404 277	4
5	3.007 139	2.990 612	2.925 984	2.863 640	2.803 473	2.745 384	5
6	3.346 254	3.325 510	3.244 615	3.166 918	3.092 254	3.020 471	6
7	3.629 439	3.604 592	3.507 946	3.415 506	3.327 036	3.242 316	7
8	3.865 920	3.837 160	3.725 576	3.619 268	3.517 916	3.421 222	8
9	4.063 399	4.030 967	3.905 434	3.786 285	3.673 102	3.565 502	9
10	4.228 308	4.192 472	4.054 078	3.923 184	3.799 270	3.681 856	10
11	4.366 019	4.327 060	4.176 924	4.035 397	3.901 846	3.775 691	11
12	4.481 018	4.439 217	4.278 450	4.127 375	3.985 240	3.851 363	12
13	4.577 051	4.532 681	4.362 355	4.202 766	4.053 041	3.912 390	13
14	4.657 245	4.610 567	4.431 698	4.264 562	4.108 163	3.961 605	14
15	4.724 213	4.675 473	4.489 007	4.315 215	4.152 978	4.001 294	15
16	4.780 136	4.729 561	4.536 369	4.356 734	4.189 413	4.033 302	16
17	4.826 836	4.774 634	4.575 512	4.390 765	4.219 035	4.059 114	17
18	4.865 834	4.812 195	4.607 861	4.418 660	4.243 118	4.079 931	18
19	4.898 400	4.843 496	4.634 596	4.441 525	4.262 698	4.096 718	19
20	4.925 595	4.869 580	4.656 691	4.460 266	4.278 616	4.110 257	20
21	4.948 305	4.891 316	4.674 951	4.475 628	4.291 558	4.121 175	21
22	4.967 269	4.909 430	4.690 042	4.488 220	4.302 079	4.129 980	22
23	4.983 106	4.924 525	4.702 514	4.498 541	4.310 634	4.137 080	23
24	4.996 330	4.937 104	4.712 822	4.507 001	4.317 588	4.142 807	24
25	5.007 374	4.947 587	4.721 340	4.513 935	4.323 243	4.147 425	25
26	5.016 596	4.956 323	4.728 380	4.519 619	4.327 839	4.151 149	26
27	5.024 297	4.963 602	4.734 199	4.524 278	4.331 577	4.154 152	27
28	5.030 729	4.969 668	4.739 007	4.528 096	4.334 615	4.156 575	28
29	5.036 099	4.974 724	4.742 981	4.531 227	4.337 086	4.158 528	29
30	5.040 584	4.978 936	4.746 265	4.533 792	4.339 094	4.160 103	30
31	5.044 329	4.982 447	4.748 980	4.535 895	4.340 727	4.161 373	31
32	5.047 456	4.985 372	4.751 223	4.537 619	4.342 054	4.162 398	32
33	5.050 068	4.987 810	4.753 077	4.539 032	4.343 134	4.163 224	33
34	5.052 249	4.989 842	4.754 609	4.540 190	4.344 011	4.163 890	34
35	5.054 070	4.991 535	4.755 875	4.541 140	4.344 724	4.164 428	35
36	5.055 591	4.992 946	4.756 922	4.541 918	4.345 304	4.164 861	36
37	5.056 861	4.994 122	4.757 786	4.542 555	4.345 776	4.165 211	37
38	5.057 921	4.995 101	4.758 501	4.543 078	4.346 159	4.165 492	38
39	5.058 807	4.995 918	4.759 092	4.543 507	4.346 471	4.165 720	39
40	5.059 546	4.996 598	4.759 580	4.543 858	4.346 724	4.165 903	40
41	5.060 164	4.997 165	4.759 984	4.544 146	4.346 930	4.166 051	41
42	5.060 680	4.997 638	4.760 317	4.544 382	4.347 098	4.166 170	42
43	5.061 110	4.998 031	4.760 593	4.544 575	4.347 234	4.166 266	43
44	5.061 470	4.998 359	4.760 820	4.544 734	4.347 345	4.166 344	44
45	5.061 770	4.998 633	4.761 008	4.544 864	4.347 435	4.166 406	45
46	5.062 021	4.998 861	4.761 164	4.544 970	4.347 508	4.166 457	46
47	5.062 231	4.999 051	4.761 293	4.545 058	4.347 567	4.166 497	47
48	5.062 406	4.999 209	4.761 399	4.545 129	4.347 616	4.166 530	48
49	5.062 552	4.999 341	4.761 487	4.545 188	4.347 655	4.166 556	49
50	5.062 674	4.999 451	4.761 559	4.545 236	4.347 687	4.166 578	50

Section 6.   Partial Payment to Amortize $1.00:

These factors represent the regular and equal payment necessary to be made at the end of each period that will repay both the interest on a loan and the original loan amount. There can be no additional withdrawals or changes in the regular (equal) payments.

In this section the following four (4) periods are presented in detail: monthly, quarterly, semiannual, and annual.

Monthly:

The factors presented on pages 148 through 155 indicate the amount of the monthly payment necessary to repay a loan and the interest. The interest is being charged at the end of each month. This is interest on the entire balance of the loan for one month (or 30 days) plus an amount of money to repay the loan.

Example K

You have a loan for $30,000.00 at 9% interest, to be repaid in 20 years. What is the monthly payment?

Turn to page 148 and locate the 9.0% interest rate column. Proceed down that column until you locate the point where the 20 year row intersects the 9.0% interest column. The number is 0.008997. Now multiply 0.008997 by $30,000.00 to get the answer of $269.91. What is the quarterly payment?

Turn to page 156 and locate the 9.0% interest column. Proceed down that column until you locate the point where the 20 years row intersects the 9.0% interest column. The number is 0.027064. Now multiply 0.027064 by $30,000.00 to get the answer $811.92. What is the semiannual payment?

Turn to page 162 and locate the 9.0% interest column. Proceed down that column until you locate the point where the 40 semi-year row intersects the 9.0% interest column. The number is 0.054343. Then, multiply 0.054343 by $30,000.00 to get the answer $1630.29.

146

What is the annual payment?

Turn to page 166 and locate the 9.0% interest column. Proceed down that column until you locate the point where the 20 year row intersects the 9.0% interest column. The number is 0.109546. Now multiply 0.109546 by $30,000.00 to get the answer $3,286.38.

For your interest, here's the formula . . .

$$\frac{1}{a_{\overline{n}|}} = \frac{i}{1 - V^n}$$

$a_{\overline{n}|}$ = Present value of $1 per period
i = interest rate per period
V^n = Present value of $1
n = number of compounding periods
$\frac{1}{a_{\overline{n}|}}$ = Partial payment to amortize $1

PARTIAL PAYMENT
TO AMORTIZE $1

MOS	7.00% ANNUAL RATE	8.00% ANNUAL RATE	9.00% ANNUAL RATE	10.00% ANNUAL RATE	10.25% ANNUAL RATE	10.50% ANNUAL RATE	MOS
1	1.005 833	1.006 667	1.007 500	1.008 333	1.008 542	1.008 750	1
2	0.504 379	0.505 006	0.505 632	0.506 259	0.506 415	0.506 572	2
3	0.337 230	0.337 788	0.338 346	0.338 904	0.339 044	0.339 184	3
4	0.253 656	0.254 181	0.254 705	0.255 230	0.255 361	0.255 493	4
5	0.203 514	0.204 018	0.204 522	0.205 028	0.205 154	0.205 280	5
6	0.170 086	0.170 577	0.171 069	0.171 561	0.171 685	0.171 808	6
7	0.146 210	0.146 692	0.147 175	0.147 659	0.147 780	0.147 901	7
8	0.128 304	0.128 779	0.129 256	0.129 733	0.129 852	0.129 972	8
9	0.114 377	0.114 848	0.115 319	0.115 792	0.115 910	0.116 029	9
10	0.103 236	0.103 703	0.104 171	0.104 640	0.104 758	0.104 875	10
11	0.094 122	0.094 586	0.095 051	0.095 517	0.095 634	0.095 751	11
12	0.086 527	0.086 988	0.087 451	0.087 916	0.088 032	0.088 149	12
13	0.080 101	0.080 561	0.081 022	0.081 485	0.081 601	0.081 717	13
14	0.074 593	0.075 051	0.075 511	0.075 973	0.076 089	0.076 205	14
15	0.069 820	0.070 277	0.070 736	0.071 197	0.071 313	0.071 428	15
16	0.065 644	0.066 100	0.066 559	0.067 019	0.067 134	0.067 250	16
17	0.061 960	0.062 415	0.062 873	0.063 333	0.063 448	0.063 563	17
18	0.058 685	0.059 140	0.059 598	0.060 057	0.060 172	0.060 288	18
19	0.055 755	0.056 210	0.056 667	0.057 127	0.057 242	0.057 357	19
20	0.053 119	0.053 574	0.054 031	0.054 490	0.054 605	0.054 720	20
21	0.050 734	0.051 188	0.051 645	0.052 105	0.052 220	0.052 335	21
22	0.048 566	0.049 020	0.049 477	0.049 937	0.050 052	0.050 168	22
23	0.046 587	0.047 041	0.047 498	0.047 958	0.048 074	0.048 189	23
24	0.044 773	0.045 227	0.045 685	0.046 145	0.046 260	0.046 376	24
25	0.043 104	0.043 559	0.044 016	0.044 477	0.044 593	0.044 708	25
26	0.041 564	0.042 019	0.042 477	0.042 938	0.043 054	0.043 170	26
27	0.040 138	0.040 593	0.041 052	0.041 513	0.041 629	0.041 745	27
28	0.038 814	0.039 270	0.039 729	0.040 191	0.040 307	0.040 423	28
29	0.037 582	0.038 038	0.038 497	0.038 960	0.039 076	0.039 192	29
30	0.036 432	0.036 888	0.037 348	0.037 811	0.037 928	0.038 044	30
31	0.035 356	0.035 813	0.036 274	0.036 737	0.036 854	0.036 971	31
32	0.034 348	0.034 805	0.035 266	0.035 731	0.035 848	0.035 965	32
33	0.033 401	0.033 859	0.034 320	0.034 786	0.034 903	0.035 020	33
34	0.032 510	0.032 968	0.033 431	0.033 896	0.034 014	0.034 131	34
35	0.031 670	0.032 129	0.032 592	0.033 058	0.033 176	0.033 293	35
36	0.030 877	0.031 336	0.031 800	0.032 267	0.032 385	0.032 502	36
37	0.030 127	0.030 587	0.031 051	0.031 519	0.031 637	0.031 755	37
38	0.029 416	0.029 877	0.030 342	0.030 811	0.030 929	0.031 047	38
39	0.028 743	0.029 204	0.029 669	0.030 139	0.030 257	0.030 375	39
40	0.028 103	0.028 564	0.029 030	0.029 501	0.029 619	0.029 738	40
41	0.027 494	0.027 956	0.028 423	0.028 894	0.029 013	0.029 132	41
42	0.026 914	0.027 377	0.027 845	0.028 317	0.028 436	0.028 555	42
43	0.026 362	0.026 825	0.027 293	0.027 767	0.027 886	0.028 005	43
44	0.025 834	0.026 298	0.026 768	0.027 242	0.027 361	0.027 480	44
45	0.025 331	0.025 795	0.026 265	0.026 740	0.026 860	0.026 979	45
46	0.024 849	0.025 314	0.025 785	0.026 261	0.026 380	0.026 501	46
47	0.024 388	0.024 854	0.025 325	0.025 802	0.025 922	0.026 042	47

YRS							
4	0.023 946	0.024 413	0.024 885	0.025 363	0.025 483	0.025 603	48
5	0.019 801	0.020 276	0.020 758	0.021 247	0.021 370	0.021 494	60
6	0.017 049	0.017 533	0.018 026	0.018 526	0.018 652	0.018 779	72
7	0.015 093	0.015 586	0.016 089	0.016 601	0.016 731	0.016 861	84
8	0.013 634	0.014 137	0.014 650	0.015 174	0.015 307	0.015 440	96
9	0.012 506	0.013 019	0.013 543	0.014 079	0.014 214	0.014 351	108
10	0.011 611	0.012 133	0.012 668	0.013 215	0.013 354	0.013 493	120
11	0.010 884	0.011 415	0.011 961	0.012 520	0.012 662	0.012 804	132
12	0.010 284	0.010 825	0.011 380	0.011 951	0.012 096	0.012 241	144
13	0.009 781	0.010 331	0.010 897	0.011 478	0.011 626	0.011 775	156
14	0.009 354	0.009 913	0.010 489	0.011 082	0.011 233	0.011 384	168
15	0.008 988	0.009 557	0.010 143	0.010 746	0.010 900	0.011 054	180
16	0.008 672	0.009 249	0.009 845	0.010 459	0.010 615	0.010 772	192
17	0.008 397	0.008 983	0.009 588	0.010 212	0.010 371	0.010 531	204
18	0.008 155	0.008 750	0.009 364	0.009 998	0.010 160	0.010 322	216
19	0.007 942	0.008 545	0.009 169	0.009 813	0.009 976	0.010 141	228
20	0.007 753	0.008 364	0.008 997	0.009 650	0.009 816	0.009 984	240
21	0.007 585	0.008 204	0.008 846	0.009 508	0.009 676	0.009 846	252
22	0.007 434	0.008 062	0.008 712	0.009 382	0.009 553	0.009 725	264
23	0.007 299	0.007 935	0.008 593	0.009 272	0.009 445	0.009 619	276
24	0.007 178	0.007 821	0.008 487	0.009 174	0.009 349	0.009 525	288
25	0.007 068	0.007 718	0.008 392	0.009 087	0.009 264	0.009 442	300
26	0.006 968	0.007 626	0.008 307	0.009 010	0.009 188	0.009 368	312
27	0.006 878	0.007 543	0.008 231	0.008 941	0.009 121	0.009 303	324
28	0.006 796	0.007 468	0.008 163	0.008 880	0.009 062	0.009 245	336
29	0.006 721	0.007 399	0.008 102	0.008 825	0.009 009	0.009 193	348
30	0.006 653	0.007 338	0.008 046	0.008 776	0.008 961	0.009 147	360

PARTIAL PAYMENT
TO AMORTIZE $1

MONTHLY
COMPOUNDING

MOS	10.75% ANNUAL RATE	11.00% ANNUAL RATE	11.25% ANNUAL RATE	11.50% ANNUAL RATE	11.75% ANNUAL RATE	12.00% ANNUAL RATE	MOS
1	1.008 958	1.009 167	1.009 375	1.009 583	1.009 792	1.010 000	1
2	0.506 729	0.506 885	0.507 042	0.507 199	0.507 356	0.507 512	2
3	0.339 323	0.339 463	0.339 603	0.339 743	0.339 882	0.340 022	3
4	0.255 624	0.255 755	0.255 887	0.256 018	0.256 150	0.256 281	4
5	0.205 407	0.205 533	0.205 660	0.205 787	0.205 913	0.206 040	5
6	0.171 931	0.172 055	0.172 178	0.172 301	0.172 425	0.172 548	6
7	0.148 022	0.148 143	0.148 264	0.148 386	0.148 507	0.148 628	7
8	0.130 091	0.130 211	0.130 331	0.130 451	0.130 570	0.130 690	8
9	0.116 147	0.116 266	0.116 384	0.116 503	0.116 622	0.116 740	9
10	0.104 993	0.105 111	0.105 228	0.105 346	0.105 464	0.105 582	10
11	0.095 868	0.095 985	0.096 102	0.096 219	0.096 337	0.096 454	11
12	0.088 265	0.088 382	0.088 498	0.088 615	0.088 732	0.088 849	12
13	0.081 833	0.081 949	0.082 065	0.082 182	0.082 298	0.082 415	13
14	0.076 320	0.076 436	0.076 552	0.076 669	0.076 785	0.076 901	14
15	0.071 544	0.071 660	0.071 775	0.071 891	0.072 008	0.072 124	15
16	0.067 365	0.067 481	0.067 597	0.067 712	0.067 828	0.067 945	16
17	0.063 679	0.063 795	0.063 910	0.064 026	0.064 142	0.064 258	17
18	0.060 403	0.060 519	0.060 634	0.060 750	0.060 866	0.060 982	18
19	0.057 473	0.057 588	0.057 704	0.057 820	0.057 936	0.058 052	19
20	0.054 836	0.054 951	0.055 067	0.055 183	0.055 299	0.055 415	20
21	0.052 451	0.052 567	0.052 682	0.052 798	0.052 914	0.053 031	21
22	0.050 283	0.050 399	0.050 515	0.050 631	0.050 747	0.050 864	22
23	0.048 305	0.048 421	0.048 537	0.048 653	0.048 769	0.048 886	23
24	0.046 492	0.046 608	0.046 724	0.046 840	0.046 957	0.047 073	24
25	0.044 824	0.044 940	0.045 057	0.045 173	0.045 290	0.045 407	25
26	0.043 286	0.043 402	0.043 518	0.043 635	0.043 752	0.043 869	26
27	0.041 861	0.041 978	0.042 095	0.042 211	0.042 328	0.042 446	27
28	0.040 539	0.040 656	0.040 773	0.040 890	0.041 007	0.041 124	28
29	0.039 309	0.039 426	0.039 543	0.039 660	0.039 777	0.039 895	29
30	0.038 161	0.038 278	0.038 395	0.038 513	0.038 630	0.038 748	30
31	0.037 088	0.037 205	0.037 322	0.037 440	0.037 558	0.037 676	31
32	0.036 082	0.036 199	0.036 317	0.036 435	0.036 553	0.036 671	32
33	0.035 137	0.035 255	0.035 373	0.035 491	0.035 609	0.035 727	33
34	0.034 248	0.034 366	0.034 484	0.034 603	0.034 721	0.034 840	34
35	0.033 411	0.033 529	0.033 647	0.033 766	0.033 885	0.034 004	35
36	0.032 620	0.032 739	0.032 857	0.032 976	0.033 095	0.033 214	36
37	0.031 873	0.031 991	0.032 110	0.032 229	0.032 349	0.032 468	37
38	0.031 165	0.031 284	0.031 403	0.031 522	0.031 642	0.031 761	38
39	0.030 494	0.030 613	0.030 732	0.030 852	0.030 972	0.031 092	39
40	0.029 857	0.029 976	0.030 095	0.030 215	0.030 335	0.030 456	40
41	0.029 251	0.029 370	0.029 490	0.029 610	0.029 730	0.029 851	41
42	0.028 674	0.028 794	0.028 914	0.029 034	0.029 155	0.029 276	42
43	0.028 125	0.028 245	0.028 365	0.028 485	0.028 606	0.028 727	43
44	0.027 600	0.027 720	0.027 841	0.027 962	0.028 083	0.028 204	44
45	0.027 100	0.027 220	0.027 341	0.027 462	0.027 583	0.027 705	45
46	0.026 621	0.026 742	0.026 863	0.026 984	0.027 106	0.027 228	46
47	0.026 163	0.026 284	0.026 405	0.026 527	0.026 649	0.026 771	47

YRS							
4	0.025 724	0.025 846	0.025 967	0.026 089	0.026 211	0.026 334	48
5	0.021 618	0.021 742	0.021 867	0.021 993	0.022 118	0.022 244	60
6	0.018 906	0.019 034	0.019 162	0.019 291	0.019 420	0.019 550	72
7	0.016 991	0.017 122	0.017 254	0.017 386	0.017 519	0.017 653	84
8	0.015 574	0.015 708	0.015 844	0.015 979	0.016 116	0.016 253	96
9	0.014 488	0.014 626	0.014 764	0.014 904	0.015 044	0.015 184	108
10	0.013 634	0.013 775	0.013 917	0.014 060	0.014 203	0.014 347	120
11	0.012 948	0.013 092	0.013 238	0.013 384	0.013 530	0.013 678	132
12	0.012 388	0.012 536	0.012 684	0.012 833	0.012 983	0.013 134	144
13	0.011 925	0.012 075	0.012 227	0.012 379	0.012 532	0.012 687	156
14	0.011 537	0.011 691	0.011 845	0.012 001	0.012 157	0.012 314	168
15	0.011 209	0.011 366	0.011 523	0.011 682	0.011 841	0.012 002	180
16	0.010 931	0.011 090	0.011 250	0.011 412	0.011 574	0.011 737	192
17	0.010 692	0.010 854	0.011 017	0.011 181	0.011 346	0.011 512	204
18	0.010 486	0.010 650	0.010 816	0.010 983	0.011 151	0.011 320	216
19	0.010 307	0.010 475	0.010 643	0.010 812	0.010 983	0.011 154	228
20	0.010 152	0.010 322	0.010 493	0.010 664	0.010 837	0.011 011	240
21	0.010 017	0.010 189	0.010 362	0.010 536	0.010 711	0.010 887	252
22	0.009 898	0.010 072	0.010 247	0.010 424	0.010 601	0.010 779	264
23	0.009 794	0.009 970	0.010 147	0.010 326	0.010 505	0.010 686	276
24	0.009 702	0.009 880	0.010 060	0.010 240	0.010 421	0.010 604	288
25	0.009 621	0.009 801	0.009 982	0.010 165	0.010 348	0.010 532	300
26	0.009 549	0.009 731	0.009 914	0.010 098	0.010 284	0.010 470	312
27	0.009 486	0.009 670	0.009 854	0.010 040	0.010 227	0.010 414	324
28	0.009 429	0.009 615	0.009 801	0.009 989	0.010 177	0.010 366	336
29	0.009 379	0.009 566	0.009 754	0.009 943	0.010 133	0.010 324	348
30	0.009 335	0.009 523	0.009 713	0.009 903	0.010 094	0.010 286	360

PARTIAL PAYMENT
TO AMORTIZE $1

MOS	12.25% ANNUAL RATE	12.50% ANNUAL RATE	12.75% ANNUAL RATE	13.00% ANNUAL RATE	13.25% ANNUAL RATE	13.50% ANNUAL RATE	MOS
1	1.010 208	1.010 417	1.010 625	1.010 833	1.011 042	1.011 250	1
2	0.507 669	0.507 826	0.507 983	0.508 140	0.508 296	0.508 453	2
3	0.340 162	0.340 302	0.340 442	0.340 581	0.340 721	0.340 861	3
4	0.256 413	0.256 544	0.256 676	0.256 807	0.256 939	0.257 071	4
5	0.206 166	0.206 293	0.206 420	0.206 547	0.206 673	0.206 800	5
6	0.172 672	0.172 796	0.172 919	0.173 043	0.173 167	0.173 290	6
7	0.148 750	0.148 871	0.148 993	0.149 114	0.149 236	0.149 358	7
8	0.130 810	0.130 930	0.131 050	0.131 170	0.131 290	0.131 411	8
9	0.116 859	0.116 978	0.117 097	0.117 216	0.117 335	0.117 454	9
10	0.105 700	0.105 818	0.105 936	0.106 055	0.106 173	0.106 291	10
11	0.096 572	0.096 689	0.096 807	0.096 924	0.097 042	0.097 160	11
12	0.088 966	0.089 083	0.089 200	0.089 317	0.089 435	0.089 552	12
13	0.082 531	0.082 648	0.082 765	0.082 882	0.082 999	0.083 116	13
14	0.077 018	0.077 134	0.077 251	0.077 368	0.077 484	0.077 601	14
15	0.072 240	0.072 357	0.072 473	0.072 590	0.072 706	0.072 823	15
16	0.068 061	0.068 177	0.068 294	0.068 410	0.068 527	0.068 644	16
17	0.064 374	0.064 491	0.064 607	0.064 724	0.064 840	0.064 957	17
18	0.061 098	0.061 215	0.061 331	0.061 448	0.061 564	0.061 681	18
19	0.058 168	0.058 284	0.058 401	0.058 518	0.058 634	0.058 751	19
20	0.055 532	0.055 648	0.055 765	0.055 881	0.055 998	0.056 115	20
21	0.053 147	0.053 264	0.053 380	0.053 497	0.053 614	0.053 731	21
22	0.050 980	0.051 097	0.051 214	0.051 331	0.051 448	0.051 565	22
23	0.049 003	0.049 119	0.049 236	0.049 354	0.049 471	0.049 588	23
24	0.047 190	0.047 307	0.047 424	0.047 542	0.047 659	0.047 777	24
25	0.045 524	0.045 641	0.045 758	0.045 876	0.045 994	0.046 111	25
26	0.043 986	0.044 103	0.044 221	0.044 339	0.044 457	0.044 575	26
27	0.042 563	0.042 681	0.042 798	0.042 916	0.043 034	0.043 153	27
28	0.041 242	0.041 360	0.041 478	0.041 596	0.041 714	0.041 833	28
29	0.040 013	0.040 131	0.040 249	0.040 368	0.040 486	0.040 605	29
30	0.038 866	0.038 984	0.039 103	0.039 222	0.039 340	0.039 460	30
31	0.037 794	0.037 912	0.038 031	0.038 150	0.038 269	0.038 389	31
32	0.036 789	0.036 908	0.037 027	0.037 146	0.037 266	0.037 385	32
33	0.035 846	0.035 965	0.036 084	0.036 204	0.036 324	0.036 443	33
34	0.034 959	0.035 078	0.035 198	0.035 317	0.035 437	0.035 558	34
35	0.034 123	0.034 242	0.034 362	0.034 482	0.034 602	0.034 723	35
36	0.033 334	0.033 454	0.033 574	0.033 694	0.033 814	0.033 935	36
37	0.032 588	0.032 708	0.032 828	0.032 949	0.033 070	0.033 191	37
38	0.031 882	0.032 002	0.032 122	0.032 243	0.032 364	0.032 486	38
39	0.031 212	0.031 333	0.031 453	0.031 575	0.031 696	0.031 818	39
40	0.030 576	0.030 697	0.030 818	0.030 940	0.031 061	0.031 183	40
41	0.029 972	0.030 093	0.030 215	0.030 336	0.030 458	0.030 581	41
42	0.029 397	0.029 518	0.029 640	0.029 762	0.029 884	0.030 007	42
43	0.028 849	0.028 971	0.029 093	0.029 215	0.029 338	0.029 461	43
44	0.028 326	0.028 448	0.028 571	0.028 693	0.028 816	0.028 939	44
45	0.027 827	0.027 949	0.028 072	0.028 195	0.028 318	0.028 442	45
46	0.027 350	0.027 473	0.027 596	0.027 719	0.027 843	0.027 967	46
47	0.026 894	0.027 017	0.027 140	0.027 264	0.027 387	0.027 512	47

YRS							
4	0.026 457	0.026 580	0.026 704	0.026 827	0.026 952	0.027 076	48
5	0.022 371	0.022 498	0.022 625	0.022 753	0.022 881	0.023 010	60
6	0.019 680	0.019 811	0.019 942	0.020 074	0.020 206	0.020 339	72
7	0.017 787	0.017 921	0.018 056	0.018 192	0.018 328	0.018 465	84
8	0.016 391	0.016 529	0.016 668	0.016 807	0.016 947	0.017 088	96
9	0.015 326	0.015 468	0.015 610	0.015 754	0.015 898	0.016 042	108
10	0.014 492	0.014 638	0.014 784	0.014 931	0.015 079	0.015 227	120
11	0.013 826	0.013 975	0.014 125	0.014 276	0.014 428	0.014 580	132
12	0.013 286	0.013 439	0.013 592	0.013 746	0.013 901	0.014 057	144
13	0.012 842	0.012 998	0.013 154	0.013 312	0.013 471	0.013 630	156
14	0.012 473	0.012 632	0.012 792	0.012 953	0.013 114	0.013 277	168
15	0.012 163	0.012 325	0.012 488	0.012 652	0.012 817	0.012 983	180
16	0.011 902	0.012 067	0.012 233	0.012 400	0.012 568	0.012 737	192
17	0.011 679	0.011 847	0.012 016	0.012 186	0.012 357	0.012 529	204
18	0.011 489	0.011 660	0.011 832	0.012 004	0.012 178	0.012 352	216
19	0.011 326	0.011 500	0.011 674	0.011 849	0.012 025	0.012 202	228
20	0.011 186	0.011 361	0.011 538	0.011 716	0.011 894	0.012 074	240
21	0.011 064	0.011 242	0.011 421	0.011 601	0.011 782	0.011 964	252
22	0.010 959	0.011 139	0.011 320	0.011 502	0.011 685	0.011 869	264
23	0.010 867	0.011 049	0.011 233	0.011 417	0.011 602	0.011 788	276
24	0.010 787	0.010 971	0.011 157	0.011 343	0.011 530	0.011 717	288
25	0.010 717	0.010 904	0.011 091	0.011 278	0.011 467	0.011 656	300
26	0.010 656	0.010 844	0.011 033	0.011 222	0.011 413	0.011 604	312
27	0.010 603	0.010 792	0.010 983	0.011 174	0.011 366	0.011 558	324
28	0.010 556	0.010 747	0.010 939	0.011 131	0.011 325	0.011 518	336
29	0.010 515	0.010 707	0.010 900	0.011 094	0.011 289	0.011 484	348
30	0.010 479	0.010 673	0.010 867	0.011 062	0.011 258	0.011 454	360

PARTIAL PAYMENT
TO AMORTIZE $1

MONTHLY
COMPOUNDING

MOS	13.75% ANNUAL RATE	14.00% ANNUAL RATE	14.25% ANNUAL RATE	14.50% ANNUAL RATE	14.75% ANNUAL RATE	15.00% ANNUAL RATE	MOS
1	1.011 458	1.011 667	1.011 875	1.012 083	1.012 292	1.012 500	1
2	0.508 610	0.508 767	0.508 924	0.509 081	0.509 238	0.509 394	2
3	0.341 001	0.341 141	0.341 281	0.341 421	0.341 561	0.341 701	3
4	0.257 202	0.257 334	0.257 466	0.257 597	0.257 729	0.257 861	4
5	0.206 927	0.207 054	0.207 181	0.207 308	0.207 435	0.207 562	5
6	0.173 414	0.173 538	0.173 662	0.173 786	0.173 910	0.174 034	6
7	0.149 479	0.149 601	0.149 723	0.149 845	0.149 967	0.150 089	7
8	0.131 531	0.131 651	0.131 772	0.131 892	0.132 013	0.132 133	8
9	0.117 574	0.117 693	0.117 812	0.117 932	0.118 051	0.118 171	9
10	0.106 410	0.106 528	0.106 647	0.106 766	0.106 884	0.107 003	10
11	0.097 278	0.097 396	0.097 514	0.097 632	0.097 750	0.097 868	11
12	0.089 670	0.089 787	0.089 905	0.090 023	0.090 140	0.090 258	12
13	0.083 233	0.083 351	0.083 468	0.083 586	0.083 703	0.083 821	13
14	0.077 718	0.077 836	0.077 953	0.078 070	0.078 188	0.078 305	14
15	0.072 940	0.073 057	0.073 174	0.073 292	0.073 409	0.073 526	15
16	0.068 761	0.068 878	0.068 995	0.069 112	0.069 229	0.069 347	16
17	0.065 074	0.065 191	0.065 308	0.065 425	0.065 543	0.065 660	17
18	0.061 798	0.061 915	0.062 032	0.062 150	0.062 267	0.062 385	18
19	0.058 868	0.058 985	0.059 103	0.059 220	0.059 338	0.059 455	19
20	0.056 232	0.056 350	0.056 467	0.056 585	0.056 703	0.056 820	20
21	0.053 849	0.053 966	0.054 084	0.054 202	0.054 319	0.054 437	21
22	0.051 683	0.051 800	0.051 918	0.052 036	0.052 154	0.052 272	22
23	0.049 706	0.049 824	0.049 942	0.050 060	0.050 178	0.050 297	23
24	0.047 895	0.048 013	0.048 131	0.048 249	0.048 368	0.048 487	24
25	0.046 230	0.046 348	0.046 466	0.046 585	0.046 704	0.046 822	25
26	0.044 693	0.044 812	0.044 930	0.045 049	0.045 168	0.045 287	26
27	0.043 271	0.043 390	0.043 509	0.043 628	0.043 747	0.043 867	27
28	0.041 952	0.042 071	0.042 190	0.042 309	0.042 429	0.042 549	28
29	0.040 724	0.040 843	0.040 963	0.041 082	0.041 202	0.041 322	29
30	0.039 579	0.039 698	0.039 818	0.039 938	0.040 058	0.040 179	30
31	0.038 508	0.038 628	0.038 748	0.038 868	0.038 989	0.039 109	31
32	0.037 505	0.037 625	0.037 746	0.037 866	0.037 987	0.038 108	32
33	0.036 564	0.036 684	0.036 805	0.036 925	0.037 047	0.037 168	33
34	0.035 678	0.035 799	0.035 920	0.036 041	0.036 162	0.036 284	34
35	0.034 844	0.034 965	0.035 086	0.035 207	0.035 329	0.035 451	35
36	0.034 056	0.034 178	0.034 299	0.034 421	0.034 543	0.034 665	36
37	0.033 312	0.033 434	0.033 556	0.033 678	0.033 800	0.033 923	37
38	0.032 608	0.032 729	0.032 852	0.032 974	0.033 097	0.033 220	38
39	0.031 940	0.032 062	0.032 184	0.032 307	0.032 430	0.032 554	39
40	0.031 306	0.031 428	0.031 551	0.031 674	0.031 798	0.031 921	40
41	0.030 703	0.030 826	0.030 949	0.031 073	0.031 197	0.031 321	41
42	0.030 130	0.030 253	0.030 377	0.030 501	0.030 625	0.030 749	42
43	0.029 584	0.029 707	0.029 831	0.029 955	0.030 080	0.030 205	43
44	0.029 063	0.029 187	0.029 311	0.029 436	0.029 560	0.029 686	44
45	0.028 566	0.028 690	0.028 815	0.028 939	0.029 065	0.029 190	45
46	0.028 091	0.028 215	0.028 340	0.028 465	0.028 591	0.028 717	46
47	0.027 636	0.027 761	0.027 886	0.028 012	0.028 138	0.028 264	47

YRS							
4	0.027 201	0.027 326	0.027 452	0.027 578	0.027 704	0.027 831	48
5	0.023 139	0.023 268	0.023 398	0.023 528	0.023 659	0.023 790	60
6	0.020 472	0.020 606	0.020 740	0.020 874	0.021 009	0.021 145	72
7	0.018 602	0.018 740	0.018 878	0.019 017	0.019 157	0.019 297	84
8	0.017 230	0.017 372	0.017 514	0.017 657	0.017 801	0.017 945	96
9	0.016 188	0.016 334	0.016 480	0.016 628	0.016 776	0.016 924	108
10	0.015 377	0.015 527	0.015 677	0.015 829	0.015 981	0.016 133	120
11	0.014 733	0.014 887	0.015 041	0.015 196	0.015 352	0.015 509	132
12	0.014 214	0.014 371	0.014 529	0.014 688	0.014 848	0.015 009	144
13	0.013 790	0.013 951	0.014 113	0.014 275	0.014 439	0.014 603	156
14	0.013 441	0.013 605	0.013 770	0.013 936	0.014 103	0.014 270	168
15	0.013 150	0.013 317	0.013 486	0.013 655	0.013 825	0.013 996	180
16	0.012 906	0.013 077	0.013 248	0.013 421	0.013 594	0.013 768	192
17	0.012 701	0.012 875	0.013 049	0.013 224	0.013 400	0.013 577	204
18	0.012 528	0.012 704	0.012 881	0.013 059	0.013 237	0.013 417	216
19	0.012 380	0.012 559	0.012 738	0.012 919	0.013 100	0.013 282	228
20	0.012 254	0.012 435	0.012 617	0.012 800	0.012 984	0.013 168	240
21	0.012 146	0.012 330	0.012 514	0.012 699	0.012 885	0.013 071	252
22	0.012 054	0.012 239	0.012 426	0.012 613	0.012 800	0.012 989	264
23	0.011 974	0.012 162	0.012 350	0.012 539	0.012 729	0.012 919	276
24	0.011 906	0.012 095	0.012 285	0.012 476	0.012 667	0.012 859	288
25	0.011 847	0.012 038	0.012 229	0.012 422	0.012 615	0.012 808	300
26	0.011 796	0.011 988	0.012 181	0.012 375	0.012 570	0.012 765	312
27	0.011 751	0.011 945	0.012 140	0.012 335	0.012 531	0.012 727	324
28	0.011 713	0.011 908	0.012 104	0.012 301	0.012 498	0.012 695	336
29	0.011 680	0.011 876	0.012 073	0.012 271	0.012 469	0.012 668	348
30	0.011 651	0.011 849	0.012 047	0.012 246	0.012 445	0.012 644	360

	15.25%	15.50%	15.75%	16.00%	16.25%	16.50%	
	ANNUAL RATE	ANNUAL RATE	ANNUAL RATE	ANNUAL RATE	ANNUAL RATE	ANNUAL RATE	
MOS							MOS
1	1.012 708	1.012 917	1.013 125	1.013 333	1.013 542	1.013 750	1
2	0.509 551	0.509 708	0.509 865	0.510 022	0.510 179	0.510 336	2
3	0.341 841	0.341 981	0.342 121	0.342 261	0.342 402	0.342 542	3
4	0.257 993	0.258 125	0.258 257	0.258 389	0.258 520	0.258 652	4
5	0.207 689	0.207 816	0.207 943	0.208 071	0.208 198	0.208 325	5
6	0.174 158	0.174 282	0.174 406	0.174 530	0.174 655	0.174 779	6
7	0.150 211	0.150 333	0.150 455	0.150 577	0.150 699	0.150 822	7
8	0.132 254	0.132 374	0.132 495	0.132 616	0.132 737	0.132 858	8
9	0.118 290	0.118 410	0.118 530	0.118 649	0.118 769	0.118 889	9
10	0.107 122	0.107 241	0.107 360	0.107 479	0.107 598	0.107 717	10
11	0.097 987	0.098 105	0.098 224	0.098 342	0.098 461	0.098 580	11
12	0.090 376	0.090 494	0.090 613	0.090 731	0.090 849	0.090 968	12
13	0.083 939	0.084 057	0.084 175	0.084 293	0.084 411	0.084 529	13
14	0.078 423	0.078 541	0.078 658	0.078 776	0.078 894	0.079 012	14
15	0.073 644	0.073 762	0.073 880	0.073 997	0.074 115	0.074 234	15
16	0.069 464	0.069 582	0.069 700	0.069 818	0.069 936	0.070 054	16
17	0.065 778	0.065 896	0.066 013	0.066 131	0.066 250	0.066 368	17
18	0.062 503	0.062 620	0.062 738	0.062 856	0.062 975	0.063 093	18
19	0.059 573	0.059 691	0.059 809	0.059 928	0.060 046	0.060 165	19
20	0.056 938	0.057 057	0.057 175	0.057 293	0.057 412	0.057 531	20
21	0.054 556	0.054 674	0.054 792	0.054 911	0.055 030	0.055 149	21
22	0.052 391	0.052 509	0.052 628	0.052 747	0.052 866	0.052 985	22
23	0.050 415	0.050 534	0.050 653	0.050 772	0.050 891	0.051 011	23
24	0.048 606	0.048 725	0.048 844	0.048 963	0.049 083	0.049 202	24
25	0.046 942	0.047 061	0.047 180	0.047 300	0.047 420	0.047 540	25
26	0.045 407	0.045 526	0.045 646	0.045 766	0.045 886	0.046 006	26
27	0.043 986	0.044 106	0.044 226	0.044 347	0.044 467	0.044 588	27
28	0.042 669	0.042 789	0.042 909	0.043 030	0.043 150	0.043 271	28
29	0.041 443	0.041 563	0.041 684	0.041 805	0.041 926	0.042 047	29
30	0.040 299	0.040 420	0.040 541	0.040 662	0.040 783	0.040 905	30
31	0.039 230	0.039 351	0.039 473	0.039 594	0.039 716	0.039 838	31
32	0.038 229	0.038 351	0.038 472	0.038 594	0.038 716	0.038 839	32
33	0.037 289	0.037 411	0.037 533	0.037 655	0.037 778	0.037 901	33
34	0.036 406	0.036 528	0.036 650	0.036 773	0.036 896	0.037 019	34
35	0.035 573	0.035 696	0.035 818	0.035 941	0.036 065	0.036 188	35
36	0.034 788	0.034 911	0.035 034	0.035 157	0.035 281	0.035 404	36
37	0.034 046	0.034 169	0.034 292	0.034 416	0.034 540	0.034 664	37
38	0.033 343	0.033 467	0.033 590	0.033 714	0.033 839	0.033 963	38
39	0.032 677	0.032 801	0.032 925	0.033 050	0.033 174	0.033 299	39
40	0.032 045	0.032 170	0.032 294	0.032 419	0.032 544	0.032 669	40
41	0.031 445	0.031 570	0.031 694	0.031 820	0.031 945	0.032 071	41
42	0.030 874	0.030 999	0.031 124	0.031 250	0.031 375	0.031 501	42
43	0.030 330	0.030 455	0.030 581	0.030 707	0.030 833	0.030 959	43
44	0.029 811	0.029 937	0.030 063	0.030 189	0.030 316	0.030 443	44
45	0.029 316	0.029 442	0.029 568	0.029 695	0.029 822	0.029 949	45
46	0.028 843	0.028 969	0.029 096	0.029 223	0.029 351	0.029 478	46
47	0.028 391	0.028 517	0.028 645	0.028 772	0.028 900	0.029 028	47
YRS							
4	0.027 958	0.028 085	0.028 212	0.028 340	0.028 468	0.028 597	48
5	0.023 921	0.024 053	0.024 185	0.024 318	0.024 451	0.024 585	60
6	0.021 281	0.021 417	0.021 554	0.021 692	0.021 830	0.021 968	72
7	0.019 437	0.019 578	0.019 720	0.019 862	0.020 005	0.020 148	84
8	0.018 090	0.018 236	0.018 382	0.018 529	0.018 676	0.018 824	96
9	0.017 074	0.017 224	0.017 374	0.017 525	0.017 677	0.017 829	108
10	0.016 287	0.016 441	0.016 596	0.016 751	0.016 907	0.017 064	120
11	0.015 667	0.015 825	0.015 984	0.016 143	0.016 303	0.016 464	132
12	0.015 170	0.015 332	0.015 495	0.015 658	0.015 822	0.015 987	144
13	0.014 768	0.014 933	0.015 100	0.015 267	0.015 435	0.015 604	156
14	0.014 439	0.014 608	0.014 778	0.014 948	0.015 120	0.015 292	168
15	0.014 167	0.014 340	0.014 513	0.014 687	0.014 862	0.015 037	180
16	0.013 942	0.014 118	0.014 294	0.014 471	0.014 649	0.014 827	192
17	0.013 755	0.013 933	0.014 112	0.014 292	0.014 472	0.014 654	204
18	0.013 597	0.013 778	0.013 960	0.014 142	0.014 326	0.014 510	216
19	0.013 465	0.013 648	0.013 833	0.014 017	0.014 203	0.014 389	228
20	0.013 353	0.013 539	0.013 725	0.013 913	0.014 100	0.014 289	240
21	0.013 258	0.013 446	0.013 635	0.013 824	0.014 014	0.014 205	252
22	0.013 178	0.013 368	0.013 559	0.013 750	0.013 942	0.014 134	264
23	0.013 110	0.013 302	0.013 494	0.013 687	0.013 881	0.014 075	276
24	0.013 052	0.013 245	0.013 439	0.013 634	0.013 829	0.014 025	288
25	0.013 003	0.013 197	0.013 393	0.013 589	0.013 785	0.013 982	300
26	0.012 960	0.013 157	0.013 353	0.013 551	0.013 749	0.013 947	312
27	0.012 924	0.013 122	0.013 320	0.013 518	0.013 717	0.013 917	324
28	0.012 894	0.013 092	0.013 291	0.013 491	0.013 691	0.013 891	336
29	0.012 867	0.013 067	0.013 267	0.013 467	0.013 668	0.013 870	348
30	0.012 845	0.013 045	0.013 246	0.013 448	0.013 649	0.013 851	360

PARTIAL PAYMENT
TO AMORTIZE $1

MONTHLY
COMPOUNDING

MOS	16.75% ANNUAL RATE	17.00% ANNUAL RATE	17.25% ANNUAL RATE	17.50% ANNUAL RATE	17.75% ANNUAL RATE	18.00% ANNUAL RATE	MOS
1	1.013 958	1.014 167	1.014 375	1.014 583	1.014 792	1.015 000	1
2	0.510 493	0.510 650	0.510 807	0.510 964	0.511 121	0.511 278	2
3	0.342 682	0.342 822	0.342 962	0.343 102	0.343 243	0.343 383	3
4	0.258 784	0.258 916	0.259 048	0.259 181	0.259 313	0.259 445	4
5	0.208 452	0.208 580	0.208 707	0.208 834	0.208 962	0.209 089	5
6	0.174 903	0.175 027	0.175 152	0.175 276	0.175 401	0.175 525	6
7	0.150 944	0.151 066	0.151 189	0.151 311	0.151 434	0.151 556	7
8	0.132 979	0.133 100	0.133 221	0.133 342	0.133 463	0.133 584	8
9	0.119 009	0.119 129	0.119 249	0.119 369	0.119 490	0.119 610	9
10	0.107 837	0.107 956	0.108 075	0.108 195	0.108 315	0.108 434	10
11	0.098 699	0.098 817	0.098 936	0.099 055	0.099 175	0.099 294	11
12	0.091 086	0.091 205	0.091 323	0.091 442	0.091 561	0.091 680	12
13	0.084 647	0.084 766	0.084 884	0.085 003	0.085 122	0.085 240	13
14	0.079 131	0.079 249	0.079 367	0.079 486	0.079 605	0.079 723	14
15	0.074 352	0.074 470	0.074 588	0.074 707	0.074 826	0.074 944	15
16	0.070 172	0.070 290	0.070 409	0.070 528	0.070 646	0.070 765	16
17	0.066 486	0.066 605	0.066 723	0.066 842	0.066 961	0.067 080	17
18	0.063 211	0.063 330	0.063 449	0.063 568	0.063 687	0.063 806	18
19	0.060 283	0.060 402	0.060 521	0.060 640	0.060 759	0.060 878	19
20	0.057 649	0.057 768	0.057 888	0.058 007	0.058 126	0.058 246	20
21	0.055 268	0.055 387	0.055 507	0.055 626	0.055 746	0.055 865	21
22	0.053 104	0.053 224	0.053 344	0.053 463	0.053 583	0.053 703	22
23	0.051 130	0.051 250	0.051 370	0.051 490	0.051 610	0.051 731	23
24	0.049 322	0.049 442	0.049 562	0.049 683	0.049 803	0.049 924	24
25	0.047 660	0.047 780	0.047 901	0.048 022	0.048 142	0.048 263	25
26	0.046 127	0.046 247	0.046 368	0.046 489	0.046 611	0.046 732	26
27	0.044 708	0.044 829	0.044 951	0.045 072	0.045 194	0.045 315	27
28	0.043 392	0.043 514	0.043 635	0.043 757	0.043 879	0.044 001	28
29	0.042 168	0.042 290	0.042 412	0.042 534	0.042 656	0.042 779	29
30	0.041 027	0.041 149	0.041 271	0.041 394	0.041 516	0.041 639	30
31	0.039 960	0.040 083	0.040 205	0.040 328	0.040 451	0.040 574	31
32	0.038 961	0.039 084	0.039 207	0.039 330	0.039 453	0.039 577	32
33	0.038 023	0.038 147	0.038 270	0.038 394	0.038 517	0.038 641	33
34	0.037 142	0.037 265	0.037 389	0.037 513	0.037 637	0.037 762	34
35	0.036 312	0.036 436	0.036 560	0.036 684	0.036 809	0.036 934	35
36	0.035 528	0.035 653	0.035 777	0.035 902	0.036 027	0.036 152	36
37	0.034 788	0.034 913	0.035 038	0.035 163	0.035 289	0.035 414	37
38	0.034 088	0.034 213	0.034 339	0.034 464	0.034 590	0.034 716	38
39	0.033 425	0.033 550	0.033 676	0.033 802	0.033 928	0.034 055	39
40	0.032 795	0.032 921	0.033 047	0.033 173	0.033 300	0.033 427	40
41	0.032 197	0.032 323	0.032 450	0.032 577	0.032 704	0.032 831	41
42	0.031 628	0.031 755	0.031 882	0.032 009	0.032 136	0.032 264	42
43	0.031 086	0.031 213	0.031 341	0.031 468	0.031 596	0.031 725	43
44	0.030 570	0.030 697	0.030 825	0.030 953	0.031 082	0.031 210	44
45	0.030 077	0.030 205	0.030 333	0.030 462	0.030 591	0.030 720	45
46	0.029 606	0.029 735	0.029 863	0.029 992	0.030 122	0.030 251	46
47	0.029 156	0.029 285	0.029 414	0.029 544	0.029 673	0.029 803	47

YRS							
4	0.028 726	0.028 855	0.028 985	0.029 114	0.029 245	0.029 375	48
5	0.024 718	0.024 853	0.024 987	0.025 122	0.025 258	0.025 393	60
6	0.022 107	0.022 246	0.022 386	0.022 526	0.022 667	0.022 808	72
7	0.020 292	0.020 436	0.020 581	0.020 726	0.020 872	0.021 018	84
8	0.018 972	0.019 121	0.019 271	0.019 421	0.019 572	0.019 723	96
9	0.017 983	0.018 136	0.018 290	0.018 445	0.018 601	0.018 757	108
10	0.017 222	0.017 380	0.017 539	0.017 698	0.017 858	0.018 019	120
11	0.016 626	0.016 788	0.016 951	0.017 115	0.017 279	0.017 444	132
12	0.016 153	0.016 319	0.016 486	0.016 654	0.016 822	0.016 991	144
13	0.015 773	0.015 943	0.016 114	0.016 285	0.016 457	0.016 630	156
14	0.015 465	0.015 638	0.015 813	0.015 988	0.016 163	0.016 340	168
15	0.015 213	0.015 390	0.015 568	0.015 746	0.015 925	0.016 104	180
16	0.015 006	0.015 186	0.015 367	0.015 548	0.015 730	0.015 913	192
17	0.014 836	0.015 018	0.015 202	0.015 386	0.015 570	0.015 756	204
18	0.014 694	0.014 879	0.015 065	0.015 252	0.015 439	0.015 627	216
19	0.014 576	0.014 764	0.014 952	0.015 141	0.015 331	0.015 521	228
20	0.014 478	0.014 668	0.014 858	0.015 049	0.015 241	0.015 433	240
21	0.014 396	0.014 588	0.014 780	0.014 973	0.015 167	0.015 361	252
22	0.014 327	0.014 521	0.014 715	0.014 910	0.015 105	0.015 300	264
23	0.014 269	0.014 465	0.014 660	0.014 857	0.015 053	0.015 250	276
24	0.014 221	0.014 418	0.014 615	0.014 812	0.015 010	0.015 209	288
25	0.014 180	0.014 378	0.014 576	0.014 775	0.014 975	0.015 174	300
26	0.014 146	0.014 345	0.014 544	0.014 744	0.014 945	0.015 146	312
27	0.014 117	0.014 317	0.014 517	0.014 718	0.014 920	0.015 122	324
28	0.014 092	0.014 293	0.014 495	0.014 697	0.014 899	0.015 101	336
29	0.014 071	0.014 273	0.014 476	0.014 679	0.014 882	0.015 085	348
30	0.014 054	0.014 257	0.014 460	0.014 663	0.014 867	0.015 071	360

PARTIAL PAYMENT
TO AMORTIZE $1

MONTHLY
COMPOUNDING

MOS	18.25% ANNUAL RATE	18.50% ANNUAL RATE	18.75% ANNUAL RATE	19.00% ANNUAL RATE	19.25% ANNUAL RATE	19.50% ANNUAL RATE	MOS
1	1.015 208	1.015 417	1.015 625	1.015 833	1.016 042	1.016 250	1
2	0.511 435	0.511 592	0.511 749	0.511 906	0.512 063	0.512 220	2
3	0.343 523	0.343 664	0.343 804	0.343 944	0.344 085	0.344 225	3
4	0.259 577	0.259 709	0.259 841	0.259 974	0.260 106	0.260 238	4
5	0.209 217	0.209 344	0.209 472	0.209 599	0.209 727	0.209 855	5
6	0.175 650	0.175 774	0.175 899	0.176 024	0.176 148	0.176 273	6
7	0.151 679	0.151 801	0.151 924	0.152 047	0.152 170	0.152 293	7
8	0.133 705	0.133 827	0.133 948	0.134 069	0.134 191	0.134 312	8
9	0.119 730	0.119 851	0.119 971	0.120 092	0.120 212	0.120 333	9
10	0.108 554	0.108 674	0.108 794	0.108 913	0.109 033	0.109 154	10
11	0.099 413	0.099 532	0.099 652	0.099 771	0.099 891	0.100 011	11
12	0.091 799	0.091 918	0.092 037	0.092 157	0.092 276	0.092 395	12
13	0.085 359	0.085 478	0.085 597	0.085 716	0.085 836	0.085 955	13
14	0.079 842	0.079 961	0.080 080	0.080 199	0.080 318	0.080 438	14
15	0.075 063	0.075 182	0.075 301	0.075 420	0.075 540	0.075 659	15
16	0.070 884	0.071 003	0.071 122	0.071 241	0.071 361	0.071 480	16
17	0.067 199	0.067 318	0.067 437	0.067 557	0.067 676	0.067 796	17
18	0.063 925	0.064 044	0.064 164	0.064 283	0.064 403	0.064 523	18
19	0.060 998	0.061 118	0.061 237	0.061 357	0.061 477	0.061 597	19
20	0.058 365	0.058 485	0.058 605	0.058 725	0.058 846	0.058 966	20
21	0.055 985	0.056 106	0.056 226	0.056 346	0.056 467	0.056 587	21
22	0.053 824	0.053 944	0.054 065	0.054 185	0.054 306	0.054 427	22
23	0.051 851	0.051 972	0.052 093	0.052 214	0.052 335	0.052 456	23
24	0.050 045	0.050 166	0.050 287	0.050 409	0.050 530	0.050 652	24
25	0.048 385	0.048 506	0.048 628	0.048 749	0.048 871	0.048 993	25
26	0.046 854	0.046 975	0.047 097	0.047 219	0.047 342	0.047 464	26
27	0.045 437	0.045 559	0.045 682	0.045 804	0.045 927	0.046 050	27
28	0.044 123	0.044 246	0.044 369	0.044 491	0.044 615	0.044 738	28
29	0.042 901	0.043 024	0.043 147	0.043 271	0.043 394	0.043 518	29
30	0.041 762	0.041 886	0.042 009	0.042 133	0.042 257	0.042 381	30
31	0.040 698	0.040 821	0.040 945	0.041 069	0.041 194	0.041 318	31
32	0.039 701	0.039 825	0.039 949	0.040 074	0.040 199	0.040 324	32
33	0.038 766	0.038 890	0.039 015	0.039 140	0.039 265	0.039 391	33
34	0.037 887	0.038 012	0.038 137	0.038 262	0.038 388	0.038 514	34
35	0.037 059	0.037 184	0.037 310	0.037 436	0.037 562	0.037 688	35
36	0.036 278	0.036 404	0.036 530	0.036 656	0.036 783	0.036 909	36
37	0.035 540	0.035 667	0.035 793	0.035 920	0.036 047	0.036 174	37
38	0.034 843	0.034 969	0.035 096	0.035 223	0.035 351	0.035 478	38
39	0.034 181	0.034 309	0.034 436	0.034 564	0.034 691	0.034 820	39
40	0.033 554	0.033 682	0.033 810	0.033 938	0.034 066	0.034 195	40
41	0.032 959	0.033 087	0.033 215	0.033 344	0.033 472	0.033 601	41
42	0.032 392	0.032 521	0.032 650	0.032 778	0.032 908	0.033 037	42
43	0.031 853	0.031 982	0.032 111	0.032 241	0.032 370	0.032 500	43
44	0.031 339	0.031 469	0.031 598	0.031 728	0.031 858	0.031 989	44
45	0.030 849	0.030 979	0.031 109	0.031 239	0.031 370	0.031 501	45
46	0.030 381	0.030 511	0.030 642	0.030 773	0.030 904	0.031 035	46
47	0.029 934	0.030 064	0.030 195	0.030 327	0.030 458	0.030 590	47

YRS							
4	0.029 506	0.029 637	0.029 768	0.029 900	0.030 032	0.030 165	48
5	0.025 530	0.025 666	0.025 803	0.025 941	0.026 078	0.026 216	60
6	0.022 949	0.023 091	0.023 234	0.023 377	0.023 520	0.023 664	72
7	0.021 165	0.021 312	0.021 460	0.021 608	0.021 757	0.021 906	84
8	0.019 875	0.020 027	0.020 180	0.020 334	0.020 488	0.020 642	96
9	0.018 914	0.019 071	0.019 229	0.019 387	0.019 546	0.019 706	108
10	0.018 180	0.018 342	0.018 504	0.018 667	0.018 831	0.018 995	120
11	0.017 610	0.017 776	0.017 943	0.018 110	0.018 278	0.018 447	132
12	0.017 161	0.017 331	0.017 502	0.017 674	0.017 846	0.018 019	144
13	0.016 803	0.016 978	0.017 152	0.017 328	0.017 504	0.017 680	156
14	0.016 516	0.016 694	0.016 872	0.017 051	0.017 231	0.017 411	168
15	0.016 284	0.016 465	0.016 647	0.016 829	0.017 011	0.017 195	180
16	0.016 096	0.016 280	0.016 464	0.016 649	0.016 835	0.017 021	192
17	0.015 942	0.016 128	0.016 315	0.016 503	0.016 691	0.016 880	204
18	0.015 815	0.016 004	0.016 194	0.016 384	0.016 574	0.016 766	216
19	0.015 711	0.015 903	0.016 094	0.016 287	0.016 479	0.016 673	228
20	0.015 626	0.015 819	0.016 013	0.016 207	0.016 402	0.016 597	240
21	0.015 555	0.015 750	0.015 945	0.016 141	0.016 338	0.016 535	252
22	0.015 497	0.015 693	0.015 890	0.016 088	0.016 286	0.016 484	264
23	0.015 448	0.015 646	0.015 845	0.016 043	0.016 243	0.016 442	276
24	0.015 408	0.015 607	0.015 807	0.016 007	0.016 207	0.016 408	288
25	0.015 374	0.015 575	0.015 776	0.015 977	0.016 178	0.016 380	300
26	0.015 347	0.015 548	0.015 750	0.015 952	0.016 154	0.016 357	312
27	0.015 324	0.015 526	0.015 729	0.015 931	0.016 135	0.016 338	324
28	0.015 304	0.015 507	0.015 711	0.015 915	0.016 118	0.016 323	336
29	0.015 288	0.015 492	0.015 696	0.015 901	0.016 105	0.016 310	348
30	0.015 275	0.015 479	0.015 684	0.015 889	0.016 094	0.016 299	360

PARTIAL PAYMENT
TO AMORTIZE $1

MONTHLY
COMPOUNDING

MOS	19.75% ANNUAL RATE	20.00% ANNUAL RATE	21.00% ANNUAL RATE	22.00% ANNUAL RATE	23.00% ANNUAL RATE	24.00% ANNUAL RATE	MOS
1	1.016 458	1.016 667	1.017 500	1.018 333	1.019 167	1.020 000	1
2	0.512 377	0.512 534	0.513 163	0.513 792	0.514 420	0.515 050	2
3	0.344 365	0.344 506	0.345 067	0.345 630	0.346 192	0.346 755	3
4	0.260 370	0.260 503	0.261 032	0.261 562	0.262 093	0.262 624	4
5	0.209 982	0.210 110	0.210 621	0.211 133	0.211 646	0.212 158	5
6	0.176 398	0.176 523	0.177 023	0.177 523	0.178 024	0.178 526	6
7	0.152 415	0.152 538	0.153 031	0.153 524	0.154 017	0.154 512	7
8	0.134 434	0.134 556	0.135 043	0.135 531	0.136 020	0.136 510	8
9	0.120 454	0.120 574	0.121 058	0.121 543	0.122 029	0.122 515	9
10	0.109 274	0.109 394	0.109 875	0.110 358	0.110 842	0.111 327	10
11	0.100 130	0.100 250	0.100 730	0.101 212	0.101 694	0.102 178	11
12	0.092 515	0.092 635	0.093 114	0.093 594	0.094 076	0.094 560	12
13	0.086 074	0.086 194	0.086 673	0.087 153	0.087 635	0.088 118	13
14	0.080 557	0.080 677	0.081 156	0.081 636	0.082 118	0.082 602	14
15	0.075 778	0.075 898	0.076 377	0.076 858	0.077 341	0.077 825	15
16	0.071 600	0.071 720	0.072 200	0.072 681	0.073 165	0.073 650	16
17	0.067 916	0.068 035	0.068 516	0.068 999	0.069 483	0.069 970	17
18	0.064 643	0.064 763	0.065 245	0.065 729	0.066 214	0.066 702	18
19	0.061 717	0.061 838	0.062 321	0.062 806	0.063 293	0.063 782	19
20	0.059 086	0.059 207	0.059 691	0.060 178	0.060 666	0.061 157	20
21	0.056 708	0.056 829	0.057 315	0.057 802	0.058 292	0.058 785	21
22	0.054 548	0.054 670	0.055 156	0.055 646	0.056 137	0.056 631	22
23	0.052 578	0.052 700	0.053 188	0.053 679	0.054 172	0.054 668	23
24	0.050 774	0.050 896	0.051 386	0.051 878	0.052 373	0.052 871	24
25	0.049 116	0.049 238	0.049 730	0.050 224	0.050 721	0.051 220	25
26	0.047 587	0.047 710	0.048 203	0.048 699	0.049 198	0.049 699	26
27	0.046 173	0.046 296	0.046 791	0.047 289	0.047 789	0.048 293	27
28	0.044 861	0.044 985	0.045 482	0.045 981	0.046 484	0.046 990	28
29	0.043 642	0.043 766	0.044 264	0.044 766	0.045 270	0.045 778	29
30	0.042 505	0.042 630	0.043 130	0.043 633	0.044 140	0.044 650	30
31	0.041 443	0.041 568	0.042 070	0.042 575	0.043 084	0.043 596	31
32	0.040 449	0.040 574	0.041 078	0.041 585	0.042 096	0.042 611	32
33	0.039 516	0.039 642	0.040 148	0.040 657	0.041 170	0.041 687	33
34	0.038 640	0.038 766	0.039 274	0.039 785	0.040 300	0.040 819	34
35	0.037 814	0.037 941	0.038 451	0.038 964	0.039 481	0.040 002	35
36	0.037 036	0.037 164	0.037 675	0.038 190	0.038 710	0.039 233	36
37	0.036 301	0.036 429	0.036 943	0.037 460	0.037 981	0.038 507	37
38	0.035 606	0.035 735	0.036 250	0.036 769	0.037 293	0.037 821	38
39	0.034 948	0.035 077	0.035 594	0.036 116	0.036 641	0.037 171	39
40	0.034 324	0.034 453	0.034 972	0.035 496	0.036 024	0.036 556	40
41	0.033 731	0.033 860	0.034 382	0.034 907	0.035 437	0.035 972	41
42	0.033 167	0.033 297	0.033 821	0.034 348	0.034 881	0.035 417	42
43	0.032 631	0.032 761	0.033 287	0.033 817	0.034 351	0.034 890	43
44	0.032 120	0.032 251	0.032 778	0.033 310	0.033 847	0.034 388	44
45	0.031 632	0.031 764	0.032 293	0.032 827	0.033 366	0.033 910	45
46	0.031 167	0.031 299	0.031 830	0.032 367	0.032 908	0.033 453	46
47	0.030 722	0.030 855	0.031 388	0.031 927	0.032 470	0.033 018	47

YRS							
4	0.030 297	0.030 430	0.030 966	0.031 506	0.032 051	0.032 602	48
5	0.026 355	0.026 494	0.027 053	0.027 619	0.028 190	0.028 768	60
6	0.023 808	0.023 953	0.024 536	0.025 126	0.025 723	0.026 327	72
7	0.022 056	0.022 206	0.022 812	0.023 426	0.024 047	0.024 676	84
8	0.020 798	0.020 953	0.021 581	0.022 217	0.022 861	0.023 513	96
9	0.019 866	0.020 027	0.020 675	0.021 332	0.021 997	0.022 671	108
10	0.019 160	0.019 326	0.019 993	0.020 670	0.021 355	0.022 048	120
11	0.018 616	0.018 786	0.019 472	0.020 166	0.020 869	0.021 581	132
12	0.018 192	0.018 366	0.019 068	0.019 779	0.020 498	0.021 226	144
13	0.017 857	0.018 035	0.018 752	0.019 478	0.020 212	0.020 954	156
14	0.017 591	0.017 773	0.018 503	0.019 243	0.019 990	0.020 745	168
15	0.017 379	0.017 563	0.018 306	0.019 058	0.019 817	0.020 583	180
16	0.017 207	0.017 395	0.018 149	0.018 911	0.019 681	0.020 457	192
17	0.017 069	0.017 259	0.018 023	0.018 795	0.019 574	0.020 358	204
18	0.016 957	0.017 149	0.017 923	0.018 703	0.019 489	0.020 281	216
19	0.016 866	0.017 060	0.017 842	0.018 629	0.019 423	0.020 221	228
20	0.016 792	0.016 988	0.017 776	0.018 571	0.019 370	0.020 174	240
21	0.016 732	0.016 929	0.017 724	0.018 524	0.019 328	0.020 137	252
22	0.016 683	0.016 882	0.017 681	0.018 486	0.019 295	0.020 108	264
23	0.016 642	0.016 843	0.017 647	0.018 456	0.019 269	0.020 085	276
24	0.016 609	0.016 811	0.017 619	0.018 432	0.019 248	0.020 067	288
25	0.016 582	0.016 785	0.017 597	0.018 412	0.019 231	0.020 053	300
26	0.016 560	0.016 763	0.017 578	0.018 397	0.019 218	0.020 042	312
27	0.016 542	0.016 746	0.017 564	0.018 384	0.019 208	0.020 033	324
28	0.016 527	0.016 731	0.017 552	0.018 374	0.019 199	0.020 026	336
29	0.016 515	0.016 720	0.017 542	0.018 366	0.019 193	0.020 020	348
30	0.016 505	0.016 710	0.017 534	0.018 360	0.019 187	0.020 016	360

PARTIAL PAYMENT
TO AMORTIZE $1

QTRS	6.50% ANNUAL RATE	7.00% ANNUAL RATE	7.50% ANNUAL RATE	8.00% ANNUAL RATE	8.50% ANNUAL RATE	9.00% ANNUAL RATE	QTRS
1	1.016 250	1.017 500	1.018 750	1.020 000	1.021 250	1.022 500	1
2	0.512 220	0.513 163	0.514 106	0.515 050	0.515 993	0.516 938	2
3	0.344 225	0.345 067	0.345 911	0.346 755	0.347 599	0.348 445	3
4	0.260 238	0.261 032	0.261 828	0.262 624	0.263 421	0.264 219	4
5	0.209 855	0.210 621	0.211 389	0.212 158	0.212 929	0.213 700	5
6	0.176 273	0.177 023	0.177 773	0.178 526	0.179 280	0.180 035	6
7	0.152 293	0.153 031	0.153 770	0.154 512	0.155 255	0.156 000	7
8	0.134 312	0.135 043	0.135 775	0.136 510	0.137 246	0.137 985	8
9	0.120 333	0.121 058	0.121 786	0.122 515	0.123 247	0.123 982	9
10	0.109 154	0.109 875	0.110 600	0.111 327	0.112 056	0.112 788	10
11	0.100 011	0.100 730	0.101 453	0.102 178	0.102 906	0.103 636	11
12	0.092 395	0.093 114	0.093 835	0.094 560	0.095 287	0.096 017	12
13	0.085 955	0.086 673	0.087 394	0.088 118	0.088 846	0.089 577	13
14	0.080 438	0.081 156	0.081 877	0.082 602	0.083 330	0.084 062	14
15	0.075 659	0.076 377	0.077 100	0.077 825	0.078 555	0.079 289	15
16	0.071 480	0.072 200	0.072 923	0.073 650	0.074 381	0.075 117	16
17	0.067 796	0.068 516	0.069 241	0.069 970	0.070 703	0.071 440	17
18	0.064 523	0.065 245	0.065 971	0.066 702	0.067 437	0.068 177	18
19	0.061 597	0.062 321	0.063 049	0.063 782	0.064 519	0.065 262	19
20	0.058 966	0.059 691	0.060 421	0.061 157	0.061 897	0.062 642	20
21	0.056 587	0.057 315	0.058 047	0.058 785	0.059 528	0.060 276	21
22	0.054 427	0.055 156	0.055 891	0.056 631	0.057 377	0.058 128	22
23	0.052 456	0.053 188	0.053 925	0.054 668	0.055 417	0.056 171	23
24	0.050 652	0.051 386	0.052 125	0.052 871	0.053 623	0.054 380	24
25	0.048 993	0.049 730	0.050 472	0.051 220	0.051 975	0.052 736	25
26	0.047 464	0.048 203	0.048 948	0.049 699	0.050 457	0.051 221	26
27	0.046 050	0.046 791	0.047 539	0.048 293	0.049 054	0.049 822	27
28	0.044 738	0.045 482	0.046 232	0.046 990	0.047 754	0.048 525	28
29	0.043 518	0.044 264	0.045 018	0.045 778	0.046 546	0.047 321	29
30	0.042 381	0.043 130	0.043 886	0.044 650	0.045 421	0.046 199	30
31	0.041 318	0.042 070	0.042 829	0.043 596	0.044 371	0.045 153	31
32	0.040 324	0.041 078	0.041 840	0.042 611	0.043 389	0.044 174	32
33	0.039 391	0.040 148	0.040 913	0.041 687	0.042 468	0.043 257	33
34	0.038 514	0.039 274	0.040 042	0.040 819	0.041 604	0.042 397	34
35	0.037 688	0.038 451	0.039 222	0.040 002	0.040 791	0.041 587	35
36	0.036 909	0.037 675	0.038 450	0.039 233	0.040 025	0.040 825	36
37	0.036 174	0.036 943	0.037 720	0.038 507	0.039 302	0.040 106	37
38	0.035 478	0.036 250	0.037 031	0.037 821	0.038 620	0.039 428	38
39	0.034 820	0.035 594	0.036 378	0.037 171	0.037 974	0.038 785	39
40	0.034 195	0.034 972	0.035 759	0.036 556	0.037 362	0.038 177	40
41	0.033 601	0.034 382	0.035 172	0.035 972	0.036 782	0.037 601	41
42	0.033 037	0.033 821	0.034 614	0.035 417	0.036 231	0.037 054	42
43	0.032 500	0.033 287	0.034 083	0.034 890	0.035 707	0.036 534	43
44	0.031 989	0.032 778	0.033 578	0.034 388	0.035 208	0.036 039	44
45	0.031 501	0.032 293	0.033 096	0.033 910	0.034 734	0.035 568	45
46	0.031 035	0.031 830	0.032 637	0.033 453	0.034 281	0.035 119	46
47	0.030 590	0.031 388	0.032 198	0.033 018	0.033 849	0.034 691	47
48	0.030 165	0.030 966	0.031 778	0.032 602	0.033 437	0.034 282	48
49	0.029 757	0.030 561	0.031 377	0.032 204	0.033 042	0.033 892	49
50	0.029 367	0.030 174	0.030 993	0.031 823	0.032 665	0.033 518	50
51	0.028 993	0.029 803	0.030 625	0.031 459	0.032 304	0.033 161	51
52	0.028 634	0.029 447	0.030 272	0.031 109	0.031 958	0.032 819	52
53	0.028 289	0.029 105	0.029 933	0.030 774	0.031 627	0.032 491	53
54	0.027 958	0.028 777	0.029 608	0.030 452	0.031 308	0.032 177	54
55	0.027 639	0.028 461	0.029 296	0.030 143	0.031 003	0.031 875	55
YRS							
14	0.027 333	0.028 158	0.028 996	0.029 847	0.030 710	0.031 585	56
15	0.026 216	0.027 053	0.027 904	0.028 768	0.029 645	0.030 535	60
16	0.025 249	0.026 098	0.026 961	0.027 839	0.028 730	0.029 634	64
17	0.024 405	0.025 266	0.026 141	0.027 032	0.027 936	0.028 855	68
18	0.023 664	0.024 536	0.025 424	0.026 327	0.027 245	0.028 177	72
19	0.023 008	0.023 892	0.024 792	0.025 708	0.026 639	0.027 585	76
20	0.022 426	0.023 321	0.024 233	0.025 161	0.026 105	0.027 064	80
21	0.021 906	0.022 812	0.023 736	0.024 676	0.025 632	0.026 604	84
22	0.021 440	0.022 357	0.023 292	0.024 244	0.025 213	0.026 197	88
23	0.021 021	0.021 949	0.022 895	0.023 859	0.024 839	0.025 836	92
24	0.020 642	0.021 581	0.022 538	0.023 513	0.024 505	0.025 514	96
25	0.020 300	0.021 249	0.022 217	0.023 203	0.024 206	0.025 226	100
26	0.019 989	0.020 948	0.021 926	0.022 923	0.023 937	0.024 968	104
27	0.019 706	0.020 675	0.021 664	0.022 671	0.023 696	0.024 737	108
28	0.019 447	0.020 426	0.021 425	0.022 443	0.023 478	0.024 530	112
29	0.019 211	0.020 200	0.021 208	0.022 236	0.023 281	0.024 343	116
30	0.018 995	0.019 993	0.021 011	0.022 048	0.023 103	0.024 174	120

PARTIAL PAYMENT
TO AMORTIZE $1

QUARTERLY
COMPOUNDING

QTRS	9.50% ANNUAL RATE	10.00% ANNUAL RATE	10.50% ANNUAL RATE	11.00% ANNUAL RATE	11.50% ANNUAL RATE	12.00% ANNUAL RATE	QTRS
1	1.023 750	1.025 000	1.026 250	1.027 500	1.028 750	1.030 000	1
2	0.517 882	0.518 827	0.519 773	0.520 718	0.521 664	0.522 611	2
3	0.349 291	0.350 137	0.350 984	0.351 832	0.352 681	0.353 530	3
4	0.265 018	0.265 818	0.266 619	0.267 421	0.268 223	0.269 027	4
5	0.214 473	0.215 247	0.216 022	0.216 798	0.217 576	0.218 355	5
6	0.180 792	0.181 550	0.182 310	0.183 071	0.183 833	0.184 598	6
7	0.156 747	0.157 495	0.158 246	0.158 997	0.159 751	0.160 506	7
8	0.138 725	0.139 467	0.140 212	0.140 958	0.141 706	0.142 456	8
9	0.124 718	0.125 457	0.126 198	0.126 941	0.127 686	0.128 434	9
10	0.113 522	0.114 259	0.114 998	0.115 740	0.116 484	0.117 231	10
11	0.104 370	0.105 106	0.105 845	0.106 586	0.107 331	0.108 077	11
12	0.096 751	0.097 487	0.098 226	0.098 969	0.099 714	0.100 462	12
13	0.090 311	0.091 048	0.091 789	0.092 533	0.093 279	0.094 030	13
14	0.084 798	0.085 537	0.086 279	0.087 025	0.087 774	0.088 526	14
15	0.080 026	0.080 766	0.081 511	0.082 259	0.083 011	0.083 767	15
16	0.075 856	0.076 599	0.077 346	0.078 097	0.078 852	0.079 611	16
17	0.072 182	0.072 928	0.073 678	0.074 432	0.075 190	0.075 953	17
18	0.068 921	0.069 670	0.070 423	0.071 181	0.071 942	0.072 709	18
19	0.066 009	0.066 761	0.067 517	0.068 278	0.069 044	0.069 814	19
20	0.063 392	0.064 147	0.064 907	0.065 672	0.066 441	0.067 216	20
21	0.061 029	0.061 787	0.062 551	0.063 319	0.064 093	0.064 872	21
22	0.058 885	0.059 647	0.060 414	0.061 186	0.061 964	0.062 747	22
23	0.056 931	0.057 696	0.058 467	0.059 244	0.060 026	0.060 814	23
24	0.055 144	0.055 913	0.056 688	0.057 469	0.058 255	0.059 047	24
25	0.053 503	0.054 276	0.055 055	0.055 840	0.056 631	0.057 428	25
26	0.051 992	0.052 769	0.053 552	0.054 341	0.055 137	0.055 938	26
27	0.050 596	0.051 377	0.052 164	0.052 958	0.053 758	0.054 564	27
28	0.049 303	0.050 088	0.050 879	0.051 677	0.052 482	0.053 293	28
29	0.048 103	0.048 891	0.049 687	0.050 489	0.051 299	0.052 115	29
30	0.046 985	0.047 778	0.048 577	0.049 384	0.050 198	0.051 019	30
31	0.045 942	0.046 739	0.047 543	0.048 355	0.049 173	0.049 999	31
32	0.044 967	0.045 768	0.046 577	0.047 393	0.048 216	0.049 047	32
33	0.044 054	0.044 859	0.045 672	0.046 493	0.047 321	0.048 156	33
34	0.043 198	0.044 007	0.044 824	0.045 649	0.046 481	0.047 322	34
35	0.042 392	0.043 206	0.044 027	0.044 856	0.045 694	0.046 539	35
36	0.041 634	0.042 452	0.043 277	0.044 111	0.044 954	0.045 804	36
37	0.040 919	0.041 741	0.042 571	0.043 410	0.044 256	0.045 112	37
38	0.040 244	0.041 070	0.041 905	0.042 748	0.043 599	0.044 459	38
39	0.039 606	0.040 436	0.041 275	0.042 123	0.042 979	0.043 844	39
40	0.039 002	0.039 836	0.040 679	0.041 532	0.042 393	0.043 262	40
41	0.038 430	0.039 268	0.040 115	0.040 972	0.041 838	0.042 712	41
42	0.037 886	0.038 729	0.039 581	0.040 442	0.041 312	0.042 192	42
43	0.037 370	0.038 217	0.039 073	0.039 939	0.040 814	0.041 698	43
44	0.036 880	0.037 730	0.038 591	0.039 461	0.040 341	0.041 230	44
45	0.036 413	0.037 268	0.038 132	0.039 007	0.039 891	0.040 785	45
46	0.035 968	0.036 827	0.037 696	0.038 575	0.039 464	0.040 363	46
47	0.035 544	0.036 407	0.037 280	0.038 164	0.039 057	0.039 961	47
48	0.035 139	0.036 006	0.036 884	0.037 772	0.038 670	0.039 578	48
49	0.034 752	0.035 623	0.036 505	0.037 398	0.038 300	0.039 213	49
50	0.034 383	0.035 258	0.036 144	0.037 041	0.037 948	0.038 865	50
51	0.034 029	0.034 909	0.035 799	0.036 700	0.037 612	0.038 534	51
52	0.033 691	0.034 574	0.035 469	0.036 374	0.037 291	0.038 217	52
53	0.033 367	0.034 254	0.035 153	0.036 063	0.036 984	0.037 915	53
54	0.033 056	0.033 948	0.034 851	0.035 765	0.036 690	0.037 626	54
55	0.032 759	0.033 654	0.034 561	0.035 480	0.036 409	0.037 349	55

YRS							
14	0.032 473	0.033 372	0.034 284	0.035 206	0.036 140	0.037 084	56
15	0.031 438	0.032 353	0.033 281	0.034 220	0.035 171	0.036 133	60
16	0.030 552	0.031 482	0.032 426	0.033 381	0.034 349	0.035 328	64
17	0.029 787	0.030 733	0.031 692	0.032 663	0.033 646	0.034 642	68
18	0.029 124	0.030 084	0.031 058	0.032 044	0.033 043	0.034 054	72
19	0.028 545	0.029 520	0.030 508	0.031 509	0.032 523	0.033 548	76
20	0.028 038	0.029 026	0.030 028	0.031 043	0.032 071	0.033 112	80
21	0.027 591	0.028 593	0.029 609	0.030 637	0.031 679	0.032 733	84
22	0.027 197	0.028 212	0.029 240	0.030 282	0.031 337	0.032 404	88
23	0.026 848	0.027 875	0.028 916	0.029 970	0.031 038	0.032 117	92
24	0.026 538	0.027 577	0.028 630	0.029 696	0.030 775	0.031 866	96
25	0.026 261	0.027 312	0.028 376	0.029 454	0.030 545	0.031 647	100
26	0.026 015	0.027 076	0.028 152	0.029 241	0.030 342	0.031 454	104
27	0.025 794	0.026 867	0.027 952	0.029 051	0.030 163	0.031 285	108
28	0.025 597	0.026 679	0.027 775	0.028 884	0.030 005	0.031 136	112
29	0.025 420	0.026 512	0.027 617	0.028 735	0.029 865	0.031 005	116
30	0.025 261	0.026 362	0.027 476	0.028 603	0.029 741	0.030 890	120

PARTIAL PAYMENT
TO AMORTIZE $1

QUARTERLY
COMPOUNDING

	12.50%	13.00%	13.50%	14.00%	14.50%	15.00%	
	ANNUAL RATE	ANNUAL RATE	ANNUAL RATE	ANNUAL RATE	ANNUAL RATE	ANNUAL RATE	
QTRS							QTRS
1	1.031 250	1.032 500	1.033 750	1.035 000	1.036 250	1.037 500	1
2	0.523 558	0.524 505	0.525 453	0.526 400	0.527 349	0.528 298	2
3	0.354 380	0.355 231	0.356 082	0.356 934	0.357 787	0.358 640	3
4	0.269 832	0.270 637	0.271 444	0.272 251	0.273 059	0.273 869	4
5	0.219 134	0.219 916	0.220 698	0.221 481	0.222 266	0.223 052	5
6	0.185 363	0.186 130	0.186 898	0.187 668	0.188 439	0.189 212	6
7	0.161 263	0.162 022	0.162 782	0.163 544	0.164 308	0.165 074	7
8	0.143 209	0.143 963	0.144 719	0.145 477	0.146 237	0.146 998	8
9	0.129 184	0.129 936	0.130 690	0.131 446	0.132 204	0.132 965	9
10	0.117 980	0.118 731	0.119 485	0.120 241	0.121 000	0.121 761	10
11	0.108 827	0.109 579	0.110 334	0.111 092	0.111 852	0.112 615	11
12	0.101 213	0.101 967	0.102 724	0.103 484	0.104 247	0.105 012	12
13	0.094 783	0.095 539	0.096 299	0.097 062	0.097 827	0.098 596	13
14	0.089 282	0.090 042	0.090 805	0.091 571	0.092 340	0.093 113	14
15	0.084 526	0.085 289	0.086 055	0.086 825	0.087 599	0.088 376	15
16	0.080 374	0.081 140	0.081 911	0.082 685	0.083 463	0.084 245	16
17	0.076 719	0.077 490	0.078 264	0.079 043	0.079 826	0.080 613	17
18	0.073 479	0.074 254	0.075 033	0.075 817	0.076 605	0.077 397	18
19	0.070 589	0.071 368	0.072 152	0.072 940	0.073 733	0.074 531	19
20	0.067 995	0.068 779	0.069 568	0.070 361	0.071 159	0.071 962	20
21	0.065 656	0.066 444	0.067 238	0.068 037	0.068 840	0.069 649	21
22	0.063 536	0.064 329	0.065 128	0.065 932	0.066 741	0.067 555	22
23	0.061 607	0.062 406	0.063 209	0.064 019	0.064 833	0.065 653	23
24	0.059 845	0.060 649	0.061 458	0.062 273	0.063 093	0.063 919	24
25	0.058 231	0.059 039	0.059 854	0.060 674	0.061 500	0.062 332	25
26	0.056 746	0.057 560	0.058 380	0.059 205	0.060 037	0.060 875	26
27	0.055 377	0.056 196	0.057 021	0.057 852	0.058 690	0.059 533	27
28	0.054 111	0.054 935	0.055 766	0.056 603	0.057 446	0.058 295	28
29	0.052 937	0.053 767	0.054 603	0.055 445	0.056 294	0.057 150	29
30	0.051 847	0.052 682	0.053 523	0.054 371	0.055 226	0.056 088	30
31	0.050 832	0.051 672	0.052 519	0.053 372	0.054 233	0.055 100	31
32	0.049 885	0.050 730	0.051 582	0.052 442	0.053 308	0.054 181	32
33	0.048 999	0.049 850	0.050 707	0.051 572	0.052 445	0.053 324	33
34	0.048 170	0.049 026	0.049 889	0.050 760	0.051 638	0.052 523	34
35	0.047 393	0.048 253	0.049 122	0.049 998	0.050 882	0.051 773	35
36	0.046 662	0.047 528	0.048 402	0.049 284	0.050 174	0.051 071	36
37	0.045 975	0.046 846	0.047 726	0.048 613	0.049 508	0.050 411	37
38	0.045 328	0.046 204	0.047 089	0.047 982	0.048 883	0.049 792	38
39	0.044 717	0.045 599	0.046 489	0.047 388	0.048 294	0.049 209	39
40	0.044 141	0.045 028	0.045 923	0.046 827	0.047 739	0.048 659	40
41	0.043 596	0.044 488	0.045 389	0.046 298	0.047 216	0.048 142	41
42	0.043 080	0.043 978	0.044 884	0.045 798	0.046 721	0.047 653	42
43	0.042 592	0.043 494	0.044 405	0.045 325	0.046 254	0.047 191	43
44	0.042 128	0.043 036	0.043 952	0.044 878	0.045 812	0.046 754	44
45	0.041 688	0.042 601	0.043 523	0.044 453	0.045 393	0.046 341	45
46	0.041 271	0.042 188	0.043 115	0.044 051	0.044 996	0.045 949	46
47	0.040 874	0.041 796	0.042 728	0.043 669	0.044 619	0.045 578	47
48	0.040 496	0.041 423	0.042 360	0.043 306	0.044 262	0.045 226	48
49	0.040 136	0.041 068	0.042 010	0.042 962	0.043 922	0.044 892	49
50	0.039 793	0.040 730	0.041 677	0.042 634	0.043 599	0.044 574	50
51	0.039 466	0.040 408	0.041 360	0.042 322	0.043 292	0.044 272	51
52	0.039 154	0.040 101	0.041 058	0.042 024	0.043 000	0.043 985	52
53	0.038 856	0.039 808	0.040 770	0.041 741	0.042 722	0.043 712	53
54	0.038 572	0.039 528	0.040 495	0.041 471	0.042 457	0.043 452	54
55	0.038 300	0.039 261	0.040 232	0.041 213	0.042 204	0.043 204	55
YRS							
14	0.038 040	0.039 006	0.039 981	0.040 967	0.041 963	0.042 968	56
15	0.037 106	0.038 090	0.039 084	0.040 089	0.041 103	0.042 127	60
16	0.036 318	0.037 319	0.038 331	0.039 353	0.040 385	0.041 427	64
17	0.035 648	0.036 666	0.037 695	0.038 734	0.039 783	0.040 841	68
18	0.035 077	0.036 110	0.037 155	0.038 210	0.039 275	0.040 349	72
19	0.034 586	0.035 635	0.036 695	0.037 765	0.038 844	0.039 934	76
20	0.034 164	0.035 227	0.036 301	0.037 385	0.038 479	0.039 582	80
21	0.033 799	0.034 876	0.035 963	0.037 060	0.038 167	0.039 283	84
22	0.033 482	0.034 572	0.035 672	0.036 782	0.037 901	0.039 029	88
23	0.033 208	0.034 309	0.035 421	0.036 543	0.037 673	0.038 812	92
24	0.032 969	0.034 082	0.035 204	0.036 337	0.037 478	0.038 627	96
25	0.032 760	0.033 884	0.035 017	0.036 159	0.037 310	0.038 469	100
26	0.032 578	0.033 711	0.034 854	0.036 006	0.037 166	0.038 333	104
27	0.032 418	0.033 561	0.034 713	0.035 873	0.037 042	0.038 217	108
28	0.032 278	0.033 430	0.034 590	0.035 759	0.036 935	0.038 117	112
29	0.032 156	0.033 315	0.034 484	0.035 659	0.036 842	0.038 032	116
30	0.032 048	0.033 215	0.034 391	0.035 573	0.036 762	0.037 958	120

PARTIAL PAYMENT
TO AMORTIZE $1

QUARTERLY
COMPOUNDING

QTRS	15.50% ANNUAL RATE	16.00% ANNUAL RATE	16.50% ANNUAL RATE	17.00% ANNUAL RATE	17.50% ANNUAL RATE	18.00% ANNUAL RATE	QTRS
1	1.038 750	1.040 000	1.041 250	1.042 500	1.043 750	1.045 000	1
2	0.529 247	0.530 196	0.531 146	0.532 096	0.533 047	0.533 998	2
3	0.359 494	0.360 349	0.361 204	0.362 060	0.362 916	0.363 773	3
4	0.274 679	0.275 490	0.276 302	0.277 115	0.277 929	0.278 744	4
5	0.223 839	0.224 627	0.225 416	0.226 207	0.226 999	0.227 792	5
6	0.189 986	0.190 762	0.191 539	0.192 317	0.193 097	0.193 878	6
7	0.165 841	0.166 610	0.167 380	0.168 152	0.168 926	0.169 701	7
8	0.147 762	0.148 528	0.149 295	0.150 065	0.150 836	0.151 610	8
9	0.133 728	0.134 493	0.135 260	0.136 029	0.136 801	0.137 574	9
10	0.122 525	0.123 291	0.124 059	0.124 830	0.125 603	0.126 379	10
11	0.113 381	0.114 149	0.114 920	0.115 693	0.116 469	0.117 248	11
12	0.105 781	0.106 552	0.107 326	0.108 103	0.108 883	0.109 666	12
13	0.099 369	0.100 144	0.100 922	0.101 703	0.102 488	0.103 275	13
14	0.093 889	0.094 669	0.095 452	0.096 238	0.097 028	0.097 820	14
15	0.089 157	0.089 941	0.090 729	0.091 520	0.092 315	0.093 114	15
16	0.085 031	0.085 820	0.086 613	0.087 410	0.088 211	0.089 015	16
17	0.081 404	0.082 199	0.082 997	0.083 800	0.084 607	0.085 418	17
18	0.078 193	0.078 993	0.079 798	0.080 607	0.081 420	0.082 237	18
19	0.075 332	0.076 139	0.076 949	0.077 764	0.078 584	0.079 407	19
20	0.072 770	0.073 582	0.074 399	0.075 220	0.076 046	0.076 876	20
21	0.070 462	0.071 280	0.072 103	0.072 931	0.073 763	0.074 601	21
22	0.068 375	0.069 199	0.070 028	0.070 862	0.071 702	0.072 546	22
23	0.066 479	0.067 309	0.068 145	0.068 986	0.069 831	0.070 682	23
24	0.064 750	0.065 587	0.066 429	0.067 276	0.068 129	0.068 987	24
25	0.063 169	0.064 012	0.064 860	0.065 715	0.066 574	0.067 439	25
26	0.061 718	0.062 567	0.063 422	0.064 283	0.065 149	0.066 021	26
27	0.060 383	0.061 239	0.062 100	0.062 967	0.063 841	0.064 719	27
28	0.059 151	0.060 013	0.060 881	0.061 755	0.062 635	0.063 521	28
29	0.058 012	0.058 880	0.059 754	0.060 635	0.061 522	0.062 415	29
30	0.056 956	0.057 830	0.058 711	0.059 598	0.060 492	0.061 392	30
31	0.055 975	0.056 855	0.057 743	0.058 637	0.059 537	0.060 443	31
32	0.055 062	0.055 949	0.056 842	0.057 743	0.058 650	0.059 563	32
33	0.054 210	0.055 104	0.056 004	0.056 911	0.057 824	0.058 745	33
34	0.053 415	0.054 315	0.055 221	0.056 135	0.057 055	0.057 982	34
35	0.052 672	0.053 577	0.054 490	0.055 410	0.056 337	0.057 270	35
36	0.051 975	0.052 887	0.053 806	0.054 732	0.055 666	0.056 606	36
37	0.051 322	0.052 240	0.053 165	0.054 097	0.055 037	0.055 984	37
38	0.050 708	0.051 632	0.052 563	0.053 502	0.054 448	0.055 402	38
39	0.050 131	0.051 061	0.051 998	0.052 944	0.053 896	0.054 856	39
40	0.049 588	0.050 523	0.051 467	0.052 418	0.053 377	0.054 343	40
41	0.049 076	0.050 017	0.050 967	0.051 924	0.052 889	0.053 862	41
42	0.048 593	0.049 540	0.050 496	0.051 459	0.052 430	0.053 409	42
43	0.048 136	0.049 090	0.050 051	0.051 021	0.051 998	0.052 982	43
44	0.047 705	0.048 665	0.049 632	0.050 607	0.051 590	0.052 581	44
45	0.047 298	0.048 262	0.049 236	0.050 217	0.051 205	0.052 202	45
46	0.046 912	0.047 882	0.048 861	0.049 848	0.050 842	0.051 845	46
47	0.046 546	0.047 522	0.048 506	0.049 499	0.050 499	0.051 507	47
48	0.046 199	0.047 181	0.048 171	0.049 169	0.050 175	0.051 189	48
49	0.045 870	0.046 857	0.047 853	0.048 856	0.049 868	0.050 887	49
50	0.045 558	0.046 550	0.047 551	0.048 560	0.049 577	0.050 602	50
51	0.045 261	0.046 259	0.047 265	0.048 279	0.049 302	0.050 332	51
52	0.044 979	0.045 982	0.046 994	0.048 013	0.049 041	0.050 077	52
53	0.044 711	0.045 719	0.046 736	0.047 761	0.048 794	0.049 835	53
54	0.044 456	0.045 469	0.046 491	0.047 521	0.048 559	0.049 605	54
55	0.044 213	0.045 231	0.046 258	0.047 293	0.048 336	0.049 388	55

YRS							
14	0.043 982	0.045 005	0.046 037	0.047 077	0.048 125	0.049 181	56
15	0.043 160	0.044 202	0.045 253	0.046 312	0.047 379	0.048 454	60
16	0.042 478	0.043 538	0.044 606	0.045 683	0.046 768	0.047 861	64
17	0.041 909	0.042 986	0.044 071	0.045 165	0.046 266	0.047 375	68
18	0.041 433	0.042 525	0.043 626	0.044 734	0.045 851	0.046 975	72
19	0.041 032	0.042 139	0.043 254	0.044 377	0.045 507	0.046 644	76
20	0.040 694	0.041 814	0.042 942	0.044 078	0.045 221	0.046 371	80
21	0.040 408	0.041 541	0.042 681	0.043 829	0.044 983	0.046 144	84
22	0.040 165	0.041 310	0.042 461	0.043 619	0.044 784	0.045 955	88
23	0.039 959	0.041 114	0.042 276	0.043 444	0.044 618	0.045 798	92
24	0.039 784	0.040 949	0.042 119	0.043 296	0.044 479	0.045 667	96
25	0.039 635	0.040 808	0.041 987	0.043 172	0.044 363	0.045 558	100
26	0.039 508	0.040 689	0.041 876	0.043 068	0.044 265	0.045 467	104
27	0.039 399	0.040 587	0.041 781	0.042 980	0.044 183	0.045 391	108
28	0.039 306	0.040 501	0.041 701	0.042 906	0.044 115	0.045 328	112
29	0.039 227	0.040 427	0.041 633	0.042 843	0.044 057	0.045 274	116
30	0.039 159	0.040 365	0.041 575	0.042 790	0.044 008	0.045 230	120

PARTIAL PAYMENT
TO AMORTIZE $1

QUARTERLY
COMPOUNDING

QTRS	18.50% ANNUAL RATE	19.00% ANNUAL RATE	19.50% ANNUAL RATE	20.00% ANNUAL RATE	20.50% ANNUAL RATE	21.00% ANNUAL RATE	QTRS
1	1.046 250	1.047 500	1.048 750	1.050 000	1.051 250	1.052 500	1
2	0.534 949	0.535 900	0.536 853	0.537 805	0.538 758	0.539 711	2
3	0.364 631	0.365 490	0.366 349	0.367 209	0.368 069	0.368 930	3
4	0.279 559	0.280 376	0.281 193	0.282 012	0.282 831	0.283 651	4
5	0.228 586	0.229 381	0.230 177	0.230 975	0.231 773	0.232 573	5
6	0.194 661	0.195 445	0.196 231	0.197 017	0.197 806	0.198 595	6
7	0.170 479	0.171 257	0.172 038	0.172 820	0.173 604	0.174 389	7
8	0.152 385	0.153 162	0.153 941	0.154 722	0.155 505	0.156 289	8
9	0.138 350	0.139 128	0.139 908	0.140 690	0.141 474	0.142 261	9
10	0.127 157	0.127 937	0.128 720	0.129 505	0.130 292	0.131 082	10
11	0.118 029	0.118 813	0.119 600	0.120 389	0.121 181	0.121 975	11
12	0.110 452	0.111 240	0.112 031	0.112 825	0.113 622	0.114 422	12
13	0.104 066	0.104 860	0.105 656	0.106 456	0.107 258	0.108 064	13
14	0.098 616	0.099 416	0.100 218	0.101 024	0.101 833	0.102 645	14
15	0.093 916	0.094 721	0.095 530	0.096 342	0.097 158	0.097 977	15
16	0.089 823	0.090 635	0.091 451	0.092 270	0.093 093	0.093 919	16
17	0.086 232	0.087 051	0.087 873	0.088 699	0.089 529	0.090 363	17
18	0.083 058	0.083 883	0.084 713	0.085 546	0.086 384	0.087 225	18
19	0.080 235	0.081 068	0.081 904	0.082 745	0.083 590	0.084 439	19
20	0.077 711	0.078 550	0.079 394	0.080 243	0.081 095	0.081 952	20
21	0.075 442	0.076 289	0.077 140	0.077 996	0.078 856	0.079 721	21
22	0.073 395	0.074 248	0.075 107	0.075 971	0.076 839	0.077 712	22
23	0.071 539	0.072 400	0.073 266	0.074 137	0.075 013	0.075 894	23
24	0.069 850	0.070 719	0.071 592	0.072 471	0.073 355	0.074 243	24
25	0.068 309	0.069 185	0.070 066	0.070 952	0.071 844	0.072 741	25
26	0.066 899	0.067 782	0.068 670	0.069 564	0.070 464	0.071 368	26
27	0.065 604	0.066 494	0.067 390	0.068 292	0.069 199	0.070 111	27
28	0.064 413	0.065 310	0.066 213	0.067 123	0.068 037	0.068 957	28
29	0.063 313	0.064 218	0.065 129	0.066 046	0.066 968	0.067 896	29
30	0.062 297	0.063 209	0.064 127	0.065 051	0.065 981	0.066 917	30
31	0.061 356	0.062 276	0.063 201	0.064 132	0.065 069	0.066 013	31
32	0.060 483	0.061 409	0.062 342	0.063 280	0.064 225	0.065 176	32
33	0.059 671	0.060 605	0.061 544	0.062 490	0.063 442	0.064 400	33
34	0.058 916	0.059 856	0.060 802	0.061 755	0.062 715	0.063 680	34
35	0.058 211	0.059 158	0.060 112	0.061 072	0.062 038	0.063 011	35
36	0.057 553	0.058 507	0.059 467	0.060 434	0.061 408	0.062 388	36
37	0.056 938	0.057 898	0.058 866	0.059 840	0.060 820	0.061 807	37
38	0.056 362	0.057 329	0.058 303	0.059 284	0.060 272	0.061 265	38
39	0.055 823	0.056 796	0.057 777	0.058 765	0.059 759	0.060 759	39
40	0.055 316	0.056 297	0.057 284	0.058 278	0.059 279	0.060 286	40
41	0.054 841	0.055 828	0.056 822	0.057 822	0.058 830	0.059 844	41
42	0.054 395	0.055 388	0.056 388	0.057 395	0.058 409	0.059 429	42
43	0.053 974	0.054 974	0.055 980	0.056 993	0.058 013	0.059 040	43
44	0.053 579	0.054 584	0.055 597	0.056 616	0.057 643	0.058 676	44
45	0.053 206	0.054 218	0.055 236	0.056 262	0.057 294	0.058 333	45
46	0.052 855	0.053 872	0.054 897	0.055 928	0.056 967	0.058 012	46
47	0.052 523	0.053 546	0.054 577	0.055 614	0.056 659	0.057 710	47
48	0.052 210	0.053 239	0.054 275	0.055 318	0.056 369	0.057 425	48
49	0.051 914	0.052 949	0.053 991	0.055 040	0.056 095	0.057 158	49
50	0.051 635	0.052 675	0.053 722	0.054 777	0.055 838	0.056 906	50
51	0.051 370	0.052 416	0.053 469	0.054 529	0.055 595	0.056 669	51
52	0.051 120	0.052 171	0.053 229	0.054 294	0.055 367	0.056 445	52
53	0.050 883	0.051 940	0.053 003	0.054 073	0.055 151	0.056 234	53
54	0.050 659	0.051 720	0.052 789	0.053 864	0.054 947	0.056 036	54
55	0.050 446	0.051 513	0.052 586	0.053 667	0.054 754	0.055 848	55

YRS							
14	0.050 245	0.051 316	0.052 395	0.053 480	0.054 572	0.055 671	56
15	0.049 537	0.050 627	0.051 724	0.052 828	0.053 939	0.055 055	60
16	0.048 961	0.050 069	0.051 183	0.052 304	0.053 431	0.054 564	64
17	0.048 491	0.049 614	0.050 744	0.051 880	0.053 022	0.054 170	68
18	0.048 105	0.049 243	0.050 387	0.051 536	0.052 692	0.053 853	72
19	0.047 788	0.048 939	0.050 095	0.051 257	0.052 425	0.053 597	76
20	0.047 527	0.048 689	0.049 857	0.051 030	0.052 208	0.053 391	80
21	0.047 311	0.048 483	0.049 661	0.050 844	0.052 032	0.053 224	84
22	0.047 132	0.048 314	0.049 501	0.050 692	0.051 888	0.053 088	88
23	0.046 984	0.048 174	0.049 369	0.050 568	0.051 771	0.052 978	92
24	0.046 861	0.048 058	0.049 260	0.050 466	0.051 676	0.052 889	96
25	0.046 759	0.047 963	0.049 171	0.050 383	0.051 598	0.052 817	100
26	0.046 674	0.047 884	0.049 098	0.050 315	0.051 535	0.052 758	104
27	0.046 603	0.047 818	0.049 037	0.050 259	0.051 483	0.052 710	108
28	0.046 544	0.047 764	0.048 987	0.050 213	0.051 441	0.052 671	112
29	0.046 495	0.047 719	0.048 946	0.050 175	0.051 406	0.052 639	116
30	0.046 455	0.047 682	0.048 912	0.050 144	0.051 378	0.052 613	120

QTRS	21.50% ANNUAL RATE	22.00% ANNUAL RATE	22.50% ANNUAL RATE	23.00% ANNUAL RATE	23.50% ANNUAL RATE	24.00% ANNUAL RATE	QTRS
1	1.053 750	1.055 000	1.056 250	1.057 500	1.058 750	1.060 000	1
2	0.540 664	0.541 618	0.542 572	0.543 527	0.544 482	0.545 437	2
3	0.369 792	0.370 654	0.371 517	0.372 381	0.373 245	0.374 110	3
4	0.284 472	0.285 294	0.286 117	0.286 941	0.287 766	0.288 591	4
5	0.233 374	0.234 176	0.234 980	0.235 784	0.236 590	0.237 396	5
6	0.199 386	0.200 179	0.200 973	0.201 768	0.202 565	0.203 363	6
7	0.175 176	0.175 964	0.176 755	0.177 546	0.178 340	0.179 135	7
8	0.157 076	0.157 864	0.158 654	0.159 446	0.160 240	0.161 036	8
9	0.143 049	0.143 839	0.144 632	0.145 427	0.146 223	0.147 022	9
10	0.131 873	0.132 668	0.133 464	0.134 263	0.135 064	0.135 868	10
11	0.122 771	0.123 571	0.124 372	0.125 177	0.125 984	0.126 793	11
12	0.115 224	0.116 029	0.116 837	0.117 648	0.118 461	0.119 277	12
13	0.108 873	0.109 684	0.110 499	0.111 316	0.112 137	0.112 960	13
14	0.103 461	0.104 279	0.105 101	0.105 926	0.106 754	0.107 585	14
15	0.098 800	0.099 626	0.100 455	0.101 288	0.102 123	0.102 963	15
16	0.094 749	0.095 583	0.096 420	0.097 260	0.098 104	0.098 952	16
17	0.091 201	0.092 042	0.092 887	0.093 736	0.094 589	0.095 445	17
18	0.088 071	0.088 920	0.089 773	0.090 630	0.091 492	0.092 357	18
19	0.085 293	0.086 150	0.087 012	0.087 877	0.088 747	0.089 621	19
20	0.082 814	0.083 679	0.084 549	0.085 423	0.086 302	0.087 185	20
21	0.080 591	0.081 465	0.082 343	0.083 226	0.084 113	0.085 005	21
22	0.078 589	0.079 471	0.080 358	0.081 249	0.082 145	0.083 046	22
23	0.076 779	0.077 670	0.078 565	0.079 465	0.080 369	0.081 278	23
24	0.075 137	0.076 036	0.076 939	0.077 848	0.078 761	0.079 679	24
25	0.073 642	0.074 549	0.075 461	0.076 378	0.077 300	0.078 227	25
26	0.072 278	0.073 193	0.074 113	0.075 039	0.075 969	0.076 904	26
27	0.071 029	0.071 952	0.072 881	0.073 814	0.074 753	0.075 697	27
28	0.069 883	0.070 814	0.071 751	0.072 693	0.073 640	0.074 593	28
29	0.068 829	0.069 769	0.070 713	0.071 663	0.072 619	0.073 580	29
30	0.067 858	0.068 805	0.069 758	0.070 716	0.071 680	0.072 649	30
31	0.066 962	0.067 917	0.068 877	0.069 843	0.070 815	0.071 792	31
32	0.066 133	0.067 095	0.068 064	0.069 038	0.070 017	0.071 002	32
33	0.065 365	0.066 335	0.067 311	0.068 292	0.069 280	0.070 273	33
34	0.064 652	0.065 630	0.066 613	0.067 603	0.068 598	0.069 598	34
35	0.063 990	0.064 975	0.065 966	0.066 963	0.067 965	0.068 974	35
36	0.063 374	0.064 366	0.065 365	0.066 369	0.067 379	0.068 395	36
37	0.062 800	0.063 800	0.064 805	0.065 817	0.066 834	0.067 857	37
38	0.062 266	0.063 272	0.064 285	0.065 303	0.066 328	0.067 358	38
39	0.061 767	0.062 780	0.063 799	0.064 825	0.065 856	0.066 894	39
40	0.061 300	0.062 320	0.063 347	0.064 379	0.065 417	0.066 462	40
41	0.060 864	0.061 891	0.062 924	0.063 963	0.065 008	0.066 059	41
42	0.060 456	0.061 489	0.062 529	0.063 574	0.064 626	0.065 683	42
43	0.060 074	0.061 113	0.062 159	0.063 211	0.064 269	0.065 333	43
44	0.059 715	0.060 761	0.061 813	0.062 872	0.063 936	0.065 006	44
45	0.059 379	0.060 431	0.061 490	0.062 554	0.063 624	0.064 700	45
46	0.059 064	0.060 122	0.061 186	0.062 256	0.063 333	0.064 415	46
47	0.058 767	0.059 831	0.060 901	0.061 978	0.063 060	0.064 148	47
48	0.058 489	0.059 559	0.060 634	0.061 716	0.062 804	0.063 898	48
49	0.058 227	0.059 302	0.060 384	0.061 471	0.062 565	0.063 664	49
50	0.057 981	0.059 061	0.060 148	0.061 241	0.062 340	0.063 444	50
51	0.057 749	0.058 835	0.059 927	0.061 025	0.062 129	0.063 239	51
52	0.057 530	0.058 622	0.059 719	0.060 823	0.061 932	0.063 046	52
53	0.057 325	0.058 421	0.059 524	0.060 632	0.061 746	0.062 866	53
54	0.057 131	0.058 232	0.059 340	0.060 453	0.061 572	0.062 696	54
55	0.056 948	0.058 055	0.059 167	0.060 285	0.061 408	0.062 537	55

YRS

YRS	21.50%	22.00%	22.50%	23.00%	23.50%	24.00%	QTRS
14	0.056 776	0.057 887	0.059 004	0.060 126	0.061 254	0.062 388	56
15	0.056 178	0.057 307	0.058 441	0.059 581	0.060 726	0.061 876	60
16	0.055 703	0.056 847	0.057 997	0.059 152	0.060 312	0.061 476	64
17	0.055 323	0.056 482	0.057 645	0.058 813	0.059 986	0.061 163	68
18	0.055 019	0.056 190	0.057 365	0.058 545	0.059 730	0.060 918	72
19	0.054 775	0.055 956	0.057 143	0.058 333	0.059 527	0.060 725	76
20	0.054 578	0.055 769	0.056 965	0.058 164	0.059 367	0.060 573	80
21	0.054 420	0.055 619	0.056 823	0.058 030	0.059 240	0.060 453	84
22	0.054 292	0.055 499	0.056 709	0.057 923	0.059 139	0.060 358	88
23	0.054 189	0.055 402	0.056 618	0.057 838	0.059 059	0.060 283	92
24	0.054 105	0.055 324	0.056 546	0.057 770	0.058 996	0.060 224	96
25	0.054 038	0.055 261	0.056 487	0.057 715	0.058 945	0.060 177	100
26	0.053 983	0.055 211	0.056 440	0.057 672	0.058 905	0.060 140	104
27	0.053 939	0.055 170	0.056 403	0.057 638	0.058 874	0.060 111	108
28	0.053 903	0.055 137	0.056 373	0.057 610	0.058 848	0.060 088	112
29	0.053 874	0.055 111	0.056 349	0.057 588	0.058 828	0.060 070	116
30	0.053 851	0.055 089	0.056 329	0.057 570	0.058 812	0.060 055	120

PARTIAL PAYMENT
TO AMORTIZE $1

SEMIANNUAL
COMPOUNDING

HALF YRS	7.00% ANNUAL RATE	8.00% ANNUAL RATE	9.00% ANNUAL RATE	10.00% ANNUAL RATE	10.50% ANNUAL RATE	11.00% ANNUAL RATE	HALF YRS
1	1.035 000	1.040 000	1.045 000	1.050 000	1.052 500	1.055 000	1
2	0.526 400	0.530 196	0.533 998	0.537 805	0.539 711	0.541 618	2
3	0.356 934	0.360 349	0.363 773	0.367 209	0.368 930	0.370 654	3
4	0.272 251	0.275 490	0.278 744	0.282 012	0.283 651	0.285 294	4
5	0.221 481	0.224 627	0.227 792	0.230 975	0.232 573	0.234 176	5
6	0.187 668	0.190 762	0.193 878	0.197 017	0.198 595	0.200 179	6
7	0.163 544	0.166 610	0.169 701	0.172 820	0.174 389	0.175 964	7
8	0.145 477	0.148 528	0.151 610	0.154 722	0.156 289	0.157 864	8
9	0.131 446	0.134 493	0.137 574	0.140 690	0.142 261	0.143 839	9
10	0.120 241	0.123 291	0.126 379	0.129 505	0.131 082	0.132 668	10
11	0.111 092	0.114 149	0.117 248	0.120 389	0.121 975	0.123 571	11
12	0.103 484	0.106 552	0.109 666	0.112 825	0.114 422	0.116 029	12
13	0.097 062	0.100 144	0.103 275	0.106 456	0.108 064	0.109 684	13
14	0.091 571	0.094 669	0.097 820	0.101 024	0.102 645	0.104 279	14
15	0.086 825	0.089 941	0.093 114	0.096 342	0.097 977	0.099 626	15
16	0.082 685	0.085 820	0.089 015	0.092 270	0.093 919	0.095 583	16
17	0.079 043	0.082 199	0.085 418	0.088 699	0.090 363	0.092 042	17
18	0.075 817	0.078 993	0.082 237	0.085 546	0.087 225	0.088 920	18
19	0.072 940	0.076 139	0.079 407	0.082 745	0.084 439	0.086 150	19
20	0.070 361	0.073 582	0.076 876	0.080 243	0.081 952	0.083 679	20
21	0.068 037	0.071 280	0.074 601	0.077 996	0.079 721	0.081 465	21
22	0.065 932	0.069 199	0.072 546	0.075 971	0.077 712	0.079 471	22
23	0.064 019	0.067 309	0.070 682	0.074 137	0.075 894	0.077 670	23
24	0.062 273	0.065 587	0.068 987	0.072 471	0.074 243	0.076 036	24
25	0.060 674	0.064 012	0.067 439	0.070 952	0.072 741	0.074 549	25
26	0.059 205	0.062 567	0.066 021	0.069 564	0.071 368	0.073 193	26
27	0.057 852	0.061 239	0.064 719	0.068 292	0.070 111	0.071 952	27
28	0.056 603	0.060 013	0.063 521	0.067 123	0.068 957	0.070 814	28
29	0.055 445	0.058 880	0.062 415	0.066 046	0.067 896	0.069 769	29
30	0.054 371	0.057 830	0.061 392	0.065 051	0.066 917	0.068 805	30
31	0.053 372	0.056 855	0.060 443	0.064 132	0.066 013	0.067 917	31
32	0.052 442	0.055 949	0.059 563	0.063 280	0.065 176	0.067 095	32
33	0.051 572	0.055 104	0.058 745	0.062 490	0.064 400	0.066 335	33
34	0.050 760	0.054 315	0.057 982	0.061 755	0.063 680	0.065 630	34
35	0.049 998	0.053 577	0.057 270	0.061 072	0.063 011	0.064 975	35
36	0.049 284	0.052 887	0.056 606	0.060 434	0.062 388	0.064 366	36
37	0.048 613	0.052 240	0.055 984	0.059 840	0.061 807	0.063 800	37
38	0.047 982	0.051 632	0.055 402	0.059 284	0.061 265	0.063 272	38
39	0.047 388	0.051 061	0.054 856	0.058 765	0.060 759	0.062 780	39
40	0.046 827	0.050 523	0.054 343	0.058 278	0.060 286	0.062 320	40
41	0.046 298	0.050 017	0.053 862	0.057 822	0.059 844	0.061 891	41
42	0.045 798	0.049 540	0.053 409	0.057 395	0.059 429	0.061 489	42
43	0.045 325	0.049 090	0.052 982	0.056 993	0.059 040	0.061 113	43
44	0.044 878	0.048 665	0.052 581	0.056 616	0.058 676	0.060 761	44
45	0.044 453	0.048 262	0.052 202	0.056 262	0.058 333	0.060 431	45
46	0.044 051	0.047 882	0.051 845	0.055 928	0.058 012	0.060 122	46
47	0.043 669	0.047 522	0.051 507	0.055 614	0.057 710	0.059 831	47
48	0.043 306	0.047 181	0.051 189	0.055 318	0.057 425	0.059 559	48
49	0.042 962	0.046 857	0.050 887	0.055 040	0.057 158	0.059 302	49
50	0.042 634	0.046 550	0.050 602	0.054 777	0.056 906	0.059 061	50
51	0.042 322	0.046 259	0.050 332	0.054 529	0.056 669	0.058 835	51
52	0.042 024	0.045 982	0.050 077	0.054 294	0.056 445	0.058 622	52
53	0.041 741	0.045 719	0.049 835	0.054 073	0.056 234	0.058 421	53
54	0.041 471	0.045 469	0.049 605	0.053 864	0.056 036	0.058 232	54
55	0.041 213	0.045 231	0.049 388	0.053 667	0.055 848	0.058 055	55
56	0.040 967	0.045 005	0.049 181	0.053 480	0.055 671	0.057 887	56
57	0.040 732	0.044 789	0.048 985	0.053 303	0.055 504	0.057 729	57
58	0.040 508	0.044 584	0.048 799	0.053 136	0.055 346	0.057 580	58
59	0.040 294	0.044 388	0.048 622	0.052 978	0.055 197	0.057 440	59

YRS

YRS	7.00%	8.00%	9.00%	10.00%	10.50%	11.00%	
30	0.040 089	0.044 202	0.048 454	0.052 828	0.055 055	0.057 307	60
31	0.039 705	0.043 854	0.048 143	0.052 552	0.054 796	0.057 064	62
32	0.039 353	0.043 538	0.047 861	0.052 304	0.054 564	0.056 847	64
33	0.039 030	0.043 249	0.047 606	0.052 081	0.054 356	0.056 654	66
34	0.038 734	0.042 986	0.047 375	0.051 880	0.054 170	0.056 482	68
35	0.038 461	0.042 745	0.047 165	0.051 699	0.054 003	0.056 328	70
36	0.038 210	0.042 525	0.046 975	0.051 536	0.053 853	0.056 190	72
37	0.037 978	0.042 323	0.046 802	0.051 390	0.053 718	0.056 067	74
38	0.037 765	0.042 139	0.046 644	0.051 257	0.053 597	0.055 956	76
39	0.037 567	0.041 969	0.046 501	0.051 138	0.053 488	0.055 858	78
40	0.037 385	0.041 814	0.046 371	0.051 030	0.053 391	0.055 769	80

PARTIAL PAYMENT
TO AMORTIZE $1

SEMIANNUAL
COMPOUNDING

	11.50%	12.00%	12.50%	13.00%	13.50%	14.00%	
	ANNUAL RATE	ANNUAL RATE	ANNUAL RATE	ANNUAL RATE	ANNUAL RATE	ANNUAL RATE	
HALF YRS							HALF YRS
1	1.057 500	1.060 000	1.062 500	1.065 000	1.067 500	1.070 000	1
2	0.543 527	0.545 437	0.547 348	0.549 262	0.551 176	0.553 092	2
3	0.372 381	0.374 110	0.375 841	0.377 576	0.379 312	0.381 052	3
4	0.286 941	0.288 591	0.290 245	0.291 903	0.293 564	0.295 228	4
5	0.235 784	0.237 396	0.239 013	0.240 635	0.242 260	0.243 891	5
6	0.201 768	0.203 363	0.204 963	0.206 568	0.208 179	0.209 796	6
7	0.177 546	0.179 135	0.180 730	0.182 331	0.183 939	0.185 553	7
8	0.159 446	0.161 036	0.162 633	0.164 237	0.165 849	0.167 468	8
9	0.145 427	0.147 022	0.148 626	0.150 238	0.151 858	0.153 486	9
10	0.134 263	0.135 868	0.137 482	0.139 105	0.140 737	0.142 378	10
11	0.125 177	0.126 793	0.128 419	0.130 055	0.131 701	0.133 357	11
12	0.117 648	0.119 277	0.120 917	0.122 568	0.124 230	0.125 902	12
13	0.111 316	0.112 960	0.114 616	0.116 283	0.117 961	0.119 651	13
14	0.105 926	0.107 585	0.109 257	0.110 940	0.112 637	0.114 345	14
15	0.101 288	0.102 963	0.104 651	0.106 353	0.108 067	0.109 795	15
16	0.097 260	0.098 952	0.100 658	0.102 378	0.104 111	0.105 858	16
17	0.093 736	0.095 445	0.097 168	0.098 906	0.100 659	0.102 425	17
18	0.090 630	0.092 357	0.094 098	0.095 855	0.097 626	0.099 413	18
19	0.087 877	0.089 621	0.091 380	0.093 156	0.094 947	0.096 753	19
20	0.085 423	0.087 185	0.088 962	0.090 756	0.092 567	0.094 393	20
21	0.083 226	0.085 005	0.086 800	0.088 613	0.090 443	0.092 289	21
22	0.081 249	0.083 046	0.084 860	0.086 691	0.088 540	0.090 406	22
23	0.079 465	0.081 278	0.083 111	0.084 961	0.086 829	0.088 714	23
24	0.077 848	0.079 679	0.081 529	3.083 398	0.085 284	0.087 189	24
25	0.076 378	0.078 227	0.080 095	0.081 981	0.083 887	0.085 811	25
26	0.075 039	0.076 904	0.078 790	0.080 695	0.082 619	0.084 561	26
27	0.073 814	0.075 697	0.077 600	0.079 523	0.081 465	0.083 426	27
28	0.072 693	0.074 593	0.076 513	0.078 453	0.080 413	0.082 392	28
29	0.071 663	0.073 580	0.075 517	0.077 474	0.079 452	0.081 449	29
30	0.070 716	0.072 649	0.074 603	0.076 577	0.078 572	0.080 586	30
31	0.069 843	0.071 792	0.073 763	0.075 754	0.077 766	0.079 797	31
32	0.069 038	0.071 002	0.072 989	0.074 997	0.077 025	0.079 073	32
33	0.068 292	0.070 273	0.072 275	0.074 299	0.076 344	0.078 408	33
34	0.067 603	0.069 598	0.071 617	0.073 656	0.075 716	0.077 797	34
35	0.066 963	0.068 974	0.071 007	0.073 062	0.075 138	0.077 234	35
36	0.066 369	0.068 395	0.070 443	0.072 513	0.074 604	0.076 715	36
37	0.065 817	0.067 857	0.069 921	0.072 005	0.074 111	0.076 237	37
38	0.065 303	0.067 358	0.069 436	0.071 535	0.073 655	0.075 795	38
39	0.064 825	0.066 894	0.068 985	0.071 099	0.073 233	0.075 387	39
40	0.064 379	0.066 462	0.068 567	0.070 694	0.072 842	0.075 009	40
41	0.063 963	0.066 059	0.068 177	0.070 318	0.072 479	0.074 660	41
42	0.063 574	0.065 683	0.067 815	0.069 968	0.072 142	0.074 336	42
43	0.063 211	0.065 333	0.067 478	0.069 644	0.071 830	0.074 036	43
44	0.062 872	0.065 006	0.067 163	0.069 341	0.071 540	0.073 758	44
45	0.062 554	0.064 700	0.066 869	0.069 060	0.071 270	0.073 500	45
46	0.062 256	0.064 415	0.066 596	0.068 797	0.071 019	0.073 260	46
47	0.061 978	0.064 148	0.066 340	0.068 553	0.070 786	0.073 037	47
48	0.061 716	0.063 898	0.066 101	0.068 325	0.070 569	0.072 831	48
49	0.061 471	0.063 664	0.065 878	0.068 112	0.070 366	0.072 639	49
50	0.061 241	0.063 444	0.065 669	0.067 914	0.070 178	0.072 460	50
51	0.061 025	0.063 239	0.065 474	0.067 729	0.070 002	0.072 294	51
52	0.060 823	0.063 046	0.065 291	0.067 556	0.069 839	0.072 139	52
53	0.060 632	0.062 866	0.065 120	0.067 394	0.069 686	0.071 995	53
54	0.060 453	0.062 696	0.064 960	0.067 243	0.069 544	0.071 861	54
55	0.060 285	0.062 537	0.064 810	0.067 101	0.069 411	0.071 736	55
56	0.060 126	0.062 388	0.064 669	0.066 969	0.069 287	0.071 620	56
57	0.059 977	0.062 247	0.064 537	0.066 846	0.069 171	0.071 512	57
58	0.059 837	0.062 116	0.064 414	0.066 730	0.069 063	0.071 411	58
59	0.059 705	0.061 992	0.064 298	0.066 622	0.068 962	0.071 317	59
YRS							
30	0.059 581	0.061 876	0.064 189	0.066 520	0.068 868	0.071 229	60
31	0.059 354	0.061 664	0.063 992	0.066 337	0.068 697	0.071 071	62
32	0.059 152	0.061 476	0.063 818	0.066 176	0.068 548	0.070 934	64
33	0.058 973	0.061 310	0.063 665	0.066 034	0.068 418	0.070 814	66
34	0.058 813	0.061 163	0.063 529	0.065 910	0.068 304	0.070 710	68
35	0.058 672	0.061 033	0.063 410	0.065 801	0.068 205	0.070 620	70
36	0.058 545	0.060 918	0.063 305	0.065 705	0.068 118	0.070 541	72
37	0.058 433	0.060 815	0.063 212	0.065 621	0.068 041	0.070 472	74
38	0.058 333	0.060 725	0.063 130	0.065 547	0.067 975	0.070 412	76
39	0.058 244	0.060 644	0.063 057	0.065 482	0.067 916	0.070 359	78
40	0.058 164	0.060 573	0.062 993	0.065 424	0.067 865	0.070 314	80

PARTIAL PAYMENT
TO AMORTIZE $1

SEMIANNUAL
COMPOUNDING

HALF YRS	14.50% ANNUAL RATE	15.00% ANNUAL RATE	15.50% ANNUAL RATE	16.00% ANNUAL RATE	16.50% ANNUAL RATE	17.00% ANNUAL RATE	HALF YRS
1	1.072 500	1.075 000	1.077 500	1.080 000	1.082 500	1.085 000	1
2	0.555 009	0.556 928	0.558 848	0.560 769	0.562 692	0.564 616	2
3	0.382 793	0.384 538	0.386 284	0.388 034	0.389 785	0.391 539	3
4	0.296 896	0.298 568	0.300 242	0.301 921	0.303 603	0.305 288	4
5	0.245 525	0.247 165	0.248 808	0.250 456	0.252 109	0.253 766	5
6	0.211 418	0.213 045	0.214 677	0.216 315	0.217 959	0.219 607	6
7	0.187 174	0.188 800	0.190 433	0.192 072	0.193 718	0.195 369	7
8	0.169 094	0.170 727	0.172 367	0.174 015	0.175 669	0.177 331	8
9	0.155 123	0.156 767	0.158 419	0.160 080	0.161 748	0.163 424	9
10	0.144 027	0.145 686	0.147 353	0.149 029	0.150 714	0.152 408	10
11	0.135 022	0.136 697	0.138 382	0.140 076	0.141 780	0.143 493	11
12	0.127 585	0.129 278	0.130 981	0.132 695	0.134 419	0.136 153	12
13	0.121 352	0.123 064	0.124 788	0.126 522	0.128 267	0.130 023	13
14	0.116 065	0.117 797	0.119 541	0.121 297	0.123 064	0.124 842	14
15	0.111 535	0.113 287	0.115 052	0.116 830	0.118 619	0.120 420	15
16	0.107 618	0.109 391	0.111 178	0.112 977	0.114 789	0.116 614	16
17	0.104 206	0.106 000	0.107 808	0.109 629	0.111 464	0.113 312	17
18	0.101 214	0.103 029	0.104 859	0.106 702	0.108 559	0.110 430	18
19	0.098 574	0.100 411	0.102 262	0.104 128	0.106 007	0.107 901	19
20	0.096 235	0.098 092	0.099 965	0.101 852	0.103 754	0.105 671	20
21	0.094 151	0.096 029	0.097 923	0.099 832	0.101 756	0.103 695	21
22	0.092 288	0.094 187	0.096 102	0.098 032	0.099 978	0.101 939	22
23	0.090 616	0.092 535	0.094 471	0.096 422	0.098 389	0.100 372	23
24	0.089 111	0.091 050	0.093 006	0.094 978	0.096 966	0.098 970	24
25	0.087 752	0.089 711	0.091 686	0.093 679	0.095 687	0.097 712	25
26	0.086 521	0.088 500	0.090 495	0.092 507	0.094 536	0.096 580	26
27	0.085 405	0.087 402	0.089 417	0.091 448	0.093 496	0.095 560	27
28	0.084 390	0.086 405	0.088 438	0.090 489	0.092 556	0.094 639	28
29	0.083 464	0.085 498	0.087 550	0.089 619	0.091 704	0.093 806	29
30	0.082 620	0.084 671	0.086 741	0.088 827	0.090 931	0.093 051	30
31	0.081 847	0.083 916	0.086 003	0.088 107	0.090 228	0.092 365	31
32	0.081 140	0.083 226	0.085 330	0.087 451	0.089 589	0.091 742	32
33	0.080 492	0.082 594	0.084 714	0.086 852	0.089 006	0.091 176	33
34	0.079 896	0.082 015	0.084 151	0.086 304	0.088 474	0.090 660	34
35	0.079 349	0.081 483	0.083 635	0.085 803	0.087 988	0.090 189	35
36	0.078 846	0.080 994	0.083 161	0.085 345	0.087 545	0.089 760	36
37	0.078 382	0.080 545	0.082 726	0.084 924	0.087 139	0.089 368	37
38	0.077 954	0.080 132	0.082 327	0.084 539	0.086 767	0.089 010	38
39	0.077 560	0.079 751	0.081 960	0.084 185	0.086 426	0.088 682	39
40	0.077 196	0.079 400	0.081 622	0.083 860	0.086 114	0.088 382	40
41	0.076 859	0.079 077	0.081 311	0.083 561	0.085 827	0.088 107	41
42	0.076 548	0.078 778	0.081 024	0.083 287	0.085 564	0.087 856	42
43	0.076 260	0.078 502	0.080 760	0.083 034	0.085 323	0.087 625	43
44	0.075 994	0.078 247	0.080 517	0.082 802	0.085 101	0.087 414	44
45	0.075 747	0.078 011	0.080 292	0.082 587	0.084 897	0.087 220	45
46	0.075 518	0.077 794	0.080 084	0.082 390	0.084 709	0.087 042	46
47	0.075 306	0.077 592	0.079 893	0.082 208	0.084 537	0.086 878	47
48	0.075 110	0.077 405	0.079 716	0.082 040	0.084 378	0.086 728	48
49	0.074 928	0.077 232	0.079 552	0.081 886	0.084 232	0.086 590	49
50	0.074 758	0.077 072	0.079 401	0.081 743	0.084 097	0.086 463	50
51	0.074 601	0.076 924	0.079 261	0.081 611	0.083 973	0.086 347	51
52	0.074 455	0.076 787	0.079 132	0.081 490	0.083 859	0.086 240	52
53	0.074 320	0.076 659	0.079 012	0.081 377	0.083 754	0.086 141	53
54	0.074 194	0.076 541	0.078 901	0.081 274	0.083 657	0.086 051	54
55	0.074 077	0.076 432	0.078 799	0.081 178	0.083 568	0.085 968	55
56	0.073 968	0.076 330	0.078 704	0.081 090	0.083 485	0.085 891	56
57	0.073 867	0.076 236	0.078 616	0.081 008	0.083 410	0.085 821	57
58	0.073 773	0.076 148	0.078 535	0.080 932	0.083 340	0.085 756	58
59	0.073 686	0.076 067	0.078 459	0.080 862	0.083 275	0.085 696	59

YRS							
30	0.073 604	0.075 991	0.078 390	0.080 798	0.083 215	0.085 641	60
31	0.073 458	0.075 856	0.078 265	0.080 683	0.083 110	0.085 544	62
32	0.073 332	0.075 740	0.078 158	0.080 585	0.083 020	0.085 462	64
33	0.073 222	0.075 639	0.078 066	0.080 501	0.082 943	0.085 392	66
34	0.073 127	0.075 553	0.077 987	0.080 429	0.082 878	0.085 333	68
35	0.073 044	0.075 478	0.077 919	0.080 368	0.082 822	0.085 282	70
36	0.072 973	0.075 413	0.077 861	0.080 315	0.082 775	0.085 240	72
37	0.072 911	0.075 357	0.077 811	0.080 270	0.082 734	0.085 204	74
38	0.072 857	0.075 309	0.077 767	0.080 231	0.082 700	0.085 173	76
39	0.072 810	0.075 267	0.077 730	0.080 198	0.082 671	0.085 147	78
40	0.072 769	0.075 231	0.077 698	0.080 170	0.082 646	0.085 125	80

PARTIAL PAYMENT
TO AMORTIZE $1

SEMIANNUAL COMPOUNDING

HALF YRS	17.50% ANNUAL RATE	18.00% ANNUAL RATE	18.50% ANNUAL RATE	19.00% ANNUAL RATE	19.50% ANNUAL RATE	20.00% ANNUAL RATE	HALF YRS
1	1.087 500	1.090 000	1.092 500	1.095 000	1.097 500	1.100 000	1
2	0.566 542	0.568 469	0.570 397	0.572 327	0.574 258	0.576 190	2
3	0.393 296	0.395 055	0.396 816	0.398 580	0.400 346	0.402 115	3
4	0.306 977	0.308 669	0.310 364	0.312 063	0.313 765	0.315 471	4
5	0.255 427	0.257 092	0.258 762	0.260 436	0.262 115	0.263 797	5
6	0.221 261	0.222 920	0.224 584	0.226 253	0.227 928	0.229 607	6
7	0.197 027	0.198 691	0.200 360	0.202 036	0.203 718	0.205 405	7
8	0.178 999	0.180 674	0.182 357	0.184 046	0.185 741	0.187 444	8
9	0.165 107	0.166 799	0.168 498	0.170 205	0.171 919	0.173 641	9
10	0.154 110	0.155 820	0.157 539	0.159 266	0.161 002	0.162 745	10
11	0.145 215	0.146 947	0.148 687	0.150 437	0.152 196	0.153 963	11
12	0.137 897	0.139 651	0.141 414	0.143 188	0.144 971	0.146 763	12
13	0.131 789	0.133 567	0.135 354	0.137 152	0.138 960	0.140 779	13
14	0.126 632	0.128 433	0.130 245	0.132 068	0.133 902	0.135 746	14
15	0.122 234	0.124 059	0.125 896	0.127 744	0.129 603	0.131 474	15
16	0.118 451	0.120 300	0.122 161	0.124 035	0.125 920	0.127 817	16
17	0.115 173	0.117 046	0.118 932	0.120 831	0.122 741	0.124 664	17
18	0.112 315	0.114 212	0.116 123	0.118 046	0.119 982	0.121 930	18
19	0.109 809	0.111 730	0.113 665	0.115 613	0.117 574	0.119 547	19
20	0.107 602	0.109 546	0.111 505	0.113 477	0.115 462	0.117 460	20
21	0.105 649	0.107 617	0.109 598	0.111 594	0.113 602	0.115 624	21
22	0.103 915	0.105 905	0.107 909	0.109 928	0.111 960	0.114 005	22
23	0.102 370	0.104 382	0.106 409	0.108 449	0.110 504	0.112 572	23
24	0.100 989	0.103 023	0.105 071	0.107 134	0.109 210	0.111 300	24
25	0.099 751	0.101 806	0.103 876	0.105 959	0.108 057	0.110 168	25
26	0.098 640	0.100 715	0.102 805	0.104 909	0.107 027	0.109 159	26
27	0.097 640	0.099 735	0.101 845	0.103 969	0.106 106	0.108 258	27
28	0.096 738	0.098 852	0.100 981	0.103 124	0.105 281	0.107 451	28
29	0.095 923	0.098 056	0.100 203	0.102 364	0.104 540	0.106 728	29
30	0.095 186	0.097 336	0.099 501	0.101 681	0.103 873	0.106 079	30
31	0.094 518	0.096 686	0.098 868	0.101 064	0.103 274	0.105 496	31
32	0.093 912	0.096 096	0.098 295	0.100 507	0.102 733	0.104 972	32
33	0.093 361	0.095 562	0.097 776	0.100 004	0.102 246	0.104 499	33
34	0.092 861	0.095 077	0.097 306	0.099 549	0.101 805	0.104 074	34
35	0.092 405	0.094 636	0.096 880	0.099 138	0.101 408	0.103 690	35
36	0.091 990	0.094 235	0.096 493	0.098 764	0.101 048	0.103 343	36
37	0.091 612	0.093 870	0.096 142	0.098 426	0.100 722	0.103 030	37
38	0.091 267	0.093 538	0.095 822	0.098 119	0.100 427	0.102 747	38
39	0.090 952	0.093 236	0.095 532	0.097 840	0.100 160	0.102 491	39
40	0.090 664	0.092 960	0.095 267	0.097 587	0.099 918	0.102 259	40
41	0.090 401	0.092 708	0.095 027	0.097 357	0.099 698	0.102 050	41
42	0.090 161	0.092 478	0.094 808	0.097 148	0.099 499	0.101 860	42
43	0.089 941	0.092 268	0.094 608	0.096 958	0.099 318	0.101 688	43
44	0.089 739	0.092 077	0.094 426	0.096 785	0.099 154	0.101 532	44
45	0.089 555	0.091 902	0.094 259	0.096 627	0.099 005	0.101 391	45
46	0.089 386	0.091 742	0.094 108	0.096 484	0.098 869	0.101 263	46
47	0.089 231	0.091 595	0.093 970	0.096 353	0.098 746	0.101 147	47
48	0.089 089	0.091 461	0.093 843	0.096 234	0.098 634	0.101 041	48
49	0.088 959	0.091 339	0.093 728	0.096 126	0.098 532	0.100 946	49
50	0.088 840	0.091 227	0.093 623	0.096 027	0.098 440	0.100 859	50
51	0.088 731	0.091 124	0.093 527	0.095 937	0.098 355	0.100 780	51
52	0.088 630	0.091 030	0.093 439	0.095 855	0.098 279	0.100 709	52
53	0.088 538	0.090 944	0.093 359	0.095 780	0.098 209	0.100 644	53
54	0.088 454	0.090 866	0.093 285	0.095 712	0.098 146	0.100 585	54
55	0.088 376	0.090 794	0.093 218	0.095 650	0.098 088	0.100 532	55
56	0.088 305	0.090 728	0.093 157	0.095 593	0.098 035	0.100 483	56
57	0.088 240	0.090 667	0.093 101	0.095 541	0.097 988	0.100 439	57
58	0.088 180	0.090 612	0.093 050	0.095 494	0.097 944	0.100 399	58
59	0.088 125	0.090 561	0.093 003	0.095 451	0.097 905	0.100 363	59

YRS	17.50%	18.00%	18.50%	19.00%	19.50%	20.00%	YRS
30	0.088 074	0.090 514	0.092 960	0.095 412	0.097 868	0.100 330	60
31	0.087 985	0.090 432	0.092 885	0.095 343	0.097 806	0.100 272	62
32	0.087 910	0.090 364	0.092 823	0.095 286	0.097 754	0.100 225	64
33	0.087 846	0.090 306	0.092 770	0.095 238	0.097 710	0.100 186	66
34	0.087 793	0.090 257	0.092 726	0.095 199	0.097 675	0.100 153	68
35	0.087 747	0.090 216	0.092 689	0.095 166	0.097 645	0.100 127	70
36	0.087 709	0.090 182	0.092 659	0.095 138	0.097 620	0.100 105	72
37	0.087 677	0.090 153	0.092 633	0.095 115	0.097 600	0.100 087	74
38	0.087 649	0.090 129	0.092 611	0.095 096	0.097 583	0.100 072	76
39	0.087 626	0.090 109	0.092 593	0.095 080	0.097 569	0.100 059	78
40	0.087 607	0.090 091	0.092 578	0.095 067	0.097 557	0.100 049	80

165

PARTIAL PAYMENT
TO AMORTIZE $1

ANNUAL
COMPOUNDING

YRS	7.00% ANNUAL RATE	8.00% ANNUAL RATE	9.00% ANNUAL RATE	10.00% ANNUAL RATE	10.25% ANNUAL RATE	10.50% ANNUAL RATE	YRS
1	1.070 000	1.080 000	1.090 000	1.100 000	1.102 500	1.105 000	1
2	0.553 092	0.560 769	0.568 469	0.576 190	0.578 124	0.580 059	2
3	0.381 052	0.388 034	0.395 055	0.402 115	0.403 886	0.405 659	3
4	0.295 228	0.301 921	0.308 669	0.315 471	0.317 180	0.318 892	4
5	0.243 891	0.250 456	0.257 092	0.263 797	0.265 484	0.267 175	5
6	0.209 796	0.216 315	0.222 920	0.229 607	0.231 292	0.232 982	6
7	0.185 553	0.192 072	0.198 691	0.205 405	0.207 099	0.208 799	7
8	0.167 468	0.174 015	0.180 674	0.187 444	0.189 153	0.190 869	8
9	0.153 486	0.160 080	0.166 799	0.173 641	0.175 370	0.177 106	9
10	0.142 378	0.149 029	0.155 820	0.162 745	0.164 497	0.166 257	10
11	0.133 357	0.140 076	0.146 947	0.153 963	0.155 740	0.157 525	11
12	0.125 902	0.132 695	0.139 651	0.146 763	0.148 565	0.150 377	12
13	0.119 651	0.126 522	0.133 567	0.140 779	0.142 607	0.144 445	13
14	0.114 345	0.121 297	0.128 433	0.135 746	0.137 601	0.139 467	14
15	0.109 795	0.116 830	0.124 059	0.131 474	0.133 355	0.135 248	15
16	0.105 858	0.112 977	0.120 300	0.127 817	0.129 725	0.131 644	16
17	0.102 425	0.109 629	0.117 046	0.124 664	0.126 599	0.128 545	17
18	0.099 413	0.106 702	0.114 212	0.121 930	0.123 891	0.125 863	18
19	0.096 753	0.104 128	0.111 730	0.119 547	0.121 533	0.123 531	19
20	0.094 393	0.101 852	0.109 546	0.117 460	0.119 470	0.121 493	20
21	0.092 289	0.099 832	0.107 617	0.115 624	0.117 659	0.119 707	21
22	0.090 406	0.098 032	0.105 905	0.114 005	0.116 063	0.118 134	22
23	0.088 714	0.096 422	0.104 382	0.112 572	0.114 653	0.116 747	23
24	0.087 189	0.094 978	0.103 023	0.111 300	0.113 403	0.115 519	24
25	0.085 811	0.093 679	0.101 806	0.110 168	0.112 292	0.114 429	25
26	0.084 561	0.092 507	0.100 715	0.109 159	0.111 304	0.113 461	26
27	0.083 426	0.091 448	0.099 735	0.108 258	0.110 422	0.112 599	27
28	0.082 392	0.090 489	0.098 852	0.107 451	0.109 634	0.111 830	28
29	0.081 449	0.089 619	0.098 056	0.106 728	0.108 929	0.111 143	29
30	0.080 586	0.088 827	0.097 336	0.106 079	0.108 298	0.110 528	30
31	0.079 797	0.088 107	0.096 686	0.105 496	0.107 731	0.109 978	31
32	0.079 073	0.087 451	0.096 096	0.104 972	0.107 222	0.109 485	32
33	0.078 408	0.086 852	0.095 562	0.104 499	0.106 765	0.109 042	33
34	0.077 797	0.086 304	0.095 077	0.104 074	0.106 354	0.108 645	34
35	0.077 234	0.085 803	0.094 636	0.103 690	0.105 983	0.108 288	35
36	0.076 715	0.085 345	0.094 235	0.103 343	0.105 649	0.107 967	36
37	0.076 237	0.084 924	0.093 870	0.103 030	0.105 349	0.107 677	37
38	0.075 795	0.084 539	0.093 538	0.102 747	0.105 077	0.107 417	38
39	0.075 387	0.084 185	0.093 236	0.102 491	0.104 832	0.107 183	39
40	0.075 009	0.083 860	0.092 960	0.102 259	0.104 611	0.106 971	40
41	0.074 660	0.083 561	0.092 708	0.102 050	0.104 411	0.106 781	41
42	0.074 336	0.083 287	0.092 478	0.101 860	0.104 230	0.106 609	42
43	0.074 036	0.083 034	0.092 268	0.101 688	0.104 067	0.106 454	43
44	0.073 758	0.082 802	0.092 077	0.101 532	0.103 919	0.106 314	44
45	0.073 500	0.082 587	0.091 902	0.101 391	0.103 786	0.106 188	45
46	0.073 260	0.082 390	0.091 742	0.101 263	0.103 665	0.106 074	46
47	0.073 037	0.082 208	0.091 595	0.101 147	0.103 555	0.105 971	47
48	0.072 831	0.082 040	0.091 461	0.101 041	0.103 456	0.105 878	48
49	0.072 639	0.081 886	0.091 339	0.100 946	0.103 367	0.105 794	49
50	0.072 460	0.081 743	0.091 227	0.100 859	0.103 285	0.105 718	50

PARTIAL PAYMENT
TO AMORTIZE $1

ANNUAL
COMPOUNDING

YRS	10.75% ANNUAL RATE	11.00% ANNUAL RATE	11.25% ANNUAL RATE	11.50% ANNUAL RATE	11.75% ANNUAL RATE	12.00% ANNUAL RATE	YRS
1	1.107 500	1.110 000	1.112 500	1.115 000	1.117 500	1.120 000	1
2	0.581 996	0.583 934	0.585 873	0.587 813	0.589 755	0.591 698	2
3	0.407 435	0.409 213	0.410 994	0.412 776	0.414 562	0.416 349	3
4	0.320 608	0.322 326	0.324 048	0.325 774	0.327 503	0.329 234	4
5	0.268 871	0.270 570	0.272 274	0.273 982	0.275 694	0.277 410	5
6	0.234 677	0.236 377	0.238 081	0.239 791	0.241 506	0.243 226	6
7	0.210 504	0.212 215	0.213 932	0.215 655	0.217 384	0.219 118	7
8	0.192 592	0.194 321	0.196 057	0.197 799	0.199 548	0.201 303	8
9	0.178 850	0.180 602	0.182 360	0.184 126	0.185 899	0.187 679	9
10	0.168 025	0.169 801	0.171 585	0.173 377	0.175 177	0.176 984	10
11	0.159 319	0.161 121	0.162 932	0.164 751	0.166 579	0.168 415	11
12	0.152 197	0.154 027	0.155 866	0.157 714	0.159 571	0.161 437	12
13	0.146 293	0.148 151	0.150 018	0.151 895	0.153 782	0.155 677	13
14	0.141 342	0.143 228	0.145 124	0.147 030	0.148 946	0.150 871	14
15	0.137 151	0.139 065	0.140 990	0.142 924	0.144 869	0.146 824	15
16	0.133 575	0.135 517	0.137 469	0.139 432	0.141 406	0.143 390	16
17	0.130 503	0.132 471	0.134 452	0.136 443	0.138 444	0.140 457	17
18	0.127 847	0.129 843	0.131 850	0.133 868	0.135 897	0.137 937	18
19	0.125 541	0.127 563	0.129 596	0.131 641	0.133 696	0.135 763	19
20	0.123 528	0.125 576	0.127 634	0.129 705	0.131 786	0.133 879	20
21	0.121 766	0.123 838	0.125 921	0.128 016	0.130 123	0.132 240	21
22	0.120 218	0.122 313	0.124 420	0.126 539	0.128 669	0.130 811	22
23	0.118 853	0.120 971	0.123 101	0.125 243	0.127 396	0.129 560	23
24	0.117 647	0.119 787	0.121 939	0.124 103	0.126 278	0.128 463	24
25	0.116 579	0.118 740	0.120 913	0.123 098	0.125 294	0.127 500	25
26	0.115 631	0.117 813	0.120 006	0.122 210	0.124 426	0.126 652	26
27	0.114 788	0.116 989	0.119 202	0.121 425	0.123 659	0.125 904	27
28	0.114 038	0.116 257	0.118 488	0.120 730	0.122 982	0.125 244	28
29	0.113 368	0.115 605	0.117 854	0.120 112	0.122 381	0.124 660	29
30	0.112 771	0.115 025	0.117 289	0.119 564	0.121 849	0.124 144	30
31	0.112 237	0.114 506	0.116 786	0.119 077	0.121 377	0.123 686	31
32	0.111 759	0.114 043	0.116 338	0.118 643	0.120 957	0.123 280	32
33	0.111 331	0.113 629	0.115 938	0.118 257	0.120 584	0.122 920	33
34	0.110 947	0.113 259	0.115 581	0.117 912	0.120 252	0.122 601	34
35	0.110 603	0.112 927	0.115 262	0.117 605	0.119 957	0.122 317	35
36	0.110 294	0.112 630	0.114 976	0.117 331	0.119 694	0.122 064	36
37	0.110 016	0.112 364	0.114 721	0.117 086	0.119 459	0.121 840	37
38	0.109 767	0.112 125	0.114 492	0.116 867	0.119 250	0.121 640	38
39	0.109 543	0.111 911	0.114 288	0.116 672	0.119 064	0.121 462	39
40	0.109 341	0.111 719	0.114 104	0.116 497	0.118 897	0.121 304	40
41	0.109 159	0.111 546	0.113 940	0.116 341	0.118 749	0.121 163	41
42	0.108 996	0.111 391	0.113 793	0.116 201	0.118 616	0.121 037	42
43	0.108 849	0.111 251	0.113 661	0.116 076	0.118 498	0.120 925	43
44	0.108 717	0.111 126	0.113 542	0.115 964	0.118 392	0.120 825	44
45	0.108 597	0.111 014	0.113 436	0.115 864	0.118 298	0.120 736	45
46	0.108 490	0.110 912	0.113 341	0.115 774	0.118 213	0.120 657	46
47	0.108 393	0.110 821	0.113 255	0.115 694	0.118 138	0.120 586	47
48	0.108 306	0.110 739	0.113 178	0.115 622	0.118 071	0.120 523	48
49	0.108 227	0.110 666	0.113 109	0.115 558	0.118 010	0.120 467	49
50	0.108 156	0.110 599	0.113 047	0.115 500	0.117 956	0.120 417	50

PARTIAL PAYMENT
TO AMORTIZE $1

ANNUAL
COMPOUNDING

YRS	12.25% ANNUAL RATE	12.50% ANNUAL RATE	12.75% ANNUAL RATE	13.00% ANNUAL RATE	13.25% ANNUAL RATE	13.50% ANNUAL RATE	YRS
1	1.122 500	1.125 000	1.127 500	1.130 000	1.132 500	1.135 000	1
2	0.593 643	0.595 588	0.597 535	0.599 484	0.601 433	0.603 384	2
3	0.418 139	0.419 931	0.421 725	0.423 522	0.425 321	0.427 122	3
4	0.330 970	0.332 708	0.334 449	0.336 194	0.337 942	0.339 693	4
5	0.279 130	0.280 854	0.282 582	0.284 315	0.286 051	0.287 791	5
6	0.244 950	0.246 680	0.248 414	0.250 153	0.251 897	0.253 646	6
7	0.220 858	0.222 603	0.224 354	0.226 111	0.227 873	0.229 641	7
8	0.203 064	0.204 832	0.206 606	0.208 387	0.210 173	0.211 966	8
9	0.189 466	0.191 260	0.193 061	0.194 869	0.196 684	0.198 505	9
10	0.178 799	0.180 622	0.182 452	0.184 290	0.186 135	0.187 987	10
11	0.170 260	0.172 112	0.173 973	0.175 841	0.177 718	0.179 602	11
12	0.163 311	0.165 194	0.167 086	0.168 986	0.170 895	0.172 811	12
13	0.157 582	0.159 496	0.161 419	0.163 350	0.165 291	0.167 240	13
14	0.152 806	0.154 751	0.156 704	0.158 667	0.160 640	0.162 621	14
15	0.148 789	0.150 764	0.152 748	0.154 742	0.156 745	0.158 757	15
16	0.145 384	0.147 388	0.149 402	0.151 426	0.153 460	0.155 502	16
17	0.142 479	0.144 512	0.146 556	0.148 608	0.150 671	0.152 743	17
18	0.139 988	0.142 049	0.144 120	0.146 201	0.148 292	0.150 392	18
19	0.137 840	0.139 928	0.142 026	0.144 134	0.146 252	0.148 380	19
20	0.135 982	0.138 096	0.140 220	0.142 354	0.144 498	0.146 651	20
21	0.134 368	0.136 507	0.138 656	0.140 814	0.142 983	0.145 161	21
22	0.132 962	0.135 125	0.137 297	0.139 479	0.141 672	0.143 873	22
23	0.131 735	0.133 919	0.136 114	0.138 319	0.140 533	0.142 757	23
24	0.130 660	0.132 866	0.135 082	0.137 308	0.139 544	0.141 788	24
25	0.129 717	0.131 943	0.134 180	0.136 426	0.138 681	0.140 945	25
26	0.128 888	0.131 134	0.133 390	0.135 655	0.137 928	0.140 211	26
27	0.128 159	0.130 423	0.132 697	0.134 979	0.137 270	0.139 570	27
28	0.127 516	0.129 797	0.132 088	0.134 387	0.136 695	0.139 010	28
29	0.126 949	0.129 246	0.131 552	0.133 867	0.136 190	0.138 521	29
30	0.126 447	0.128 760	0.131 081	0.133 411	0.135 748	0.138 092	30
31	0.126 004	0.128 331	0.130 666	0.133 009	0.135 360	0.137 717	31
32	0.125 612	0.127 952	0.130 300	0.132 656	0.135 019	0.137 388	32
33	0.125 265	0.127 617	0.129 978	0.132 345	0.134 719	0.137 100	33
34	0.124 957	0.127 321	0.129 693	0.132 071	0.134 456	0.136 847	34
35	0.124 684	0.127 059	0.129 441	0.131 829	0.134 224	0.136 624	35
36	0.124 442	0.126 827	0.129 218	0.131 616	0.134 020	0.136 429	36
37	0.124 227	0.126 621	0.129 022	0.131 428	0.133 840	0.136 258	37
38	0.124 036	0.126 439	0.128 848	0.131 262	0.133 682	0.136 107	38
39	0.123 867	0.126 278	0.128 694	0.131 116	0.133 543	0.135 974	39
40	0.123 716	0.126 134	0.128 558	0.130 986	0.133 420	0.135 858	40
41	0.123 582	0.126 007	0.128 437	0.130 872	0.133 312	0.135 755	41
42	0.123 463	0.125 895	0.128 331	0.130 771	0.133 216	0.135 665	42
43	0.123 357	0.125 795	0.128 236	0.130 682	0.133 132	0.135 585	43
44	0.123 263	0.125 706	0.128 153	0.130 603	0.133 058	0.135 515	44
45	0.123 179	0.125 627	0.128 078	0.130 534	0.132 992	0.135 454	45
46	0.123 105	0.125 557	0.128 013	0.130 472	0.132 934	0.135 400	46
47	0.123 039	0.125 495	0.127 955	0.130 417	0.132 883	0.135 352	47
48	0.122 980	0.125 440	0.127 903	0.130 369	0.132 838	0.135 310	48
49	0.122 927	0.125 391	0.127 857	0.130 327	0.132 799	0.135 273	49
50	0.122 880	0.125 347	0.127 817	0.130 289	0.132 764	0.135 241	50

YRS	13.75% ANNUAL RATE	14.00% ANNUAL RATE	14.25% ANNUAL RATE	14.50% ANNUAL RATE	14.75% ANNUAL RATE	15.00% ANNUAL RATE	YRS
1	1.137 500	1.140 000	1.142 500	1.145 000	1.147 500	1.150 000	1
2	0.605 336	0.607 290	0.609 244	0.611 200	0.613 158	0.615 116	2
3	0.428 926	0.430 731	0.432 539	0.434 350	0.436 162	0.437 977	3
4	0.341 447	0.343 205	0.344 965	0.346 729	0.348 496	0.350 265	4
5	0.289 535	0.291 284	0.293 036	0.294 792	0.296 552	0.298 316	5
6	0.255 399	0.257 157	0.258 920	0.260 688	0.262 460	0.264 237	6
7	0.231 414	0.233 192	0.234 976	0.236 766	0.238 560	0.240 360	7
8	0.213 765	0.215 570	0.217 381	0.219 198	0.221 021	0.222 850	8
9	0.200 333	0.202 168	0.204 010	0.205 858	0.207 713	0.209 574	9
10	0.189 847	0.191 714	0.193 588	0.195 469	0.197 357	0.199 252	10
11	0.181 494	0.183 394	0.185 302	0.187 217	0.189 139	0.191 069	11
12	0.174 736	0.176 669	0.178 610	0.180 559	0.182 516	0.184 481	12
13	0.169 198	0.171 164	0.173 138	0.175 121	0.177 112	0.179 110	13
14	0.164 611	0.166 609	0.168 616	0.170 632	0.172 656	0.174 688	14
15	0.160 779	0.162 809	0.164 848	0.166 896	0.168 952	0.171 017	15
16	0.157 554	0.159 615	0.161 685	0.163 764	0.165 852	0.167 948	16
17	0.154 825	0.156 915	0.159 015	0.161 124	0.163 241	0.165 367	17
18	0.152 502	0.154 621	0.156 749	0.158 886	0.161 032	0.163 186	18
19	0.150 517	0.152 663	0.154 818	0.156 982	0.159 155	0.161 336	19
20	0.148 814	0.150 986	0.153 167	0.155 357	0.157 555	0.159 761	20
21	0.147 348	0.149 545	0.151 750	0.153 964	0.156 186	0.158 417	21
22	0.146 084	0.148 303	0.150 531	0.152 768	0.155 013	0.157 266	22
23	0.144 990	0.147 231	0.149 481	0.151 739	0.154 005	0.156 278	23
24	0.144 041	0.146 303	0.148 573	0.150 851	0.153 137	0.155 430	24
25	0.143 218	0.145 498	0.147 787	0.150 084	0.152 388	0.154 699	25
26	0.142 501	0.144 800	0.147 106	0.149 420	0.151 742	0.154 070	26
27	0.141 877	0.144 193	0.146 516	0.148 846	0.151 183	0.153 526	27
28	0.141 334	0.143 664	0.146 003	0.148 348	0.150 699	0.153 057	28
29	0.140 859	0.143 204	0.145 556	0.147 915	0.150 280	0.152 651	29
30	0.140 444	0.142 803	0.145 168	0.147 539	0.149 917	0.152 300	30
31	0.140 082	0.142 453	0.144 830	0.147 213	0.149 602	0.151 996	31
32	0.139 764	0.142 147	0.144 535	0.146 929	0.149 328	0.151 733	32
33	0.139 487	0.141 880	0.144 278	0.146 682	0.149 091	0.151 505	33
34	0.139 244	0.141 646	0.144 054	0.146 467	0.148 884	0.151 307	34
35	0.139 030	0.141 442	0.143 858	0.146 279	0.148 705	0.151 135	35
36	0.138 844	0.141 263	0.143 687	0.146 116	0.148 549	0.150 986	36
37	0.138 680	0.141 107	0.143 538	0.145 974	0.148 413	0.150 857	37
38	0.138 536	0.140 970	0.143 408	0.145 850	0.148 295	0.150 744	38
39	0.138 410	0.140 850	0.143 294	0.145 742	0.148 193	0.150 647	39
40	0.138 299	0.140 745	0.143 195	0.145 647	0.148 103	0.150 562	40
41	0.138 202	0.140 653	0.143 108	0.145 565	0.148 025	0.150 489	41
42	0.138 117	0.140 573	0.143 031	0.145 493	0.147 958	0.150 425	42
43	0.138 042	0.140 502	0.142 965	0.145 431	0.147 899	0.150 369	43
44	0.137 976	0.140 440	0.142 907	0.145 376	0.147 847	0.150 321	44
45	0.137 919	0.140 386	0.142 856	0.145 328	0.147 803	0.150 279	45
46	0.137 868	0.140 338	0.142 811	0.145 287	0.147 764	0.150 242	46
47	0.137 823	0.140 297	0.142 773	0.145 250	0.147 730	0.150 211	47
48	0.137 784	0.140 260	0.142 738	0.145 218	0.147 700	0.150 183	48
49	0.137 750	0.140 228	0.142 709	0.145 191	0.147 674	0.150 159	49
50	0.137 719	0.140 200	0.142 683	0.145 167	0.147 652	0.150 139	50

PARTIAL PAYMENT
TO AMORTIZE $1

ANNUAL
COMPOUNDING

YRS	15.25% ANNUAL RATE	15.50% ANNUAL RATE	15.75% ANNUAL RATE	16.00% ANNUAL RATE	16.25% ANNUAL RATE	16.50% ANNUAL RATE	YRS
1	1.152 500	1.155 000	1.157 500	1.160 000	1.162 500	1.165 000	1
2	0.617 076	0.619 037	0.620 999	0.622 963	0.624 928	0.626 894	2
3	0.439 794	0.441 613	0.443 434	0.445 258	0.447 084	0.448 911	3
4	0.352 038	0.353 814	0.355 593	0.357 375	0.359 160	0.360 948	4
5	0.300 083	0.301 855	0.303 630	0.305 409	0.307 192	0.308 979	5
6	0.266 018	0.267 804	0.269 595	0.271 390	0.273 189	0.274 993	6
7	0.242 166	0.243 976	0.245 792	0.247 613	0.249 439	0.251 270	7
8	0.224 685	0.226 526	0.228 372	0.230 224	0.232 082	0.233 946	8
9	0.211 442	0.213 316	0.215 196	0.217 082	0.218 975	0.220 874	9
10	0.201 154	0.203 063	0.204 979	0.206 901	0.208 830	0.210 766	10
11	0.193 006	0.194 951	0.196 902	0.198 861	0.200 826	0.202 799	11
12	0.186 453	0.188 433	0.190 420	0.192 415	0.194 417	0.196 426	12
13	0.181 117	0.183 132	0.185 154	0.187 184	0.189 222	0.191 266	13
14	0.176 729	0.178 777	0.180 834	0.182 898	0.184 970	0.187 049	14
15	0.173 090	0.175 171	0.177 260	0.179 358	0.181 462	0.183 575	15
16	0.170 052	0.172 165	0.174 285	0.176 414	0.178 550	0.180 694	16
17	0.167 501	0.169 643	0.171 794	0.173 952	0.176 118	0.178 292	17
18	0.165 349	0.167 520	0.169 698	0.171 885	0.174 079	0.176 281	18
19	0.163 526	0.165 723	0.167 929	0.170 142	0.172 362	0.174 590	19
20	0.161 976	0.164 199	0.166 429	0.168 667	0.170 912	0.173 165	20
21	0.160 655	0.162 901	0.165 155	0.167 416	0.169 684	0.171 960	21
22	0.159 526	0.161 795	0.164 070	0.166 353	0.168 642	0.170 938	22
23	0.158 560	0.160 848	0.163 144	0.165 447	0.167 756	0.170 071	23
24	0.157 730	0.160 038	0.162 352	0.164 673	0.167 001	0.169 334	24
25	0.157 018	0.159 343	0.161 675	0.164 013	0.166 357	0.168 707	25
26	0.156 405	0.158 746	0.161 094	0.163 447	0.165 807	0.168 172	26
27	0.155 877	0.158 233	0.160 595	0.162 963	0.165 336	0.167 715	27
28	0.155 421	0.157 791	0.160 167	0.162 548	0.164 934	0.167 325	28
29	0.155 028	0.157 411	0.159 799	0.162 192	0.164 589	0.166 992	29
30	0.154 689	0.157 083	0.159 482	0.161 886	0.164 294	0.166 707	30
31	0.154 396	0.156 800	0.159 209	0.161 623	0.164 041	0.166 463	31
32	0.154 142	0.156 556	0.158 975	0.161 397	0.163 824	0.166 254	32
33	0.153 923	0.156 345	0.158 772	0.161 203	0.163 637	0.166 075	33
34	0.153 733	0.156 164	0.158 598	0.161 036	0.163 477	0.165 922	34
35	0.153 569	0.156 006	0.158 448	0.160 892	0.163 340	0.165 791	35
36	0.153 426	0.155 871	0.158 318	0.160 769	0.163 222	0.165 678	36
37	0.153 303	0.155 753	0.158 206	0.160 662	0.163 121	0.165 582	37
38	0.153 196	0.155 652	0.158 110	0.160 571	0.163 034	0.165 499	38
39	0.153 104	0.155 564	0.158 027	0.160 492	0.162 959	0.165 428	39
40	0.153 024	0.155 488	0.157 955	0.160 424	0.162 895	0.165 368	40
41	0.152 954	0.155 422	0.157 893	0.160 365	0.162 839	0.165 315	41
42	0.152 894	0.155 366	0.157 839	0.160 315	0.162 792	0.165 271	42
43	0.152 842	0.155 316	0.157 793	0.160 271	0.162 751	0.165 232	43
44	0.152 796	0.155 274	0.157 753	0.160 234	0.162 716	0.165 199	44
45	0.152 757	0.155 237	0.157 718	0.160 201	0.162 686	0.165 171	45
46	0.152 723	0.155 205	0.157 689	0.160 174	0.162 660	0.165 147	46
47	0.152 694	0.155 178	0.157 663	0.160 150	0.162 637	0.165 126	47
48	0.152 668	0.155 154	0.157 641	0.160 129	0.162 618	0.165 108	48
49	0.152 646	0.155 133	0.157 622	0.160 111	0.162 602	0.165 093	49
50	0.152 626	0.155 115	0.157 605	0.160 096	0.162 587	0.165 080	50

PARTIAL PAYMENT
TO AMORTIZE $1

ANNUAL
COMPOUNDING

YRS	16.75% ANNUAL RATE	17.00% ANNUAL RATE	17.25% ANNUAL RATE	17.50% ANNUAL RATE	17.75% ANNUAL RATE	18.00% ANNUAL RATE	YRS
1	1.167 500	1.170 000	1.172 500	1.175 000	1.177 500	1.180 000	1
2	0.628 861	0.630 829	0.632 799	0.634 770	0.636 742	0.638 716	2
3	0.450 741	0.452 574	0.454 408	0.456 245	0.458 083	0.459 924	3
4	0.362 739	0.364 533	0.366 330	0.368 130	0.369 933	0.371 739	4
5	0.310 770	0.312 564	0.314 362	0.316 163	0.317 969	0.319 778	5
6	0.276 802	0.278 615	0.280 432	0.282 254	0.284 080	0.285 910	6
7	0.253 106	0.254 947	0.256 793	0.258 645	0.260 501	0.262 362	7
8	0.235 815	0.237 690	0.239 570	0.241 456	0.243 348	0.245 244	8
9	0.222 779	0.224 691	0.226 608	0.228 531	0.230 460	0.232 395	9
10	0.212 708	0.214 657	0.216 612	0.218 573	0.220 541	0.222 515	10
11	0.204 779	0.206 765	0.208 758	0.210 757	0.212 764	0.214 776	11
12	0.198 442	0.200 466	0.202 496	0.204 533	0.206 577	0.208 628	12
13	0.193 319	0.195 378	0.197 445	0.199 518	0.201 599	0.203 686	13
14	0.189 136	0.191 230	0.193 332	0.195 440	0.197 556	0.199 678	14
15	0.185 695	0.187 822	0.189 957	0.192 098	0.194 247	0.196 403	15
16	0.182 845	0.185 004	0.187 170	0.189 343	0.191 523	0.193 710	16
17	0.180 473	0.182 662	0.184 857	0.187 060	0.189 269	0.191 485	17
18	0.178 490	0.180 706	0.182 929	0.185 159	0.187 396	0.189 639	18
19	0.176 825	0.179 067	0.181 316	0.183 572	0.185 834	0.188 103	19
20	0.175 424	0.177 690	0.179 963	0.182 243	0.184 528	0.186 820	20
21	0.174 242	0.176 530	0.178 825	0.181 126	0.183 433	0.185 746	21
22	0.173 241	0.175 550	0.177 865	0.180 187	0.182 514	0.184 846	22
23	0.172 393	0.174 721	0.177 055	0.179 395	0.181 740	0.184 090	23
24	0.171 674	0.174 019	0.176 370	0.178 726	0.181 088	0.183 454	24
25	0.171 062	0.173 423	0.175 790	0.178 161	0.180 538	0.182 919	25
26	0.170 542	0.172 917	0.175 298	0.177 683	0.180 073	0.182 467	26
27	0.170 099	0.172 487	0.174 881	0.177 278	0.179 681	0.182 087	27
28	0.169 721	0.172 121	0.174 526	0.176 935	0.179 348	0.181 765	28
29	0.169 399	0.171 810	0.174 225	0.176 644	0.179 067	0.181 494	29
30	0.169 124	0.171 545	0.173 969	0.176 398	0.178 829	0.181 264	30
31	0.168 889	0.171 318	0.173 751	0.176 188	0.178 628	0.181 070	31
32	0.168 688	0.171 126	0.173 566	0.176 010	0.178 457	0.180 906	32
33	0.168 517	0.170 961	0.173 409	0.175 859	0.178 312	0.180 767	33
34	0.168 370	0.170 821	0.173 274	0.175 730	0.178 189	0.180 650	34
35	0.168 245	0.170 701	0.173 160	0.175 621	0.178 085	0.180 550	35
36	0.168 137	0.170 599	0.173 063	0.175 528	0.177 996	0.180 466	36
37	0.168 046	0.170 512	0.172 980	0.175 450	0.177 921	0.180 395	37
38	0.167 967	0.170 437	0.172 909	0.175 382	0.177 858	0.180 335	38
39	0.167 900	0.170 373	0.172 849	0.175 325	0.177 804	0.180 284	39
40	0.167 842	0.170 319	0.172 797	0.175 277	0.177 758	0.180 240	40
41	0.167 793	0.170 273	0.172 753	0.175 236	0.177 719	0.180 204	41
42	0.167 751	0.170 233	0.172 716	0.175 200	0.177 686	0.180 172	42
43	0.167 715	0.170 199	0.172 684	0.175 171	0.177 658	0.180 146	43
44	0.167 684	0.170 170	0.172 657	0.175 145	0.177 634	0.180 124	44
45	0.167 658	0.170 145	0.172 634	0.175 123	0.177 614	0.180 105	45
46	0.167 635	0.170 124	0.172 614	0.175 105	0.177 597	0.180 089	46
47	0.167 616	0.170 106	0.172 597	0.175 089	0.177 582	0.180 075	47
48	0.167 599	0.170 091	0.172 583	0.175 076	0.177 570	0.180 064	48
49	0.167 585	0.170 078	0.172 571	0.175 065	0.177 559	0.180 054	49
50	0.167 573	0.170 066	0.172 560	0.175 055	0.177 550	0.180 046	50

PARTIAL PAYMENT
TO AMORTIZE $1

ANNUAL
COMPOUNDING

YRS	18.25% ANNUAL RATE	18.50% ANNUAL RATE	18.75% ANNUAL RATE	19.00% ANNUAL RATE	19.25% ANNUAL RATE	19.50% ANNUAL RATE	YRS
1	1.182 500	1.185 000	1.187 500	1.190 000	1.192 500	1.195 000	1
2	0.640 690	0.642 666	0.644 643	0.646 621	0.648 600	0.650 581	2
3	0.461 767	0.463 612	0.465 459	0.467 308	0.469 159	0.471 012	3
4	0.373 547	0.375 359	0.377 174	0.378 991	0.380 811	0.382 634	4
5	0.321 590	0.323 407	0.325 227	0.327 050	0.328 877	0.330 708	5
6	0.287 745	0.289 584	0.291 427	0.293 274	0.295 126	0.296 982	6
7	0.264 228	0.266 099	0.267 974	0.269 855	0.271 740	0.273 630	7
8	0.247 147	0.249 054	0.250 967	0.252 885	0.254 808	0.256 737	8
9	0.234 336	0.236 282	0.238 234	0.240 192	0.242 156	0.244 125	9
10	0.224 495	0.226 481	0.228 473	0.230 471	0.232 475	0.234 485	10
11	0.216 796	0.218 821	0.220 853	0.222 891	0.224 935	0.226 985	11
12	0.210 685	0.212 749	0.214 819	0.216 896	0.218 979	0.221 068	12
13	0.205 780	0.207 881	0.209 988	0.212 102	0.214 222	0.216 349	13
14	0.201 807	0.203 943	0.206 086	0.208 235	0.210 390	0.212 551	14
15	0.198 565	0.200 734	0.202 910	0.205 092	0.207 280	0.209 475	15
16	0.195 904	0.198 104	0.200 310	0.202 523	0.204 743	0.206 968	16
17	0.193 708	0.195 937	0.198 173	0.200 414	0.202 662	0.204 916	17
18	0.191 889	0.194 145	0.196 407	0.198 676	0.200 950	0.203 229	18
19	0.190 378	0.192 658	0.194 945	0.197 238	0.199 536	0.201 839	19
20	0.189 118	0.191 421	0.193 731	0.196 045	0.198 365	0.200 691	20
21	0.188 065	0.190 390	0.192 719	0.195 054	0.197 395	0.199 740	21
22	0.187 184	0.189 528	0.191 876	0.194 229	0.196 588	0.198 950	22
23	0.186 446	0.188 806	0.191 172	0.193 542	0.195 916	0.198 295	23
24	0.185 826	0.188 202	0.190 582	0.192 967	0.195 356	0.197 750	24
25	0.185 305	0.187 695	0.190 089	0.192 487	0.194 890	0.197 296	25
26	0.184 866	0.187 269	0.189 675	0.192 086	0.194 500	0.196 917	26
27	0.184 497	0.186 911	0.189 329	0.191 750	0.194 174	0.196 602	27
28	0.184 186	0.186 610	0.189 037	0.191 468	0.193 902	0.196 339	28
29	0.183 924	0.186 357	0.188 793	0.191 232	0.193 674	0.196 119	29
30	0.183 702	0.186 144	0.188 588	0.191 034	0.193 484	0.195 936	30
31	0.183 516	0.185 964	0.188 415	0.190 869	0.193 324	0.195 782	31
32	0.183 358	0.185 813	0.188 270	0.190 729	0.193 191	0.195 654	32
33	0.183 225	0.185 686	0.188 149	0.190 612	0.193 079	0.195 547	33
34	0.183 113	0.185 578	0.188 045	0.190 514	0.192 985	0.195 458	34
35	0.183 018	0.185 488	0.187 959	0.190 432	0.192 907	0.195 383	35
36	0.182 938	0.185 411	0.187 886	0.190 363	0.192 841	0.195 320	36
37	0.182 870	0.185 347	0.187 825	0.190 305	0.192 786	0.195 268	37
38	0.182 813	0.185 293	0.187 774	0.190 256	0.192 740	0.195 224	38
39	0.182 765	0.185 247	0.187 731	0.190 215	0.192 701	0.195 188	39
40	0.182 724	0.185 208	0.187 694	0.190 181	0.192 668	0.195 157	40
41	0.182 689	0.185 176	0.187 663	0.190 152	0.192 641	0.195 131	41
42	0.182 660	0.185 148	0.187 638	0.190 128	0.192 618	0.195 110	42
43	0.182 635	0.185 125	0.187 616	0.190 107	0.192 599	0.195 092	43
44	0.182 614	0.185 106	0.187 598	0.190 090	0.192 583	0.195 077	44
45	0.182 597	0.185 089	0.187 582	0.190 076	0.192 570	0.195 064	45
46	0.182 582	0.185 075	0.187 569	0.190 064	0.192 559	0.195 054	46
47	0.182 569	0.185 063	0.187 558	0.190 053	0.192 549	0.195 045	47
48	0.182 558	0.185 054	0.187 549	0.190 045	0.192 541	0.195 038	48
49	0.182 549	0.185 045	0.187 541	0.190 038	0.192 535	0.195 032	49
50	0.182 542	0.185 038	0.187 535	0.190 032	0.192 529	0.195 026	50

YRS	19.75% ANNUAL RATE	20.00% ANNUAL RATE	21.00% ANNUAL RATE	22.00% ANNUAL RATE	23.00% ANNUAL RATE	24.00% ANNUAL RATE	YRS
1	1.197 500	1.200 000	1.210 000	1.220 000	1.230 000	1.240 000	1
2	0.652 563	0.654 545	0.662 489	0.670 450	0.678 430	0.686 429	2
3	0.472 868	0.474 725	0.482 175	0.489 658	0.497 173	0.504 718	3
4	0.384 460	0.386 289	0.393 632	0.401 020	0.408 451	0.415 926	4
5	0.332 542	0.334 380	0.341 765	0.349 206	0.356 700	0.364 248	5
6	0.298 842	0.300 706	0.308 203	0.315 764	0.323 389	0.331 074	6
7	0.275 525	0.277 424	0.285 067	0.292 782	0.300 568	0.308 422	7
8	0.258 671	0.260 609	0.268 415	0.276 299	0.284 259	0.292 293	8
9	0.246 099	0.248 079	0.256 053	0.264 111	0.272 249	0.280 465	9
10	0.236 501	0.238 523	0.246 665	0.254 895	0.263 208	0.271 602	10
11	0.229 042	0.231 104	0.239 411	0.247 807	0.256 289	0.264 852	11
12	0.223 164	0.225 265	0.233 730	0.242 285	0.250 926	0.259 648	12
13	0.218 481	0.220 620	0.229 234	0.237 939	0.246 728	0.255 598	13
14	0.214 719	0.216 893	0.225 647	0.234 491	0.243 418	0.252 423	14
15	0.211 675	0.213 882	0.222 766	0.231 738	0.240 791	0.249 919	15
16	0.209 199	0.211 436	0.220 441	0.229 530	0.238 697	0.247 936	16
17	0.207 175	0.209 440	0.218 555	0.227 751	0.237 021	0.246 359	17
18	0.205 515	0.207 805	0.217 020	0.226 313	0.235 676	0.245 102	18
19	0.204 148	0.206 462	0.215 769	0.225 148	0.234 593	0.244 098	19
20	0.203 021	0.205 357	0.214 745	0.224 202	0.233 720	0.243 294	20
21	0.202 089	0.204 444	0.213 906	0.223 432	0.233 016	0.242 649	21
22	0.201 318	0.203 690	0.213 218	0.222 805	0.232 446	0.242 132	22
23	0.200 678	0.203 065	0.212 652	0.222 294	0.231 984	0.241 716	23
24	0.200 147	0.202 548	0.212 187	0.221 877	0.231 611	0.241 382	24
25	0.199 705	0.202 119	0.211 804	0.221 536	0.231 308	0.241 113	25
26	0.199 338	0.201 762	0.211 489	0.221 258	0.231 062	0.240 897	26
27	0.199 033	0.201 467	0.211 229	0.221 030	0.230 863	0.240 723	27
28	0.198 778	0.201 221	0.211 015	0.220 843	0.230 701	0.240 583	28
29	0.198 566	0.201 016	0.210 838	0.220 691	0.230 570	0.240 470	29
30	0.198 390	0.200 846	0.210 692	0.220 566	0.230 463	0.240 379	30
31	0.198 242	0.200 705	0.210 572	0.220 464	0.230 376	0.240 305	31
32	0.198 120	0.200 587	0.210 472	0.220 380	0.230 306	0.240 246	32
33	0.198 017	0.200 489	0.210 390	0.220 311	0.230 249	0.240 198	33
34	0.197 932	0.200 407	0.210 322	0.220 255	0.230 202	0.240 160	34
35	0.197 860	0.200 339	0.210 266	0.220 209	0.230 164	0.240 129	35
36	0.197 801	0.200 283	0.210 220	0.220 171	0.230 133	0.240 104	36
37	0.197 751	0.200 235	0.210 182	0.220 140	0.230 109	0.240 084	37
38	0.197 710	0.200 196	0.210 150	0.220 115	0.230 088	0.240 068	38
39	0.197 675	0.200 163	0.210 124	0.220 094	0.230 072	0.240 055	39
40	0.197 646	0.200 136	0.210 103	0.220 077	0.230 058	0.240 044	40
41	0.197 622	0.200 113	0.210 085	0.220 063	0.230 047	0.240 035	41
42	0.197 602	0.200 095	0.210 070	0.220 052	0.230 039	0.240 029	42
43	0.197 585	0.200 079	0.210 058	0.220 043	0.230 031	0.240 023	43
44	0.197 571	0.200 066	0.210 048	0.220 035	0.230 025	0.240 019	44
45	0.197 559	0.200 055	0.210 040	0.220 029	0.230 021	0.240 015	45
46	0.197 550	0.200 046	0.210 033	0.220 023	0.230 017	0.240 012	46
47	0.197 541	0.200 038	0.210 027	0.220 019	0.230 014	0.240 010	47
48	0.197 535	0.200 032	0.210 022	0.220 016	0.230 011	0.240 008	48
49	0.197 529	0.200 026	0.210 018	0.220 013	0.230 009	0.240 006	49
50	0.197 524	0.200 022	0.210 015	0.220 011	0.230 007	0.240 005	50

DEPRECIATION

	STRAIGHT LINE		125% S/L		150% S/L		200% S/L		SUM YEARS DIGITS		
YEAR	ANN. %	CUM. %	ANN. %	CUM. %	ANN. %	CUM. %	ANN. %	CUM. %	ANN. %	CUM. %	YEAR
					5 YEAR USEFUL LIFE						
1	20.0	20.0	25.0	25.0	30.0	30.0	40.0	40.0	33.3	33.3	1
2	20.0	40.0	18.8	43.8	21.0	51.0	24.0	64.0	26.7	60.0	2
3	20.0	60.0	14.1	57.8	14.7	65.7	14.4	78.4	20.0	80.0	3
4	20.0	80.0	10.5	68.4	10.3	76.0	8.6	87.0	13.3	93.3	4
5	20.0	100.0	7.9	76.3	7.2	83.2	5.2	92.2	6.7	100.0	5
					10 YEAR USEFUL LIFE						
1	10.0	10.0	12.5	12.5	15.0	15.0	20.0	20.0	18.2	18.2	1
2	10.0	20.0	10.9	23.4	12.8	27.7	16.0	36.0	16.4	34.5	2
3	10.0	30.0	9.6	33.0	10.8	38.6	12.8	48.8	14.5	49.1	3
4	10.0	40.0	8.4	41.4	9.2	47.8	10.2	59.0	12.7	61.8	4
5	10.0	50.0	7.3	48.7	7.8	55.6	8.2	67.2	10.9	72.7	5
6	10.0	60.0	6.4	55.1	6.7	62.3	6.6	73.8	9.1	81.8	6
7	10.0	70.0	5.6	60.7	5.7	67.9	5.2	79.0	7.3	89.1	7
8	10.0	80.0	4.9	65.6	4.8	72.8	4.2	83.2	5.5	94.5	8
9	10.0	90.0	4.3	69.9	4.1	76.8	3.4	86.6	3.6	98.2	9
10	10.0	100.0	3.8	73.7	3.5	80.3	2.7	89.3	1.8	100.0	10
					15 YEAR USEFUL LIFE						
1	6.7	6.7	8.3	8.3	10.0	10.0	13.3	13.3	12.5	12.5	1
2	6.7	13.3	7.6	16.0	9.0	19.0	11.6	24.9	11.7	24.2	2
3	6.7	20.0	7.0	23.0	8.1	27.1	10.0	34.9	10.8	35.0	3
4	6.7	26.7	6.4	29.4	7.3	34.4	8.7	43.6	10.0	45.0	4
5	6.7	33.3	5.9	35.3	6.6	41.0	7.5	51.1	9.2	54.2	5
6	6.7	40.0	5.4	40.7	5.9	46.9	6.5	57.6	8.3	62.5	6
7	6.7	46.7	4.9	45.6	5.3	52.2	5.7	63.3	7.5	70.0	7
8	6.7	53.3	4.5	50.1	4.8	57.0	4.9	68.2	6.7	76.7	8
9	6.7	60.0	4.2	54.3	4.3	61.3	4.2	72.4	5.8	82.5	9
10	6.7	66.7	3.8	58.1	3.9	65.1	3.7	76.1	5.0	87.5	10
					20 YEAR USEFUL LIFE						
1	5.0	5.0	6.3	6.3	7.5	7.5	10.0	10.0	9.5	9.5	1
2	5.0	10.0	5.9	12.1	6.9	14.4	9.0	19.0	9.0	18.6	2
3	5.0	15.0	5.5	17.6	6.4	20.9	8.1	27.1	8.6	27.1	3
4	5.0	20.0	5.1	22.8	5.9	26.8	7.3	34.4	8.1	35.2	4
5	5.0	25.0	4.8	27.6	5.5	32.3	6.6	41.0	7.6	42.9	5
6	5.0	30.0	4.5	32.1	5.1	37.4	5.9	46.9	7.1	50.0	6
7	5.0	35.0	4.2	36.3	4.7	42.1	5.3	52.2	6.7	56.7	7
8	5.0	40.0	4.0	40.3	4.3	46.4	4.8	57.0	6.2	62.9	8
9	5.0	45.0	3.7	44.1	4.0	50.4	4.3	61.3	5.7	68.6	9
10	5.0	50.0	3.5	47.6	3.7	54.1	3.9	65.1	5.2	73.8	10
					25 YEAR USEFUL LIFE						
1	4.0	4.0	5.0	5.0	6.0	6.0	8.0	8.0	7.7	7.7	1
2	4.0	8.0	4.7	9.7	5.6	11.6	7.4	15.4	7.4	15.1	2
3	4.0	12.0	4.5	14.3	5.3	16.9	6.8	22.1	7.1	22.2	3
4	4.0	16.0	4.3	18.5	5.0	21.9	6.2	28.4	6.8	28.9	4
5	4.0	20.0	4.1	22.6	4.7	26.6	5.7	34.1	6.5	35.4	5
6	4.0	24.0	3.9	26.5	4.4	31.0	5.3	39.4	6.2	41.5	6
7	4.0	28.0	3.7	30.2	4.1	35.2	4.9	44.2	5.8	47.4	7
8	4.0	32.0	3.5	33.7	3.9	39.0	4.5	48.7	5.5	52.9	8
9	4.0	36.0	3.3	37.0	3.7	42.7	4.1	52.8	5.2	58.2	9
10	4.0	40.0	3.2	40.1	3.4	46.1	3.8	56.6	4.9	63.1	10

DEPRECIATION

	METHOD										
	STRAIGHT LINE		125% S/L		150% S/L		200% S/L		SUM YEARS DIGITS		
YEAR	ANN. %	CUM. %	ANN. %	CUM. %	ANN. %	CUM. %	ANN. %	CUM. %	ANN. %	CUM. %	YEAR

30 YEAR USEFUL LIFE

YEAR	ANN. %	CUM. %	ANN. %	CUM. %	ANN. %	CUM. %	ANN. %	CUM. %	ANN. %	CUM. %	YEAR
1	3.3	3.3	4.2	4.2	5.0	5.0	6.7	6.7	6.5	6.5	1
2	3.3	6.7	4.0	8.2	4.7	9.7	6.2	12.9	6.2	12.7	2
3	3.3	10.0	3.8	12.0	4.5	14.3	5.8	18.7	6.0	18.7	3
4	3.3	13.3	3.7	15.7	4.3	18.5	5.4	24.1	5.8	24.5	4
5	3.3	16.7	3.5	19.2	4.1	22.6	5.1	29.2	5.6	30.1	5
6	3.3	20.0	3.4	22.5	3.9	26.5	4.7	33.9	5.4	35.5	6
7	3.3	23.3	3.2	25.8	3.7	30.2	4.4	38.3	5.2	40.6	7
8	3.3	26.7	3.1	28.9	3.5	33.7	4.1	42.4	4.9	45.6	8
9	3.3	30.0	3.0	31.8	3.3	37.0	3.8	46.3	4.7	50.3	9
10	3.3	33.3	2.8	34.7	3.2	40.1	3.6	49.8	4.5	54.8	10

33 1/3 YEAR USEFUL LIFE

YEAR	ANN. %	CUM. %	ANN. %	CUM. %	ANN. %	CUM. %	ANN. %	CUM. %	ANN. %	CUM. %	YEAR
1	3.0	3.0	3.8	3.7	4.5	4.5	6.0	6.0	5.8	5.8	1
2	3.0	6.0	3.6	7.4	4.3	8.8	5.6	11.6	5.7	11.5	2
3	3.0	9.0	3.5	10.8	4.1	12.9	5.3	16.9	5.5	17.0	3
4	3.0	12.0	3.3	14.2	3.9	16.8	5.0	21.9	5.3	22.3	4
5	3.0	15.0	3.2	17.4	3.7	20.6	4.7	26.6	5.1	27.4	5
6	3.0	18.0	3.1	20.5	3.6	24.1	4.4	31.0	5.0	32.3	6
7	3.0	21.0	3.0	23.5	3.4	27.6	4.1	35.2	4.8	37.1	7
8	3.0	24.0	2.9	26.3	3.3	30.8	3.9	39.0	4.6	41.7	8
9	3.0	27.0	2.8	29.1	3.1	33.9	3.7	42.7	4.4	46.1	9
10	3.0	30.0	2.7	31.8	3.0	36.9	3.4	46.1	4.3	50.4	10

35 YEAR USEFUL LIFE

YEAR	ANN. %	CUM. %	ANN. %	CUM. %	ANN. %	CUM. %	ANN. %	CUM. %	ANN. %	CUM. %	YEAR
1	2.9	2.9	3.6	3.6	4.3	4.3	5.7	5.7	5.6	5.6	1
2	2.9	5.7	3.4	7.0	4.1	8.4	5.4	11.1	5.4	11.0	2
3	2.9	8.6	3.3	10.3	3.9	12.3	5.1	16.2	5.2	16.2	3
4	2.9	11.4	3.2	13.5	3.8	16.1	4.8	21.0	5.1	21.3	4
5	2.9	14.3	3.1	16.6	3.6	19.7	4.5	25.5	4.9	26.2	5
6	2.9	17.1	3.0	19.6	3.4	23.1	4.3	29.7	4.8	31.0	6
7	2.9	20.0	2.9	22.5	3.3	26.4	4.0	33.8	4.6	35.6	7
8	2.9	22.9	2.8	25.2	3.2	29.6	3.8	37.5	4.4	40.0	8
9	2.9	25.7	2.7	27.9	3.0	32.6	3.6	41.1	4.3	44.3	9
10	2.9	28.6	2.6	30.5	2.9	35.5	3.4	44.5	4.1	48.4	10

40 YEAR USEFUL LIFE

YEAR	ANN. %	CUM. %	ANN. %	CUM. %	ANN. %	CUM. %	ANN. %	CUM. %	ANN. %	CUM. %	YEAR
1	2.5	2.5	3.1	3.1	3.8	3.7	5.0	5.0	4.9	4.9	1
2	2.5	5.0	3.0	6.2	3.6	7.4	4.7	9.7	4.8	9.6	2
3	2.5	7.5	2.9	9.1	3.5	10.8	4.5	14.3	4.6	14.3	3
4	2.5	10.0	2.8	11.9	3.3	14.2	4.3	18.5	4.5	18.8	4
5	2.5	12.5	2.8	14.7	3.2	17.4	4.1	22.6	4.4	23.2	5
6	2.5	15.0	2.7	17.3	3.1	20.5	3.9	26.5	4.3	27.4	6
7	2.5	17.5	2.6	19.9	3.0	23.5	3.7	30.2	4.1	31.6	7
8	2.5	20.0	2.5	22.4	2.9	26.3	3.5	33.7	4.0	35.6	8
9	2.5	22.5	2.4	24.9	2.8	29.1	3.3	37.0	3.9	39.5	9
10	2.5	25.0	2.3	27.2	2.7	31.8	3.2	40.1	3.8	43.3	10

50 YEAR USEFUL LIFE

YEAR	ANN. %	CUM. %	ANN. %	CUM. %	ANN. %	CUM. %	ANN. %	CUM. %	ANN. %	CUM. %	YEAR
1	2.0	2.0	2.5	2.5	3.0	3.0	4.0	4.0	3.9	3.9	1
2	2.0	4.0	2.4	4.9	2.9	5.9	3.8	7.8	3.8	7.8	2
3	2.0	6.0	2.4	7.3	2.8	8.7	3.7	11.5	3.8	11.5	3
4	2.0	8.0	2.3	9.6	2.7	11.5	3.5	15.1	3.7	15.2	4
5	2.0	10.0	2.3	11.9	2.7	14.1	3.4	18.5	3.6	18.8	5
6	2.0	12.0	2.2	14.1	2.6	16.7	3.3	21.7	3.5	22.4	6
7	2.0	14.0	2.1	16.2	2.5	19.2	3.1	24.9	3.5	25.8	7
8	2.0	16.0	2.1	18.3	2.4	21.6	3.0	27.9	3.4	29.2	8
9	2.0	18.0	2.0	20.4	2.4	24.0	2.9	30.7	3.3	32.5	9
10	2.0	20.0	2.0	22.4	2.3	26.3	2.8	33.5	3.2	35.7	10